Machine Learning Fundamentals

This lucid, accessible introduction to supervised machine learning presents core concepts in a focused and logical way that is easy for beginners to follow. The author assumes basic calculus, linear algebra, probability and statistics but no prior exposure to machine learning. Coverage includes widely used traditional methods such as SVMs, boosted trees, HMMs, and LDAs, plus popular deep learning methods such as convolution neural nets, attention, transformers, and GANs. Organized in a coherent presentation framework that emphasizes the big picture, the text introduces each method clearly and concisely "from scratch" based on the fundamentals. All methods and algorithms are described by a clean and consistent style, with a minimum of unnecessary detail. Numerous case studies and concrete examples demonstrate how the methods can be applied in a variety of contexts.

Hui Jiang is a Professor of Electrical Engineering and Computer Science at York University, where he has been since 2002. His main research interests include machine learning, particularly deep learning, and its applications to speech and audio processing, natural language processing, and computer vision. Over the past 30 years, he has worked on a wide range of research problems from these areas and published hundreds of technical articles and papers in the mainstream journals and top-tier conferences. His works have won the prestigious IEEE Best Paper Award and the ACL Outstanding Paper honor.

Simplicity is the ultimate sophistication.

—Leonardo da Vinci

Machine Learning Fundamentals

A Concise Introduction

Hui Jiang

York University, Toronto

CAMBRIDGE
UNIVERSITY PRESS

University Printing House, Cambridge CB2 8BS, United Kingdom

One Liberty Plaza, 20th Floor, New York, NY 10006, USA

477 Williamstown Road, Port Melbourne, VIC 3207, Australia

314–321, 3rd Floor, Plot 3, Splendor Forum, Jasola District Centre,
New Delhi – 110025, India

103 Penang Road, #05–06/07, Visioncrest Commercial, Singapore 238467

Cambridge University Press is part of the University of Cambridge.

It furthers the University's mission by disseminating knowledge in the pursuit of education, learning, and research at the highest international levels of excellence.

www.cambridge.org
Information on this title: www.cambridge.org/9781108837040
DOI: 10.1017/9781108938051

First published 2021

Printed in the United Kingdom by TJ Books Limited, Padstow Cornwall

A catalogue record for this publication is available from the British Library.

ISBN 978-1-108-83704-0 Hardback
ISBN 978-1-108-94002-3 Paperback

Contents

Preface

Machine learning used to be a niche area originating out of pattern classification in electrical engineering and artificial intelligence in computer science. Today, machine learning has grown into a very diverse discipline spanning a variety of topics in mathematics, science, and engineering. Because of the widespread use and increased power of computers, machine learning has found a plethora of relevant applications in almost all engineering domains and has made a huge impact on our society. In particular, with the boom of deep learning in recent years, thousands of new researchers and practitioners across academia and industry join forces every year to tackle machine learning and its applications. In many universities, machine learning has become one of the most popular advanced elective courses, highly demanded by senior undergraduates and graduates in almost all computer science and electrical engineering programs. The number of industrial job positions in machine learning, deep learning, and data science has dramatically increased in recent years, and this trend is expected to continue for at least the next 10 years due to the availability of a huge amount of data over the internet and personal devices.

Why This Book?

There are already plenty of well-written textbooks for machine learning, most of which exhaustively cover a wide range of topics in machine learning. In teaching my machine learning courses, I found that they are too challenging for beginners because of the vast range of presented topics and the overwhelming technical details associated with them. Many beginners have trouble with the heavy mathematical notation and equations, whereas others drown in all the technical details and fail to grasp the essence of these machine learning methods.

In contrast, this book is intended to present the fundamental machine learning concepts, algorithms, and principles in a concise and lucid manner, without heavy mathematical machinery and excess detail. I have been selective in terms of the topics so that it can all be covered in an introductory course, rather than making it comprehensive enough to cover all machine learning topics. I chose to cover only relatively mature topics primarily related to supervised learning, which I believe are not only fundamental to the field of machine learning but also significant enough to have made an impact in both academia and industry. In other words, some satisfactory and feasible solutions have already been developed for these topics so that they are able to address not just toy problems but many interesting problems arising in the real world. At the same time, I have tried to omit many minor issues surrounding the central topics so that beginners will not be distracted by these purely technical details.

Instead of covering the selected topics separately, one after another, I have tried to organize all machine learning topics into a coherent structure to give readers a big picture of the entire field. All topics are arranged into coherent groups, and the individual chapters are dedicated to covering all logically relevant methods in each group. After reading each chapter, readers can immediately understand the differences between them, grasp their relevance, and also know how these methods fit into the big picture of machine learning.

This book also aims to reflect the latest advancements in the field. I have included significant coverage on several important recent techniques, such as *transformers*, which have come to dominate many natural-language-processing tasks; *batch norm* and *ADAM optimization*, which are popular in learning large and deep neural networks; and recently popular deep generative models such as *variational autoencoders (VAEs)* and *generative adversarial nets (GANs)*.

For all topics in this book, I provide enough technical depth to explain the motivation, principles, and methodology in a professional manner. As much as possible, I derive the machine learning methods from scratch using rigorous mathematics to highlight the core ideas behind them. For critical theoretical results, I have included many important theorems and some light proofs. The important mathematical topics and methods that modern machine learning methods are built on are thoroughly reviewed in Chapter 2. However, readers do need a good background in *calculus*, *linear algebra*, and *probability and statistics* to be able to follow the descriptions and discussions in this book. Throughout the book, I have also done my best to present all technical content using clean and consistent mathematical notations and represent all algorithms in this book as concise linear algebra formulas, which can be translated almost line by line into efficient code using a programming language supporting vectorization, such as MATLAB or Python.

Whom Is This Book For?

This book is primarily written as a textbook for an introductory course on machine learning for senior undergraduate students in computer science and computer/ software/electrical engineering programs or first-year graduate students in many science, engineering, and applied mathematics programs who are interested in basic machine learning methods for their own research problems. I also hope it will be useful as a self-study or reference book for researchers who wish to apply machine learning methods to solve their own problems, as well as industrial practitioners who want to understand the concepts and principles behind the popular machine learning methods they implement. Given the large number of machine learning software programs and toolkits freely available today, it is often not hard to write code to run fairly complicated machine learning algorithms. However, in many cases, knowledge of the principles and mathematics behind these algorithms is required to tune these algorithms in order to deliver optimal results for the task at hand.

Online Resources

This book is accompanied by the following GitHub repository:

`https://github.com/iNCML/MachineLearningBook`

This website provides a variety of supplementary materials to support this book, including the following:

- Lecture slides per chapter
- Code samples for some lab projects (MATLAB or Python)

Meanwhile, readers and instructors can also provide their feedback, suggestions, and comments on this book as *issues* through the GitHub repository. I will reply to these requests as much as possible.

How to Use This Book

I have made much effort to keep this book succinct and only cover the most important issues for each selected topic. I encourage readers to read all chapters in order because I have tried my best to arrange a wide range of machine learning topics in a coherent structure. For each machine learning method, I have thoroughly covered the motivation, main ideas, concepts, methodology, and algorithms in the main text and sometimes have left extensive issues and extra technical details or extensions as chapter-end exercises. Readers may optionally follow these links to work on these exercises and practice the main ideas discussed in the text.

- **For a Semester-Long Course**
  Instructors may use this book as the primary or alternate textbook for a standard semester-long introductory course (about 10–12 weeks) on machine learning in the fourth year of a computer science, engineering, or applied mathematics program. I suggest covering the following topics in order:

- Chapter 1: Introduction (0.5 week)
- Chapter 2: Mathematical Foundation (1.5 weeks)
- Chapter 4: Feature Extraction (1 week)
- Chapter 5: Statistical Learning Theory (0.5 week)
  - §5.1 Formulation of Discriminative Models
  - §5.2 Learnability
- Chapter 6: Linear Models (1.5 weeks)
- Chapter 7: Learning Discriminative Models (1 week)
  - §7.1 General Framework
  - §7.2 Ridge and LASSO
  - §7.3 Matrix Factorization
- Chapter 8: Neural Networks (2 weeks)
- Chapter 9: Ensemble Learning (1 week)
- Chapter 10: Overview of Generative Models (1 week)
- Chapter 11: Unimodal Models (1 week)
  - §11.1 Gaussian Models
  - §11.2 Multinomial Models
  - §11.3 Markov Chain Models
- Chapter 12 Mixture Models (1 week)
  - §12.1 Formulation
  - §12.2 EM Method
  - §12.3 Gaussian Mixture Models

► **For a Year-Long Full Course**

Instructors may also use this book as the primary or alternate textbook for a year-long full course on machine learning (20–24 weeks) to give balanced coverage of both discriminative and generative models. The first half focuses on the mathematical preparation and discriminative models, whereas the second half gives full exposure to a variety of topics in generative models, including Chapter 13: Entangled Models, Chapter 14: Bayesian Learning, and Chapter 15: Graphical Models.

If time is tight, instructors may skip some optional topics, such as §4.3 Manifold Learning, §7.4 Dictionary Learning, §11.4 Generalized Linear Models, §12.4 Hidden Markov Models, or §14.4 Gaussian Processes.

► **For Self-Study**

All self-study readers are strongly recommended to go through the book in order. This will give a smooth transition from one topic to another, generally progressing gradually from easy topics to hard ones. Depending on one's own interests, readers may choose to skip any of the following advanced topics without affecting the understanding of other parts:

- §4.3 Manifold Learning
- §7.4 Dictionary Learning
- §11.4 Generalized Linear Models
- §12.4 Hidden Markov Models
- §14.4 Gaussian Processes

Acknowledgments

Writing a textbook is a very challenging task. This book would not have been possible without help and supports from a large number of people.

Most content in this book evolved from the lecture notes I have used for many years to teach a machine learning course in the Department of Electrical Engineering and Computer Science at York University in Toronto, Canada. I am grateful to York University for the long-standing support of my teaching and research there.

I also thank Zoubin Ghahramani, David Blei, and Huy Vu for granting permission to use their materials in this book.

Many people have helped to significantly improve this book by proofreading the early draft and providing valuable comments and suggestions, including Dong Yu, Kelvin Jiang, Behnam Asadi, Jia Pan, Yong Ge, William Fu, Xiaodan Zhu, Chao Wang, Jiebo Luo, Hanjia Lyu, Joyce Luo, Qiang Huo, Chunxiao Zhou, Wei Zhang, Maria Koshkina, Zhuoran Li, Junfei Wang, and Parham Eftekhar. My special thanks to all of them!

Finally, I would like to thank my family, Iris and Kelvin, and my parents for their endless support and love throughout the time of writing this book as well as my career and life.

Notation

This list describes some of the symbols that are used within this book.

$\boldsymbol{\mu}$	The mean vector of a multivariate Gaussian
$\boldsymbol{\Sigma}$	The covariance matrix of a multivariate Gaussian
$\mathbb{E}[\,\cdot\,]$	The expectation or the mean
$\mathbb{E}_X[\,\cdot\,]$	The expectation with respect to X
$\mathbb{H}$	Model space
$\mathbb{N}$	The set of natural numbers
$\mathbb{R}$	The set of real numbers
$\mathbb{R}^n$	The set of n-dimensional real vectors
$\mathbb{R}^{m\times n}$	The set of $m \times n$ real matrices
$\mathbb{W}$	The set of all parameters in a neural network
$\mathbf{S}$	The sample covariance matrix
$\mathbf{w} * \mathbf{x}$	The convolution sum of $\mathbf{w}$ and $\mathbf{x}$
$\mathbf{w} \cdot \mathbf{x}$	The inner product of two vectors $\mathbf{w}$ and $\mathbf{x}$
$\mathbf{w} \odot \mathbf{x}$	The element-wise multiplication of $\mathbf{w}$ and $\mathbf{x}$
$\mathbf{W}$	A weight matrix
$\mathbf{w}$	A weight vector
$\mathbf{x}$	A feature vector
$\nabla f(\mathbf{x})$	The gradient of a function $f(\mathbf{x})$
$\Pr(A)$	The probability of an event A
$\|\mathbf{w}\|$	The norm (or L_2 norm) of a vector $\mathbf{w}$
$\|\mathbf{w}\|_p$	The L_p norm of a vector $\mathbf{w}$
$f(\mathbf{x};\boldsymbol{\theta})$	A function of $\mathbf{x}$ with the parameter $\boldsymbol{\theta}$
$f_{\boldsymbol{\theta}}(\mathbf{x})$	A function of $\mathbf{x}$ with the parameter $\boldsymbol{\theta}$
$l(\boldsymbol{\theta})$	A log-likelihood function of the model parameter $\boldsymbol{\theta}$
$m \ll n$	m is much less than n
$p(\mathbf{x},\mathbf{y})$	A joint distribution of $\mathbf{x}$ and $\mathbf{y}$
$p(\mathbf{y}\,\vert\,\mathbf{x})$	A conditional distribution of $\mathbf{y}$ given $\mathbf{x}$
$p_{\boldsymbol{\theta}}(\mathbf{x})$	A probability distribution of $\mathbf{x}$ with the parameter $\boldsymbol{\theta}$
$Q(\mathbb{W};\mathbf{x})$	An objective function of the model parameters $\mathbb{W}$ given the data $\mathbf{x}$
$\boldsymbol{\theta}$	Model parameter

Summary of the General Notation Rules

Notation	Meaning	Examples
Lowercase letters	A scalar	x, y, n, m, x_i, x_{ij}
	A function	$f(\cdot), p(\cdot), g(\cdot), h(\cdot)$
Lowercase letters in bold	A column vector	$\mathbf{w}, \mathbf{x}, \mathbf{y}, \mathbf{z}, \mathbf{a}, \mathbf{b}$ $\boldsymbol{\mu}, \boldsymbol{\nu}$
Uppercase letters	A random variable	X, Y, X_i, X_j
	A function	$Q(\cdot), \Phi(\cdot, \cdot)$
Uppercase letters in bold	A matrix	$\mathbf{A}, \mathbf{W}, \mathbf{S}$ $\boldsymbol{\Sigma}, \boldsymbol{\Phi}$
Uppercase letters in blackboard bold	A set of numbers	$\mathbb{N}, \mathbb{R}$
	A set of parameters	$\mathbb{B}, \mathbb{W}, \mathbb{V}$
Uppercase letters in calligraphy	A set of data	$\mathcal{D}, \mathcal{D}_N$

Introduction | 1

This first chapter briefly reviews how the field of machine learning has evolved into a major discipline in computer science and engineering in the past decades. Afterward, it takes a descriptive approach and provides some simple examples to introduce basic concepts and general principles in machine learning to give readers a big picture of machine learning, as well as some general expectations on the topics that will be covered in this book. Finally, this introductory chapter concludes with a list of advanced topics in machine learning, which are currently pursued as active research topics in the machine learning community.

1.1 What Is Machine Learning?

Since its inception several decades ago, the digital computer has constantly amazed us with its unprecedented capability for computation and data storage. On the other hand, people are also extremely interested in investigating the limits on what a computer is able to do beyond the basic skills of computing and storing. The most interesting question along this line is whether the human-made machinery of digital computers can perform complex tasks that normally require human intelligence. For example, can computers be taught to play complex board games like chess and Go, transcribe and understand human speech, translate text documents from one language to another, and autonomously operate cars? These research pursuits have been normally categorized as a broad discipline in computer science and engineering under the umbrella of *artificial intelligence* (AI). However, artificial intelligence is a loosely defined term and is used colloquially to describe computers that mimic cognitive functions associated with the human mind, such as learning, perception, reasoning, and problem solving [207]. Traditionally, we tended to follow the same idea of computer programming to tackle an AI task because it was believed that we could write a large program to teach a computer to accomplish any complex task. Roughly speaking, such a program is essentially composed of a large number of "if-then" statements that are used to instruct the computer to take certain actions under certain conditions. These if-then statements are often called *rules*. All rules in an AI system are collectively called a *knowledge base* because they are often handcrafted based on the knowledge of human experts. Furthermore, some mathematical tools, such as logic and graphs, can also be adopted into some AI systems as

The term *artificial intelligence* (AI) was coined at a workshop at Dartmouth College in 1956 by John McCarthy, who was an MIT computer scientist and a founder of the AI field.

more advanced methods for knowledge representation. Once the knowledge base is established, some well-known search strategies can be used to explore all available rules in the knowledge base to make decisions for each observation. These methods are often called *symbolic* approaches [207]. Symbolic approaches were dominant in the early stage of AI because mathematically sound inference algorithms can be used to derive some highly explainable results through a transparent decision process, such as the *expert systems* popular in the 1970s and 1980s [110].

The key to the success of these knowledge-based (or rule-based) symbolic approaches lies in how to construct all necessary rules in the knowledge base. Unfortunately, this has turned out to be an insurmountable obstacle for any realistic task. First of all, the process of explicitly articulating human knowledge using some well-formulated rules is not straightforward. For example, when you see a picture of a cat, you can immediately recognize a cat, but it is difficult to express what rules you might have used to make your judgment. Second, the real world is often so complicated that it requires using an endless number of rules to cover all the different conditions in any realistic scenario. Constructing these rules manually is a tedious and daunting task. Third, even worse, as the number of rules increases in the knowledge base, it becomes impossible to maintain them. For example, some rules may contradict each other under some conditions, and we often have no good ways to detect these contradictions in a large knowledge base. Moreover, whenever we need to make an adjustment to a particular rule, this change may affect many other rules, which are not easy to identify as well. Fourth, rule-based symbolic systems do not know how to make decisions based on partial information and often fail to handle uncertainty in the decision-making process. As we know, neither partial information nor uncertainty is a major hurdle in human intelligence.

On the other hand, an alternative approach toward AI is to design learning algorithms by which computers can automatically improve their capability on any particular AI task through experience [165]. The past experience is fed to a learning algorithm as the so-called "training data" for the algorithm to learn from. The design of these learning algorithms has been motivated by different strategies, from biologically inspired learning machines [200, 206, 205] to probability-based statistical learning methods [56, 9, 112, 38]. Since the 1980s, the study of these automatic learning algorithms has quickly emerged as a prominent subfield in AI, under the name *machine learning*. The nature of automatic learning prevents machine learning from suffering the aforementioned drawbacks of the symbolic approaches. As opposed to the knowledge-based symbolic approaches, data-driven machine learning algorithms focus more on how to automatically exploit the training data to build some mathematical models in order to make decisions without having explicit programming to do so [212]. With the help of machine learning algorithms, the major burden in

The term *machine learning* was first coined in a 1959 paper [212] by Arthur Samuel, who was an IBM researcher and pioneer in the field of AI.

building an AI system has moved from the extremely challenging task of manual knowledge representation to a relatively feasible procedure of data collection. After initial success in some real-world AI applications during the 1970s and 1980s (e.g., speech recognition [9, 112] and machine translation [38]), a major paradigm shift occurred in the field of artificial intelligence—namely, the data-driven machine learning methods have replaced the traditional rule-based symbolic approaches to become the mainstream methodology for AI. As the computation power of modern computers constantly improves, machine learning has found a plethora of relevant applications in almost all engineering domains and has made a huge impact on our society.

Figure 1.1: An illustration of the pipeline of building a machine learning system, consisting of three major steps of data collection, feature generation, and model training.

As shown in Figure 1.1, the pipeline of building a successful machine learning system normally consists of three key steps. In the first stage, we need to collect a sufficient amount of training data to represent the previous experience from which computers can learn. Ideally, the training data should be collected under the same conditions in which the system will be eventually deployed. The data collected in this way are often called *in-domain* data. Many learning algorithms also require human annotators to manually label the data in such a way to facilitate the learning algorithms. As a result, it is a fairly costly process to collect in-domain training data in practice. However, the final performance of a machine learning system in any practical task is largely determined by the amount of available in-domain training data. In most cases, accessing more in-domain data is the most effective way to boost performance for any real-world application. In the second stage, we usually need to apply some domain-specific procedures to extract the so-called features out of the raw data. The features should be compact but also retain the most important information in the raw data. The feature-extraction procedures need to be manually designed based on the nature of the data and the domain knowledge, and they often vary from one domain to another. For example, a good feature to represent speech signals should be derived based on our understanding of speech itself, and it should drastically differ from a good feature to represent an image. In the final stage, we choose a learning algorithm to build some mathematical models from the extracted feature representations of the training data. The machine learning research in the past few decades has provided us with a wide range of choices in terms of which learning algorithms to use and which models to build. The main purpose of this book is to introduce different choices of machine learning methods in a systematic way. Most of these learning methods are generic enough for a variety of

A recent trend in machine learning is to replace the handcrafted features with some automatic feature extraction algorithms. The recent *end-to-end learning* tends to combine the last two steps of feature extraction and modeling into a single uniform module that can be jointly learned from the training data. We will discuss the end-to-end learning in Section 8.5.

problems and applications, and they are usually independent of domain knowledge. Therefore, most learning methods and their corresponding models can be introduced in a general manner without restricting their use to any particular application.

1.2 Basic Concepts in Machine Learning

In this section, we will use some simple examples to explain some common terminology, as well as several basic concepts widely used in machine learning.

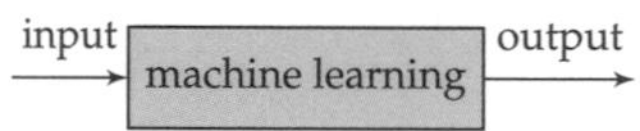

Figure 1.2: A system view of any machine learning problem.

Generally speaking, it is useful to take the system view of input and output to examine any machine learning problem, as shown in Figure 1.2. For any machine learning problem at hand, it is important to understand what its input and output are, respectively. For example, in a speech-recognition problem, the system's input is speech signals captured by a microphone, and the output is the words/sentences embedded in the signals. In an English-to-French machine translation problem, the input is a text document in English, and the output is the corresponding French translation. In a self-driving problem, the input is the videos and signals of the surrounding scenes of the car, captured by cameras and various sensors, and the output is the control signals generated to guide the steering wheel and brakes.

The system view in Figure 1.2 can also help us explain several popular machine learning terminologies.

1.2.1 Classification versus Regression

Depending on the type of the system outputs, machine learning problems can be broken down into two major categories. If the output is continuous—namely, it can take any real value within an interval—it is a *regression* problem. On the other hand, if the output is discrete—namely, it can only take a value out of a finite number of predefined choices—it is said to be a *classification* problem. For instance, speech recognition is a classification problem because the output must be constructed using a finite number of words allowed in the language. On the other hand, image generation is a regression problem because the pixels of an output image can take any arbitrary values. It is fundamentally similar in principle to solve classification and regression problems, but they often need slightly different treatments in problem formulation.

In some machine learning problems, the outputs are structured objects. These problems are referred to as *structured learning* (a.k.a. *structured prediction*) [10]. Some examples are when the output is a binary tree or a sentence following certain grammar rules.

1.2.2 Supervised versus Unsupervised Learning

As we know, all machine learning methods require collecting training data in the first place. *Supervised learning* deals with those problems where both the input and output shown in Figure 1.2 can be accessed in data collection. In other words, the training data in supervised learning consist of input–output pairs. For each input in the training data, we know its corresponding output, which can be used to guide learning algorithms as a supervision signal. Supervised learning methods are well studied in machine learning and usually guarantee good performance, as long as sufficient numbers of input–output pairs are available. However, collecting the input–output pairs for supervised learning often requires human annotation, which may be expensive in practice.

In contrast, *unsupervised learning* methods deal with the problems where we can only access the input shown in Figure 1.2 when collecting the training data. A good unsupervised learning algorithm should be able to figure out some criteria to group similar inputs together using only the information of all possible inputs, where two inputs are said to be similar only when they are expected to yield the same output label. The fundamental difficulty in unsupervised learning lies in how to know which inputs are similar when their output labels are unavailable. Unsupervised learning is a much harder problem because of the lack of supervision information. In unsupervised learning, it is usually cheaper to collect training data because it does not require extra human efforts to label each input with the corresponding output. However, unsupervised learning largely remains an open problem in machine learning. We desperately need good unsupervised learning strategies that can effectively learn from unlabeled data.

In many circumstances, unsupervised learning is also called *clustering* [66].

In between these two extremes, we can combine a small amount of labeled data with a large amount of unlabeled data during training. These learning methods are often called *semisupervised learning*. In other cases, if the true outputs shown in Figure 1.2 are too difficult or expensive to obtain, we can use other readily available information, which is only partially relevant to the true outputs, as some weak supervision signals in learning. These methods are called *weakly supervised learning*.

We know that it is difficult and costly to annotate the precise meaning of each word in text documents. However, due to the distribution hypothesis [91] in linguistics (i.e., "words that are close in meaning will occur in similar pieces of text"), the surrounding words can be used as weak supervision signals to learn the meanings of words. See Example 7.3.2.

1.2.3 Simple versus Complex Models

In machine learning, we run learning algorithms over training data to build some mathematical models for decision making. In terms of choosing the specific model to be used in learning, we usually have to make a sensible choice between simple models and complex models. The complexity of a model depends on the functional form of the model as well as the number of free parameters. In general, linear models are treated as simple models, whereas nonlinear models are viewed as complex models because nonlinear models can capture much more complicated patterns in data distributions than linear ones. A simple model requires much less computing resources and can be reliably learned from a much smaller training set. In many cases, we can derive a full theoretical analysis for simple models, which gives us a better understanding of the underlying learning process. However, the performance of simple models often saturates quickly as more training data become available. In many practical cases, simple models can only yield mediocre performance because they fail to handle complicated patterns, which are the norm in almost all real-world applications. On the other hand, complex models require much more computing resources in learning, and we need to prepare much more training data to reliably learn them. Due to their complex functional forms, there does not exist any theoretical analysis for many complex models. Hence, learning complex models is often a very awkward black-box process and usually requires many inexplicable tricks to yield optimal results.

We will introduce linear models in Chapter 6 and more complex models in Chapter 8.

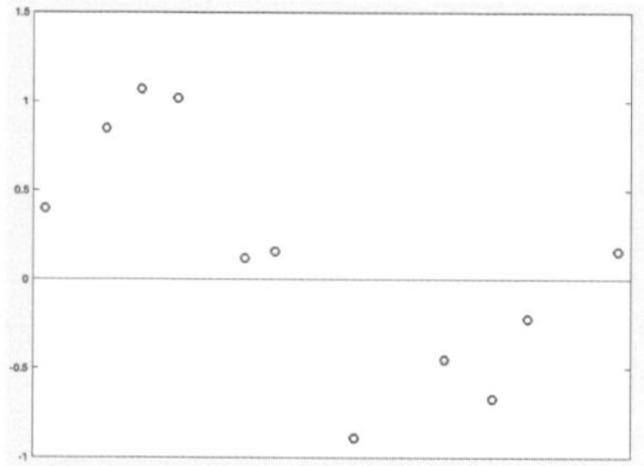

Figure 1.3: An illustration of a curve-fitting problem, which can be viewed as a regression problem in machine learning.

Example 1.2.1 *Curve Fitting*

There exists an unknown function $y = f(x)$. Assume we can only observe its function values at several isolated points, indicated by blue circles in Figure 1.3. Show how to determine its values for all other points in the interval.

This is a standard curve-fitting problem in mathematics, which requires constructing a curve, or mathematical function, to best fit these observed points. From the perspective of machine learning, this curve-fitting problem is a regression problem because it requires us to estimate the function value y, which is continuous, for any x in the interval. The observed points serve as the training data for this regression problem. Because we can access both input x and output y in the training data, it is a supervised learning problem.

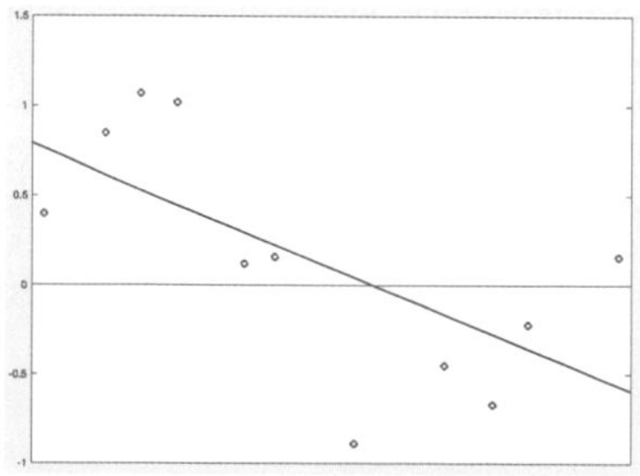

Figure 1.4: An illustration of using a linear model for the curve-fitting problem shown in Figure 1.3.

First of all, assume we construct a linear function for this problem:

$$f(x) = a_0 + a_1\, x.$$

Through a learning process that determines the two unknown coefficients (to be introduced in the later chapters), we can construct the best-fit linear function in Figure 1.4. We can see that this best-fit linear function yields values quite different from most of the observed points and has failed to capture the "up-and-down wiggly pattern" shown in the training data. This indicates that linear models may be too simple for this task. In fact, this problem can be easily solved by choosing a more complex model. A natural choice here is to use a higher-order polynomial function. We can choose a fourth-order polynomial function, as follows:

$$f(x) = a_0 + a_1\,x + a_2\,x^2 + a_3\,x^3 + a_4\,x^4.$$

After we determine all five unknown coefficients, we can find the best-fit fourth-order polynomial function, as shown in Figure 1.5. From that, we can see that this model captures the pattern in the data much better despite still yielding slightly different values at the observed points. ♦

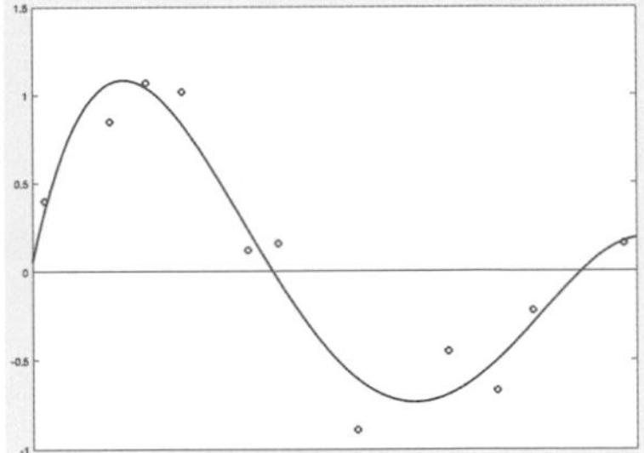

Figure 1.5: An illustration of using a fourth-order polynomial function for the curve-fitting problem.

Example 1.2.2 *Fruits Recognition*

Assume we want to teach a computer to recognize different fruits based on some observed characteristics, such as *size, color, shape,* and *taste.* Consider a suitable model that can be used for this purpose.

This is a typical classification problem because the output is discrete: it must be a known fruit (e.g., *apple, grape*). Among many choices, we can implement the tree-structured model shown in Figure 1.6 for this classification problem. In this model, each internal node is associated with a binary question regarding one aspect of the characteristics, and each leaf node corresponds to one class of fruits. For each unknown object, the decision process is simple: We start from the root node and ask the associated question for the unknown object. We then move down to a different child node based on the answer to this question. This process is repeated until a leaf node is reached. The class label of the reached leaf node is the classification result for the unknown object. This model is normally called a *decision tree* in the literature [34]. If this tree is manually constructed according to human knowledge, it is just a convenient way to represent various rules in a knowledge base. However, if we can automatically learn such a tree model from training data, it is considered to be an interesting method in machine learning, known as *decision trees.* ♦

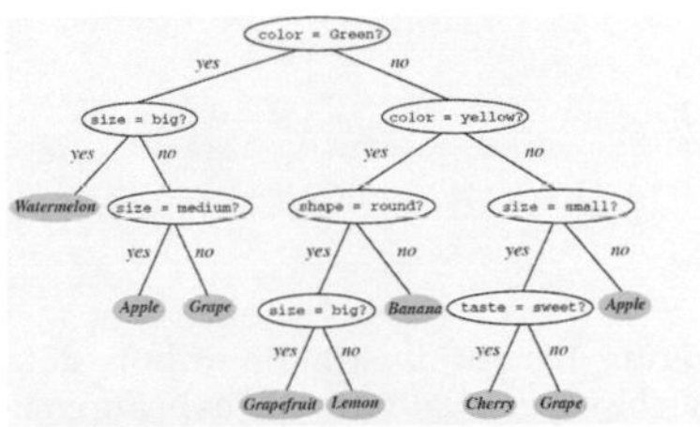

Figure 1.6: An illustration of using a decision tree to recognize various fruits based on some measured features. (Source: [57].)

We will introduce various learning methods for decision trees in Chapter 9.

1.2.4 Parametric versus Nonparametric Models

When we choose a model for a machine learning problem, there are two different types. The so-called *parametric models* (a.k.a. *finite-dimensional models*) are models that take a presumed functional form and are completely determined by a fixed set of model parameters. In the previous curve-fitting example, once we choose to use a linear model (or a fourth-order polynomial model), it can be fully specified by two (or five) coefficients. By definition, both linear and polynomial models are parametric models. In contrast, the so-called *nonparametric models* (a.k.a. *distribution-free models*) do not assume the functional form of the underlying model, and more importantly, the complexity of such a model is not fixed and may depend on the available data. In other words, a nonparametric model cannot be fully specified by a fixed number of parameters. For example, the decision tree is a typical nonparametric model. When we use a decision tree, we do not presume the functional form of the model, and the tree size is usually not fixed as well. If we have more training data, it may allow us to build a larger decision tree. Another well-known nonparametric model is the histogram. When we use a histogram to estimate a data distribution, we do not constrain the shape of the distribution, and the histogram can dramatically change as more and more samples become available.

Generally speaking, it is easier to handle parametric models than nonparametric models because we can always focus on estimating a fixed set of parameters for any parametric model. Parameter estimation is always a much simpler problem than estimating an arbitrary model without knowing of its form.

1.2.5 Overfitting versus Underfitting

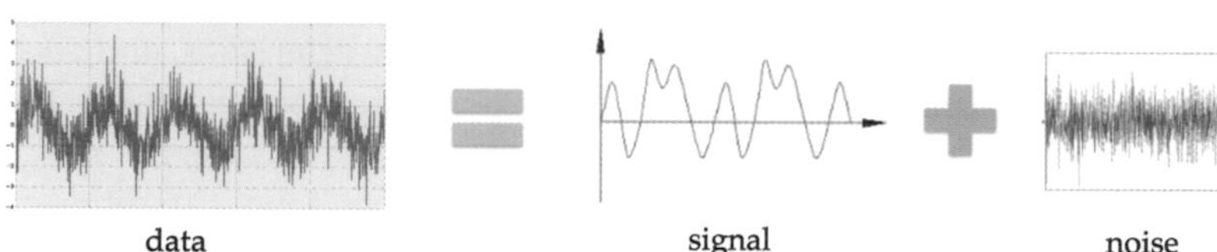

Figure 1.7: An illustration of how data can be conceptually viewed as being composed of signal and noise components.

All machine learning methods rely on training data. Intuitively speaking, training data contain the important information on certain regularities we want to learn with a model, which we informally call the *signal* component. On the other hand, training data also inevitably include some irrelevant or even distracting information, called the *noise* component. A major source of noise is the sampling variations exhibited in any finite set of random samples. If we randomly draw some samples, even from the same distribution, twice, we will not obtain identical samples. This variation can be conceptually viewed as a noise component in the collected data. Of course, noise may also come from measurement or recording errors. In general, we can conceptually represent any collected training data as a combination of two components:

$$\text{data} = \text{signal} + \text{noise}.$$

This decomposition concept is also illustrated in Figure 1.7, where we can see that the signal component represents some regularities in the data, whereas the noise component represents some unpredictable, highly fluctuating residuals. Once we have this conceptual view in mind, we can easily understand two important concepts in machine learning, namely, *underfitting* and *overfitting*.

We will formally introduce the theory behind overfitting in Chapter 5.

Assume we learn a simple model from a set of training data. If the used model is too simple to capture all regularities in the signal component, the learned model will yield very poor results even in the training data, not to mention any unseen data, which is normally called *underfitting*. Figure 1.4 clearly shows an underfitting case, where a linear function is too simple to capture the "up-and-down wiggly pattern" evident in the given data points. On the other hand, if the used model is too complex, the learning process may force a powerful model to perfectly fit the random noise component while trying to catch the regularities in the signal component. Moreover, perfectly fitting the noise component may obstruct the model from capturing all regularities in the signal component because the highly fluctuating noise can distract the learning outcome more when a complex model is used. Even worse, it is useless to perfectly fit the noise component because we will face a completely different noise component in another set of data samples. This will lead to the notorious phenomenon of *overfitting* in machine learning. Continuing with the curve fitting as an example, assume that we use a 10th-order polynomial to fit the given data points in Figure 1.3. After we learn all 11 coefficients, we can create the best-fit 10th-order polynomial model shown in Figure 1.8. As we can see, this model perfectly fits all given training samples but behaves wildly. Our intuition tells us that it yields a much poorer explanation of the data than the model in Figure 1.5.

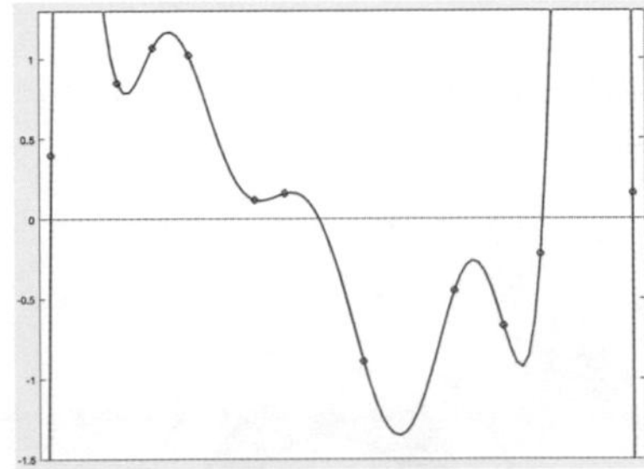

Figure 1.8: An illustration of using a 10th-order polynomial function for the previous curve-fitting problem. The best-fit model behaves wildly because the overfitting happened in the learning process.

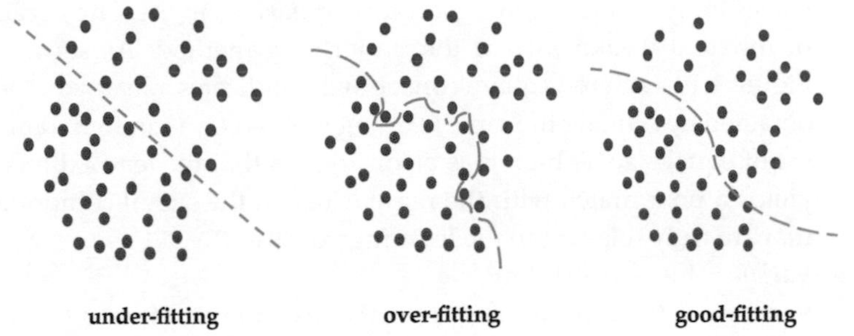

Figure 1.9: An illustration of underfitting and overfitting in a binary classification problem of two classes; the colors indicate class labels.

Not limited to regression, underfitting and overfitting can also occur in classification problems. In the simple classification problem of two classes shown in Figure 1.9, if a simple model is used for learning, it leads to a straight separation boundary between the two classes in the left figure, indicating an underfitting case because many training samples are located on the wrong side of the boundary. On the other hand, if we use a complex model in learning, it may end up with the complicated separation boundary shown in the middle figure. This implies an overfitting case because this boundary perfectly separates all training samples but is not a natural explanation of the data. Finally, among these three cases, the model on the right seems to provide the best explanation of the data set.

We should avoid underfitting and overfitting as much as possible in any machine learning problem because they both hurt the learning performance in one way or another. Underfitting occurs when the learning performance is not satisfactory even in the training set. We can easily get rid of the underfitting problem by increasing the model complexity (i.e., either increasing the number of free parameters or changing to a more complex model). On the other hand, we can identify the overfitting problem if we notice a nearly perfect performance in the training set but a fairly poor performance in another unseen evaluation set. Similarly, we can mitigate overfitting in machine learning either by augmenting more training data, or by reducing the model complexity, or by using so-called *regularization* techniques during the learning process.

We will formally discuss *regularization* in Chapter 7.

1.2.6 Bias–Variance Trade-Off

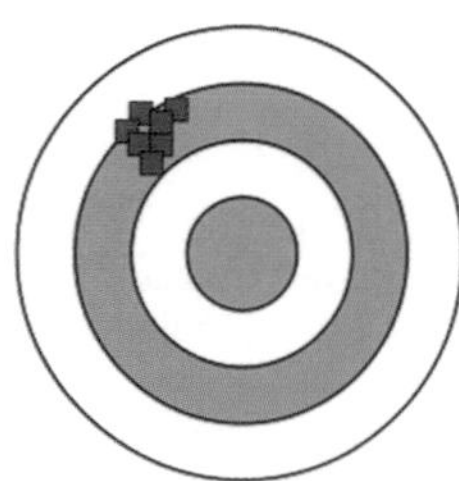

High Bias

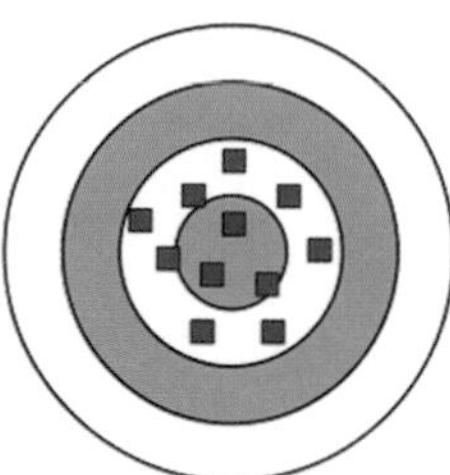

High Variance

Figure 1.10: An illustration of high bias errors versus high variances in machine learning, where each square represents a learned model from a random training set, and the center of the circles indicates the true regularities to be learned. (Image credit: Sebastian Raschka/CC-BY-SA-4.0.)

Generally speaking, the total expected error of a machine learning algorithm on an unseen data set can be decomposed into the following two sources:

- *Bias* due to underfitting:
  The bias error quantifies the inability of a learned model to capture all regularities in the signal component due to erroneous assumptions in the used model. High biases indicate that the learned model consistently misses some important regularities in the data because of inherent weaknesses of the underlying method. As shown in Figure 1.10, each red square conceptually indicates a learned model obtained by running the same learning method on a random training set of equal size. A high bias error implies that the learned model yields a poor match with the regularities in the signal component that are truly relevant to the learning goal.
- *Variance* due to overfitting:
  Variance is the error arising from the learning sensitivity to small fluctuations in the training data. In other words, variance quantifies the overfitting error of a learning method when the learned model is forced to mistakenly capture the randomness in the noise component. As shown in Figure 1.10, when variance is high, all learning results randomly deviate from the true target in a different way because each training set contains a different noise component. High variance indicates that the learned model gives a weak match with the regularities in the signal component as it randomly deviates from the true learning target from one case to another.

We will formally prove the bias and variance decomposition

$$\text{error} = \text{bias}^2 + \text{variance}.$$

in Example 2.2.2.

In precise terms, we can show that the average error of a learning algorithm can be mathematically decomposed as follows:

$$\text{learning error} = \text{bias}^2 + \text{variance}$$

As shown in Figure 1.11, when we have chosen a particular method to learn for a given problem from *a fixed amount* of training data, we cannot reduce the two sources of error at the same time. When we choose a simple model, it usually yields a low variance but a high bias error as a result of underfitting. On the other hand, when we choose a complex model, it can reduce the bias error but leads to higher variance as a result of overfitting. This phenomenon is often called the *bias–variance trade-off* in machine learning. For any particular learning problem, we can usually adjust the model complexity to find the optimal model choice that results in the lowest total learning error.

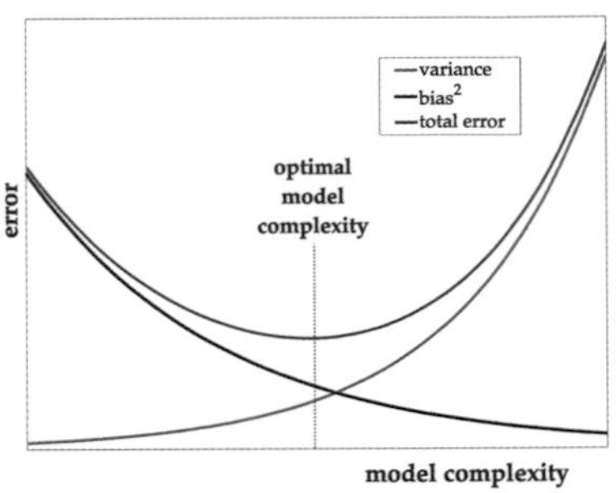

Figure 1.11: An illustration of how to manage the bias–variance trade-off by choosing the optimal model complexity in machine learning.

1.3 General Principles in Machine Learning

In this section, we will cover several general principles in machine learning, providing important insights necessary for understanding some fundamental ideas in machine learning.

1.3.1 Occam's Razor

Occam's razor is a general problem-solving principle in philosophy and science. It is sometimes paraphrased by a statement akin to "the simplest solution is most likely the right one." In the context of machine learning, Occam's razor means a preference for simplicity in model selection. If two different models are observed to yield similar performance on training data, we should prefer the simpler model to the more complicated one. Moreover, the principle of *minimum description length* (MDL) [198] is a formalization of Occam's razor in machine learning, which states that all machine learning methods aim to find regularities in data, and the best model (or hypothesis) to describe the regularities in data is also the one that can compress the data the most.

1.3.2 No-Free-Lunch Theorem

In the context of machine learning, the *no-free-lunch* theorem [253, 57, 220] states that no learning method is universally superior to other methods for all possible learning problems. Given any two machine learning algorithms, if we use them to learn all possible learning problems we can imagine, the average performance of these two algorithms must be the same. Or even worse, their average performance is no better than random guessing.

We can use the earlier curve-fitting problem as an example to explain why the no-free-lunch theorem makes sense. Given the training samples in Figure 1.3, our goal is to create a model to predict function values for other x points. No matter what learning method we use, we eventually end up with an estimated model, such as the red curve in Figure 1.12. Because we have no knowledge of the ground-truth function $y = f(x)$ other than the training samples, theoretically speaking, the ground-truth function $y = f(x)$ could take any arbitrary value for a new point, which is not in the training set. When we use the estimated model to predict function values at some new points, say, x_1 and x_2, it is easy to see that the estimated model yields a good prediction if the ground-truth function $y = f(x)$ happens to yield "good" values (as indicated by green dots in Figure 1.12). However, we can always imagine another scenario where the ground-truth function yields "bad" values (as indicated by red squares in Figure 1.12), for which the estimated model will give a very poor prediction. This is true no matter what learning algorithm we use to estimate the model. If we average the prediction performance of any estimated model over all possible scenarios for the ground-truth function, the average performance is close to a random guess because for each good-prediction case, we can also come up with any number of bad-prediction cases.

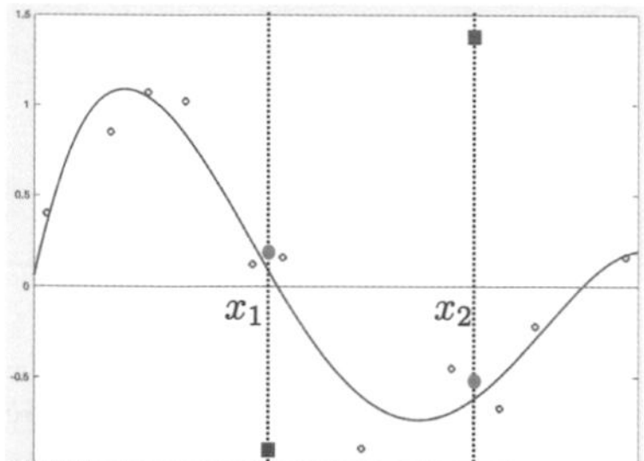

Figure 1.12: An illustration of the no-free-lunch theorem in a simple curve-fitting problem: when an estimated model (red curve) is used to predict function values at x_1 and x_2, it works well for some target functions (green dots), but meanwhile, it will work poorly for other functions (red squares).

The no-free-lunch theorem simply says that no machine learning algorithm can learn anything useful *merely* from the training data. If a machine learning method works well for some problems, the method must have explicitly or implicitly used other knowledge of the underlying problems beyond the training data.

1.3.3 Law of the Smooth World

Despite the aforementioned no-free-lunch theorem, a fundamental reason why many machine learning methods thrive in practice is that our physical world is always smooth. Because of the hard constraints that exist in reality, such as energy and power, any physical process in the macro world is smooth in nature (e.g., audios, images, videos). Furthermore, our intuition and perception are all built on top of the *law of the smooth world*. Therefore, if we use machine learning to tackle any problems arising from the real world, the law of the smooth world is always applicable, dramatically simplifying many of our learning problems at hand.

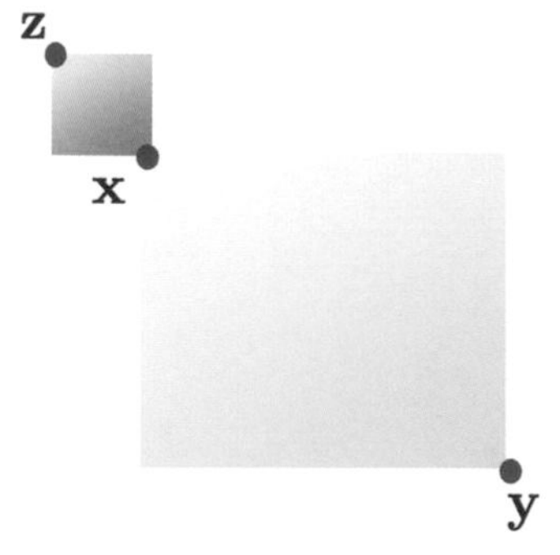

Figure 1.13: An illustration of why the law of the smooth world can simplify a machine learning problem.

For example, as shown in Figure 1.13, assume that a training set contains some measurements of a physical process at three points in the space, that is, **x**, **y**, and **z**, where **x** and **y** are located far apart, whereas **x** and **z** are close by. If we need to learn a model to predict the process in the yellow region between **x** and **y**, it is a hard problem because the training data do not provide any information for this, and many unpredictable things could happen within such a wide range. On the other hand, if we need to predict this process in the blue region between two nearby points, it should be relatively simple because the law of the smooth world significantly restricts the behavior of the process within such a narrow region given the two observations at **x** and **z**. In fact, some machine learning models can be built to give fairly accurate predictions in the blue region by simply interpolating these two observations at **x** and **z**. The exact prediction accuracy actually depends on the smoothness of the underlying process. In machine learning, such smoothness is often mathematically quantified using the concept of *Lipschitz continuity* (see margin note) or a more recent notion of *bandlimitedness* [115].

A function $f(x)$ is said to be *Lipschitz continuous* if there exists a real constant $L > 0$, for any two x_1 and x_2, where

$$\left|f(x_1) - f(x_2)\right| \leq L \left|x_1 - x_2\right|$$

always holds.

Moreover, let us go back to the no-free-lunch example in Figure 1.12. If we have enough training samples to ensure that the gaps between all samples are small enough, then many "bad" values as assumed by the no-free-lunch theorem will not actually occur in practice because they violate the law of the smooth world. As a result, when we only average all plausible scenarios in practice, suitable machine learning methods achieve much better prediction accuracy than random guessing.

Furthermore, the law of the smooth world immediately suggests a simple strategy for machine learning. Given any unknown observation, if we search over all known samples in the training set, the prediction for the unknown can be made based on the nearest sample in the training set. This leads to the famous *nearest neighbors* (NN) algorithm. In order to deal with some possible outliers in the training set, this algorithm can be extended to a more robust version, namely, the k-*nearest neighbors* (k-NN) algorithm.

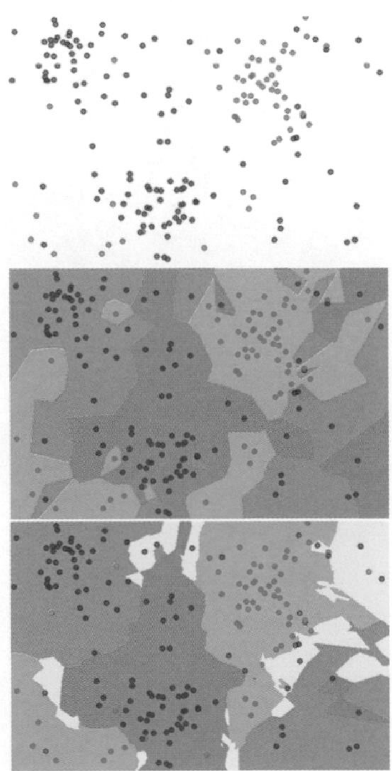

Figure 1.14: An illustration of the decision boundary of the k-nearest neighbors (k-NN) algorithm for classification:
Top panel: Three-class data (labeled by color). Middle panel: Boundary of 1-NN ($k = 1$). Bottom panel: Boundary of 5-NN ($k = 5$). (Image credit: Agor153/CC-BY-SA-3.0.)

Example 1.3.1 k-NN for Classification

For each unknown object, we search the whole training set to find the top k nearest neighbors, where k is a small positive integer to be manually specified beforehand. The class label of the unknown object is determined by a majority vote of these k-NN. If we choose $k = 1$, the object is simply assigned the class of the single nearest neighbor.

The k-NN method is conceptually simple and intuitive, and it can yield the decision boundary in the entire space based on any given training set, as shown in Figure 1.14. In many cases, the simple k-NN method can yield satisfactory classification performance. In general, the success of the k-NN method depends on two factors:

- Whether we have a good similarity measure to properly compute the distance between any two objects in the space. This topic is usually studied in a subfield of machine learning called *metric learning* [255, 136].

- Whether we have enough samples in the training set to sufficiently cover all regions in the space.

In terms of how many samples are needed to ensure good performance for the k-NN method, some theoretical analysis [220] has shown that if we want to achieve an error rate below ϵ $(0 < \epsilon < 1)$, the minimum number of training samples N required by the k-NN algorithm increases exponentially with the dimensionality of the space, denoted as d, as follows:

See Exercise Q1.1.

$$N \propto \left(\frac{\sqrt{d}}{\epsilon}\right)^{d+1}.$$

Assume we need 100 samples to achieve an error rate $\epsilon = 0.01$ for a problem in a low-dimension space (e.g., $d = 3$). But for some similar problems in a higher-dimensional space, we need a huge number of training samples in order to achieve the same performance. For example, we may need roughly 2×10^8 training samples for a similar problem in a 10-dimension space and about 7×10^{123} training samples for a similar problem in a 100-dimension space. Obviously, these numbers are prohibitively large for any practical system. This result shows that the k-NN method can effectively solve problems in a low-dimensional space but will encounter challenges when the dimensionality of problems increases. In fact, this problem is not just limited to the k-NN method but implies another general principle in machine learning, known as the *curse of dimensionality*. ♦

1.3.4 Curse of Dimensionality

In machine learning, the *curse of dimensionality* refers to the dilemma of learning in high-dimensional spaces. As shown in the previous k-NN example, as the dimensionality of learning problems grows, the volume of the underlying space increases exponentially. This typically requires an exponentially increasing amount of training data and computing resources to ensure the effectiveness of any learning methods. Moreover, our intuition of the three-dimensional physical world often fails in high dimensions [54]. The similarity-based reasoning breaks down in high dimensions as the distance measures become unreliable and counterintuitive. For example, if many samples are uniformly placed inside a unit hypercube in a high-dimensional space, it is proven that most of these samples are closer to a face of the hypercube than to their nearest neighbors.

However, the worst-case scenarios predicted by the curse of dimensionality normally occur when the data are uniformly distributed in high-dimensional spaces. Most real-world learning problems involve high-dimensional data, but the good news is that real-world data never spread evenly throughout the high-dimensional spaces. This observation is often referred to as the *blessing of nonuniformity* [54]. The blessing of nonuniformity essentially allows us to be able to effectively learn these high-dimensional problems using a reasonable amount of training data and computing resources. A nonuniform data distribution suggests that all dimensions of the data are not independent but highly correlated in such a way that many dimensions are redundant. In other words, many dimensions can be discarded without losing much information about the data distribution. This idea motivates a group of machine learning methods called *dimensionality reduction*. Alternatively, a nonuniform distribution in a high-dimensional space also suggests that the real data are only concentrated in a linear subspace or a lower-dimensional nonlinear subspace, which is often called a *manifold*. In machine learning, the so-called *manifold learning* aims to identify such lower-dimensional topological spaces where high-dimensional data are congregated.

We will introduce various dimensionality-reduction methods and manifold learning in Chapter 4.

1.4 Advanced Topics in Machine Learning

This book aims to introduce only the basic principles and methods of machine learning, mainly focusing on the well-established supervised learning methods. Chapter 3 further sketches out these topics. This section briefly lists other advanced topics in machine learning that will not be fully covered in this book. These short summaries serve as an entry point for interested readers to further explore these topics in future study.

1.4.1 Reinforcement Learning

Reinforcement learning [234] is an area in machine learning that is concerned with how to teach a computer agent to take the best possible actions in a long interaction course with an unknown environment. Different from the standard supervised learning, the learning agent in a reinforcement learning setting does not receive any strong supervision from the environment regarding what the best action is at each step. Instead, the agent only occasionally receives some numerical rewards (positive or negative). The goal in reinforcement learning is to learn what action should be taken under each condition, often called *policy*, in order to maximize the notion of a cumulative reward over the long term. Traditionally, some numerical tables are used to represent the expected cumulative rewards of various actions under each policy, leading to the so-called *Q-learning* [248]. More recently, neural networks have been used as a function approximator to compute the expected cumulative rewards. These methods are sometimes called *deep reinforcement learning* (a.k.a. *deep Q-learning*) [166].

Reinforcement learning represents a general learning framework, but it is regarded as an extremely challenging task because a learning agent must learn how to explore potentially huge search spaces only based on weak reward signals. With the help of neural networks, the deep reinforcement learning methods have recently achieved some notable successes in several closed-ended gaming settings, such as Atari video games [167] and the ancient board game Go [224], but it still remains unclear how to extend these methods to cope with open-ended tasks in a real-world environment.

1.4.2 Meta-Learning

Meta-learning (a.k.a. *learning to learn*) is a subfield of machine learning that studies how to design automatic learning algorithms to improve the performance of existing learning algorithms or to learn the algorithm itself based on some meta-data about previous learning experiments. The meta-data may include hyperparameter settings, model structures (e.g., pipeline compositions or network architectures), the learned model parameters, accuracy, and training time, as well as other measurable properties of the learning tasks [241]. Next, another optimizer, also called the *meta-learner*, is used to learn from the meta-data in order to extract knowledge and guide the search for optimal models for new tasks.

The hyperparameters of a learning algorithm are the parameters that must be manually specified prior to automatic learning (e.g., the value of k in the k-NN algorithm).

1.4.3 Causal Inference

As we know, humans often rationalize the world in terms of cause and effect, that is, the so-called causal relations between variables or events. On the other hand, typical machine learning methods can only examine the statistical correlations in data. It is well known that correlation is not equal to causation. *Causal inference* is an area of machine learning that focuses on the process of drawing causal connections between variables in order to gain a better understanding of the physical world [183, 184, 186].

1.4.4 Other Advanced Topics

Transfer learning [190] is another subfield in machine learning that focuses on how to efficiently adapt an existing machine learning model, which has learned to perform well in one domain, to a different but related domain. Hence, it is also called *domain adaption* [143, 19], which was initially studied extensively for speaker adaption in speech recognition in the 1980s [37, 77, 144].

Online learning methods [105] focus on scenarios where training data become available in a sequential order. In this case, each data sample is used to update the model as soon as it becomes available. Ideally, an online learning method does not need to store all previous data after the model has been updated so that it can also be used in some learning problems where it is computationally infeasible to train over the entire data set.

Active learning methods [219, 58] study a special case of machine learning in which a learning algorithm can interactively query a teacher to obtain necessary supervision information for desired inputs. The goal in active learning is to make the best use of proactive queries in order to learn models in the most efficient way.

Imitation learning techniques [106] aim to mimic human behaviors for a given task. A learning agent is trained to perform a task from some demonstrations by learning a mapping between observations and actions. Like reinforcement learning, imitation learning also aims to learn how to make a sequence of decisions in an unknown environment. The difference is that it is learned by observing some demonstrations rather than maximizing a cumulative reward. Therefore, imitation learning is often used in cases where the proper reward signals are difficult to specify.

Exercises

Q1.1 Is the k-NN method parametric or nonparametric? Explain why.

Q1.2 A real-valued function $f(x)$ $(x \in \mathbb{R})$ is said to be Lipschitz continuous if there exists a real constant $L > 0$, for any two points $x_1 \in \mathbb{R}$ and $x_2 \in \mathbb{R}$, where

$$\left|f(x_1) - f(x_2)\right| \leq L \left|x_1 - x_2\right|$$

always holds. If $f(x)$ is differentiable, prove that $f(x)$ is Lipschitz continuous if and only if

$$\left|f'(x)\right| \leq L$$

holds for all $x \in \mathbb{R}$.

Mathematical Foundation | 2

Before we dig into any particular machine learning method, we will first review some important subjects in mathematics and statistics because they form the foundation for almost all machine learning methods. In particular, we will cover some relevant topics in *linear algebra*, *probability and statistics*, *information theory*, and *mathematical optimization*. This chapter stresses the mathematical knowledge that is required to understand the following chapters, and meanwhile, it presents many examples to prepare readers for the notation used in this book. Moreover, the coverage in this chapter is intended to be as self-contained as possible so that readers can study it without referring to other materials. All readers are encouraged to go over this chapter first so as to become acquainted with the mathematical background as well as the notation used in the book.

2.1 Linear Algebra

2.1.1 Vectors and Matrices

A *scalar* is a single number, often denoted by a lowercase letter, such as x or n. We also use $x \in \mathbb{R}$ to indicate that x is a real-valued scalar and $n \in \mathbb{N}$ for that n is a natural number. A *vector* is a list of numbers arranged in order, denoted by a lowercase letter in bold, such as $\mathbf{x}$ or $\mathbf{y}$. All numbers in a vector can be aligned in a row or column, called a *row vector* or *column vector*, accordingly. We use $\mathbf{x} \in \mathbb{R}^n$ to indicate that $\mathbf{x}$ is an n-dimensional vector containing n real numbers. This book adopts the convention of writing a vector in a column, such as the following:

$$\mathbf{x} = \begin{bmatrix} x_1 \\ x_2 \\ \vdots \\ x_n \end{bmatrix} \qquad \mathbf{y} = \begin{bmatrix} y_1 \\ y_2 \\ \vdots \\ y_m \end{bmatrix}.$$

A *matrix* is a group of numbers arranged in a two-dimensional array, often denoted by an uppercase letter in bold, such as $\mathbf{A}$ or $\mathbf{B}$. For example, a matrix containing m rows and n columns is called an $\mathrm{m} \times \mathrm{n}$ *matrix*, represented as

$$\mathbf{A} = \begin{bmatrix} a_{11} & a_{12} & \cdots & a_{1n} \\ a_{21} & a_{22} & \cdots & a_{2n} \\ \vdots & \vdots & \ddots & \vdots \\ a_{m1} & a_{m2} & \cdots & a_{mn} \end{bmatrix}.$$

Along the same lines, we can arrange a group of numbers in a three-dimensional or higher-dimensional array, which is often called a *tensor*.

We use $\mathbf{A} \in \mathbb{R}^{m \times n}$ to indicate that $\mathbf{A}$ is an $m \times n$ matrix containing all real numbers.

2.1.2 Linear Transformation as Matrix Multiplication

A common question that beginners have is why we need vectors and matrices and what we can do with them. We can easily spot that vectors may be viewed as special matrices. However, it must be noted that vectors and matrices represent very different concepts in mathematics. An n-dimensional vector can be viewed as a point in an n-dimensional space if we interpret each number in the vector as the coordinate along an axis. Each axis in turn can be viewed as some measurement of one particular characteristic of an object. In other words, vectors can be viewed as an abstract way to represent objects in mathematics. On the other hand, a matrix represents a motion of all points in a space (i.e., one particular way to move any point in a space into a different position in another space). Alternatively, a matrix can be viewed as a particular way to transform the representations of objects from one space to another. More importantly, the exact algorithm to implement such motion is to take advantage of a matrix operation, called *matrix multiplication*, which is defined as shown in Figure 2.1.

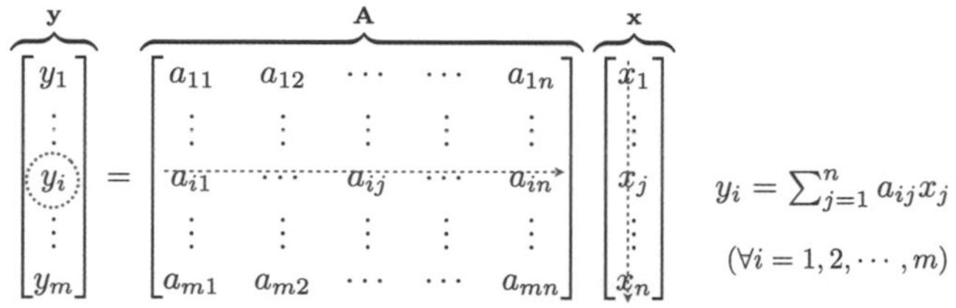

$$\overbrace{\begin{bmatrix} y_1 \\ \vdots \\ y_i \\ \vdots \\ y_m \end{bmatrix}}^{\mathbf{y}} = \overbrace{\begin{bmatrix} a_{11} & a_{12} & \cdots & \cdots & a_{1n} \\ \vdots & \vdots & \vdots & \vdots & \vdots \\ a_{i1} & \cdots & a_{ij} & \cdots & a_{in} \\ \vdots & \vdots & \vdots & \vdots & \vdots \\ a_{m1} & a_{m2} & \cdots & \cdots & a_{mn} \end{bmatrix}}^{\mathbf{A}} \overbrace{\begin{bmatrix} x_1 \\ \vdots \\ x_j \\ \vdots \\ x_n \end{bmatrix}}^{\mathbf{x}} \qquad y_i = \sum_{j=1}^{n} a_{ij} x_j \quad (\forall i = 1, 2, \cdots, m)$$

Figure 2.1: An illustration of how to implement linear transformation using matrix multiplication.

We denote this as $\mathbf{y} = \mathbf{A}\mathbf{x}$ for short. Using the matrix multiplication, any point $\mathbf{x}$ in the first space $\mathbb{R}^n$ is transformed into another point $\mathbf{y}$ in a different space $\mathbb{R}^m$. The exact mapping between $\mathbf{x}$ and $\mathbf{y}$ depends on all numbers in the matrix $\mathbf{A}$. If $\mathbf{A}$ is a square matrix in $\mathbb{R}^{n \times n}$, this mapping can also be viewed as transforming one point $\mathbf{x} \in \mathbb{R}^n$ into another point $\mathbf{y}$ in the same space $\mathbb{R}^n$.

However, this matrix multiplication cannot implement any arbitrary mapping between two spaces. The matrix multiplication actually can only implement a small subset of all possible mappings called *linear transformations*. As shown in Figure 2.2, a linear transformation is a mapping from the first space $\mathbb{R}^n$ to another space $\mathbb{R}^m$ that must satisfy two conditions: (i) the origin in $\mathbb{R}^n$ is mapped to the origin in $\mathbb{R}^m$; (ii) every straight line in $\mathbb{R}^n$ is always mapped to a straight line (or a single point) in $\mathbb{R}^m$. Other mappings that do not satisfy these two conditions are called *nonlinear transformations*, which must be implemented by other methods rather than matrix multiplication.

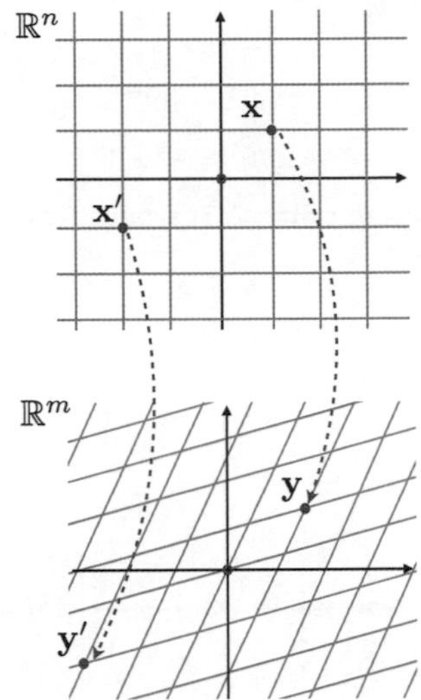

Figure 2.2: An illustration of mapping a point from one space $\mathbb{R}^n$ to another space $\mathbb{R}^m$ through a linear transformation.

This matrix multiplication method can be done between two matrices. For example, we can have the following:

$$\underbrace{\begin{bmatrix} c_{11} & \cdots & c_{1n} \\ \vdots & c_{ij} & \vdots \\ c_{m1} & \cdots & c_{mn} \end{bmatrix}}_{\mathbf{C}} = \text{i-th row} \underbrace{\begin{bmatrix} a_{11} & \cdots & a_{1r} \\ \vdots & a_{ik} & \vdots \\ a_{m1} & \cdots & a_{mr} \end{bmatrix}}_{\mathbf{A}} \overset{\text{j-th column}}{\underbrace{\begin{bmatrix} b_{11} & \cdots & b_{1n} \\ \vdots & b_{kj} & \vdots \\ b_{r1} & \cdots & b_{rn} \end{bmatrix}}_{\mathbf{B}}} \qquad \begin{array}{c} c_{ij} = \sum_{k=1}^{r} a_{ik} b_{kj} \\ \forall i = 1, 2, \cdots, m \\ \forall j = 1, 2, \cdots, n \end{array}$$

We denote this as $\mathbf{C} = \mathbf{AB}$ for short. Note that the column number of the first matrix $\mathbf{A}$ must match the row number of the second matrix $\mathbf{B}$ so that they can be multiplied together.

Conceptually speaking, this matrix multiplication corresponds to a composition of two linear transformations. As shown in Figure 2.3, $\mathbf{A}$ represents a linear transformation from the first space $\mathbb{R}^n$ to the second space $\mathbb{R}^r$, and $\mathbf{B}$ represents another linear transformation from the second space $\mathbb{R}^r$ to the third space $\mathbb{R}^m$. The matrix multiplication $\mathbf{C} = \mathbf{AB}$ composes these two transformations to derive a direct linear transformation from the first space $\mathbb{R}^n$ to the third one $\mathbb{R}^m$. Because this process has to go through the same space in the middle, these two matrices must match each other in their dimensions, as described previously.

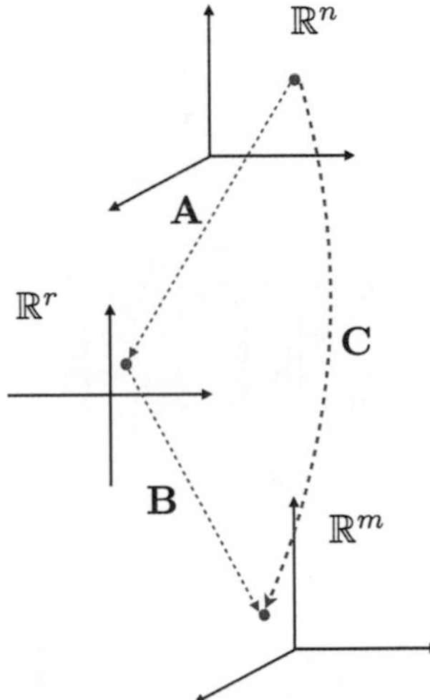

Figure 2.3: An illustration of composing two linear transformations into another linear transformation by matrix multiplication.

2.1.3 Basic Matrix Operations

The transpose of a matrix $\mathbf{A}$ is an operator that flips the matrix over its diagonal so that all rows become columns, and vice versa. The new matrix is denoted as $\mathbf{A}^\intercal$. If $\mathbf{A}$ is an $m \times n$ matrix, then $\mathbf{A}^\intercal$ will be an $n \times m$ matrix.

$$\mathbf{A} = \begin{bmatrix} a_{11} & a_{12} & \cdots & \cdots & a_{1n} \\ \vdots & \vdots & \vdots & \vdots & \vdots \\ a_{i1} & \cdots & a_{ij} & \cdots & a_{in} \\ \vdots & \vdots & \vdots & \vdots & \vdots \\ a_{m1} & a_{m2} & \cdots & \cdots & a_{mn} \end{bmatrix} \Longrightarrow \mathbf{A}^\intercal = \begin{bmatrix} a_{11} & a_{21} & \cdots & \cdots & a_{m1} \\ \vdots & \vdots & \vdots & \vdots & \vdots \\ a_{1i} & \cdots & a_{ji} & \cdots & a_{mi} \\ \vdots & \vdots & \vdots & \vdots & \vdots \\ a_{1n} & a_{2n} & \cdots & \cdots & a_{mn} \end{bmatrix}$$

We have

$$(\mathbf{A}^\intercal)^\intercal = \mathbf{A}$$
$$(\mathbf{A}\mathbf{B})^\intercal = \mathbf{B}^\intercal\mathbf{A}^\intercal$$
$$(\mathbf{A} \pm \mathbf{B})^\intercal = \mathbf{A}^\intercal \pm \mathbf{B}^\intercal$$

A square matrix $\mathbf{A}$ is symmetric if and only if

$$\mathbf{A}^\intercal = \mathbf{A}.$$

$$\mathbf{w} = \begin{bmatrix} w_1 \\ w_2 \\ \vdots \\ w_n \end{bmatrix} \implies \mathbf{w}^\intercal = \begin{bmatrix} w_1 & w_2 & \cdots & w_n \end{bmatrix}.$$

For any square matrix $\mathbf{A} \in \mathbb{R}^{n \times n}$, we can compute a real number for it, called the *determinant*, denoted as $|\mathbf{A}|$ ($\in \mathbb{R}$). As we know, a square matrix $\mathbf{A}$ represents a linear transformation from $\mathbb{R}^n$ to $\mathbb{R}^n$, and it will transform any unit hypercube in the original space into a polyhedron in the new space. The determinant $|\mathbf{A}|$ represents the volume of the polyhedron in the new space.

$$\mathbf{I} = \begin{bmatrix} 1 & 0 & \cdots & 0 \\ 0 & 1 & \vdots & 0 \\ \vdots & \vdots & \ddots & \vdots \\ 0 & 0 & \cdots & 1 \end{bmatrix}$$

For any $\mathbf{A} \in \mathbb{R}^{n \times n}$, we have

$$\mathbf{A}\mathbf{I} = \mathbf{I}\mathbf{A} = \mathbf{A}.$$

We can verify that

$$|\mathbf{A}^{-1}| = \frac{1}{|\mathbf{A}|}.$$

We often use $\mathbf{I}$ to represent a special square matrix, called an *identity* matrix, that has all 1s in its diagonal and 0s everywhere else. For a square matrix $\mathbf{A}$, if we can find another square matrix, denoted as $\mathbf{A}^{-1}$, that satisfies

$$\mathbf{A}^{-1}\mathbf{A} = \mathbf{A}\mathbf{A}^{-1} = \mathbf{I},$$

we call $\mathbf{A}^{-1}$ the inverse matrix of $\mathbf{A}$. We say $\mathbf{A}$ is invertible if its inverse matrix $\mathbf{A}^{-1}$ exists.

$$\mathbf{w} = \begin{bmatrix} w_1 \\ w_2 \\ \vdots \\ w_n \end{bmatrix} \qquad \mathbf{x} = \begin{bmatrix} x_1 \\ x_2 \\ \vdots \\ x_n \end{bmatrix}$$

The inner product between any two n-dimensional vectors (e.g., $\mathbf{w} \in \mathbb{R}^n$ and $\mathbf{x} \in \mathbb{R}^n$) is defined as the sum of all element-wise multiplications between them, denoted as $\mathbf{w} \cdot \mathbf{x}$ ($\in \mathbb{R}$) . We can further represent the inner product using the matrix transpose and multiplication as follows:

$$\mathbf{w} \cdot \mathbf{x} \triangleq \sum_{i=1}^{n} w_i x_i = \mathbf{w}^\intercal \mathbf{x} = \mathbf{x}^\intercal \mathbf{w}.$$

The norm of a vector $\mathbf{w}$ (a.k.a. the L_2 norm), denoted as $\|\mathbf{w}\|$, is defined as the square root of the inner product with itself. The meaning of the norm $\|\mathbf{w}\|$ represents the length of the vector $\mathbf{w}$ in the Euclidean space:

$$\|\mathbf{w}\|^2 = \mathbf{w} \cdot \mathbf{w} = \sum_{i=1}^{n} w_i^2 = \mathbf{w}^\intercal \mathbf{w}.$$

Example 2.1.1 Given two n-dimensional vectors, $\mathbf{x} \in \mathbb{R}^n$ and $\mathbf{z} \in \mathbb{R}^n$, and an $n \times n$ matrix $\mathbf{A} \in \mathbb{R}^{n \times n}$, reparameterize the following norms using matrix multiplication:

$$\|\mathbf{z} - \mathbf{x}\|^2 \qquad \text{and} \qquad \|\mathbf{z} - \mathbf{A}\mathbf{x}\|^2.$$

$$\|\mathbf{z} - \mathbf{x}\|^2 = (\mathbf{z} - \mathbf{x})^\intercal (\mathbf{z} - \mathbf{x}) = (\mathbf{z}^\intercal - \mathbf{x}^\intercal)(\mathbf{z} - \mathbf{x}) = \mathbf{z}^\intercal \mathbf{z} + \mathbf{x}^\intercal \mathbf{x} - 2\,\mathbf{z}^\intercal \mathbf{x}.$$

$$\begin{aligned}\|\mathbf{z}-\mathbf{A}\mathbf{x}\|^2 &= (\mathbf{z}-\mathbf{A}\mathbf{x})^\intercal(\mathbf{z}-\mathbf{A}\mathbf{x}) = (\mathbf{z}^\intercal-\mathbf{x}^\intercal\mathbf{A}^\intercal)(\mathbf{z}-\mathbf{A}\mathbf{x})\\ &= \mathbf{z}^\intercal\mathbf{z}+\mathbf{x}^\intercal\mathbf{A}^\intercal\mathbf{A}\mathbf{x}-2\,\mathbf{z}^\intercal\mathbf{A}\mathbf{x}\end{aligned}$$

♦

We can verify:

$$\mathbf{z}^\intercal\mathbf{x} = \mathbf{x}^\intercal\mathbf{z}$$

$$\mathbf{z}^\intercal\mathbf{A}\mathbf{x} = \mathbf{x}^\intercal\mathbf{A}^\intercal\mathbf{z}$$

because we have the following:

1. Both sides of each question are symmetric to each other because transposing the left-hand side leads to the right.
2. All of them are actually scalars.

Example 2.1.2 Given an n-dimensional vector, $\mathbf{x} \in \mathbb{R}^n$, compare $\mathbf{x}^\intercal\mathbf{x}$ with $\mathbf{x}\,\mathbf{x}^\intercal$.

We can first show that

$$\mathbf{x}^\intercal\mathbf{x} = \begin{bmatrix} x_1 & x_2 & \cdots & x_n\end{bmatrix}\begin{bmatrix} x_1\\ x_2\\ \vdots\\ x_n\end{bmatrix} = \sum_{i=1}^{n} x_i^2.$$

On the other hand, we have

$$\mathbf{x}\,\mathbf{x}^\intercal = \begin{bmatrix} x_1\\ x_2\\ \vdots\\ x_n\end{bmatrix}\begin{bmatrix} x_1 & x_2 & \cdots & x_n\end{bmatrix} = \begin{bmatrix} x_1^2 & x_1x_2 & \cdots & x_1x_n\\ x_1x_2 & x_2^2 & \cdots & x_2x_n\\ \vdots & \vdots & \ddots & \vdots\\ x_1x_n & x_2x_n & \cdots & x_n^2\end{bmatrix}.$$

Therefore, $\mathbf{x}\,\mathbf{x}^\intercal$ is actually an $n \times n$ symmetric matrix. ♦

The trace of a square matrix $\mathbf{A} \in \mathbb{R}^{n\times n}$ is defined to be the sum of all elements on the main diagonal of $\mathbf{A}$, denoted as $\mathrm{tr}(\mathbf{A})$; we thus have

$$\mathrm{tr}(\mathbf{A}) = \sum_{i=1}^{n} a_{ii}.$$

We can verify that $\mathbf{x}^\intercal\mathbf{x} = \mathrm{tr}(\mathbf{x}\,\mathbf{x}^\intercal)$ in this example.

For any two matrices, $\mathbf{A} \in \mathbb{R}^{m\times n}$ and $\mathbf{B} \in \mathbb{R}^{m\times n}$, we can verify that

$$\begin{aligned}\mathrm{tr}(\mathbf{A}^\intercal\mathbf{B}) &= \mathrm{tr}(\mathbf{A}\mathbf{B}^\intercal)\\ &= \mathrm{tr}(\mathbf{B}\mathbf{A}^\intercal) = \mathrm{tr}(\mathbf{B}^\intercal\mathbf{A})\\ &= \sum_{i=1}^{m}\sum_{j=1}^{n} a_{ij}b_{ij}.\end{aligned}$$

For any two square matrices (i.e., $\mathbf{X} \in \mathbb{R}^{n\times n}$ and $\mathbf{Y} \in \mathbb{R}^{n\times n}$), we can also verify

$$\mathrm{tr}(\mathbf{X}\mathbf{Y}) = \mathrm{tr}(\mathbf{Y}\mathbf{X}).$$

2.1.4 Eigenvalues and Eigenvectors

Given a square matrix $\mathbf{A} \in \mathbb{R}^{n\times n}$, we can find a nonzero vector $\mathbf{u} \in \mathbb{R}^n$ that satisfies

$$\mathbf{A}\,\mathbf{u} = \lambda\,\mathbf{u},$$

where λ is a scalar. We call $\mathbf{u}$ an *eigenvector* of $\mathbf{A}$, and λ is an *eigenvalue* corresponding to $\mathbf{u}$. As we have learned, a square matrix $\mathbf{A}$ can be viewed as a linear transformation that maps any point in a space $\mathbb{R}^n$ into another point in the same space. An eigenvector $\mathbf{u}$ represents a special point in the space whose direction is not changed by this linear transformation. Depending on the corresponding eigenvalue λ, it can be stretched or contracted along the original direction. If the eigenvalue λ is negative, it is flipped into the opposite direction after the mapping. The eigenvalues and eigenvectors are completely determined by matrix **A** itself and are considered as an inherent characteristic of matrix **A**.

Any two vectors, $\mathbf{u}_i$ and $\mathbf{u}_j$, are orthogonal if and only if

$$\mathbf{u}_i \cdot \mathbf{u}_j = 0.$$

Example 2.1.3 Given $\mathbf{A} \in \mathbb{R}^{n \times n}$, assume we can find n orthogonal eigenvectors $\mathbf{u}_i$ ($i = 1, 2, \cdots, n$) as follows:

$$\mathbf{A}\,\mathbf{u}_i = \lambda_i\,\mathbf{u}_i \quad (\text{assuming } \|\mathbf{u}_i\|^2 = 1),$$

where λ_i is the eigenvalue corresponding to $\mathbf{u}_i$. Show that the matrix **A** can be factorized.

First, we align both sides of the equations column by column:

$$\begin{bmatrix} | & | & & | \\ \mathbf{A}\mathbf{u}_1 & \mathbf{A}\mathbf{u}_2 & \cdots & \mathbf{A}\mathbf{u}_n \\ | & | & & | \end{bmatrix} = \begin{bmatrix} | & | & & | \\ \lambda_1\mathbf{u}_1 & \lambda_2\mathbf{u}_2 & \cdots & \lambda_n\mathbf{u}_n \\ | & | & & | \end{bmatrix}.$$

Next, we can move **A** out in the left-hand side and arrange the right-hand side into two matrices according to the multiplication rule:

$$\mathbf{A}\underbrace{\begin{bmatrix} | & | & & | \\ \mathbf{u}_1 & \mathbf{u}_2 & \cdots & \mathbf{u}_n \\ | & | & & | \end{bmatrix}}_{\mathbf{U}} = \underbrace{\begin{bmatrix} | & | & & | \\ \mathbf{u}_1 & \mathbf{u}_2 & \cdots & \mathbf{u}_n \\ | & | & & | \end{bmatrix}}_{\mathbf{U}} \underbrace{\begin{bmatrix} \lambda_1 & 0 & \cdots & 0 \\ 0 & \lambda_2 & \cdots & 0 \\ \vdots & \vdots & \ddots & \vdots \\ 0 & 0 & \cdots & \lambda_n \end{bmatrix}}_{\mathbf{\Lambda}},$$

A diagonal matrix has nonzero elements only on the main diagonal.

where the matrix $\mathbf{U} \in \mathbb{R}^{n \times n}$ is constructed by using all eigenvectors as its columns, and $\mathbf{\Lambda} \in \mathbb{R}^{n \times n}$ is a diagonal matrix with all eigenvalues aligned on the main diagonal. Because all eigenvectors are normed to 1 and they are orthogonal to each other, we have

$$\mathbf{u}_i^\intercal \mathbf{u}_j = \begin{cases} 1 & i = j \\ 0 & i \neq j \end{cases}.$$

Therefore, we can show that $\mathbf{U}^\intercal\mathbf{U} = \mathbf{I}$. This means that $\mathbf{U}^{-1} = \mathbf{U}^\intercal$. If we multiply the previous equation by this from the right, we finally derive

$$\mathbf{A} = \mathbf{U}\,\mathbf{\Lambda}\,\mathbf{U}^\intercal.$$

♦

The idea of eigenvalues can be extended to nonsquare matrices, leading to the so-called *singular values*. A nonsquare matrix $\mathbf{A} \in \mathbb{R}^{m \times n}$ can be similarly factorized using the *singular value decomposition (SVD)* method. (See Section 7.3 for more.)

A square matrix $\mathbf{A} \in \mathbb{R}^{n \times n}$ is said to be *positive definite* (or *positive semidefinite*) if $\mathbf{x}^\intercal\mathbf{A}\mathbf{x} > 0$ (or ≥ 0) holds for any $\mathbf{x} \in \mathbb{R}^n$, denoted as $\mathbf{A} \succ 0$ (or $\mathbf{A} \succeq 0$). A symmetric matrix **A** is positive definite (or semidefinite) if and only if all of its eigenvalues are positive (or nonnegative).

2.1.5 Matrix Calculus

In mathematics, matrix calculus is a specialized notation to conduct multivariate calculus with respect to vectors or matrices. If y is a function involving all elements of a vector $\mathbf{x}$ (or a matrix $\mathbf{A}$), then $\partial y/\partial \mathbf{x}$ (or $\partial y/\partial \mathbf{A}$) is defined as a vector (or a matrix) in the same size as $\mathbf{x}$ (or $\mathbf{A}$), where each element is defined as a partial derivative of y with respect to the corresponding element in $\mathbf{x}$ (or $\mathbf{A}$).

Assuming we are given

$$\mathbf{x} = \begin{bmatrix} x_1 \\ x_2 \\ \vdots \\ x_n \end{bmatrix} \quad \text{and} \quad \mathbf{A} = \begin{bmatrix} a_{11} & a_{12} & \cdots & a_{1n} \\ a_{21} & a_{22} & \cdots & a_{2n} \\ \vdots & \vdots & \ddots & \vdots \\ a_{m1} & a_{m2} & \cdots & a_{mn} \end{bmatrix},$$

then we have

$$\frac{\partial y}{\partial \mathbf{x}} \triangleq \begin{bmatrix} \frac{\partial y}{\partial x_1} \\ \frac{\partial y}{\partial x_2} \\ \vdots \\ \frac{\partial y}{\partial x_n} \end{bmatrix} \quad \text{and} \quad \frac{\partial y}{\partial \mathbf{A}} \triangleq \begin{bmatrix} \frac{\partial y}{\partial a_{11}} & \frac{\partial y}{\partial a_{12}} & \cdots & \frac{\partial y}{\partial a_{1n}} \\ \frac{\partial y}{\partial a_{21}} & \frac{\partial y}{\partial a_{22}} & \cdots & \frac{\partial y}{\partial a_{2n}} \\ \vdots & \vdots & \ddots & \vdots \\ \frac{\partial y}{\partial a_{m1}} & \frac{\partial y}{\partial a_{m2}} & \cdots & \frac{\partial y}{\partial a_{mn}} \end{bmatrix}.$$

Example 2.1.4 Given $\mathbf{x} \in \mathbb{R}^n$ and $\mathbf{A} \in \mathbb{R}^{n\times n}$, show the following identities:

$$\frac{\partial}{\partial \mathbf{x}}\left(\mathbf{x}^\intercal \mathbf{A}\mathbf{x}\right) = \mathbf{A}\mathbf{x} + \mathbf{A}^\intercal \mathbf{x} \qquad \frac{\partial}{\partial \mathbf{A}}\left(\mathbf{x}^\intercal \mathbf{A}\mathbf{x}\right) = \mathbf{x}\mathbf{x}^\intercal.$$

Let's denote $y = \mathbf{x}^\intercal \mathbf{A}\mathbf{x}$; we thus have

$$y = \begin{bmatrix} x_1 & \cdots & x_n \end{bmatrix} \begin{bmatrix} a_{11} & \cdots & a_{1n} \\ \vdots & \ddots & \vdots \\ a_{n1} & \cdots & a_{nn} \end{bmatrix} \begin{bmatrix} x_1 \\ \vdots \\ x_n \end{bmatrix} = \sum_{i=1}^{n}\sum_{j=1}^{n} x_i a_{ij} x_j.$$

For any $t \in \{1, 2, \cdots, n\}$, we have

$$\frac{\partial y}{\partial x_t} = \underbrace{\sum_{j=1}^{n} a_{tj} x_j}_{\text{when } i=t} + \underbrace{\sum_{i=1}^{n} x_i a_{it}}_{\text{when } j=t}.$$

If we denote $\mathbf{A}\mathbf{x} + \mathbf{A}^\intercal \mathbf{x}$ as a column vector:

$$\mathbf{A}\mathbf{x} + \mathbf{A}^\intercal \mathbf{x} = \begin{bmatrix} z_1 & z_2 & \cdots & z_n \end{bmatrix}^\intercal,$$

$$\mathbf{A}\mathbf{x} + \mathbf{A}^\intercal \mathbf{x} = \begin{bmatrix} z_1 \\ z_2 \\ \vdots \\ z_n \end{bmatrix}$$

then for any $t \in \{1, 2, \cdots, n\}$, we can compute

$$z_t = \sum_{j=1}^{n} a_{tj} x_j + \sum_{i=1}^{n} x_i a_{it}.$$

Therefore, we have proved that $(\partial/\partial\mathbf{x})(\mathbf{x}^\intercal\mathbf{A}\mathbf{x}) = \mathbf{A}\mathbf{x} + \mathbf{A}^\intercal\mathbf{x}$.

Similarly, we can compute

$$\frac{\partial y}{\partial a_{ij}} = x_i x_j \qquad (\forall i, j \in \{1, 2, \cdots, n\}).$$

Then we have

$$\frac{\partial y}{\partial \mathbf{A}} = \begin{bmatrix} x_1^2 & x_1 x_2 & \cdots & x_1 x_n \\ x_1 x_2 & x_2^2 & \cdots & x_2 x_n \\ \vdots & \vdots & \ddots & \vdots \\ x_1 x_n & x_2 x_n & \cdots & x_n^2 \end{bmatrix}.$$

As shown in Example 2.1.2, this matrix equals to $\mathbf{x}\mathbf{x}^\intercal$. Therefore, we have shown that $(\partial/\partial\mathbf{A})(\mathbf{x}^\intercal\mathbf{A}\mathbf{x}) = \mathbf{x}\mathbf{x}^\intercal$ holds. ♦

The following box lists all matrix calculus identities that will be used in the remainder of this book. Readers are encouraged to examine them for future reference.

Matrix Calculus Identities for Machine Learning

$$\frac{\partial}{\partial \mathbf{x}}\left(\mathbf{x}^\intercal\mathbf{x}\right) = 2\mathbf{x}$$

$$\frac{\partial}{\partial \mathbf{x}}\left(\mathbf{x}^\intercal\mathbf{y}\right) = \mathbf{y}$$

$$\frac{\partial}{\partial \mathbf{x}}\left(\mathbf{x}^\intercal\mathbf{A}\mathbf{x}\right) = \mathbf{A}\mathbf{x} + \mathbf{A}^\intercal\mathbf{x}$$

$$\frac{\partial}{\partial \mathbf{x}}\left(\mathbf{x}^\intercal\mathbf{A}\mathbf{x}\right) = 2\mathbf{A}\mathbf{x} \quad (\text{symmetric } \mathbf{A})$$

$$\frac{\partial}{\partial \mathbf{A}}\left(\mathbf{x}^\intercal\mathbf{A}\mathbf{y}\right) = \mathbf{x}\mathbf{y}^\intercal$$

$$\frac{\partial}{\partial \mathbf{A}}\left(\mathbf{x}^\intercal\mathbf{A}^{-1}\mathbf{y}\right) = -(\mathbf{A}^\intercal)^{-1}\mathbf{x}\mathbf{y}^\intercal(\mathbf{A}^\intercal)^{-1} \quad (\text{square } \mathbf{A})$$

$$\frac{\partial}{\partial \mathbf{A}}\left(\ln|\mathbf{A}|\right) = (\mathbf{A}^{-1})^\intercal = (\mathbf{A}^\intercal)^{-1} \quad (\text{square } \mathbf{A})$$

$$\frac{\partial}{\partial \mathbf{A}}\left(\mathrm{tr}(\mathbf{A})\right) = \mathbf{I} \quad (\text{square } \mathbf{A})$$

2.2 Probability and Statistics

Probability theory is a mathematical tool to deal with uncertainty. Probability is a real number between 0 and 1, assigned to indicate how likely an event is to occur in an experiment. The higher the probability of an event, the more likely it is the event will occur. A sample space is defined as a collection of all possible outcomes in an experiment. Any subset of the sample space can be viewed as an event. The probability of a null event is 0, and that of the full sample space is 1. For example, in an experiment of tossing a fair six-faced dice only once, the sample space includes six outcomes in total: $\{1, 2, \cdots, 6\}$. We can define many events for this experiment, such as A = "observing an even number," B = "observing the digit 6," C = "observing a natural number," and D = "observing a negative number". We can easily calculate the probabilities for these events as $\Pr(A) = 1/2$, $\Pr(B) = 1/6$, $\Pr(C) = 1$, and $\Pr(D) = 0$.

2.2.1 Random Variables and Distributions

Random variables are a formal tool to study a random phenomenon in mathematics. A *random variable* is defined as a variable whose values depend on the outcomes of a random experiment. In other words, a random variable could take different values in different probabilities based on the experimental outcomes. Depending on all possible values a random variable can take, there are two types of random variables: discrete and continuous. A *discrete random variable* can take on only a finite set of distinct values. For example, if we define a random variable X to indicate the digit observed in the previous dice-tossing experiment, X is a discrete random variable that can take only six different values. On the other hand, a *continuous random variable* may take an infinite number of possible values. For example, if we define another random variable Y to indicate a temperature measurement by a thermometer, Y is continuous because it may take any real number.

If we want to fully specify a random variable, we have to state two ingredients for it: (i) its *domain*, the set of all possible values that the random variable can take, and (ii) its *probability distribution*, how likely it is that the random variable may take each possible value. In probability theory, these two ingredients are often characterized by a probability function.

For any discrete random variable X, we can specify these two ingredients with the so-called *probability mass function (p.m.f.)*, which is defined on the domain of X (i.e., $\{x_1, x_2, \cdots\}$) as follows:

$$p(x) = \Pr(X = x) \quad \text{for all} \quad x \in \{x_1, x_2, \cdots\}.$$

x	x_1	x_2	x_3	x_4
$p(x)$	0.4	0.3	0.2	0.1

A p.m.f. of a random variable X that takes four distinct values (i.e. $\{x_1, x_2, x_3, x_4\}$) in the probabilities specified in the table.

If we sum $p(x)$ over all values in the domain, it satisfies the sum-to-1 constraint:

$$\sum_x p(x) = 1. \tag{2.1}$$

A p.m.f. can be conveniently represented in a table. The table shown in the left margin represents a simple p.m.f. of a random variable that can take four distinct values.

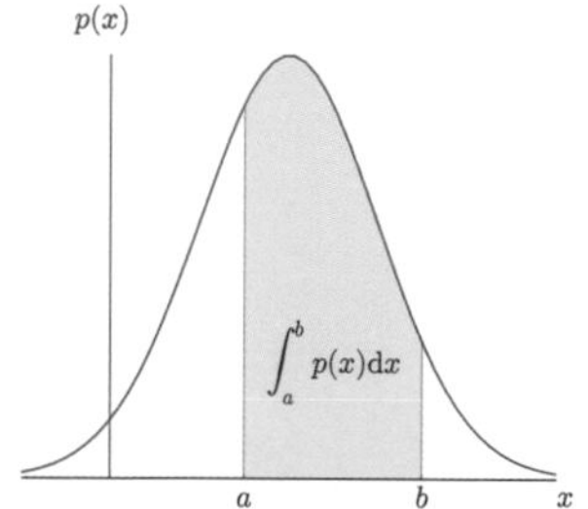

Figure 2.4: An illustration of a simple probability density function (p.d.f.) of a continuous random variable taking values in $(-\infty, +\infty)$.

For any continuous random variable, we cannot define its probability of taking a single value. This probability will end up with 0s for all values because a continuous random variable can take an infinite number of different values. In probability theory, we instead consider the probability for a continuous random variable to fall within any interval. For example, given a continuous random variable X and any interval $[a, b]$ inside its domain, we try to measure the probability $\Pr(a \le X \le b)$, which is often nonzero. As shown in Figure 2.4, we define a function $p(x)$ in such a way that this probability equals to the area of the shaded region under the function $p(x)$ between a and b. In other words, we have

$$\Pr(a \le X \le b) = \int_a^b p(x)\,dx,$$

which holds for any interval $[a, b]$ inside the domain of the random variable. We usually call $p(x)$ the *probability density function (p.d.f.)* of X (see the margin note for an explanation). If we choose the entire domain as the interval, by definition, the probability must be 1. Therefore, we have the sum-to-1 constraint

$$\int_{-\infty}^{+\infty} p(x)\,dx = 1, \tag{2.2}$$

which holds for any probability density function.

By definition, we have

$$\begin{aligned} p(x) &= \lim_{\Delta x \to 0} \frac{\Pr\left(x \le X \le x + \Delta x\right)}{\Delta x} \\ &= \frac{\text{probability}}{\text{interval}} \\ &= \text{probability density.} \end{aligned}$$

In addition to p.d.f., we can also define another probability function for any continuous random variable X as

$$F(x) = \Pr\left(X \le x\right) \quad (\forall x),$$

which is often called the *cumulative distribution function (c.d.f.)*. By definition, we have

$$\lim_{x \to -\infty} F(x) = 0 \quad \text{and} \quad \lim_{x \to +\infty} F(x) = 1,$$

and

$$F(x) = \int_{-\infty}^{x} p(x)\,dx$$

$$p(x) = \frac{d}{dx} F(x).$$

2.2.2 Expectation: Mean, Variance, and Moments

As we know, a random variable is fully specified by its probability function. In other words, the probability function gives the full knowledge on the random variable, and we are able to compute any statistics of it from the probability function. Here, let us look at how to compute some important statistics for random variables from a p.d.f. or p.m.f. Thereafter, we will use $p(x)$ to represent the p.m.f. for a discrete random variable and the p.d.f. for a continuous random variable.

Given a continuous random variable X, for any function $f(X)$ of the random variable, we can define the *expectation* of $f(X)$ as follows:

$$\mathbb{E}\big[f(X)\big] = \int_{-\infty}^{+\infty} f(x)\,p(x)\,dx.$$

If X is a discrete random variable, we replace the integral with summation as follows:

$$\mathbb{E}\big[f(X)\big] = \sum_{x} f(x)\,p(x).$$

Because X is a random variable, the function $f(X)$ also yields different values in different probabilities. The expectation $\mathbb{E}\big[f(X)\big]$ gives the average of all possible values of $f(X)$. Relying on the expectation, we may define some statistics for random variables. For example, the *mean* of a random variable is defined as the expectation of the random variable itself (i.e., $\mathbb{E}\big[X\big]$). The rth moment of a random variable is defined as the expectation of its rth power (i.e., $\mathbb{E}\big[X^r\big]$; for any $r \in \mathbb{N}$). The *variance* of a random variable is defined as follows:

$$\text{var}(X) = \mathbb{E}\big[(X - \mathbb{E}[X])^2\big].$$

Intuitively speaking, the mean of a random variable indicates the center of its distribution, and the variance tells how much it may deviate from the center on average.

Example 2.2.1 For any random variable X, show that

$$\text{var}(X) = \mathbb{E}\big[X^2\big] - \big(\mathbb{E}[X]\big)^2.$$

For any constant c irrelevant of X, it is easy to show

$$\mathbb{E}[c] = c$$

$$\mathbb{E}[c \cdot X] = c \cdot \mathbb{E}[X].$$

$$\begin{aligned}
\text{var}(X) &= \mathbb{E}\big[(X - \mathbb{E}[X])^2\big] = \mathbb{E}\Big[X^2 - 2 \cdot X \cdot \mathbb{E}[X] + \big(\mathbb{E}[X]\big)^2\Big] \\
&= \mathbb{E}\big[X^2\big] - 2\mathbb{E}[X] \cdot \mathbb{E}[X] + \big(\mathbb{E}[X]\big)^2 \\
&= \mathbb{E}\big[X^2\big] - \big(\mathbb{E}[X]\big)^2.
\end{aligned}$$

$\mathbb{E}[X]$ can be viewed as a constant because it is a fixed value for any random variable X.

♦

Next, let us revisit the general principle of the *bias–variance trade-off* discussed in the previous chapter. In any machine learning problem, we basically need to estimate a model from some training data. The true model is usually unknown but fixed, denoted as f. Hence, we can treat the true model f as an unknown constant. Imagine that we can repeat the model estimation many times. At each time, we randomly collect some training data and run the same learning algorithm to derive an estimate, denoted as $\hat{f}$. The estimate $\hat{f}$ can be viewed as a random variable because we may derive a different estimate each time depending on the training data used, which differ from one collection to another. Generally speaking, we are interested in the average learning error between an estimate $\hat{f}$ and the true model f:

$$\text{error} = \mathbb{E}\big[(\hat{f} - f)^2\big].$$

The bias of a learning method is defined as the difference between the true model and the mean of all possible estimates derived from this method:

$$\text{bias} = \Big|f - \mathbb{E}\big[\hat{f}\big]\Big|.$$

The variance of an estimate is as defined previously:

$$\text{variance} = \text{var}\big(\hat{f}\big) = \mathbb{E}\Big[\big(\hat{f} - \mathbb{E}[\hat{f}]\big)^2\Big].$$

Example 2.2.2 The Bias-Variance Trade-Off

Show that the bias and variance decomposition holds as follows:

$$\text{error} = \text{bias}^2 + \text{variance}.$$

$$\begin{aligned} \text{error} &= \mathbb{E}[(f - \hat{f})^2] = \mathbb{E}\Big[\big(f - \mathbb{E}[\hat{f}] - \hat{f} + \mathbb{E}[\hat{f}]\big)^2\Big] \\ &= \mathbb{E}\Big[\big(f - \mathbb{E}[\hat{f}]\big)^2\Big] + \mathbb{E}\Big[\big(\hat{f} - \mathbb{E}[\hat{f}]\big)^2\Big] \\ &\quad -2 \cdot \mathbb{E}\Big[\big(f - \mathbb{E}[\hat{f}]\big)\big(\hat{f} - \mathbb{E}[\hat{f}]\big)\Big] \\ &= \underbrace{\big(f - \mathbb{E}[\hat{f}]\big)^2}_{\text{bias}^2} + \underbrace{\mathbb{E}\Big[\big(\hat{f} - \mathbb{E}[\hat{f}]\big)^2\Big]}_{\text{variance}}. \end{aligned}$$

Because both f and $\mathbb{E}[\hat{f}]$ are constants, we have

$$\begin{aligned} &\mathbb{E}\Big[\big(f - \mathbb{E}[\hat{f}]\big)\big(\hat{f} - \mathbb{E}[\hat{f}]\big)\Big] \\ =\ & \big(f - \mathbb{E}[\hat{f}]\big)\mathbb{E}\big[\hat{f} - \mathbb{E}[\hat{f}]\big] \\ =\ & \big(f - \mathbb{E}[\hat{f}]\big)\underbrace{\big(\mathbb{E}[\hat{f}] - \mathbb{E}[\hat{f}]\big)}_{=0} \\ =\ & 0. \end{aligned}$$

♦

2.2.3 Joint, Marginal, and Conditional Distributions

We have discussed the probability functions for a single random variable. If we need to consider multiple random variables at the same time, we can similarly define some probability functions for them in the product space of their separate domains.

Assume the domains of two random variables, X and Y, are

$$X \in \{x_1, x_2\} \quad \text{and} \quad Y \in \{y_1, y_2\}.$$

The product space of X and Y includes all pairs like the following:

$$\Big\{(x_1, y_1), (x_1, y_2), (x_2, y_1), (x_2, y_2)\Big\}.$$

If we have multiple discrete random variables, a multivariate function can be defined in the product space of their domains as follows:

$$p(x, y) = \Pr(X = x, Y = y) \quad \forall x \in \{x_1, x_2, \cdots\}, y \in \{y_1, y_2, \cdots\},$$

$y \setminus x$	x_1	x_2	x_3
y_1	0.03	0.24	0.17
y_2	0.23	0.11	0.22

where $p(x, y)$ is often called the *joint distribution* of two random variables X and Y. The joint distributions of discrete random variables can also be represented with some multidimensional tables. For example, a joint distribution $p(x, y)$ of two discrete random variables, X and Y, is shown in the left margin, where each entry indicates the probability for X and

Y to take the corresponding values. If we sum over all entries in a joint distribution, it must satisfy the sum-to-1 constraint $\sum_x \sum_y p(x,y) = 1$.

For multiple continuous random variables, we can follow the same idea of the p.d.f. to define a joint distribution, as in Figure 2.5, to ensure that the probability for them to fall into any region Ω in their product space can be computed by the following multiple integral:

$$\Pr\Big((x,y) \in \Omega\Big) = \int \cdots \int_{\Omega} p(x,y)\,dxdy.$$

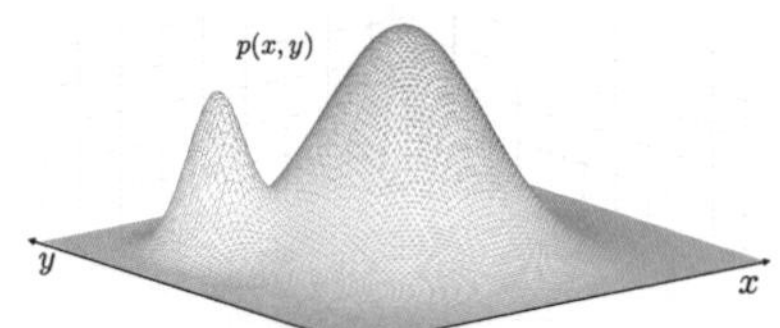

Figure 2.5: An illustration of a joint distribution (p.d.f.) of two continuous random variables $p(x,y)$.

Similarly, if we integrate the joint distribution over the entire space, it satisfies the sum-to-1 constraint: $\int_{-\infty}^{+\infty} \int_{-\infty}^{+\infty} p(x,y)\,dxdy = 1$.

A joint distribution fully specifies all underlying random variables. From a joint distribution, we should be able to derive any information regarding each underlying random variable. From a joint distribution of multiple random variables, we can derive the distribution function of any subset of these random variables by an operation called *marginalization*. The derived distribution of a subset is often called a *marginal distribution*. A marginal distribution is derived by marginalizing all irrelevant random variables, namely, integrating out each continuous random variable or summing out each discrete random variable. For example, given a joint distribution of two random variables $p(x,y)$, we can derive the marginal distribution of one random variable by marginalizing out the other one:

$$p(x) = \int_{-\infty}^{+\infty} p(x,y)dy,$$

if y is a continuous random variable, or

$$p(x) = \sum_{y} p(x,y),$$

if y is a discrete random variable. This marginalization can be applied to any joint distribution to derive a marginal distribution of any subset of random variables that we are interested in. This marginalization is often called the *rule of sum* in probability.

Moreover, we can further define the so-called *conditional distributions* among multiple random variables. For example, the conditional distribution of x given y is defined as follows:

$$p(x \mid y) \triangleq \frac{p(x,y)}{p(y)} = \frac{p(x,y)}{\int p(x,y)\,dx}.$$

If x is a discrete random variable, we have

$$p(x \mid y) = \frac{p(x,y)}{p(y)} = \frac{p(x,y)}{\sum_x p(x,y)}$$

The conditional distribution $p(x \mid y)$ is a function of x, and it only describes how x is distributed when y is known to take a particular value. Using a conditional distribution, we can compute the conditional expectation of

$f(X)$ when Y is given as $Y = y_0$:

$$\mathbb{E}_X\Big[f(X)\,\big|\,Y = y_0\Big] = \int_{-\infty}^{+\infty} f(x) \cdot p(x \mid y_0)\, dx.$$

If X is discrete, we have

$$\mathbb{E}_X\Big[f(X)\,\big|\,Y = y_0\Big] = \sum_x f(x) \cdot p(x \mid y_0).$$

Example 2.2.3 Assuming the joint distribution of two continuous random variables, X and Y, is given as $p(x, y)$, compare the regular mean of X (i.e., $\mathbb{E}\big[X\big]$) and a conditional mean of X when $Y = y_0$ (i.e., $\mathbb{E}_X\big[X\,\big|\,Y = y_0\big]$).

$$\mathbb{E}\big[X\big] = \int_{-\infty}^{+\infty} x \cdot p(x)\, dx = \int_{-\infty}^{+\infty}\int_{-\infty}^{+\infty} x \cdot p(x, y)\, dxdy$$

$$\begin{aligned} \mathbb{E}_X\big[X\,\big|\,Y = y_0\big] &= \int_{-\infty}^{+\infty} x \cdot p(x \mid y_0)\, dx = \int_{-\infty}^{+\infty} x \cdot \frac{p(x, y_0)}{p(y_0)}\, dx \\ &= \frac{\int_{-\infty}^{+\infty} x \cdot p(x, y_0)\, dx}{\int_{-\infty}^{+\infty} p(x, y_0)\, dx}. \end{aligned}$$

From this, we can see that both means can be computed from the joint distribution, but they are two different quantities. ♦

Two random variables, X and Y, are said to be *independent* if and only if their joint distribution $p(x, y)$ can be factorized as a product of their own marginal distributions:

$$p(x, y) = p(x)\, p(y) \quad (\forall x, y).$$

From the previous definition of conditional distributions, we can see that X and Y are independent if and only if $p(x|y) = p(x)$ holds for all y.

For any two random variables, X and Y, we can define the *covariance* between them as

$$\begin{aligned} \text{cov}(X, Y) &= \mathbb{E}\Big[\big(X - \mathbb{E}[X]\big)\big(Y - \mathbb{E}[Y]\big)\Big] \\ &= \int_{-\infty}^{+\infty}\int_{-\infty}^{+\infty} \big(x - \mathbb{E}[X]\big)\big(y - \mathbb{E}[Y]\big)\, p(x, y)\, dxdy. \end{aligned}$$

If X and Y are discrete,

$$\text{cov}(X, Y) = \sum_x \sum_y \big(x - \mathbb{E}[X]\big)\big(y - \mathbb{E}[Y]\big)\, p(x, y).$$

If $\text{cov}(X, Y) = 0$, we say that two random variables, X and Y, are *uncorrelated*. Note that *uncorrelatedness* is a much weaker condition than independence. If two random variables are independent, we can show from the previous definition that they must be uncorrelated. However, it is generally not true the other way around.

Relying on the concept of the conditional distribution, we can factorize any joint distribution involving many random variables by following a particular order of these variables. For example, we have

$$p(x_1, x_2, x_3, x_4, \cdots) = p(x_1)\,p(x_2|x_1)\,p(x_3|x_1, x_2)\,p(x_4|x_1, x_2, x_3)\cdots$$

For example, we can also do the following:

$$p(x_1, x_2, x_3, x_4, \cdots) = p(x_3)\,p(x_1|x_3)$$
$$p(x_4|x_1, x_3)\,p(x_2|x_1, x_3, x_4)\cdots$$

Note that there exist many different ways to correctly factorize any joint distribution as long as the probability of each variable is conditioned on all previous variables prior to the current one in the order. In probability theory, this factorization rule is often called the *multiplication rule* of probability, also known as the *general product rule* of probability.

When we have a joint distribution of a large number of random variables, for notational convenience, we often group some related random variables into random vectors so that we represent it as a joint distribution of random vectors:

$$p(\underbrace{x_1, x_2, x_3}_{\mathbf{x}}, \underbrace{y_1, y_2, y_3, y_4}_{\mathbf{y}}) = p(\mathbf{x}, \mathbf{y}).$$

We can use the same rule as previously to similarly derive the marginal and conditional distributions for random vectors, as follows:

$$p(\mathbf{x}) = \int p(\mathbf{x}, \mathbf{y})\, d\mathbf{y}$$

$$p(\mathbf{x} \,|\, \mathbf{y}) \triangleq \frac{p(\mathbf{x}, \mathbf{y})}{p(\mathbf{y})}.$$

If $\mathbf{y}$ is discrete, we have

$$p(\mathbf{x}) = \sum_{\mathbf{y}} p(\mathbf{x}, \mathbf{y}).$$

The mean of a random vector $\mathbf{x}$ is a vector, denoted as $\mathbb{E}[\mathbf{x}]$:

$$\mathbb{E}\big[\mathbf{x}\big] = \int \mathbf{x}\, p(\mathbf{x})\, d\mathbf{x} = \int\!\!\int \mathbf{x}\, p(\mathbf{x}, \mathbf{y})\, d\mathbf{x} d\mathbf{y}.$$

If $\mathbf{x}$ and $\mathbf{y}$ are both discrete, we have

$$\mathbb{E}\big[\mathbf{x}\big] = \sum_{\mathbf{x}}\sum_{\mathbf{y}} \mathbf{x}\, p(\mathbf{x}, \mathbf{y}).$$

The covariance between two random vectors, $\mathbf{x}$ and $\mathbf{y}$, becomes a matrix, which is often called the *covariance matrix*:

$$\begin{aligned} \text{cov}(\mathbf{x}, \mathbf{y}) &= \mathbb{E}\Big[(\mathbf{x} - \mathbb{E}[\mathbf{x}])(\mathbf{y} - \mathbb{E}[\mathbf{y}])^\intercal\Big] \\ &= \int\!\!\int (\mathbf{x} - \mathbb{E}[\mathbf{x}])(\mathbf{y} - \mathbb{E}[\mathbf{y}])^\intercal\, p(\mathbf{x}, \mathbf{y})\, d\mathbf{x} d\mathbf{y}. \end{aligned}$$

$$\text{cov}(\mathbf{x}, \mathbf{y}) = \sum_{\mathbf{x}}\sum_{\mathbf{y}} (\mathbf{x} - \mathbb{E}[\mathbf{x}])(\mathbf{y} - \mathbb{E}[\mathbf{y}])^\intercal\, p(\mathbf{x}, \mathbf{y}).$$

Finally, the general product rule of probability can be equally applied to factorize a joint distribution of random vectors as well.

$$p(\mathbf{x}, \mathbf{y}, \mathbf{z}) = p(\mathbf{x})\, p(\mathbf{y}|\mathbf{x})\, p(\mathbf{z}|\mathbf{x}, \mathbf{y}).$$

2.2.4 Common Probability Distributions

Here, let us review some popular probability functions often used to represent the distributions of random variables. For each of these probability functions, we need to know not only its functional form but also what physical phenomena it can be used to describe. Moreover, we need to clearly distinguish parameters from random variables in the mathematical formula and correctly identify the domain of the underlying random variables (a.k.a. the *support* of the distribution), as well as the valid range of the parameters.

Binomial Distribution

The binomial distribution is the discrete probability distribution of the number of outcomes in a sequence of N independent binary experiments. Each binary experiment has two different outcomes. We use the binomial distribution to compute the probabilities of observing r ($r \in \{0, 1, \cdots, N\}$) times of one particular outcome from all N experiments—for example, the probability of seeing r heads when a coin is tossed N times in a row. When we use a discrete random variable X to represent the number of an outcome, and assuming the probability of observing this outcome is $p \in [0, 1]$ in one experiment, the binomial distribution takes the following formula:

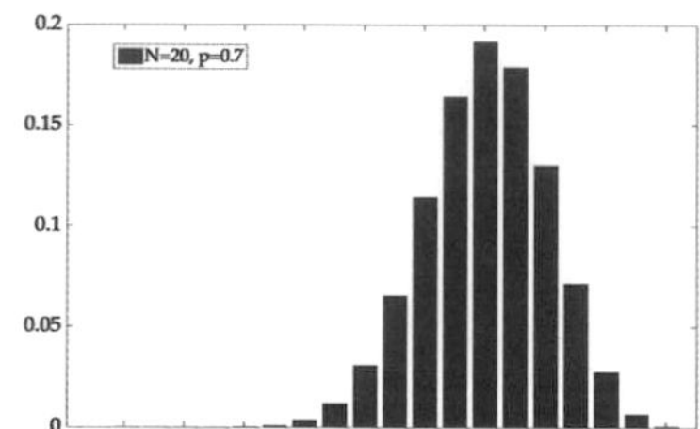

Figure 2.6: An illustration the binomial distribution $\mathrm{B}(r \mid N, p)$ with $p = 0.7$ and $N = 20$.

$$\mathrm{B}(r \mid N, p) \triangleq \Pr(X = r) = \frac{N!}{r!\,(N-r)!}\, p^r (1-p)^{N-r},$$

where N and p denote two parameters of the distribution.

We summarize some key properties for the binomial distribution as follows:

- Parameters: $N \in \mathbb{N}$ and $p \in [0, 1]$.
- Support: The domain of the random variable is $r \in \{0, 1, \cdots N\}$.
- Mean and variance: $\mathbb{E}[X] = Np$ and $\mathrm{var}(X) = Np(1-p)$.
- The sum-to-1 constraint: $\sum_{r=0}^{N} \mathrm{B}(r \mid N, p) = 1$.

Figure 2.6 shows an example of the binomial distribution for $p = 0.7$ and $N = 20$.

When only one binary experiment is done ($N = 1$),

$$\mathrm{B}(r \mid N = 1, p) = p^r (1-p)^{1-r}$$

is also called the Bernoulli distribution, where $r \in \{0, 1\}$.

Multinomial Distribution

The multinomial distribution can be viewed as an extension of the binomial distribution when each experiment is not binary but has m distinct outcomes. In each experiment, the probabilities of observing all possible outcomes are denoted as $\{p_1, p_2, \cdots, p_m\}$, where we have the sum-to-1 constraint $\sum_{i=1}^{m} p_i = 1$. When we independently repeat the experiment N times, we introduce m different random variables to represent the number of each outcome from all N experiments (i.e., $\{X_1, X_2, \cdots, X_m\}$). The joint distribution of these m random variables is the multinomial distribution, computed as follows:

$$\begin{aligned}
&\text{Mult}(r_1, r_2, \cdots, r_m \mid N, p_1, p_2, \cdots, p_m) \\
\triangleq\ & \Pr(X_1 = r_1, X_2 = r_2, \cdots, X_m = r_m) \\
=\ & \frac{N!}{r_1!\, r_2! \cdots r_m!}\, p_1^{r_1} p_2^{r_2} \cdots p_m^{r_m},
\end{aligned}$$

where $\sum_{i=1}^m r_i = N$ holds because N experiments are conducted in total.

We summarize some properties for the multinomial distribution as follows:

- Parameters: $N \in \mathbb{N}$; $0 \le p_i \le 1$ $(\forall i = 1, 2, \cdots, m)$ and $\sum_{i=1}^m p_i = 1$.
- Support (the domain of m random variables): $r_i \in \{0, 1, \cdots N\}$ $(\forall i = 1, \cdots, m)$ and $\sum_{i=1}^m r_i = N$.
- Means, variances, and covariances:

$$\mathbb{E}\big[X_i\big] = Np_i \ \text{ and } \ \text{var}(X_i) = Np_i(1 - p_i) \qquad (\forall i)$$
$$\text{cov}(X_i, X_j) = -Np_i p_j \qquad (\forall i, j).$$

- The sum-to-1 constraint:

$$\sum_{r_1 \cdots r_m} \text{Mult}(r_1, r_2, \cdots, r_m \mid N, p_1, p_2, \cdots, p_m) = 1.$$

When we conduct only one experiment $(N = 1)$,

$$\begin{aligned}
&\text{Mult}(r_1, \cdots, r_m \mid N = 1, p_1, \cdots, p_m) \\
&= p_1^{r_1} p_2^{r_2} \cdots p_m^{r_m}
\end{aligned}$$

is also called the categorical distribution, where we have $r_i \in \{0, 1\}$ $(\forall i)$ and

$$\sum_{i=1}^m r_i = 1.$$

As we will learn, the multinomial distribution is the main building block for constructing any statistical model for discrete random variables in machine learning.

Beta Distribution

The beta distribution is used to describe a continuous random variable, X, that takes a probability-like value $x \in \mathbb{R}$ and $0 \le x \le 1$.The beta distribution takes the following functional form:

$$\text{Beta}(x \mid \alpha, \beta) = \frac{\Gamma(\alpha + \beta)}{\Gamma(\alpha)\Gamma(\beta)}\, x^{\alpha-1}\, (1 - x)^{\beta-1},$$

where $\Gamma(\cdot)$ denotes the gamma function, and α and β are two positive parameters of the beta distribution. Similarly, we can summarize some key properties for the beta distribution as follows:

The gamma function is defined as follows:

$$\Gamma(x) = \int_0^{+\infty} t^{x-1}\, e^{-t}\, dt \quad (\forall x > 0).$$

$\Gamma(x)$ is often considered as a generalization of the factorial to noninteger numbers because of the following property:

$$\Gamma(x + 1) = x\,\Gamma(x)$$

- Parameters: $\alpha > 0$ and $\beta > 0$.
- Support (the domain of the continuous random variable):

$$x \in \mathbb{R} \quad \text{and} \quad 0 \le x \le 1.$$

► Mean and variance:

$$\mathbb{E}\big[X\big] = \frac{\alpha}{\alpha+\beta} \qquad \text{var}(X) = \frac{\alpha\beta}{(\alpha+\beta)^2(\alpha+\beta+1)}.$$

► The sum-to-1 constraint:

$$\int_0^1 \text{Beta}\big(x \mid \alpha, \beta\big)\, dx = 1.$$

We can recognize that the beta distribution shares the same functional form as the binomial distribution. They differ only in terms of swapping the roles of the parameters and random variables. Therefore, these two distributions are said to be *conjugate* to each other. In this sense, the beta distribution can be viewed as a distribution of the parameter p in the binomial distribution. As we will learn, this viewpoint plays an important role in Bayesian learning (refer to Chapter 14).

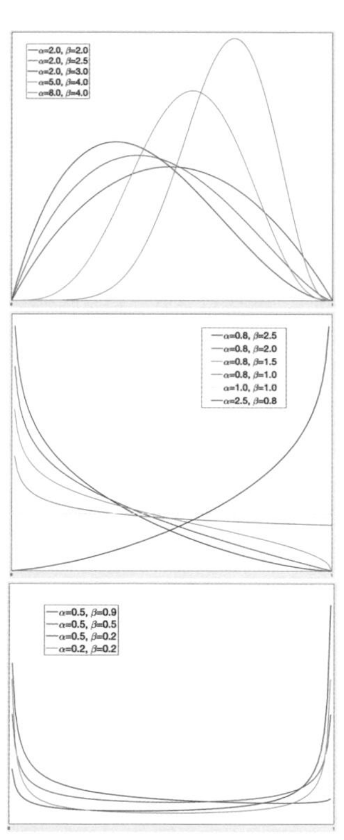

Figure 2.7: An illustration of some beta distributions when two parameters α and β take different values: (i) $\alpha > 1$ and $\beta > 1$; (ii) $0 < \alpha < 1 < \beta$ or $0 < \beta < 1 < \alpha$; (iii) $0 < \alpha, \beta < 1$.

Depending on the choices of the two parameters α and β, the beta distribution behaves quite differently. As shown in Figure 2.7, when both parameters are larger than 1, the beta distribution is a unimodal bell-shaped distribution between 0 and 1. The mode of the distribution can be computed as $(\alpha-1)/(\alpha+\beta-2)$ in this case. It becomes a monotonic distribution when one parameter is larger than 1 and the other is smaller than 1, particularly monotonically decaying if $0 < \alpha < 1 < \beta$ and monotonically increasing if $0 < \beta < 1 < \alpha$. At last, if both parameters are smaller than 1, the beta distribution is bimodal between 0 and 1, peaking at the two ends.

Dirichlet Distribution

The Dirichlet distribution is a multivariate generalization of the beta distribution that is used to describe multiple continuous random variables $\{X_1, X_2, \cdots, X_m\}$, taking values on the probabilities of observing a complete set of mutually exclusive events. As a result, the values of these random variables are always summed to 1 because these events are complete. For example, if we use some biased dice in a tossing experiment, we can define six random variables, each of which represents the probability of observing each digit when tossing a die. For each biased die, these six random variables take different probabilities, but they always sum to 1 for each die. These six random variables from all biased dice can be assumed to follow the Dirichlet distribution.

In general, the Dirichlet distribution takes the following functional form:

$$\text{Dir}\big(p_1, p_2, \cdots, p_m \,\big|\, r_1, r_2, \cdots, r_m\big)$$

$$= \frac{\Gamma(r_1 + \cdots + r_m)}{\Gamma(r_1) \cdots \Gamma(r_m)} p_1^{r_1-1} p_2^{r_2-1} \cdots p_m^{r_m-1},$$

where $\{r_1, r_2, \cdots, r_m\}$ denote m positive parameters of the distribution. We can similarly summarize some key properties for the Dirichlet distribution as follows:

- Parameters: $r_i > 0$ ($\forall i = 1, \cdots, m$).
- Support: The domain of m random variables is an m-dimensional simplex that can be represented as

$$0 < p_i < 1 \ (\forall i = 1, \cdots, m) \quad \text{and} \quad \sum_{i=1}^{m} p_i = 1.$$

  For example, Figure 2.8 shows a three-dimensional simplex for the Dirichlet distribution of three random variables $\{p_1, p_2, p_3\}$ when $m = 3$.
- Means, variances, and covariances:

$$\mathbb{E}\big[X_i\big] = \frac{r_i}{r_0} \qquad \mathrm{var}\big(X_i\big) = \frac{r_i(r_0 - r_i)}{r_0^2(r_0 + 1)}$$

$$\mathrm{cov}\big(X_i, X_j\big) = -\frac{r_i r_j}{r_0^2(r_0 + 1)},$$

  where we denote $r_0 = \sum_{i=1}^{m} r_i$.
- The sum-to-1 constraint holds inside the simplex:

$$\int \cdots \int_{p_1 \cdots p_m} \mathrm{Dir}\big(p_1, p_2, \cdots p_m \,\big|\, r_1, r_2, \cdots, r_m\big)\, dp_1 \cdots dp_m = 1.$$

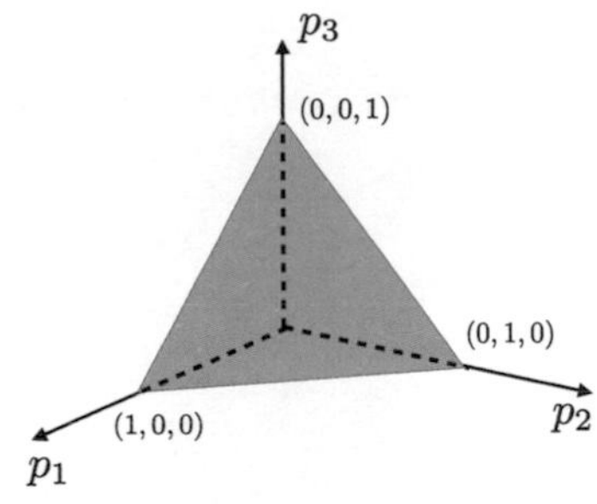

Figure 2.8: An illustration of the three-dimensional simplex of the Dirichlet distribution of three random variables.

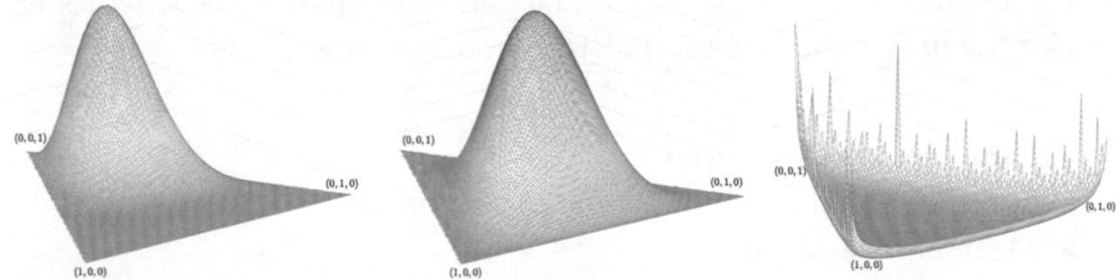

Figure 2.9: An illustration of three Dirichlet distributions in the three-dimensional simplex with various choices of parameters:
1. Regular: $r_1 = 2.0, r_2 = 4.0, r_3 = 10.0$
2. Symmetric: $r_1 = r_2 = r_3 = 4.0$
3. Sparse: $r_1 = 0.7, r_2 = 0.8, r_3 = 0.9$

The shape of a Dirichlet distribution also heavily depends on the choice of its parameters. Figure 2.9 plots the Dirichlet distribution in the triangle simplex for three typical choices of its parameters. Generally speaking, if we choose all parameters to be larger than 1, the Dirichlet distribution is a unimodal distribution centering somewhere in the simplex. In this case, the mode of the distribution is located at $\big[\hat{p}_1 \ \hat{p}_2 \ \cdots \ \hat{p}_m\big]^\intercal$, where $\hat{p}_i = (r_i - 1)/(r_0 - m)$ for all $i = 1, 2, \cdots, m$. If we force all parameters to be the same value, it leads to a symmetric distribution centering at the center of the simplex. On the other hand, if we choose all parameters to be smaller than 1, it results in a distribution that yields a large probability mass only near the vertices and edges of the simplex. It is easy to verify that the vertices or edges correspond to the cases where some random variables p_i take 0 values. In other words, this choice of parameters favors sparse choices of random variables, leading to the so-called *sparse* Dirichlet distribution.

Moreover, we can also identify that the Dirichlet distribution shares the same functional form as the multinomial distribution. Therefore, these two distributions are also conjugate to each other. Similarly, the Dirichlet distribution can be viewed as a distribution of all parameters of a multinomial distribution. Because the multinomial distribution is the main building block for any statistical model of discrete random variables, the Dirichlet distribution is often said to be a distribution of all distributions of discrete random variables. Similar to the beta distribution, the Dirichlet distribution also plays an important role in Bayesian learning for multinomial-related models (see Chapter 14).

Gaussian Distribution

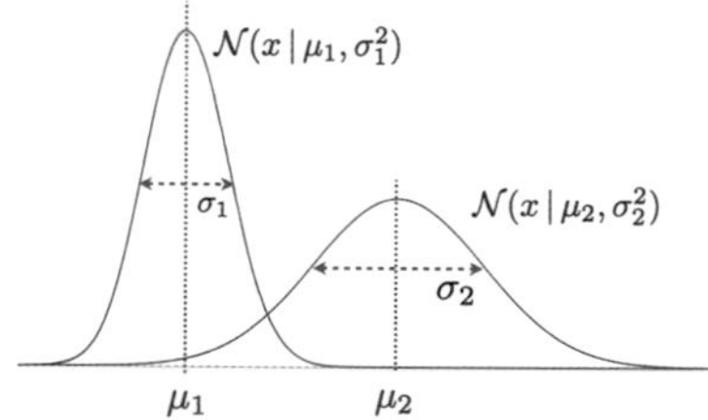

Figure 2.10: An illustration of two univariate Gaussian distributions with various parameters ($\sigma_2 > \sigma_1$).

The univariate Gaussian distribution (a.k.a. the *normal distribution*) is often used to describe a continuous random variable X that can take any real value in $\mathbb{R}$. The general form of a Gaussian distribution is

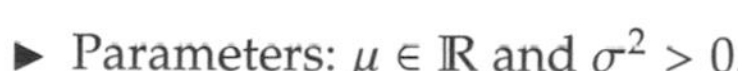

$$\mathcal{N}\left(x \mid \mu, \sigma^2\right) = \frac{1}{\sqrt{2\pi\sigma^2}} \, e^{-\frac{(x-\mu)^2}{2\sigma^2}},$$

where μ and σ^2 are two parameters. We can summarize some key properties for the univariate Gaussian distribution as follows:

- Parameters: $\mu \in \mathbb{R}$ and $\sigma^2 > 0$.
- Support: The domain of the random variable is $x \in \mathbb{R}$.
- Mean and variance:

$$\mathbb{E}[X] = \mu \quad \text{and} \quad \text{var}(X) = \sigma^2.$$

- The sum-to-1 constraint:

$$\int_{-\infty}^{+\infty} \mathcal{N}(x \mid \mu, \sigma) \, dx = 1.$$

Several important identities related to the univariate Gaussian distribution are as follows:

$$\int_{-\infty}^{+\infty} e^{-\frac{(x-\mu)^2}{2\sigma^2}} \, dx = \sqrt{2\pi\sigma^2},$$

$$\int_{-\infty}^{+\infty} x \, e^{-\frac{(x-\mu)^2}{2\sigma^2}} \, dx = \mu\sqrt{2\pi\sigma^2},$$

$$\int_{-\infty}^{+\infty} x^2 \, e^{-\frac{(x-\mu)^2}{2\sigma^2}} \, dx = (\sigma^2 + \mu^2)\sqrt{2\pi\sigma^2}.$$

The Gaussian distribution is the well-known unimodal bell-shaped curve. As shown in Figure 2.10, the first parameter μ equals to the mean, indicating the center of the distribution, whereas the second parameters σ equals to the standard deviation, indicating the spread of the distribution.

Multivariate Gaussian Distribution

The multivariate Gaussian distribution extends the univariate Gaussian distribution to represent a joint distribution of multiple continuous random variables $\{X_1, X_2, \cdots, X_n\}$, each of which can take any real value in $\mathbb{R}$. If we arrange these random variables as an n-dimensional random vector, the multivariate Gaussian distribution takes the following compact form:

$$\mathcal{N}(\mathbf{x} \mid \boldsymbol{\mu}, \boldsymbol{\Sigma}) = \frac{1}{\sqrt{(2\pi)^n |\boldsymbol{\Sigma}|}} e^{-\frac{(\mathbf{x}-\boldsymbol{\mu})^\intercal \boldsymbol{\Sigma}^{-1} (\mathbf{x}-\boldsymbol{\mu})}{2}},$$

where the vector $\boldsymbol{\mu} \in \mathbb{R}^n$ and the symmetric matrix $\boldsymbol{\Sigma} \in \mathbb{R}^{n \times n}$ denote two parameters of the distribution. Note that the exponent in the multivariate Gaussian distribution is computed as follows:

$$\left[(\mathbf{x}-\boldsymbol{\mu})^\intercal\right]_{1\times d} \left[\quad \boldsymbol{\Sigma}^{-1} \quad \right]_{d\times d} \left[\mathbf{x}-\boldsymbol{\mu} \right]_{d\times 1} = [\,\cdot\,]_{1\times 1}.$$

We can summarize some key properties for the multivariate Gaussian distribution as follows:

Some important identities related to the multivariate Gaussian distribution are as follows:

$$\int \mathcal{N}(\mathbf{x} \mid \boldsymbol{\mu}, \boldsymbol{\Sigma})\, d\mathbf{x} = 1,$$

$$\int \mathbf{x}\, \mathcal{N}(\mathbf{x} \mid \boldsymbol{\mu}, \boldsymbol{\Sigma})\, d\mathbf{x} = \boldsymbol{\mu},$$

$$\int \mathbf{x}\mathbf{x}^\intercal\, \mathcal{N}(\mathbf{x} \mid \boldsymbol{\mu}, \boldsymbol{\Sigma})\, d\mathbf{x} = \boldsymbol{\Sigma} + \boldsymbol{\mu}\boldsymbol{\mu}^\intercal.$$

- Parameters: $\boldsymbol{\mu} \in \mathbb{R}^n$; $\boldsymbol{\Sigma} \in \mathbb{R}^{n \times n} \succ 0$ is symmetric, positive definite, and invertible.
- Support: The domain of all random variables: $\mathbf{x} \in \mathbb{R}^n$.
- Mean vector and covariance matrix:

  $$\mathbb{E}\left[\mathbf{x}\right] = \boldsymbol{\mu} \quad \text{and} \quad \text{cov}\left(\mathbf{x}, \mathbf{x}\right) = \boldsymbol{\Sigma}.$$

  Therefore, the first parameter $\boldsymbol{\mu}$ is called the *mean vector*, and the second parameter $\boldsymbol{\Sigma}$ is called the *covariance matrix*. The inverse covariance matrix $\boldsymbol{\Sigma}^{-1}$ is often called the *precision* matrix.
- The sum-to-1 constraint:

  $$\int \mathcal{N}(\mathbf{x} \mid \boldsymbol{\mu}, \boldsymbol{\Sigma})\, d\mathbf{x} = 1.$$

- Any marginal distribution or conditional distribution of these n random variables is also Gaussian. (See Exercise Q2.8.)

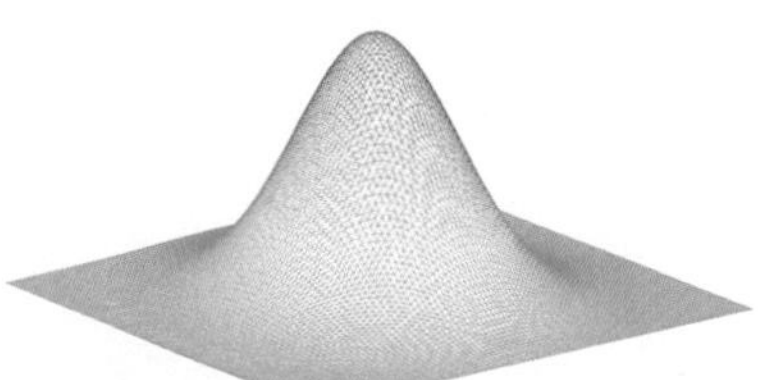

Figure 2.11: An illustration of a unimodal multivariate Gaussian distribution in a two-dimensional space.

As shown in Figure 2.11, the multivariate Gaussian is a unimodal distribution in the n-dimensional space, centering at the mean vector $\boldsymbol{\mu}$. The shape of the distribution depends on the eigenvalues (all positive) of the covariance matrix $\boldsymbol{\Sigma}$.

In order not to make this section further lengthy, the description of other probability distributions, including the uniform, Poisson, gamma, inverse-Wishart, and von Mises–Fisher distributions, are provided in Appendix A as a reference for readers.

2.2.5 Transformation of Random Variables

Assume we have a set of n continuous random variables, denoted as $\{X_1, X_2, \cdots, X_n\}$. If we arrange their values as a vector $\mathbf{x} \in \mathbb{R}^n$, we can represent their joint distribution (p.d.f.) as $p(\mathbf{x})$. We can apply some transformations to convert them into another set of n continuous random variables as follows:

$$\begin{aligned} Y_1 &= f_1(X_1, X_2, \cdots, X_n) \\ Y_2 &= f_2(X_1, X_2, \cdots, X_n) \\ &\vdots \\ Y_n &= f_n(X_1, X_2, \cdots, X_n). \end{aligned}$$

$$\mathbf{x} = \begin{bmatrix} x_1 \\ x_2 \\ \vdots \\ x_n \end{bmatrix} \xrightarrow{f} \mathbf{y} = \begin{bmatrix} y_1 \\ y_2 \\ \vdots \\ y_n \end{bmatrix}$$

We similarly arrange the values of the new random variables $\{Y_1, Y_2, \cdots, Y_n\}$ as another vector $\mathbf{y} \in \mathbb{R}^n$, and we further represent the transformations as a single vector-valued and multivariate function:

$$\mathbf{y} = f(\mathbf{x}) \qquad (\mathbf{x} \in \mathbb{R}^n, \mathbf{y} \in \mathbb{R}^n).$$

$$\mathbf{y} = \begin{bmatrix} y_1 \\ y_2 \\ \vdots \\ y_n \end{bmatrix} \xrightarrow{f^{-1}} \mathbf{x} = \begin{bmatrix} x_1 \\ x_2 \\ \vdots \\ x_n \end{bmatrix}$$

If this function is continuously differentiable and invertible, we can represent the inverse function as $\mathbf{x} = f^{-1}(\mathbf{y})$. Under these conditions, we are able to conveniently derive the joint distribution for these new random variables, that is, $p(\mathbf{y})$.

We first need to define the so-called Jacobian matrix for these inverse transformations $\mathbf{x} = f^{-1}(\mathbf{y})$, as follows:

$$\mathbf{J}(\mathbf{y}) = \left[\frac{\partial x_i}{\partial y_j} \right]_{n \times n} = \begin{bmatrix} \frac{\partial x_1}{\partial y_1} & \frac{\partial x_1}{\partial y_2} & \cdots & \frac{\partial x_1}{\partial y_n} \\ \frac{\partial x_2}{\partial y_1} & \frac{\partial x_2}{\partial y_2} & \cdots & \frac{\partial x_2}{\partial y_n} \\ \vdots & \vdots & \ddots & \vdots \\ \frac{\partial x_n}{\partial y_1} & \frac{\partial x_n}{\partial y_2} & \cdots & \frac{\partial x_n}{\partial y_n} \end{bmatrix}.$$

According to Bertsekas [21], the joint distribution of the new random variables can be derived as

$$p(\mathbf{y}) = \left|\mathbf{J}(\mathbf{y})\right| p(\mathbf{x}) = \left|\mathbf{J}(\mathbf{y})\right| p\big(f^{-1}(\mathbf{y})\big), \tag{2.3}$$

where $\left|\mathbf{J}(\mathbf{y})\right|$ denotes the determinant of the Jacobian matrix.

Example 2.2.4 Assume the joint distribution (p.d.f.) of n continuous random variables is given as $p(\mathbf{x})$ ($\mathbf{x} \in \mathbb{R}^n$), and we use an $n \times n$ orthogonal matrix $\mathbf{U}$ to linearly transform $\mathbf{x}$ into another set of n random variables as $\mathbf{y} = \mathbf{U}\mathbf{x}$. Show that $p(\mathbf{y}) = p(\mathbf{x})$ in this case.

$$\mathbf{y} = \mathbf{U}\mathbf{x} \implies \mathbf{x} = \mathbf{U}^{-1}\mathbf{y}.$$

According to the definition of an orthogonal matrix, we know that $\mathbf{U}^{-1} = \mathbf{U}^{\intercal}$. Moreover, because the inverse function is linear, we can verify that the Jacobian matrix

$$\mathbf{J}(\mathbf{y}) = \mathbf{U}^{-1} = \mathbf{U}^{\intercal}.$$

Because $\mathbf{U}$ is an orthogonal matrix, we have $|\mathbf{U}^{\intercal}| = |\mathbf{U}| = 1$. According to the previous result, we can derive $p(\mathbf{y}) = p(\mathbf{x})$ due to $\big|\mathbf{J}(\mathbf{y})\big| = 1$. ♦

An interesting conclusion from this example is that any orthogonal linear transformation of some random variables does not affect their joint distribution.

An *orthogonal matrix* (a.k.a. *orthonormal matrix*) $\mathbf{U}$ is a real square matrix whose column (or row) vectors are normalized to 1 and orthogonal to each other. That is,

$$\mathbf{U}^{\intercal}\mathbf{U} = \mathbf{U}\mathbf{U}^{\intercal} = \mathbf{I}.$$

An orthogonal matrix represents a special linear transformation of rotating the coordinate system.

2.3 Information Theory

Information theory was founded by Claude Shannon in 1948 as a discipline to study the quantification, storage, and communication of information. In the past decades, it has played a critical role in modern communication as well as many other applications in engineering and computer science. This section reviews information theory from the perspective of machine learning and emphasizes only the concepts and results relevant to machine learning, particularly *mutual information* [222] and the *Kullback–Leibler (KL) divergence* [137].

2.3.1 Information and Entropy

The first fundamental problem in information theory is how to quantitatively measure information. The most significant progress to address this issue is attributed to Shannon's brilliant idea of using probabilities. The amount of information that a message delivers solely depends on the probability of observing this message rather than its real content or anything else. This treatment allows us to establish a general mathematical framework to handle information independent of application domains. According to Shannon, if the probability of observing an event A is $\Pr(A)$, the amount of information delivered by this event A is calculated as follows:

$$I(A) = \log_2\left(\frac{1}{\Pr(A)}\right) = -\log_2\big(\Pr(A)\big).$$

When we use the binary logarithm $\log_2(\cdot)$, the unit of the calculated information is the bit. Shannon's definition of information is intuitive and consistent with our daily experience. A small-probability event will surprise us because it contains more information, whereas a common event that happens every day is not telling us anything new.

Shannon's idea can be extended to measure information for random variables. As we know, a random variable may take different values in different probabilities, and we can define the so-called *entropy* for a discrete random variable X as the expectation of the information for it to take different values:

$$H(X) = \mathbb{E}\big[-\log_2 \Pr(X=x)\big] = -\sum_x p(x)\log_2 p(x),$$

where $p(x)$ is the p.m.f. of X. Intuitively speaking, the entropy $H(X)$ represents the amount of uncertainty associated with the random variable X, namely, the amount of information we need to fully resolve this random variable.

The entropy of a continuous random variable X is similarly defined as

$$H(X) = \mathbb{E}\big[-\log_2 p(x)\big] = -\int_x p(x)\log_2 p(x)dx,$$

where $p(x)$ denotes the p.d.f. of X.

Example 2.3.1 Calculate the entropy for a binary random variable X that takes $x = 1$ in the probability of p and $x = 0$ in the probability of $1-p$, where $p \in [0,1]$.

x	1	0
$p(x)$	p	$1-p$

$$H(X) = -\sum_{x=0,1} p(x)\log_2 p(x) = -p\log_2 p - (1-p)\log_2(1-p).$$

We define $0 \times \log_2 0 = 0$.

Figure 2.12 shows $H(X)$ as a function of p and shows that $H(X) = 0$ when $p = 1$ or $p = 0$. In these cases, the entropy $H(X)$ equals to 0 because X surely takes the value of 1 (or 0) when $p = 1$ (or $p = 0$). On the other hand, X achieves the maximum entropy value when $p = 0.5$. In this case, X contains the highest level of uncertainty because it may take either value equiprobably. ♦

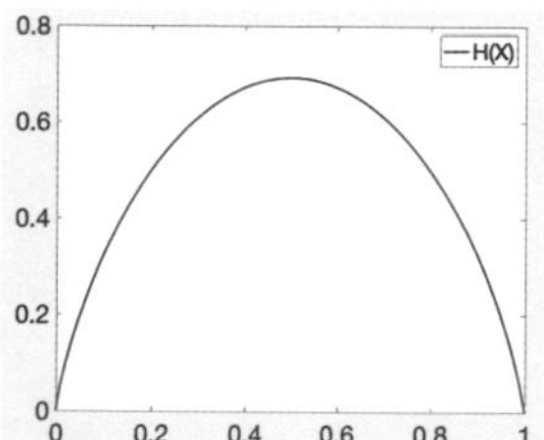

Figure 2.12: An illustration of entropy $H(X)$ as a function of p for a binary random variable.

Example 2.3.2 Calculate the entropy for a continuous random variable X that follows a Gaussian distribution $\mathcal{N}(x \mid \mu_0, \sigma_0^2)$.

$$\begin{aligned} H(X) &= -\int_x \mathcal{N}(x \mid \mu_0, \sigma_0^2)\log_2 \mathcal{N}(x \mid \mu_0, \sigma_0^2)\,dx \\ &= \frac{\log_2(e)}{2}\int_x \Big[\log(2\pi\sigma_0^2) + \frac{(x-\mu_0)^2}{\sigma_0^2}\Big]\mathcal{N}(x \mid \mu_0, \sigma_0^2)\,dx \\ &= \frac{1}{2}\big[\log_2(2\pi\sigma_0^2) + \log_2(e)\big] = \frac{1}{2}\log_2(2\pi e\sigma_0^2). \end{aligned}$$

Refer to the identities of the univariate Gaussian distribution for how to solve this integral.

And we have

$$\log \mathcal{N}(\mu_0, \sigma_0^2) = \frac{\log_2 \mathcal{N}(\mu_0, \sigma_0^2)}{\log_2(e)}.$$

The entropy of a Gaussian variable solely depends on its variance. A larger variance indicates a higher entropy because the random variable scatters more widely. Note that the entropy of a Gaussian variable may become negative when its variance is very small (i.e., $\sigma_0^2 < 1/2\pi e$). ♦

The concept of entropy can be further extended to multiple random variables based on their joint distribution. For example, assuming the joint distribution of two discrete random variables, X and Y, is given as $p(x, y)$, we can define the *joint entropy* for them as follows:

$$H(X,Y) = \mathbb{E}_{X,Y}\big[-\log_2 \Pr(X = x, Y = y)\big] = -\sum_x \sum_y p(x,y) \log_2 p(x,y).$$

If X and Y are continuous random variables, we calculate their joint entropy by replacing the summations with integrals:

$$H(X,Y) = -\int\int p(x,y) \log_2 p(x,y)\, dx dy.$$

Intuitively speaking, the joint entropy represents the total amount of uncertainty associated with these two random variables, namely, the total amount of information we need to resolve both of them.

Furthermore, we can define the so-called *conditional entropy* for two random variables, X and Y, based on their conditional distribution $p(y|x)$ as follows:

$$H(Y|X) = \mathbb{E}_{X,Y}\big[-\log_2 \Pr(Y = y|X = x)\big] = -\sum_x \sum_y p(x,y) \log_2 p(y|x).$$

Intuitively speaking, the conditional entropy $H(Y|X)$ indicates the amount of uncertainty associated with Y after X is known, namely, the amount of information we still need to resolve Y even after X is known. Similarly, we can define the conditional entropy $H(X|Y)$ based on the conditional distribution $p(x|y)$ as follows:

$$H(X|Y) = \mathbb{E}_{X,Y}\big[-\log_2 \Pr(X = x|Y = y)\big] = -\sum_x \sum_y p(x,y) \log_2 p(x|y).$$

If X and Y are continuous, we have

$$H(Y|X) = -\int\int p(x,y) \log_2 p(y|x)\, dx dy$$

and

$$H(X|Y) = -\int\int p(x,y) \log_2 p(x|y)\, dx dy.$$

In the same way, $H(X|Y)$ indicates the amount of uncertainty associated with X after Y is known, namely, the amount of information we still need to resolve X after Y is known.

If two random variables X and Y are independent, we have

$$H(X,Y) = H(X) + H(Y)$$

$$H(X|Y) = H(X) \quad \text{and} \quad H(Y|X) = H(Y).$$

See Exercise Q2.10.

2.3.2 Mutual Information

As we have learned, the entropy $H(X)$ represents the amount of uncertainty related to the random variable X, and the conditional entropy $H(X|Y)$ represents the amount of uncertainty related to the same variable X after another random variable Y is known. Therefore, the difference $H(X) - H(X|Y)$ represents the uncertainty reduction about X before and after Y is known. In other words, it indicates the amount of information another random variable Y can provide for X. We often define this uncertainty reduction as the *mutual information* between these two random

If X and Y are continuous,

$$I(X,Y) = \int\int p(x,y)\log_2 \frac{p(x,y)}{p(x)p(y)}\, dxdy.$$

See Exercise Q2.11.

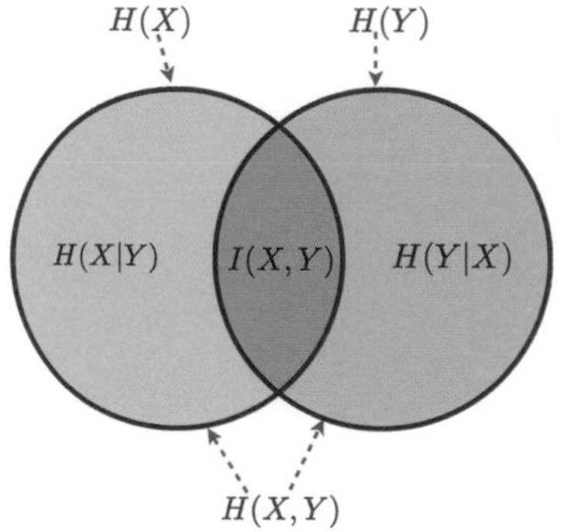

Figure 2.13: An illustration of how mutual information is related to entropy, joint entropy, and conditional entropy.

variables:

$$\begin{aligned} I(X,Y) &= H(X) - H(X|Y) \\ &= \sum_x \sum_y p(x,y)\log_2\left(\frac{p(x,y)}{p(x)p(y)}\right). \end{aligned}$$

Of course, we have several different ways to measure the uncertainty reduction between two random variables, and they all lead to the same mutual information as defined previously:

$$\begin{aligned} I(X,Y) &= H(Y) - H(Y|X) \\ &= H(X) + H(Y) - H(X,Y). \end{aligned}$$

In general, we can conceptually describe the relations among all of these quantities as shown in Figure 2.13. This diagram is useful to visualize all the aforementioned equations related to mutual information.

In the following discussion, we summarize several important properties of mutual information:

- Mutual information is symmetrical (i.e., $I(X,Y) = I(Y,X)$).
- Mutual information is always nonnegative (i.e., $I(X,Y) \geq 0$).
- $I(X,Y) = 0$ if and only if X and Y are independent.

We can easily verify the first property of symmetry from the definition of mutual information. We will prove the other two properties in the next section. From these, we can see that mutual information is guaranteed to be nonnegative for any random variables. In contrast, entropy is nonnegative only for discrete random variables, and it may become negative for continuous random variables (see Example 2.3.2).

Finally, the next example explains how to use mutual information for feature selection in machine learning.

Example 2.3.3 Mutual Information for Keyword Selection

In many real-world text-classification tasks, we often need to filter out noninformative words in text documents before we build classification models. Mutual information is often used as a popular data-driven criterion to select keywords that are informative.

Assume we want to build a text classifier to automatically classify a news article into one of the predefined topics, such as *sports*, *politics*, *business*, or *science*. We first need to collect some news articles from each of these categories. However, these news articles often contain a large number of distinct words. It will definitely complicate the model learning process if we keep all words used in the text documents. Moreover, in natural languages, there are many common words that are used everywhere, so they do not provide much information in terms of distinguishing news topics. In natural language processing, it is a common practice to filter out all noninformative words in an initial preprocessing stage. Mutual information serves as a popular criterion to calculate the correlation between each word and a news topic for this purpose.

As we have learned, mutual information is defined for random variables. We need to specify random variables before we can actually compute mutual information. Let us first pick up a word (e.g., *score*) and a topic (e.g., "sports"); we define two binary random variables:

$X \in \{0,1\}$: whether a document's topic is "sports" or not,
$Y \in \{0,1\}$: whether a document contains the word *score* or not.

We can go over the entire text corpus to compute a joint distribution for X and Y, as shown in the margin. The probabilities in the table are computed based on the counts for each case. For example, we can do the following counts:

$p(x,y)$	$y=0$	$y=1$	$p(x)$
$x=0$	0.80	0.02	0.82
$x=1$	0.11	0.07	0.18
$p(y)$	0.91	0.09	

$$p(X=1,Y=1) = \frac{\text{\# of docs with topic "sports" and containing } score}{\text{total \# of docs in the corpus}}$$

$$p(X=1,Y=0) = \frac{\text{\# of docs with topic "sports" but not containing } score}{\text{total \# of docs in the corpus}}$$

$$p(X=0,Y=0) = \frac{\text{\# of docs without topic "sports" and not containing } score}{\text{total \# of docs in the corpus}}$$

$$p(X=0,Y=1) = \frac{\text{\# of docs without topic "sports" but containing } score}{\text{total \# of docs in the corpus}}.$$

Once all probabilities are computed for the joint distribution, the mutual information $I(X,Y)$ can be computed as

$$I(X,Y) = \sum_{x\in\{0,1\}} \sum_{y\in\{0,1\}} p(x,y) \log_2 \frac{p(x,y)}{p(x)p(y)} = 0.126.$$

$$\begin{aligned} I(X,Y) &= \\ &0.80 \times \log_2 \frac{0.80}{0.82\times 0.91} \\ &+0.02 \times \log_2 \frac{0.02}{0.82\times 0.09} \\ &+0.11 \times \log_2 \frac{0.11}{0.18\times 0.91} \\ &+0.07 \times \log_2 \frac{0.07}{0.18\times 0.09} \\ &= 0.126 \end{aligned}$$

The mutual information $I(X,Y)$ reflects the correlation between the word *score* and the topic "sports." If we repeat this procedure for another word, *what*, and the topic "sports," we may obtain the corresponding $I(X,Y) =$ 0.00007. From these two cases, we can tell that the word *score* is much more informative than *what* in relation to the topic "sports." Finally, we just need to repeat these steps of mutual information computation for all combinations of words and topics, then filter out all words that yield low mutual-information values with respect to all topics. ♦

2.3.3 KL Divergence

Kullback–Leibler (KL) divergence is a criterion to measure the difference between two probability distributions that have the same support. Given any two distributions (e.g., $p(x)$ and $q(x)$), if the domains of their underlying random variables are the same, the KL divergence is defined as the expectation of the logarithm difference between two distributions over the entire domain:

$$\log\left(\frac{p(x)}{q(x)}\right) = \log p(x) - \log q(x).$$

$$\mathrm{KL}\Big(p(x)\,\|\,q(x)\Big) \triangleq \mathbb{E}_{x\sim p(x)}\left[\log\left(\frac{p(x)}{q(x)}\right)\right].$$

Note that the expectation is computed with respect to the first distribution in the KL divergence. As a result, the KL divergence is not symmetric; that is, $\mathrm{KL}(q(x)\,||\,p(x)) \neq \mathrm{KL}(p(x)\,||\,q(x))$.

By definition, we have

$$\mathrm{KL}\Big(q(x)\,\|\,p(x)\Big) \triangleq \mathbb{E}_{x\sim q(x)}\left[\log\left(\frac{q(x)}{p(x)}\right)\right].$$

For discrete random variables, we can calculate the KL divergence as follows:

$$\mathrm{KL}\Big(p(x)\,\|\,q(x)\Big) = \sum_x p(x)\,\log\left(\frac{p(x)}{q(x)}\right).$$

On the other hand, if the random variables are continuous, the KL divergence is computed with the integral as follows:

$$\mathrm{KL}\Big(p(x)\,\|\,q(x)\Big) = \int p(x)\,\log\left(\frac{p(x)}{q(x)}\right)dx.$$

Regarding the property of the KL divergence, we have the following result from mathematical statistics:

Theorem 2.3.1 *The KL divergence is always nonnegative:*

$$\mathrm{KL}\Big(p(x)\,\|\,q(x)\Big) \geq 0.$$

Furthermore, $\mathrm{KL}\Big(p(x)\,\|\,q(x)\Big) = 0$ *if and only if* $p(x) = q(x)$ *holds almost everywhere in the domain.*

Proof:

Step 1: Reviewing Jensen's inequality

Let's first review Jensen's inequality [114] because this theorem can be derived as a corollary from Jensen's inequality. As shown in Figure 2.14, a real-valued function is called *convex* if the line segment between any two points on the graph of the function lies above or on the graph. If $f(x)$ is convex, for any two points x_1 and x_2, we have

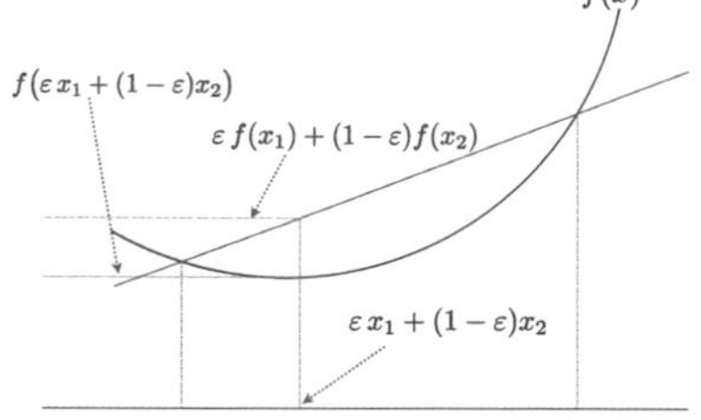

Figure 2.14: An illustration of Jensen's inequality for two points of a convex function. (Image credit: Eli Osherovich/CC-BY-SA-3.0.)

$$f(\varepsilon x_1 + (1-\varepsilon)x_2) \leq \varepsilon f(x_1) + (1-\varepsilon)f(x_2).$$

for any $\varepsilon \in [0,1]$. Jensen's inequality generalizes the statement that the secant line of a convex function lies above the graph of the function from two points to any number of points. In the context of probability theory, Jensen's inequality states that if X is a random variable and $f(\cdot)$ is a convex function, then we have

$$f\big(\mathbb{E}[X]\big) \leq \mathbb{E}\big[f(X)\big]$$

The complete proof of Jensen's inequality is not shown here because its complexity is beyond the scope of this book.

Step 2: Showing the function $-\log(x)$ is strictly convex

We know that any twice-differentiable function is convex if it has positive second-order derivatives everywhere. It is easy to show that $-\log(x)$ has positive second-order derivatives (see margin note).

We have

$$\frac{d^2}{dx^2}\Big(-\log(x)\Big) = \frac{1}{x^2} > 0$$

for all $x > 0$.

Step 3: Applying Jensen's inequality to $-\log(x)$

$$\begin{aligned}
\mathrm{KL}\Big(p(x)\,\|\,q(x)\Big) &= \mathbb{E}_{x\sim p(x)}\left[\log\left(\frac{p(x)}{q(x)}\right)\right] = \mathbb{E}_{x\sim p(x)}\left[-\log\left(\frac{q(x)}{p(x)}\right)\right] \\
&\geq -\log\left(\mathbb{E}_{x\sim p(x)}\left[\frac{q(x)}{p(x)}\right]\right) = -\log\left(\int p(x)\frac{q(x)}{p(x)}\,dx\right) \\
&= -\log\int q(x)\,dx = -\log(1) = 0.
\end{aligned}$$

$q(x)$ satisfies the sum-to-1 constraint because it is a probability distribution.

According to Jensen's inequality, equality holds if and only if $\log\big(p(x)/q(x)\big)$ is a constant. Because both $p(x)$ and $q(x)$ satisfy the sum-to-1 condition, this leads to $p(x)/q(x) = 1$ almost everywhere in the domain. ■

Because of the property stated in the theorem, the KL divergence is often used as a measure of how one probability distribution differs from another reference probability distribution, analogous to the Euclidean distance for two points in a space. Intuitively speaking, the KL divergence $\mathrm{KL}\big(q(x)\,||\,p(x)\big)$ represents the amount of information lost when we replace one probability distribution $p(x)$ with another distribution $q(x)$. However, we have to note that the KL divergence does not qualify as a formal statistical metric because the KL divergence is not symmetric, and it does not satisfy the triangle inequality.

In the context of machine learning, the KL divergence is often used as a loss measure when we use a simple statistical model $q(x)$ to approximate a complicated model $p(x)$. In this case, the best-fit simple model, denoted as $q^*(x)$, can be derived by minimizing the KL divergence between them:

$$q^*(x) = \arg\min_{q(x)} \ \mathrm{KL}\big(q(x)\,||\,p(x)\big).$$

The best-fit model $q^*(x)$ found here is optimal because the minimum amount of information is lost when a complicated model is approximated by a simple one. We will come back to discuss this idea further in Chapter 13 and Chapter 14.

Finally, we can also see that mutual information $I(X,Y)$ can be cast as the KL divergence of the following form:

$$I(X,Y) = \mathrm{KL}\Big(p(x,y) \,\big\|\, p(x)p(y)\Big).$$

This formulation first proves that mutual information $I(X,Y)$ is always nonnegative because it is a special kind of the KL divergence. We can also see that $I(X,Y) = 0$ if and only if $p(x,y) = p(x)p(y)$ holds for all x and y, which implies that X and Y are independent. Therefore, mutual information can be viewed as an information gain from the assumption that random variables are independent.

Example 2.3.4 Compute the KL divergence between two univariate Gaussian distributions with a common variance σ^2: $\mathcal{N}(x \mid \mu_1, \sigma^2)$ and $\mathcal{N}(x \mid \mu_2, \sigma^2)$.

Based on the definition of the KL divergence, we have

Note that

$$\int x\mathcal{N}(x \mid \mu_1, \sigma^2)\, dx = \mu_1$$

$$\begin{aligned}
&\mathrm{KL}\Big(\mathcal{N}(x \mid \mu_1, \sigma^2) \,\big\|\, \mathcal{N}(x \mid \mu_2, \sigma^2)\Big) \\
&= \int \mathcal{N}(x \mid \mu_1, \sigma^2) \log \frac{\mathcal{N}(x \mid \mu_1, \sigma^2)}{\mathcal{N}(x \mid \mu_2, \sigma^2)}\, dx \\
&= -\frac{1}{2\sigma^2} \int \mathcal{N}(x \mid \mu_1, \sigma^2) \Big[(\mu_1^2 - \mu_2^2) - 2x(\mu_1 - \mu_2)\Big]\, dx \\
&= -\frac{1}{2\sigma^2} \Big[(\mu_1^2 - \mu_2^2) - 2\mu_1(\mu_1 - \mu_2)\Big] = \frac{(\mu_1 - \mu_2)^2}{2\sigma^2}.
\end{aligned}$$

We can see that the KL divergence is nonnegative and equals to 0 only when these two Gaussian distributions are identical (i.e., $\mu_1 = \mu_2$). ♦

2.4 Mathematical Optimization

Many real-world problems in engineering and science require us to find the best-fit candidate among a family of feasible choices in that it satisfies certain design criteria in an optimal way. These problems can be cast as a universal problem in mathematics, called *mathematical optimization* (or *optimization* for short). In an optimization problem, we always start with a criterion and formulate an objective function that can quantitatively measure the underlying criterion as a function of all available choices. The optimization problem is solved by just finding the variables that maximize or minimize the objective function among all feasible choices. The feasibility of a choice is usually specified by some constraints in the optimization problem. The following discussion first introduces a general formulation for all mathematical optimization problems, along with some related concepts and terminologies. Next, some analytic results regarding optimality conditions for this general optimization problem under several typical scenarios are presented. As we will see, for many simple optimization problems, we can handily derive closed-form solutions based on these optimality conditions. However, for other sophisticated optimization problems arising from practical applications, we will have to rely on numerical methods to derive a satisfactory solution in an iterative manner. Finally, some popular numerical optimization methods that play an important role in machine learning, such as a variety of gradient descent methods, will be introduced.

2.4.1 General Formulation

We first assume each candidate in an optimization problem can be specified by a bunch of free variables that are collectively represented as a vector $\mathbf{x} \in \mathbb{R}^n$, and the underlying objective function is given as $f(\mathbf{x})$. All kinds of constraints on a feasible choice can always be described by another set of functions of $\mathbf{x}$, among which we may have equality and/or inequality constraints. Without losing generality, any mathematical optimization problem can be formulated as follows:

If we need to maximize $f(\mathbf{x})$, we convert it into minimization as follows:

$$\arg\max_{\mathbf{x}} f(\mathbf{x}) \Leftrightarrow \arg\min_{\mathbf{x}} -f(\mathbf{x}).$$

Similarly, we have

$$g_j(\mathbf{x}) \geq 0 \Leftrightarrow -g_j(\mathbf{x}) \leq 0.$$

$$\mathbf{x}^* = \arg\min_{\mathbf{x}} \ f(\mathbf{x}), \tag{2.4}$$

subject to

$$h_i(\mathbf{x}) = 0 \quad (i = 1, 2, \cdots, m), \tag{2.5}$$

$$g_j(\mathbf{x}) \leq 0 \quad (j = 1, 2, \cdots, n). \tag{2.6}$$

The m equality constraints in Eq. (2.5) and the n inequality constraints in Eq. (2.6) collectively define a feasible set Ω for the free variable $\mathbf{x}$. We assume that these constraints are specified in a meaningful way so that the resultant feasible set Ω is nonempty. An optimization problem essentially requires us to search for all values of $\mathbf{x}$ in Ω so as to yield the best value $\mathbf{x}^*$ that minimizes the objective function in Ω.

This formulation is general enough to accommodate almost all optimization problems. However, without further assumptions on the amenability of the objective function $f(\mathbf{x})$ and all constraint functions $\{h_i(\mathbf{x}), g_j(\mathbf{x})\}$, the optimization problem is in general unsolvable [172]. In the history of mathematical optimization, *linear programming* is the first category of optimization problems that has been extensively studied. The optimization is said to be a linear programming problem if all functions in the formulation, including $f(\mathbf{x})$ and $\{h_i(\mathbf{x}), g_j(\mathbf{x})\}$, are linear or affine. Linear programming problems are considered to be easy to solve, and plenty of efficient numerical methods have been developed to solve all sorts of linear programming problems with reasonable theoretical guarantees.

A linear function takes the form of

$$y = \mathbf{a}^\top \mathbf{x},$$

and an affine function takes the form:

$$y = \mathbf{a}^\top \mathbf{x} + b.$$

During the past decades, the research in mathematical optimization has mainly focused on a more general group of optimization problems called *convex optimization* [28, 172]. The optimization is a convex optimization problem if the objective function $f(\mathbf{x})$ is a convex function (see Figure 2.14) and the feasible set Ω defined by all constraints is a convex set (see margin note). All convex optimization problems have the nice property that a locally optimal solution is guaranteed to be globally optimal. Because of this, convex optimization problems can be efficiently solved by many local search algorithms, which are theoretically guaranteed to converge at a reasonable speed. Compared with linear programming, convex optimization represents a much wider range of optimization problems, including linear programming, quadratic programming, second-order cone programming, and semidefinite programming. Many real-world problems can be formulated or approximated as a convex optimization problem. As we will see, convex optimization also plays an important role in machine learning. The learning problems of many useful models are actually convex optimization. The nice properties of convex optimization ensure that these models can be efficiently learned in practice.

A set is said to be convex if for any two points in the set, the line segment joining them lies entirely within the set.

2.4.2 Optimality Conditions

Here, we will first review the necessary and/or sufficient conditions for any $\mathbf{x}^*$ that is an optimal solution to the optimization problem in Eq. (2.4). These optimality conditions will not only provide us with a good understanding of optimization problems in theory but also help to derive a closed-form solution for some relatively simple problems. We will discuss the optimality conditions for three different scenarios of the optimization problem in Eq. (2.4), namely, without any constraint, under only equality constraints, and under both equality and inequality constraints.

Unconstrained Optimization

Let's start with the cases where we aim to minimize an objective function without any constraint. In general, an unconstrained optimization problem can be represented as follows:

$$\mathbf{x}^* = \arg\min_{\mathbf{x} \in \mathbb{R}^n} f(\mathbf{x}). \tag{2.7}$$

For any function $f(\mathbf{x})$, we can define the following concepts relevant to the optimality conditions of Eq. (2.7):

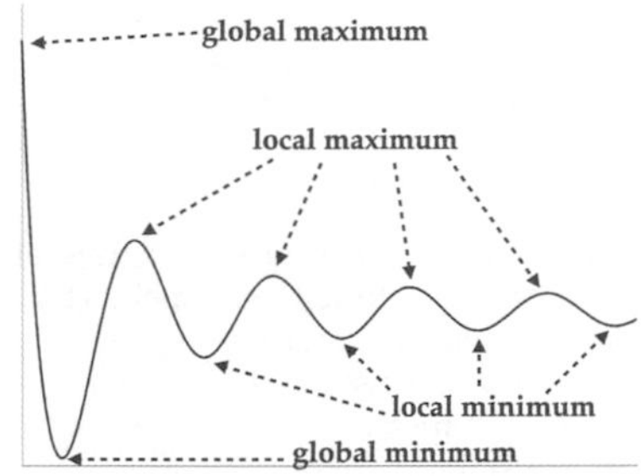

Figure 2.15: An illustration of global minimum (maximum) points versus local minimum (maximum) points.

- **Global minimum (maximum)**
  A point $\hat{\mathbf{x}}$ is said to be a global minimum (or maximum) of $f(\mathbf{x})$ if $f(\hat{\mathbf{x}}) \le f(\mathbf{x})$ (or $f(\hat{\mathbf{x}}) \ge f(\mathbf{x})$) holds for any $\mathbf{x}$ in the domain of the function $f(\mathbf{x})$; see Figure 2.15.
- **Local minimum (maximum)**
  A point $\hat{\mathbf{x}}$ is said to be a local minimum (or maximum) of $f(\mathbf{x})$ if $f(\hat{\mathbf{x}}) \le f(\mathbf{x})$ (or $f(\hat{\mathbf{x}}) \ge f(\mathbf{x})$) holds for all $\mathbf{x}$ within a local neighborhood of $\hat{\mathbf{x}}$; that is, $\|\mathbf{x} - \hat{\mathbf{x}}\| \le \epsilon$ for some $\epsilon > 0$, as shown in Figure 2.15. All local minimum and maximum points are also called *local extreme points*.
- **Stationary point**
  If a function $f(\mathbf{x})$ is differentiable, we can compute partial derivatives with respect to each element in $\mathbf{x}$. These partial derivatives are often arranged as the so-called *gradient* vector, denoted as follows:

$$\mathbf{x} = \begin{bmatrix} x_1 \\ x_2 \\ \vdots \\ x_n \end{bmatrix}$$

$$\nabla f(\mathbf{x}) \stackrel{\Delta}{=} \frac{\partial f(\mathbf{x})}{\partial \mathbf{x}} = \begin{bmatrix} \frac{\partial f(\mathbf{x})}{\partial x_1} \\ \frac{\partial f(\mathbf{x})}{\partial x_2} \\ \vdots \\ \frac{\partial f(\mathbf{x})}{\partial x_n} \end{bmatrix}.$$

  The gradient can be computed for any $\mathbf{x}$ in the function domain. If the gradient $\nabla f(\mathbf{x})$ is nonzero, it points to the direction of the fastest increase of the function value at $\mathbf{x}$. On the other hand, a point $\hat{\mathbf{x}}$ is said to be a stationary point of $f(\mathbf{x})$ if all partial derivatives are 0 at $\hat{\mathbf{x}}$; that is, the gradient vanishes at $\hat{\mathbf{x}}$:

$$\nabla f(\hat{\mathbf{x}}) \stackrel{\Delta}{=} \nabla f(\mathbf{x})\Big|_{\mathbf{x}=\hat{\mathbf{x}}} = 0.$$

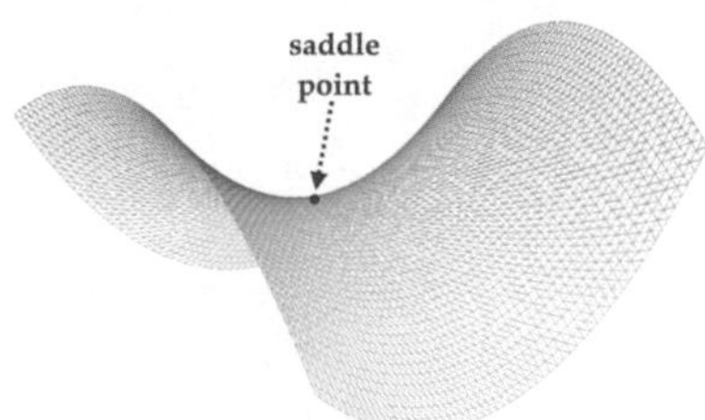

Figure 2.16: An illustration of a saddle point at $x = 0, y = 0$ on the surface of $f(x, y) = x^2 - y^2$. It is not an extreme point, but we can verify that the gradient vanishes there.

- **Critical point**
  A point $\hat{\mathbf{x}}$ is a critical point of a function if it is either a stationary point or a point where the gradient is undefined. For a general function, critical points include all stationary points and all singular points where the function is not differentiable. On the other hand, if the function is differentiable everywhere, every critical point is also a stationary point.
- **Saddle point**
  If a point $\hat{\mathbf{x}}$ is a critical point but it is not a local extreme point of the function $f(\mathbf{x})$, it is called a *saddle point*. There are usually a large number of saddle points on the high-dimensional surface of a multivariate function, as shown in Figure 2.16.

Figure 2.17 summarizes the relationship between all of the previously discussed concepts for a differentiable function.

Figure 2.17: A diagram to illustrate all concepts related to stationary points for a differentiable function:
1. $A \implies B$ means A is B.
2. $A \not\Longleftrightarrow B$ means A and B are not the same (disjoint).
3. $A \iff B$ means A and B are equivalent.

Strictly speaking, only a global minimum point constitutes an optimal solution to the optimization problem in Eq. (2.7). *Global optimization* methods aim to find a global minimum for the optimization problem in Eq. (2.7). However, for most objective functions, finding a global optimal point is an extremely challenging task, in which the computational complexity often exponentially grows with the number of free variables. As a result, we often have to relax to resort to a *local optimization* strategy, where a local optimization algorithm can only find a local minimum for the optimization problem in Eq. (2.7).

For any differentiable objective function, we have the following necessary condition for any locally optimal solution:

Theorem 2.4.1 (necessary condition for unconstrained optimization) *Assume the objective function $f(\mathbf{x})$ is differentiable everywhere. If $\mathbf{x}^*$ is a local minimum of Eq. (2.7), then $\mathbf{x}^*$ must be a stationary point; that is, the gradient vanishes at $\mathbf{x}^*$ as $\nabla f(\mathbf{x}^*) = 0$.*

This theorem suggests a simple strategy to solve any unconstrained optimization problem in Eq. (2.7). If we can compute the gradient of the objective function $\nabla f(\mathbf{x})$, we can vanish it by solving the following:

$$\nabla f(\mathbf{x}) = 0,$$

which results in a group of n equations. If we can solve these equations explicitly, their solution may be a locally optimal solution to the original unconstrained optimization problem. Because the previous theorem only states a necessary condition, the found solution may also be a local maximum or a saddle point of the original problem. In practice, we will have to verify whether the solution found by vanishing the gradient is indeed a true local minimum to the original problem.

If the objective function is twice differentiable, we can establish stronger optimality conditions based on the second-order derivatives. In particular, we can compute all second-order partial derivatives for the objective function $f(\mathbf{x})$ in the following $n \times n$ matrix:

$$\mathbf{H}(\mathbf{x}) = \left[\frac{\partial^2 f(\mathbf{x})}{\partial x_i \partial x_j} \right]_{n \times n} = \begin{bmatrix} \frac{\partial^2 f(\mathbf{x})}{\partial x_1^2} & \frac{\partial^2 f(\mathbf{x})}{\partial x_1 \partial x_2} & \cdots & \frac{\partial^2 f(\mathbf{x})}{\partial x_1 \partial x_n} \\ \frac{\partial^2 f(\mathbf{x})}{\partial x_1 \partial x_2} & \frac{\partial^2 f(\mathbf{x})}{\partial x_2^2} & \cdots & \frac{\partial^2 f(\mathbf{x})}{\partial x_2 \partial x_n} \\ \vdots & \vdots & \ddots & \vdots \\ \frac{\partial^2 f(\mathbf{x})}{\partial x_1 \partial x_n} & \frac{\partial^2 f(\mathbf{x})}{\partial x_2 \partial x_n} & \cdots & \frac{\partial^2 f(\mathbf{x})}{\partial x_n^2} \end{bmatrix},$$

where $\mathbf{H}(\mathbf{x})$ is often called the *Hessian* matrix. Similar to the gradient, we can compute the Hessian matrix at any point $\mathbf{x}$ for a twice-differentiable function. The Hessian matrix $\mathbf{H}(\mathbf{x})$ describes the local curvature of the function surface $f(\mathbf{x})$ at $\mathbf{x}$.

If we have obtained a stationary point $\mathbf{x}^*$ by vanishing the gradient as $\nabla f(\mathbf{x}^*) = 0$, we can know more about $\mathbf{x}^*$ by examining the Hessian matrix at $\mathbf{x}^*$. If $\mathbf{H}(\mathbf{x}^*)$ contains both positive and negative eigenvalues (neither positive nor negative definite), $\mathbf{x}^*$ must be a saddle point, as in Figure 2.16, where the function value increases along some directions and decreases along other directions. If $\mathbf{H}(\mathbf{x}^*)$ contains all positive eigenvalues (positive definite), $\mathbf{x}^*$ is a strict isolated local minimum, where the function value increases along all directions, as in Figure 2.18. If $\mathbf{H}(\mathbf{x}^*)$ only contains both positive and 0 eigenvalues (positive semidefinite), $\mathbf{x}^*$ is still a local minimum, but it is located at a flat valley in Figure 2.18, where the function value remains constant along some directions related to 0 eigenvalues. Finally, if the Hessian matrix also vanishes (i.e., $\mathbf{H}(\mathbf{x}^*) = 0$), $\mathbf{x}^*$ is located on a plateau of the function surface.

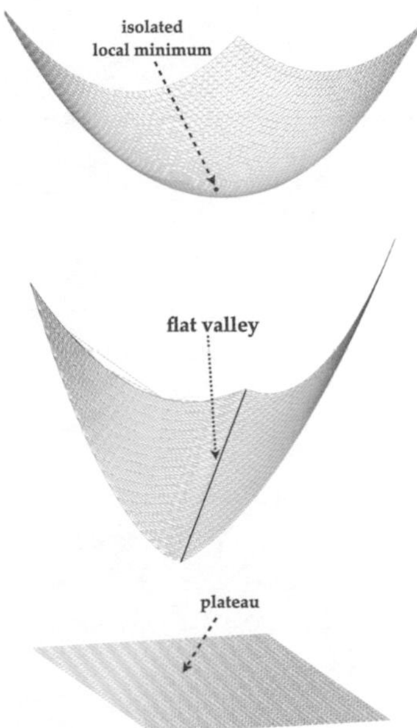

Figure 2.18: An illustration of several different scenarios of a stationary point, where the curvature of the surface is indicated by the Hessian matrix:
1. Isolated minimum: $\mathbf{H}(\mathbf{x}) \succ 0$
2. Flat valley: $\mathbf{H}(\mathbf{x}) \succeq 0$ and $\mathbf{H}(\mathbf{x}) \neq 0$
3. Plateau: $\mathbf{H}(\mathbf{x}) = 0$

Based on the Hessian matrix, we can establish the following second-order necessary or sufficient condition for any local optimal solution of Eq. (2.7) as follows:

Theorem 2.4.2 (second-order necessary condition) *Assume the objective function $f(\mathbf{x})$ is twice differentiable. If $\mathbf{x}^*$ is a local minimum of Eq. (2.7), then*

$$\nabla f(\mathbf{x}^*) = 0 \quad \textit{and} \quad \mathbf{H}(\mathbf{x}^*) \succeq 0.$$

Theorem 2.4.3 (second-order sufficient condition) *Assume the objective function $f(\mathbf{x})$ is twice differentiable. If a point $\mathbf{x}^*$ satisfies*

$$\nabla f(\mathbf{x}^*) = 0 \quad \textit{and} \quad \mathbf{H}(\mathbf{x}^*) \succ 0,$$

then $\mathbf{x}^*$ is an isolated local minimum of Eq. (2.7).

The proofs of Theorems 2.4.1, 2.4.2, and 2.4.3 are straightforward, and they are left for Exercise Q2.14.

Equality Constraints

Let's further discuss the optimality conditions for an optimization problem under only equality constraints, such as

$$\mathbf{x}^* = \arg\min_{\mathbf{x}} \; f(\mathbf{x}), \tag{2.8}$$

subject to

$$h_i(\mathbf{x}) = 0 \quad (i = 1, 2, \cdots, m). \tag{2.9}$$

Generally speaking, stationary points of the objective function $f(\mathbf{x})$ usually are not the optimal solution anymore because these stationary points may not satisfy the constraints in Eq. (2.9). The Lagrange multiplier theorem establishes a first-order necessary condition for the optimization under equality constraints as follows:

Theorem 2.4.4 (Lagrange necessary conditions) *Assume the objective function $f(\mathbf{x})$ and all constraint functions $\{h_i(\mathbf{x})\}$ in Eq. (2.9) are differentiable. If a point $\mathbf{x}^*$ is a local optimal solution to the problem in Eq. (2.8), then the gradients of these functions are linearly dependent at $\mathbf{x}^*$:*

$$\nabla f(\mathbf{x}^*) + \sum_{i=1}^{m} \lambda_i \, \nabla h_i(\mathbf{x}^*) = 0,$$

where $\lambda_i \in \mathbb{R}$ $(i = 1, 2, \cdots, m)$ are called the Lagrange multipliers.

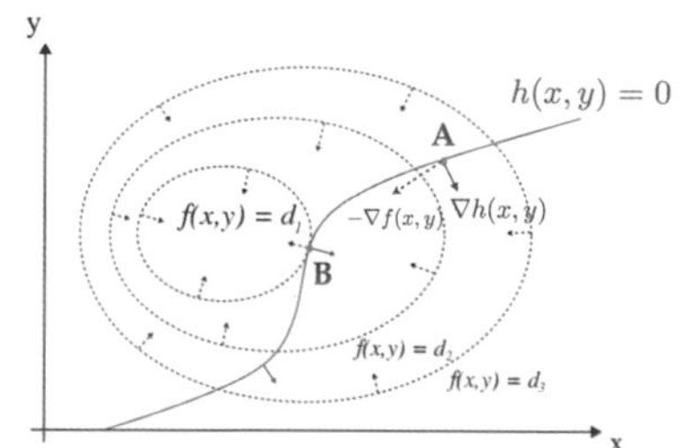

Figure 2.19: An illustration of the Lagrange necessary conditions for an objective function of two free variables $f(x,y)$, which is displayed with the contours, under one equality constraint $h(x,y) = 0$, which is plotted as the red curve.

$$\min_{x,y} \; f(x,y),$$

subject to

$$h(x,y) = 0.$$

We can intuitively explain the Lagrange necessary conditions with the simple example shown in Figure 2.19, where we minimize a function of two variables (i.e., $f(x,y)$) under one equality constraint $h(x,y) = 0$ (plotted as the red curve). Looking at an arbitrary point A on the constraint curve, the negative gradient (i.e., $-\nabla f(x,y)$) points to a direction of the fastest decrease of the function value, and $\nabla h(x,y)$ indicates the norm vector of the curve at A. Imagine we want to move A along the constraint curve to further decrease the function value; we can always project the negative gradient to the tangent plane perpendicular to the norm vector. If we move A slightly along this projected direction, the function value will decrease accordingly. As a result, A cannot be a local optimal point to the original optimization problem. We can continue to move A until it reaches the point B, where the negative gradient is in the same space of the norm vector so that the projection is not possible anymore. This indicates that B may be a local optimal point, and we can verify that the Lagrange condition holds at B.

The Lagrange necessary conditions suggest a convenient treatment to handle equality constraints in any optimization problem in Eq. (2.8) and Eq.

(2.9). For each equality constraint $h_i(\mathbf{x}) = 0$, we introduce a new free variable λ, called a *Lagrange multiplier*, and construct the so-called *Lagrangian* function:

$$L(\mathbf{x}, \{\lambda_i\}) = f(\mathbf{x}) + \sum_{i=1}^{m} \lambda_i \, h_i(\mathbf{x}).$$

If we can optimize the Lagrangian function with respect to the original variables $\mathbf{x}$ and all Lagrange multipliers, we can derive the solution to the original constrained optimization in Eq. (2.8). We can see that the Lagrangian function is a useful technique to convert a constrained optimization problem into an unconstrained one.

$$\min_{\mathbf{x},\{\lambda_i\}} L(\mathbf{x}, \{\lambda_i\})$$

$$\Longrightarrow \frac{\partial L(\mathbf{x}, \{\lambda_i\})}{\partial \mathbf{x}} = 0.$$

This further leads to the same Lagrange conditions in Theorem 2.4.4:

$$\nabla f(\mathbf{x}) + \sum_{i=1}^{m} \lambda_i \, \nabla h_i(\mathbf{x}) = 0.$$

Example 2.4.1 As shown in Figure 2.20, compute the distance from a point $\mathbf{x}_0 \in \mathbb{R}^n$ to a hyperplane $\mathbf{w}^\intercal \mathbf{x} + b = 0$ in the space $\mathbf{x} \in \mathbb{R}^n$, where $\mathbf{w} \in \mathbb{R}^n$ and $b \in \mathbb{R}$ are given.

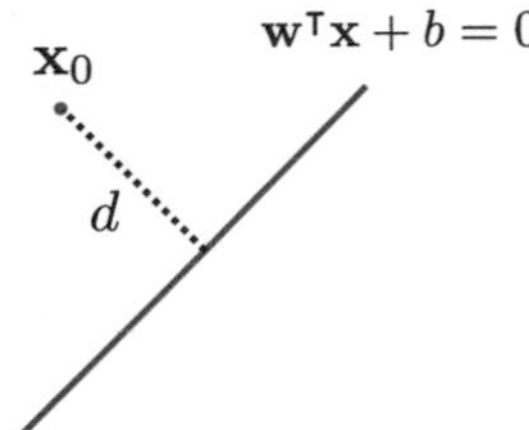

Figure 2.20: An illustration of the distance from any point $\mathbf{x}_0$ to a hyperplane $\mathbf{w}^\intercal \mathbf{x} + b = 0$.

We can formulate this problem as the following constrained optimization problem:

$$d^2 = \min_{\mathbf{x}} \|\mathbf{x} - \mathbf{x}_0\|^2,$$

subject to

$$\mathbf{w}^\intercal \mathbf{x} + b = 0.$$

We introduce a Lagrange multiplier λ for this equality constraint and further construct the Lagrangian function as follows:

$$\begin{aligned} L(\mathbf{x}, \lambda) &= \|\mathbf{x} - \mathbf{x}_0\|^2 + \lambda \left(\mathbf{w}^\intercal \mathbf{x} + b\right) \\ &= \left(\mathbf{x} - \mathbf{x}_0\right)^\intercal \left(\mathbf{x} - \mathbf{x}_0\right) + \lambda \left(\mathbf{w}^\intercal \mathbf{x} + b\right) \end{aligned}$$

$$\begin{aligned} \frac{\partial L(\mathbf{x}, \lambda)}{\partial \mathbf{x}} = 0 \quad &\Longrightarrow \quad 2\left(\mathbf{x} - \mathbf{x}_0\right) + \lambda \mathbf{w} = 0 \\ &\Longrightarrow \quad \mathbf{x}^* = \mathbf{x}_0 - \frac{\lambda^*}{2} \mathbf{w}, \end{aligned}$$

Substituting it into the constraint $\mathbf{w}^\intercal \mathbf{x}^* + b = 0$, we can solve for λ^* as follows:

$$\lambda^* = \frac{2\left(\mathbf{w}^\intercal \mathbf{x}_0 + b\right)}{\mathbf{w}^\intercal \mathbf{w}} = \frac{2\left(\mathbf{w}^\intercal \mathbf{x}_0 + b\right)}{\|\mathbf{w}\|^2}.$$

Finally, we have

$$d^2 = \|\mathbf{x}^* - \mathbf{x}_0\|^2 = \frac{\lambda^{*2}}{4} \|\mathbf{w}\|^2 = \frac{|\mathbf{w}^\intercal \mathbf{x}_0 + b|^2}{\|\mathbf{w}\|^2}$$

$$\Longrightarrow d = \frac{|\mathbf{w}^\intercal \mathbf{x}_0 + b|}{\|\mathbf{w}\|}.$$

♦

Inequality Constraints

$$\mathbf{x}^* = \arg\min_{\mathbf{x}} f(\mathbf{x}),$$

subject to

$$h_i(\mathbf{x}) = 0 \quad (i = 1, 2, \cdots, m)$$

$$g_j(\mathbf{x}) \leq 0 \quad (j = 1, 2, \cdots, n).$$

We assume all these constraints define a nonempty feasible set for $\mathbf{x}$, denoted as Ω.

In this section, we will investigate how to establish the optimality conditions for the general optimization problems in Eq. (2.4) (copied at left), which involves both equality and inequality constraints.

First of all, following a similar idea as before, we introduce a Lagrange multiplier λ_i ($\forall i$) for each equality constraint function and a *nonnegative* Lagrange multiplier $\nu_j \geq 0$ ($\forall j$) for each inequality constraint function to construct a Lagrangian function as follows:

$$\begin{aligned} L\Big(\mathbf{x}, \{\lambda_i, \nu_j\}\Big) &= f(\mathbf{x}) + \sum_{i=1}^{m} \overbrace{\lambda_i\, h_i(\mathbf{x})}^{=0} + \sum_{j=1}^{n} \overbrace{\nu_j\, g_j(\mathbf{x})}^{\leq 0} \\ &\leq f(\mathbf{x}) \qquad (\forall \mathbf{x} \in \Omega). \end{aligned}$$

Because of the constraints $\nu_j \geq 0$ ($\forall j$), this Lagrangian is a lower bound of the original objective function $f(\mathbf{x})$ in the feasible set Ω. We can further minimize out the original variables $\mathbf{x}$ inside Ω so as to derive a function of all Lagrange multipliers:

inf is a generalization of min for open sets.

$$L^*\Big(\{\lambda_i, \nu_j\}\Big) = \inf_{\mathbf{x}\in\Omega} L\Big(\mathbf{x}, \{\lambda_i, \nu_j\}\Big).$$

This function is often called the *Lagrange dual function*. From the above definitions, we can easily show that the dual function is also a lower bound of the original objective function:

$$L^*\Big(\{\lambda_i, \nu_j\}\Big) \leq L\Big(\mathbf{x}, \{\lambda_i, \nu_j\}\Big) \leq f(\mathbf{x}) \qquad (\mathbf{x} \in \Omega).$$

In other words, the Lagrange dual function is below the original objective function $f(\mathbf{x})$ for all $\mathbf{x}$ in Ω. Assuming $\mathbf{x}^*$ is an optimal solution to the original optimization problem in Eq. (2.4), we still have

$$L^*\Big(\{\lambda_i, \nu_j\}\Big) \leq f(\mathbf{x}^*). \tag{2.10}$$

An interesting thing to do is to further optimize all Lagrange multipliers to maximize the dual function in order to close the gap as much as possible, which leads to a new optimization problem, as follows:

$$\{\lambda_i^*, \nu_j^*\} = \arg\max_{\{\lambda_i, \nu_j\}} L^*\Big(\{\lambda_i, \nu_j\}\Big),$$

subject to

$$\nu_j \geq 0 \qquad (j = 1, 2, \cdots, n).$$

This new optimization problem is called the *Lagrange dual problem*. In contrast, the original optimization problem in Eq. (2.4) is called the *primal problem*. From Eq. (2.10), we can immediately derive

$$L^*\Big(\{\lambda_i^*, \nu_j^*\}\Big) \leq f(\mathbf{x}^*).$$

If the original primary problem is convex optimization and some minor qualification conditions (such as Slater's condition [225]) are met, the gap becomes 0, and the equality

$$L^*\Big(\{\lambda_i^*, \nu_j^*\}\Big) = f(\mathbf{x}^*)$$

holds, which is called *strong duality*. When strong duality holds, $\mathbf{x}^*$ and $\{\lambda_i^*, \nu_j^*\}$ form a saddle point of the Lagrangian $L(\mathbf{x}, \{\lambda_i, \nu_j\})$, as shown in Figure 2.21, where the Lagrangian increases with respect to **x** but decreases with respect to $\{\lambda_i, \nu_j\}$. In this case, both the primary and dual problems are equivalent because they lead to the same optimal solution at the saddle point.

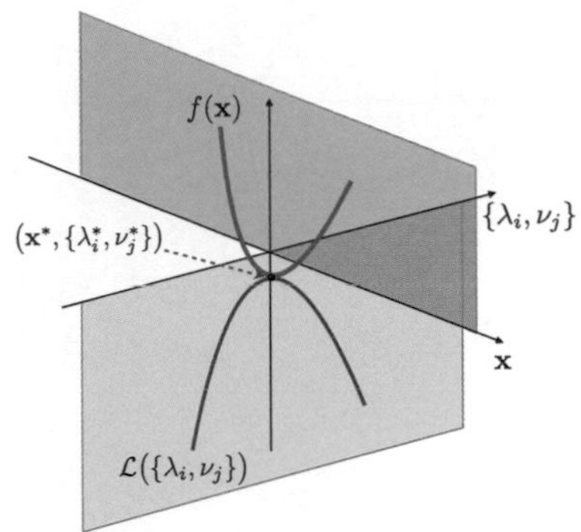

Figure 2.21: An illustration of strong duality occurring in a saddle point of the Lagrangian function.

When strong duality holds, we have

$$\begin{aligned} f(\mathbf{x}^*) &= L^*\Big(\{\lambda_i^*, \nu_j^*\}\Big) \leq L\Big(\mathbf{x}^*, \{\lambda_i^*, \nu_j^*\}\Big) \\ &= f(\mathbf{x}^*) + \sum_{i=1}^{m} \underbrace{\lambda_i^* h_i(\mathbf{x}^*)}_{=0} + \sum_{j=1}^{n} \nu_j^* g_j(\mathbf{x}^*). \end{aligned}$$

From this, we can see that $\sum_{j=1}^n \nu_j^* g_j(\mathbf{x}^*) \geq 0$. On the other hand, by definition, we have $\nu_j^* g_j(\mathbf{x}^*) \leq 0$ for all $j = 1, 2 \cdots, n$. These results further suggest the so-called *complementary slackness* conditions:

$$\nu_j^* g_j(\mathbf{x}^*) = 0 \quad (j = 1, 2, \cdots, n).$$

Finally, we summarize all of the previous results, called Karush–Kuhn–Tucker (KKT) conditions [124, 135], in the following theorem:

Theorem 2.4.5 (KKT necessary conditions) *If* $\mathbf{x}^*$ *and* $\{\lambda_i^*, \nu_j^*\}$ *form a saddle point of the Lagrangian function* $L(\mathbf{x}, \{\lambda_i, \nu_j\})$*, then* $\mathbf{x}^*$ *is an optimal solution to the problem in Eq. (2.4). The saddle point satisfies the following conditions:*
1. Stationariness:

$$\nabla f(\mathbf{x}^*) + \sum_{i=1}^{m} \lambda_i^* \nabla h_i(\mathbf{x}^*) + \sum_{j=1}^{n} \nu_j^* \nabla g_j(\mathbf{x}^*) = 0.$$

2. Primal feasibility:

$$h_i(\mathbf{x}^*) = 0 \;\; and \;\; g_j(\mathbf{x}^*) \leq 0 \quad (\forall i = 1, 2, \cdots, m; j = 1, 2, \cdots, n).$$

Note that the stationariness condition is derived as such because the saddle point is a stationary point, where the gradient vanishes.

3. *Dual feasibility:*

$$\nu_j^* \geq 0 \qquad (\forall j = 1, 2, \cdots, n).$$

4. *Complementary slackness:*

$$\nu_j^* g_j(\mathbf{x}^*) = 0 \qquad (\forall j = 1, 2, \cdots, n).$$

Next, we will use an example to show how to apply the KKT conditions to solve an optimization problem under inequality constraints.

Example 2.4.2 Compute the distance from a point $\mathbf{x}_0 \in \mathbb{R}^n$ to a half-space $\mathbf{w}^\intercal\mathbf{x} + b \leq 0$ in the space $\mathbf{x} \in \mathbb{R}^n$, where $\mathbf{w} \in \mathbb{R}^n$ and $b \in \mathbb{R}$ are given.

Similar to Example 2.4.1, we can formulate this problem as the following constrained optimization problem:

$$d^2 = \min_{\mathbf{x}} \ \|\mathbf{x} - \mathbf{x}_0\|^2,$$

subject to

$$\mathbf{w}^\intercal\mathbf{x} + b \leq 0.$$

We introduce a Lagrange multiplier ν for the inequality constraint. As opposed to Example 2.4.1, because this is an inequality constraint, we have the complementary slackness and dual-feasibility conditions:

$$\nu^* \big(\mathbf{w}^\intercal\mathbf{x}^* + b\big) = 0 \qquad \text{and} \qquad \nu^* \geq 0.$$

Accordingly, we can conclude that the optimal solution $\mathbf{x}^*$ and ν^* must be one of the following two cases:

$$(a)\ \mathbf{w}^\intercal\mathbf{x}^* + b = 0 \quad \text{and} \quad \nu^* \geq 0,$$

$$(b)\ \nu^* = 0 \quad \text{and} \quad \mathbf{w}^\intercal\mathbf{x}^* + b \leq 0.$$

For case (a), where $\mathbf{w}^\intercal\mathbf{x}^* + b = 0$ must hold, we can derive from the stationariness condition in the same way as in Example 2.4.1:

$$L(\mathbf{x}, \nu) = \|\mathbf{x} - \mathbf{x}_0\|^2 + \nu\,\big(\mathbf{w}^\intercal\mathbf{x} + b\big),$$

$$\frac{\partial L(\mathbf{x}, \nu)}{\partial \mathbf{x}} = 0 \implies \nu^* = \frac{2\big(\mathbf{w}^\intercal\mathbf{x}_0 + b\big)}{\|\mathbf{w}\|^2}.$$

If $\mathbf{w}^\intercal\mathbf{x}_0 + b \geq 0$, corresponding to the case where the half-space does not contain $\mathbf{x}_0$ (see the left side in Figure 2.22), we have $\nu^* \geq 0$ for this case. This leads to the same problem as Example 2.4.1. We can finally derive $d = (\mathbf{w}^\intercal\mathbf{x}_0 + b)/\|\mathbf{w}\|$ for this case. However, if $\mathbf{w}^\intercal\mathbf{x}_0 + b < 0$, corresponding to the case where the half-space contains $\mathbf{x}_0$ (see the right side in Figure

2.22), then we have $\nu^* < 0$. This result is invalid because it violates the dual-feasibility condition.

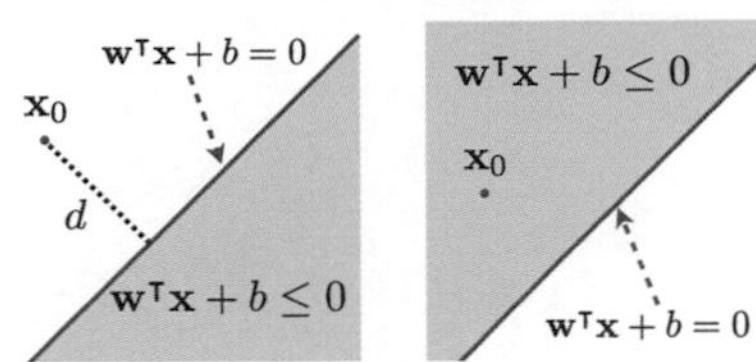

Figure 2.22: An illustration of two cases when computing the distance from a point $\mathbf{x}_0$ to a half-space $\mathbf{w}^\intercal\mathbf{x} + b \le 0$:
1. Left: $\mathbf{x}_0$ not in the half-space
2. Right: $\mathbf{x}_0$ in the half-space

Moreover, let us consider case (b), where $\nu^* = 0$ and $\mathbf{w}^\intercal\mathbf{x}^* + b \le 0$ must hold. After substituting $\nu^* = 0$ into the stationariness condition, we can derive $\mathbf{x}^* = \mathbf{x}_0$ and $d = 0$ immediately for this case. This is the correct result for the case where the half-space contains $\mathbf{x}_0$ in the right side of Figure 2.22.

Finally, we can summarize these results as follows:

$$d = \begin{cases} \frac{\mathbf{w}^\intercal\mathbf{x}_0 + b}{\|\mathbf{w}\|} & \text{if } \ \mathbf{w}^\intercal\mathbf{x}_0 + b \ge 0 \\ 0 & \text{if } \ \mathbf{w}^\intercal\mathbf{x}_0 + b \le 0. \end{cases}$$

♦

2.4.3 Numerical Optimization Methods

For many optimization problems arising from real-world applications, the analytic methods based on the optimality conditions do not always lead to a useful closed-form solution. For these practical problems, we have to rely on numerical methods to derive a reasonable solution in an iterative fashion. Depending on what information is used in each iteration of these numerical methods, they can be roughly classified into several categories, namely, the *zero-order*, *first-order*, and *second-order* methods. In this section, we will briefly review some common methods from each category but focus more on the first-order methods because they are the most popular choices in machine learning. For simplicity, we will use the unconstrained optimization problem

$$\arg\min_{\mathbf{x}\in\mathbb{R}^n} \ f(\mathbf{x})$$

as an example to introduce these numerical methods, but many numerical methods can be easily adapted to deal with constraints.

For example, we can project an unconstrained gradient into the feasible set for all first-order methods, leading to the so-called *projected gradient descent* method.

Zero-Order Methods

The zero-order methods only rely on the zero-order information of the objective function, namely, the function value $f(\mathbf{x})$. We usually need to build a coordinate grid for all free variables in $f(\mathbf{x})$ and then use the grid search strategy to exhaustively check the function value at each point until a satisfactory solution is found. This method is simple, but it suffers from the curse of dimensionality because the number of points in a grid exponentially grows with the number of free parameters. In machine learning, the zero-order methods are mainly used only for the cases where we have a small number of variables (less than 10), such as hyperparameter optimization.

First-Order Methods

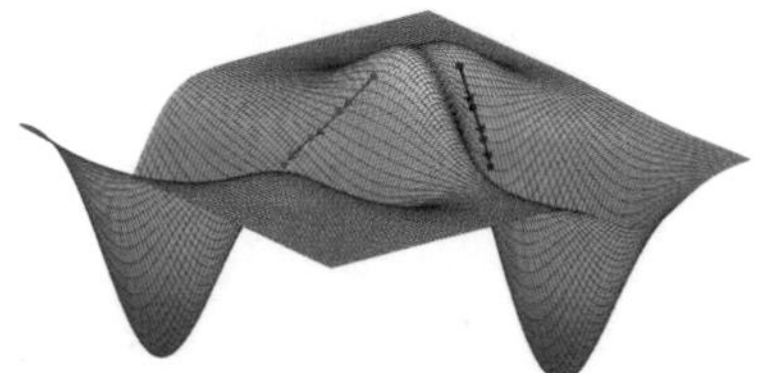

Figure 2.23: An illustration of the gradient descent method, where two trajectories indicate two initial points used by the algorithm.

The first-order methods can access both the zero-order and the first-order information of the objective function, namely, the function value $f(\mathbf{x})$ and the gradient $\nabla f(\mathbf{x})$. As we have learned, the gradient $\nabla f(\mathbf{x})$ points to a direction of the fastest increase of the function value at $\mathbf{x}$. As shown in Figure 2.23, starting from any point on the function surface, if we move a sufficiently small step along the direction of the negative gradient, it is guaranteed that the function value will be more or less decreased. We can repeat this step over and over until it converges to any stationary point. This idea leads to a simple iterative optimization method, called *gradient descent* (a.k.a. *steepest descent*), shown in Algorithm 2.1.

Algorithm 2.1 Gradient Descent Method

randomly choose $\mathbf{x}^{(0)}$, and set η_0
set $n = 0$
while not converged **do**
  update: $\mathbf{x}^{(n+1)} = \mathbf{x}^{(n)} - \eta_n \nabla f(\mathbf{x}^{(n)})$
  adjust: $\eta_n \rightarrow \eta_{n+1}$
  $n = n + 1$
end while

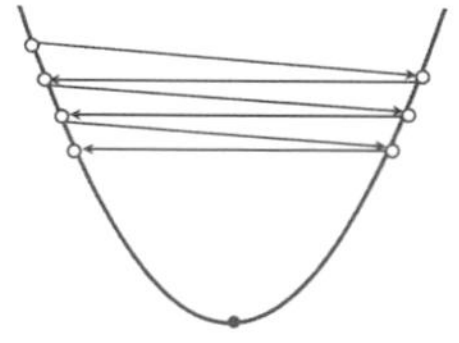

Figure 2.24: An illustration of how a large step size may affect the convergence of the gradient descent method.

Because the gradient cannot tell us how much we should move along the direction, we have to use a manually specified *step size* η_n for each move. The key in the gradient descent method is how to properly choose the step size for each iteration. If the step sizes are too small, the convergence will be slow because it needs to run too many updates to reach any stationary point. On the other hand, if the step sizes are too large, each update may overshoot the target and cause the fluctuation shown in Figure 2.24. As we come close to a stationary point, we usually need to use an even smaller step size to ensure the convergence. As a result, we need to follow a schedule to adjust the step size at the end of each iteration. When we run gradient descent Algorithm 2.1 from any starting point $\mathbf{x}^{(0)}$, it will generate a trajectory $\{\mathbf{x}^{(0)}, \mathbf{x}^{(1)}, \mathbf{x}^{(2)}, \cdots\}$ on the function surface, which gradually converges to a stationary point of the objective function. As shown in Figure 2.23, each trajectory heavily depends on the initial point. In other words, if we start from a different initial point $\mathbf{x}^{(0)}$ at the beginning, we may eventually end up with a different solution. Choosing a good initial point is another key factor in ensuring the success of the gradient descent method.

The gradient descent method is conceptually simple and only needs to use the gradient, which can be easily computed for almost any meaningful objective function. As a result, the gradient descent method becomes a very popular numerical optimization method in practice. If the objective function is smooth and differentiable, we can theoretically prove that the gradient descent algorithm is guaranteed to converge to a stationary point as long as a sufficiently small step size is used at each iteration (see Exercise Q2.16). However, the convergence rate is relatively slow (a *sublinear* rate). If we want to achieve $\|\nabla f(\mathbf{x}^{(n)})\| \leq \epsilon$, we need to run at least $O(1/\epsilon^2)$ iterations. However, if we can make stronger assumptions on the objective function, such as $f(\mathbf{x})$ is convex and at least twice differentiable and its derivatives are sufficiently smooth, we can prove that the gradient descent algorithm is guaranteed to converge to a local minimum $\mathbf{x}^*$ if small enough steps are used. Under these conditions, the gradient descent method can achieve a much faster convergence rate (a *linear* rate). If we want to achieve $\|\mathbf{x}^{(n)} - \mathbf{x}^*\| \leq \epsilon$, we just need to run approximately $O(\ln(1/\epsilon))$ iterations.

If a sequence $\{x_k\}$ converges to the limit x^*: $\lim_{k\to\infty} x_k = x^*$. The rate of convergence is defined as

$$\mu = \lim_{k\to\infty} \frac{|x_{k+1} - x^*|}{|x_k - x^*|}.$$

The convergence is said to be

$$\begin{cases} \text{superlinear} & \text{if } \mu = 0, \\ \text{linear} & \text{if } 0 < \mu < 1, \\ \text{sublinear} & \text{if } \mu = 1. \end{cases}$$

Example 1: For a sequence of exponentially decaying errors:

$$|x_k - x^*| = C\rho^k,$$

where $0 < \rho < 1$. We can verify its convergence rate is linear because

$$\mu = \frac{|x_{k+1} - x^*|}{|x_k - x^*|} = \rho.$$

For any error tolerance $\epsilon > 0$, if we want to achieve $|x_k - x^*| \leq \epsilon$, we have to access x_k with

$$k \geq \frac{\ln C + \ln \frac{1}{\epsilon}}{\ln \frac{1}{\rho}} \approx O(\ln \frac{1}{\epsilon}).$$

Example 2: For another sequence of decaying errors:

$$|x_k - x^*| = \frac{C}{\sqrt{k}},$$

its convergence rate is sublinear as

$$\mu = \lim_{k\to\infty} \frac{\sqrt{k}}{\sqrt{k+1}} = 1.$$

To achieve $|x_k - x^*| \leq \epsilon$, we need

$$k \geq \frac{C^2}{\epsilon^2} \approx O(\frac{1}{\epsilon^2}).$$

In machine learning, we often need to optimize an objective function that can be decomposed as a sum of many homogeneous components:

$$f(\mathbf{x}) = \frac{1}{N} \sum_{i=1}^{N} f_i(\mathbf{x}).$$

For example, the objective function $f(\mathbf{x})$ represents the average loss measured on all samples in a training set, and each $f_i(\mathbf{x})$ indicates the loss measure on each training sample. If we use the gradient descent Algorithm 2.1 to minimize this objective function, at each iteration, we need to go through all training samples to compute the gradient as follows:

$$\nabla f(\mathbf{x}) = \frac{1}{N} \sum_{i=1}^{N} \nabla f_i(\mathbf{x}).$$

If the training set is large, this step is extremely expensive. To address this issue, we often adopt a stochastic approximation strategy to compute the gradient, where the gradient is approximated as $\nabla f_k(\mathbf{x})$ using a randomly chosen sample k rather than being averaged over all samples. This idea leads to the well-known stochastic gradient descent (SGD) method [24], as shown in Algorithm 2.2.

In Algorithm 2.2, each $\nabla f_k(\mathbf{x})$ can be viewed as a noisy estimate of the true gradient $\nabla f(\mathbf{x})$. Because $\nabla f_k(\mathbf{x})$ can be computed in a relatively cheap way in SGD, we can afford to run much more iterations using a much smaller step size than in the regular gradient descent method. By doing so, the SGD algorithm can converge to a reasonable solution, even in a much shorter training time. Moreover, many empirical results have shown that

Algorithm 2.2 Stochastic Gradient Descent (SGD) Method

randomly choose $\mathbf{x}^{(0)}$, and set η_0
set $n = 0$
while not converged **do**
  randomly choose a sample k
  update: $\mathbf{x}^{(n+1)} = \mathbf{x}^{(n)} - \eta_n \nabla f_k(\mathbf{x}^{(n)})$
  adjust: $\eta_n \rightarrow \eta_{n+1}$
  $n = n + 1$
end while

small noises in gradient estimation can even help to converge to a better solution because small noises make the algorithm escape from poor local minimums or saddle points.

Along these lines, an enhanced SGD version is proposed in Algorithm 2.3, where the gradient is estimated at each step, not using only a single sample but from a small subset of randomly chosen samples. Each subset is often called a *mini-batch*. The samples in a mini-batch are randomly chosen every time to ensure all training samples are accessed equally. In Algorithm 2.3, called *mini-batch SGD*, we can choose the size of all mini-batches to control how much noise is injected into each gradient estimation.

Algorithm 2.3 Mini-Batch SGD

randomly choose $\mathbf{x}^{(0)}$, and set η_0
set $n = 0$
while not converged **do**
  randomly shuffle all training samples into mini-batches
  for each mini-batch B **do**
    update: $\mathbf{x}^{(n+1)} = \mathbf{x}^{(n)} - \frac{\eta_n}{|B|} \sum_{k \in B} \nabla f_k(\mathbf{x})$
    adjust $\eta_n \rightarrow \eta_{n+1}$
    $n = n + 1$
  end for
end while

$|B|$ denotes the number of samples in B.

The mini-batch SGD algorithm is a very flexible optimization method because we can always choose several key hyperparameters properly, such as the mini-batch size, the initial learning rate, and the strategy to adjust the learning rate at the end of each step, to make the optimization process converge to a reasonable solution for a large number of practical problems. Therefore, the mini-batch SGD is often regarded as one of the most popular optimization methods in machine learning.

Second-Order Methods

The second-order optimization methods require the use of the zero-order, first-order, and second-order information of the objective function, namely, the function value $f(\mathbf{x})$, the gradient $\nabla f(\mathbf{x})$, and the Hessian matrix $\mathbf{H}(\mathbf{x})$.

For a multivariate function $f(\mathbf{x})$, we can use Taylor's theorem to expand it around any fixed point $\mathbf{x}_0$, as follows:

$$f(\mathbf{x}) = f(\mathbf{x}_0) + (\mathbf{x} - \mathbf{x}_0)^\intercal \nabla f(\mathbf{x}_0) + \frac{1}{2}(\mathbf{x} - \mathbf{x}_0)^\intercal \mathbf{H}(\mathbf{x}_0)(\mathbf{x} - \mathbf{x}_0) + o(\|\mathbf{x} - \mathbf{x}_0\|^2).$$

If we ignore all high-order terms, we can derive the stationary point by vanishing the gradient $\mathbf{x}^*$, as follows:

$$\nabla f(\mathbf{x}) = \frac{\partial f(\mathbf{x})}{\partial \mathbf{x}} = 0 \quad \Longrightarrow \quad \mathbf{x}^* = \mathbf{x}_0 - \mathbf{H}^{-1}(\mathbf{x}_0)\,\nabla f(\mathbf{x}_0).$$

We first compute the gradient as

$$\nabla f(\mathbf{x}) = \frac{\partial f(\mathbf{x})}{\partial \mathbf{x}} = \nabla f(\mathbf{x}_0) + \mathbf{H}(\mathbf{x}_0)(\mathbf{x} - \mathbf{x}_0).$$

Then we vanish the gradient $\nabla f(\mathbf{x}) = 0$:

$$\nabla f(\mathbf{x}_0) + \mathbf{H}(\mathbf{x}_0)(\mathbf{x} - \mathbf{x}_0) = 0$$

$$\Longrightarrow \mathbf{x}^* = \mathbf{x}_0 - \mathbf{H}^{-1}(\mathbf{x}_0)\nabla f(\mathbf{x}_0).$$

If $f(\mathbf{x})$ is a quadratic function, no matter where we start, we can use this formula to derive the stationary point in one step. For a general objective function $f(\mathbf{x})$, we can still use the updating rule

$$\mathbf{x}^{(n+1)} = \mathbf{x}^{(n)} - \mathbf{H}^{-1}(\mathbf{x}^{(n)})\,\nabla f(\mathbf{x}^{(n)})$$

in an iterative algorithm, as in Algorithm 2.1, which leads to the *Newton method*. If the objective function is convex and at least twice differentiable and its derivatives are sufficiently smooth, the Newton method is guaranteed to converge to a local minimum $\mathbf{x}^*$, and it can achieve a *superlinear* rate. If we want to achieve $\|\mathbf{x}^{(n)} - \mathbf{x}^*\| \leq \epsilon$, we just need to run approximately $O(\ln\ln(1/\epsilon))$ iterations.

The Newton method is fast in terms of how many iterations are needed to converge. However, each iteration in the Newton method is actually extremely expensive because it involves computing, maintaining, and even inverting a large Hessian matrix. In most machine learning problems, it is impossible to handle the Hessian matrix because we usually have a large number of free variables in $\mathbf{x}$. This is why the Newton method is seldom used in machine learning. Alternatively, there are many approximate second-order methods, called *quasi-Newton* methods, that aim to approximate the Hessian matrix in certain ways (e.g., using some diagonal or block-diagonal matrices to approximate the real Hessian so as to make matrix inversion possible in the updating formula). The popular quasi-Newton methods include the DFP [65], the BFGS [65], Quickprop [60], and the Hessian-free method [175, 160].

Exercises

Q2.1 Given two matrices, $\mathbf{A} \in \mathbb{R}^{m\times n}$ and $\mathbf{B} \in \mathbb{R}^{m\times n}$, prove that

$$\mathrm{tr}(\mathbf{A}^\intercal\mathbf{B}) = \mathrm{tr}(\mathbf{A}\mathbf{B}^\intercal) = \mathrm{tr}(\mathbf{B}\mathbf{A}^\intercal) = \mathrm{tr}(\mathbf{B}^\intercal\mathbf{A}) = \sum_{i=1}^{m}\sum_{j=1}^{n} a_{ij}b_{ij},$$

where a_{ij} and b_{ij} denote an element in the matrices $\mathbf{A}$ and $\mathbf{B}$, respectively.

Q2.2 For any two square matrices, $\mathbf{X} \in \mathbb{R}^{n\times n}$ and $\mathbf{Y} \in \mathbb{R}^{n\times n}$, show that

a. $\mathrm{tr}(\mathbf{XY}) = \mathrm{tr}(\mathbf{YX})$, and
b. $\mathrm{tr}(\mathbf{X}^{-1}\mathbf{YX}) = \mathrm{tr}(\mathbf{Y})$ if $\mathbf{X}$ is invertible.

Q2.3 Given two sets of m vectors, $\mathbf{x}_i \in \mathbb{R}^n$ and $\mathbf{y}_i \in \mathbb{R}^n$ for all $i = 1, 2, \cdots, m$, verify that the summations $\sum_{i=1}^m \mathbf{x}_i\mathbf{x}_i^\intercal$ and $\sum_{i=1}^m \mathbf{x}_i\mathbf{y}_i^\intercal$ can be vectorized as the following matrix multiplications:

$$\sum_{i=1}^{m} \mathbf{x}_i\mathbf{x}_i^\intercal = \mathbf{X}\mathbf{X}^\intercal \quad \text{and} \quad \sum_{i=1}^{m} \mathbf{x}_i\mathbf{y}_i^\intercal = \mathbf{X}\mathbf{Y}^\intercal,$$

where $\mathbf{X} = \begin{bmatrix}\mathbf{x}_1\, \mathbf{x}_2\, \cdots\, \mathbf{x}_m\end{bmatrix} \in \mathbb{R}^{n\times m}$ and $\mathbf{Y} = \begin{bmatrix}\mathbf{y}_1\, \mathbf{y}_2\, \cdots\, \mathbf{y}_m\end{bmatrix} \in \mathbb{R}^{n\times m}$.

Q2.4 Given $\mathbf{x} \in \mathbb{R}^n$, $\mathbf{z} \in \mathbb{R}^m$, and $\mathbf{A} \in \mathbb{R}^{m\times n}$ $(m < n)$,

a. prove that $\mathbf{z}^\intercal\mathbf{A}\mathbf{x} = \mathrm{tr}\big(\mathbf{x}\,\mathbf{z}^\intercal\mathbf{A}\big)$,
b. compute the derivative $(\partial/\partial\mathbf{x})\, \|\mathbf{z} - \mathbf{A}\mathbf{x}\|^2$, and
c. compute the derivative $(\partial/\partial\mathbf{A})\, \|\mathbf{z} - \mathbf{A}\mathbf{x}\|^2$.

Q2.5 For any matrix $\mathbf{A} \in \mathbb{R}^{n\times n}$, if we use $\mathbf{a}_i$ $(i = 1, 2, \ldots, n)$ to denote the ith column of the matrix $\mathbf{A}$ and use $g_{ij} = |\cos\theta_{ij}| = |\mathbf{a}_i \cdot \mathbf{a}_j|/(\|\mathbf{a}_i\|\|\mathbf{a}_j\|)$ to denote the absolute cosine of the angle θ_{ij} between any two vectors $\mathbf{a}_i$ and $\mathbf{a}_j$ (for all $1 \le i, j \le n$), show that

$$\frac{\partial}{\partial\mathbf{A}}\left(\sum_{i=1}^{n}\sum_{j=i+1}^{n} g_{ij}\right) = (\mathbf{D} - \mathbf{B})\mathbf{A},$$

where $\mathbf{D}$ is an $n \times n$ matrix with its elements computed as $d_{ij} = \mathrm{sign}(\mathbf{a}_i \cdot \mathbf{a}_j)/(\|\mathbf{a}_i\|\|\mathbf{a}_j\|)$ $(1 \le i, j \le n)$, and $\mathbf{B}$ is an $n \times n$ diagonal matrix with its diagonal elements computed as $b_{ii} = (\sum_{j=1} g_{ij})/\|\mathbf{a}_i\|^2$ $(1 \le i \le n)$.

Q2.6 Consider a multinomial distribution of m discrete random variables as follows:

$$\begin{aligned}\Pr(X_1 = r_1, X_2 = r_2, \ldots, X_m = r_m) &= \mathrm{Mult}\big(r_1, r_2, \ldots, r_m \,\big|\, N, p_1, p_2, \ldots, p_m\big) \\ &= \frac{N!}{r_1!\, r_2! \cdots r_m!}\, p_1^{r_1}\, p_2^{r_2} \cdots p_m^{r_m}\end{aligned}$$

a. Prove that the multinomial distribution satisfies the sum-to-1 constraint $\sum_{X_1,\cdots,X_m} \Pr(X_1 = r_1, X_2 = r_2, \cdots, X_m = r_m) = 1$.
b. Show the procedure to derive the mean and variance for each X_i $(\forall i = 1, 2, \ldots, m)$ and the covariance for any two X_i and X_j $(\forall i, j = 1, 2, \ldots, m)$.

Q2.7 Assume m continuous random variables $\{X_1, X_2, \ldots, X_m\}$ follow the Dirichlet distribution as follows:

$$\text{Dir}\big(p_1, p_2, \cdots, p_m \,\big|\, r_1, r_2, \ldots, r_m\big) = \frac{\Gamma(r_1 + \cdots + r_m)}{\Gamma(r_1) \cdots \Gamma(r_m)} p_1^{r_1 - 1} \times p_2^{r_2 - 1} \times \cdots \times p_m^{r_m - 1}.$$

Derive the following results:

$$\mathbb{E}[X_i] = \frac{r_i}{r_0} \qquad \text{var}(X_i) = \frac{r_i(r_0 - r_i)}{r_0^2(r_0 + 1)} \qquad \text{cov}\big(X_i, X_j\big) = -\frac{r_i r_j}{r_0^2(r_0 + 1)},$$

where we denote $r_0 = \sum_{i=1}^{m} r_i$.
Hints: $\Gamma(x + 1) = x \cdot \Gamma(x)$.

Q2.8 Assume n continuous random variables $\{X_1, X_2, \cdots, X_n\}$ jointly follow a multivariate Gaussian distribution $\mathcal{N}(\mathbf{x} \mid \boldsymbol{\mu}, \Sigma)$.

a. For any random variable X_i $(\forall i)$, derive its marginal distribution $p(X_i)$.
b. For any two random variables X_i and X_j $(\forall i, j)$, derive the conditional distribution $p(X_i | X_j)$.
c. For any subset of these random variables S, derive the marginal distribution for S.
d. Split all n random variables into two disjoint subsets S_1 and S_2, and then derive the conditional distribution $p(S_1 | S_2)$.

Hints: Some identities for the inversion and determinant of a symmetric block matrix, where $\boldsymbol{\Sigma}_{11} \in \mathbb{R}^{p \times p}$, $\boldsymbol{\Sigma}_{12} \in \mathbb{R}^{p \times q}$, $\boldsymbol{\Sigma}_{22} \in \mathbb{R}^{q \times q}$, are as follows:

$$\begin{bmatrix} \boldsymbol{\Sigma}_{11} & \boldsymbol{\Sigma}_{12} \\ \boldsymbol{\Sigma}_{12}^{\intercal} & \boldsymbol{\Sigma}_{22} \end{bmatrix}^{-1} = \begin{bmatrix} \boldsymbol{\Sigma}_{11}^{-1} - \mathbf{N}\mathbf{M}^{-1}\mathbf{N}^{\intercal} & -\mathbf{N}\mathbf{M}^{-1} \\ -(\mathbf{N}\mathbf{M}^{-1})^{\intercal} & \mathbf{M}^{-1} \end{bmatrix}$$

$$\left| \begin{bmatrix} \boldsymbol{\Sigma}_{11} & \boldsymbol{\Sigma}_{12} \\ \boldsymbol{\Sigma}_{12}^{\intercal} & \boldsymbol{\Sigma}_{22} \end{bmatrix} \right| = \left|\boldsymbol{\Sigma}_{11}\right| \left|\mathbf{M}\right|,$$

where $\mathbf{M} = \left(\boldsymbol{\Sigma}_{22} - \boldsymbol{\Sigma}_{12}^{\intercal}\boldsymbol{\Sigma}_{11}^{-1}\boldsymbol{\Sigma}_{12}\right)$, and $\mathbf{N} = \boldsymbol{\Sigma}_{11}^{-1}\boldsymbol{\Sigma}_{12}$.

Q2.9 Assume a random vector $\mathbf{x} \in \mathbb{R}^n$ follows a multivariate Gaussian distribution (i.e., $p(\mathbf{x}) = \mathcal{N}\big(\mathbf{x} \,\big|\, \boldsymbol{\mu}, \Sigma\big)$). If we apply an invertible linear transformation to convert $\mathbf{x}$ into another random vector as $\mathbf{y} = \mathbf{A}\mathbf{x} + \mathbf{b}$ ($\mathbf{A} \in \mathbb{R}^{n \times n}$ and $\mathbf{b} \in \mathbb{R}^n$), prove that the joint distribution $p(\mathbf{y})$ is also a multivariate Gaussian distribution, and compute its mean vector and covariance matrix.

Q2.10 Show that any two random variables X and Y are independent if and only if any one of the following equations holds:

$$H(X, Y) = H(X) + H(Y)$$
$$H(X|Y) = H(X)$$
$$H(Y|X) = H(Y)$$

Q2.11 Show that mutual information satisfies the following:

$$\begin{aligned} I(X,Y) &= H(X) - H(X|Y) \\ &= H(Y) - H(Y|X) \\ &= H(X) + H(Y) - H(X,Y). \end{aligned}$$

Q2.12 Assume a random vector $\mathbf{x} = \begin{bmatrix} x_1 \\ x_2 \end{bmatrix}$ follows a bivariate Gaussian distribution: $\mathcal{N}(\mathbf{x} \,|\, \boldsymbol{\mu}, \boldsymbol{\Sigma})$, where $\boldsymbol{\mu} = \begin{bmatrix} \mu_1 \\ \mu_2 \end{bmatrix}$ is the mean vector and $\boldsymbol{\Sigma} = \begin{bmatrix} \sigma_1^2 & \rho\sigma_1\sigma_2 \\ \rho\sigma_1\sigma_2 & \sigma_2^2 \end{bmatrix}$ is the covariance matrix. Derive the formula to compute mutual information between x_1 and x_2 (i.e., $I(x_1, x_2)$).

Q2.13 Given two multivariate Gaussian distributions: $\mathcal{N}(\mathbf{x} \,|\, \boldsymbol{\mu}_1, \boldsymbol{\Sigma}_1)$ and $\mathcal{N}(\mathbf{x} \,|\, \boldsymbol{\mu}_2, \boldsymbol{\Sigma}_2)$, where $\boldsymbol{\mu}_1$ and $\boldsymbol{\mu}_2$ are the mean vectors, and $\boldsymbol{\Sigma}_1$ and $\boldsymbol{\Sigma}_2$ are the covariance matrices, derive the formula to compute the KL divergence between these two Gaussian distributions.

Q2.14 Prove Theorems 2.4.1, 2.4.2, and 2.4.3.

Q2.15 Compute the distance of a point $\mathbf{x}_0 \in \mathbb{R}^n$ to

a. the surface of a unit ball: $\|\mathbf{x}\| = 1$;
b. a unit ball $\|\mathbf{x}\| \leq 1$;
c. an elliptic surface $\mathbf{x}^\intercal \mathbf{A} \mathbf{x} = 1$, where $\mathbf{A} \in \mathbb{R}^{n \times n}$ and $\mathbf{A} \succ 0$; and
d. an ovoid $\mathbf{x}^\intercal \mathbf{A} \mathbf{x} \leq 1$, where $\mathbf{A} \in \mathbb{R}^{n \times n}$ and $\mathbf{A} \succ 0$.

Hints: Give a numerical procedure if no closed-form solution exists.

Q2.16 Assume a differentiable objective function $f(\mathbf{x})$ is Lipschitz continuous; namely, there exists a real constant $L > 0$, and for any two points $\mathbf{x}_1$ and $\mathbf{x}_2$, $\left|f(\mathbf{x}_1) - f(\mathbf{x}_2)\right| \leq L \,\|\mathbf{x}_1 - \mathbf{x}_2\|$ always holds. Prove that the gradient descent Algorithm 2.1 always converges to a stationary point, namely, $\lim_{n\to\infty} \|\nabla f(\mathbf{x}^{(n)})\| = 0$, as long as all used step sizes are small enough, satisfying $\eta_n < 1/L$.

3 Supervised Machine Learning (in a Nutshell)

When we talk about machine learning in an application-oriented context, we mostly mean supervised machine learning because it is currently regarded as the most mature machine learning technique and has already made significant commercial impacts in many real-world tasks. Under the conditions of big data and big models, when we can access plenty of labeled training data as well as sufficient computing resources to build very large models, supervised machine learning is said to be a solved problem because today's supervised learning methods yield acceptable performance for these scenarios. This chapter outlines all supervised learning methods, from a high level to give a big picture; technical details follow in the subsequent chapters.

See the definition of *supervised learning* in Section 1.2.2.

3.1 Overview

From a technical perspective, every machine learning problem is composed of several key choices to be made in a standard pipeline of five steps.

Step 1: Feature Extraction (Optional)
Derive compact and uncorrelated features to represent raw data.

All machine learning techniques heavily rely on training data. In order to build a well-performing machine learning system, it is critical to collect enough (actually, it's never enough—the more, the better) in-domain training samples under the same (or close enough) conditions that exist where the system will be eventually deployed. However, raw data collected from

Feature extraction is discussed in Chapter 4.

most real-world applications are of high dimension, and the dimensions are always highly correlated. To facilitate the following steps, sometimes we may apply certain automatic **dimensionality-reduction** methods to derive more compact and uncorrelated features to represent raw data. Alternatively, we may explore domain knowledge to manually extract representative features from raw data, which is quite heuristic in nature and normally called **feature engineering**.

See dimensionality reduction in Section 4.1.3.

See feature engineering in Section 4.1.1.

It is worth mentioning that many recent deep learning methods based on neural networks demonstrate the strong capability to directly take high-dimensional raw data as input, which totally bypasses feature extraction as an explicit step. These methods are usually called **end-to-end learning**, and they are still actively studied at present.

See end-to-end learning in Section 8.5.

Step 2: Choose a proper model from List A.

Based on the nature of the given problem, choose a good machine learning model from the candidates listed in List A.

Machine learning has been an active research area for decades and has provided a rich set of model choices for a variety of data types and problems. List A presents a list of impactful models that have been extensively studied in the literature. Throughout this book, a distinction is made between two categories of these models, namely, **discriminative models** and **generative models**.

See the definition of *discriminative models* in Section 5.1 and that of *generative models* in Section 10.1.

Supervised machine learning problems deal with labeled data, where each input sample, represented by its feature vector $\mathbf{x} \in \mathbb{R}^d$, is labeled as a desirable target output y. Discriminative models take a deterministic approach to this learning problem. We simply assume all input samples and their corresponding output labels are generated by an unknown but fixed target function (i.e., $y = f(\mathbf{x})$). Different discriminative models attempt to estimate the target function from a different function family, ranging from simple linear functions and bilinear/quadratic functions to neural networks (as universal function approximators). On the other hand, generative models take a probabilistic approach to this learning problem. We assume both input $\mathbf{x}$ and output y are random variables that follow an unknown joint distribution (i.e., $p(\mathbf{x}, y)$). Once the joint distribution is estimated, the relation between input $\mathbf{x}$ and output y may be determined based on the corresponding conditional distribution $p(y|\mathbf{x})$. Generative models aim to estimate the joint data distribution from the given training data. Different generative models search for the best estimate of the unknown joint distribution from a different family of probabilistic models, ranging from simple uniform models (Gaussian/multinomial) and complex mixture/entangled models to very general graphical models. In particular, some advanced probabilistic models are suitable for modeling sequential data, such as Markov chain models, hidden Markov models, and state-space models.

List A: Machine Learning Models

- ▶ **Discriminative models**:
  - Linear models (§6)
  - Bilinear models, quadratic models (§7.3, §7.4)
  - Logistic sigmoid, softmax, probit (§6.4)
  - Nonlinear kernels (§6.5.3)
  - Decision trees (§9.1.1)
  - Neural networks (§8):
    - ∗ Full-connection neural networks (FCNNs)
    - ∗ Convolutional neural networks (CNNs)
    - ∗ Recurrent neural networks (RNNs)
    - ∗ Long short-term memory (LSTM)
    - ∗ Transformers, and so on
- ▶ **Generative models:**
  - Gaussian models (§11.1)
  - Multinomial models (§11.2)
  - Markov chain models (§11.3)
  - Mixture models (§12)
    - ∗ Gaussian mixture models (§12.3)
    - ∗ Hidden Markov models (§12.4)
  - Entangled models (§13)
  - Deep generative models (§13.4)
    - ∗ Variational autoencoders (§13.4.1)
    - ∗ Generative adversarial nets (§13.4.2)
  - Graphical models (§15):
    - ∗ Bayesian networks (§15.2; naïve Bayes, latent Dirichlet allocation [LDA])
    - ∗ Markov random fields (§15.3; e.g., conditional random field, restricted Boltzmann machine)
  - Gaussian processes (§14.4)
  - State-space (dynamic) models [122]

Step 3: Choose a learning criterion from List B.

Choose an appropriate learning criterion from List B and (if necessary) a regularization term, which forms an objective function of model parameters.

List B: Machine Learning Criteria

- **For discriminative models**:
  - Least-square error (§5.1)
  - Minimum classification error (§6.3)
  - Maximum margin (§6.5.1)
  - Minimum L_p norm (§7.1.2)
  - Minimum cross-entropy (§8.3.1)
- **For generative models:**
  - Maximum likelihood (§10.4.1)
  - Maximum conditional likelihood (§15.3.2)
  - Maximum a posteriori (§14.1.2)
  - Maximum marginal likelihood (§14.2.1)
  - Minimum KL divergence (§14.3.2)

For discriminative models, once we have constrained the function family to be learned from, we already know the functional form of the chosen models, and what remains undetermined has been reduced to the unknown parameters related to the chosen models. We can choose certain criteria to measure some empirical error counts of the selected models over the training data as a function of unknown model parameters. The popular ways to measure training errors include square error, classification error, cross-entropy, and so forth. Furthermore, in order to combat *overfitting*, in many cases, we may also include some regularization-related penalty terms to make the learning less aggressive, such as a maximum margin term and minimum L_p norm terms.

See the definition of *likelihood* in Section 10.4.1.

For generative models, once we have constrained the family of probabilistic models to be used to learn the unknown joint distribution, the only unknown things are similarly reduced to be the parameters of the probabilistic models. In these cases, some likelihood-related criteria can be chosen to measure how the chosen probabilistic models match the given training data, which are believed to be randomly drawn from the unknown joint distribution. The selected likelihood measure is essentially a function of unknown model parameters. Here, if necessary, some regularization terms may also be added to alleviate *overfitting* in learning, such as Bayes priors.

Step 4: Choose an optimization algorithm from list C.

Considering the characteristics of the derived objective function, use an appropriate optimization algorithm from List C to learn the model parameters.

List C: Optimization Methods

- Grid search (§2.4.3)
- Gradient descent (§2.4.3)
- SGD (§2.4.3)
- Subgradient methods [223]
- Newton method (§2.4.3)
- Quasi-Newton methods (§2.4.3):
  - Quickprop, R-prop
  - Broyden–Fletcher–Goldfarb–Shannon (BFGS), limited-memory BFGS (L-BFGS)
- EM (§12.2)
- Sequential line search [27]
- ADMM [29]
- Gradient boosting (§9.3.1)

Once the objective functions are determined, machine learning is turned into a standard optimization problem, where the objective function needs to be maximized or minimized with respect to the unknown model parameters. Unfortunately, no closed-form solution is available for most machine learning problems. We have to rely on some numerical methods to iteratively optimize the underlying objective function to derive the model parameters. In many cases, we can use generic optimization methods, such as gradient descent and quasi-Newton methods. For some particular models, we have the choice to use specialized algorithms that are more efficient, such as expectation-maximization (EM), line search, and alternating direction method of multipliers (ADMM).

For many real-world problems, where we have to use very large models to accommodate a huge amount of training data, this step usually leads to some extremely large-scale optimization problems that may involve millions or even billions of free variables. The primary concern in choosing a suitable optimization method is whether it is efficient enough in terms of both running time and memory consumption. This is why the simplest optimization methods, such as stochastic gradient descent (SGD) and its variants, thrive in practice.

Step 5: Perform empirical evaluation and (optional) derive theoretical guarantees.

Use held-out data to empirically evaluate the performance of learned models, and if possible, derive theoretical guarantees on whether/why the learning method converges to a good solution and whether/why the learned model generalizes well to all unseen data.

The ultimate goal in machine learning is to develop good models that perform well not only with the given training data but for any new unseen samples that are statistically similar to the training data. In practice, the performance of the learned models can always be empirically evaluated based on a held-out data set that is not used anywhere in the earlier steps. The held-out test set should match the real conditions where the machine learning systems will eventually operate. Also, the test set needs to be sufficiently large to provide statistically significant results. Finally, the same test set should not be repeatedly used to evaluate the same learning method because this may result in overfitting.

Empirical evaluation is easy, but it may not be fully satisfactory for many reasons. If possible, it is better to seek strong theoretical guarantees on whether and why the learning method converges to a good solution and whether and why the learned model generalizes well to all possible unseen data. Strict theoretical analysis is challenging for many popular machine learning methods, but it should be stressed further as a critical research goal in machine learning.

3.2 Case Studies

Every machine learning problem involves three critical choices to be made from Lists A, B, and C. Of course, not all combinations from these lists make technical sense. The following list highlights some popular machine learning methods that have been extensively studied in the past few decades and explains how we make good choices from among the three dimensions of the representative machine learning methods.

See linear regression in Section 6.2.

- **Linear regression** = (**linear model**) × (**least-square error**)
  Linear regression adopts the simplest model form and the most tractable criterion to measure loss so that it enjoys a simple closed-form solution. Linear regression is probably the most straightforward machine learning method. It works well for small data sets, and its results may be intuitively interpreted. As a result, linear regression plays an important role in finance, economics, and other social sciences.

See ridge regression in Section 7.2.

- **Ridge regression** = (**linear model**) × (**least-square error + min L_2 norm**)
  Ridge regression is a regularization method that imposes a simple L_2 norm-minimization on top of the linear regression formula. A simple closed-form solution can also be derived for ridge regression. It may help to mitigate some estimation problems in linear regression with a large number of parameters, such as overfitting.

- **LASSO = (linear model) × (least-square error + min L_1 norm) × (gradient descent)**
  LASSO, standing for *least absolute shrinkage and selection operator*, is another regularized regression analysis that operates by imposing L_1 norm minimization on top of linear regression. There is no closed-form solution to LASSO, and we have to use iterative numerical methods, such as gradient descent. Alternatively, we can also use subgradient methods to solve it because the L_1 norm is not strictly differentiable. As a result of the L_1 norm regularization, LASSO yields sparse solutions to regression analysis. Therefore, LASSO may be used for variable selection and penalized estimation.

See LASSO in Section 7.2.

- **Logistic regression = (linear model + logistic sigmoid) × (maximum likelihood) × (gradient descent)**
  Logistic regression embeds a linear model into a logistic sigmoid function to generate probability-like outputs between 0 and 1, which can be combined to generate a likelihood function for any given training set. Because of the nonlinearity of the sigmoid function, we have to rely on gradient descent methods to iteratively solve logistic regression. Logistic regression is particularly useful for many simple two-class binary classification problems, which involve a large number of features derived from feature engineering.

See logistic regression in Sections 6.4 and 11.4.

- **Linear SVM = (linear model) × (maximum margin) × (gradient descent)** Linear support vector machines (SVMs) estimate a linear model based on the maximum margin criterion, equivalent to minimizing the L_2 norm, for linearly separable two-class classification problems. The formulation of SVM is elegant because it possesses a unique globally optimal solution, which can be easily found by many optimization methods, such as gradient descents.

See linear SVM in Section 6.5.1.

- **Nonlinear SVM = (nonlinear kernels + linear model) × (maximum margin) × (gradient descent)**
  Nonlinear SVMs use the famous *kernel trick* to introduce a nonlinear kernel function on top of a linear SVM formulation. As a result, nonlinear SVMs may result in highly nonlinear boundaries to separate classes. The beauty of the kernel trick is that nonlinear SVMs share the same mathematical simplicity as linear SVMs. Therefore, nonlinear SVMs can be solved by the same optimization methods, such as gradient descents.

See nonlinear SVM in Section 6.5.3.

- **Soft SVM = (kernels + linear model) × (minimum linear error + maximum margin) × (gradient descent)**
  Soft SVMs extend regular SVMs into some hard pattern-classification problems, where different classes are not linearly separable. Soft SVMs combine the maximum-margin criterion with the minimiza-

See soft SVM in Section 6.5.2.

tion of a *linear tolerable error* count. This specialized linear error term is introduced in such a way that the combined objective function still maintains the nice property of having a unique globally optimal solution. Therefore, soft SVMs can still be numerically solved with similar optimization methods as regular SVMs.

See matrix factorization in Section 7.3.

- **Matrix factorization** = (**bilinear model**) × (**least-square error + min L_2 norm**) × (**gradient descent**)
Matrix factorization uses a bilinear model to reconstruct a very large matrix based on the product of two lower-rank matrices. In recommendation systems, this method leads to a class of the so-called *collaborative filtering* algorithms, where the large matrix is the partially observed user–item interaction matrix. Some gradient descent methods can be used to learn the two lower-rank matrices by minimizing the reconstruction error and some L_2 regularization terms. This method is also used for natural language processing, called *vector space model* or *latent semantic analysis*, where the large matrix is the term-document matrix computed from a large text corpus.

See dictionary learning in Section 7.4.

- **Dictionary learning** = (**bilinear model**) × (**least-square error + minimum L_1 norm**) × (**gradient descent**)
Dictionary learning is also called *sparse representation learning* or *sparse approximating*. It adopts a simple idea that all real-world observations can be reconstructed based on a huge dictionary and some sparse codes. A bilinear model is usually used to combine the large dictionary with a sparse code to generate each real observation. The large dictionary and sparse codes are jointly learned from many observations by minimizing the L_1 norm of the codes under a tolerable range of reconstruction errors. Similar to LASSO, the L_1 norm is imposed to ensure the sparseness of the learned codes. In practice, sparse coding can be used to learn representations for visual or acoustic signals, such as images, speech, audio.

See topic modeling in Section 15.2.6.

- **Topic modeling** = (**LDA**) × (**maximum marginal likelihood**) × (**EM algorithm**)
Topic modeling adopts a specially structured graphical model, LDA, to model text documents. The hierarchical structure of LDA helps to discover the abstract *topics* that occur in a collection of text documents. The parameters of LDA can be estimated by maximizing the so-called *marginal likelihood*, where all intermediate variables are first marginalized. The marginal likelihood of LDA contains some intractable integrals, and a lower bound of the marginal likelihood is instead optimized with a specific optimization method, the EM algorithm, in an iterative way. LDA is a popular graphical model that has so far shown practical impacts in some real-world applications.

- **Boosted trees** = (**decision trees**) × (**least-square error**) × (**gradient boosting**)
  Tree boosting is a popular ensemble learning method that sequentially trains a large number of decision trees based on the famous gradient-boosting algorithm, where each new base model is estimated along a functional gradient in the model space, and all base models are eventually combined as an ensemble model for the final decision. Several tree-boosting methods have achieved excellent performance on a variety of practical machine learning tasks, including both regression and classification problems. In boosted regression trees, the least-square error is often used as the objective function in gradient boosting.

See boosted trees in Section 9.3.3.

- **Deep learning** = (**neural networks**) × (**minimum cross-entropy error**) × (**SGD or its variants**)
  Deep learning is currently the dominant method for machine learning, and it has already demonstrated unprecedented impact in many real-world artificial intelligence (AI) problems. Deep learning relies on artificial neural networks, whose unknown weights can be estimated by optimizing a special cross-entropy error function. Neural networks can be flexibly arranged as complex structures, consisting of a variety of basic structures designed for some particular purposes, such as *fully connected* multilayer structures for universal function approximation, *convolution* structures for weight sharing and locality modeling, *recurrent* structures for sequence modeling, and *attention* structures for catching long-span dependency. Moreover, by simply expanding their size in depth and width, neural networks have shown excellent capability in accommodating enormous sets of training data. No matter what network structures are used, the learning can be done by a very simple SGD-based iterative method, the so-called error *back-propagation*. Of course, the success of learning competitive neural networks also heavily depends on many engineering tricks, which cannot be fully explained yet. At last, neural networks are also criticized as *black-box* approaches because the learned networks cannot be intuitively understood or interpreted by humans. Many theoretical problems related to neural networks remain open, which calls for more serious research efforts in deep learning.

See deep learning in Chapter 8.

Feature Extraction | 4

This chapter discusses some important issues related to feature extraction in the pipeline of machine learning. As we have seen, feature extraction often varies from one task to another because it requires domain knowledge in order to extract good representations for any particular type of raw data at hand. The following section briefly introduces some general concepts in feature extraction and then focuses on the domain-independent methods of *dimensionality reduction* that play an important role in building a successful machine learning system. The chapter presents a variety of dimension-reduction methods, ranging from linear methods to nonlinear ones, and the key ideas behind them.

4.1 Feature Extraction: Concepts

Generally speaking, feature extraction involves three distinct but related topics, namely, *feature engineering*, *feature selection*, and *dimensionality reduction*. The following subsections briefly introduce them one by one.

4.1.1 Feature Engineering

Feature engineering is the process of using domain knowledge to extract new variables, often called *features*, from raw data that can facilitate model building in machine learning problems. For example, we often use a normalized short-time energy distribution over all frequency bands, that is, the so-called mel-frequency cepstrum (MFC) [49], to represent speech, music, and other audio signals. We may use the scale-invariant feature transformation (SIFT) [149] to detect local features to represent images in computer vision. We often use the so-called *bag-of-words* features [91] to represent a text document in natural language processing and information retrieval. In general, we cannot fully understand these domain-specific features without learning the characteristics of each data type. The following discussion uses the relatively intuitive bag-of-words features as an example to explain how to extract a feature vector to represent raw data.

Example 4.1.1 Bag-of-Words Features for Text Documents

Assuming we can ignore the word order and grammar structure, show how to represent a text document as the bag of its words.

Figure 4.1: An illustration of representing a text document as a fixed-size bag-of-words feature vector.

First of all, we have to specify a vocabulary that includes all distinct words used in all documents in the corpus. For each document, we ignore internal linguistic structure, such as word order and grammar, and keep only the counts of how many times each word appears in the document. As shown in Figure 4.1, any variable-length document can always be represented with a fixed-size vector of all word counts, denoted as $\mathbf{x}$, which is normally called the *bag-of-words* feature. The dimension of the bag-of-word feature vector $\mathbf{x}$ equals to the number of distinct words in the vocabulary, which can reach hundreds of thousands or even millions for real text documents. Furthermore, the plain bag-of-words features can be normalized based on how frequently each word appears across different documents, leading to the so-called term frequency-inverse document frequency (tf-idf) feature [117]. The tf-idf feature vector has the same dimension as the plain bag-of-words feature vector, but it gives more weight to the more meaningful words. Moreover, some ordinal encoding schemes, such as fixed-size ordinally-forgetting encoding (FOFE) [264], can also be used to enhance the plain bag-of-words feature to retain the word-order information in each text document. ♦

In feature engineering, after we have extracted various features, we normally need to use a proper scaling method to normalize the dynamic range of each independent feature to ensure all dimensions in a feature vector have zero mean and unit variance. It has been found that this simple normalization step can significantly facilitate the optimization process in model learning.

4.1.2 Feature Selection

If the number of different features derived from the previously described feature-engineering procedure is too high, we usually have to reduce the dimension of feature vectors to avoid the curse of dimensionality and alleviate overfitting in order to improve generalization. The premise is that some of the manually extracted features may be redundant or insignificant, so we can remove them without incurring much loss of information.

In machine learning, *feature selection* is the process of selecting a subset of relevant features for use in model construction and discarding the others [88]. A feature-selection algorithm aims to produce the best feature subset using a search technique to propose different feature combinations and relying on an evaluation measure to score the usefulness of each feature subset. We normally divide all feature-selection strategies into three categories: wrapper, filter, and embedded methods. In the most efficient filter methods, we tend to use a fast proxy measure to score each feature subset. The proxy measure is chosen in such a way that it is fast to compute while still capturing the usefulness of the features, such as mutual information (see Example 2.3.3) and Pearson's correlation coefficient (see margin note).

For any two random variables x and y, Pearson's correlation coefficient is the covariance of two variables divided by the product of their standard deviations:

$$\begin{aligned}\rho &= \frac{\text{cov}(x, y)}{\sigma_x \sigma_y} \\ &= \frac{\mathbb{E}\big[(x - \mu_x)(y - \mu_y)\big]}{\sigma_x \sigma_y},\end{aligned}$$

where the variables are as follows:
μ_x: the mean of x,
μ_y: the mean of y,
σ_x: the standard deviation of x, and
σ_y: the standard deviation of y.

4.1.3 Dimensionality Reduction

In contrast to feature selection, we use *dimensionality reduction* to refer to another group of techniques that utilize a mapping function to convert a high-dimensional feature vector to a lower-dimensional one while retaining the distribution information in the original high-dimensional space as much as possible. Due to the aforementioned "blessing of nonuniformity," we know this is always possible for high-dimensional feature vectors arising from real-world applications.

As shown in Figure 4.2, a function $f(\cdot) : \mathbb{R}^n \to \mathbb{R}^m$ maps any point in an n-dimensional space to a point in an m-dimensional space, where $m \ll n$. We can use different functional forms for $f(\cdot)$ (e.g., linear functions, piece-wise linear functions, or other general nonlinear functions). On the other hand, we also need to choose a learning criterion in terms of what information is retained during this mapping. Depending on our choices, we can end up with a variety of different dimension-reduction methods in machine learning. The following sections introduce some representative methods from several typical categories.

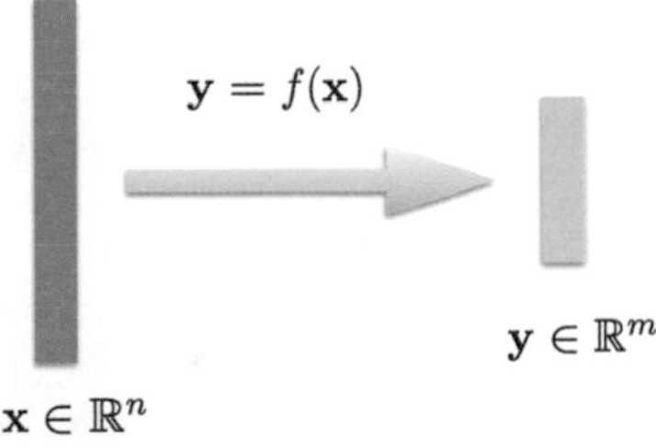

Figure 4.2: An illustration of dimension-reduction methods that use a mapping function $f(\cdot)$ to convert a high-dimensional feature vector to a lower-dimensional one.

4.2 Linear Dimension Reduction

This section first introduces the simplest dimension-reduction method, that is, *linear dimension reduction*, where we are constrained to use a linear mapping function, as shown in Figure 4.2. As we know, any linear function from $\mathbb{R}^n$ to $\mathbb{R}^m$ can be represented by an $m \times n$ matrix $\mathbf{A}$ as follows:

$$\mathbf{y} = f(\mathbf{x}) = \mathbf{A}\,\mathbf{x},$$

where $\mathbf{A} \in \mathbb{R}^{m \times n}$ denotes all parameters of this linear function that need to be estimated. The following subsections introduce two popular methods that estimate the matrix $\mathbf{A}$ in a different way.

$$\overbrace{\begin{bmatrix} y_1 \\ \vdots \\ y_m \end{bmatrix}}^{\mathbf{y}} = \underbrace{\begin{bmatrix} a_{11} & \cdots & a_{1n} \\ \vdots & a_{ij} & \vdots \\ a_{m1} & \cdots & a_{mn} \end{bmatrix}}_{\mathbf{A}} \underbrace{\begin{bmatrix} x_1 \\ \vdots \\ x_n \end{bmatrix}}_{\mathbf{x}}$$

4.2.1 Principal Component Analysis

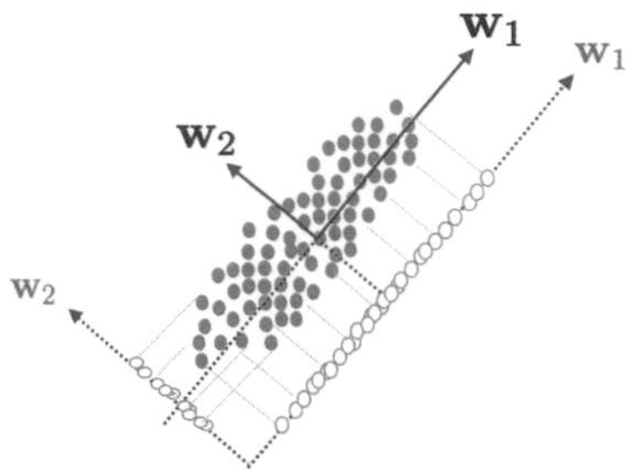

Figure 4.3: An illustration of a simple example of PCA in a 2D space. Each blue dot indicates a 2D feature vector, and each blue circle indicates a projection in a 1D subspace.

Principal component analysis (PCA) is probably the most popular linear dimension-reduction technique in machine learning [185, 103]. Let's first use a simple example to explain the main idea behind PCA. Assume we have some feature vectors distributed in a two-dimensional (2D) space, as shown in Figure 4.3. If we want to use a linear method to reduce dimensionality, it essentially means that we need to project these 2D vectors to a straight line in the space. Each straight line is indicated by a directional vector. Figure 4.3 shows two orthogonal directional vectors, denoted as $\mathbf{w}_1$ and $\mathbf{w}_2$. If we project all 2D feature vectors into each of these two directions, we end up with two different linear methods to project all feature vectors into one-dimensional (1D) space. The example in Figure 4.3 displays a striking difference between these two projections. When we project all vectors in the direction of $\mathbf{w}_1$, all projections scatter widely along the line of $\mathbf{w}_1$. In other words, the projections have a larger variance in the 1D space along the line of $\mathbf{w}_1$. On the other hand, if we project all 2D vectors into the direction of $\mathbf{w}_2$, all projections heavily congregate within a small interval. This indicates that they have a smaller variance along the line of $\mathbf{w}_2$. An interesting question is which projection is better in terms of retaining the distribution information of all original 2D vectors. The answer is the projection that achieves a larger variance. When we project vectors from a 2D space into a 1D space, basically, we will have to lose some information about the original data distribution. However, the projection achieving a larger variance tends to maintain more variations than the one yielding a smaller variance. If the projections have a smaller variance, it means that these projections can be better represented by a single point in the space, namely, the mean of these projections. This tells us that it retains less information on the data distribution.

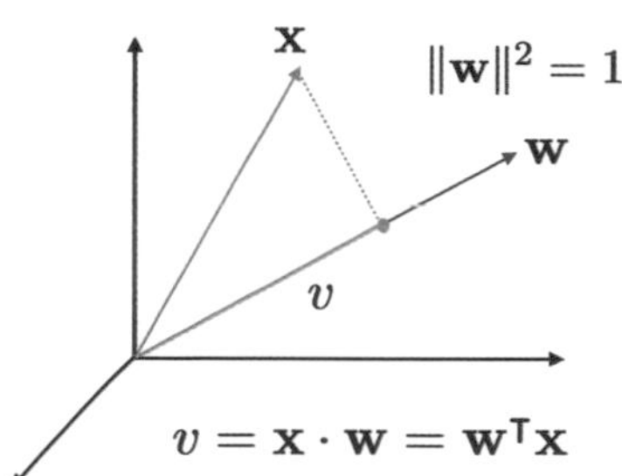

Figure 4.4: An illustration of projecting a high-dimensional vector **x** into a straight line specified by the directional vector **w**.

PCA aims to search for some orthogonal projection directions in the space that can achieve the maximum variance. These directions are often called the *principal components* of the original data distribution. PCA uses these principal components as the basis vectors to construct a linear subspace for dimensionality reduction. In the following, we will first look at how to find a principal component that maximizes the projection variance.

As shown in Figure 4.4, assume we want to project a vector in an n-dimensional space $\mathbf{x} \in \mathbb{R}^n$ into 1D space, that is, a line indicated by a directional vector $\mathbf{w}$. We further assume the directional vector $\mathbf{w}$ is of unit length:

$$\|\mathbf{w}\|^2 = \mathbf{w}^\intercal \mathbf{w} = 1. \tag{4.1}$$

If we project $\mathbf{x}$ into the line of $\mathbf{w}$, its coordinate in the line, denoted as v, can be computed by the inner product of these two vectors (see margin note):

$$v = \mathbf{x} \cdot \mathbf{w} = \mathbf{w}^\intercal \mathbf{x} \qquad (4.2)$$

If we use θ to denote the angle between $\mathbf{x}$ and $\mathbf{w}$ in Figure 4.4, we have

$$v = \|\mathbf{x}\| \cos\theta.$$

According to the definition of the inner product in a Euclidean space, we have

$$\cos\theta = \frac{\mathbf{x} \cdot \mathbf{w}}{\|\mathbf{x}\|\,\|\mathbf{w}\|}.$$

Therefore, we have

$$v = \frac{\mathbf{x} \cdot \mathbf{w}}{\|\mathbf{w}\|} = \mathbf{x} \cdot \mathbf{w}$$

because $\|\mathbf{w}\| = 1$.

Assume we are given a set of N vectors in the n-dimensional space:

$$\mathcal{D} = \{\mathbf{x}_1, \mathbf{x}_2, \cdots, \mathbf{x}_N\}.$$

Let us investigate how to find the direction that achieves the maximum projection variance for all vectors in $\mathcal{D}$. If we project all vectors in $\mathcal{D}$ into a line of $\mathbf{w}$, according to Eq. (4.2), we have their coordinates in the line as follows:

$$\{v_1, v_2, \cdots, v_N\},$$

where $v_i = \mathbf{w}^\intercal \mathbf{x}_i$ for all $i = 1, 2, \cdots, N$. We can compute the variance of these projection coordinates as

$$\sigma^2 = \frac{1}{N} \sum_{i=1}^{N} (v_i - \bar{v})^2,$$

where $\bar{v} = \frac{1}{N} \sum_{i=1}^{N} v_i$ denotes the mean of these projection coordinates. We can verify that (see margin note)

$$\bar{v} = \mathbf{w}^\intercal \bar{\mathbf{x}},$$

$$\bar{v} = \frac{1}{N} \sum_{i=1}^{N} v_i = \frac{1}{N} \sum_{i=1}^{N} \mathbf{w}^\intercal \mathbf{x}_i = \mathbf{w}^\intercal \left[\frac{1}{N} \sum_{i=1}^{N} \mathbf{x}_i \right] = \mathbf{w}^\intercal \bar{\mathbf{x}}.$$

with $\bar{\mathbf{x}} = \frac{1}{N} \sum_{i=1}^{N} \mathbf{x}_i$ indicating the mean of all vectors in $\mathcal{D}$.

We can further compute the variance as follows:

$$\begin{aligned}
\sigma^2 &= \frac{1}{N} \sum_{i=1}^{N} (v_i - \bar{v})(v_i - \bar{v}) \\
&= \frac{1}{N} \sum_{i=1}^{N} (\mathbf{w}^\intercal \mathbf{x}_i - \mathbf{w}^\intercal \bar{\mathbf{x}})(\mathbf{w}^\intercal \mathbf{x}_i - \mathbf{w}^\intercal \bar{\mathbf{x}}) \\
&= \frac{1}{N} \sum_{i=1}^{N} \mathbf{w}^\intercal (\mathbf{x}_i - \bar{\mathbf{x}})\, \mathbf{w}^\intercal (\mathbf{x}_i - \bar{\mathbf{x}}) \\
&= \frac{1}{N} \sum_{i=1}^{N} \mathbf{w}^\intercal (\mathbf{x}_i - \bar{\mathbf{x}})\, (\mathbf{x}_i - \bar{\mathbf{x}})^\intercal \mathbf{w} \\
&= \mathbf{w}^\intercal \underbrace{\left[\frac{1}{N} \sum_{i=1}^{N} (\mathbf{x}_i - \bar{\mathbf{x}})\, (\mathbf{x}_i - \bar{\mathbf{x}})^\intercal \right]}_{\mathbf{S}} \mathbf{w},
\end{aligned}$$

Note that

$$\mathbf{w}^\intercal \mathbf{x} = \mathbf{x}^\intercal \mathbf{w}$$

holds for any two n-dimensional vectors $\mathbf{w}$ and $\mathbf{x}$.

where the matrix $\mathbf{S} \in \mathbb{R}^{n \times n}$ is the sample covariance matrix of the data set $\mathcal{D}$. The principal component can be derived by maximizing the variance as follows:

$$\mathbf{S} = \frac{1}{N} \sum_{i=1}^{N} (\mathbf{x}_i - \bar{\mathbf{x}})\, (\mathbf{x}_i - \bar{\mathbf{x}})^\intercal. \qquad (4.3)$$

$$\hat{\mathbf{w}} = \arg\max_{\mathbf{w}} \; \mathbf{w}^\intercal \mathbf{S}\, \mathbf{w},$$

subject to

$$\mathbf{w}^\intercal \mathbf{w} = 1.$$

We further introduce a Lagrange multiplier λ for the previous equality constraint and derive the Lagrangian of $\mathbf{w}$ as

Note that we have

$$\frac{\partial}{\partial \mathbf{x}}\left(\mathbf{x}^\intercal \mathbf{x}\right) = 2\mathbf{x}$$

$$\frac{\partial}{\partial \mathbf{x}}\left(\mathbf{x}^\intercal A\mathbf{x}\right) = 2A\mathbf{x} \quad \text{(symmetric } A\text{)}.$$

$$L(\mathbf{w}) = \mathbf{w}^\intercal \mathbf{S}\,\mathbf{w} + \lambda \cdot \left(1 - \mathbf{w}^\intercal \mathbf{w}\right).$$

We can compute the partial derivative with respect to $\mathbf{w}$ as

$$\frac{\partial L(\mathbf{w})}{\partial \mathbf{w}} = 2\mathbf{S}\mathbf{w} - 2\lambda\mathbf{w}.$$

After vanishing the gradient $\frac{\partial L(\mathbf{w})}{\partial \mathbf{w}} = 0$, we can derive that the principal component $\hat{\mathbf{w}}$ must satisfy the following condition:

$$\mathbf{S}\,\hat{\mathbf{w}} = \lambda\,\hat{\mathbf{w}}.$$

In other words, the principal component $\hat{\mathbf{w}}$ must be an eigenvector of the sample covariance matrix $\mathbf{S}$ while the Lagrange multiplier λ equals to the corresponding eigenvalue. In an n-dimensional space, we can have at most n such eigenvectors that are all orthogonal. When we substitute any of these eigenvectors into the previous objective function, we can derive that the projection variance equals to the corresponding eigenvalue, as follows:

$$\sigma^2 = \hat{\mathbf{w}}^\intercal \mathbf{S}\hat{\mathbf{w}} = \hat{\mathbf{w}}^\intercal \lambda\,\hat{\mathbf{w}} = \lambda \cdot \|\hat{\mathbf{w}}\|^2 = \lambda.$$

This result suggests that if we want to maximize the projection variance, we just use the eigenvector corresponding to the largest eigenvalue.

We can further extend this result to the case where we want to map a vector $\mathbf{x} \in \mathbb{R}^n$ into a lower-dimensional space $\mathbb{R}^m$ ($m \ll n$) (see Exercise Q4.1). In this case, we should use the m eigenvectors corresponding to the top m largest eigenvalues of $\mathbf{S}$, denoted as $\left\{\hat{\mathbf{w}}_1, \hat{\mathbf{w}}_2, \cdots, \hat{\mathbf{w}}_m\right\}$, to construct the matrix $\mathbf{A}$ in the mapping function $\mathbf{y} = \mathbf{A}\mathbf{x}$:

$$\mathbf{A} = \begin{bmatrix} - & \hat{\mathbf{w}}_1^\intercal & - \\ - & \hat{\mathbf{w}}_2^\intercal & - \\ & \vdots & \\ - & \hat{\mathbf{w}}_m^\intercal & - \end{bmatrix}_{m \times n},$$

where each eigenvector forms a row of $\mathbf{A}$.

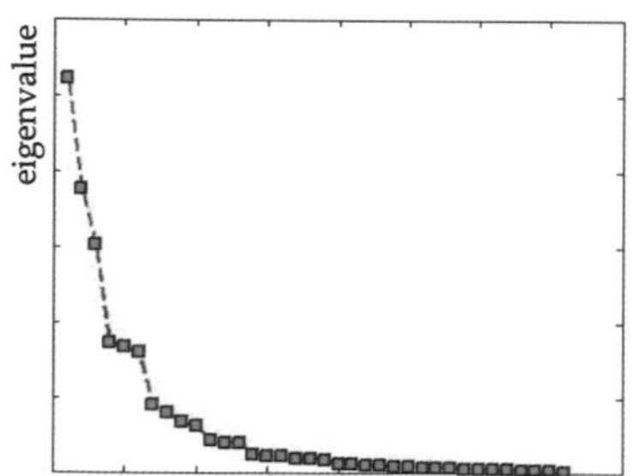

Figure 4.5: An illustration of the distribution of all n eigenvalues of a sample covariance matrix.

When we have a sufficient amount of training samples (i.e., $N \geq n$), the sample covariance matrix $\mathbf{S}$ is symmetric and has full rank. Therefore, we can compute n different mutually orthogonal eigenvectors for $\mathbf{S}$ corresponding to n nonzero eigenvalues. As shown in Figure 4.5, when we plot all eigenvalues of a typical sample covariance matrix $\mathbf{S}$ from the largest to the smallest, we can see that the first few components normally dominate the total variance. As a result, we can always use a small number of top eigenvectors to construct a PCA matrix that can retain a significant portion of the total variance in the original data distribution. After the PCA mapping, $\mathbf{y}$ serves as a compact representation in a lower-dimensional linear subspace for the original high-dimensional vector $\mathbf{x}$.

Here, we can summarize the whole PCA procedure as follows:

PCA Procedure

Assume the training data are given as $\mathcal{D} = \{\mathbf{x}_1, \mathbf{x}_2, \cdots, \mathbf{x}_N\}$.

1. Compute the sample covariance matrix $\mathbf{S}$ in Eq. (4.3).
2. Calculate the top m eigenvectors of $\mathbf{S}$.
3. Form $\mathbf{A} \in \mathbb{R}^{m \times n}$ with an eigenvector in a row.
4. For any $\mathbf{x} \in \mathbb{R}^n$, map it to $\mathbf{y} \in \mathbb{R}^m$ as $\mathbf{y} = \mathbf{A}\mathbf{x}$.

At last, let us consider how to reconstruct the original $\mathbf{x}$ from its PCA representation $\mathbf{y}$. First of all, let's assume that we maintain all eigenvectors in the PCA matrix $\mathbf{A}$; in this case, we have $m = n$, $\mathbf{A}$ is an $n \times n$ orthogonal matrix, and the PCA mapping corresponds to a rotation in the n-dimensional space. As a result, we can perfectly reconstruct $\mathbf{x}$ from $\mathbf{y}$ as follows:

$$\tilde{\mathbf{x}} = \mathbf{A}^\intercal \mathbf{y} = \underbrace{\mathbf{A}^\intercal \mathbf{A}}_{\mathbf{I}} \mathbf{x} = \mathbf{x}.$$

When $m = n$, $\mathbf{A}$ is an orthogonal matrix; thus, we have

$$\mathbf{A}^\intercal \mathbf{A} = \mathbf{I}.$$

However, when $m < n$, $\mathbf{A}$ is an $m \times n$ matrix, and $\mathbf{A}^\intercal \mathbf{A}$ is still an $n \times n$ matrix, but we can verify that

$$\mathbf{A}^\intercal \mathbf{A} \neq \mathbf{I}.$$

However, in a regular PCA procedure, we normally do not keep all eigenvectors in $\mathbf{A}$ in order to reduce dimensionality. In this case, $\mathbf{A}$ is an $m \times n$ matrix. For simplicity, we still can use the same formula

$$\tilde{\mathbf{x}} = \mathbf{A}^\intercal \mathbf{y}$$

to reconstruct an n-dimensional vector from an m-dimensional PCA representation $\mathbf{y}$. However, we can see that $\tilde{\mathbf{x}} \neq \mathbf{x}$ in this case (see margin note). In other words, we cannot perfectly recover the original high-dimensional vector because of the truncated eigenvectors. As shown in Figure 4.6,

Refer to Exercise Q4.3 for a better way to reconstruct $\mathbf{x}$ from $\mathbf{y}$:

$$\tilde{\mathbf{x}} = \mathbf{A}^\intercal \mathbf{y} + (\mathbf{I} - \mathbf{A}^\intercal \mathbf{A})\bar{\mathbf{x}}$$

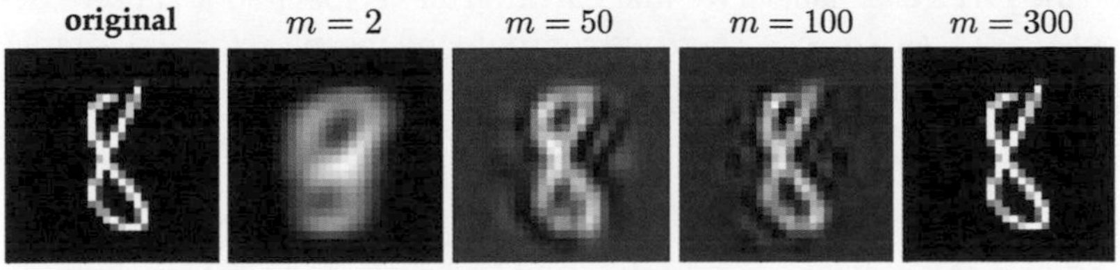

original $m = 2$ $m = 50$ $m = 100$ $m = 300$

Figure 4.6: An illustration of reconstructed images ($n = 784$) from some lower-dimensional PCA projections ($m = 2, 50, 100, 300$). (Courtesy of Huy Vu.)

where the original image of a handwritten digit is $28 \times 28 = 784$ in size, we have shown some reconstructed images from its lower-dimensional PCA projections ($m = 2, 50, 100, 300$). When m is small, we can restore only the main shape of the digit, having lost many fine details of the original image.

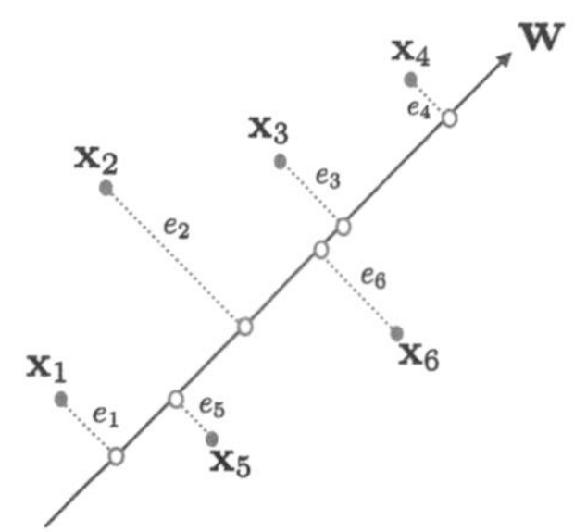

Figure 4.7: An illustration of the minimum-distortion-error formulation for PCA.

There exists a different formulation to derive the PCA method by minimizing the total distortion when we project high-dimensional vectors into a low-dimensional space. As shown in Figure 4.7, when we project a high-dimensional vector $\mathbf{x}_i$ into a straight line indicated by the directional vector $\mathbf{w}$, we essentially introduce a distortion error indicated by e_i. We can formulate PCA by searching for the best projection direction $\mathbf{w}$ to ensure the total introduced error is minimized over the training set. This formulation leads to the same result as we have discussed before. Please refer to Exercises Q4.2 and Q4.3 for more details on this formulation.

4.2.2 Linear Discriminant Analysis

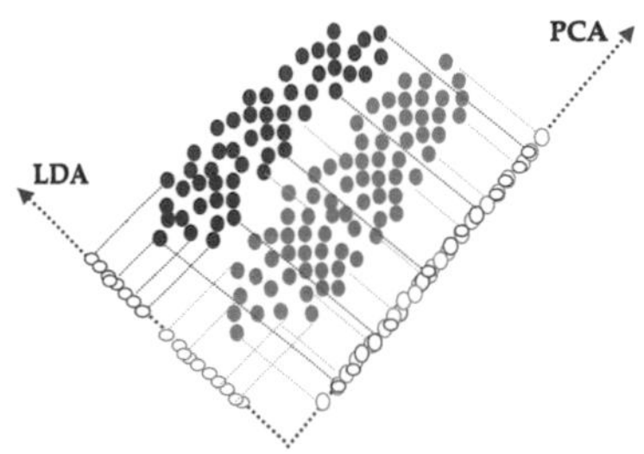

Figure 4.8: A comparison of PCA versus linear discriminant analysis (LDA) in a simple two-class example, where color indicates the class label of each feature vector.

As we know, PCA aims to project high-dimensional data along the principal components to maximize the variance. In some cases, when we know the data come from several different classes, we may want to project the data into a lower-dimensional space in such a way that the separation between different classes is maximized. Generally speaking, PCA cannot achieve this goal. For example, assume some feature vectors from two different classes (labeled by color) are distributed as shown in Figure 4.8. If we use the PCA method, the data will be projected to the line PCA, where the variance of all vectors is maximized. As we can see, the variance is maximized along this direction, but two classes are mapped to the same region, and they become highly overlapped after this dimension reduction. From the perspective of maintaining class separation, this projection direction is not ideal. On the other hand, if we project the data along the line LDA, the separation between two classes can be well maintained in the low-dimensional space.

This section introduces a general method to derive a projection direction that can achieve the maximum separation between different classes. Assume all high-dimensional vectors come from K different classes. Based on the given class labels, we first partition all vectors into K subsets, denoted as $C_1, C_2, \cdots, C_K$. Then, we compute the mean vector and sample covariance matrix for each subset, as follows:

$|C_k|$ denotes the number of vectors in the subset C_k.

$$\boldsymbol{\mu}_k = \frac{1}{|C_k|} \sum_{\mathbf{x}_i \in C_k} \mathbf{x}_i$$

$$\mathbf{S}_k = \frac{1}{|C_k|} \sum_{\mathbf{x}_i \in C_k} (\mathbf{x}_i - \boldsymbol{\mu}_k)(\mathbf{x}_i - \boldsymbol{\mu}_k)^\top,$$

for all $k = 1, 2, \cdots, K$.

If we still adopt a linear projection method as done previously, we will project all vectors into a line of directional vector $\mathbf{w}$. If we want to achieve the maximum class separation between different classes, conceptually speaking, all projections from the same class should stay close, whereas different classes should be mapped into some far-apart regions. To accommodate these two goals at the same time, Fisher's *linear discriminant analysis* (LDA) [64] aims to derive a projection direction $\mathbf{w}$ by maximizing the following ratio:

$$\max_{\mathbf{w}} \underbrace{\frac{\mathbf{w}^\intercal \mathbf{S}_b \mathbf{w}}{\mathbf{w}^\intercal \mathbf{S}_w \mathbf{w}}}_{J(\mathbf{w})}.$$

The numerator is used to measure the separation between different classes with the so-called *between-class scatter matrix* $\mathbf{S}_b \in \mathbb{R}^{n \times n}$, which is computed by the mean vectors of all classes as follows:

$$\mathbf{S}_b = \sum_{k=1}^{K} |C_k| \left(\boldsymbol{\mu}_k - \boldsymbol{\mu}\right)\left(\boldsymbol{\mu}_k - \boldsymbol{\mu}\right)^\intercal,$$

where $\boldsymbol{\mu}$ denotes the mean vector of all vectors from all different classes.

Meanwhile, the denominator is used to measure the closeness of all projections from the same class with the so-called *within-class scatter matrix* $\mathbf{S}_w \in \mathbb{R}^{n \times n}$, which is defined as the sum of all individual sample covariance matrices:

$$\mathbf{S}_w = \sum_{k=1}^{K} \mathbf{S}_k.$$

Furthermore, we can verify that maximizing the ratio $J(\mathbf{w})$ is equivalent to the following constrained optimization problem (see margin note):

$$\mathbf{w}^* = \arg\max_{\mathbf{w}} \; \mathbf{w}^\intercal \mathbf{S}_b \mathbf{w},$$

subject to

$$\mathbf{w}^\intercal \mathbf{S}_w \mathbf{w} = 1.$$

Assume $\mathbf{w}_1$ is a solution to maximize the ratio $J(\mathbf{w})$, but $\mathbf{w}_1^\intercal \mathbf{S}_w \mathbf{w}_1 \neq 1$. We can always scale $\mathbf{w}_1$ as

$$\mathbf{w}_2 = \alpha \mathbf{w}_1$$

to make $\mathbf{w}_2^\intercal \mathbf{S}_w \mathbf{w}_2 = 1$. This scaling does not change the value of $J(\mathbf{w})$ because the scaling factor α cancels out from the numerator and denominator. Therefore, the constraint

$$\mathbf{w}^\intercal \mathbf{S}_w \mathbf{w} = 1$$

does not affect the optimization problem because the scaled $\mathbf{w}_2$ is as good as $\mathbf{w}_1$.

Using the same method of Lagrange multipliers, we can derive that the solution to the LDA problem must be an eigenvector of the matrix $\mathbf{S}_w^{-1}\mathbf{S}_b$ (see Exercise Q4.4). Therefore, LDA is very similar to the PCA procedure, except we compute the eigenvectors from another $n \times n$ matrix $\mathbf{S}_w^{-1}\mathbf{S}_b$.

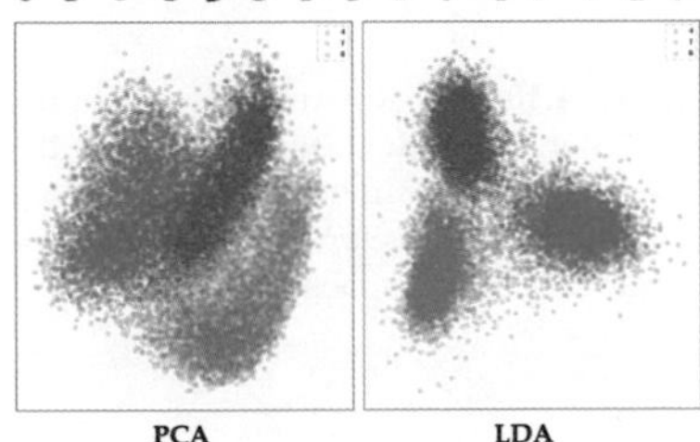

Figure 4.9: An illustration of projecting some images of handwritten digits (i.e., 4, 7, and 8) into 2D space using PCA and LDA. (courtesy of Huy Vu.)

As an example, Figure 4.9 compares LDA with PCA by plotting their projections in a 2D space for some 28×28 images of three handwritten digits of 4, 7, and 8. As we can see, the LDA projection can achieve much better class separation than PCA because LDA can leverage the information about class labels.

K is the number of different classes in data.

Finally, LDA can be viewed as a supervised learning method for dimension reduction because it requires class labels, whereas PCA is an unsupervised learning method because it can derive the principal components from unlabeled data. Another major difference between them is that LDA can only find at most $K - 1$ projection directions. The reason is that the between-class scatter matrix $\mathbf{S}_b$ does not have full rank. It is derived from only K different class-dependent mean vectors, and we can verify that its rank cannot exceed $K - 1$. As a result, the rank of the matrix $\mathbf{S}_w^{-1}\mathbf{S}_b$ does not exceed $K - 1$ as well, and thus in LDA, we can only derive at most $K - 1$ mutually orthogonal eigenvectors corresponding to $K - 1$ nonzero eigenvalues.

4.3 Nonlinear Dimension Reduction (I): Manifold Learning

The linear methods for dimension reduction are often intuitive in concept and simple in computation. For example, both PCA and LDA can be solved with a closed-form solution. However, linear methods make sense only when the low-dimensional structure in the data distribution can be well captured by some linear subspaces. For example, in Figure 4.10, we can see the data are distributed in a 1D nonlinear structure, but we cannot use any straight line to represent it precisely. We have to use a nonlinear dimension-reduction method to capture this structure. In mathematics, such nonlinear structures in a lower-dimensional topological space are often called *manifolds*.

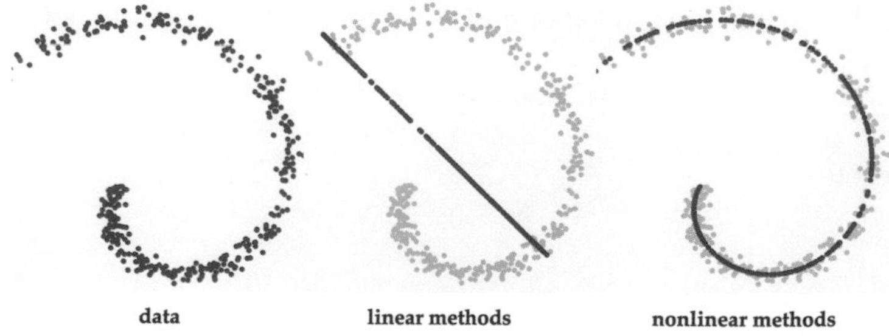

Figure 4.10: An illustration of nonlinear dimension-reduction methods for the case where high-dimensional vectors are distributed in a lower-dimensional nonlinear topological space.

In this section, we will introduce some representative nonlinear methods from the literature of *manifold learning*. These methods try to identify the underlying low-dimensional manifold using some nonparametric approaches, where we do not assume the functional form for the nonlinear mapping function $f(\cdot)$ but directly estimate the coordinates $\mathbf{y}$ in the low-dimensional space for all high-dimensional vectors. The next section introduces a parametric approach that uses neural networks to approximate the underlying nonlinear mapping function.

4.3.1 Locally Linear Embedding

Locally linear embedding (LLE) [201] aims to capture the underlying manifold with a piece-wise linear method. Within any small neighborhood in the manifold, we assume the data can be locally modeled by a linear function. As shown in Figure 4.11, any vector $\mathbf{x}_i$ in the high-dimensional space can be linearly reconstructed from some nearby vectors within a sufficiently small neighborhood, denoted as N_i, as follows:

$$\mathbf{x}_i \approx \sum_{j \in N_i} w_{ij} \mathbf{x}_j,$$

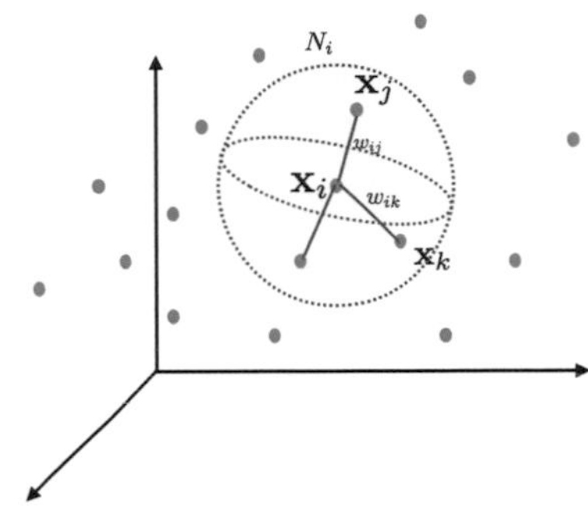

Figure 4.11: An illustration of the local linear structure of LLE in the high-dimensional space.

where w_{ij} denotes a linear contribution weight when we reconstruct $\mathbf{x}_i$ using $\mathbf{x}_j$. The weights are nonzero only for the nearby vectors within the neighborhood N_i. In LLE, a convenient way to specify the neighborhood N_i is to use k nearest neighbors of $\mathbf{x}_i$. We further assume the total contribution from all nearby vectors in each neighborhood is constant (i.e., $\sum_j w_{ij} = 1$). All pair-wise weights can be derived by minimizing the total reconstruction error over all $\mathbf{x}_i$:

$$\{\hat{w}_{ij}\} = \arg\min_{\{w_{ij}\}} \sum_i \left\| \mathbf{x}_i - \sum_{j \in N_i} w_{ij} \mathbf{x}_j \right\|^2,$$

subject to $\sum_j w_{ij} = 1 \quad (\forall i)$.

Furthermore, when we map all high-dimensional vectors to a low-dimensional space, we try to maintain the locally linear structure in the high-dimensional space. In other words, we assume all pair-wise linear weights $\{\hat{w}_{ij}\}$ obtained in the high-dimensional space can be directly applied to the low-dimensional space to locally associate their projections in the same linear way, as shown in Figure 4.12. Based on this assumption, we can derive all low-dimensional projections by minimizing the reconstruction error in the low-dimensional space:

$$\{\hat{\mathbf{y}}_i\} = \arg\min_{\{\mathbf{y}_i\}} \sum_i \left\| \mathbf{y}_i - \sum_{j \in N_i} \hat{w}_{ij} \mathbf{y}_j \right\|^2.$$

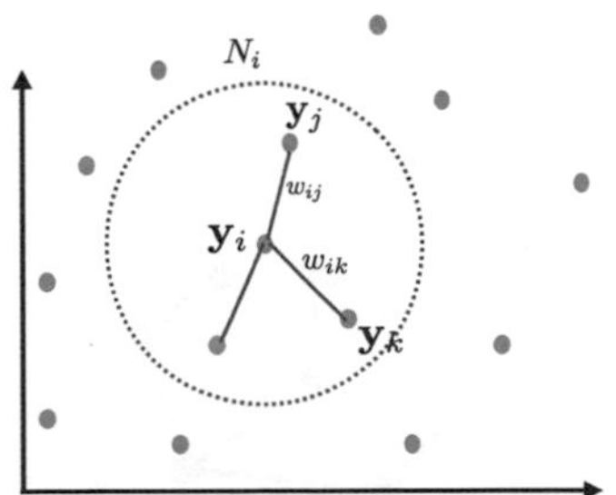

Figure 4.12: An illustration of the local linear structure of LLE in the low-dimensional space.

Interestingly enough, both optimization problems can be solved with a closed-form solution (see Exercise Q4.5). This makes LLE one of the most efficient nonlinear methods for dimension reduction.

4.3.2 Multidimensional Scaling

The key idea behind the so-called *multidimensional scaling* (MDS) [163] is to preserve all pair-wise distances when we project high-dimensional vectors into a low-dimensional space. If two vectors are nearby in the high-dimensional space, their projections should be close in the low-dimensional space as well, and vice versa.

In MDS, we first use a metric to compute the pair-wise distances of all high-dimensional vectors, for example, computing the Euclidean distance $d_{ij} = \|\mathbf{x}_i - \mathbf{x}_j\|$ for all i and j.

Next, we derive the coordinates of all projections in a low-dimensional space by minimizing the total difference between the corresponding pair-wise distances:

$$\{\hat{\mathbf{y}}_i\} = \arg\min_{\{\mathbf{y}_i\}} \sum_i \sum_{j>i} \Big(\|\mathbf{y}_i - \mathbf{y}_j\| - d_{ij}\Big)^2.$$

A major issue in this optimization is that it focuses on matching far-apart vectors because a long distance contributes much more in this objective function than a short distance. A simple fix is to use Sammon mapping [211] to normalize the distance difference to weigh more on the nearby pairs:

$$\{\hat{\mathbf{y}}_i\} = \arg\min_{\{\mathbf{y}_i\}} \sum_i \sum_{j>i} \left(\frac{\|\mathbf{y}_i - \mathbf{y}_j\| - d_{ij}}{d_{ij}}\right)^2.$$

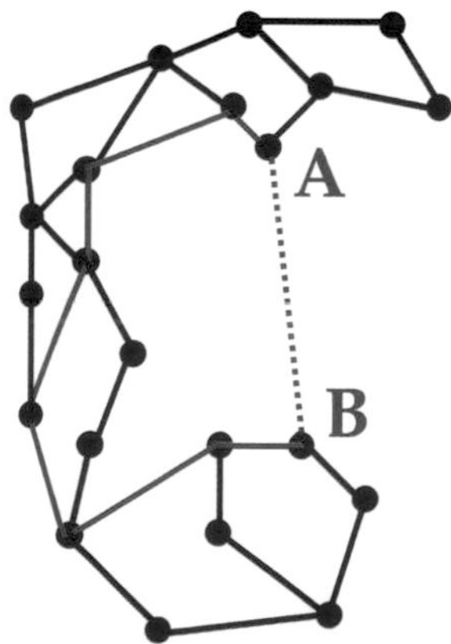

Figure 4.13: An illustration of using a weighted graph to compute the distance for far-apart vectors in Isomap. The distance between A and B is computed by the shortest path (solid red lines) in the graph rather than the direct distance in the space (dashed red line).

There is no easy way to solve these optimization problems in MDS. We will have to rely on numerical optimization methods, such as the gradient descent method. As a result, the computational complexity of MDS is fairly high.

Another interesting idea to further improve MDS is the so-called *isometric feature mapping* (Isomap) method [235], where we only compute pair-wise distances for nearby vectors in the high-dimensional space. These nearby vectors are further connected to form a sparse graph in the high-dimensional space, as shown in Figure 4.13. Each edge in the graph is weighted by the corresponding pair-wise distance. For any pair of far-apart vectors (e.g., A and B), their distance is computed by the shortest path in the weighted graph (solid red lines) rather than the direct distance between them in the space (dashed red line). By doing this, Isomap can significantly improve the capability of capturing local structures in the data distribution. We also note that Isomap is even more costly to run than the regular MDS because it is very expensive to traverse a large graph to compute the shortest paths.

4.3.3 Stochastic Neighborhood Embedding

Stochastic neighborhood embedding (SNE) [98] is a probabilistic local mapping method that relies on some pair-wise conditional probabilities computed from local distances. First of all, for any two high-dimensional vectors, $\mathbf{x}_i$ and $\mathbf{x}_j$ $(i \neq j)$, we define a conditional probability using a Gaussian kernel as follows:

$$p_{ij} = \frac{\exp\left(-\gamma_i \|\mathbf{x}_i - \mathbf{x}_j\|^2\right)}{\sum_k \exp\left(-\gamma_i \|\mathbf{x}_i - \mathbf{x}_k\|^2\right)} \qquad (\forall i, j \;\; i \neq j),$$

The function

$$\Phi(\mathbf{x}_i, \mathbf{x}_j) = \exp\left(-\gamma \|\mathbf{x}_i - \mathbf{x}_j\|^2\right)$$

is called a *Gaussian kernel* because it resembles the Gaussian distribution.

where γ_i is a control parameter that needs to be manually specified. Intuitively speaking, we can view p_{ij} as the probability of picking $\mathbf{x}_j$ as a neighbor of $\mathbf{x}_i$. Because of the sum-to-1 constraint $\sum_j p_{ij} = 1$, we know that $P_i = \{p_{ij} \,|\, \forall j\}$ forms a multinomial distribution.

Similarly, we can define pair-wise conditional probabilities based on the projections in a low-dimensional space as follows:

$$q_{ij} = \frac{\exp\left(-\|\mathbf{y}_i - \mathbf{y}_j\|^2\right)}{\sum_k \exp\left(-\|\mathbf{y}_i - \mathbf{y}_k\|^2\right)} \qquad (\forall i, j).$$

Here, $Q_i = \{q_{ij} \,|\, \forall j\}$ also forms a multinomial distribution. The key idea behind SNE is to derive all low-dimensional projections by minimizing the Kullback–Leibler (KL) divergence between these multinomial distributions:

$$\begin{aligned} \{\hat{\mathbf{y}}_i\} &= \arg\min_{\{\mathbf{y}_i\}} \sum_i \mathrm{KL}(P_i \,\|\, Q_i) \\ &= \arg\min_{\{\mathbf{y}_i\}} \sum_i \sum_j p_{ij} \ln \frac{p_{ij}}{q_{ij}}. \end{aligned}$$

Refer to Section 2.3.3 for KL divergence.

Once again, we have to rely on iterative numerical methods to solve this optimization problem.

The t-*distributed stochastic neighbor embedding* (t-SNE) method [150] is an extension of SNE. Instead of using the sharp Gaussian kernel, t-SNE uses a heavy-tailed Student's t-distribution with 1 degree of freedom to define the conditional probabilities in a low-dimensional space:

$$q_{ij} = \frac{\left(1 + \|\mathbf{y}_i - \mathbf{y}_j\|^2\right)^{-1}}{\sum_{k \neq i} \left(1 + \|\mathbf{y}_i - \mathbf{y}_k\|^2\right)^{-1}} \qquad (\forall i, j).$$

When we use t-SNE to project high-dimensional data into a low-dimensional space of two or three dimensions, it has been found that t-SNE is particularly good at displaying clusters. As a result, t-SNE is a very popular tool for data visualization. For example, when we use t-SNE to plot the images of three handwritten digits (i.e., 4, 7, and 8) in Figure 4.14, it shows a better clustering effect than the two linear methods in Figure 4.9.

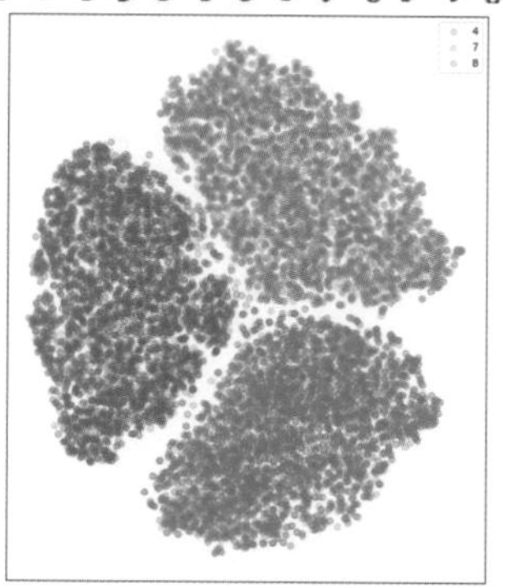

Figure 4.14: An illustration of using t-SNE to project some images of the handwritten digits 4, 7, and 8 into 2D space. (courtesy of Huy Vu.)

4.4 Nonlinear Dimension Reduction (II): Neural Networks

This section briefly introduces another group of nonlinear dimension-reduction methods that use neural networks to approximate the general nonlinear mapping function $f(\cdot)$ in Figure 4.2. As opposed to the nonparametric manifold learning approaches discussed in the previous section, these methods can be considered as parametric approaches for nonlinear dimension reduction because the nonlinear mapping function can be determined by the underlying neural network, which in turn is fully specified by a fixed set of parameters (i.e., all connection weights in the network). Neural networks are not fully covered until Chapter 8. This section describes the basic ideas of using neural networks for nonlinear dimension reduction. Readers need to refer to Chapter 8 for implementation details in terms of how to configure network structure and how to learn parameters.

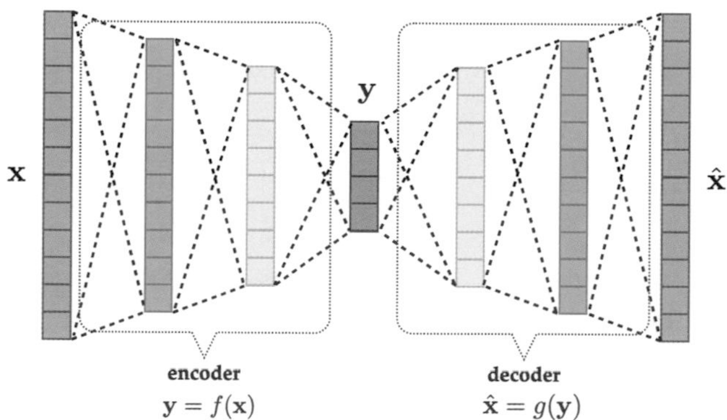

Figure 4.15: An illustration of an autoencoder that uses neural networks as an encoder and a decoder to learn how to project high-dimensional vectors $\mathbf{x}$ into a low-dimensional space $\mathbf{y}$.

4.4.1 Autoencoder

As shown in Figure 4.15, an *autoencoder* [132] relies on two neural networks: one as an encoder and the other as a decoder. The encoder network serves as the nonlinear mapping function $\mathbf{y} = f(\mathbf{x})$ in Figure 4.2, mapping high-dimensional vectors $\mathbf{x}$ into a low-dimensional space $\mathbf{y}$. On the other hand, the decoder network aims to learn an inverse transformation to recover the original high-dimensional vector from its low-dimensional representation: $\hat{\mathbf{x}} = g(\mathbf{y})$. Both encoder and decoder networks are jointly trained by minimizing the difference between the input and output (i.e., $\|\hat{\mathbf{x}} - \mathbf{x}\|^2$). In this way, an autoencoder can be learned from unlabeled data so that it is an unsupervised learning method for nonlinear dimension reduction. Due to this, an autoencoder can be viewed as a nonlinear extension of PCA [11].

4.4.2 Bottleneck Features

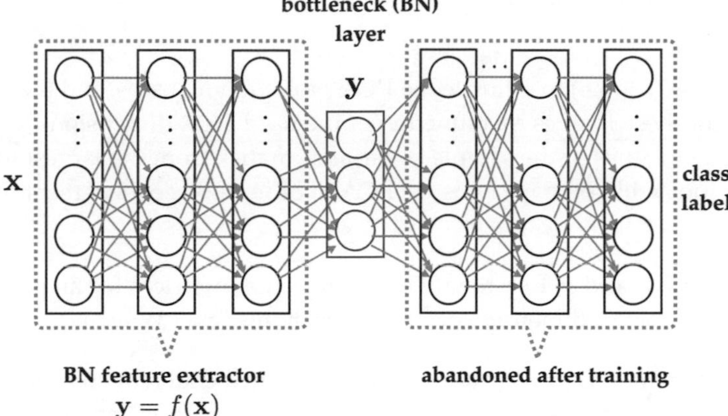

Figure 4.16: An illustration of using a bottleneck layer in a deep neural network to learn how to project high-dimensional vectors $\mathbf{x}$ into a low-dimensional space $\mathbf{y}$.

If we have access to class labels of data, we can build a deep neural network to map high-dimensional vectors $\mathbf{x}$ into their corresponding class labels. As shown in Figure 4.16, we can deliberately insert a narrow layer in the middle of the deep network, which is often called a *bottleneck layer*. After the entire deep network is trained using labeled data, we can use the first part of the network (prior to the bottleneck layer) as a nonlinear mapping function to transform any high-dimensional vector into a low-dimensional representation: $\mathbf{y} = f(\mathbf{x})$, where $\mathbf{y}$ is often called the *bottleneck (BN) feature*. Similar to LDA, we need to use class labels to learn the BN feature extractor. Hence, we can view BN features as a nonlinear extension of LDA. The BN features have been successfully used to learn compact representations for speech signals in speech recognition [94, 86].

Lab Project I

In this project, you will implement several feature-extraction methods. You may choose to use any programming language for your own convenience. You are only allowed to use libraries for linear algebra operations, such as matrix multiplication, matrix inversion, matrix factorization, and so forth. You are not allowed to use any existing machine learning or statistics toolkits or libraries or any open-source codes for this project.

In this project, you will use the MNIST data set [142], which is a handwritten digit set containing 60,000 training images and 10,000 test images. Each image is 28 by 28 in size. The MNIST data set can be downloaded from `http://yann.lecun.com/exdb/mnist/`. In this project, for simplicity, you just use pixels as raw features for the following methods:

a. Use all training images of three digits (4, 7, and 8) to estimate the PCA projection matrices, and then plot the total distortion error in Eq. (4.5) of these images as a function of the used PCA dimensions (e.g., 2, 10, 50, 100, 200, 300). Also, plot all eigenvalues of the sample covariance matrix from the largest to the smallest. At least how many dimensions will you have to use in PCA in order to keep 98 percent of the total variance in data?

b. Use all training images of three digits (4, 7, and 8) to estimate LDA projection matrices for all possible LDA dimensions. What are the maximum LDA dimensions you can use in this case? Why?

c. Use PCA and LDA to project all images into 2D space, and plot each digit in a different color for data visualization. Compare these two linear methods with a popular nonlinear method, namely, t-SNE (`https://lvdmaaten.github.io/tsne/`). You do not need to implement t-SNE and can directly download the t-SNE code from the website and run it on your data to compare with PCA and LDA. Based on your results, explain how these three methods differ in data visualization.

d. If you have enough computing resources, repeat the previous steps using the training images of all 10 digits in MNIST.

Exercises

Q4.1 Use proof by induction to show that the m-dimensional PCA corresponds to the linear projection defined by the m eigenvectors of the sample covariance matrix $\mathbf{S}$ corresponding to the m largest eigenvalues. Use Lagrange multipliers to enforce the orthogonality constraints.

Q4.2 Deriving the PCA under the minimum error formulation (I): Formulate each distance e_i in Figure 4.7, and search for $\mathbf{w}$ to minimize the total error $\sum_i e_i^2$.

Q4.3 Deriving the PCA under the minimum error formulation (II): Given a set of N vectors in an n-dimensional space: $\mathcal{D} = \{\mathbf{x}_1, \mathbf{x}_2, \cdots, \mathbf{x}_N\}$ ($\mathbf{x}_i \in \mathbb{R}^n$), we search for a complete orthonormal set of basis vectors $\{\mathbf{w}_j \in \mathbb{R}^n \mid j = 1, 2, \cdots, n\}$, satisfying $\mathbf{w}_j^\intercal \mathbf{w}_{j'} = \begin{cases} 1 & j = j' \\ 0 & j \neq j' \end{cases}$. We know that each data point $\mathbf{x}_i$ in $\mathcal{D}$ can be represented by this set of basis vectors as $\mathbf{x}_i = \sum_{j=1}^{n} (\mathbf{w}_j^\intercal \mathbf{x}_i)\,\mathbf{w}_j$. Our goal is to approximate $\mathbf{x}_i$ using a representation involving only $m < n$ dimensions as follows:

$$\tilde{\mathbf{x}}_i = \sum_{j=1}^{m} (\mathbf{w}_j^\intercal \mathbf{x}_i)\,\mathbf{w}_j + \overbrace{\sum_{j=m+1}^{n} b_j \mathbf{w}_j}^{\text{residual}}, \tag{4.4}$$

where $\{b_j \mid j = m+1, \cdots, n\}$ in the residual represents the common biases for all data points in $\mathcal{D}$. If we minimize the total distortion error

$$E = \sum_{i=1}^{N} \|\mathbf{x}_i - \tilde{\mathbf{x}}_i\|^2 \tag{4.5}$$

with respect to both $\{\mathbf{w}_1, \mathbf{w}_2, \cdots, \mathbf{w}_m\}$ and $\{b_j\}$:

a. Show that the m optimal basis vectors $\{\mathbf{w}_j\}$ lead to the same matrix $\mathbf{A}$ in PCA.
b. Show that using the optimal biases $\{b_j\}$ in Eq. (4.4) leads to a new reconstruction formula converting the m-dimensional PCA projection $\mathbf{y} = \mathbf{A}\mathbf{x}$ to the original $\mathbf{x}$, as follows:

$$\tilde{\mathbf{x}} = \mathbf{A}^\intercal \mathbf{y} + (\mathbf{I} - \mathbf{A}^\intercal \mathbf{A})\bar{\mathbf{x}},$$

where $\bar{\mathbf{x}} = \frac{1}{N}\sum_{i=1}^{N} \mathbf{x}_i$ denotes the mean of all training samples in $\mathcal{D}$.

Q4.4 Use the method of Lagrange multipliers to derive the LDA solution.

Q4.5 Derive the closed-form solutions for two error-minimization problems in LLE.

DISCRIMINATIVE MODELS

5 Statistical Learning Theory

Before introducing any particular discriminative model in detail, this chapter first presents a general framework to formally describe all discriminative models. Next, some important concepts and results in statistical learning theory are introduced, which can be used to answer some fundamental questions related to machine learning (ML) approaches using discriminative models.

5.1 Formulation of Discriminative Models

Any ML model can be viewed as a system (see margin note) that takes feature vectors $\mathbf{x}$ as input and generates target labels y as output. We further assume input vectors $\mathbf{x}$ are n-dimensional vectors from an *input space*, denoted as $\mathbb{X}$; thus, we have $\mathbf{x} \in \mathbb{X}$. Some examples for $\mathbb{X}$ are as follows: (i) $\mathbb{R}^n$ for unconstrained continuous inputs; (ii) a hypercube $[0, 1]^n$ for constrained continuous inputs; (iii) and $\mathbb{X}$, which may be a finite or countable set for discrete inputs. Without losing generality, we assume outputs y are scalar, coming from an *output space*, denoted as $\mathbb{Y}$. Depending on whether the output y is continuous or discrete, the ML problem is called a *regression* or *classification problem*.

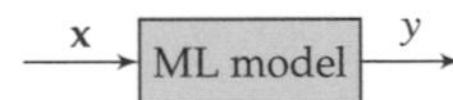

For all discriminative models, we always assume the inputs $\mathbf{x}$ are *random variables*, drawn from an unknown probability distribution $p(\mathbf{x})$ (i.e., $\mathbf{x} \sim p(\mathbf{x})$). However, for each input $\mathbf{x}$, the corresponding output y is generated by an unknown *deterministic* function (i.e., $y = \bar{f}(\mathbf{x})$), which is normally called the *target function*. When using any discriminative models in ML,

Refer to Section 10.1 for generative models. Compare the basic assumptions with those of discriminative models.

our goal is to learn the target function from a prespecified function family, called *model space* $\mathbb{H}$ (a.k.a., hypothesis space), based on a training set consisting of a finite number of sample pairs:

$$\mathcal{D}_N = \left\{(\mathbf{x}_i, y_i) \mid i = 1, \cdots, N\right\},$$

See page 151 for the definition of L^p functions.

where $\mathbf{x}_i$ is an independent sample drawn from the distribution $p(\mathbf{x})$ (i.e., $\mathbf{x}_i \sim p(\mathbf{x})$), and $y_i = \bar{f}(\mathbf{x}_i)$ for all $i = 1, 2, \cdots, N$. The model space $\mathbb{H}$ could be any valid function space, such as all linear functions, all quadratic functions, all polynomial functions, or all L^p functions.

Because the target function is unknown, what we can do in ML is to find the best estimate of the target function inside $\mathbb{H}$. To do so, we also need to introduce a loss function $l(y, y')$ to specify the way we count errors in ML. For pattern-classification problems, it makes sense to count the total number of misclassification errors for any data set: one error is counted when the model predicts a class that differs from the true label, and zero error is counted otherwise. In this case, we normally adopt the so-called zero–one loss function, as follows:

$$l(y, y') = \begin{cases} 0 & (y = y') \\ 1 & (y \neq y'). \end{cases} \tag{5.1}$$

On the other hand, for regression problems, it makes sense to use the so-called square-error loss function to count prediction deviations:

$$l(y, y') = (y - y')^2. \tag{5.2}$$

Based on the selected loss function $l(y, y')$, for any model candidate $f \in \mathbb{H}$, we can compute the average loss between f and the target function $\bar{f}$ in two different ways. The first one is computed based on all samples in the training set $\mathcal{D}_N$, usually called the *empirical loss* (a.k.a., empirical risk or in-sample error):

$$R_{\text{emp}}(f|\mathcal{D}_N) = \frac{1}{N}\sum_{i=1}^{N} l\big(y_i, f(\mathbf{x}_i)\big), \tag{5.3}$$

where we know $y_i = \bar{f}(\mathbf{x}_i)$ for all i. The second one is computed for all possible samples in the entire input space, that is, the so-called *expected risk*:

$$R(f) = \mathbb{E}_{\mathbf{x}\sim p(\mathbf{x})}\Big[l\big(\bar{f}(\mathbf{x}), f(\mathbf{x})\big)\Big] = \int_{\mathbf{x}\in\mathbb{X}} l\big(\bar{f}(\mathbf{x}), f(\mathbf{x})\big)p(\mathbf{x})\, d\mathbf{x}. \tag{5.4}$$

It is easy to see that $R(f) \neq R_{\text{emp}}(f|\mathcal{D}_N)$. The expected risk $R(f)$ represents the true expectation of the loss function over the entire input space, whereas $R_{\text{emp}}(f|\mathfrak{D}_N)$ represents the sample mean of the loss function on the training set. If we sample $\mathbf{x}_i \sim p(\mathbf{x})$ and generate $y_i = \bar{f}(\mathbf{x}_i)$ for all i, then based on the law of large numbers, we have

$$\lim_{N\to\infty} R_{\text{emp}}(f|\mathfrak{D}_N) = R(f). \tag{5.5}$$

5.2 Learnability

The ultimate goal of ML is to learn effective models based on a finite training set that perform well not only with the same training data but also with any new unseen samples that are statistically similar to the training data (i.e., for any $\mathbf{x} \sim p(\mathbf{x})$). Ideally, we should seek for a model $f(\cdot)$ inside $\mathbb{H}$ that yields the lowest possible expected loss $R(f)$. However, this is not a feasible task because $R(f)$ is not computable in practice. Note that $R(f)$ in Eq. (5.4) involves two unknown things, namely, the target function $\bar{f}(\cdot)$ and the true data distribution $p(\mathbf{x})$.

Without an alternative, for any ML problem, we will have to seek a model f inside $\mathbb{H}$ that yields a low empirical loss $R_{\text{emp}}(f|\mathfrak{D}_N)$ because $R_{\text{emp}}(f|\mathfrak{D}_N)$ can be computed solely based on a training set $\mathfrak{D}_N$. For example, we can seek a model inside $\mathbb{H}$ that yields the lowest empirical loss $R_{\text{emp}}(f|\mathfrak{D}_N)$:

$$f^* = \arg\min_{f\in\mathbb{H}} R_{\text{emp}}(f|\mathfrak{D}_N). \tag{5.6}$$

Generally speaking, this empirical risk minimization (ERM) could be easily achieved. For example, we can take a simple database approach, as follows in Example 5.2.1.

Example 5.2.1 Naive Memorization Using an Unbounded Database

We first store all training samples $(\mathbf{x}_i, y_i)$ in $\mathfrak{D}_N$ in a large database. We treat the database as our learned model. For any new sample $\mathbf{x}$, we query the database: if an *exact match* $(\mathbf{x}_i, y_i)$ is found when $\mathbf{x}_i = \mathbf{x}$, we return the corresponding y_i as output; otherwise, we return *unknown* or a random guess as output. ♦

The memorization approach in Example 5.2.1 gives the lowest possible $R_{\text{emp}}(f|\mathfrak{D}_N) = 0$ for any $\mathfrak{D}_N$ as long as the database is large enough to hold all training samples. However, we do not consider this approach a good ML method because it learns nothing beyond the given samples.

Example 5.2.1 suggests that ERM alone is not sufficient to guarantee meaningful learning. When we minimize or reduce the empirical risk, if we can ensure the expected risk is also minimized or at least significantly reduced, then we say the problem is *learnable*. Otherwise, if the expected risk always remains unchanged or even becomes worse when the empirical risk is reduced, we say this problem is not learnable. Evidently, the *learnability* depends on the gap

$$\left|R(f^*) - R_{\text{emp}}(f^*|\mathcal{D}_N)\right|, \tag{5.7}$$

where f^* denotes the model found in the ERM procedure.

5.3 Generalization Bounds

For any fixed model from the model space (i.e., $f \in \mathbb{H}$), the gap

$$\left|R(f) - R_{\text{emp}}(f|\mathcal{D}_N)\right|$$

can be computed based on Hoeffding's inequality in Eq. (5.8). Assuming we adopt the zero–one loss function in Eq. (5.1) for pattern classification, the quantity $l\big(\bar{f}(\mathbf{x}), f(\mathbf{x})\big)$ can be viewed as a binary random variable, taking a value of 0 or 1 for any $\mathbf{x}$. After replacing X with $l\big(\bar{f}(\mathbf{x}), f(\mathbf{x})\big)$ and $p(x)$ with the data distribution $p(\mathbf{x})$ in Eq. (5.8), we can derive that

Hoeffding's inequality:
Assuming $\{x_1, x_2, \cdots, x_N\}$ are N independent and identically distributed (i.i.d.) samples of a random variable X whose distribution function is given as $p(x)$, and $a \le x_i \le b$ for all $i = 1, 2, \cdots, N$. $\forall \epsilon > 0$, we have

$$\Pr\left[\left|\mathbb{E}[X] - \frac{1}{N}\sum_{i=1}^{N} x_i\right| > \epsilon\right] \le 2e^{-\frac{2N\epsilon^2}{(b-a)^2}}. \tag{5.8}$$

$$\Pr\left[\left|R(f) - R_{\text{emp}}(f|\mathcal{D}_N)\right| > \epsilon\right] \le 2e^{-2N\epsilon^2}. \tag{5.9}$$

Note that $0 \le l\big(\bar{f}(\mathbf{x}), f(\mathbf{x})\big) \le 1$ holds for any $\mathbf{x}$ because we use the zero–one loss function.

However, Eq. (5.9) holds for a fixed model in $\mathbb{H}$, but it does not apply to f^* derived from ERM because f^* depends on $\mathcal{D}_N$. For a different training set of the same size N, ERM may end up with a different model in $\mathbb{H}$ even when the same optimization algorithm is run for ERM. In order to derive the bound for any one model in $\mathbb{H}$, we will have to consider the following uniform deviation:

$$B(N, \mathbb{H}) = \sup_{f \in \mathbb{H}} \left|R(f) - R_{\text{emp}}(f|\mathcal{D}_N)\right|, \tag{5.10}$$

because we have $\left|R(f^*) - R_{\text{emp}}(f^*|\mathcal{D}_N)\right| \le B(N, \mathbb{H})$ as long as $f^* \in \mathbb{H}$. We can see that $B(N, \mathbb{H})$ depends on the chosen model space $\mathbb{H}$. Next, we will consider how to derive $B(N, \mathbb{H})$ for two different types of $\mathbb{H}$.

5.3.1 Finite Model Space: $|\mathbb{H}|$

Assume model space $\mathbb{H}$ consists of a finite number of distinct models, denoted as $\mathbb{H} = \left\{f_1, f_2, \cdots, f_{|\mathbb{H}|}\right\}$, where $|\mathbb{H}|$ denotes the number of all distinct models in $\mathbb{H}$. According to the definition of $B(N, \mathbb{H})$ in Eq. (5.10),

$\forall \epsilon > 0$, if $B(N, \mathbb{H}) > \epsilon$ holds, it means that there exists *at least* one model f_i in $\mathbb{H}$ that must satisfy

$$\left|R(f_i) - R_{\text{emp}}(f_i|\mathcal{D}_N)\right| > \epsilon.$$

In other words, if $B(N, \mathbb{H}) > \epsilon$ holds, it is equivalent to say that

$$\left|R(f_1) - R_{\text{emp}}(f_1|\mathcal{D}_N)\right| > \epsilon \quad \text{or} \quad \left|R(f_2) - R_{\text{emp}}(f_2|\mathcal{D}_N)\right| > \epsilon \quad \text{or} \quad \cdots$$

$$\cdots \quad \text{or} \quad \left|R(f_{|\mathbb{H}|}) - R_{\text{emp}}(f_{|\mathbb{H}|}|\mathcal{D}_N)\right| > \epsilon.$$

Because we know that the bound in Eq. (5.9) holds for every f_i in $\mathbb{H}$, based on the union bound in Eq. (5.11), we can immediately derive

$$\Pr\Big(B(N, \mathbb{H}) > \epsilon\Big) \leq 2|\mathbb{H}|e^{-2N\epsilon^2}. \tag{5.12}$$

Equivalently, we can rearrange this as

$$\Pr\Big(B(N, \mathbb{H}) \leq \epsilon\Big) \geq 1 - 2|\mathbb{H}|e^{-2N\epsilon^2},$$

which means that $B(N, \mathbb{H}) \leq \epsilon$ holds at least in probability $1 - 2|\mathbb{H}|e^{-2N\epsilon^2}$.

If we denote $\delta = 2|\mathbb{H}|e^{-2N\epsilon^2}$, which leads to $\epsilon = \sqrt{\frac{\ln|\mathbb{H}| + \ln\frac{2}{\delta}}{2N}}$, then we can say the same thing in a different way, as follows:

$$B(N, \mathbb{H}) \leq \sqrt{\frac{\ln|\mathbb{H}| + \ln\frac{2}{\delta}}{2N}}$$

holds at least in probability $1 - \delta$ ($\forall \delta \in (0, 1]$).

Due to the fact that $f^* \in \mathbb{H}$, we have $\left|R(f^*) - R_{\text{emp}}(f^*|\mathcal{D}_N)\right| \leq B(N, \mathbb{H})$. Based on the bound for $B(N, \mathbb{H})$, we can conclude the upper bound for $R(f^*)$ as follows:

$$R(f^*) \leq R_{\text{emp}}(f^*|\mathcal{D}_N) + \sqrt{\frac{\ln|\mathbb{H}| + \ln\frac{2}{\delta}}{2N}} \tag{5.13}$$

holds at least in probability $1 - \delta$. This is our first generalization bound for a finite model space. If we perform ERM over a finite model space based on a training set of N samples, the gap between the expected risk and the minimized empirical risk is at most of order $O(\sqrt{\frac{\ln|\mathbb{H}|}{N}})$. When we choose a large model space, the achieved empirical risk $R_{\text{emp}}(f^*|\mathcal{D}_N)$ may be lower, but the gap may also increase. On the other hand, if we choose a small model space, the achieved empirical risk $R_{\text{emp}}(f^*|\mathcal{D}_N)$ may be higher, but the gap is guaranteed to be tighter.

Union bound:
For a countable set of events

$$A_1, A_2, \cdots,$$

we have

$$\Pr\Big(\bigcup_i A_i\Big) \leq \sum_i \Pr(A_i). \tag{5.11}$$

For any ϵ, we have

$$\Pr\Big(B(N, \mathbb{H}) \leq \epsilon\Big) +$$

$$\Pr\Big(B(N, \mathbb{H}) > \epsilon\Big) = 1.$$

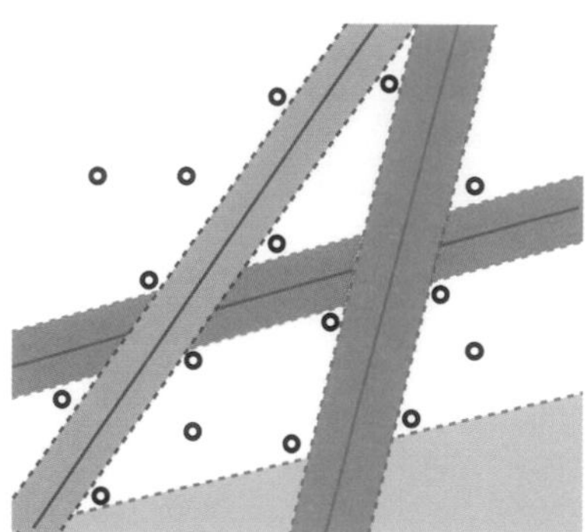

Figure 5.1: All training samples are plotted as dots in space. All models within each shaded area separate these samples in the same way.

5.3.2 Infinite Model Space: VC Dimension

If model space $\mathbb{H}$ is continuous, consisting of an infinite number of distinct models, the previously described generalization bound does not hold because the union bound cannot be directly applied as in Eq. (5.12). The basic intuition is as follows: if all training samples are given, not every model in a continuous model space $\mathbb{H}$ will make a difference in terms of separating these samples. For example, as shown in Figure 5.1, all models within each color-shaded area separate these data samples (plotted as dots) in the same way so that all models within each color-shaded area should be counted as only one *effective model* for this data set. Hence, the generalization bound for an infinite model space should only depend on the maximum number of effective models rather than the total number of all possible models.

Vapnik–Chervonenkis (VC) theory [242, 243, 25] has been developed to count the total number of effective models in a continuous model space in terms of separating a finite number of data samples. A popular tool developed for this purpose is the so-called *VC dimension*. The VC dimension is defined based on the concept of *shattering* a data set: given a data set of N samples, for every possible label combination of these N samples, if we can always find at least one model out of $\mathbb{H}$ to generate this label combination, we say that $\mathbb{H}$ shatters this data set. In binary classification, each sample can have two possible labels, and we have a total of 2^N possible label combinations for every N samples. If we can find a model out of $\mathbb{H}$ to generate each of these 2^N possible label combinations, $\mathbb{H}$ is said to shatter this set of N samples. For example, if we assume $\mathbb{H}$ is a two-dimensional (2D) linear model space, containing all straight lines in a 2D space, given the set of three points in Figure 5.2, we have in total $2^3 = 8$ possible label combinations. As shown in Figure 5.2, we can find at least one straight line to separate these three points to generate every possible label combination.

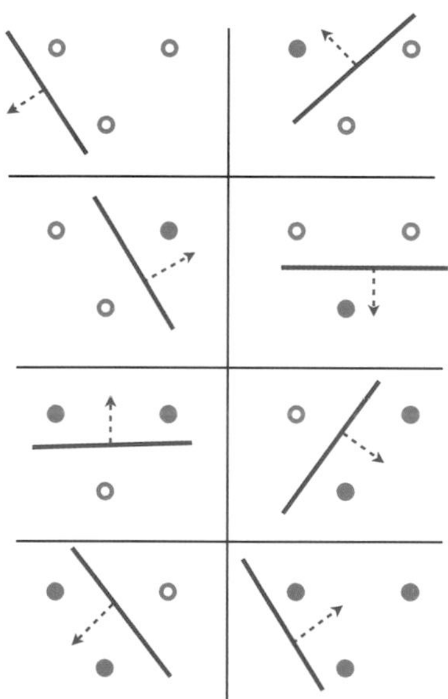

Figure 5.2: A set of three data points is *shattered* by $\mathbb{H}$, consisting of all 2D linear models.

The VC dimension of $\mathbb{H}$ is defined as the maximum number of points that can be shattered by $\mathbb{H}$. If the VC dimension of $\mathbb{H}$ is known to be H, it means that $\mathbb{H}$ can shatter at least one set of H points (no need to shatter all sets of H points), but $\mathbb{H}$ cannot shatter any set of $H + 1$ points.

Example 5.3.1 The VC Dimension of 2D Linear Models Is 3—Why?

1. The 2D linear models can shatter a set of three points, as shown in Figure 5.2.
2. If we have another set of three points that are aligned in a straight line, all 2D linear models actually cannot shatter this set. Verify it and explain why this does not matter.

3. If we have four points in a 2D space, verify that 2D linear models cannot shatter any four points no matter how we arrange them. ♦

A general extension of this example is that the VC dimension of linear models in $\mathbb{R}^n$ is $n+1$. The VC dimension is a nice single numeric measure that conveniently quantifies the overall modeling capacity of model space $\mathbb{H}$. The VC dimension of simple models is small, whereas that of complex models should be large. However, in practice, it is still hard to accurately estimate the VC dimension for most complex models, such as neural networks. For many amenable models that are practically useful in machine learning, we have the following *rule of thumb*:

$$\text{VC dimension} \approx \text{number of free parameters.}$$

Many exceptions exist. For example, the model space $y = f(x) = \sin(x/a)$ with one parameter $a \in \mathbb{R}$ is said to have a VC dimension of ∞ because the behavior of $f(x)$ gets wild as $a \to 0$.

As shown in [242, 243, 25], once we know the VC dimension of model space $\mathbb{H}$ is H, the total number of effective models in $\mathbb{H}$ for a set of N points is upper-bounded by

$$\begin{cases} = 2^N & \text{if } N < H \\ \leq \left(\frac{eN}{H}\right)^H & \text{if } N \geq H. \end{cases}$$

As the data size increases, the number of effective models in $\mathbb{H}$ grows exponentially only for small data sets, and it slows down as a polynomial growth after its size exceeds the VC dimension of $\mathbb{H}$. Based on this result, a VC generalization bound for $\mathbb{H}$ with a VC dimension of H can be derived as follows [242, 243]:

We have skipped some cumbersome details that are needed to derive the result in Eq. (5.14). Interested readers may refer to [25, 210].

$$R(f^*) \leq R_{\text{emp}}(f^* | \mathcal{D}_N) + \sqrt{\frac{8H(\ln\frac{2N}{H}+1) + 8\ln\frac{4}{\delta}}{N}} \tag{5.14}$$

holds at least in probability $1-\delta$ ($\forall\delta \in (0,1]$) for any large data set ($N \geq H$). In this case, the gap between the expected risk and the minimized empirical risk is roughly at the order of $O\left(\sqrt{\frac{H}{N}}\right)$.

One striking advantage of the above VC bound is that it is totally problem-independent and the same bounds hold for any data distributions. However, this may also be viewed as a major drawback since the bounds are extremely loose for most problems.

Example 5.3.2 Limitations of the VC Generalization Bound

1. Case A: ASSUME we use $N = 1{,}000$ data samples (the feature dimension is 100) to learn a linear classifier ($H = 101$). We have observed that the training error rate is 1 percent, and the test error rate in a large held-out set is 2.4 percent. Now let us set $\delta = 0.001$

(with a 99.9 percent chance of being correct) and use the VC bound to estimate the expected loss. We have

$$R(f^*) \leq 0.01 + \mathbf{1.8123} = 182.23\% \quad (\gg 2.4\%).$$

2. Case B: Same as case A, except $N = 10,000$, and the test error rate is 1.1 percent.

$$R(f^*) \leq 0.01 + \mathbf{0.7174} = 72.74\% \quad (\gg 1.1\%)$$

3. Case C: Same as case A, except the feature dimension is 1,000 (thus $H = 1,001$), and the test error rate is 3.8 percent.

$$R(f^*) \leq 0.01 + \mathbf{3.690} = 370.0\% \quad (\gg 3.8\%)$$ ♦

The test error rates in this example serve as a good estimate for the expected risk $R(f)$ in each case because they are evaluated on some fairly large unseen data sets. Example 5.3.2 clearly shows how loose the VC bounds are for real problems. In some cases, the predicted upper bounds are even beyond the natural range $[0, 1]$ for zero–one loss. These cases explain why the VC bound has an elegant form that can be intuitively explained in theory but fails to provide any impacts for real-world problems. This calls for more research efforts in these areas to derive much tighter generalization bounds (probably problem specific) for real ML problems.

In summary, the main conclusions from the previous theoretical analysis are as follows:

- ERM does not always result in good ML models that generalize well on unseen data.
- In general, we have

$$\text{expected risk} \leq \text{empirical loss} + \text{generation bound}.$$

- Generalization bounds depend on the chosen model space in ERM.

When simple models are used, the generalization bound is relatively tight, but we may not be able to achieve a low enough empirical loss. When complex models are used, the empirical loss can be easily reduced, but meanwhile, the so-called *regularization* techniques must be applied to control generalization. The central idea of regularization is to enforce some constraints to ensure ERM is conducted only over a subspace of $\mathbb{H}$ rather than the whole allowed space of $\mathbb{H}$. By doing so, the total number of effective models considered in ERM decreases indirectly, and so does the generalization bound. The following chapters will show how to combine ERM with regularization to actually estimate popular discriminative models, such as linear models and neural networks.

Exercises

Q5.1 Based on the concept of the VC dimension, explain why the memorization approach using an unbounded database in Example 5.2.1 is not learnable.

Q5.2 Estimate the VC dimensions for the following simple model spaces:

a. A model space of N distinct models, $\{A_1, A_2, \cdots, A_N\}$
b. An interval $[a, b]$ on the real line with $a \leq b$
c. Two intervals $[a, b]$ and $[c, d]$ on the real line with $a \leq b \leq c \leq d$
d. Discs in $\mathbb{R}^2$
e. Triangles in $\mathbb{R}^2$
f. Rectangles in $\mathbb{R}^2$
g. Convex hulls in $\mathbb{R}^2$
h. Closed balls in $\mathbb{R}^d$
i. Hyper-rectangles in $\mathbb{R}^d$

Q5.3 In an ML problem as specified in Section 5.1, we use f^* to denote the model obtained from the ERM procedure in Eq. (5.6):

$$f^* = \arg\min_{f \in \mathbb{H}} R_{\text{emp}}(f | \mathfrak{D}_N),$$

and we use $\hat{f}$ to denote the best possible model in the model space $\mathbb{H}$, that is:

$$\hat{f} = \arg\min_{f \in \mathbb{H}} R(f)$$

We further assume the unknown target function is denoted as $\bar{f}$. By definition, we have $R(\bar{f}) = 0$ and $R_{\text{emp}}(\bar{f} | \mathfrak{D}_N) = 0$. We can define several types of errors in ML as follows:

- Generalization error E_g:

$$E_g = \left| R(f^*) - R_{\text{emp}}(f^* | \mathfrak{D}_N) \right|$$

- Estimation error E_e:

$$E_e = \left| R(f^*) - R(\hat{f}) \right|$$

- Approximation error E_a:

$$E_a = \left| R(\hat{f}) - R(\bar{f}) \right| = R(\hat{f})$$

Use words to explain the physical meanings of these errors.
Section 5.3 showed that $E_g \leq B(N, \mathbb{H})$, where $B(N, \mathbb{H})$ is the generalization bound defined in Eq. (5.10). In this exercise, prove the following properties:

a. $R(f^*) \leq E_e + E_a$
b. $R_{\text{emp}}(f^* | \mathfrak{D}_N) \leq E_g + E_e + E_a$
c. $E_e \leq 2 \cdot B(N, \mathbb{H})$

Linear Models | 6

This chapter first focuses on a family of the simplest functions for discriminative models, namely, linear models. This discussion treats linear function $y = \mathbf{w}^\intercal\mathbf{x}$ or affine function $y = \mathbf{w}^\intercal\mathbf{x} + b$ equally because both behave similarly in most machine learning problems. Throughout this book, linear models include both linear and affine functions. This chapter mainly uses simple two-class binary classification problems as an example to discuss how to use different machine learning methods to solve binary classification with a linear model and briefly discusses how to extend it to deal with multiple classes at the end of each section. Finally, this chapter also briefly introduces the famous *kernel trick* to extend linear models into nonlinear models.

The function $y = \mathbf{w}^\intercal\mathbf{x} + b$ is traditionally called an *affine function* because it does not strictly satisfy the definition of linear functions, such as zero input leading to zero output.
However, an affine function can be reformulated as a linear function in a higher-dimensional space. For example, denoting $\bar{\mathbf{x}} = [\mathbf{x}; 1]$ and $\bar{\mathbf{w}} = [\mathbf{w}; b]$, then we have

$$y = \mathbf{w}^\intercal\mathbf{x} + b = \bar{\mathbf{w}}^\intercal\bar{\mathbf{x}}.$$

Generally speaking, a binary classification problem is normally formulated as follows. Assume a set of training data is given as

$$\mathcal{D}_N = \big\{(\mathbf{x}_i, y_i) \mid i = 1, 2, \cdots N\big\},$$

where each feature vector is a d-dimensional vector $\mathbf{x}_i \in \mathbb{R}^d$, and each binary label $y_i \in \{+1, -1\}$ equals to +1 for one class and −1 for another. Based on $\mathcal{D}_N$, we need to learn a linear model $y = \mathbf{w}^\intercal\mathbf{x} + b$ (or $y = \mathbf{w}^\intercal\mathbf{x}$), where $\mathbf{w} \in \mathbb{R}^d$ and $b \in \mathbb{R}$, to separate these two classes. Depending on the given training set $\mathcal{D}_N$, we have two scenarios (as shown in Figure 6.1):

1. *Linearly separable* cases, where at least one linear hyperplane exists to perfectly separate all samples in the training set
2. *Linearly nonseparable* cases, where no linear hyperplane exists to perfectly separate all samples

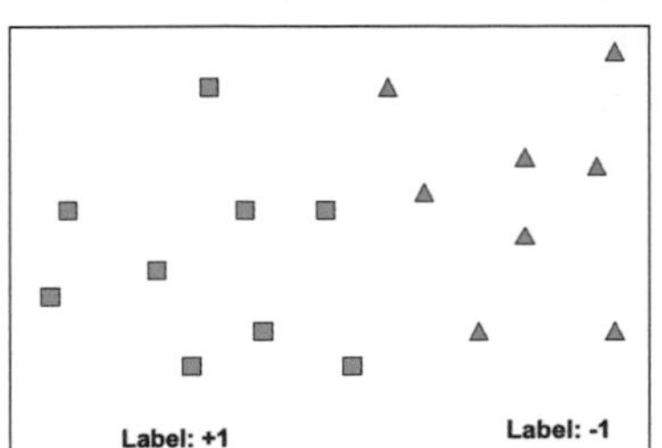

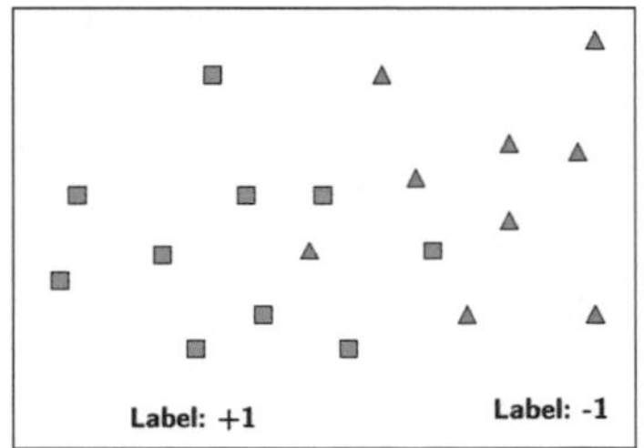

Figure 6.1: Linearly separable (left) versus nonseparable (right) cases in binary classification, where each sample is plotted as a point, and its color indicates its class label.

The following sections discuss how to use different learning algorithms to learn linear models for these two scenarios. These algorithms include the early *perceptron*, simple *linear regression*, *minimum classification error* estimation, the popular *logistic regression*, and the famous *support vector machines (SVMs)*. We will highlight the differences among these learning methods and discuss their pros and cons.

6.1 Perceptron

The perceptron is one of the earliest machine learning algorithms and was initially proposed by F. Rosenbaltt in 1957 [200]. A solid theoretical guarantee was also established for linearly separable cases by A. Novikoff in 1962 [176]. Because of its simplicity, it led to excitement in the field and eventually triggered the first boom of neural networks in the early 1960s.

The perceptron is a simple iterative algorithm to learn a linear model from a training set $\mathcal{D}_N$ to separate two classes. A linear model is used to assign any input $\mathbf{x}$ to one of two classes according to the sign of the linear function:

$$y = \text{sign}(\mathbf{w}^\intercal \mathbf{x}) = \begin{cases} +1 & \text{if } \mathbf{w}^\intercal \mathbf{x} > 0 \\ -1 & \text{otherwise.} \end{cases} \tag{6.1}$$

The perceptron algorithm is shown in Algorithm 6.4. First, it initializes the weight vector for the linear model. Next, it uses the linear model to iterate over all samples in the training set: whenever a mistake is found, the weight vector is immediately updated according to a simple rule. This process continues until no mistake is found in the training set. If the training set is linearly separable, the perceptron algorithm is guaranteed to terminate after a finite number of updates, and it will return a linear model that perfectly classifies the training set (see the following discussion for why).

Algorithm 6.4 Perceptron

> initialize $\mathbf{w}^{(0)} = 0$, $n = 0$
> **loop**
>   randomly choose a sample $(\mathbf{x}_i, y_i)$ in $\mathcal{D}_N$
>   calculate the actual output $h_i = \text{sign}(\mathbf{w}^{(n)\intercal}\mathbf{x}_i)$
>   **if** upon a mistake: $h_i \neq y_i$ **then**
> $\mathbf{w}^{(n+1)} = \mathbf{w}^{(n)} + y_i\mathbf{x}_i$
> $n = n + 1$
>   **else if** no mistake is found **then**
>   return $\mathbf{w}^{(n)}$ and terminate
>   **end if**
> **end loop**

Despite the perceptron algorithm being one of the first major machine learning algorithms created more than 60 years ago, it clearly shares some similarities with many modern learning algorithms. However, there are two important differences worth mentioning. First, the perceptron algorithm does not rely on any hyperparameter. The algorithm may scan the training set differently and result in a different sequence of updates, but no hyperparameter is needed in the updating formula. This will make the learning easy and reproducible, unlike many modern learning methods that heavily rely on sensitive hyperparameters. Second, at least for linearly separable cases where optimal solutions exist, the perceptron algorithm is theoretically guaranteed to terminate and return one of those optimal solutions. The theoretical proof for the perceptron algorithm is very intuitive and elegant. It is regarded as a pioneering work in learning theory. Although it only considers some extremely simple cases, many mathematical techniques used in this proof (e.g., margin bound) can still be widely found in many recent theoretical works in machine learning.

In machine learning, a hyperparameter is a parameter whose value must be set manually before the learning process starts.

The following discussion briefly introduces this important work and tries to give readers a taste of theoretical analysis for a learning algorithm.

If the training set $\mathcal{D}_N$ is given, we can always normalize all feature vectors to ensure that all of them are located inside a unit sphere:

$$||\mathbf{x}_i|| \leq 1 \quad \forall i = \{1, 2, \cdots, N\}. \tag{6.2}$$

Moreover, if training set $\mathcal{D}_N$ is linearly separable, it means that there exists some gap between the samples from two classes. This gap can be mathematically defined as an optimal separating hyperplane that achieves the *maximum* margin from all training samples, as shown in Figure 6.2. This maximum margin hyperplane, denoted as $\hat{\mathbf{w}}^\intercal \mathbf{x} = 0$, is unique for each linearly separable set. Furthermore, $\hat{\mathbf{w}}$ is scaled to be of unit length (i.e., $||\hat{\mathbf{w}}|| = 1$). Note that the location of the hyperplane does not change when $\hat{\mathbf{w}}$ is scaled by a real number.

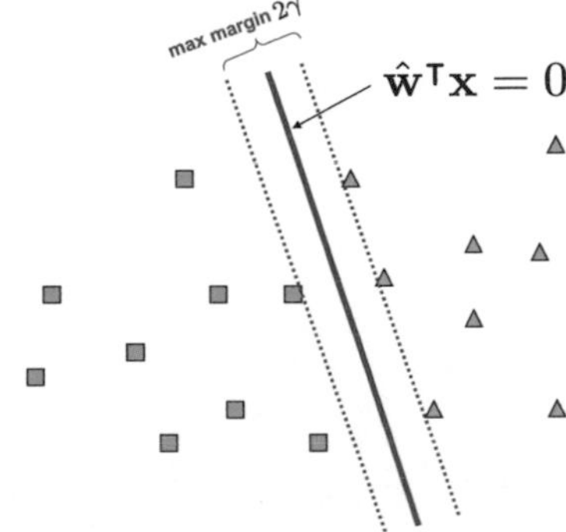

Figure 6.2: The optimal separating hyperplane achieves the maximum separation margin from all data samples.

According to the formula to compute the distance from a point to a hyperplane in geometry in Figure 6.3, the separation margin can be expressed as follows:

$$\gamma = \min_{\mathbf{x}_i \in \mathcal{D}_N} \frac{|\hat{\mathbf{w}}^\intercal \mathbf{x}_i|}{||\hat{\mathbf{w}}||} = \min_{\mathbf{x}_i \in \mathcal{D}_N} |\hat{\mathbf{w}}^\intercal \mathbf{x}_i|. \tag{6.3}$$

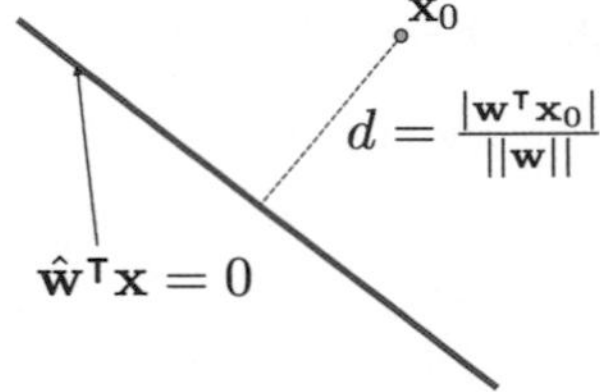

Figure 6.3: The distance formula from a point to a hyperplane (refer to Example 2.4.1).

If the training set $\mathcal{D}_N$ is linearly separable, the optimal maximum-margin hyperplane $\hat{\mathbf{w}}$ exists, and the gap between two classes can be quantitatively measured as 2γ.

Theorem 6.1.1 *If the perceptron algorithm is run on a linearly separable training set $\mathcal{D}_N$, the number of mistakes made on $\mathcal{D}_N$ is at most $1/\gamma^2$. In other words, the perceptron algorithm will terminate after at most $\lceil 1/\gamma^2 \rceil$ updates and return a hyperplane that perfectly separates $\mathcal{D}_N$.*

Proof:

Step 1:

Based on the margin definition in Eq. (6.3), for any $\mathbf{x}_i \in \mathcal{D}_N$, we have

$$|\hat{\mathbf{w}}^\intercal \mathbf{x}_i| \geq \gamma.$$

Because $\hat{\mathbf{w}}$ perfectly separates all samples in $\mathcal{D}_N$, we can get rid of the absolute sign by multiplying its own label:

$$y_i \hat{\mathbf{w}}^\intercal \mathbf{x}_i \geq \gamma \quad \forall i, (\mathbf{x}_i, y_i) \in \mathcal{D}_N. \tag{6.4}$$

Step 2:

When we run the perceptron algorithm on $\mathcal{D}_N$, we record all mistakes (all pairs of sample and label) made by the algorithm as follows:

$$\mathcal{M} = \{(\mathbf{x}^{(1)}, y^{(1)}), (\mathbf{x}^{(2)}, y^{(2)}), \cdots, (\mathbf{x}^{(M)}, y^{(M)})\},$$

where each pair is from $\mathcal{D}_N$, and the number of mistakes is M. The number of mistakes, M, could be very large because the same sample in $\mathcal{D}_N$ could be repeatedly recorded in $\mathcal{M}$.

Because of Eq. (6.4), we have

$$\sum_{n \in \mathcal{M}} y^{(n)} \hat{\mathbf{w}}^\intercal \mathbf{x}^{(n)} \geq M \cdot \gamma. \tag{6.5}$$

Furthermore, we have

$$\begin{aligned} M \cdot \gamma &\leq \sum_{n \in \mathcal{M}} y^{(n)} \hat{\mathbf{w}}^\intercal \mathbf{x}^{(n)} \\ &= \hat{\mathbf{w}}^\intercal \Big(\sum_{n \in \mathcal{M}} y^{(n)} \mathbf{x}^{(n)} \Big) \\ &\leq \|\hat{\mathbf{w}}\| \cdot \Big\| \sum_{n \in \mathcal{M}} y^{(n)} \mathbf{x}^{(n)} \Big\| \quad \text{(Cauchy–Schwarz inequality)} \\ &= \Big\| \sum_{n \in \mathcal{M}} y^{(n)} \mathbf{x}^{(n)} \Big\| \quad (\|\hat{\mathbf{w}}\| = 1 \text{ by definition}). \end{aligned} \tag{6.6}$$

Cauchy–Schwarz inequality:

$$|\mathbf{u}^\intercal \mathbf{v}| \leq \|\mathbf{u}\| \cdot \|\mathbf{v}\|.$$

Step 3:

In the perceptron algorithm, every mistake $(\mathbf{x}^{(n)}, y^{(n)})$ is used to update the weight vector from $\mathbf{w}^{(n)}$ to $\mathbf{w}^{(n+1)}$:

$$\mathbf{w}^{(n+1)} = \mathbf{w}^{(n)} + y^{(n)} \mathbf{x}^{(n)}.$$

Therefore, we have

$$\begin{aligned}
\Big\|\sum_{n\in\mathcal{M}} y^{(n)}\mathbf{x}^{(n)}\Big\| &= \Big\|\sum_{n\in\mathcal{M}} \big(\mathbf{w}^{(n+1)} - \mathbf{w}^{(n)}\big)\Big\| = \big\|\mathbf{w}^{(M+1)} - \mathbf{w}^{(0)}\big\| = \big\|\mathbf{w}^{(M+1)}\big\| \\
&= \sqrt{\|\mathbf{w}^{(M+1)}\|^2} = \sqrt{\sum_{n\in\mathcal{M}} \big(\|\mathbf{w}^{(n+1)}\|^2 - \|\mathbf{w}^{(n)}\|^2\big)} \\
&= \sqrt{\sum_{n\in\mathcal{M}} \big(\|\mathbf{w}^{(n)} + y^{(n)}\mathbf{x}^{(n)}\|^2 - \|\mathbf{w}^{(n)}\|^2\big)} \\
&= \sqrt{\sum_{n\in\mathcal{M}} \Big(\cancel{\|\mathbf{w}^{(n)}\|^2} + \underbrace{2y^{(n)}\mathbf{w}^{(n)\top}\mathbf{x}^{(n)}}_{<0} + \overbrace{\cancel{(y^{(n)})^2}}^{(\pm1)^2}\|\mathbf{x}^{(n)}\|^2 - \cancel{\|\mathbf{w}^{(n)}\|^2}\Big)} \\
&< \sqrt{\sum_{n\in\mathcal{M}} \|\mathbf{x}^{(n)}\|^2} \le \sqrt{M}. \qquad (6.7)
\end{aligned}$$

Note that we initialize $\mathbf{w}^{(0)} = 0$.

By definition, $(\mathbf{x}^{(n)}, y^{(n)})$ was a mistake when being evaluated by the model $\mathbf{w}^{(n)}$; thus, we have

$$y^{(n)}(\mathbf{w}^{(n)})^\top\mathbf{x}^{(n)} < 0.$$

Otherwise, this was not a mistake.

We have $\|\mathbf{x}^{(n)}\|^2 \le 1$ after data normalization.

Step 4:

By combining Eqs. (6.6) and (6.7), we have

$$M\cdot\gamma \le \Big\|\sum_{n\in\mathcal{M}} y^{(n)}\mathbf{x}^{(n)}\Big\| < \sqrt{M}.$$

Finally, we derive

$$M < (1/\gamma)^2.$$

In other words, the total number of mistakes made by the algorithm cannot exceed $(1/\gamma)^2$. ■

In summary, if we run the perceptron algorithm on a linear separable data set, the convergence of the algorithm is theoretically guaranteed. The algorithm will converge to some hyperplane that will perfectly separate two classes. The total number of model updates cannot exceed an upper bound, $(1/\gamma)^2$, where 2γ indicates the minimum gap between the training samples of two classes. Note that the converged model is not necessarily the maximum-margin hyperplane $\hat{\mathbf{w}}$ in Figure 6.2 [221]. On the other hand, the perceptron Algorithm 6.4 can be slightly modified to approximately achieve the maximum separation margin, leading to the so-called *margin perceptron algorithm* (see Exercise Q6.2 for more details on this). However, if the data set is not linearly separable, the behavior of the perceptron algorithm is unpredictable, and the algorithm may update the model back and forth and never terminate (see Freund and Schapire [69] for more).

The following sections discuss other machine learning methods for linear models that can be applied to nonseparable cases.

6.2 Linear Regression

Linear regression is a popular method for solving high-dimensional function-fitting problems, but we can still apply the idea of linear regression to classification problems as well. As will be shown later, the advantage of linear regression is that model estimation is relatively simple, and it can be solved by a closed-form solution without using an iterative algorithm.

The basic idea in linear regression is to establish a linear mapping from input feature vectors $\mathbf{x}$ to output targets $y = \mathbf{w}^\intercal\mathbf{x}$. The only difference for two-class classification is that output targets are binary: $y = \pm 1$. The popular criterion to estimate the mapping function is to minimize the total square error in a given training set, as follows:

$$\mathbf{w}^* = \arg\min_{\mathbf{w}} E(\mathbf{w}) = \arg\min_{\mathbf{w}} \sum_{i=1}^{N} (\mathbf{w}^\intercal\mathbf{x}_i - y_i)^2, \tag{6.8}$$

This learning criterion is called the *least-square error* or *minimum mean-squared error*.

where the objective function $E(\mathbf{w})$ measures the total reconstruction error in the training set when the linear model is used to construct each output from its corresponding input.

By constructing the following two matrices:

$$\mathbf{X} = \begin{bmatrix} \mathbf{x}_1^\intercal \\ \mathbf{x}_2^\intercal \\ \vdots \\ \mathbf{x}_N^\intercal \end{bmatrix}_{N\times d} \qquad \mathbf{y} = \begin{bmatrix} y_1 \\ y_2 \\ \vdots \\ y_N \end{bmatrix}_{N\times 1}$$

we can represent the objective function $E(\mathbf{w})$ as follows:

$$\begin{aligned} E(\mathbf{w}) &= \left\|\mathbf{X}\mathbf{w} - \mathbf{y}\right\|^2 = (\mathbf{X}\mathbf{w} - \mathbf{y})^\intercal(\mathbf{X}\mathbf{w} - \mathbf{y}) \\ &= \mathbf{w}^\intercal\mathbf{X}^\intercal\mathbf{X}\mathbf{w} - 2\mathbf{w}^\intercal\mathbf{X}^\intercal\mathbf{y} + \mathbf{y}^\intercal\mathbf{y}. \end{aligned}$$

By diminishing the gradient $\frac{\partial E(\mathbf{w})}{\partial \mathbf{w}} = 0$, we have

$$2\mathbf{X}^\intercal\mathbf{X}\mathbf{w} - 2\mathbf{X}^\intercal\mathbf{y} = 0.$$

Next, we derive the following closed-form solution for the linear regression problem:

$$\mathbf{w}^* = \left(\mathbf{X}^\intercal\mathbf{X}\right)^{-1}\mathbf{X}^\intercal\mathbf{y}, \tag{6.9}$$

In practice, we often use a gradient descent method to solve linear regressions to avoid the matrix inversion. See Exercise Q6.6.

where we need to invert a $d \times d$ matrix $\mathbf{X}^\intercal\mathbf{X}$, which is expensive for high-dimensional problems.

Once the linear model $\mathbf{w}^*$ is estimated as in Eq. (6.9), we can assign a label to any new data $\mathbf{x}$ based on the sign of the linear function:

$$y = \text{sign}(\mathbf{w}^{*\intercal}\mathbf{x}) = \begin{cases} +1 & \text{if } \mathbf{w}^{*\intercal}\mathbf{x} > 0 \\ -1 & \text{otherwise.} \end{cases} \tag{6.10}$$

Linear regression can be easily solved by a closed-form solution, but it may not yield good performance for classification problems. The main reason is that the square error used in training models does not match well with our goal in classification. For classification problems, our primary concern is to reduce the misclassification errors rather than the reconstruction error. The following sections discuss other machine learning methods that allow us to measure the classification errors in certain ways.

6.3 Minimum Classification Error

For classification problems, empirical risk minimization (ERM) suggests minimizing the zero–one classification errors on the training set. This section discusses how to construct a sensible objective function that counts the 0-1 training errors.

If the classification rule in Eq. (6.10) is used, given any linear model $f(\mathbf{x}) = \mathbf{w}^\intercal\mathbf{x}$, then for each training sample $(\mathbf{x}_i, y_i)$ in the training set, whether it leads to a misclassification error actually depends on the following quantity:

$$-y_i\mathbf{w}^\intercal\mathbf{x}_i = \begin{cases} > 0 & \Longrightarrow \text{misclassification} \\ < 0 & \Longrightarrow \text{correct classification.} \end{cases} \tag{6.11}$$

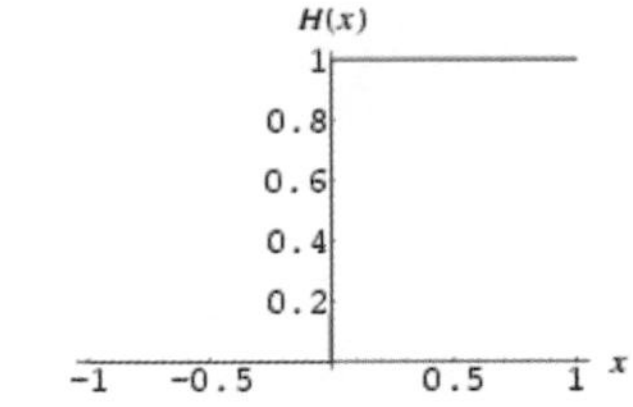

Figure 6.4: The step function $H(x)$.

This quantity can be embedded into the step function $H(\cdot)$ (as shown in Figure 6.4) to count the 0-1 misclassification error for $(\mathbf{x}_i, y_i)$ as $H(-y_i\mathbf{w}^\intercal\mathbf{x}_i)$. Furthermore, it can be summed over all samples in the training set to result in the following objective function:

$$E_0(\mathbf{w}) = \sum_{i=1}^{N} H(-y_i\mathbf{w}^\intercal\mathbf{x}_i),$$

which strictly counts the 0-1 training errors for any given model $\mathbf{w}$. However, this objective function is extremely difficult to optimize because the derivatives of the step function $H(\cdot)$ are 0 almost everywhere except the origin. A common trick to solve this problem is to use a smooth function to approximate the step function. The best candidate for this purpose is

the well-known *sigmoid* function (a.k.a., *logistic sigmoid*):

$$l(x) = \frac{1}{1+e^{-x}}, \tag{6.12}$$

where the sigmoid function $l(x)$ is differentiable everywhere, and it can approximate the step function fairly well as long as its slope is made to be sharp enough (by scaling x), as shown in Figure 6.5.

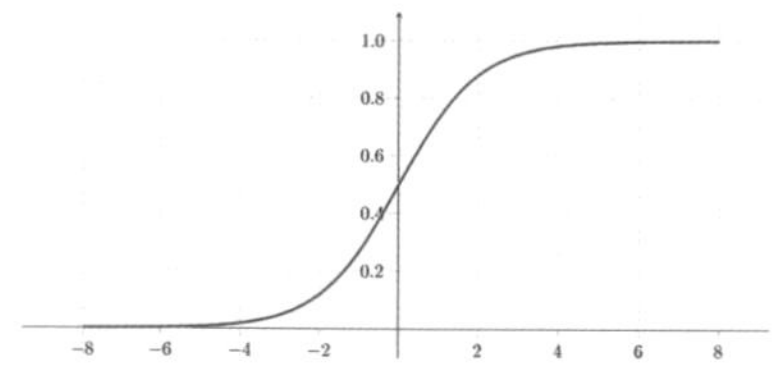

Figure 6.5: The sigmoid function $l(x)$.

If we use the sigmoid function $l(\cdot)$ to replace the step function $H(\cdot)$ in the previous objective function, we derive a differential objective function as follows:

$$E_1(\mathbf{w}) = \sum_{i=1}^{N} l(-y_i \mathbf{w}^\intercal \mathbf{x}_i), \tag{6.13}$$

where $l(-y_i \mathbf{w}^\intercal \mathbf{x}_i)$ is a quantity between 0 and 1, which is sometimes called a *soft error*, as opposed to either a 0 or 1 hard error measured by the step function. Therefore, the objective function $E_1(\mathbf{w})$ actually measures the total *soft errors* on the training set. The learning algorithm that minimizes $E_1(\mathbf{w})$ is usually called the *minimum classification error* (MCE) method. The gradient of $E_1(\mathbf{w})$ can be easily computed as follows:

Note that the minus sign in $l(-y_i \mathbf{w}^\intercal \mathbf{x}_i)$ can be merged with $\mathbf{w}$, which simplifies the formula but does not change the learned model. In this case,

$$E_1(\mathbf{w}) = \sum_{i=1}^{N} l(y_i \mathbf{w}^\intercal \mathbf{x}_i).$$

$$\frac{\partial E_1(\mathbf{w})}{\partial \mathbf{w}} = \sum_{i=1}^{N} y_i l(y_i \mathbf{w}^\intercal \mathbf{x}_i)\Big(1 - l(y_i \mathbf{w}^\intercal \mathbf{x}_i)\Big)\mathbf{x}_i. \tag{6.14}$$

$$\begin{aligned}\frac{dl(x)}{dx} &= \frac{e^{-x}}{(1+e^{-x})^2} \\ &= l(x)(1-l(x)).\end{aligned} \tag{6.15}$$

In MCE, this gradient is used to minimize the soft error $E_1(\mathbf{w})$ iteratively based on any gradient descent or stochastic gradient descent (SGD) method.

6.4 Logistic Regression

Logistic regression is a very popular and simple method for many practical classification tasks. Logistic regression is widely used when feature vectors are manually derived in feature engineering. Logistic regression may be derived under several contexts (see Section 11.4). This section will show that logistic regression is actually closely related to the MCE method described in the previous section.

$$\begin{aligned}1 - l(-x) &= 1 - \frac{1}{1+e^{x}} \\ &= \frac{e^{x}}{1+e^{x}} \\ &= \frac{1}{e^{-x}+1} \\ &= l(x).\end{aligned}$$

In MCE, the quantity $l(-y_i \mathbf{w}^\intercal \mathbf{x}_i)$ in Eq. (6.13) is interpreted as a soft error count of misclassifying one training sample. Because $l(-y_i \mathbf{w}^\intercal \mathbf{x}_i)$ is a real number between 0 and 1, it is also possible to view $l(-y_i \mathbf{w}^\intercal \mathbf{x}_i)$ as the probability of making an error on the training sample $(\mathbf{x}_i, y_i)$ using the model $\mathbf{w}$. In this case, the probability of making a correct classification on $(\mathbf{x}_i, y_i)$ equals to $1 - l(-y_i \mathbf{w}^\intercal \mathbf{x}_i) = l(y_i \mathbf{w}^\intercal \mathbf{x}_i)$. Assuming all samples in the training set are independent and identically distributed (i.i.d.), the joint probability of making a correct classification for all samples in the training set can be expressed as follows:

$$L(\mathbf{w}) = \prod_{i=1}^{N} l(y_i \mathbf{w}^\intercal \mathbf{x}_i).$$

Logistic regression aims to learn a linear model $\mathbf{w}$ to maximize the joint probability of correct classification. Because the logarithm is a monotonic function, it is equivalent to maximizing

$$\ln L(\mathbf{w}) = \sum_{i=1}^{N} \ln l(y_i \mathbf{w}^\intercal \mathbf{x}_i). \tag{6.16}$$

Then, we can derive the gradient for logistic regression as follows:

$$\frac{\partial \ln L(\mathbf{w})}{\partial \mathbf{w}} = \sum_{i=1}^{N} y_i \Big(1 - l(y_i \mathbf{w}^\intercal \mathbf{x}_i)\Big)\mathbf{x}_i, \tag{6.17}$$

and a gradient descent or SGD method can be used to minimize $-\ln L(\mathbf{w})$ to derive the solution to the logistic regression.

When we compare the MCE gradients in Eq. (6.14) with the gradients of the logistic regression in Eq. (6.17), we can notice that they are closely related. However, as shown in Figure 6.6, the MCE gradient weights (in red) indicate that the MCE learning focuses more on the boundary cases, where $|y_i \mathbf{w}^\intercal \mathbf{x}_i|$ is close to 0, because only the training samples near the decision boundary generate large gradients. On the other hand, the gradient weights of the logistic regression (in blue) show that the logistic regression generates significant gradients for all misclassified samples, where $y_i \mathbf{w}^\intercal \mathbf{x}_i$ is small. As a result, logistic regression may be quite sensitive to outliers in the training set. Generally speaking, logistic regression generates larger gradients so that it may converge faster than MCE.

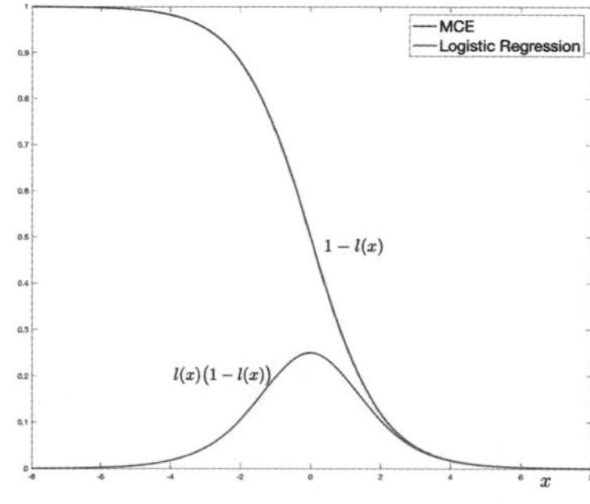

Figure 6.6: Comparison of gradient weights of MCE and logistic regression.

Finally, we can extend the previous formulations of the logistic regression and the MCE training to multiple-class classification problems by simply replacing the previous sigmoid function with the following function from $\mathbf{x}$ ($\in \mathbb{R}^n$) to $\mathbf{z}$ ($\in \mathbb{R}^n$):

$$z_i = \frac{e^{x_i}}{\sum_{j=1}^{n} e^{x_j}} \quad \forall i = \{1, 2, \cdots, n\}, \tag{6.18}$$

where the outputs are all positive and satisfy the sum-to-1 constraint. This function is traditionally called the *softmax* function [36, 35]. Its output behaves like a discrete probability distribution over n classes. Refer to

Exercises Q6.4 and Q6.5 for how to derive MCEs and logistic regressions for multiple-class problems.

6.5 Support Vector Machines

This section introduces SVMs, an important family of discriminative models. The initial concept of SVMs stems from deriving the maximum margin separating hyperplane for linearly separable cases, similar to what we have discussed for the perceptron algorithm. Unlike the perceptron, the power of SVMs lies in the fact that SVMs can be nicely extended to complicated scenarios. First, the so-called *soft margin* is introduced and extended to the nonseparable cases, which is called *soft SVM* formulation. Second, the kernel trick is used to extend the SVM formulation from linear models to nonlinear ones, where a preselected nonlinear kernel function can be applied to data prior to linear models. The beauty of SVMs is that all of these different SVM formulations actually end up with the same optimization problem, namely, *quadratic programming*, which can be solved cleanly because of its theoretically guaranteed convexity. More importantly, a deeper investigation of the SVM formulation actually suggests a more general learning framework for discriminative models, which will be discussed in detail in the next chapter.

6.5.1 Linear SVM

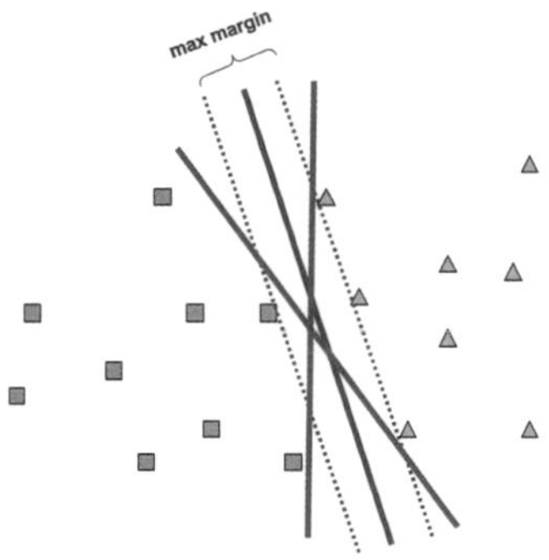

Figure 6.7: The maximum-margin hyperplane (in red) versus other hyperplanes (in blue) perfectly separating samples.

As we know, for linearly separable cases, we can use the simple perceptron algorithm to derive a hyperplane that perfectly separates the training samples. We also know that the perceptron algorithm does not normally lead to the maximum-margin hyperplane $\hat{\mathbf{w}}$ shown in Figure 6.2. The central problem in the initial SVM formulation is how to design a learning method to derive this maximum-margin hyperplane for any linearly separable case. According to geometry, it is known that there always exists only one such maximum-margin hyperplane for any linearly separable case. As shown in Figure 6.7, in terms of separating the training samples, this maximum margin hyperplane (in red) is equivalent to any other hyperplane (in blue) found by the perceptron because all of them give the lowest empirical loss. However, when being used to classify unseen data, this maximum-margin hyperplane tends to show some advantages. For example, it achieves the maximum separation distance from all training samples, so it may be more robust to noises in the data, where small perturbations in the data are unlikely to push them to cross the decision boundary to result in misclassification errors. Also, it is often said that this maximum-margin hyperplane has better generalization capability with new, unseen data than others because of its tighter generalization bound.

In this part, we first derive the initial SVM formulation, called the *linear SVM*, which finds the maximum separation hyperplane for any linearly separable case. To be consistent with most SVM derivations in the literature, we will use the affine function $y = \mathbf{w}^\intercal \mathbf{x} + b$ instead of the linear function $y = \mathbf{w}^\intercal \mathbf{x}$ for all SVMs. Of course, the mathematical differences between the two are minor.

It is well known that the distance from any sample $\mathbf{x}_i$ to a hyperplane $y = \mathbf{w}^\intercal \mathbf{x} + b$ is calculated as $\frac{|\mathbf{w}^\intercal \mathbf{x}_i + b|}{||\mathbf{w}||}$. If this sample is correctly classified by the hyperplane, we can use its label y_i to get rid of the absolute sign in the numerator as $\frac{y_i(\mathbf{w}^\intercal \mathbf{x}_i + b)}{||\mathbf{w}||}$. If a hyperplane $y = \mathbf{w}^\intercal \mathbf{x} + b$ perfectly separates all samples in a linearly separable training set $\mathcal{D}_N$, the minimum separation distance of this hyperplane from all samples can be expressed as follows:

$$\gamma = \min_{\mathbf{x}_i \in \mathcal{D}_N} \frac{y_i(\mathbf{w}^\intercal \mathbf{x}_i + b)}{||\mathbf{w}||}.$$

This maximum-margin hyperplane can be found by searching for the maximum separation distance, which leads to the following *maxmin* optimization problem:

$$\{\mathbf{w}^*, b^*\} = \arg\max_{\mathbf{w},b} \gamma = \arg\max_{\mathbf{w},b} \min_{\mathbf{x}_i \in \mathcal{D}_N} \frac{y_i(\mathbf{w}^\intercal \mathbf{x}_i + b)}{||\mathbf{w}||}. \quad (6.19)$$

If we treat the unknown maximum margin γ as a new free variable, we can reformulate the previous maxmin optimization problem into a standard constrained optimization problem, as follows:

Problem **SVM0**:

$$\max_{\gamma,\mathbf{w},b} \gamma$$

subject to

$$\frac{y_i(\mathbf{w}^\intercal \mathbf{x}_i + b)}{||\mathbf{w}||} \geq \gamma \quad \forall i \in \{1, 2, \cdots, N\}$$

The difficulties in solving the optimization problem of SVM0 are as follows: (i) it contains a large number of constraints, each of which corresponds to one training sample in $\mathcal{D}_N$; (ii) each constraint contains a fraction of two complex parts.

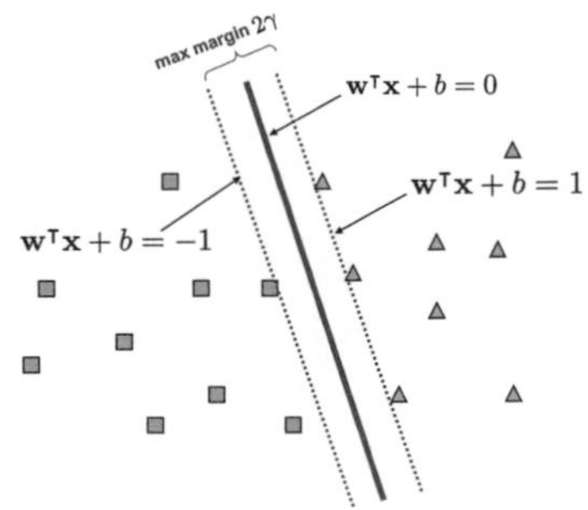

Figure 6.8: The maximum-margin hyperplane is scaled.

Next, let us see how to apply some mathematical tricks to simplify this optimization problem into some more tractable formats. First of all, if we scale both $\mathbf{w}$ and b in a hyperplane $y = \mathbf{w}^\intercal \mathbf{x} + b$ with any real number, it does not change the location of the hyperplane in the space. For the maximum-margin hyperplane, we can always scale $\{\mathbf{w}, b\}$ properly to ensure the closest data points from both sides yield $\mathbf{w}^\intercal\mathbf{x} + b = \pm 1$, as shown in Figure 6.8. In this case, the maximum margin is equal to the distance between the two parallel hyperplanes (shown as two dashed lines): $2\gamma = \frac{2}{||\mathbf{w}||}$ (because the numerator in the distance formula is equal to 1 after scaling). Also, maximizing the margin 2γ is the same as minimizing $||\mathbf{w}||^2 = \mathbf{w}^\intercal\mathbf{w}$. Finally, another condition for $2\gamma = \frac{2}{||\mathbf{w}||}$ to hold is to ensure that none of the training samples is located between these two dashed lines, that is, $y_i(\mathbf{w}^\intercal\mathbf{x}_i + b) \geq 1$, for all $\mathbf{x}_i$ in the training set.

Putting it all together, we reformulate the optimization problem of SVM0 into the following equivalent optimization problem:

Problem **SVM1**:

$$\min_{\mathbf{w},b} \quad \frac{1}{2}\mathbf{w}^\intercal\mathbf{w}$$

subject to

$$y_i(\mathbf{w}^\intercal\mathbf{x}_i + b) \geq 1 \quad \forall i \in \{1, 2, \cdots, N\}$$

In SVM1, $\frac{1}{2}$ is added for notation convenience, to be shown later.

In order to get rid of a large number of constraints in SVM1, we consider the Lagrange duality of SVM1. For each inequality constraint in SVM1, we introduce a Lagrange multiplier, $\alpha_i \geq 0$ ($\forall i \in \{1, 2, \cdots, N\}$) and derive the Lagrangian as follows:

$$L\big(\mathbf{w}, b, \{\alpha_i\}\big) = \frac{1}{2}\mathbf{w}^\intercal\mathbf{w} + \sum_{i=1}^{N} \alpha_i\Big(1 - y_i(\mathbf{w}^\intercal\mathbf{x}_i + b)\Big). \tag{6.20}$$

And the Lagrange dual function can be obtained by minimizing the Lagrangian over $\mathbf{w}$ and b:

$$L^*(\{\alpha_i\}) = \inf_{\mathbf{w},b} \; L\big(\mathbf{w}, b, \{\alpha_i\}\big).$$

In this case, the Lagrange dual function can be derived in a closed form by diminishing the following gradients:

$$\begin{aligned} & \frac{\partial}{\partial \mathbf{w}} L\big(\mathbf{w}, b, \{\alpha_i\}\big) = 0 \\ \Longrightarrow \quad & \mathbf{w} - \sum_{i=1}^{N} \alpha_i y_i \mathbf{x}_i = 0 \\ \Longrightarrow \quad & \mathbf{w}^* = \sum_{i=1}^{N} \alpha_i y_i \mathbf{x}_i. \end{aligned} \tag{6.21}$$

$$\frac{\partial}{\partial b} L\big(\mathbf{w}, b, \{\alpha_i\}\big) = 0.$$

$$\Longrightarrow \quad \sum_{i=1}^{N} \alpha_i y_i = 0 \tag{6.22}$$

Substituting Eqs. (6.21) and (6.22) into the Lagrangian in Eq. (6.20), we have the Lagrange dual function as follows:

$$L^*(\{\alpha_i\}) = \sum_{i=1}^{N} \alpha_i - \frac{1}{2} \sum_{i=1}^{N} \sum_{j=1}^{N} \alpha_i \alpha_j y_i y_j \mathbf{x}_i^\top \mathbf{x}_j. \tag{6.23}$$

See the margin note for some intermediate steps if necessary.

If we introduce the following vectors and matrix:

$$\boldsymbol{\alpha} = \begin{bmatrix} \alpha_1 \\ \vdots \\ \alpha_N \end{bmatrix}_{N\times 1}$$

$$\mathbf{y} = \begin{bmatrix} y_1 \\ \vdots \\ y_N \end{bmatrix}_{N\times 1}$$

$$\mathbf{1} = \begin{bmatrix} 1 \\ \vdots \\ 1 \end{bmatrix}_{N\times 1}$$

and

$$\mathbf{Q} = \Big[Q_{ij} \Big]_{N\times N} = \Big[\mathbf{y}\mathbf{y}^\top \Big]_{N\times N} \odot \begin{bmatrix} \mathbf{x}_1^\top \mathbf{x}_1 & \cdots & \mathbf{x}_1^\top \mathbf{x}_N \\ \vdots & \mathbf{x}_i^\top \mathbf{x}_j & \vdots \\ \mathbf{x}_N^\top \mathbf{x}_1 & \cdots & \mathbf{x}_N^\top \mathbf{x}_N \end{bmatrix}_{N\times N}$$

where $\odot$ denotes element-wise multiplication (see the margin note), we can represent the Lagrange dual function as the following quadratic form:

$$L^*(\boldsymbol{\alpha}) = \mathbf{1}^\top \boldsymbol{\alpha} - \frac{1}{2} \boldsymbol{\alpha}^\top \mathbf{Q} \boldsymbol{\alpha}.$$

Because SVM1 satisfies the strong duality condition, it is equivalent to maximizing the Lagrange dual function with respect to (w.r.t.) $\boldsymbol{\alpha}$, subject to the constraint in Eq. (6.22) (i.e., $\mathbf{y}^\top \boldsymbol{\alpha} = 0$ and $\alpha_i \geq 0$ for all i). Therefore, we have the following equivalent dual problem for linear SVMs:

1. We know

$$\frac{1}{2}\mathbf{w}^\top \mathbf{w} = \frac{1}{2}\Big(\sum_{i=1}^{N} \alpha_i y_i \mathbf{x}_i\Big)^\top \sum_{i=1}^{N} \alpha_i y_i \mathbf{x}_i = \frac{1}{2} \sum_{i=1}^{N}\sum_{j=1}^{N} \alpha_i \alpha_j y_i y_j \mathbf{x}_i^\top \mathbf{x}_j.$$

2. Because of Eq. (6.22),

$$b \sum_{i=1}^{N} \alpha_i y_i = 0.$$

3. We have

$$-\sum_{i=1}^{N} \alpha_i y_i \mathbf{w}^\top \mathbf{x}_i = -\mathbf{w}^\top \sum_{i=1}^{N} \alpha_i y_i \mathbf{x}_i = -\Big(\sum_{i=1}^{N} \alpha_i y_i \mathbf{x}_i\Big)^\top \sum_{i=1}^{N} \alpha_i y_i \mathbf{x}_i = -\sum_{i=1}^{N}\sum_{j=1}^{N} \alpha_i \alpha_j y_i y_j \mathbf{x}_i^\top \mathbf{x}_j.$$

$$\mathbf{x} = \begin{bmatrix} x_1 \\ x_2 \\ \vdots \\ x_N \end{bmatrix}_{N\times 1} \qquad \mathbf{y} = \begin{bmatrix} y_1 \\ y_2 \\ \vdots \\ y_N \end{bmatrix}_{N\times 1}$$

$$\mathbf{x} \odot \mathbf{y} = \begin{bmatrix} x_1 y_1 \\ x_2 y_2 \\ \vdots \\ x_N y_N \end{bmatrix}_{N\times 1}$$

$$\Big[a_{ij} \Big]_{M\times N} \odot \Big[b_{ij} \Big]_{M\times N} = \Big[a_{ij} b_{ij} \Big]_{M\times N}$$

Problem **SVM2**:

$$\max_{\alpha} \; \mathbf{1}^\intercal \alpha - \frac{1}{2}\alpha^\intercal \mathbf{Q}\alpha$$

subject to

$$\mathbf{y}^\intercal \alpha = 0$$

$$\alpha \geq 0$$

Problem SVM2 is a standard quadratic programming problem that can be directly solved by many off-the-shelf optimizers. A specific method for solving this quadratic programming for SVMs is presented on page 126. Once the solution to SVM2 is found as

$$\alpha^* = \begin{bmatrix} \alpha_1^* \\ \alpha_2^* \\ \vdots \\ \alpha_N^* \end{bmatrix},$$

the maximum-margin hyperplane can be constructed using $\boldsymbol{\alpha}^*$. According to Eq. (6.21), we have

$$\mathbf{w}^* = \sum_{i=1}^{N} \alpha_i^* y_i \mathbf{x}_i.$$

Next, let us look at an important property of $\boldsymbol{\alpha}^*$: the optimal solution to SVM2 is normally sparse. In other words, α^* usually contains only a small number of nonzero elements, whereas the most elements in $\boldsymbol{\alpha}^*$ are actually zeros. This can be explained by the Karush–Kuhn–Tucker (KKT) conditions of the prime-dual problem in SVM1 and SVM2. If we have found the optimal solution to the Lagrangian in Eq. (6.20) as $\mathbf{w}^*, b^*, \boldsymbol{\alpha}^*$, $\forall i \in \{1, 2, \cdots, N\}$, we know that the following complementary slackness conditions hold:

$$\alpha_i^*(1 - y_i \mathbf{w}^{*\intercal}\mathbf{x}_i - y_i b^*) = 0. \tag{6.24}$$

In other words, for any i, either $\alpha_i^* = 0$ or $y_i(\mathbf{w}^{*\intercal}\mathbf{x}_i + b^*) = 1$ must hold for the optimal solution. As shown in Figure 6.8, only a small number of samples that lie in either of two dashed lines satisfy $y_i(\mathbf{w}^{*\intercal}\mathbf{x}_i + b^*) = 1$; thus, their corresponding $\alpha_i^* \neq 0$. For other samples that are located outside the margin range (i.e., $y_i(\mathbf{w}^{*\intercal}\mathbf{x}_i + b^*) > 1$), the corresponding $\alpha_i^* = 0$. Therefore, the maximum-margin hyperplane $\mathbf{w}^*$ depends only on those samples located on either of the dashed lines because they are the only samples having nonzero α_i^*. These training samples are called *support vectors*. For the rest of the training samples, they do not affect the maximum-margin hyperplane because they all have $\alpha_i^* = 0$. This tells us that even if we remove them from the training set, we will end up with the same maximum-margin hyperplane for linear SVMs. Of course, we usually do not know which samples are support vectors until conducting the optimization. The quadratic programming in SVM2 will help us to identify which training samples are support vectors and which are not.

Because the final solution to the SVM depends on only a small number of training samples, SVMs are sometimes called *sparse* models or machines. Intuitively speaking, sparse models are usually not prone to outliers and overfitting.

Finally, let us determine the bias b^* for the maximum-margin hyperplane. After we have obtained the optimal solution α^* to Problem SVM2, we can choose any nonzero element $\alpha_i^* > 0$. Based on Eq. (6.24), the corresponding sample $(\mathbf{x}_i, y_i)$ has to be a support vector, which satisfies $y_i(\mathbf{w}^{*\mathsf{T}}\mathbf{x}_i + b^*) = 1$. Thus, we compute b^* as follows:

As $y_i \in \{+1, -1\}$,

$$y_i(\mathbf{w}^{*\mathsf{T}}\mathbf{x}_i + b^*) = 1$$

$$\Longrightarrow \mathbf{w}^{*\mathsf{T}}\mathbf{x}_i + b^* = y_i.$$

$$b^* = y_i - \mathbf{w}^{*\mathsf{T}}\mathbf{x}_i. \tag{6.25}$$

6.5.2 Soft SVM

The linear SVM formulation discussed previously makes sense only for linearly separable data. If the training samples are not linearly separable, the maximum-margin hyperplane does not exist. However, the SVM formulation can be extended to nonseparable cases based on a concept called the *soft margin*.

As shown in Figure 6.9, if we cannot perfectly separate all training samples with a strict margin measure, then we allow some samples to cross the margin boundaries (shown as dashed lines). In this case, we will introduce a nonnegative error term ξ for every sample in the training set. For each sample that has crossed the margin boundary, the error term ξ is used to measure the distance that it has passed the margin boundary. For those samples located on the correct side of the margin boundary, their error terms ξ should be 0. For each hyperplane $y = \mathbf{w}^{\mathsf{T}}\mathbf{x} + b$, the concept of the

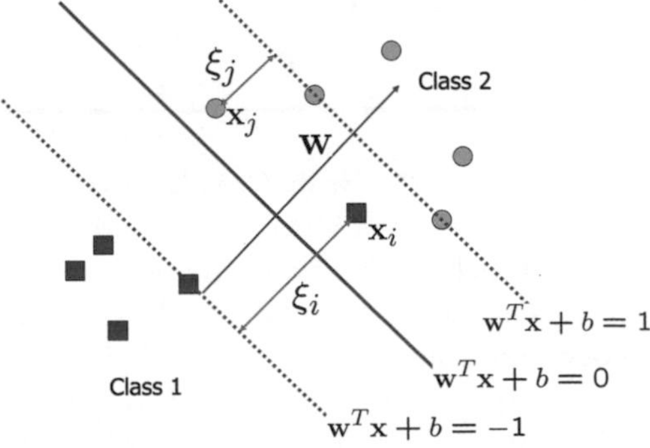

Figure 6.9: The soft-margin formulation for SVMs.

soft margin is introduced to account for two things: (i) the margin of the hyperplane, which is the same as before and equal to the distance between the two dashed lines (as shown in Figure 6.9), and (ii) the total errors introduced by this hyperplane on the whole training set. The *soft SVM* formulation aims to optimize a linear combination of the two; namely, it tries to maximize the margin as much as possible and simultaneously tries to minimize the total introduced errors as well. By doing so, the soft SVM can be applied to any training set. If the training set is linearly separable, it may result in the same maximum-margin hyperplane as the linear SVM formulation. However, if the training set is nonseparable, the soft SVM formulation still leads to a hyperplane that optimizes the soft margin.

After slightly extending the formulation of SVM1 to take into account the soft margin in the objective function, we have the primary problem for the soft SVM formulation as follows:

Problem **SVM3**:

$$\min_{\mathbf{w},b,\xi_i} \frac{1}{2}\mathbf{w}^\intercal\mathbf{w} + C\sum_{i=1}^{N}\xi_i$$

subject to

$$y_i(\mathbf{w}^\intercal\mathbf{x}_i + b) \geq 1 - \xi_i \quad \text{and} \quad \xi_i \geq 0 \quad \forall i \in \{1, 2, \cdots, N\}$$

C is a hyperparameter to control the trade-off between the margin and error terms in the soft margin.

We can apply the same Lagrangian technique as previously and derive the dual problem for the soft SVM formulation as follows:

Problem **SVM4**:

$$\max_{\boldsymbol{\alpha}} \mathbf{1}^\intercal\boldsymbol{\alpha} - \frac{1}{2}\boldsymbol{\alpha}^\intercal\mathbf{Q}\boldsymbol{\alpha}$$

subject to

$$\mathbf{y}^\intercal\boldsymbol{\alpha} = 0$$

$$0 \leq \boldsymbol{\alpha} \leq C$$

Here we use

$$0 \leq \boldsymbol{\alpha} \leq C$$

to indicate that every element in vector $\boldsymbol{\alpha}$ is constrained in $[0, C]$.

We leave the derivation of SVM4 from SVM3 as Exercise Q6.7. It is quite surprising that SVM4 for the soft SVM is almost identical to SVM2. The only difference is that each dual variable in $\boldsymbol{\alpha}$ is currently restricted in a closed interval $[0, C]$. Of course, SVM4 can be solved by the same optimizer as SVM2. Moreover, the solution to SVM4 will also be sparse and will contain nonzero α_i^* only for a small number of support vectors, which in this case are defined as those samples that either lie on the dashed lines

$(0 < \alpha_i^* < C)$ or introduce a nonzero error ξ_i $(\alpha_i^* = C)$. See Exercise Q6.7 for details on this.

6.5.3 Nonlinear SVM: The Kernel Trick

One limitation of the SVM formulation is that we can only learn a linear model to separate two classes in the input space. Of course, in many cases, especially for some hard problems in practice, we are interested in learning some nonlinear separating boundaries for pattern classification. An interesting idea for doing so is that we first map the original inputs $\mathbf{x}$ into another feature space of much higher dimensions using a carefully chosen nonlinear function: $\hat{\mathbf{x}} = h(\mathbf{x})$. As shown in Figure 6.10, even though the original data set is linearly nonseparable in the original input space, it may become linearly separable in a much higher-dimensional space. Conceptually speaking, this is very likely to happen because we have more power to apply a linear model in a higher-dimensional space due to the increased model parameters. If the mapping function $h(\mathbf{x})$ is invertible, the linear boundary in the high-dimensional space actually corresponds to a nonlinear boundary in the original input space because of the nonlinearity introduced by the mapping function $h(\mathbf{x})$.

Note that nonlinear SVMs are not a linear model anymore. They are included in this chapter because they are highly relevant to linear SVMs and can be solved using the same optimization methods.

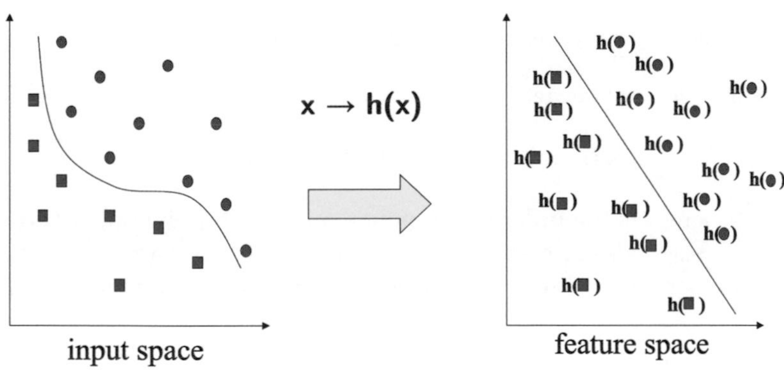

Figure 6.10: Nonlinear mapping function from the input space to a much higher-dimensional feature space for nonlinear SVMs.

The key idea of nonlinear SVMs is that we first select a nonlinear function $h(\mathbf{x})$ to map each input $\mathbf{x}_i$ into $h(\mathbf{x}_i)$ in a higher-dimensional space, and then we follow the same SVM procedure as previously to derive the maximum margin (or soft-margin) hyperplane in the mapped feature space. We still solve the dual problem of this SVM formulation in the mapped feature space. As shown in Eq. (6.23), the dual problem of the SVM formulation only depends on the inner product of any two training samples (i.e., $\mathbf{x}_i^\intercal \mathbf{x}_j$). In this case, it corresponds to the inner product of any two mapped vectors in the feature space (i.e., $h^\intercal(\mathbf{x}_i)h(\mathbf{x}_j)$). In other words, as long as we know how to compute $h^\intercal(\mathbf{x}_i)h(\mathbf{x}_j)$, we will be able to construct the dual program to learn the SVM model in the high-dimensional feature space and then derive the corresponding nonlinear model in the original input space. There is no need for us to know the exact form of $h(\mathbf{x}_j)$.

In many cases, it is beneficial to directly specify $h^\intercal(\mathbf{x}_i)h(\mathbf{x}_j)$ rather than $h(\mathbf{x}_j)$, which is usually called the *kernel function*, denoted as

$$\Phi(\mathbf{x}_i, \mathbf{x}_j) = h^\intercal(\mathbf{x}_i)h(\mathbf{x}_j).$$

Because $h(\mathbf{x}_j)$ is a mapping from a low-dimensional space to a higher-dimensional space, it is usually awkward and inefficient to specify it directly. On the other hand, the kernel function is a function mapping from two inputs in the low-dimension space to a real number in $\mathbb{R}$; thus, it is much more convenient to specify the kernel function than the mapping function itself. Theoretically speaking, we can specify any function as the kernel function $\Phi(\mathbf{x}_i, \mathbf{x}_j)$ as long as it satisfies the so-called *Mercer's condition* (see margin note). If $\Phi(\mathbf{x}_i, \mathbf{x}_j)$ satisfies Mercer's condition, it always corresponds to a valid mapping function $h(\mathbf{x}_j)$, which we may not know explicitly [45].

Mercer's condition:
For any set of N samples in the input space (e.g., $\{\mathbf{x}_1, \mathbf{x}_2, \cdots, \mathbf{x}_N\}$), if the following $N \times N$ matrix

$$\left[\Phi(\mathbf{x}_i, \mathbf{x}_j)\right]_{N\times N}$$

is always symmetric and positive definite, then we says $\Phi(\mathbf{x}_i, \mathbf{x}_j)$ satisfies Mercer's condition.

In practice, we usually choose one of the following functions for $\Phi(\mathbf{x}_i, \mathbf{x}_j)$:

- **Linear kernel**:

  $$\Phi(\mathbf{x}_i, \mathbf{x}_j) = \mathbf{x}_i^\intercal \mathbf{x}_j,$$

  which corresponds to an identity-mapping function.

- **Polynomial kernel**:

  $$\Phi(\mathbf{x}_i, \mathbf{x}_j) = (\mathbf{x}_i^\intercal \mathbf{x}_j)^p \quad \text{or} \quad \Phi(\mathbf{x}_i, \mathbf{x}_j) = (\mathbf{x}_i^\intercal \mathbf{x}_j + 1)^p,$$

  where p is the order of the polynomial. Each polynomial kernel corresponds to a mapping function from the input space into a much higher-dimensional feature space; see Exercise Q6.9 for more details on this.

- **Gaussian (or RBF) kernel**:

  $$\Phi(\mathbf{x}_i, \mathbf{x}_j) = \exp(-\gamma||\mathbf{x}_i - \mathbf{x}_j||^2),$$

  where γ is a hyperparameter to control the variance of the Gaussian. We can show that an RBF kernel corresponds to a mapping from the input space into a feature space that has an infinite number of dimensions. See Exercise Q6.10 for more.

RBF kernel stands for *radial basis function* kernel.

In addition, many other kernel functions can be designed to handle special data types, such as sequences and graphs. This kernel technique to extend linear SVMs into nonlinear ones can actually be applied to many machine learning methods, where we can extend some well-established linear methods to nonlinear cases. Therefore, it is named the *kernel trick* in the literature.

Another application of the kernel trick in machine learning is the *kernel PCA* method; see Schölkopf et al. [216] for details.

Interestingly enough, once the kernel trick is applied, the nonlinear SVM formulation leads to the same optimization problem as SVM4. The only difference is that we compute the $\mathbf{Q}$ matrix using the selected kernel function $\Phi(\mathbf{x}_i, \mathbf{x}_j)$, as follows:

$$\mathbf{Q} = \begin{bmatrix} Q_{ij} \end{bmatrix}_{N\times N} = \begin{bmatrix} \mathbf{y}\mathbf{y}^\intercal \end{bmatrix}_{N\times N} \odot \begin{bmatrix} \Phi(\mathbf{x}_1, \mathbf{x}_1) & \cdots & \Phi(\mathbf{x}_1, \mathbf{x}_N) \\ \vdots & \Phi(\mathbf{x}_i, \mathbf{x}_j) & \vdots \\ \Phi(\mathbf{x}_N, \mathbf{x}_1) & \cdots & \Phi(\mathbf{x}_N, \mathbf{x}_N) \end{bmatrix}_{N\times N}$$

Once the optimal solution to the quadratic programming is found as $\boldsymbol{\alpha}^* = [\alpha_1^*, \cdots, \alpha_N^*]^\intercal$, which is also sparse, the nonlinear SVM model can be constructed accordingly. For any new input $\mathbf{x}$, the output is computed as follows (see margin note):

In this case, the SVM in the feature space is first constructed as follows:

$$\mathbf{w}^* = \sum_{i=1}^{N} \alpha_i^* y_i h(\mathbf{x}_i).$$

Then we have

$$y = (\mathbf{w}^*)^\intercal h(\mathbf{x}) + b^* = \sum_{i=1}^{N} \alpha_i^* y_i \Phi(\mathbf{x}_i, \mathbf{x}) + b^*.$$

$$y = \text{sign}\Big(\sum_{i=1}^{N} \alpha_i^* y_i \Phi(\mathbf{x}_i, \mathbf{x}) + b^*\Big). \tag{6.26}$$

Similar to Eq. (6.25), the bias b^* can be computed based on any support vector $(\mathbf{x}_k, y_k)$, where $\alpha_k^* \neq 0$ and $\alpha_k^* \neq C$, as follows:

$$b^* = y_k - \sum_{i=1}^{N} \alpha_i^* y_i \Phi(\mathbf{x}_i, \mathbf{x}_k).$$

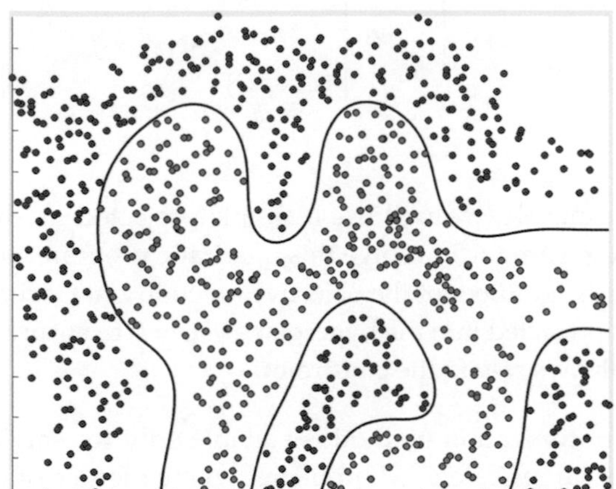

Figure 6.11: The separating boundary of a nonlinear SVM using the RBF kernel [41].

As an example, if we use the RBF kernel to compute the matrix $\mathbf{Q}$ for some hard binary classification data set, the final decision boundary for Eq. (6.26) is as shown in Figure 6.11. It is clear to see that the separating boundary between two classes in the input space is highly nonlinear because of the nonlinear RBF kernel function. The complexity of this separating boundary also demonstrates that nonlinear SVMs are actually very powerful models if a suitable kernel function is used.

6.5.4 Solving Quadratic Programming

As we have discussed, various SVM formulations lead to solving some types of dense quadratic programming as follows:

$$\min_{\alpha} \overbrace{\frac{1}{2}\alpha^{\intercal}\mathbf{Q}\alpha - \mathbf{1}^{\intercal}\alpha}^{L(\alpha)},$$

subject to $\mathbf{y}^{\intercal}\alpha = 0, 0 \leq \alpha \leq C$, where

$$\alpha = \begin{bmatrix} \alpha_1 \\ \vdots \\ \alpha_N \end{bmatrix}_{N\times 1}$$

are the optimization variables, and the following matrices are built from the training data:

$$\mathbf{y} = \begin{bmatrix} y_1 \\ \vdots \\ y_N \end{bmatrix}_{N\times 1} \qquad \mathbf{1} = \begin{bmatrix} 1 \\ \vdots \\ 1 \end{bmatrix}_{N\times 1}$$

$$\mathbf{Q} = \begin{bmatrix} Q_{ij} \end{bmatrix}_{N\times N} = \begin{bmatrix} \mathbf{y}\mathbf{y}^{\intercal} \end{bmatrix}_{N\times N} \odot \begin{bmatrix} \Phi(\mathbf{x}_1, \mathbf{x}_1) & \cdots & \Phi(\mathbf{x}_1, \mathbf{x}_N) \\ \vdots & \Phi(\mathbf{x}_i, \mathbf{x}_j) & \vdots \\ \Phi(\mathbf{x}_N, \mathbf{x}_1) & \cdots & \Phi(\mathbf{x}_N, \mathbf{x}_N) \end{bmatrix}_{N\times N}$$

$\odot$ denotes element-wise multiplication between two matrices of equal size.

Here, as an example, we will use a simple projected gradient descent method in Algorithm 6.5 to solve this quadratic programming problem. At each step, the gradient of the objective function $L(\alpha)$ is first computed, and then it is projected into the hyperplane $\mathbf{y}^{\intercal}\alpha = 0$ to ensure the updated parameters always satisfy the constraint.

This simple optimization method is suitable only for small-scale SVM problems. For large-scale SVM problems, where the size of the $\mathbf{Q}$ matrix may become extremely large, there are many other memory-efficient methods. One such example is the coordinate descent algorithm that optimizes only a single α_i at a time. In this case, we do not need to save the entire matrix $\mathbf{Q}$ in memory all the time. As another example, refer to Exercise Q6.12 for a popular optimization method called *sequential minimization*

Algorithm 6.5 Projected Gradient Descent Algorithm for SVM

initialize $\boldsymbol{\alpha}^{(0)} = 0$, and set $n = 0$
while not converged **do**
(1) compute the gradient:

$$\nabla L(\boldsymbol{\alpha}^{(n)}) = \mathbf{Q}\boldsymbol{\alpha}^{(n)} - \mathbf{1}$$

(2) project the gradient to the hyperplane $\mathbf{y}^\intercal \boldsymbol{\alpha} = 0$:

$$\tilde{\nabla} L(\boldsymbol{\alpha}^{(n)}) = \nabla L(\boldsymbol{\alpha}^{(n)}) - \frac{\mathbf{y}^\intercal \nabla L(\boldsymbol{\alpha}^{(n)})}{||\mathbf{y}||^2}\mathbf{y}$$

(3) projected gradient descent:

$$\boldsymbol{\alpha}^{(n+1)} = \boldsymbol{\alpha}^{(n)} - \eta_n \cdot \tilde{\nabla} L(\boldsymbol{\alpha}^{(n)})$$

(4) clip $\boldsymbol{\alpha}^{(n+1)}$ to $[0, C]$
(5) $n = n + 1$
end while

η_n denotes the step sizes used in the gradient descent.

A simple way to clip $\boldsymbol{\alpha}^{(n+1)}$ in step (4): for all $i = 1, \cdots, N$

$$\alpha_i^{(n+1)} = \begin{cases} 0 & \text{if } \alpha_i^{(n+1)} < 0 \\ C & \text{if } \alpha_i^{(n+1)} > C. \end{cases}$$

Also, see Exercise Q6.11 for a better way to clip $\boldsymbol{\alpha}^{(n+1)}$.

optimization (SMO) [188], proposed particularly for SVMs in the literature, that aims to optimize two variables α_i and α_j at a time.

6.5.5 Multiclass SVM

Although the previously described SVM formulations are restricted to two-class binary-classification problems, they can be easily extended to solve multiclass pattern-classification problems. A simple way to do so is to construct many binary SVMs. For example, a binary SVM is built to separate each pair of classes in the multiclass problem, which is called the *one-versus-one* strategy. Alternatively, a binary SVM can be built to separate each class from all other classes, called the *one-versus-all* strategy. In the decision stage, a new unknown input is tested against all binary SVMs, and the final decision is based on a majority-voting result among all binary classifiers. This method is simple and effective, but it needs to maintain a large number of binary SVMs, which is inconvenient. See [189] for another method to combine multiple binary SVMs for multiclass problems. Another method is to redefine margins or soft margins for multiclass cases and directly extend the SVM learning formulation to multiclass problems; see Weston and Watkins [250] and Crammer and Singer [46] for more details.

In summary, we have gone through a long process to derive several SVM formulations for various scenarios. As we have seen, the kernel trick has largely enhanced the power of SVM models. The nice part of SVM models is that all different formulations lead to the same quadratic programming problem, which can be solved by the same optimizer. Another advantage is that learning an SVM involves only a small number of hyperparameters, such as C and usually one or two more for the chosen kernel function. As a result, the learning procedure for SVMs is actually quite straightforward, as summarized in the following box.

SVM Learning Procedure (in a Nutshell)

Given a training set as $\mathcal{D}_N = \{(\mathbf{x}_1, y_1), (\mathbf{x}_2, y_2), \cdots, (\mathbf{x}_N, y_N)\}$:

1. Choose a kernel function $\Phi(\mathbf{x}_i, \mathbf{x}_j)$.
2. Build the matrices $\mathbf{Q}$, $\mathbf{y}$, and $\mathbf{e}$ from $\mathcal{D}_N$ and $\Phi(\mathbf{x}_i, \mathbf{x}_j)$.
3. Solve the quadratic programming problem to get

$$\boldsymbol{\alpha}^* = [\alpha_1^*, \cdots \alpha_N^*]^\intercal \text{ and } b^*.$$

4. Evaluate the learned model as follows:

$$y = \text{sign}\Big(\sum_{i=1}^{N} \alpha_i^* y_i \Phi(\mathbf{x}_i, \mathbf{x}) + b^*\Big).$$

Lab Project II

In this project, you will implement several discriminative models for pattern classification. You can choose to use any programming language for your own convenience. You are only allowed to use libraries for linear algebra operations, such as matrix multiplication, matrix inversion, matrix factorization, and so forth. You are not allowed to use any existing machine learning or statistics toolkits or libraries or any open-source codes for this project. You will have to implement most of the model learning and testing algorithms yourself to practice the various algorithms learned in this chapter. That is the purpose of this project.

Once again, you will use the MNIST data set [142] for this project, which is a handwritten digit set containing 60,000 training images and 10,000 test images. Each image is 28 by 28 in size. The MNIST data set can be downloaded from `http://yann.lecun.com/exdb/mnist/`. In this project, for simplicity, you just use pixels as raw features for the following models.

a. **Linear Regression**:
   Use the linear regression method to build a linear classifier to separate the digits 5 and 8 based on all training data of these two digits. Evaluate the performance of the built model. Repeat for the pair of 6 and 7, and discuss why the performance differs from that of 5 and 8.

b. **MCE and logistic regression**:
   Use the MCE method and logistic regression to build two linear models to separate digits 5 and 8 based on all training data of these two digits. Compare the performance of the MCE and logistic regression on both training and test sets and discuss how these two learning methods differ. You may choose to use any iterative optimization algorithm. Don't just call any off-the-shelf optimizer: implement the optimizer yourself.

c. **SVM**:
   Use all training data for two digits 5 and 8 to learn two binary classifiers using linear SVM and nonlinear SVM (with Gaussian RBF kernel), and compare and discuss the performance and efficiency of the linear SVM and nonlinear SVM methods for these two digits. Next, use the one-versus-one strategy to build binary SVM classifiers for all 10 digits, and report the best classification performance in the held-out test images. Don't call any off-the-shelf optimizers. Implement the SVM optimizer yourself using either the projected gradient descent in Algorithm 6.5 or the sequential minimization optimization method in Exercise Q6.12.

Exercises

Q6.1 Extend the perceptron algorithm to an affine function $y = \mathbf{w}^\intercal \mathbf{x} + b$; also, revise the proof of Theorem 6.1.1 to accommodate the bias term b.

Q6.2 Given a training set $\mathfrak{D}$ with a separation margin γ_0, the original perceptron algorithm predicts a mistake when $y\,\mathbf{w}^{(n)\intercal}\mathbf{x} < 0$. As we have discussed in Section 6.1, this algorithm converges to a linear classifier that can perfectly separate $\mathfrak{D}$ but does not necessarily achieve the maximum margin. The *margin perceptron algorithm* extends Algorithm 6.4 to approximately maximize the margin in the perceptron algorithm, where it is considered to be a mistake when $\frac{y\,\mathbf{w}^{(n)\intercal}\mathbf{x}}{\|\mathbf{w}^{(n)}\|} < \frac{\gamma}{2}$, where $\gamma > 0$ is a parameter. Prove that the number of mistakes made by the margin perceptron algorithm is at most $8/\gamma_0^2$ if $\gamma \leq \gamma_0$.

Q6.3 Given a training set $\mathfrak{D}_N = \{(\mathbf{x}_i, y_i) \mid i = 1, 2, \cdots N\}$ with $\mathbf{x}_i \in \mathbb{R}^n$ and $y_i \in \{+1, -1\}$ for all i, assume we want to use a quadratic function $y = \mathbf{x}^\intercal \mathbf{A} \mathbf{x} + \mathbf{b}^\intercal \mathbf{x} + c$, where $\mathbf{A} \in \mathbb{R}^{n \times n}$, $\mathbf{b} \in \mathbb{R}^n$, and $c \in \mathbf{R}$, to map from each input $\mathbf{x}_i$ to each output y_i in $\mathfrak{D}_N$, often called *quadratic regression*. Derive the closed-form formula to estimate all parameters $\{\mathbf{A}, \mathbf{b}, c\}$ based on the least-square-error criterion.

Q6.4 Extend the MCE method in Section 6.3 to deal with pattern-classification problems involving $K > 2$ classes.

Q6.5 Extend the logistic regression method in Section 6.4 to deal with pattern-classification problems involving $K > 2$ classes.

Q6.6 Derive stochastic gradient descent algorithms to optimize the following linear models:

a. Linear regression
b. Logistic regression
c. MCE
d. Linear SVMs (Problem SVM1)
e. Soft SVMs (Problem SVM3)

Q6.7 Based on the Lagrange dual function, show the procedure to derive dual problems for soft SVMs:

a. Derive SVM4 from SVM3.
b. Explain how to determine which training samples are support vectors in soft SVMs. Which support vectors lie on the margin boundaries? Which support vectors introduce nonzero error terms?
c. Derive b^* for soft SVMs (also consider the case where all nonzero α_i equal to C).

Q6.8 Derive an efficient way to compute the matrix $\mathbf{Q}$ in the SVM formulation using the vectorization method (only involving vector/matrix operations without any loop or summation) for the following kernel functions:

a. The linear kernel function
b. The polynomial kernel function
c. The RBF kernel function

Q6.9 Show that the second-order polynomial kernel (i.e., $\Phi(\mathbf{x}_i, \mathbf{x}_j) = (\mathbf{x}_i^\intercal \mathbf{x}_j + 1)^2$) corresponds to the following mapping function $h(\mathbf{x})$ from $\mathbb{R}^d$ to $\mathbb{R}^{d(d+1)}$:

$$\mathbf{x} = \begin{bmatrix} x_1 \\ x_2 \\ \vdots \\ x_d \end{bmatrix} \mapsto \begin{bmatrix} x_1^2 \\ \vdots \\ x_d^2 \\ \sqrt{2}x_1x_2 \\ \vdots \\ \sqrt{2}x_{d-1}x_d \\ \sqrt{2}x_1 \\ \vdots \\ \sqrt{2}x_d \end{bmatrix}.$$

Then, consider the mapping function for a third-order polynomial kernel and a general pth order polynomial kernel.

Q6.10 Show the mapping function corresponding to the RBF kernel (i.e., $\Phi(\mathbf{x}_i, \mathbf{x}_j) = \exp(-\frac{1}{2}||\mathbf{x}_i - \mathbf{x}_j||^2)$).

Q6.11 Algorithm 6.5 is not optimal because it attempts to satisfy two constraints alternatively in each iteration. A better way is to compute an optimal step size η^* at each step, which satisfies both constraints:

$$\eta^* = \arg\max_{\eta} \ \eta,$$

subject to

$$0 \leq \alpha^{(n)} - \eta \cdot \tilde{\nabla} L(\alpha^{(n)}) \leq C$$

$$0 \leq \eta \leq \eta_n.$$

use the KKT conditions to derive a closed-form solution to compute the optimal step size η^*.

Q6.12 In Problem SVM4, if we only optimize two multipliers α_i and α_j and keep all other multipliers constant, we can derive a closed-form solution to update α_i and α_j. This idea leads to the famous SMO for SVMs, which selects only two multipliers to update at each iteration. Derive the closed-form solution to update any two α_i and α_j for Problem SVM4.

7 Learning Discriminative Models in General

As discussed in Chapter 5, when we learn a discriminative model from given training samples, if we strictly follow the idea of empirical risk minimization (ERM) and consider ERM as the only goal in learning, it may not lead to the best possible performance as a result of overfitting. This chapter introduces a more general learning framework for discriminative models, namely, minimizing the *regularized* empirical risk. It discusses a variety of ways to formulate the regularized empirical risk for different learning tasks and explains why regularization is important for machine learning (ML). Moreover, it introduces how to apply this general method to several interesting ML tasks, such as regularized linear regression (ridge and least absolute shrinkage and selection operator [LASSO]), matrix factorization, and dictionary learning.

7.1 A General Framework to Learn Discriminative Models

The primary problem of soft SVM (SVM3):

$$\min_{\mathbf{w},b,\xi_i} \quad \frac{1}{2}\mathbf{w}^\intercal\mathbf{w} + C\sum_{i=1}^{N}\xi_i,$$

subject to

$$y_i(\mathbf{w}^\intercal\mathbf{x}_i + b) \geq 1 - \xi_i \quad \text{and} \quad \xi_i \geq 0$$

$$\forall i \in \{1, 2, \cdots, N\}.$$

First of all, let us revisit the primary problem of the soft support vector machine (SVM) formulation (see margin note), that is, Problem SVM3 discussed on page 122. Based on the two constraints in SVM3 for each variable ξ_i (for all $i = 1, 2, \cdots, N$), we have

$$\xi_i \geq 1 - y_i(\mathbf{w}^\intercal\mathbf{x}_i + b)$$

$$\xi_i \geq 0.$$

We may equivalently combine the two inequalities into a compact expression, as follows:

$$\xi_i \geq \max\Big(0, 1 - y_i(\mathbf{w}^\intercal \mathbf{x}_i + b)\Big).$$

We define a new function:

$$H_1(x) = \max(0, 1 - x),$$

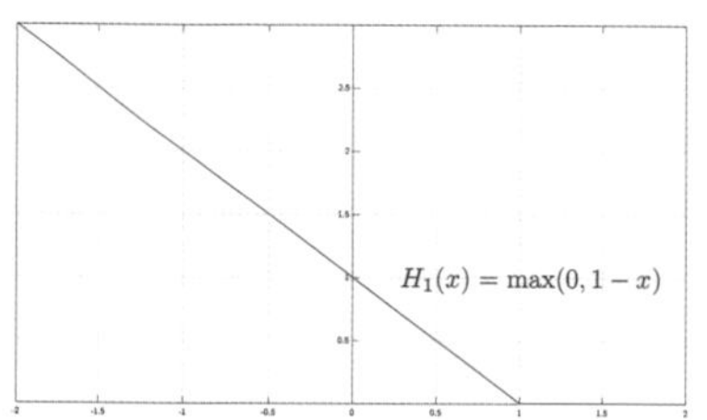

Figure 7.1: The hinge function $H_1(x)$.

which is normally called the *hinge function*. As shown in Figure 7.1, the hinge function $H_1(x)$ is a monotonically nonincreasing piece-wise linear function. We can represent each ξ_i using the hinge function as follows:

$$\xi_i \geq H_1\Big(y_i(\mathbf{w}^\intercal \mathbf{x}_i + b)\Big).$$

As shown in SVM3, because we minimize the summation of all ξ_i in the objective function, the minimization will force all ξ_i to take the lower bounds specified by the hinge function. Therefore, we can immediately derive the optimal value for each ξ_i in SVM3 as

$$\xi_i^* = H_1\Big(y_i(\mathbf{w}^\intercal \mathbf{x}_i + b)\Big) \quad \forall i = 1, 2, \cdots, N.$$

Recall that the binary-classification setting, as in Eq. (6.11), $y_i(\mathbf{w}^\intercal \mathbf{x}_i + b)$ indicates whether the training sample $(\mathbf{x}_i, y_i)$ leads to a misclassification error or not:

$$y_i(\mathbf{w}^\intercal \mathbf{x}_i + b)$$

$$\begin{cases} < 0 & \Longrightarrow \text{misclassification} \\ > 0 & \Longrightarrow \text{correct classification.} \end{cases}$$

Therefore, $H_1\left(y_i(\mathbf{w}^\intercal \mathbf{x}_i + b)\right)$ indicates one particular way to count errors using the hinge function $H_1(\cdot)$ as the loss function.

After we substitute these optimal values ξ_i^* into SVM3, and because $\mathbf{w}^\intercal \mathbf{w} = \|\mathbf{w}\|^2$, we can reformulate the soft SVM problem as the following unconstrained optimization problem:

$$\min_{\mathbf{w},b} \left[\underbrace{\sum_{i=1}^{N} H_1\Big(y_i(\mathbf{w}^\intercal \mathbf{x}_i + b)\Big)}_{\text{empirical loss}} + \underbrace{\lambda \cdot \|\mathbf{w}\|^2}_{\text{regularization term}} \right], \tag{7.1}$$

where the regularization parameter λ is a hyperparameter used to balance the contribution of the regularization term.

This formulation provides us with another perspective to view soft SVM models. In the soft SVMs, we essentially learn a linear model by minimizing a regularized empirical loss, consisting of two terms:

1. The first term is the regular empirical loss summed over all training samples when evaluated using the hinge function as the loss function.
2. The second term is a regularization term based on the L_2 norm of the model parameters.

As shown in Problem SVM1 on page 118, at least for linear models, the criterion of the *maximum margin* is equivalent to applying the L_2 norm regularization in learning.

More importantly, this formulation also suggests a fairly general framework for us to learn discriminative models for various ML problems. We may vary at least three dimensions in the previous formulation to result in different ML problems. First, we may replace the linear model in Eq. (7.1) with more sophisticated models, such as bilinear models (see Sections 7.3 and 7.4), quadratic models, or neural networks (see Chapter 8). Second, we may use other loss functions rather than the hinge loss function $H_1(x)$. Third, we may consider imposing other types of regularization terms instead of the L_2 norm. For example, we can extend it to a general L_p norm for various $p > 0$. The following section first introduces many possible loss functions that may be used to evaluate the empirical loss in Eq. (7.1) and their pros and cons. Next, the chapter discusses why regularization can help to avoid overfitting and also investigates the property of the L_p norm for all $p > 0$ when it is used as a regularization term in ML.

7.1.1 Common Loss Functions in Machine Learning

If we inspect all objective functions discussed in Chapter 6, we can easily derive the underlying loss functions used in those ML methods. For example, considering the objective function of logistic regression in Eq. (6.16), we can identify that the loss function used in logistic regression is $-\ln l(x) = \ln(1 + e^{-x})$. Similarly, for the objective function of the linear regression in Eq. (6.8), we can derive that its loss function is actually the quadratic function $(1 - x)^2$ (see margin note for why). Table 7.1 summarizes many popular loss functions used to evaluate the empirical risk in ML. Interested readers are encouraged to verify these results.

Given $y_i \in \{+1, -1\}$, it is easy to verify the following:

$$\left(y_i - (\mathbf{w}^\intercal \mathbf{x}_i + b)\right)^2$$

$$= \left(1 - y_i(\mathbf{w}^\intercal \mathbf{x}_i + b)\right)^2.$$

Table 7.1: Various loss functions used in different ML methods.

ML method	Loss function
—	0-1 loss: $H(x) = \begin{cases} 1 & x \le 0 \\ 0 & x > 0 \end{cases}$
Perceptron	Rectified linear loss: $H_0(x) = \max(0, -x)$
MCE	Sigmoid loss: $l(x) = \frac{1}{1+e^x}$
Logistic Regression	Logistic loss: $H_{lg}(x) = \ln(1 + e^{-x})$
Linear Regression	Square loss: $H_2(x) = (1 - x)^2$
Soft SVM	Hinge loss: $H_1(x) = \max(0, 1 - x)$
Boosting	Exponential loss: $H_e(x) = e^{-x}$

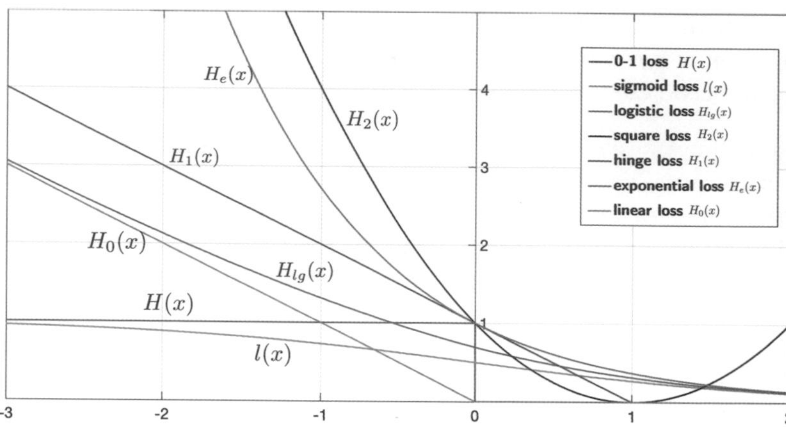

Figure 7.2: An illustration of popular loss functions used in various ML methods.

A function is *convex* if the line segment between any two points on the graph of the function lies above or on the graph.

Moreover, Figure 7.2 plots these loss functions for comparison. The loss function specifies the way to count errors in an ML problem, and it plays an important role when we construct the objective function for an ML problem. There are a few issues we want to take into account when choosing a loss function for our ML tasks. First, we need to consider whether the loss function itself is convex or not. If we choose a convex loss function, we may have a good chance of formulating the whole learning as a convex optimization problem, which is easier to solve. Among the loss functions in Table 7.1, we can easily verify that most of them are actually convex, except the ideal 0-1 loss and the sigmoid loss $l(x)$ used in MCE. The second issue we need to consider in choosing the loss function is the monotonic nonincreasing property; that is, a good loss function should monotonically increase as $x \to -\infty$, whereas it should approach 0 for $x > 0$. In other words, a good loss function should penalize misclassification errors and reward correct classifications. As shown in Figure 7.2, most loss functions are indeed monotonically nonincreasing, except the quadratic loss $H_2(x)$ used in linear regression, which begins to increase for $x > 1$. This explains why linear regression normally does not yield good performance in classification because it may penalize correct classifications for $x > 1$. On the other hand, some loss functions increase substantially when $x \to -\infty$, such as exponential loss $H_e(x)$. This property may make the learned models prone to outliers in the training data because their error counts may dominate the underlying objective function.

7.1.2 Regularization Based on L_p Norm

Let us first consider what role the regularization term in Eq. (7.1) actually plays and then study how to extend it to a more general way to do regularization in ML.

Generally speaking, when a suitable regularization parameter λ is used, the unconstrained optimization problem in Eq. (7.1) is somewhat similar to the following constrained optimization problem:

$$\min_{\mathbf{w},b} \sum_{i=1}^{N} H_1\Big(y_i(\mathbf{w}^\mathsf{T}\mathbf{x}_i + b)\Big),$$

subject to

$$\|\mathbf{w}\|^2 \leq 1.$$

It is evident that the regularization term forces it to learn a model only in a constrained region instead of the entire valid model space. In this case, the constrained region is inside the unit L_2 hyper-sphere. According to the theoretical analysis in Chapter 5, when the model space is constrained, we essentially limit the total number of effective models considered in a learning problem. This will implicitly tighten the generalization bound so that it can eventually prevent the learned model from overfitting.

As we have shown, when the L_2 norm regularization term is used in the objective function for learning, it essentially constrains the learning to search for the optimal model only inside an L_2 hyper-sphere in the model space. A natural way to extend this idea of regularization is to consider a more general L_p norm for some other $p > 0$. For any positive real number $p > 0$, the L_p norm is defined as follows:

$$\|\mathbf{w}\|_p = \Big(|w_1|^p + |w_2|^p + \cdots + |w_n|^p\Big)^{\frac{1}{p}}.$$

When $p = 2$, the L_2 norm is the usual Euclidean norm. It is also interesting to consider a few special cases, such as $p = 1$, $p = 0$, and $p = \infty$ (see margin note). If we use the L_p norm as the regularization term in Eq. (7.1), we essentially constrain the model learning only inside the following unit L_p hyperball in the model space:

$$\|\mathbf{w}\|_p \leq 1.$$

As an example, Figure 7.3 plots what a unit L_p hyperball looks like in a three-dimensional (3D) space for several typical p values. It is straightforward to verify the shapes of the unit L_p hyperballs in Figure 7.3 when p takes these special values. For example, $\|\mathbf{w}\|_\infty = 1$ corresponds to the unit hypercube in the high-dimensional space, $\|\mathbf{w}\|_2 = 1$ represents the regular hyper-sphere, and $\|\mathbf{w}\|_1 = 1$ is the octahedron-like shape in the high-dimensional space. It is noticeable that the volume of a unit L_p hyperball shrinks as we decrease p toward 0. When $p = 0$, $\|\mathbf{w}\|_0 = 1$ degenerates into some isolated line segments along all coordinate axes that are intersecting only in the origin. In other words, when the L_p regularization term is used

L_2 norm:

$$\|\mathbf{w}\|_2 = \sqrt{|w_1|^2 + \cdots + |w_n|^2}.$$

L_1 norm:

$$\|\mathbf{w}\|_1 = |w_1| + \cdots + |w_n|.$$

L_0 norm:

$$\|\mathbf{w}\|_0 = |w_1|^0 + \cdots + |w_n|^0.$$

Note that $\|\mathbf{w}\|_0$ ($\in \mathbb{Z}$) equals to the number of nonzero elements in $\mathbf{w}$.

L_∞ norm:

$$\|\mathbf{w}\|_\infty = \max\Big(|w_1|, \cdots, |w_n|\Big).$$

Note that $\|\mathbf{w}\|_\infty$ equals to the largest magnitude of all elements in $\mathbf{w}$.

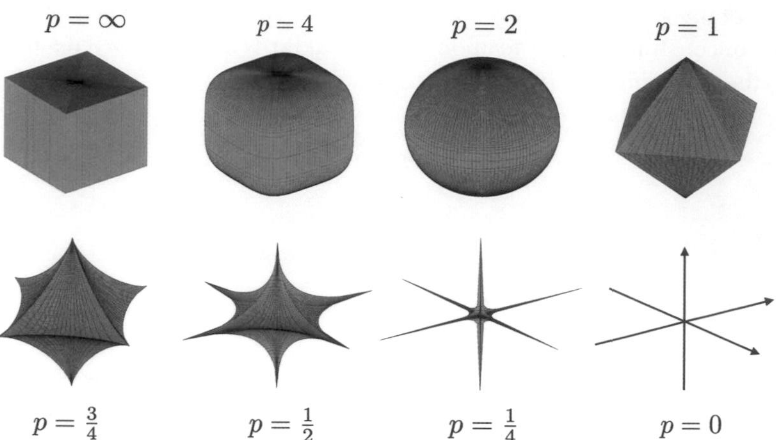

Figure 7.3: An illustration of L_p unit hyperballs, $\|\mathbf{w}\|_p \leq 1$, in a 3D space for some typical p values.

in ML, a smaller p value usually implies that stronger regularization is imposed.

Another important property of the L_p hyperballs is that $\|\mathbf{w}\|_p \leq 1$ represents a convex set when $p \geq 1$, but it becomes nonconvex for $0 \leq p < 1$. As we know, a set is convex when the line segment joining any two points in the set lies completely within the set. Therefore, $p = 1$ is usually the smallest p value used in practice because the nonconvexity for $0 \leq p < 1$ imposes a huge challenge in the underlying optimization process.

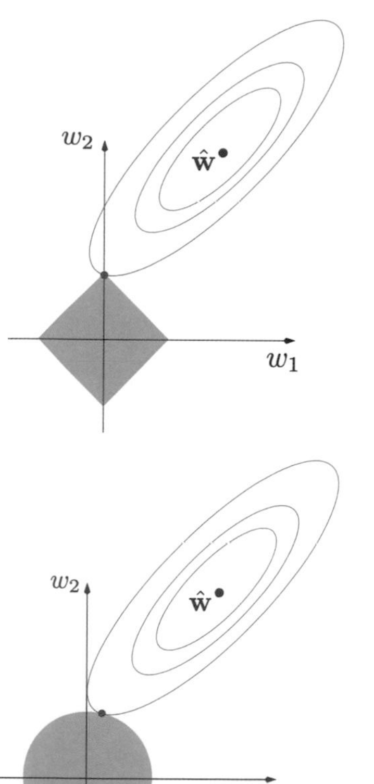

Figure 7.4: An illustration of the difference between the L_1 and L_2 regularization in a quadratic optimization problem. (Source: [92].)

An intriguing property of L_1 regularization is that it normally leads to some sparse solutions. Figure 7.4 shows the differences between L_1 regularization and L_2 regularization when they are used to optimize a quadratic objective function. When L_1 regularization is used, the optimal solution to the constrained optimization usually occurs in one of the vertexes of the L_1 hyperball because gradient descent may slide over the flat surfaces until it ends up at a vertex. These vertices correspond to some sparse solutions because some coordinates of these vertices are 0. On the other hand, when L_2 regularization is used, the constrained optimization usually finishes with a tangentially contacted point between two quadratic surfaces, which normally corresponds to a dense solution.

Another way to explain why L_1 regularization leads to sparsity is to consider the gradient of the L_1 norm:

$$\frac{\partial \|\mathbf{w}\|_1}{\partial w_i} = \text{sgn}(w_i) = \begin{cases} 1 & w_i > 0 \\ 0 & w_i = 0 \\ -1 & w_i < 0. \end{cases} \tag{7.2}$$

Because the magnitude of the gradients for any model parameter w_i remains constant unless $w_i = 0$, the gradient descent algorithm tends to continuously decrease the magnitude of all small parameters until they actually become 0. On the other hand, the gradient of the L_2 norm is computed as follows:

$$\frac{\partial \|\mathbf{w}\|_2^2}{\partial w_i} = 2w_i.$$

As w_i gets closer to 0, the magnitude of its gradient also becomes smaller. In other words, L_2 regularization tends to modify w_i values that are far away from 0 rather than those w_i values that are already small in magnitude. As a result, L_2 regularization normally leads to a solution containing many small but nonzero w_i values.

The remainder of the chapter looks at how to apply the general idea of regularized ERM to learn discriminative models for some interesting ML problems.

7.2 Ridge Regression and LASSO

In Section 6.2, we studied a standard linear regression problem, where a linear function is used to fit a given training set by minimizing the reconstruction error, which is measured with a square loss function. As we have seen, a closed-form solution can be derived for this standard linear regression. In this section, let us look at how to apply L_p norm regularization to the standard linear regression problem. Regularization is important in linear regression, especially when we need to estimate a high-dimensional linear model from a relatively small training set.

First, when L_2 norm regularization is used for linear regression, it leads to the so-called *ridge regression* [87] in statistics. With the help of L_2 regularization, ridge regression is particularly useful for deriving more reliable estimates when the number of model parameters is large. Similar to the settings in Section 6.2, a linear function $y = \mathbf{w}^\intercal \mathbf{x}$ is used to fit a training set: $\mathcal{D}_N = \{(\mathbf{x}_i, y_i) \mid i = 1, 2, \cdots, N\}$. In ridge regression, we estimate the model parameter $\mathbf{w}$ by minimizing the following regularized empirical loss:

$$\mathbf{w}^*_{\text{ridge}} = \arg\min_{\mathbf{w}} \left[\sum_{i=1}^{N} (\mathbf{w}^\intercal \mathbf{x}_i - y_i)^2 + \lambda \cdot \|\mathbf{w}\|_2^2 \right].$$

Following a treatment similar to that in Section 6.2, we can derive the closed-form solution to the ridge regression as follows:

$$\mathbf{w}^*_{\text{ridge}} = \left(\mathbf{X}^\intercal \mathbf{X} + \lambda \cdot \mathbf{I}\right)^{-1} \mathbf{X}^\intercal \mathbf{y}, \tag{7.3}$$

where $\mathbf{I}$ denotes the identity matrix, and the ridge parameter λ serves as a positive constant shifting the diagonals to stabilize the condition number of the matrix $\mathbf{X}^\intercal\mathbf{X}$.

The *condition number* of a square matrix is defined as the ratio of its largest to smallest eigenvalue. A matrix with a high condition number is said to be *ill-conditioned*.

Second, when we apply L_1 norm regularization to linear regression, it leads to another famous approach in statistics, LASSO [236]. In LASSO, the model parameters are estimated by minimizing the following regularized empirical loss:

$$\mathbf{w}^*_{\text{lasso}} = \arg\min_{\mathbf{w}} \underbrace{\left[\frac{1}{2}\sum_{i=1}^{N}(\mathbf{w}^\intercal\mathbf{x}_i - y_i)^2 + \lambda \cdot \|\mathbf{w}\|_1 \right]}_{Q_{\text{lasso}}(\mathbf{w})}. \tag{7.4}$$

Unfortunately, no closed-form solution exists to solve this optimization problem because the objective function is not differentiable everywhere. Some iterative gradient descent methods, such as the subgradient method or coordinate descent method, must be used to compute $\mathbf{w}^*_{\text{lasso}}$ (see the margin note for more details). With the help of L_1 norm regularization, LASSO normally leads to a sparse solution. Therefore, LASSO can improve the accuracy of the linear regression models as a result of the strong L_1 regularization. Meanwhile, the derived sparse solution usually selects a subset of features rather than using all features, which may provide a better interpretation of the underlying regression problem.

The gradient of the LASSO objective function can be represented as follows:

$$\frac{\partial Q_{\text{lasso}}(\mathbf{w})}{\partial \mathbf{w}} = \Big(\sum_{i=1}^{N}\mathbf{x}_i\mathbf{x}_i^\intercal\Big)\mathbf{w} - \sum_{i=1}^{N} y_i\mathbf{x}_i + \lambda \cdot \text{sgn}(\mathbf{w}),$$

where $\text{sgn}(\cdot)$ denotes the three-value sign function in Eq. (7.2). In the coordinate descent method [75], at each time point, an element w_i in $\mathbf{w}$ is selected and updated based on the computed gradient. This process is repeated until it converges.

7.3 Matrix Factorization

Because many real-world applications require us to factorize a gigantic matrix into a product of two smaller matrices, matrix factorization serves as the technical foundation to solve many important real-world problems. As we know, many traditional linear algebra methods can be used to factorize matrices, such as the well-known *singular value decomposition (SVD)*. In SVD, an $n \times m$ rectangular matrix $\mathbf{X}$ (assuming $n > m$) can be decomposed into a product of three matrices:

$$\Big[\ \mathbf{X}\ \Big]_{n\times m} = \Big[\ \mathbf{U}\ \Big]_{n\times m} \Big[\ \mathbf{\Sigma}\ \Big]_{m\times m} \Big[\ \mathbf{V}\ \Big]_{m\times m},$$

where $\mathbf{U} \in \mathbb{R}^{n\times m}$, $\mathbf{V} \in \mathbb{R}^{m\times m}$, and $\mathbf{\Sigma}$ is an $m \times m$ diagonal matrix and its nonzero diagonal elements are called *singular values* of $\mathbf{X}$. We can merge $\mathbf{\Sigma}$ with either $\mathbf{U}$ or $\mathbf{V}$ so that $\mathbf{X}$ is factorized as a product of two matrices as follows:

$$\Big[\ \mathbf{X}\ \Big]_{n\times m} = \Big[\ \mathbf{U}\ \Big]_{n\times m} \Big[\ \mathbf{V}\ \Big]_{m\times m}.$$

In this case, the matrices $\mathbf{U}$ and $\mathbf{V}$ are not much smaller than $\mathbf{X}$. However, the size of $\mathbf{U}$ and $\mathbf{V}$ can be trimmed based on the magnitudes of those singular values in $\mathbf{\Sigma}$. As shown in Figure 7.5, if we only keep the top k ($\ll m$) most significant singular values and ignore the other smaller singular values in $\mathbf{\Sigma}$, then we end up truncating the corresponding columns in $\mathbf{U}$ and the corresponding rows in $\mathbf{V}$. In doing so, we will be able to approximate the original $n \times m$ matrix $\mathbf{X}$ by a product of two much smaller matrices:

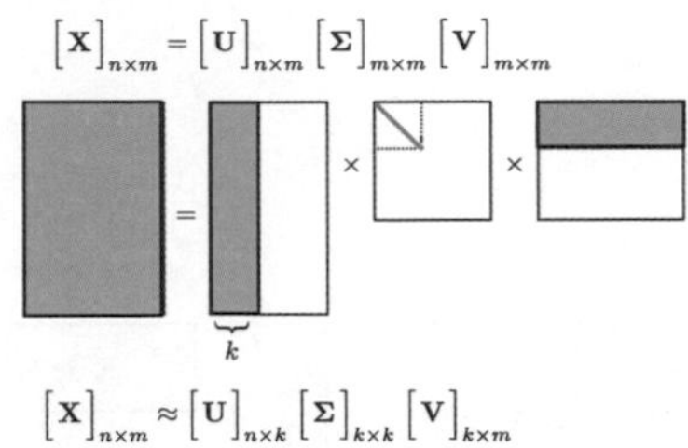

$[\mathbf{X}]_{n\times m} = [\mathbf{U}]_{n\times m} [\mathbf{\Sigma}]_{m\times m} [\mathbf{V}]_{m\times m}$
=
×
×
k
$[\mathbf{X}]_{n\times m} \approx [\mathbf{U}]_{n\times k} [\mathbf{\Sigma}]_{k\times k} [\mathbf{V}]_{k\times m}$

Figure 7.5: An Illustration of using SVD and truncated SVD to factorize an $n \times m$ matrix $\mathbf{X}$.

$$\Big[\ \mathbf{X}\ \Big]_{n\times m} \approx \Big[\ \mathbf{U}\ \Big]_{n\times k} \Big[\ \mathbf{V}\ \Big]_{k\times m} \quad (k \ll m, k \ll n).$$

This method is normally called *truncated SVD*, which is a conventional method to factorize a huge matrix into two much smaller matrices in an approximate way.

Here, let us first consider two interesting problems originating from some real-world applications that rely on the matrix-factorization technique for their solutions. The first example is the famous *collaborative filtering* that is the core technology in most online recommendation systems. The second example is the so-called *latent semantic analysis* in natural language processing.

Example 7.3.1 Collaborative Filtering for Recommendation

In many online e-commerce platforms, if the platform can keep track of all historical interactions between users and products (e.g., which user bought which products or which user rated [liked or disliked] which movies), this information becomes extremely useful for the platform to know the characteristics of the users and products. Based on the historical data, the platform will be able to develop automatic methods to recommend relevant products to each user to boost its revenue. The core technique behind the automatic recommendation is matrix factorization, which is usually called *collaborative filtering* in this context [197].

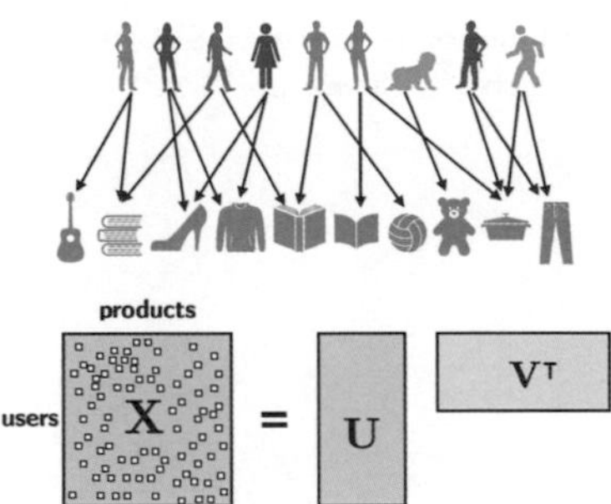

Figure 7.6: An illustration of collaborative filtering for recommendation.

In collaborative filtering, all historical interactions are first represented with a huge user–product matrix $\mathbf{X}$, as shown in Figure 7.6. Each row of $\mathbf{X}$ represents a distinct user, and each column a distinct product. Each element in $\mathbf{X}$ represents the interaction between a user and a product (e.g., how many times this user bought this product). We want to factorize this large, sparse matrix into a product of two smaller, dense matrices, $\mathbf{U}$ and $\mathbf{V}$, as in Figure 7.6. Each row vector of $\mathbf{U}^\intercal$ may be viewed as a compact representation of each user. By computing the distances between these row vectors, we will be able to know the similarity between these users. Similarly, each column vector of $\mathbf{V}$ may be viewed as a compact representation of a product, and the distances between these column vectors represent the similarity between these products. Based on these similarity measures, the platform will be able to recommend to a user some products that are similar to the products previously bought by this user or recommend some products previously bought by other users similar to this user. ♦

Example 7.3.2 Latent Semantic Analysis

Latent semantic analysis (LSA) is a technique to learn semantic representations for words and documents in a natural language process [50]. The key assumption behind LSA is the distributional hypothesis in linguistics—that is, "words that are close in meaning will occur in similar pieces of text" [91].

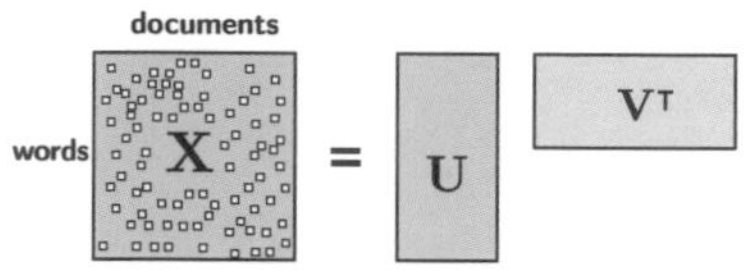

Figure 7.7: An illustration of LSA to learn semantic word representations.

As shown in Figure 7.7, we first construct a word–document matrix **X** from a large text corpus. The rows of matrix **X** represent the unique words in a language, and the columns represent all documents in the corpus. The elements in **X** contain word counts per document or other normalized frequency measures [240]. Similarly, assume we can factorize the large matrix **X** into a product of **U** and **V**. Each row vector in $\mathbf{U}^\intercal$ can be viewed as a compact semantic representation for a word, and the distances between them represent semantic similarity between different words. On the other hand, all column vectors in **V** may be treated as compact, fixed-size representations for all documents in the corpus, which usually vary in length. ♦

The time complexity to do SVD on an $n \times m$ matrix is $O(n^2m + nm^2 + m^3)$.

In principle, the traditional SVD algorithm in linear algebra can be used to factorize any matrix, as previously described. However, there are several difficulties when we apply the SVD method to real-world problems, as in Examples 7.3.1 and 7.3.2. First of all, the traditional SVD algorithm is computationally expensive in terms of both running time and memory usage. Most matrices arising from real-world applications are extremely large in size. For example, in the case of collaborative filtering, it is normal to have hundreds of millions of users and hundreds of thousands of products. In this case, the user–product matrix is normally very sparse, but it is extremely large in size. It may be very inefficient to run the standard SVD algorithm on these huge, sparse matrices. Second, many matrices originating from practical applications are usually partially observed. In other words, we only know some elements in matrix **X**, and the remaining ones are missing or unknown. For example, if matrix **X** is used to represent the ratings (like or dislike) of a large number of users on many movies, we cannot expect each user to rate all available movies because they may not have a chance to watch most movies. No linear algebra method can be used to factorize a partially observed matrix. On the other hand, if we can factorize a partially observed matrix **X** into two smaller matrices **U** and **V**, we essentially have filled all missing elements in **X** because any missing element can be estimated by a product of a row vector in **U** and a column vector in **V**. Therefore, factorization of partially observed matrices is sometimes also called *matrix completion*.

In the following, we will formulate matrix factorization as an ML problem, where the matrix **X** or its observed part is treated as training data, and two smaller matrices **U** and **V** are treated as unknown parameters to be learned [131]. As we will see, the solution to this ML problem tends to be much more efficient than the traditional SVD method for large, sparse matrices, and more importantly, it is equally applicable to both fully observed and partially observed matrices.

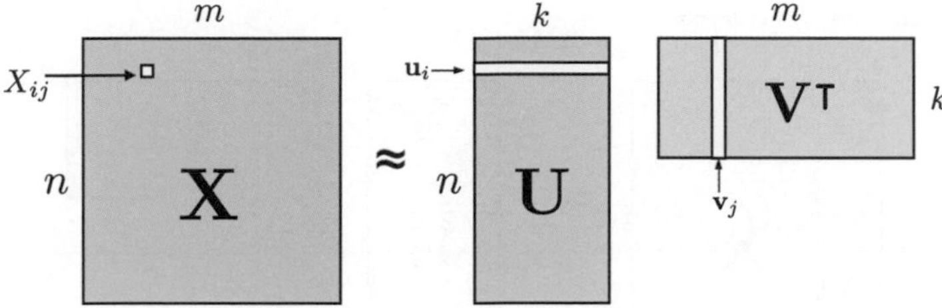

Figure 7.8: Matrix factorization as an ML problem.

Given an $n \times m$ matrix **X**, as shown in Figure 7.8, we want to learn two matrices **U** ($\in \mathbb{R}^{k\times n}$) and **V** ($\in \mathbb{R}^{k\times m}$) to approximate **X** as

$$\mathbf{X} \approx \mathbf{U}^\intercal \mathbf{V},$$

where k is a hyperparameter, usually $k \ll n, m$. If **X** is partially observed, we denote the indices of all observed elements in **X** as a set $\Omega = \{(i,j)\}$. Furthermore, we use Ω_i^r to denote all column indices of observed elements in the ith row of **X**, and we use Ω_j^c for all row indices of observed elements in the jth column of **X**, as shown in Figure 7.9.

If **X** is fully observed, Ω simply contains all element indices.

If we want $\mathbf{U}^\intercal\mathbf{V}$ to be as close to **X** as possible, we may define a squared loss over all observed elements in **X**:

$$\sum_{(i,j)\in\Omega} \left(x_{ij} - \mathbf{u}_i^\intercal \mathbf{v}_j\right)^2,$$

where $\mathbf{u}_i$ denotes the ith column vector in **U**, and $\mathbf{v}_j$ denotes the jth column vector in **V**.

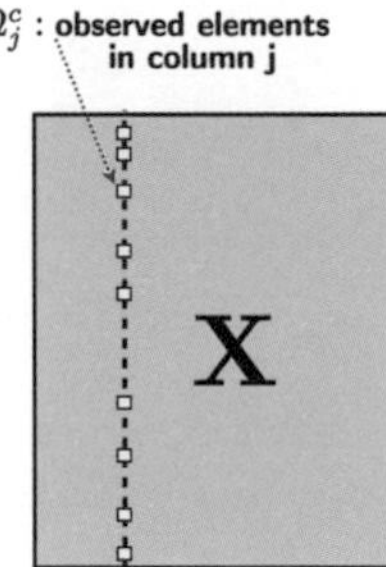

Figure 7.9: The row indices of all observed elements in column j is denoted as Ω_j^c.

Moreover, we can impose L_2 norm regularization on all row vectors of **U** and **V**. Therefore, we formulate the objective function of this matrix factorization problem as follows:

$$Q(\mathbf{U},\mathbf{V}) = \sum_{(i,j)\in\Omega} \left(x_{ij} - \mathbf{u}_i^\intercal \mathbf{v}_j\right)^2 + \lambda_1 \sum_{i=1}^{n} \|\mathbf{u}_i\|_2^2 + \lambda_2 \sum_{j=1}^{m} \|\mathbf{v}_j\|_2^2.$$

In this ML problem, we essentially try to learn a so-called *bilinear function* (see the margin note) to fit all observed elements of **X**. The objective function is constructed based on the mean-squared error and the L_2 norm regularization. Because of the nonconvexity introduced by the bilinear

If both $\mathbf{U}$ and $\mathbf{V}$ are free variables,

$$\mathbf{X} = \mathbf{U}^\intercal \mathbf{V}$$

is a bilinear function, which is a special form of quadratic function. It is called as such because it becomes a linear function when either $\mathbf{U}$ or $\mathbf{V}$ is fixed.

function, it is not easy to optimize $\mathbf{u}_i$ and $\mathbf{v}_j$ jointly. However, the bilinear function has a nice linear property if we fix either $\mathbf{U}$ or $\mathbf{V}$. Therefore, if we only optimize one variable at a time, it becomes a fairly simple convex optimization problem. In other words, it is possible to derive a simple formula to solve $\mathbf{u}_i$ and $\mathbf{v}_j$ in an alternating fashion. For example, let us consider how to solve for one particular $\mathbf{v}_j$ only, when all $\mathbf{u}_i$ and other $\mathbf{v}_{j'}$ are assumed to be fixed.

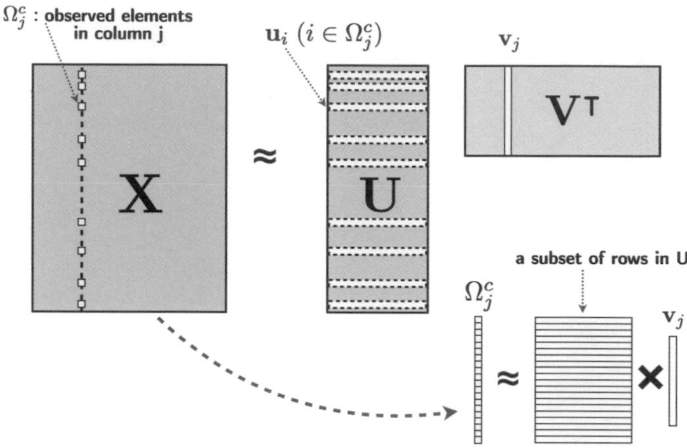

Figure 7.10: An alternate way to solve matrix factorization [195]: solving only one column vector in $\mathbf{V}$.

As shown in Figure 7.10, after we collect only the terms related to $\mathbf{v}_j$, the previous optimization problem can be simplified as a ridge regression problem for $\mathbf{v}_j$:

$$\arg\min_{\mathbf{v}_j} \sum_{i\in\Omega_j^c} \left(x_{ij} - \mathbf{u}_i^\intercal \mathbf{v}_j\right)^2 + \lambda_2 \cdot \|\mathbf{v}_j\|_2^2.$$

Similar to Eq. (7.3), this optimization problem can be solved with the following closed-form solution:

$$\mathbf{v}_j = \left(\sum_{i\in\Omega_j^c} \mathbf{u}_i\mathbf{u}_i^\intercal + \lambda_2\,\mathbf{I}\right)^{-1}\left(\sum_{i\in\Omega_j^c} x_{ij}\mathbf{u}_i\right).$$

In the same way, if we assume other vectors are fixed, we can solve for any particular $\mathbf{u}_i$ as follows:

$$\mathbf{u}_i = \left(\sum_{j\in\Omega_i^r} \mathbf{v}_j\mathbf{v}_j^\intercal + \lambda_1\,\mathbf{I}\right)^{-1}\left(\sum_{j\in\Omega_i^r} x_{ij}\mathbf{v}_i\right).$$

Putting it all together, we have a complete algorithm in Algorithm 7.6 for factorizing any partially observed matrix $\mathbf{X}$. Note that Algorithm 7.6 can be run in parallel in a distributed computing system if more processors are available. At each iteration, we update all $\mathbf{u}_i$ (or all $\mathbf{v}_j$) on different processors in parallel. However, each update in Algorithm 7.6 requires us to invert a $k \times k$ matrix, which has the computational complexity of $O(k^3)$. This becomes quite expensive when k is large.

Algorithm 7.6 Alternating Algorithm for Matrix Factorization

set $t = 0$
randomly initialize $\mathbf{v}_j^{(0)}$ $(j = 1, 2, \cdots, m)$
while not converged **do**
  for $i = 1, \cdots, n$ **do**

$$\mathbf{u}_i^{(t+1)} = \Big(\sum_{j \in \Omega_i^r} \mathbf{v}_j^{(t)} (\mathbf{v}_j^{(t)})^\intercal + \lambda_1 \mathbf{I} \Big)^{-1} \Big(\sum_{j \in \Omega_i^r} x_{ij} \mathbf{v}_i^{(t)} \Big)$$

  end for
  for $j = 1, \cdots, m$ **do**

$$\mathbf{v}_j^{(t+1)} = \Big(\sum_{i \in \Omega_j^c} \mathbf{u}_i^{(t+1)} (\mathbf{u}_i^{(t+1)})^\intercal + \lambda_2 \mathbf{I} \Big)^{-1} \Big(\sum_{i \in \Omega_j^c} x_{ij} \mathbf{u}_j^{(t+1)} \Big)$$

  end for
  $t = t + 1$
end while

In the literature, other more efficient algorithms have also been proposed to solve matrix factorization. For example, a faster algorithm can be derived using stochastic gradient descent (SGD). At each iteration, a random element x_{ij} $(\in \Omega)$ is selected, and its corresponding $\mathbf{u}_i$ and $\mathbf{v}_j$ are updated separately based on gradient descent. In this case, the gradient for either $\mathbf{u}_i$ or $\mathbf{v}_j$ may be computed in a very efficient way without using matrix inversion. We leave this as Exercise Q7.6 for interested readers.

7.4 Dictionary Learning

Dictionary learning [202, 157], also known as *sparse representation learning*, is a representational learning method for high-dimensional data that exploits the sparsity property prevalent in most signals that naturally occur in the physical world. The basic assumption is that all real-world data can be broken down into many basic elements from a presumably large but finite *dictionary*. Each element in the dictionary is called an *atom*. Even though this dictionary may contain a large number of atoms, every data sample can be constructed with only a few atoms from the dictionary. Every data sample needs to use a different subset of the atoms in the dictionary, but each subset for any sample is fairly small in size. Moreover, this assumption is also supported by some empirical successes in the approach of *compressed sensing* (also known as *sparse sampling*) in signal

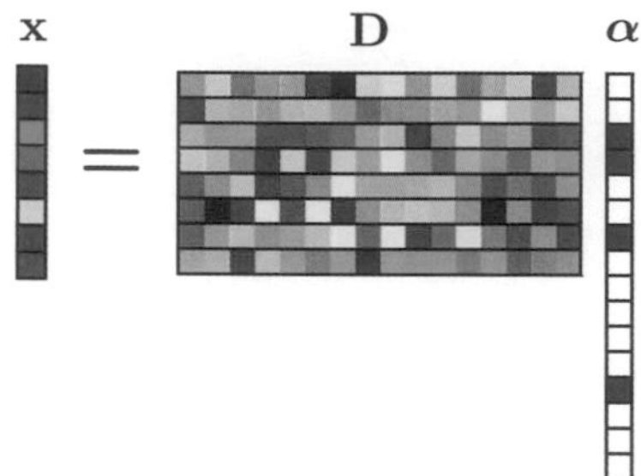

Figure 7.11: Sparse coding represents each data sample as a linear combination of a dictionary and a sparse code.

processing [39, 67]. For example, there are presumably a large number of possible objects existing in the world. However, when we take a picture of any natural scene, we usually only see a few coherent objects appearing in it. When we take a picture of another natural scene, we may see a few other objects. Generally speaking, it is unnatural to have a large number of incoherent objects appearing in the same scene.

In particular, as shown in Figure 7.11, we further assume that each data sample $\mathbf{x}$ ($\in \mathbb{R}^d$) can be represented as a linear combination of all atoms in the dictionary $\mathbf{D}$ ($\in \mathbb{R}^{d\times n}$) based on a very sparse code $\boldsymbol{\alpha}$ ($\in \mathbb{R}^n$), most of whose elements are 0. We usually use a large dictionary (i.e., $n \gg d$). That is,

$$\mathbf{x} = \begin{bmatrix} | & & | \\ \mathbf{d}_1 & \cdots & \mathbf{d}_n \\ | & & | \end{bmatrix}_{d\times n} \begin{bmatrix} \alpha_1 \\ \vdots \\ \alpha_n \end{bmatrix} = \mathbf{D}\,\boldsymbol{\alpha},$$

where each column vector in $\mathbf{D}$ (i.e., $\mathbf{d}_i \in \mathbb{R}^d$ $(i = 1, 2, \cdots, n)$) denotes an atom in the dictionary. The sparse code $\boldsymbol{\alpha}$ may be used as a feature vector to represent the original data input $\mathbf{x}$. Moreover, $\boldsymbol{\alpha}$ may be viewed as an intuitive interpretation for the original data $\mathbf{x}$ because it contains only a few nonzero elements. In practice, the dictionary itself must be learned jointly with these sparse codes from available training data.

Assume a training set is given as $\{\mathbf{x}_1, \mathbf{x}_2, \cdots, \mathbf{x}_N\}$, and we denote the unknown sparse codes for all of them as $\{\boldsymbol{\alpha}_1, \boldsymbol{\alpha}_2, \cdots, \boldsymbol{\alpha}_N\}$. We may represent all training samples and their sparse codes as a $d \times N$ matrix and an $n \times N$ matrix, respectively, as follows:

$$\mathbf{X} = \begin{bmatrix} | & & | \\ \mathbf{x}_1 & \cdots & \mathbf{x}_N \\ | & & | \end{bmatrix}_{d\times N} \qquad \mathbf{A} = \begin{bmatrix} | & & | \\ \boldsymbol{\alpha}_1 & \cdots & \boldsymbol{\alpha}_N \\ | & & | \end{bmatrix}_{n\times N}.$$

Similar to matrix factorization, we formulate dictionary learning as an ML problem where both $\mathbf{D}$ and $\mathbf{A}$ are jointly learned from the given training samples $\mathbf{X}$. In this case, we use the mean-squared error to measure the loss between each data sample and its sparse code. We also impose L_2 norm regularization on each atom in the dictionary to alleviate overfitting and L_1 norm regularization on each code to promote sparsity. Therefore, the final optimization problem in dictionary learning can be formulated as follows:

$$\arg\min_{\mathbf{D},\mathbf{A}} \underbrace{\frac{1}{2}\sum_{i=1}^{N}\left\|\mathbf{x}_i - \mathbf{D}\,\boldsymbol{\alpha}_i\right\|_2^2 + \lambda_1 \sum_{i=1}^{N}\left\|\boldsymbol{\alpha}_i\right\|_1 + \frac{\lambda_2}{2}\sum_{j=1}^{n}\left\|\mathbf{d}_j\right\|_2^2}_{Q(\mathbf{D},\mathbf{A})}.$$

Here, $\frac{1}{2}$ is added for notation convenience.

Similar to matrix factorization, we also use a bilinear model in dictionary learning to combine the dictionary and sparse codes to generate the raw data. The difference here is that different regularization terms are used, promoting sparsity in this case.

In the following, we consider a gradient descent algorithm to solve the optimization problem for dictionary learning. First of all, we can compute the gradient for each sparse code $\boldsymbol{\alpha}_i$ (for all $i = 1, 2, \cdots, N$) as follows:

$$\frac{\partial Q(\mathbf{D},\mathbf{A})}{\partial \boldsymbol{\alpha}_i} = \mathbf{D}^{\intercal}\mathbf{D}\boldsymbol{\alpha}_i - \mathbf{D}^{\intercal}\mathbf{x}_i + \lambda_1 \cdot \mathrm{sgn}\big(\boldsymbol{\alpha}_i\big). \tag{7.5}$$

Note that we may reparameterize

$$\left\|\mathbf{x}_i - \mathbf{D}\,\boldsymbol{\alpha}_i\right\|_2^2 = \Big(\mathbf{D}\,\boldsymbol{\alpha}_i - \mathbf{x}_i\Big)^{\intercal}\Big(\mathbf{D}\,\boldsymbol{\alpha}_i - \mathbf{x}_i\Big).$$

If we align the left-hand side of this equation as a column to form a single matrix for all $\boldsymbol{\alpha}_i$, we obtain $\frac{\partial Q(\mathbf{D},\mathbf{A})}{\partial \mathbf{A}}$. Similarly, we may pack the corresponding right-hand sides into another matrix and finally derive:

$$\frac{\partial Q(\mathbf{D},\mathbf{A})}{\partial \mathbf{A}} = \mathbf{D}^{\intercal}\mathbf{D}\mathbf{A} - \mathbf{D}^{\intercal}\mathbf{X} + \lambda_1 \cdot \mathrm{sgn}\big(\mathbf{A}\big),$$

where $\mathrm{sgn}(\cdot)$ applies Eq. (7.2) to a vector or matrix element-wise.

Similarly, we may compute the gradient for $\mathbf{D}$ (see margin note) as follows:

$$\frac{\partial Q(\mathbf{D},\mathbf{A})}{\partial \mathbf{D}} = \mathbf{D}\mathbf{A}\mathbf{A}^{\intercal} - \mathbf{X}\mathbf{A}^{\intercal} + \lambda_2 \cdot \mathbf{D}.$$

$$Q(\mathbf{D},\mathbf{A}) = \frac{1}{2}\sum_{i=1}^{N}(\mathbf{D}\,\boldsymbol{\alpha}_i - \mathbf{x}_i)^{\intercal}(\mathbf{D}\,\boldsymbol{\alpha}_i - \mathbf{x}_i) + \frac{\lambda_2}{2}\sum_{j=1}^{n}\|\mathbf{d}_j\|_2^2 + \cdots$$
$$\Longrightarrow \frac{\partial Q(\mathbf{D},\mathbf{A})}{\partial \mathbf{D}} = \sum_{i=1}^{N}(\mathbf{D}\,\boldsymbol{\alpha}_i - \mathbf{x}_i)\boldsymbol{\alpha}_i^{\intercal} + \lambda_2\mathbf{D}$$
$$= \mathbf{D}\underbrace{\sum_{i=1}^{N}\boldsymbol{\alpha}_i\boldsymbol{\alpha}_i^{\intercal}}_{\mathbf{A}\mathbf{A}^{\intercal}} - \underbrace{\sum_{i=1}^{N}\mathbf{x}_i\boldsymbol{\alpha}_i^{\intercal}}_{\mathbf{X}\mathbf{A}^{\intercal}} + \lambda_2\mathbf{D}.$$

(See Exercise Q2.3.)

Using these computed gradients, we have a complete gradient descent algorithm to learn the dictionary $\mathbf{D}$ from all training data $\mathbf{X}$ in Algorithm 7.7.

Once we have learned the dictionary $\mathbf{D}$ from the training data as previously described, for any new datum $\mathbf{x}$ that is not in the training set, we can derive its sparse code $\boldsymbol{\alpha}$ by solving the following optimization:

$$\boldsymbol{\alpha}^* = \arg\min_{\boldsymbol{\alpha}} \underbrace{\frac{1}{2}\left\|\mathbf{x} - \mathbf{D}\,\boldsymbol{\alpha}\right\|_2^2 + \lambda_1 \cdot \left\|\boldsymbol{\alpha}\right\|_1}_{Q'(\boldsymbol{\alpha})}.$$

This problem is similar to the LASSO problem in Eq. (7.4), and it can be solved with the gradient descent or the coordinate descent method as

Algorithm 7.7 Gradient Descent for Dictionary Learning

set $t = 0$ and η_0
randomly initialize $\mathbf{D}^{(0)}$ and $\mathbf{A}^{(0)}$
while not converged **do**
  update $\mathbf{A}$:

$$\mathbf{A}^{(t+1)} = \mathbf{A}^{(t)} - \eta_t \Big((\mathbf{D}^{(t)})^\intercal \mathbf{D}^{(t)} \mathbf{A}^{(t)} - (\mathbf{D}^{(t)})^\intercal \mathbf{X} + \lambda_1 \cdot \mathrm{sgn}\big(\mathbf{A}^{(t)}\big) \Big)$$

  update $\mathbf{D}$:

$$\mathbf{D}^{(t+1)} = \mathbf{D}^{(t)} - \eta_t \Big(\mathbf{D}^{(t)} \mathbf{A}^{(t+1)} \big(\mathbf{A}^{(t+1)}\big)^\intercal - \mathbf{X}\big(\mathbf{A}^{(t+1)}\big)^\intercal + \lambda_2 \cdot \mathbf{D}^{(t)} \Big)$$

  adjust $\eta_t \rightarrow \eta_{t+1}$
  $t = t + 1$
end while

described on page 140. Referring to Eq. (7.5), we can compute the gradient for the previous objective function as follows:

$$\frac{\partial Q'(\boldsymbol{\alpha})}{\partial \boldsymbol{\alpha}} = \mathbf{D}^\intercal \mathbf{D}\, \boldsymbol{\alpha} - \mathbf{D}^\intercal \mathbf{x} + \lambda_1 \cdot \mathrm{sgn}(\boldsymbol{\alpha}).$$

Finally, the sparse code $\boldsymbol{\alpha}^*$ can be derived iteratively using any gradient descent method.

Lab Project III

In this project, you will use a text corpus, called the English Wikipedia Dump [156, 146], to construct document–word matrices and then use the LSA technique to factorize the matrices to derive word representations, also known as *word embeddings* or *word vectors*. You will first use the derived word vectors to investigate semantic similarity between different words based on the Pearson's correlation coefficient obtained by comparing the cosine distance between word vectors and human-assigned similarity scores in the WordSim353 data set [62] (`http://www.cse.yorku.ca/~hj/wordsim353_human_scores.txt`). Furthermore, the derived word vectors will be visualized in a two-dimensional (2D) space using the t-distributed stochastic neighbor embedding (t-SNE) method to inspect the semantic relationship among English words. In this project, you will implement several ML methods to factorize large, sparse matrices to study how to produce meaningful word representations for natural language processing.

a. Use the small enwiki8 data set (download from `http://www.cse.yorku.ca/~hj/enwiki8.txt.zip`) to construct a document–word frequency matrix like that in Figure 7.7. In this experiment, you should treat each paragraph in a line as a document. Construct the matrix in a sparse format for the top 10,000 most frequent words in enwiki8 and all words in WordSim353.

b. First, use a standard SVD procedure from a linear algebra library to factorize the sparse document–word matrix, and truncate it to $k = 20, 50, 100$. Examine the run-in time and memory consumption for the SVD.

c. Implement the alternating Algorithm 7.6 to factorize the document–word matrix for $k = 20, 50, 100$. Examine the run-in time and memory consumption for this method.

d. Implement the SGD method in Exercise Q7.6 to factorize the document–word matrix for $k = 20, 50, 100$. Examine the run-in time and memory consumption.

e. Investigate the quality of the previously derived word vectors based on the correlation with some human-assigned similarity scores. For each pair of words in WordSim353, compute the cosine distance between their word vectors, and then compute the Pearson's correlation coefficient between these cosine distances and human scores, tuning your learning hyperparameters toward higher correlation.

f. Visualize the previous word representations for the top 300 most frequent words in enwiki8 using the t-SNE method by projecting each set into a 2D space. Investigate how these 300 word representations are distributed, and inspect whether the semantically relevant words are located closer in the space. Explain why or why not.

g. Refer to [240] to reconstruct the document–word matrix based on the positive point-wise mutual information (PPMI). Repeat the previous steps to see how much the performance is improved.

h. If you have enough computing resources, optimize your implementations and run the previous steps on a larger data set, the enwiki9 (`http://www.cse.yorku.ca/~hj/enwiki9.txt.zip`), to investigate how much a larger text corpus can improve the quality of the derived word representations.

Exercises

Q7.1 Explain why the loss function is the rectified linear loss $H_0(x)$ in perceptron and the sigmoid loss $l(x)$ in MCE.

Q7.2 Derive the closed-form solution to the ridge regression in Eq. (7.3).

Q7.3 Derive and compare the solutions to the ridge regression for the following two variants:

a. The constrained norm:

$$\min_{\mathbf{w}} \sum_{i=1}^{N} (\mathbf{w}^\intercal \mathbf{x}_i - y_i)^2,$$

subject to

$$\|\mathbf{w}\|_2^2 \leq 1.$$

b. The scaled norm:

$$\min_{\mathbf{w}} \left[\sum_{i=1}^{N} (\mathbf{w}^\intercal \mathbf{x}_i - y_i)^2 + \lambda \cdot \|\mathbf{w}\|_2^2 \right],$$

where $\lambda > 0$ is a preset constant.

Q7.4 The coordinate descent algorithm aims to optimize the objective function with respect to one free variable at a time. Derive the coordinate descent algorithm to solve LASSO.

Q7.5 Derive the gradient descent methods to solve the ridge regression and LASSO.

Q7.6 In addition to the alternating Algorithm 7.6, derive the SGD algorithm to solve matrix factorization for any sparse matrix **X**. Assume **X** is huge but very sparse.

Q7.7 Run *linear regression*, *ridge regression*, and *LASSO* on a small data set (e.g., the Boston Housing Dataset; `https://www.cs.toronto.edu/~delve/data/boston/bostonDetail.html`) to experimentally compare the regression models obtained from these methods.

Neural Networks | 8

Chapter 6 discussed various methods to learn linear models for machine learning tasks and also described how to use the kernel trick to extend them to some specific nonlinear models. Chapter 7 presented a general framework to learn discriminative models. An interesting question that follows is how to learn nonlinear discriminative models in a general way. One natural path for pursuing this idea is to explore high-degree polynomial functions. However, we usually deal with high-dimensional feature vectors in most machine learning problems, and multivariate polynomial functions are known to be seriously plagued by the curse of dimensionality. As a result, only quadratic functions are occasionally used under certain settings for some machine learning tasks, such as matrix factorization and sparse coding. Other higher-order polynomial functions beyond those are rarely used in machine learning.

On the other hand, *artificial neural networks* (ANNs), which have been theoretically shown to represent a rich family of nonlinear models, have recently been successfully applied to machine learning, particularly supervised learning. ANNs were initially inspired by the biological neuron networks in animals and humans, but some strong mathematical justifications have also been found to support them in theory. For example, under some minor conditions, it has been proved that well-structured and sufficiently large neural networks can approximate, up to any arbitrary precision, any function from some well-known function families, such as continuous functions or L^p functions (see margin note). These function families are very general and include pretty much all realistic functions (either linear or nonlinear) that we may encounter in real-world applications. Moreover, ANNs are so flexible that many structures can be constructed to accommodate various types of real-world data, such as static patterns, multidimensional inputs, and sequential data. Under the support of today's powerful computing resources, large-scale neural networks can be reliably learned from a huge amount of training data to yield excellent performance for many real-world tasks, ranging from speech recognition and image classification to machine translation. At present, neural networks have become the dominant machine learning models for supervised learning. Under the umbrella of *deep learning*, many deep and multilayer structures have been proposed for neural networks in a variety of practical applications related to speech/music/audio, image/video, text, and other sensory data.

The function $f(\mathbf{x})$ is called an L^p function if its p-norm ($p > 0$) is finite; that is:

$$\int_{\mathbf{x}} |f(\mathbf{x})|^p \, d\mathbf{x} < \infty.$$

One example is the L^2 function space where $p = 2$, which is a Hilbert space. It includes all possible nonlinear functions as long as they are either energy limited or bounded and of a finite domain. It is safe to say that any function arising from a physical process belongs to L^2.

This chapter discusses various topics related to ANNs, including basic formulations, common building blocks for network construction, popular network structures, the error back-propagation learning algorithm based on automatic differentiation, and some critical engineering tricks to fine-tune hyperparameters.

8.1 Artificial Neural Networks

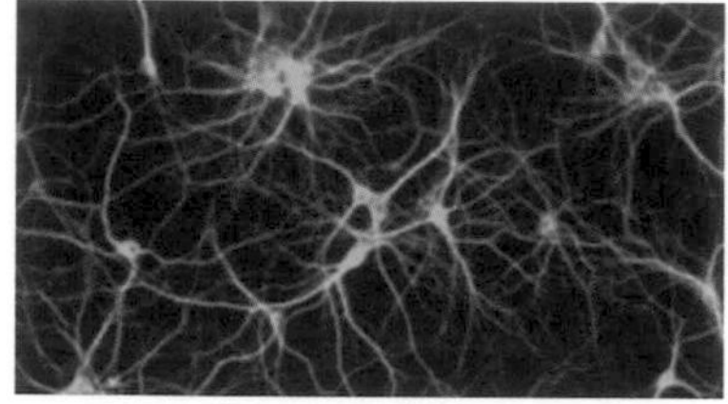

Figure 8.1: An illustration of a part of a biological neuronal network.

The development of ANNs has been largely inspired by the biological neuronal networks in animals and humans. In most animals, as well as humans, the biological neuronal network is enormous and consists of a huge number of cells called *neurons*. We believe the huge neuronal networks in their brains are responsible for their intelligence. How these large neuronal networks function as a whole still remains mostly unclear to us, but the behavior of each neuron is well known. As shown in Figure 8.1, each neuron is connected to hundreds or thousands of other neurons in the network through their *axons* and *dendrites*. Most importantly, the strength of each connection depends on a *synapse*, which may be adjusted or learned. Each neuron receives impulse signals from other neurons through these weighted connections and then combines and processes them nonlinearly to generate an output signal (either helping or hindering firing), which will be sent to other connected neurons, as shown in Figure 8.2. What a single biological neuron does is fairly straightforward, but the whole neuronal network can conduct extremely complex functions through the collective activities of a huge number of neurons. The overall function of the whole neuronal network largely depends on how these neurons are linked and the connection strengths of these links. The key idea of ANNs is to build mathematical models for computers to simulate the behavior of a biological neuronal network in order to achieve artificial intelligence (AI).

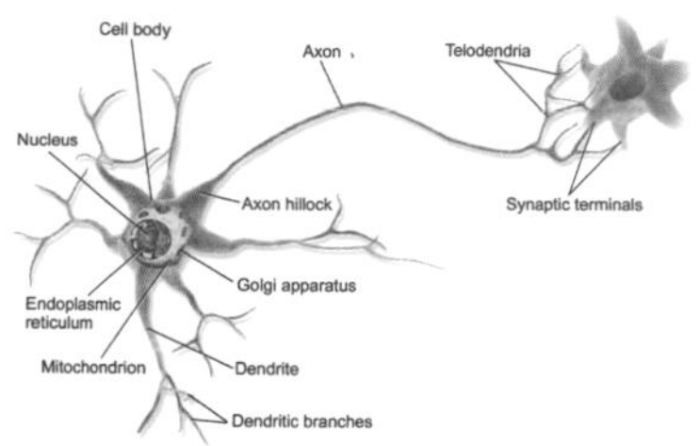

Figure 8.2: An illustration of a biological neuron. (Image credit: BruceBlaus/ CC-BY-3.0.)

8.1.1 Basic Formulation of Artificial Neural Networks

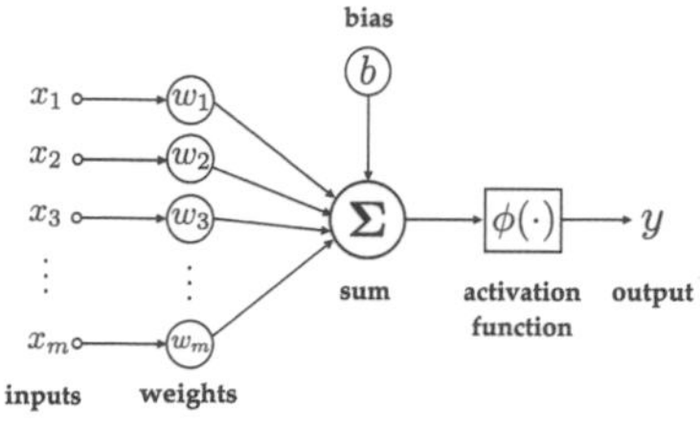

Figure 8.3: An artificial neuron: a simple mathematical model to simulate a biological neuron.

The first step in the simulation is to use a computational model to mimic each biological neuron in computers. Based on the behavior of biological neurons described previously, a simple mathematical model has been proposed to simulate it, which is usually called an *artificial neuron* (or *neuron* for short hereafter). As shown in Figure 8.3, each neuron takes multiple inputs (e.g., $\mathbf{x} = [x_1; x_2; \cdots; x_m]$) and computes a linearly weighted sum of these inputs using some adjustable parameters (e.g., some weights $\mathbf{w} = [w_1; w_2; \cdots; w_m]$ and a bias b). The sum is passed through a nonlinear activation function $\phi(\cdot)$ to generate the output of this neuron as y. If we put all of these together, we can represent the computation of each neuron as $y = \phi(\mathbf{w}^\intercal \mathbf{x} + b)$. If we use the step function in Figure 6.4 as the activation function, this neuron behaves exactly like the perceptron model discussed in Section 6.1. The modeling power of a single neuron like this is very limited because we know that the perceptron model works only for simple cases such as linearly separable classes. Back in the 1960s, it was already well known that the modeling power could be significantly enhanced by combining multiple neurons in certain ways. However, the simple perceptron algorithm in Algorithm 6.4 cannot be extended for a group of neurons, and the simple gradient-based optimization methods cannot be used to learn multiple cascaded neurons because the derivative of the step function is 0 almost everywhere except the origin. The learning problem of multiple neurons had not been solved for some time until researchers [249, 204] realized that the step function in neurons could be replaced by some more amenable nonlinear functions, such as the sigmoid function and the hyperbolic tangent function (tanh) (as shown in Figure 8.4). The key idea in this learning algorithm, currently known as *back-propagation*, is similar to the trick that replaces the step function with a smoother approximation, as discussed for the minimum classification error (MCE) in Section 6.3. A differentiable function, such as sigmoid or tanh, is often used to approximate the step function so that the gradients can be computed for the parameters of all neurons.

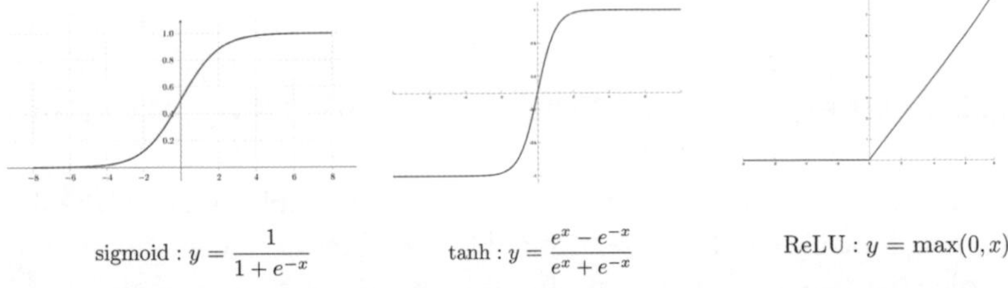

sigmoid : $y = \frac{1}{1+e^{-x}}$
tanh : $y = \frac{e^{x} - e^{-x}}{e^{x} + e^{-x}}$
ReLU : $y = \max(0, x)$

Figure 8.4: Some popular nonlinear activation functions used for ANNs.

More recently, a new nonlinear activation function $y = \max(0, x)$, called the *rectified linear (ReLU) function* (see Figure 8.4), has been proposed for ANNs [111, 168, 82]. The ReLU function is a convex piece-wise linear function. When the ReLU activation function was initially proposed, it was quite a surprise because the ReLU function is actually unbounded. In fact, this is not a problem because the input x is always bounded in practice, so only the central portion of the ReLU function is relevant. The advantage of the ReLU activation function is that it normally leads to much larger gradients than other activation functions. This becomes extremely important in learning very large and deep neural networks. As a result, the ReLU function has become the dominant choice for the nonlinear activation functions in neural networks these days.

After we know how to construct a single neuron, we will be able to build ANNs by connecting multiple neurons. When doing this, each neuron takes outputs from other neurons or information from the outside world as its own inputs. Then, it processes all inputs with its own parameters to generate a single output, which is in turn sent out to another neuron as another input or the outside world as an overall result. We may follow an arbitrary structure to connect a large number of neurons to form a very large neural network. If we view this neural network as a whole, as shown in Figure 8.5, it can be considered as a multivariate and vector-valued function that maps the input vector **x** to output vector **y**. In the context of machine learning, the input vectors represent some features related to an observed pattern, and the outputs represent some target labels of this pattern.

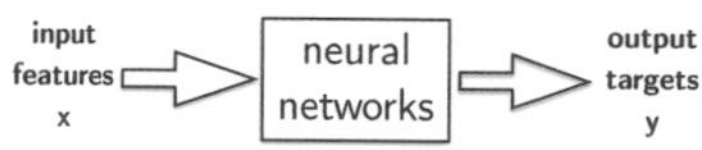

Figure 8.5: Neural networks are primarily used as a function approximator between any input **x** and output **y**.

Before we introduce various possible structures that we can use to systematically build large neural networks, one may want to ask a fundamental question: How powerful could a constructed model potentially become if it is built by just combining some relatively simple neurons? To answer this question, we will briefly review some theoretical results regarding the expressiveness of neural networks, which were developed in the early 1990s. The conclusion is quite striking: we can build a neural network to approximate any function from some broad function families as long as we have the resources to use as many neurons as we want and we follow a meaningful way to connect these neurons. This work is normally referred to as the *universal approximator theory* in the literature.

8.1.2 Mathematical Justification: Universal Approximator

The universal approximator theory was initially established by Cybenko [47] and Hornik [102]. In the original work, they only consider a very simple structure to combine multiple neurons, which is colloquially referred to as a *multilayer perceptron* (MLP), as shown in Figure 8.6. In an MLP structure, all neurons are aligned in a middle layer (called the *hidden layer*), and each neuron takes all inputs from outside and processes them with its own parameters to generate an output. The overall output of the MLP is just the sum of the outputs from all neurons. An MLP may be viewed as a multivariate function $y = f(x_1, x_2, \cdots, x_m)$, which depends on the parameters of all neurons in the hidden layer. A different set of parameters will result in a different function. Assume we use N neurons in the hidden layer, so if we vary all possible parameters of these N neurons, this MLP could represent many different functions. Let us represent all of these functions as a set, denoted as Λ_N. If we use more neurons in the hidden layer (i.e., $N' > N$), an MLP may be able to represent more functions, namely, $\Lambda_N \subseteq \Lambda_{N'}$.

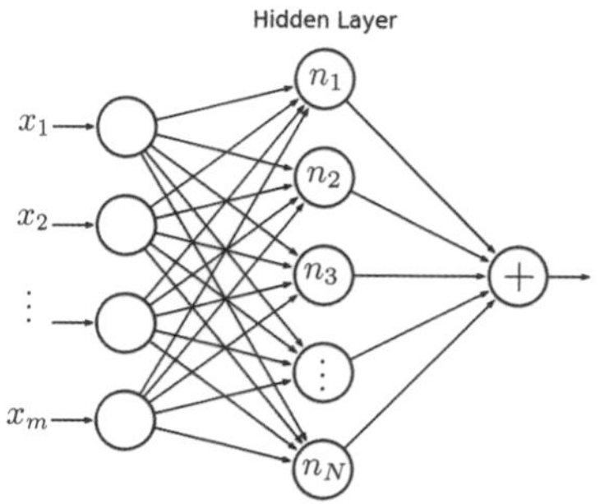

Figure 8.6: An illustration of an MLP of N neurons in the hidden layer.

The universal approximator theory states that if we are allowed to use a large number of neurons in the hidden layer and we select a suitable common nonlinear activation for all neurons, an MLP can approximate any function up to arbitrary precision. The following discussion presents two major results in the universal approximator theory without proof. The proofs are out of the scope of this book because they require many techniques from modern analysis. Interested readers may refer to Hornik [102] and Asadi and Jiang [3] for more details.

Theorem 8.1.1 *Denote all continuous functions on $\mathbb{R}^m$ as C. If the nonlinear activation function $\phi(\cdot)$ is continuous, bounded, and nonconstant, then Λ_N is dense in C as $N \to \infty$ (i.e., $\lim_{N\to\infty} \Lambda_N = C$).*

This theorem applies to the cases where we use sigmoid or tanh as the activation function for the neurons in the hidden layer. As Theorem 8.1.1 states, as we use more and more neurons in the hidden layer, the MLP will be able to represent any continuous function on $\mathbb{R}^m$.

Theorem 8.1.2 *Denote all L^p functions on $\mathbb{R}^m$ as L^p. If the nonlinear activation function $\phi(\cdot)$ is the ReLU function, then Λ_N is dense in L^p as $N \to \infty$ (i.e., $\lim_{N\to\infty} \Lambda_N = L^p$).*

Theorem 8.1.2 states that as we use more and more ReLU neurons in the hidden layer, the MLP will be able to represent any L^p function ($p > 1$). As previously mentioned, any function arising from a physical process must belong to L^2 because of the limited-energy constraint. Roughly speaking, an MLP consisting of a large number of ReLU neurons in the hidden layer will be able to represent any function we encounter in real-world applications, regardless of whether it is linear or nonlinear.

A conceptual way to understand the universal approximator theory is shown in Figure 8.7. If we represent the sets of functions that can be represented by an MLP using $N = 1, 2, \cdots$ neurons in the hidden layer as $\Lambda_1, \Lambda_2, \cdots$, under some minor conditions (e.g., the parameters of all neurons are bounded), each of these sets constitutes a subset inside the whole function space (either C or L^p depending on the choice of the activation function). These sets form a nested structure because an MLP can represent more functions after each new neuron is added. As we add more and more neurons, the modeling power of MLP keeps growing, and it will eventually occupy the whole function space.

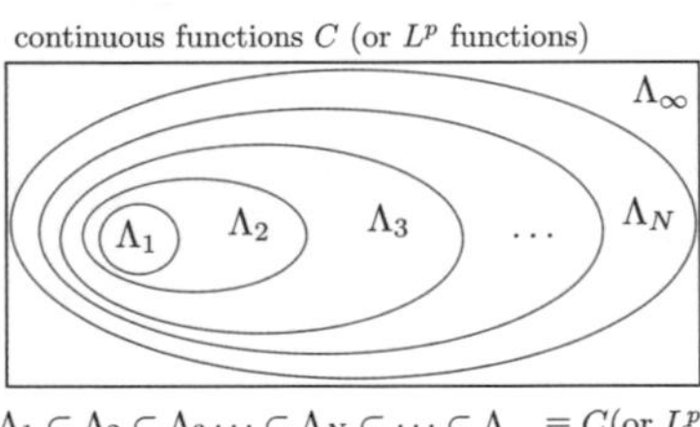

Figure 8.7: An illustration of the nested structure of function approximators using MLPs.

As we have seen, the universal approximator theory only considers a very simple structure to construct neural networks, namely, the MLP in Figure 8.6. As we will see later, there are many other structures for constructing neural networks. Some of those structures include MLP as a special case, such as deep structures of multiple hidden layers. Some of them may be viewed as special cases of MLPs, such as convolutional layers. Generally speaking, the universal approximator theory equally applies to these well-defined network structures. The key message here is that well-structured and sufficiently large neural networks are able to represent any function we are interested in for all real-world problems. Therefore, ANNs represent a very general class of nonlinear models for machine learning. The next section introduces some popular network structures we can use to construct large-scale neural networks.

8.2 Neural Network Structures

In our brains, our biological neuronal networks grow from scratch after we are born, and the network structures are constantly changing as we learn. However, we have not found any effective machine learning methods that can automatically learn a network structure from data. When we use ANNs, we have to first predetermine the network structure based on the nature of the data, as well as our domain knowledge. After that, some powerful learning algorithms are used to learn all parameters in the neural network to yield a good model for our underlying tasks. This section presents some common structures for neural networks and the reasons we may choose each particular structure.

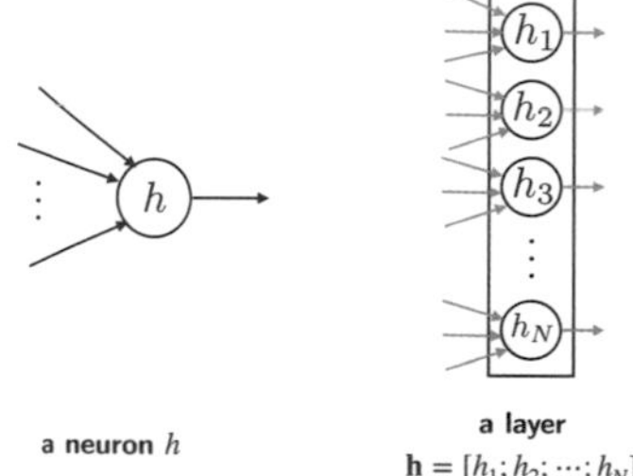

Figure 8.8: An illustration of a neuron versus a layer of neurons: a neuron represents a scalar, and a layer represents a vector.

As we have discussed, a neuron is the basic unit for building all neural networks. Mathematically speaking, each neuron represents a variable that indicates the status of a hidden unit in the network or an intermediate result in computation. In practice, we prefer to group multiple neurons into a larger unit, called a *layer*, for network construction. As shown in Figure 8.8, a layer consists of any number of neurons. All neurons in a layer are normally not interconnected to each other but instead may be connected to other layers. Mathematically speaking, each layer of neurons represents a vector in computation. As we will see, all common neural network structures can be constructed by organizing different layers of neurons in a certain way. Therefore, in the following, we will treat a layer of neurons as the basic unit to build all sorts of neural networks.

8.2.1 Basic Building Blocks to Connect Layers

Let us first introduce some basic operations that can be used to connect two different layers in a neural network. These simple operations constitute the basic building blocks for any complex neural network.

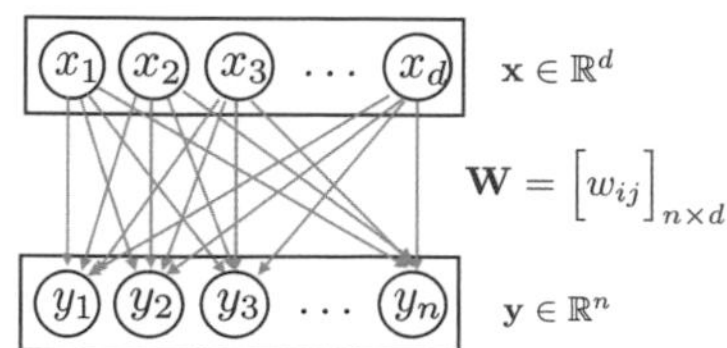

Figure 8.9: An illustration of two layers fully connected through a linear transformation.

- **Full connection**
  A straightforward way to connect two layers is to use full linear connections between them. The output from every neuron in the first layer is connected to every neuron in the second layer through a weighted link along with a bias, as shown in Figure 8.9. In this case, the input to each node in the second layer is a linear combination

of all outputs from the first layer. The computation in such a full connection can be represented as the following matrix form:

$$\mathbf{y} = \mathbf{W}\mathbf{x} + \mathbf{b},$$

where $\mathbf{W} \in \mathbb{R}^{n \times d}$ and $\mathbf{b} \in \mathbb{R}^n$ denote all parameters used to make such a full connection. We need in total $n \times (d+1)$ parameters to fully connect a layer of d neurons to another layer of n neurons. The total number of parameters to make a full connection is quadratic to the size of the layers. The computational complexity of such a full connection is $O(n \times d)$.

As we have seen in the MLP example, the fully connected layers are particularly suitable in constructing neural networks for *universal function approximation*. In practice, instead of using one very large hidden layer as in the MLP, we can also cascade many narrower layers through several full-connection operations (of course, each linear connection is followed by a nonlinear activation function). It is believed that these cascaded layers require far fewer parameters than one really wide layer for the same approximation precision.

▶ **Convolution**

The convolution sum is a well-known linear operation in digital signal processing. This operation can also be used to connect two layers in a neural network [76, 141]. As shown in Figure 8.10, we use a *kernel* (a.k.a. *filter* in signal processing) $\mathbf{w} \in \mathbb{R}^f$ to scan through all positions in the first layer. At each position, an output is computed by element-wise multiplications and summed:

$$y_j = \sum_{i=1}^{f} w_i \times x_{j+i-1} \quad (\forall j = 1, 2, \cdots, n).$$

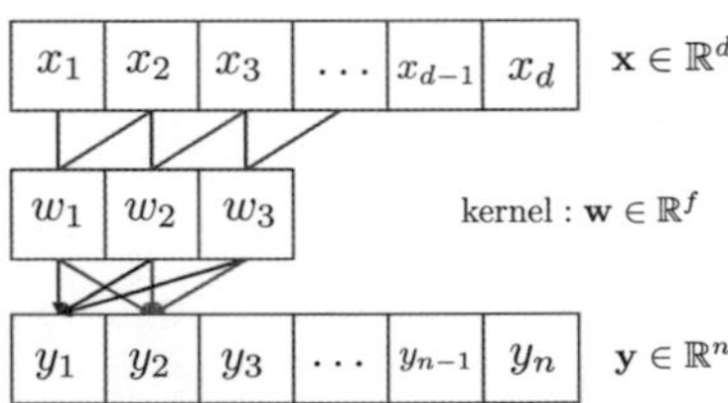

Figure 8.10: An illustration of two layers that are connected by a convolution sum using one kernel.

$$y_1 = w_1 \cdot x_1 + w_2 \cdot x_2 + w_3 \cdot x_3 + \cdots$$

$$y_2 = w_1 \cdot x_2 + w_2 \cdot x_3 + w_3 \cdot x_4 + \cdots$$

$$y_3 = w_1 \cdot x_3 + w_2 \cdot x_4 + w_3 \cdot x_5 + \cdots$$

$$\vdots$$

For convenience, we may also use a generic notation to represent the convolution operation as

$$\mathbf{y} = \mathbf{x} * \mathbf{w} \quad (\mathbf{x} \in \mathbb{R}^d, \ \mathbf{w} \in \mathbb{R}^f, \ \mathbf{y} \in \mathbb{R}^n),$$

where the kernel $\mathbf{w}$ represents the learnable parameters in each convolution connection.

When we use the convolution operation to connect two layers of neurons, the number of neurons in the second layer cannot be arbitrary. For example, if we have d neurons in the first layer and use a kernel of f weights, we can easily calculate the number of neurons in the second layer to be $n = d - f + 1$. Of course, we can change the number of outputs of convolution by slightly varying the operation. For example, when we slide the kernel through the first layer, we

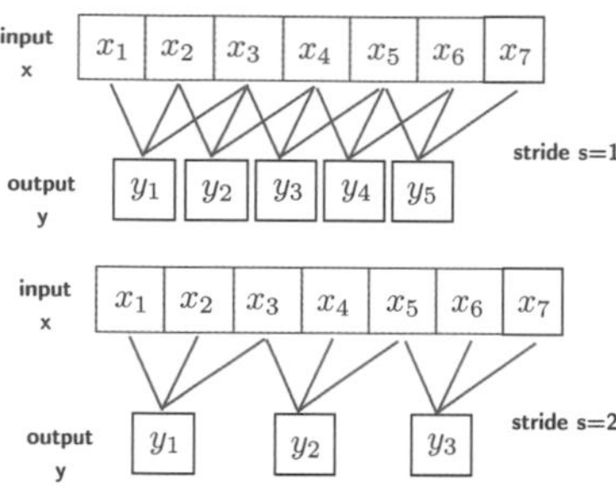

Figure 8.11: An illustration of two different strides ($s = 1, 2$) in a convolution operation connecting two layers ($d = 7$ and $f = 3$).

can take a different *stride* $s = 1, 2, \cdots$, as shown in Figure 8.11. When a larger stride $s > 1$ is used, we will get fewer outputs. On the other hand, we may *pad* some 0s in both ends of the input layer so that we can slide the kernel beyond the original ends of the input layer when the convolution sum is conducted. This will result in more outputs for the second layer. No matter what, when we use convolution to connect two layers, the number of neurons in the second layer must match the setting used for convolution. Moreover, we can see that the computation complexity in this convolution operation is $O(d \times f)$.

Compared with full connection, convolution has two unique properties. First, convolution is suitable for *locality modeling*. Each output in the second layer only depends on a local region in the input layer. When a proper kernel is used, convolution is good at capturing a certain local feature in the input. On the other hand, in fully connected layers, every output neuron depends on all neurons in the input layer. Secondly, convolution allows *weight sharing* among output neurons. Each output neuron is generated with the same set of weights on different inputs. Because of this, when we connect a layer of d neurons to another layer of n neurons as in Figure 8.10, we only need to use a kernel of f weights ($f < d$). If we connect the same layers with a full connection, we need to use $n \times (d + 1)$ parameters. This is a huge saving in model parameters.

Furthermore, we can show that convolution may be viewed as a special case of full connection, where many of the connections have 0 weights. Alternatively, a full connection can also be viewed as a convolution using specially chosen kernels. These are left as Exercise Q8.1.

- **Nonlinear activation**

As we have seen, each neuron includes a nonlinear activation function $\phi(\cdot)$ as part of its computation. We may apply this activation function to all neurons in a layer jointly, as shown in Figure 8.12. In this case, the two layers have the same number of neurons, and the activation function is applied to each pair as follows: $y_i = \phi(x_i)$ ($\forall i = 1, 2, \cdots, n$). We represent this as a compact vector form:

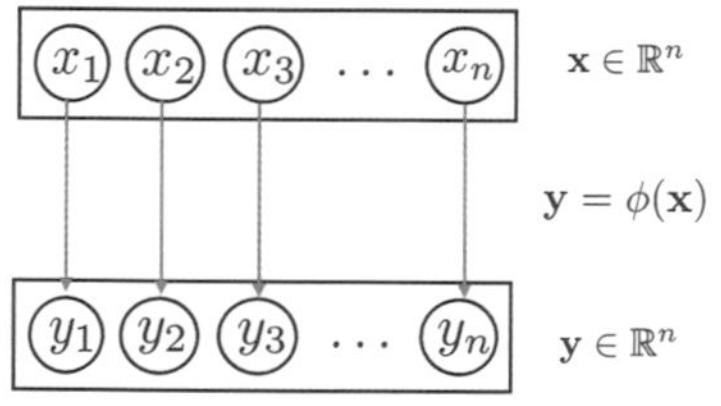

Figure 8.12: An illustration of two layers that are connected by a nonlinear activation function.

$$\mathbf{y} = \phi(\mathbf{x}),$$

where the activation function $\phi(\cdot)$ is applied to the input vector $\mathbf{x}$ element-wise. We may choose ReLU, sigmoid, or tanh for $\phi(\cdot)$. No matter which one we use, there is no learnable parameter in this activation connection.

► **Softmax**

As shown in Eq. (6.18), *softmax* is a special function that maps an n-dimensional vector $\mathbf{x}$ ($\mathbf{x} \in \mathbb{R}^n$) into another n-dimensional vector $\mathbf{y}$ inside the hypercube $[0,1]^n$ [36, 35]. Every element in $\mathbf{y}$ is a positive number between $[0,1]$, and all elements of $\mathbf{y}$ sum to 1. Thus, $\mathbf{y}$ behaves similarly as a discrete probability distribution over n classes. As shown in Figure 8.13, we use the softmax function to connect two layers with the same number of neurons. This connection is usually represented as the following compact vector form:

$$\mathbf{y} = \text{softmax}(\mathbf{x}).$$

The softmax connection is usually used as the last layer of a neural network so that the neural network is made to generate probability-like outputs. Similar to the activation connection, the connection using the softmax function does not have any learnable parameters.

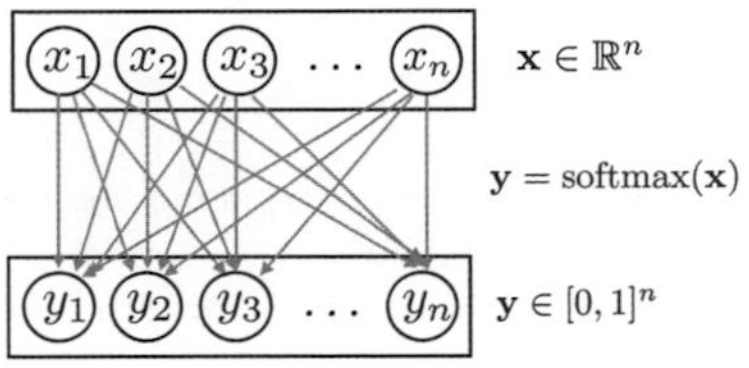

Figure 8.13: An illustration of two layers that are connected by the softmax function.

Note that in a softmax function $\mathbf{y} = \text{softmax}(\mathbf{x})$, for all $i = 1, 2, \cdots, n$, we have

$$y_i = \frac{e^{x_i}}{\sum_{j=1}^{n} e^{x_j}}.$$

► **Max-pooling**

Max-pooling is a convenient way to shrink the size of a layer [254]. In the max-pooling operation by m, a window of m neurons is slid over the input layer with a stride of m, and the maximum value within the window is computed as the output at each position. If the input layer contains n neurons, then the output layer will have $\frac{n}{m}$ neurons, each of which keeps the maximum value at each window position. This operation is usually represented as the following vector form:

$$\mathbf{y} = \text{maxpool}_{/m}(\mathbf{x}) \quad (\mathbf{x} \in \mathbb{R}^n, \mathbf{y} \in \mathbb{R}^{\frac{n}{m}}).$$

The max-pooling operation does not have any learnable parameters as well, and the window size m needs to be set as a hyperparameter. As we can see, the max-pooling operation helps to make the output less sensitive to small translation variations in input.

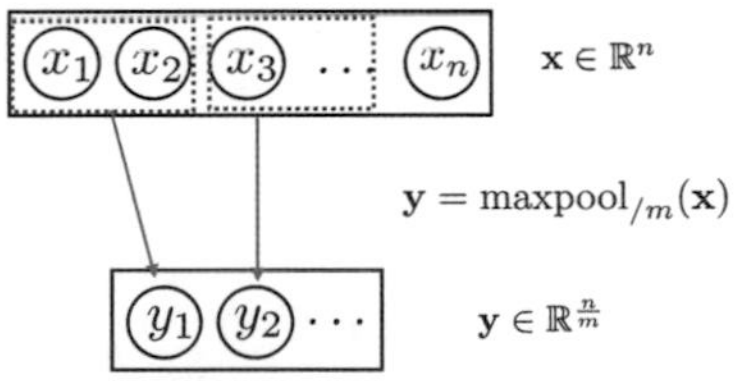

Figure 8.14: An illustration of two layers that are connected by the max-pooling function by m.

► **Normalization**

In deep neural networks, some normalization operations are introduced to normalize the dynamic ranges of neuron outputs. In a very deep neural network, the outputs of some neurons may vastly differ from that of others in a different part of the network if their inputs flow through very different paths. It is believed that a good normalization helps to smooth out the loss function of the neural networks so that it will significantly facilitate the learning of neural networks. These normalization operations are usually based on some local statistics as well as a few rescaling parameters to be learned. Due to the computational efficiency, the local statistics are usually

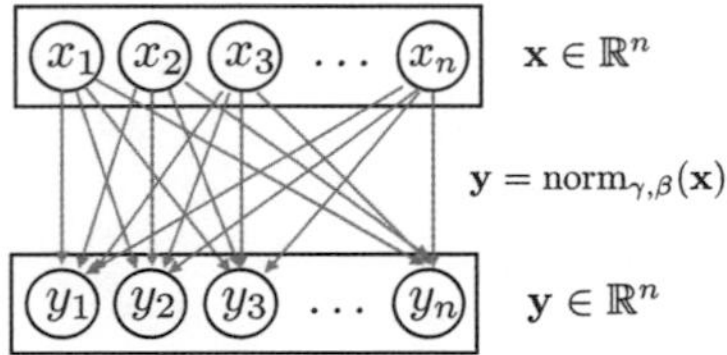

Figure 8.15: An illustration of two layers that are connected by a normalization function with two rescaling parameters $\boldsymbol{\gamma}$ and $\boldsymbol{\beta}$.

accumulated from the current mini-batch because all results for the current mini-batch are readily available in memory. The most popular normalization is the so-called *batch normalization* [108]. As shown in Figure 8.15, batch normalization will normalize each dimension x_i in an input vector $\mathbf{x}$ ($\in \mathbb{R}^n$) into the corresponding element y_i in the output vector $\mathbf{y}$ ($\in \mathbb{R}^n$) using the following two steps:

Note that $\mu_{\text{B}}(i)$ and $\sigma^2_{\text{B}}(i)$ stand for the sample mean and the sample variance of ith dimension x_i of input $\mathbf{x}$ over the current mini-batch B:

$$\mu_{\text{B}}(i) = \frac{1}{|B|}\sum_{\mathbf{x}\in B} x_i$$

$$\sigma^2_{\text{B}}(i) = \frac{1}{|B|}\sum_{\mathbf{x}\in B} (x_i - \mu_{\text{B}}(i))^2.$$

A small positive number $\epsilon > 0$ is used here to stabilize the cases where the sample variances become very small.

$$\text{normalize:} \quad \hat{x}_i = \frac{x_i - \mu_{\text{B}}(i)}{\sqrt{\sigma^2_{\text{B}}(i) + \epsilon}} \quad (\forall i \in \{1, 2, \cdots n\})$$

$$\text{rescaling :} \quad y_i = \gamma_i \hat{x}_i + \beta_i \quad (\forall i \in \{1, 2, \cdots n\}),$$

where $\mu_{\text{B}}(i)$ and $\sigma^2_{\text{B}}(i)$ denote the sample mean and the sample variance over the current mini-batch, respectively (see margin note), and $\boldsymbol{\gamma}$ ($\in \mathbb{R}^n$) and $\boldsymbol{\beta}$ ($\in \mathbb{R}^n$) are two learnable parameter vectors in each batch-normalization connection. This batch normalization is usually expressed as the following compact vector form:

$$\mathbf{y} = \text{BN}_{\boldsymbol{\gamma},\boldsymbol{\beta}}(\mathbf{x}) \quad (\mathbf{x}, \mathbf{y} \in \mathbb{R}^n). \tag{8.1}$$

When very small mini-batches are used in training, the local statistics estimated from such a small sample set may become unreliable. To solve this problem, there is a slightly different normalization operation, called *layer normalization* [7], where local statistics are estimated over all dimensions in each input vector $\mathbf{x}$:

$$\mu = \frac{1}{n}\sum_{i=1}^{n} x_i \qquad \sigma^2 = \frac{1}{n}\sum_{i=1}^{n}(x_i - \mu)^2.$$

Then μ and σ^2 are used in the previously described two-step normalization for the current input $\mathbf{x}$ in place of $\mu_B(i)$ and $\sigma^2_B(i)$. The layer normalization is similarly represented by the following compact vector form:

$$\mathbf{y} = \text{LN}_{\boldsymbol{\gamma},\boldsymbol{\beta}}(\mathbf{x}) \quad (\mathbf{x}, \mathbf{y} \in \mathbb{R}^n).$$

As we already discussed, the main reason why we use the normalization connections is to facilitate the learning of neural networks because these normalization operations can make the loss function much smoother. In these cases, some larger learning rates may be used in training, and in turn, the learning will converge much faster. We will come back to these issues when we discuss the learning algorithms for neural networks.

Relying on the aforementioned operations to connect various layers, we can already construct many very powerful feed-forward neural networks that map each fixed-sized input to another fixed-sized output. The drawback of these networks is that they are usually memoryless. In other words, the current output solely depends on the current input. This makes these networks unsuitable for handling variable-length sequential data because there is no easy way to feed them to these networks. The following discussion introduces several common operations that will add memory mechanisms to neural networks. After these operations are added, a neural network will be able to memorize historical information so that the current output depends on not only the current input but also on all inputs in the previous time instances.

- **Time-delayed feedback**
A simple strategy to introduce the memory mechanism into neural networks is to add some time-delayed feedback paths. As shown in Figure 8.16, a time-delayed path (in red) is used to send the status of a layer $\mathbf{y}$ back to a previous layer (closer to the input end) as a part of its next input. The time-delayed unit is represented as

$$\mathbf{y}_{t-1} = z^{-1}(\mathbf{y}_t),$$

where $\mathbf{y}_t$ and $\mathbf{y}_{t-1}$ denote the values of the layer $\mathbf{y}$ at time instances t and $t-1$, and z^{-1} indicates a time-delay unit, which is physically implemented as a memory unit storing the current value of $\mathbf{y}$ for the next time instance. At any time instance t, the lower-level layer $\mathbf{x}$ usually takes both $\mathbf{y}_{t-1}$ and the new input to produce its output. The time-delayed feedback paths introduce cycles into the network. The neural networks containing such feedback paths are usually called *recurrent neural networks (RNNs)*. RNNs can remember the past history because the old information may flow along these cycles over and over. We know recurrent feedbacks are abundant in biological neuronal networks as one of the major mechanisms for short-term memory. However, these feedback paths impose some significant challenges in the learning of ANNs. RNNs are discussed in detail on page 170.

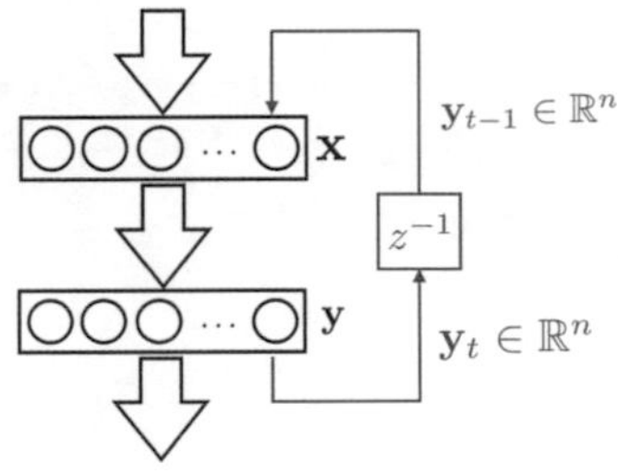

Figure 8.16: An illustration of how to use a time-delayed path (in red) to introduce recurrent feedback in neural networks.

- **Tapped delay line**
Another possible way to introduce memory mechanisms into neural networks without using any recurrent feedback is to use a structure called a *tapped delay line* [246, 262, 265], which is essentially a number of synchronized memory units aligned in a line. As shown in Figure 8.17, these memory units are synchronized to store the values of the layer $\mathbf{y}$ at all previous time instances (i.e., $\{\mathbf{y}_t, \mathbf{y}_{t-1}, \mathbf{y}_{t-2}, \cdots\}$). At the next time instance $t+1$, all values saved in these memory units are shifted right by 1 unit. The number of the saved historical values depends on the length of the tapped delay line, that is, the

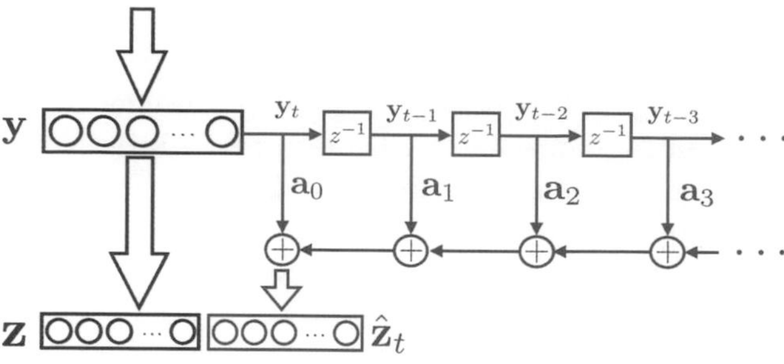

Figure 8.17: An illustration of nonrecurrent memory module using a tapped-delay-line structure (in red), where $\hat{\mathbf{z}}_t$ and $\mathbf{z}$ are concatenated to feed to the next layer.

total number of memory units in the line. In some cases, we can use a large number of memory units to store all historical values in an input sequence. At each time instance t, all stored values in the tapped delay line are linearly combined through some learnable parameters (i.e., $\{\mathbf{a}_0, \mathbf{a}_1, \mathbf{a}_2, \cdots\}$) to generate a new layer of outputs, denoted as $\hat{\mathbf{z}}_t$:

$$\hat{\mathbf{z}}_t = \sum_{i=0}^{L-1} \mathbf{a}_i \otimes \mathbf{y}_{t-i},$$

where L denotes the length of the tapped delay line. Here, each of the learnable parameters, $\mathbf{a}_i$, may be chosen as a scalar, vector, or matrix. If $\mathbf{a}_i$ is a scalar, $\otimes$ stands for multiplication; if $\mathbf{a}_i$ is a vector, $\otimes$ stands for element-wise multiplication between two vectors; if $\mathbf{a}_i$ is a matrix, $\otimes$ stands for matrix multiplication. An important aspect of this structure is that the generated vector $\hat{\mathbf{z}}_t$ will be sent to the next layer (closer to the output end) so that it will not introduce any cycle into the network. The overall network remains as a nonrecurrent feed-forward structure, but it possesses strong memory capability as a result of the introduced memory units in the tapped delay line. The learning algorithm for these network structures is the same as that of other feed-forward networks.
As another note is that if we are allowed to delay the decision at time t to $t + L'$, the tapped delay line can even look ahead. In this case, when the decision for time t is made, the tapped delay line already stores all values of $\mathbf{y}$ from time $t - L$ to $t + L'$. The future information in the look-ahead window $[t + 1, t + L']$ is also incorporated into the output vector $\hat{\mathbf{z}}_t$.

▶ **Attention**
In the tapped-delay-line structure, the coefficients $\{\mathbf{a}_0, \mathbf{a}_1, \mathbf{a}_2, \cdots\}$ are all learnable parameters. Once these parameters are learned, they remain constant, just like other network parameters. The attention mechanism aims to dynamically adjust these coefficients to select the most prominent features from all saved historical information based on the current input condition from outside and/or the present in-

ternal status of the network. An attention mechanism is critical in modeling long-span dependency in very long sequences [8]. The long-span dependency is widespread in natural language. For example, the interpretation of a word may depend on another word or phrase located far away in the context.

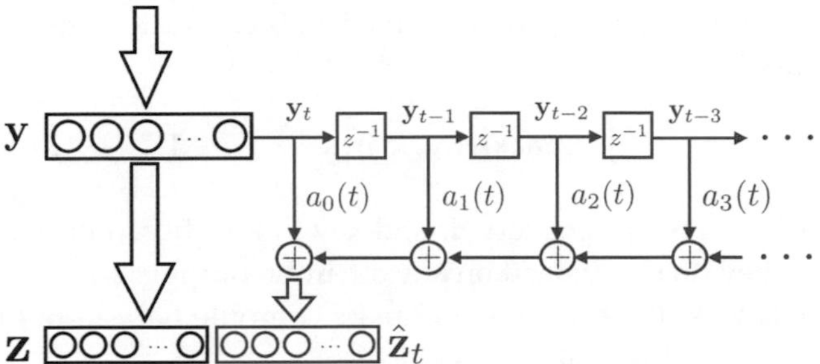

Figure 8.18: An illustration of the attention mechanism (in red) in neural networks, where time-variant coefficients $\{a_0(t), a_1(t), \cdots\}$ are used to combine all saved historical values $\{\mathbf{y}_t, \mathbf{y}_{t-1}, \cdots\}$ to generate $\hat{\mathbf{z}}_t$ at each time t.

The attention mechanism is usually implemented using a special tapped-delay-line structure, as shown in Figure 8.18, where we use time-variant scalar coefficients $\{a_0(t), a_1(t), \cdots\}$ to combine all saved historical values $\{\mathbf{y}_t, \mathbf{y}_{t-1}, \cdots\}$. These time-variant scalar coefficients are dynamically computed by an attention function $g(\cdot)$ at each time instance t, which will take the current input condition from outside and the present internal status of the network as two inputs to generate a set of scalars, as follows:

The attention function $g(\mathbf{q}_t, \mathbf{k}_t) \in \mathbb{R}^L$ takes two vectors as input and generates an L-dimensional vector as output.

$$\mathbf{c}_t \stackrel{\Delta}{=} \begin{bmatrix} c_0(t) & c_1(t) & \cdots & c_{L-1}(t) \end{bmatrix}^\intercal = g(\mathbf{q}_t, \mathbf{k}_t),$$

where the two vectors $\mathbf{q}_t$ and $\mathbf{k}_t$ denote the current input condition and the internal system status at time t, which are sometimes called the *query* $\mathbf{q}_t \in \mathbb{R}^l$ and the *key* $\mathbf{k}_t \in \mathbb{R}^l$. Next, these outputs from the attention function are usually normalized by the softmax function to ensure all attention coefficients are positive and summed to 1:

$$\mathbf{a}_t \stackrel{\Delta}{=} \begin{bmatrix} a_0(t) & a_1(t) & \cdots & a_{L-1}(t) \end{bmatrix}^\intercal = \text{softmax}(\mathbf{c}_t).$$

At each time t, the attention module generates the output $\hat{\mathbf{z}}_t$ as

In short, the attention mechanism can be viewed as a dynamic way to generate time-variant coefficients in the tapped delay line for each t as follows:

$$\mathbf{a}_t = \text{softmax}\big(g(\mathbf{q}_t, \mathbf{k}_t)\big).$$

$$\hat{\mathbf{z}}_t = \sum_{i=0}^{L-1} a_i(t)\mathbf{y}_{t-i} = \begin{bmatrix} \mathbf{y}_t \; \mathbf{y}_{t-1} & \cdots & \mathbf{y}_{t-L+1} \end{bmatrix} \mathbf{a}_t.$$

This attention mechanism is pretty flexible because we can choose a different attention function $g(\cdot)$ and also select different vectors as the query and key for various modeling purposes. Similarly, the look-ahead window can be used here to make sure that the attention mechanism can select features not just from the past but also from the future. If we have enough resources to make the tapped delay line very long, for any input sequence of total T items, we can store all $\mathbf{y} \in \mathbb{R}^n$ of the sequence as a large matrix:

$$\mathbf{V} = \begin{bmatrix} \mathbf{y}_T & \mathbf{y}_{T-1} & \cdots & \mathbf{y}_1 \end{bmatrix}_{n \times T}$$

where this matrix V is sometimes called a *value matrix*. In this case, at any time t, the attention mechanism is conducted over all saved values in $\mathbf{V}$:

$$\hat{\mathbf{z}}_t = \mathbf{V} \begin{bmatrix} \text{softmax}\big(g(\mathbf{q}_t, \mathbf{k}_t)\big) \end{bmatrix}_{T \times 1} \quad (\forall t \in 1, 2, \cdots, T). \tag{8.2}$$

Furthermore, if the query $\mathbf{q}_t$ and key $\mathbf{k}_t$ are chosen in such a way that they do not depend on any attention outputs $\hat{\mathbf{z}}_t$, all queries $\mathbf{q}_t$ and keys $\mathbf{k}_t$ ($\forall t \in 1, 2, \cdots, T$) can be computed ahead of time and packed into two matrices as follows:

$$\mathbf{Q} \triangleq \begin{bmatrix} \mathbf{q}_T & \mathbf{q}_{T-1} & \cdots & \mathbf{q}_1 \end{bmatrix}_{l \times T}$$

$$\mathbf{K} \triangleq \begin{bmatrix} \mathbf{k}_T & \mathbf{k}_{T-1} & \cdots & \mathbf{k}_1 \end{bmatrix}_{l \times T}$$

where $\mathbf{Q}$ and $\mathbf{K}$ are normally called the *query* and *key* matrices. Therefore, the attention operations for all time instances $t = 1, 2, \cdots, T$ can be represented as the following compact matrix form:

In this context, the attention function $g(\cdot)$ takes two matrices as input and generates a $T \times T$ matrix as output. Each column of the output matrix is computed as previously based on one column from each input matrix (i.e., $g(\mathbf{q}_t, \mathbf{k}_t)$).

$$\hat{\mathbf{Z}} = \mathbf{V} \ \text{softmax}\big(g(\mathbf{Q}, \mathbf{K})\big), \tag{8.3}$$

where $\hat{\mathbf{Z}} \triangleq \begin{bmatrix} \hat{\mathbf{z}}_T \cdots \hat{\mathbf{z}}_2 \ \hat{\mathbf{z}}_1 \end{bmatrix}$ and the softmax function is applied to $g(\mathbf{Q}, \mathbf{K})$ ($\in \mathbb{R}^{T \times T}$) column-wise.
Therefore, the attention mechanism represents a very flexible and complex computation in neural networks, and it depends on how we choose the following four elements:

1. **Attention function** $g(\cdot)$
2. **Value matrix V**
3. **Query matrix Q**
4. **Key matrix K**

Unlike other introduced operations that are used to link only two layers of neurons, the attention mechanism involves many layers in a network. The attention mechanism plays an important role in a popular neural network structure recently proposed to handle long text sequences, called *transformers* [244], to be introduced later on page 172.

Now that we have covered the most basic building blocks that we can use to connect layers of neurons to construct various architectures for large neural networks, the next sections present several popular neural network models as our case studies. In particular, we will explore the traditional fully connected deep neural networks, convolutional neural networks, recurrent neural networks, and the more recent transformers.

8.2.2 Case Study I: Fully Connected Deep Neural Networks

Fully connected deep neural networks are the most traditional architecture for deep learning, which usually consist of one input layer at the beginning, one output layer at the end, and any number of hidden layers in between. As shown in Figure 8.19, these feed-forward networks are memoryless, and they take a fixed-size vector as input and sequentially process the input through several fully connected hidden layers until the final output is generated from the output layer.

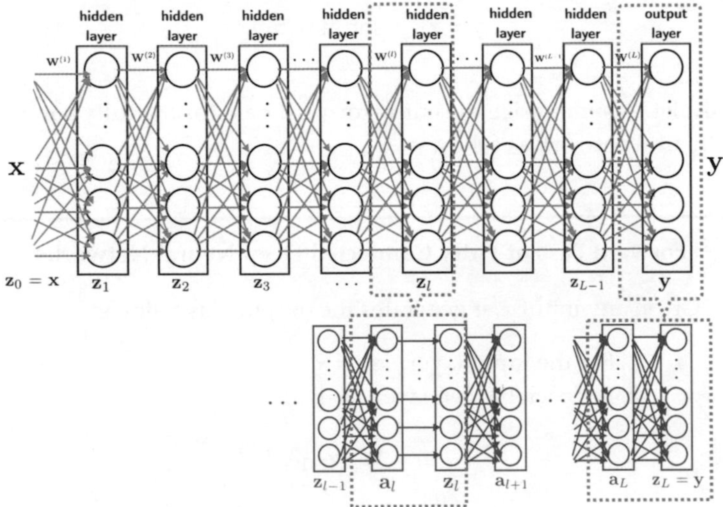

Figure 8.19: An illustration of a fully connected neural network consisting of $L-1$ hidden layers and one softmax output layer.

The input layer simply takes an input vector $\mathbf{x}$ and sends it to the first hidden layer. Each hidden layer is essentially composed of two sublayers, which we name as the *linear sublayer* and the *nonlinear sublayer*, denoted as $\mathbf{a}_l$ and $\mathbf{z}_l$ for the lth hidden layer. As shown in Figure 8.19, the linear sublayer $\mathbf{a}_l$ is connected to the previous nonlinear sublayer $\mathbf{z}_{l-1}$ through a full connection:

$$\mathbf{a}_l = \mathbf{W}^{(l)}\mathbf{z}_{l-1} + \mathbf{b}^{(l)} \quad (\forall l = 1, 2, \cdots, L-1),$$

where $\mathbf{W}^{(l)}$ and $\mathbf{b}^{(l)}$ denote the weight matrix and the bias vector of the full connection in the lth hidden layer, respectively. On the other hand, the linear sublayer $\mathbf{a}_l$ is connected to $\mathbf{z}_l$ through a nonlinear activation operation. If we use ReLU as the activation function $\phi(\cdot)$ for all hidden layers, then we have

$$\mathbf{z}_l = \text{ReLU}(\mathbf{a}_l) \quad (\forall l = 1, 2, \cdots, L-1).$$

Many hidden layers can be cascaded in this way to form a deep neural network. Finally, the last layer is the output layer that generates the final output $\mathbf{y}$ for this deep neural network. If the network is used for classification, the output layer usually uses the softmax function to yield probability-like outputs for all different classes. Therefore, the output layer can also be broken down into two sublayers (i.e., $\mathbf{a}_L$ and $\mathbf{z}_L$). Here, $\mathbf{a}_L$ is connected to the previous $\mathbf{z}_{L-1}$ through a full connection in the same way as previously:

$$\mathbf{a}_L = \mathbf{W}^{(L)}\mathbf{z}_{L-1} + \mathbf{b}^{(L)},$$

but $\mathbf{a}_L$ is connected to $\mathbf{z}_L$, being equal to the final output of the whole network, through a softmax operation as follows:

$$\mathbf{y} = \mathbf{z}_L = \text{softmax}(\mathbf{a}_L).$$

Finally, let us summarize the entire forward pass for the fully connected deep neural network as follows:

Forward Pass of Fully Connected Deep Neural Networks

Given any input $\mathbf{x}$, it generates the output $\mathbf{y}$ as follows:

1. For the input layer: $\mathbf{z}_0 = \mathbf{x}$
2. For each hidden layer $l = 1, 2, \cdots, L-1$:

$$\mathbf{a}_l = \mathbf{W}^{(l)}\mathbf{z}_{l-1} + \mathbf{b}^{(l)}$$

$$\mathbf{z}_l = \text{ReLU}(\mathbf{a}_l)$$

3. For the output layer:

$$\mathbf{a}_L = \mathbf{W}^{(L)}\mathbf{z}_{L-1} + \mathbf{b}^{(L)}$$

$$\mathbf{y} = \mathbf{z}_L = \text{softmax}(\mathbf{a}_L)$$

8.2.3 Case Study II: Convolutional Neural Networks

Another popular architecture for neural networks is the so-called *convolutional neural networks (CNNs)*. At present, CNNs are the dominant machine learning models to handle visual data, such as images and videos. CNNs are also periodically applied to many other applications involving sequential data, such as speech, audio, and text. Conceptually speaking, CNNs take advantage of the basic idea behind the convolution sum to perform locality modeling over high-dimensional data. Compared with fully connected neural networks, the convolution operation forces CNNs to focus more on the local features in high-dimensional data, which is more akin to human perception. The aforementioned one-dimensional (1D) convolution connection by itself is too simple and needs to be significantly expanded along several dimensions to be able to handle real-world data. The following list introduces four major extensions on top of the simple 1D convolution sum and shows how these extensions eventually lead to the popular CNN structures.

- **Extension 1: allow multiple feature plies in input**
  In the simple 1D convolution sum shown in Figure 8.10, we assume there is only one feature at each input location. However, many real-world data may contain multiple features at each position. For example, each pixel in a color image is represented by three values (R/G/B). Therefore, we can extend the previous setting to allow multiple features at each input location. These different features form multiple *plies* (a.k.a. *maps*) in the input. As shown in Figure 8.20, if we assume the input $\mathbf{x}$ contains p feature plies, the input data become a $p \times d$ matrix. In order to handle the multiple plies in input, we also need to extend the kernel into a $p \times f$ matrix. When we conduct the convolution sum, we still slide the kernel $\mathbf{w}$ over the input $\mathbf{x}$. At each position, the kernel $\mathbf{w}$ covers a $p \times f$ chunk of the input, and an output is still computed by element-wise multiplication and summation. By default, the total number of outputs is $n = d - f + 1$. Similarly, we may change the number of outputs by varying the stride and zero-padding settings. This convolution can be represented as follows:

$$y_j = \sum_{k=1}^{p} \sum_{i=1}^{f} w_{i,k} \times x_{j+i-1,k} \qquad (\forall j = 1, 2, \cdots, n).$$

  We also use the following generic matrix notation to represent this convolution:

$$\mathbf{y} = \mathbf{x} * \mathbf{w} \qquad (\mathbf{x} \in \mathbb{R}^{d \times p},\ \mathbf{w} \in \mathbb{R}^{f \times p},\ \mathbf{y} \in \mathbb{R}^{n}).$$

  We can calculate that the computational complexity of this convolution is $O(d \cdot f \cdot p)$. The number of parameters we need to connect input and output is $p \times f$. The kernel still focuses on local features along the input dimension, but the local features are computed over all feature plies.

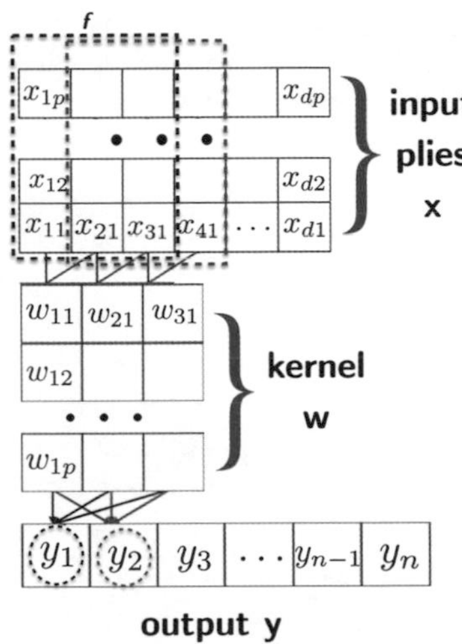

Figure 8.20: An illustration of the 1D convolution sum involving multiple input feature plies.

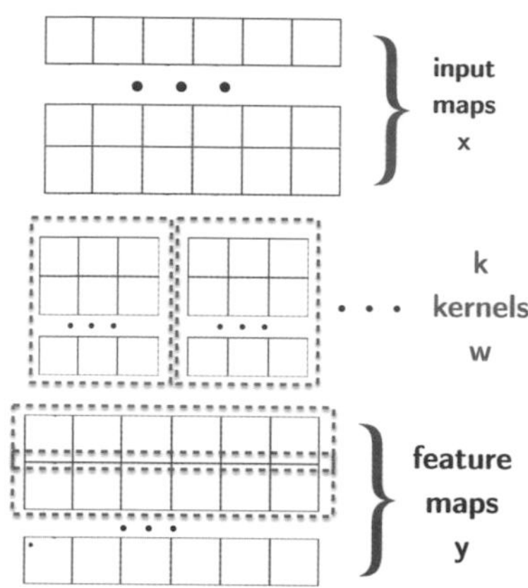

Figure 8.21: An illustration of the 1D convolution sum involving multiple input feature plies and multiple kernels.

▶ **Extension 2: allow multiple kernels**
If all parameters of the kernel are set properly, the kernel can capture only one particular local feature in the input. If we are interested in capturing multiple local features in the input, we can extend the model to use multiple kernels in the convolution. As shown in Figure 8.21, each kernel is slid over the input maps to generate a sequence of outputs. Assuming we use k different kernels, we will end up with k different output sequences, each of which contains n values as before. This $k \times n$ output is sometimes called the *feature map*. Meanwhile, all k kernels may be represented as an $f \times p \times k$ tensor. In this case, the convolution is computed as follows:

$$y_{j_1,j_2} = \sum_{i_2=1}^{p} \sum_{i_1=1}^{f} w_{i_1,i_2,j_2} \times x_{j_1+i_1-1,i_2} \qquad (\forall j_1 = 1, \cdots, n;\ j_2 = 1, \cdots, k).$$

Similarly, this convolution may be represented by the following compact form:

$$\mathbf{y} = \mathbf{x} * \mathbf{w} \qquad (\mathbf{x} \in \mathbb{R}^{d \times p},\ \mathbf{w} \in \mathbb{R}^{f \times p \times k},\ \mathbf{y} \in \mathbb{R}^{n \times k}).$$

The computational complexity of this convolution is $O(d \cdot f \cdot p \cdot k)$. The total number of parameters increases to $f \times p \times k$.

▶ **Extension 3: allow multiple input dimensions**
In the previous discussions, we always assume the input $\mathbf{x}$ is a 1D signal from 1 to d. Of course, we may expand the input dimension to handle multidimensional data, such as images (two-dimensional [2D]) and videos (three-dimensional [3D]). Here, let us consider how to extend the input $\mathbf{x}$ from 1D to 2D. In this case, the input $\mathbf{x}$ becomes a $d \times d \times p$ tensor, as shown in Figure 8.22. We also have to extend each kernel into an $f \times f \times p$ tensor. As shown in Figure 8.22, when we convolve the kernel with the input, we slide the kernel over the entire 2D space. At each position, an output is generated by the similar element-wise multiplication and summation. The result of the convolution using one kernel is an $n \times n$ map. If we have k different kernels, all of these kernels can be represented as an $f \times f \times p \times k$ tensor, and the output of the convolution becomes an $n \times n \times k$ tensor, accordingly. This 2D convolution is exactly computed as follows:

$$y_{j_1,j_2,j_3} = \sum_{i_3=1}^{p} \sum_{i_2=1}^{f} \sum_{i_1=1}^{f} w_{i_1,i_2,i_3,j_3} \times x_{j_1+i_1-1,j_2+i_2-1,i_3} \tag{8.4}$$

$$(j_1 = 1, \cdots, n;\ j_2 = 1, \cdots, n;\ j_3 = 1, \cdots, k).$$

Similarly, we represent this 2D convolution as the following compact tensor form:

$$\mathbf{y} = \mathbf{x} * \mathbf{w} \quad (\mathbf{x} \in \mathbb{R}^{d \times d \times p},\ \mathbf{w} \in \mathbb{R}^{f \times f \times p \times k},\ \mathbf{y} \in \mathbb{R}^{n \times n \times k}). \tag{8.5}$$

The computational complexity of this convolution is $O(d^2 \cdot f^2 \cdot p \cdot k)$, and the total number of parameters is $f^2 \times p \times k$. The property of locality modeling is still applicable to the 2D convolution, but in this case, the 2D local features are actually captured and modeled.

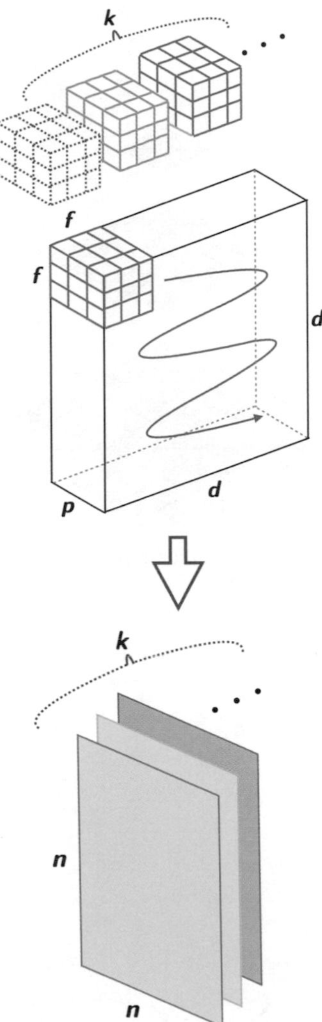

Figure 8.22: An illustration of 2D convolution involving one kernel over multiple input feature plies. (Source: [208].)

- **Extension 4: stack many convolution layers**
  The final step in constructing a typical CNN is to stack many convolutional layers, as described previously, to form a deep structure. Because convolution is a linear operation, each convolution layer is normally followed by a nonlinear ReLU layer before it is cascaded to the next convolution layer. By doing so, we can significantly increase the modeling power after many such layers are stacked. Note that a composition of two linear functions is still a linear function. Sometimes we also insert max-pooling layers in between to reduce the size of the maps to be passed to the following layers. A typical CNN structure for image classification is shown in Figure 8.23.
  At each convolution layer, the input/kernel/output tensors must match with each other in their sizes based on the definition of the 2D convolution operation in Eq. (8.5). When we stack many convolution layers like this, each layer conducts locality modeling on the output of the previous layer. The hierarchical structure of many convolution layers recursively combines the local features extracted at each level to form higher-level features. This makes sense when handling visual data such as images: the low-level convolution kernels first consider small local regions to extract low-level features based on nearby pixels of an image, and the high-level convolution layers will try to locally combine these smaller local features to consider much larger regions in the image.

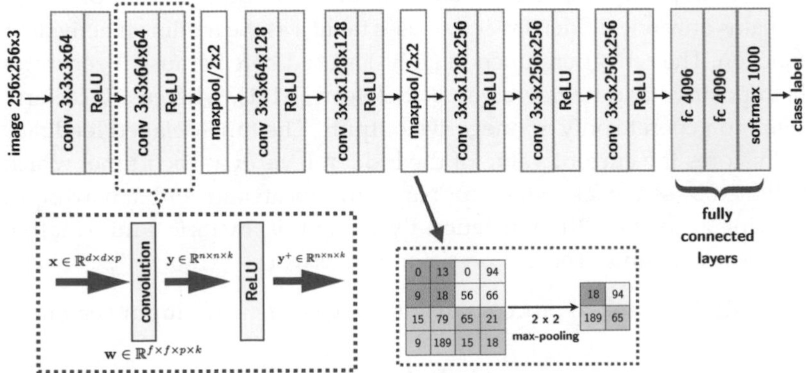

Figure 8.23: An illustration of a typical CNN consisting of convolution layers, ReLU layers, max-pooling layers, and fully connected layers.

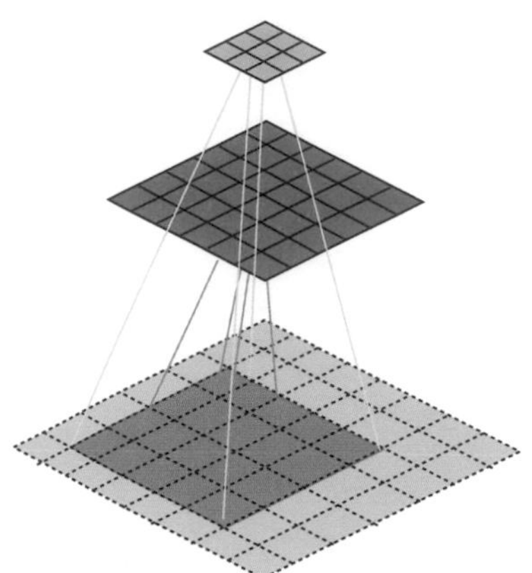

Figure 8.24: An illustration of receptive fields in CNNs.

As shown in Figure 8.24, each location of an output feature map from a convolution layer is locally computed based on a small region in the previous layer. If we keep tracking this backward to the original input image, we will identify a local region of the image that contributes to the computation of this location. This local region in the input is usually called the *receptive field* of this feature map. As we can see, the receptive fields get larger and larger as we move to the higher layers in the hierarchy of a CNN.

As shown in Figure 8.23, several fully connected layers and a softmax layer are usually added at the top of this hierarchy to map the locally extracted features to the final image labels. The entire CNN structure may be broken down into two parts:

1. The stacked convolution layers responsible for visual feature extraction
2. The fully connected layers as a universal function approximator to map these features to the target labels

Now that we have covered two feed-forward neural network structures for fixed-size input data, in the following, we will examine two popular structures that are suitable for handling variable-length sequences. The first structure is based on recurrent feedback and is called a *recurrent neural network (RNN)*. We will briefly examine a standard structure for RNNs. The second structure, called a *transformer*, relies on nonrecurrent structures using the attention mechanism. As we will see, transformers are very expensive in computational complexity and memory consumption but are good at capturing long-span dependency in long sequences.

8.2.4 Case Study III: Recurrent Neural Networks (RNNs)

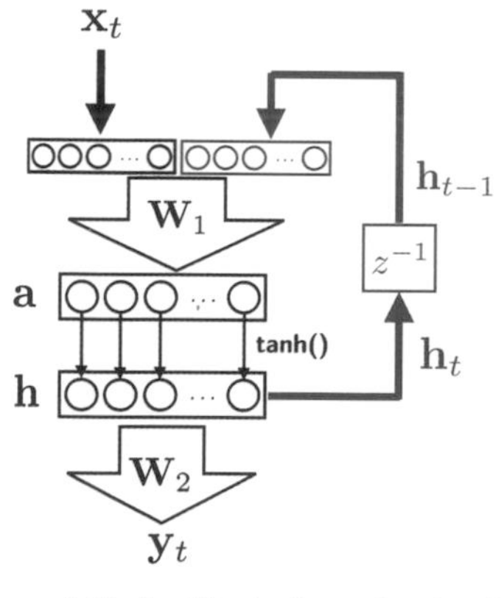

Figure 8.25: An illustration of a simple RNN structure.

As already mentioned, RNNs are neural networks that contain recurrent feedback that typically results in some cycles in the network. Figure 8.25 shows a simple recurrent structure for RNNs that was proposed early on and has been extensively studied in the literature. This simple RNN contains only one hidden layer that uses $\tanh(\cdot)$ as the nonlinear activation function. The activation function $\tanh(\cdot)$ is used here because it generates both positive and negative values between $[-1, 1]$, whereas ReLU and sigmoid generate only nonnegative outputs. The time-delayed feedback path stores the current value of the hidden layer $\mathbf{h}$ at each time, which will then be sent back to the input layer to concatenate with a new input arriving at the next time instance. By doing this, historical information will flow over and over and persist in the network.

If this RNN is used to process the following sequence of input vectors:

$$\{\mathbf{x}_1, \mathbf{x}_2, \cdots, \mathbf{x}_T\},$$

and we assume that the initial status of the hidden layer is $\mathbf{h}_0$, the RNN will operate for $t = 1, 2, \cdots T$ as follows:

Here, $[\mathbf{x}_t;\ \mathbf{h}_{t-1}]$ denotes that two column vectors (i.e., $\mathbf{x}_t$ and $\mathbf{h}_{t-1}$) are concatenated into a longer column vector.

$$\mathbf{a}_t = \mathbf{W}_1 \big[\mathbf{x}_t;\ \mathbf{h}_{t-1}\big] + \mathbf{b}_1$$

$$\mathbf{h}_t = \tanh(\mathbf{a}_t)$$

$$\mathbf{y}_t = \mathbf{W}_2 \mathbf{h}_t + \mathbf{b}_2,$$

where $\mathbf{W}_1$, $\mathbf{b}_1$, $\mathbf{W}_2$, and $\mathbf{b}_2$ denote the parameters used in the two full connections of the RNN.

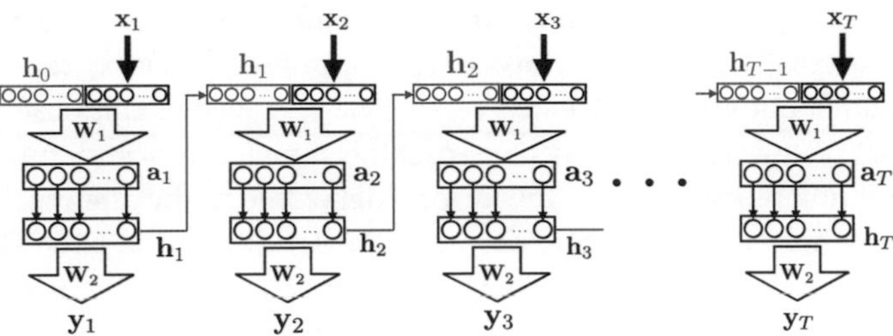

Figure 8.26: Unfolding an RNN into a nonrecurrent structure.

A convenient way to analyze the behavior of the recurrent feedback in an RNN is to unfold the recursive computation along the time steps for the whole input sequence. For example, if we unfold the feedback along time, the recursive computation is equivalent to the nonrecurrent network shown in Figure 8.26. By doing this, any RNN may be viewed as duplicating the same nonrecurrent network for every time instance, each passing a message to its successor (as shown in red in Figure 8.26). If the RNN is used to process a long input sequence, this nonrecurrent network becomes a very deep structure. Just consider the path from the first input $\mathbf{x}_1$ to the last output $\mathbf{y}_T$ if T is large. Theoretically speaking, RNNs are very powerful models suitable for all sequences. However, in practice, the learning of RNNs turns out to be extremely difficult because of the deep structure introduced by the recurrent feedback. Empirical results have shown that simple RNN structures, such as that shown in Figure 8.25, are only good at modeling short-term dependency in sequences but fail to capture any dependency that spans a long distance in input sequences. To solve this issue, many structure variations have been proposed for RNNs, such as long short-term memory (LSTM) [101, 177], gated recurrent units (GRUs) [43], and higher-order recurrent neural networks (HORNNs) [228, 95]. The basic idea in these methods is to introduce some shortcut paths in the deep structures in various ways so that the signals can flow more smoothly in the deep networks, which will significantly improve the learning of RNNs. Another possible way to enhance RNNs is to use the so-called *bidirectional recurrent neural networks* [217], where each output is computed based on both the left and right sides of the context in a sequence. Interested readers may refer to the original articles for those improved recurrent structures.

8.2.5 Case Study IV: Transformer

As previously discussed, RNNs were originally designed to handle sequences in a sequential way, taking one input item at a time and generating an output item based on the current input and internal status. By doing this recursively from beginning to end, RNNs are able to map any input sequence into an output sequence. However, if we unfold an RNN, as shown in Figure 8.26, we may view this unfolded network as a single nonrecurrent structure that transforms an input sequence $\{\mathbf{x}_1, \mathbf{x}_2, \cdots, \mathbf{x}_T\}$ into another output sequence $\{\mathbf{y}_1, \mathbf{y}_2, \cdots, \mathbf{y}_T\}$ as a whole. This observation suggests that we may actually construct this nonrecurrent structure using any building blocks, such as the tapped delay line or the attention mechanism, rather than just unfolding an RNN. The limitation of an RNN is evident from its unfolded structure in Figure 8.26: when the RNN computes the output $\mathbf{y}_t$ at time step t, $\mathbf{x}_t$ needs to flow through one copy of the subnetwork, $\mathbf{x}_{t-1}$ through two copies, $\mathbf{x}_{t-3}$ through three copies, and so on. The contribution from far-back history decays significantly because it needs to flow through a long path to reach the current output.

On the other hand, if we use the attention mechanism in Eq. (8.2) to compute the output $\mathbf{y}_t$, the relation with all historical information or even future information can be any way we prefer, depending on how we choose the attention function $g(\cdot)$, the query $\mathbf{q}_t$, and the key $\mathbf{k}_t$ to compute the attention coefficients. From this perspective, attention is a better way to capture long-span dependency in sequences.

In the following, we will explore a popular network structure designed with this idea in mind. This network structure, called the *transformer* [244], relies on the attention mechanism discussed in Eq. (8.3) as its main building block. The transformer is a very powerful model that relies on the so-called *self-attention* mechanism to transform any input sequence into a context-aware output sequence that can encode long-span dependencies. The reason it is called *self-attention* is that the transformer adopts a special structure for the attention mechanism in Eq. (8.3), where the three matrices $\mathbf{V}$, $\mathbf{Q}$, and $\mathbf{K}$ are all derived from the same input sequence. The transformer is a very popular machine learning model for long text documents, and it has demonstrated tremendous successes in a wide range of natural-language-processing tasks.

Let us assume each vector in the input sequence is a d-dimension vector: $\mathbf{x}_t \in \mathbb{R}^d$ $(\forall t = 1, 2, \cdots, T)$. We align all input vectors to form the following $d \times T$ matrix:

$$\mathbf{X} = \begin{bmatrix} \mathbf{x}_T & \cdots & \mathbf{x}_2 & \mathbf{x}_1 \end{bmatrix}.$$

Next, we define three matrices $\mathbf{A} \in \mathbb{R}^{l \times d}$, $\mathbf{B} \in \mathbb{R}^{l \times d}$, and $\mathbf{C} \in \mathbb{R}^{o \times d}$ to be the learnable parameters of the transformer. These three matrices will be used as three linear transformations to transform the input sequence $\mathbf{X}$ into query matrix $\mathbf{Q}$, key matrix $\mathbf{K}$, and value matrix $\mathbf{V}$:

$$\mathbf{Q} = \mathbf{A}\mathbf{X} \qquad \mathbf{K} = \mathbf{B}\mathbf{X} \qquad \mathbf{V} = \mathbf{C}\mathbf{X},$$

where $\mathbf{Q}, \mathbf{K} \in \mathbb{R}^{l \times T}$, and $\mathbf{V} \in \mathbb{R}^{o \times T}$. We further define the attention function as the following bilinear function:

$$g(\mathbf{Q}, \mathbf{K}) = \mathbf{Q}^{\intercal}\mathbf{K},$$

where $g(\mathbf{Q}, \mathbf{K}) \in \mathbb{R}^{T \times T}$.

Under this setting, we simply use the attention formula in Eq. (8.3) to transform $\mathbf{X}$ into another matrix $\mathbf{Z} \in \mathbb{R}^{o \times T}$, as follows:

$$\mathbf{Z} = (\mathbf{C}\mathbf{X}) \ \text{softmax}\Big((\mathbf{A}\mathbf{X})^{\intercal}(\mathbf{B}\mathbf{X})\Big),$$

where the softmax function is applied to each column to ensure all entries are positive and each column sums to 1. The process of self-attention is also depicted in Figure 8.27.

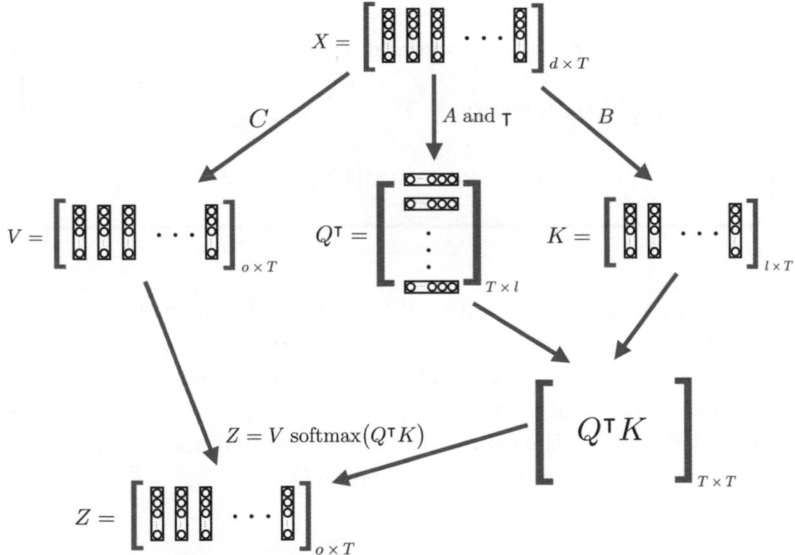

Figure 8.27: An illustration of the computation flowchart of a single-head transformer.

Moreover, the transformer can be further empowered by using multiple sets of parameters **A**, **B**, and **C**. Each set is called a *head* of the transformer. The outputs **Z** from all heads are concatenated and then sent to a nonlinear module, consisting of a fully connected layer and a ReLU activation layer, to generate the final output of the multihead transformer. In Vaswani et al. [244], all dimensions of these matrices are chosen carefully to ensure that the final output has the same size as the input $\mathbf{X}$. In this way, many such multihead transformers can be easily stacked one after another to construct a deep model, which can flexibly transform any input sequence into another context-aware output sequence.

The following box briefly summarizes how such a multihead transformer works:

Multihead Transformer

Choose $d = 512$, $o = 64$, a multihead transformer will transform an input sequence $\mathbf{X} \in \mathbb{R}^{512\times T}$ into $\mathbf{Y} \in \mathbb{R}^{n\times T}$:

- Multihead transformer: use eight sets of parameters:

$$\mathbf{A}^{(j)}, \mathbf{B}^{(j)} \in \mathbb{R}^{l\times 512}, \mathbf{C}^{(j)} \in \mathbb{R}^{64\times 512} \quad (j = 1, 2, \cdots, 8).$$

- For $j = 1, 2, \cdots, 8$:

$$\mathbf{Z}^{(j)} \in \mathbb{R}^{64\times T} = \left(\mathbf{C}^{(j)}\mathbf{X}\right) \text{ softmax}\Big(\left(\mathbf{A}^{(j)}\mathbf{X}\right)^\intercal \left(\mathbf{B}^{(j)}\mathbf{X}\right)\Big).$$

- Concatenate all heads:

$$\mathbf{Z} \in \mathbb{R}^{512\times T} = \text{concat}\left(\mathbf{Z}^{(1)}, \mathbf{Z}^{(2)}, \cdots, \mathbf{Z}^{(8)}\right).$$

- Apply nonlinearity:

$$\mathbf{Y} = \text{feedforward}\Big(\text{LN}_{\gamma,\beta}(\mathbf{X} + \mathbf{Z})\Big).$$

Note that we use

$$\mathbf{Y} = \text{feed-forward}(\mathbf{X})$$

as a shorthand for a fully connected neural network of one hidden layer. Here, we send each column of $\mathbf{X}$, denoted as $\mathbf{x}_t$, through a full connection layer of parameters $\mathbf{W}$ and $\mathbf{b}$ and then a ReLU nonlinear layer:

$$\mathbf{y}_t = \text{ReLU}(\mathbf{W}\mathbf{x}_t + \mathbf{b}).$$

And all outputs are concatenated as follows:

$$\mathbf{Y} = \left[\mathbf{y}_1\ \mathbf{y}_2\ \cdots\ \mathbf{y}_T\right].$$

From this description, we can easily see that the transformer is an extremely expensive model in terms of computational complexity because it involves multiplications of several large matrices at each step. Moreover, it also requires a fairly large memory space to store these matrices and other intermediate results. The estimation of the computational complexity of the multihead transformer is left to Exercise Q8.9.

8.3 Learning Algorithms for Neural Networks

So far, we have thoroughly discussed how to construct various neural network structures, and we also know how to compute network outputs from any inputs, provided all network parameters are given. Now, we will discuss how to learn these network parameters. Once a network's structure is determined, using $\mathbb{W}$ to denote all parameters, a neural network can be viewed as a multivariate and vector-valued function as follows:

$$\mathbf{y} = f(\mathbf{x}; \mathbb{W}).$$

Just like other discriminative models, the neural network parameters $\mathbb{W}$ must be learned from a training set, which usually consists of many input–output pairs, as follows:

$$\mathcal{D}_N = \Big\{(\mathbf{x}_1, \mathbf{r}_1), (\mathbf{x}_2, \mathbf{r}_2), \cdots, (\mathbf{x}_N, \mathbf{r}_N)\Big\},$$

where each $\mathbf{x}_i$ denotes an input sample, and $\mathbf{r}_i$ is its correct label.

8.3.1 Loss Function

First, let us explore some common loss functions that can be used to construct the objective function for learning neural networks.

If a neural network is used for any regression problem, the best loss function is the mean-square error (MSE). In this case, the objective function can be easily formed as follows:

$$Q_{\text{MSE}}(\mathbb{W}; \mathcal{D}_N) = \sum_{i=1}^{N} \|f(\mathbf{x}_i; \mathbb{W}) - \mathbf{r}_i\|^2.$$

Next, let us consider the cases where a neural network is used for pattern-classification problems. In a classification problem, we normally assume all different classes (assuming K classes in total) are mutually exclusive. In other words, any input can only be assigned to one of these classes. For mutually exclusive classes, we usually use the so-called 1-of-K *one-hot* strategy to encode the correct label for each training sample $\mathbf{x}_i$. Its corresponding label $\mathbf{r}_i$ is a K-dimension vector, containing all 0s but a single 1 in the position corresponding to the correct class. We use a scalar r_i to indicate the position of 1 in $\mathbf{r}_i$, where $r_i \in \{1, 2, \cdots, K\}$.

If the underlying classes in a classification problem are not mutually exclusive, they can always be broken down to some separate classification problems. For example, say we want to recognize whether an image contains *a cat* or *a dog*. Obviously, it is possible to have some images containing both cats and dogs. This problem can be formulated as two separate binary classification problems, namely, *"whether an image contains a cat? (yes/no)"* and *"whether an image contains a dog? (yes/no)."* The output layer of the neural network can be reconfigured to accommodate both problems at the same time. This is left as Exercise Q8.2.

For mutually exclusive classes, we normally use a softmax output layer in neural networks to yield probability-like outputs. Meanwhile, each one-hot encoding label $\mathbf{r}_i$ can be viewed as the desired probability distribution over all classes: the correct class is 1, and everything else is 0.

In this case, we use the Kullback–Leibler (KL) divergence between $\mathbf{r}_i$ and the neural network output $\mathbf{y}_i = f(\mathbf{x}_i; \mathbb{W})$ to measure the loss for each data sample $\mathbf{x}_i$, usually called the *cross-entropy (CE) error*. Because $\mathbf{r}_i$ is a one-hot

It is easy to verify:

$$\mathrm{KL}(\{\mathbf{r}_i\}||\{\mathbf{y}_i\}) = -\ln\left[\mathbf{y}_i\right]_{r_i}.$$

vector containing only one 1 at position r_i, we have

$$Q_{\mathrm{CE}}(\mathbb{W};\mathcal{D}_N) = -\sum_{i=1}^{N} \ln\left[\mathbf{y}_i\right]_{r_i} = -\sum_{i=1}^{N} \ln\left[f(\mathbf{x}_i;\mathbb{W})\right]_{r_i} \tag{8.6}$$

where $[\cdot]_r$ denotes the rth element of a vector.

8.3.2 Automatic Differentiation

If we want to learn the network parameters $\mathbb{W}$ by optimizing the objective function $Q(\mathbb{W})$, we need to know how to compute the gradient of the objective function (i.e., $\frac{\partial Q(\mathbb{W})}{\partial \mathbb{W}}$). This section introduces the automatic differentiation (AD) technique [145], which is guaranteed to compute the gradient in the most efficient way for any network structure. This technique also leads to the famous *error back-propagation* algorithm for neural networks [249, 204]. The key idea behind automatic differentiation is the simple chain rule in calculus. Any neural network can be viewed as a composition of many simpler functions, each of which is represented by a smaller network module. AD essentially passes some key "messages" along the network so that all gradients can be computed locally from these messages. AD has two different accumulation modes: forward and reverse. In the following, we will explore how to use the reverse-accumulation mode to compute the gradients for neural networks, which is colloquially called the *error back-propagation algorithm*.

First of all, let us use a simple example to show the essence of the reverse-accumulation mode in AD. As shown in Figure 8.28, assume that we have a module in a neural network, which represents a function $y = f_{\mathbf{w}}(x)$ that takes $x \in \mathbb{R}$ as input and generates $y \in \mathbb{R}$ as output. All learnable parameters inside this module are denoted as $\mathbf{w}$. For any objective function $Q(\cdot)$, suppose we already know its partial derivative with respect to the immediate output of this module, which is usually called the *error signal* of this module, denoted as $e = \frac{\partial Q}{\partial y}$. According to the chain rule, we can easily compute the gradient of all learnable parameters in this module as follows:

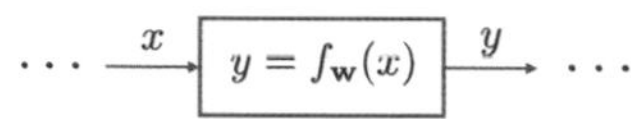

Figure 8.28: An illustration of a module in neural networks representing a simple function.

$$\frac{\partial Q}{\partial \mathbf{w}} = \frac{\partial Q}{\partial y}\frac{\partial y}{\partial \mathbf{w}} = e\frac{\partial f_{\mathbf{w}}(x)}{\partial \mathbf{w}},$$

where $\frac{\partial f_{\mathbf{w}}(x)}{\partial \mathbf{w}}$ can be computed locally based on the function itself. In other words, as long as we know the error signal of this module, the gradient of all learnable parameters of this module can be computed locally, independent of other parts of the neural network. In order to generate error signals for all modules in a network, we have to propagate it in a certain way. From the perspective of this module, we at least have to propagate it from the output end to the input end, to be used as the error signal for the module immediately before. In other words, we need to derive the partial derivative with respect to (w.r.t.) the input of this module (i.e., $\frac{\partial Q}{\partial x}$). We will continue this process until we reach the first module of the whole network. Once again, according to the chain rule, the propagation of the error signal from the output end to the input end is another simple task that can be done locally:

$$\frac{\partial Q}{\partial x} = \frac{\partial Q}{\partial y}\frac{\partial y}{\partial x} = e\frac{df_{\mathbf{w}}(x)}{dx},$$

where $\frac{df_{\mathbf{w}}(x)}{dx}$ can be computed solely from the function itself.

This idea can be extended to a more general case, where the underlying module represents a vector-input and vector-output function (i.e., $\mathbf{y} = f_{\mathbf{w}}(\mathbf{x})$ ($\mathbf{x} \in \mathbb{R}^m$ and $\mathbf{y} \in \mathbb{R}^n$)), as shown in Figure 8.29. In this case, the two local derivatives are represented by two Jacobian matrices, $J_{\mathbf{w}}$ and $J_{\mathbf{x}}$, as follows:

$$\cdots \xrightarrow{\mathbf{x} \in \mathbb{R}^m} \boxed{\mathbf{y} = f_{\mathbf{w}}(\mathbf{x})} \xrightarrow{\mathbf{y} \in \mathbb{R}^n} \cdots$$

Figure 8.29: An illustration of a module in neural networks representing a vector-input and vector-output function.

$$J_{\mathbf{w}} = \begin{bmatrix} \frac{\partial y_1}{\partial w_1} & \frac{\partial y_2}{\partial w_1} & \cdots & \frac{\partial y_n}{\partial w_1} \\ \frac{\partial y_1}{\partial w_2} & \frac{\partial y_2}{\partial w_2} & \cdots & \frac{\partial y_n}{\partial w_2} \\ \vdots & \vdots & \vdots & \vdots \\ \frac{\partial y_1}{\partial w_k} & \frac{\partial y_2}{\partial w_k} & \cdots & \frac{\partial y_n}{\partial w_k} \end{bmatrix}_{k\times n} = \left[\frac{\partial y_j}{\partial w_i}\right]_{k\times n}$$

where y_j denotes jth element of the output vector $\mathbf{y}$, w_i denotes the ith element of the parameter vector $\mathbf{w}$ ($\in \mathbb{R}^k$), and

$$J_{\mathbf{x}} = \begin{bmatrix} \frac{\partial y_1}{\partial x_1} & \frac{\partial y_2}{\partial x_1} & \cdots & \frac{\partial y_n}{\partial x_1} \\ \frac{\partial y_1}{\partial x_2} & \frac{\partial y_2}{\partial x_2} & \cdots & \frac{\partial y_n}{\partial x_2} \\ \vdots & \vdots & \vdots & \vdots \\ \frac{\partial y_1}{\partial x_m} & \frac{\partial y_2}{\partial x_m} & \cdots & \frac{\partial y_n}{\partial x_m} \end{bmatrix}_{m\times n} = \left[\frac{\partial y_j}{\partial x_i}\right]_{m\times n}$$

$$\mathbf{y} = \begin{bmatrix} y_1 \\ y_2 \\ \vdots \\ y_n \end{bmatrix} \quad \mathbf{x} = \begin{bmatrix} x_1 \\ x_2 \\ \vdots \\ x_m \end{bmatrix} \quad \mathbf{w} = \begin{bmatrix} w_1 \\ w_2 \\ \vdots \\ w_k \end{bmatrix}$$

where x_i denotes ith element of the input vector $\mathbf{x}$.

These two Jacobian matrices can be both computed locally based on this network module alone. Once again, assume we already know the error signal of this module, which is similarly defined as the partial derivatives of the objective function $Q(\cdot)$ w.r.t. the immediate output of this module. In this case, the error signal is a vector because this module generates a vector output:

$$\mathbf{e} \triangleq \frac{\partial Q}{\partial \mathbf{y}} \quad (\mathbf{e} \in \mathbb{R}^n).$$

Similarly, we may perform the two steps required by the reverse accumulation of AD as two simple matrix multiplications:

1. **Back-propagation:**
$$\frac{\partial Q}{\partial \mathbf{x}} = J_{\mathbf{x}}\, \mathbf{e}. \tag{8.7}$$
2. **Local gradients:**
$$\frac{\partial Q}{\partial \mathbf{w}} = J_{\mathbf{w}}\, \mathbf{e}. \tag{8.8}$$

Now, let us consider how to perform these two steps for the common building blocks of neural networks that we have discussed previously.

► **Full connection**
As shown in Figure 8.9, full connection is a linear transformation that connects input $\mathbf{x} \in \mathbb{R}^d$ to output $\mathbf{y} \in \mathbb{R}^n$ as $\mathbf{y} = \mathbf{W}\mathbf{x} + \mathbf{b}$, where $\mathbf{W} \in \mathbb{R}^{n\times d}$, and $\mathbf{b} \in \mathbb{R}^n$. Assume that we have the error signal of this module (i.e., $\mathbf{e} = \frac{\partial Q}{\partial \mathbf{y}}$). Let us consider how to conduct back-propagation and compute local gradients for this module.
First, because we have $\mathbf{y} = \mathbf{W}\mathbf{x} + \mathbf{b}$, it is easy to derive the following Jacobian matrix:
$$J_{\mathbf{x}} = \left[\frac{\partial y_j}{\partial x_i}\right]_{d\times n} = \mathbf{W}^\intercal.$$
Therefore, we have the following formula to back-propagate the error signal to the input end:
$$\frac{\partial Q}{\partial \mathbf{x}} = \mathbf{W}^\intercal \mathbf{e}. \tag{8.9}$$
Second, if we use $\mathbf{w}_i^\intercal$ to denote the ith row of the weight matrix $\mathbf{W}$ and b_i for the ith element of the bias $\mathbf{b}$, we have $y_i = \mathbf{w}_i^\intercal \mathbf{x} + b_i$. Furthermore, $\mathbf{w}_i$ and b_i are not related to any other elements in $\mathbf{y}$ except y_i.
Therefore, for any $i \in \{1, 2, \cdots, n\}$, we have
$$\frac{\partial Q}{\partial \mathbf{w}_i} = \frac{\partial Q}{\partial y_i}\frac{\partial y_i}{\partial \mathbf{w}_i} = \mathbf{x}\frac{\partial Q}{\partial y_i},$$
and
$$\frac{\partial Q}{\partial b_i} = \frac{\partial Q}{\partial y_i}\frac{\partial y_i}{\partial b_i} = \frac{\partial Q}{\partial y_i}.$$
We may arrange these results for all i into the following compact matrix form to compute the local gradients of all parameters for the

full-connection module:

For each row vector of $\mathbf{W}$, we have

$$\frac{\partial Q}{\partial \mathbf{w}_i^\mathsf{T}} = \frac{\partial Q}{\partial y_i}\mathbf{x}^\mathsf{T}.$$

$$\frac{\partial Q}{\partial \mathbf{W}} = \begin{bmatrix} \frac{\partial Q}{\partial y_1} \\ \vdots \\ \frac{\partial Q}{\partial y_n} \end{bmatrix} \mathbf{x}^\mathsf{T} = \mathbf{e}\,\mathbf{x}^\mathsf{T}. \tag{8.10}$$

$$\frac{\partial Q}{\partial \mathbf{b}} = \mathbf{e}. \tag{8.11}$$

- **Nonlinear activation**

As shown in Figure 8.12, a nonlinear activation is an operation to connect $\mathbf{x}$ ($\in \mathbb{R}^n$) to $\mathbf{y}$ ($\in \mathbb{R}^n$) as $\mathbf{y} = \phi(\mathbf{x})$, where the nonlinear activation function $\phi(\cdot)$ is applied to the input vector $\mathbf{x}$ element-wise: $y_i = \phi(x_i)$ ($\forall i = 1, 2, \cdots, n$).

Because there are no learnable parameters in the nonlinear activation module, we have no need to compute local gradients. For each of such modules, the only thing we need to do is to back-propagate the error signal from the output end to the input end. Because the activation function is applied to each input component element-wise to generate each output element, the Jacobian matrix $\mathbf{J_x}$ is a diagonal matrix:

$$\mathbf{J_x} = \left[\frac{\partial y_j}{\partial x_i}\right]_{n\times n} = \begin{bmatrix} \phi'(x_1) & & \\ & \ddots & \\ & & \phi'(x_n) \end{bmatrix}_{n\times n}$$

where we denote $\phi'(x) \stackrel{\Delta}{=} \frac{d}{dx}\phi(x)$.

Assuming $\mathbf{e} = \frac{\partial Q}{\partial \mathbf{y}}$ denotes the error signal of this module, the back-propagation formula can be expressed in a compact way using element-wise multiplication between two vectors in place of matrix multiplication:

$$\frac{\partial Q}{\partial \mathbf{x}} = \mathbf{J_x}\mathbf{e} = \phi'(\mathbf{x}) \odot \mathbf{e},$$

where $\phi'(\mathbf{x})$ denotes a column vector $\left[\phi'(x_1); \cdots; \phi'(x_n)\right]$, and $\odot$ stands for element-wise multiplication.

For a ReLU activation module, we have

$$\frac{\partial Q}{\partial \mathbf{x}} = H(\mathbf{x}) \odot \mathbf{e}, \tag{8.12}$$

where $H(\cdot)$ stands for the step function, as shown in Figure 6.4.

We have

$$\frac{d}{dx}\mathrm{ReLU}(x) = \begin{cases} 0 & \text{if } x < 0 \\ 1 & \text{otherwise} \end{cases}$$
$$= H(x).$$

For a sigmoid activation module, we have

Referring to Eq. (6.15), we have

$$\frac{d}{dx}l(x) = l(x)(1 - l(x)).$$

$$\frac{\partial Q}{\partial \mathbf{x}} = l(\mathbf{x}) \odot \big(\mathbf{1} - l(\mathbf{x})\big) \odot \mathbf{e}, \tag{8.13}$$

where $l(\mathbf{x})$ denotes that the sigmoid function $l(\cdot)$ is applied to $\mathbf{x}$ element-wise, and $\mathbf{1}$ is an $n \times 1$ vector consisting of all 1s.

► **Softmax**

As shown in Figure 8.13, *softmax* is a special function that maps an n-dimensional vector $\mathbf{x}$ ($\in \mathbb{R}^n$) into another n-dimensional vector $\mathbf{y}$ inside the hypercube $[0, 1]^n$. Similar to nonlinear activation, the softmax function does not have any learnable parameters. For each softmax module, we only need to back-propagate the error signal from the output end to the input end.

As in Eq. (6.18), the softmax function is defined as

$$y_j = \frac{e^{x_j}}{\sum_{i=1}^n e^{x_i}}.$$

For any diagonal element, $\frac{\partial y_j}{\partial x_i}$ ($j = i$), we have

$$\frac{\partial y_i}{\partial x_i} = \frac{\partial}{\partial x_i} \frac{e^{x_i}}{\sum_{i=1}^n e^{x_i}}$$
$$= \frac{e^{x_i}\left(\sum_{i=1}^n e^{x_i}\right) - e^{x_i} e^{x_i}}{\left(\sum_{i=1}^n e^{x_i}\right)^2}$$
$$= y_i(1 - y_i).$$

For any off-diagonal element, $\frac{\partial y_j}{\partial x_i}$ ($j \neq i$), we have

$$\frac{\partial y_j}{\partial x_i} = \frac{\partial}{\partial x_i} \frac{e^{x_j}}{\sum_{i=1}^n e^{x_i}}$$
$$= \frac{-e^{x_j} e^{x_i}}{\left(\sum_{i=1}^n e^{x_i}\right)^2}$$
$$= -y_j y_i.$$

Based on the softmax function in Eq. (6.18), we derive its Jacobian matrix as follows (see margin note):

$$\mathbf{J_x} = \left[\frac{\partial y_j}{\partial x_i}\right]_{n\times n} = \begin{bmatrix} y_1(1-y_1) & -y_1y_2 & \cdots & -y_1y_n \\ -y_1y_2 & y_2(1-y_2) & \cdots & -y_2y_n \\ \vdots & \vdots & \vdots & \vdots \\ -y_1y_n & -y_2y_n & \cdots & y_n(1-y_n) \end{bmatrix}_{n\times n}$$

$$\triangleq J_{\text{sm}}.$$

Assume the error signal of a softmax module is given as $\mathbf{e} = \frac{\partial Q}{\partial \mathbf{y}}$; then we back-propagate it to the input end as follows:

$$\frac{\partial Q}{\partial \mathbf{x}} = J_{\text{sm}}\mathbf{e}. \tag{8.14}$$

► **Convolution**

Let us first consider the simple convolution sum in Figure 8.10, which connects an input vector $\mathbf{x}$ ($\in \mathbb{R}^d$) to an output vector $\mathbf{y}$ ($\in \mathbb{R}^n$) by $\mathbf{y} = \mathbf{x} * \mathbf{w}$ with $\mathbf{w} \in \mathbb{R}^f$.

As we know, the convolution sum is computed as follows:

$$y_j = \sum_{i=1}^{f} w_i \times x_{j+i-1},$$

for all $j = 1, 2 \cdots, n$.
It is easy to derive the Jacobian matrix $\mathbf{J_x}$ as follows:

$$\mathbf{J_x} = \left[\frac{\partial y_j}{\partial x_i}\right]_{d\times n} = \begin{bmatrix} w_1 & & & \\ w_2 & w_1 & & \\ \vdots & \vdots & \ddots & \\ w_f & w_{f-1} & \ddots & w_1 \\ & w_f & & w_2 \\ & & \ddots & \vdots \\ & & & w_f \end{bmatrix}_{d\times n}$$

Assume the error signal is given as $\mathbf{e} = \frac{\partial Q}{\partial \mathbf{y}}$; we have

$$\frac{\partial Q}{\partial \mathbf{x}} = \mathbf{J_x e} = \begin{bmatrix} w_1 & & & \\ w_2 & w_1 & & \\ \vdots & \vdots & \ddots & \\ w_f & w_{f-1} & \ddots & w_1 \\ & w_f & & w_2 \\ & & \ddots & \vdots \\ & & & w_f \end{bmatrix} \begin{bmatrix} \frac{\partial Q}{\partial y_1} \\ \frac{\partial Q}{\partial y_2} \\ \vdots \\ \frac{\partial Q}{\partial y_n} \end{bmatrix} = \begin{bmatrix} w_1 \frac{\partial Q}{\partial y_1} \\ w_2 \frac{\partial Q}{\partial y_1} + w_1 \frac{\partial Q}{\partial y_2} \\ \vdots \\ w_f \frac{\partial Q}{\partial y_n} \end{bmatrix}$$

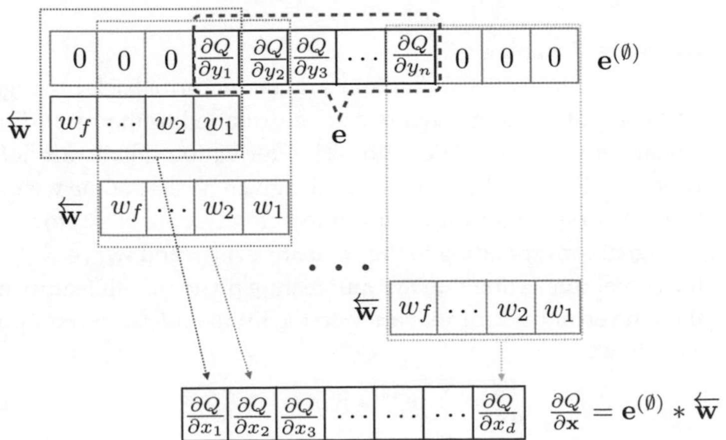

Figure 8.30: Representing the error back-propagation of a convolution sum as another convolution sum.

After some inspections, as shown in Figure 8.30, we can see that the matrix multiplication can be represented by the following convolution sum:

$$\frac{\partial Q}{\partial \mathbf{x}} = \mathbf{e}^{(\emptyset)} * \overleftarrow{\mathbf{w}}, \tag{8.15}$$

where $\mathbf{e}^{(\emptyset)}$ denotes $\mathbf{e}$ with both ends padded with $f-1$ 0s, and $\overleftarrow{\mathbf{w}}$ denotes $\mathbf{w}$ with elements in reverse order: $\overleftarrow{\mathbf{w}} = [w_f \ \cdots \ w_2 \ w_1]^\intercal$.

Next, let us look at how to compute the local gradients for kernel $\mathbf{w}$ based on the error signal $\mathbf{e}$. In this case, the Jacobian matrix w.r.t. $\mathbf{w}$ can be computed as follows:

$$\mathbf{J_w} = \left[\frac{\partial y_j}{\partial w_i}\right]_{f\times n} = \begin{bmatrix} x_1 & x_2 & \cdots & x_n \\ x_2 & x_3 & \cdots & x_{n+1} \\ \vdots & \vdots & \ddots & \vdots \\ x_f & x_{f+1} & \cdots & x_{n+f-1} \end{bmatrix}_{f\times n}$$

The local gradient $\frac{\partial Q}{\partial \mathbf{w}}$ is computed as follows:

$$\frac{\partial Q}{\partial \mathbf{w}} = \mathbf{J_w e} = \begin{bmatrix} x_1 & x_2 & \cdots & x_n \\ x_2 & x_3 & \cdots & x_{n+1} \\ \vdots & \vdots & \ddots & \vdots \\ x_f & x_{f+1} & \cdots & x_{n+f-1} \end{bmatrix} \begin{bmatrix} \frac{\partial Q}{\partial y_1} \\ \frac{\partial Q}{\partial y_2} \\ \vdots \\ \frac{\partial Q}{\partial y_n} \end{bmatrix} = \begin{bmatrix} \sum_{i=1}^n x_i \, e_i \\ \sum_{i=1}^n x_{i+1} \, e_i \\ \vdots \\ \sum_{i=1}^n x_{i+f-1} \, e_i \end{bmatrix}$$

Similarly, this matrix multiplication can be represented as the following convolution sum:

$$\frac{\partial Q}{\partial \mathbf{w}} = \mathbf{x} * \mathbf{e}, \tag{8.16}$$

where $\mathbf{x} \in \mathbb{R}^d$, and $\mathbf{e} \in \mathbb{R}^n$.

The idea of using convolution sums to conduct error back-propagation and compute local gradients can be extended to the multidimensional convolution in Eq. (8.5). The derivation details are left as Exercise Q8.6, and the final results are given here. Assume we use $\mathbf{x}_i$ ($\in \mathbb{R}^{d\times d}$) to stand for the ith input feature ply, $\mathbf{e}_j$ ($\in \mathbb{R}^{n\times n}$) for the error signal corresponding to the jth feature map, and $\mathbf{w}_{ij}$ ($\in \mathbb{R}^{f\times f}$) for the kernel connecting the ith input feature ply to the jth feature map; then the error back-propagation to the input end can be computed as follows:

$$\frac{\partial Q}{\partial \mathbf{x}_i} = \sum_{j=1}^{k} \mathbf{e}_j{}^{(\emptyset)} * \overleftarrow{\mathbf{w}_{ij}} \quad (i = 1, 2 \cdots p). \tag{8.17}$$

In this case, zero padding and order reversal are done similarly for

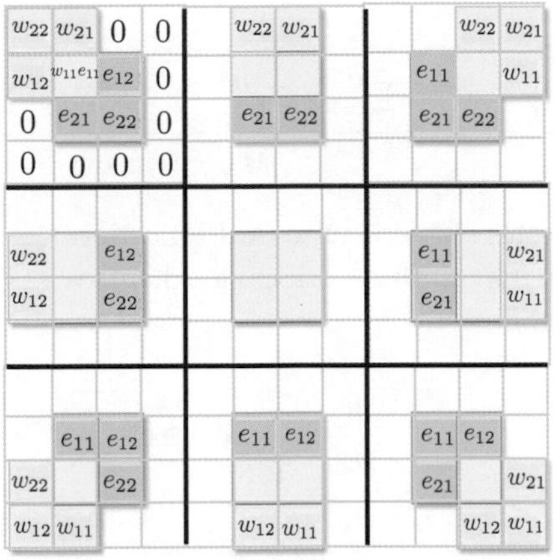

Figure 8.31: Representing the error back-propagation of 2D convolution as another convolution for one feature map and its corresponding kernel. Here, we have $f = 2, d = 3, n = 2$.

2D matrices, as shown by a simple example in Figure 8.31.
Furthermore, for the local gradients w.r.t. the kernel, we have

$$\frac{\partial Q}{\partial \mathbf{w}_{ij}} = \mathbf{x}_i * \mathbf{e}_j \quad (i = 1, 2 \cdots p; \; j = 1, 2 \cdots k), \tag{8.18}$$

where $\mathbf{x}_i \in \mathbb{R}^{d \times d}$, and $\mathbf{e}_j \in \mathbb{R}^{n \times n}$.

► **Normalization**
Normalization is an important technique to train very deep neural networks. We can still apply the Jacobian matrix method to derive the formula to back-propagate the error signal as well as to compute the local gradients for the normalization parameters.
Here, we take *batch normalization* as an example. As shown on page 160, each input element x_i is first normalized to $\hat{x}_i$ based on the local mean $\mu_B(i)$ and variance $\sigma_B^2(i)$ estimated in the current mini-batch B, and then it is rescaled to the corresponding output element y_i based on two learnable normalization parameters, γ and β. Suppose that the current mini-batch B consists of M samples as $B = \{\mathbf{x}^{(1)}, \mathbf{x}^{(2)}, \cdots, \mathbf{x}^{(M)}\}$, and the corresponding output for $\mathbf{x}^{(m)}$ is denoted as $\mathbf{y}^{(m)} = \text{BN}_{\gamma,\beta}(\mathbf{x}^{(m)})$, and we denote its corresponding error signal as

$$\mathbf{e}^{(m)} = \frac{\partial Q}{\partial \mathbf{y}^{(m)}} \quad (m = 1, 2 \cdots M).$$

In order to back-propagate the error signal to the input end, we need to compute the Jacobian matrix $\mathbf{J}_\mathbf{x}$. It is easy to verify that $\mathbf{J}_\mathbf{x}$ is a diagonal matrix, but it depends on all samples in the current mini-batch B. After some mathematical derivations (see margin note), we have the error back-propagation formula for each $\mathbf{x}^{(m)}$ in B, as

Given any $\mathbf{x}^{(m)}$ in B, when we consider $\frac{\partial Q}{\partial x_i^{(m)}}$ for each element $i = 1, 2, \cdots, n$, we know all $\hat{x}_i^{(k)}$ in B ($k = 1, \cdots M$) depend on $x_i^{(m)}$, and these $\hat{x}_i^{(k)}$ also depend on $\mu_B(i)$ and $\sigma_B^2(i)$, each of which is in turn a function of $x_i^{(m)}$. Moreover, $\sigma_B^2(i)$ also depends on $\mu_B(i)$. Therefore, we may compute

$$\frac{\partial Q}{\partial x_i^{(m)}} = \sum_{k=1}^{M} \frac{\partial Q}{\partial y_i^{(k)}} \frac{\partial y_i^{(k)}}{\partial \hat{x}_i^{(k)}} \left[\frac{\partial \hat{x}_i^{(k)}}{\partial x_i^{(m)}} + \frac{\partial \hat{x}_i^{(k)}}{\partial \mu_B(i)} \frac{\partial \mu_B(i)}{\partial x_i^{(m)}} + \frac{\partial \hat{x}_i^{(k)}}{\partial \sigma_B^2(i)} \left(\frac{\partial \sigma_B^2(i)}{\partial \mu_B(i)} \frac{\partial \mu_B(i)}{\partial x_i^{(m)}} + \frac{\partial \sigma_B^2(i)}{\partial x_i^{(m)}} \right) \right].$$

Based on the definition of batch normalization on page 160, we may compute all partial derivatives in this equation. After some mathematical manipulations, we may derive $\frac{\partial Q}{\partial x_i^{(m)}}$ as follows:

$$\frac{\gamma_i M e_i^{(m)} - \gamma_i \sum_{k=1}^{M} e_i^{(k)} - \gamma_i \hat{x}_i^{(m)} \sum_{k=1}^{M} e_i^{(k)} \hat{x}_i^{(k)}}{M \sqrt{\sigma_B^2(i) + \epsilon}}$$

$$(\forall i = 1, 2 \cdots, n).$$

See Zakka [259] for more details.

follows:

$$\frac{\partial Q}{\partial \mathbf{x}^{(m)}} = \frac{M\boldsymbol{\gamma} \odot \mathbf{e}^{(m)} - \sum_{k=1}^{M} \boldsymbol{\gamma} \odot \mathbf{e}^{(k)} - \boldsymbol{\gamma} \odot \hat{\mathbf{x}}^{(m)} \odot \left(\sum_{k=1}^{M} \mathbf{e}^{(k)} \odot \hat{\mathbf{x}}^{(k)} \right)}{M\sqrt{\sigma_{\mathrm{B}}^2(i) + \epsilon}},$$

where $\odot$ denotes element-wise multiplication.
Similarly, we may derive the local gradients w.r.t. $\boldsymbol{\gamma}$ and $\boldsymbol{\beta}$ (see margin note) as follows:

$$\frac{\partial Q}{\partial \gamma_i} = \sum_{k=1}^{M} \frac{\partial Q}{\partial y_i^{(k)}} \frac{\partial y_i^{(k)}}{\partial \gamma_i} = \sum_{k=1}^{M} e_i^{(k)} \hat{x}_i^{(k)}$$

$$\frac{\partial Q}{\partial \beta_i} = \sum_{k=1}^{M} \frac{\partial Q}{\partial y_i^{(k)}} \frac{\partial y_i^{(k)}}{\partial \beta_i} = \sum_{k=1}^{M} e_i^{(k)}.$$

$$\frac{\partial Q}{\partial \boldsymbol{\gamma}} = \sum_{k=1}^{M} \hat{\mathbf{x}}^{(k)} \odot \mathbf{e}^{(k)}$$

$$\frac{\partial Q}{\partial \boldsymbol{\beta}} = \sum_{k=1}^{M} \mathbf{e}^{(k)}.$$

We may extend this technique to other normalization methods, such as layer normalization. This is left as Exercise Q8.7.

- **Max-pooling**
Max-pooling is a simple function that chooses the maximum value within each sliding window and discards the other values. Max-pooling does not have any learnable parameters, so for each max-pooling module, we only need to back-propagate the error signal to the input end. In order to do this, we need to keep track of the location where each maximum value comes from the input. That is, for each element y_j in the output, we keep track of the location of its corresponding maximum value in the input $\mathbf{x}$ as $\hat{j}$ (i.e., $y_j = x_{\hat{j}}$), as shown in Figure 8.32. Assuming the error signal is $\mathbf{e} = \frac{\partial Q}{\partial \mathbf{y}}$, we back-propagate the error signal using the following simple rule:

$$\frac{\partial Q}{\partial x_i} = \begin{cases} \frac{\partial Q}{\partial y_j} & \text{if } i = \hat{j} \\ 0 & \text{otherwise.} \end{cases}$$

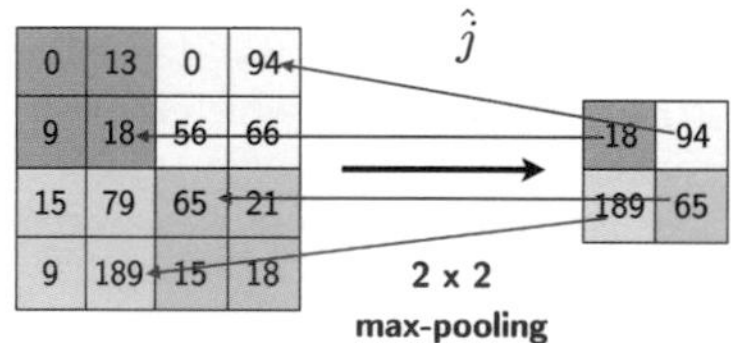

Figure 8.32: Keep track of indexes of maximum values for back-propagation in max-pooling.

Finally, the Jacobian-matrix-based methods can be similarly used to back-propagate error signals and to compute local gradients for the remaining building blocks of neural networks, including *time-delayed feedback*, *tapped delay line*, and *attention*. Once again, these are left as Exercises Q8.8 for interested readers.

When we back-propagate error signals, if the modules in a network are not connected serially, we need to handle some branching cases. Here, we consider the following two branching cases:

- **Merged input**

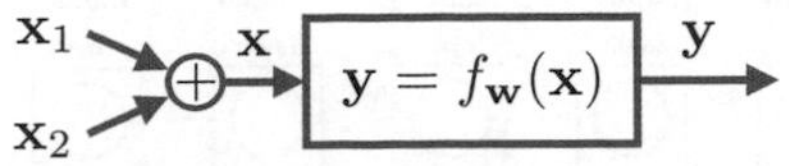

Figure 8.33: An illustration of a module with a merged input.

As shown in Figure 8.33, if a module receives a merged input from two preceding models (i.e., $\mathbf{x} = \mathbf{x}_1 + \mathbf{x}_2$), we use the same back-propagation method to propagate the error signal from the immediate input end (i.e., $\frac{\partial Q}{\partial \mathbf{x}}$). And we immediately have

$$\frac{\partial Q}{\partial \mathbf{x}_1} = \frac{\partial Q}{\partial \mathbf{x}_2} = \frac{\partial Q}{\partial \mathbf{x}}. \tag{8.19}$$

▶ **Split output**

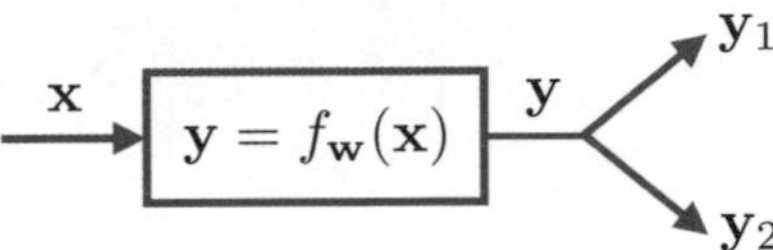

Figure 8.34: An illustration of a module with a split output

As shown in Figure 8.34, consider the case where the output of a module is branched out to two different paths (i.e., $\mathbf{y}_1 = \mathbf{y}_2 = \mathbf{y}$). Assume that the error signals have been propagated to $\mathbf{y}_1$ and $\mathbf{y}_2$, and we already know the partial derivatives $\frac{\partial Q}{\partial \mathbf{y}_1}$ and $\frac{\partial Q}{\partial \mathbf{y}_2}$. Based on the chain rule (see margin note), we just need to compute

$$\frac{\partial Q}{\partial \mathbf{y}} = \frac{\partial Q}{\partial \mathbf{y}_1} + \frac{\partial Q}{\partial \mathbf{y}_2} \tag{8.20}$$

before we propagate it to the input end $\mathbf{x}$.

According to the chain rule, we have

$$\frac{\partial}{\partial \mathbf{y}} Q(\mathbf{y}_1, \mathbf{y}_2) = \frac{\partial}{\partial \mathbf{y}_1} Q(\mathbf{y}_1, \mathbf{y}_2) \frac{\partial \mathbf{y}_1}{\partial \mathbf{y}} + \frac{\partial}{\partial \mathbf{y}_2} Q(\mathbf{y}_1, \mathbf{y}_2) \frac{\partial \mathbf{y}_2}{\partial \mathbf{y}}.$$

If we substitute $\mathbf{y}_1 = \mathbf{y}$ and $\mathbf{y}_2 = \mathbf{y}$, we derive Eq. (8.20).

Relying on these back-propagation results, we are able to derive the full AD procedure to compute the gradients of all model parameters in any neural network structure. Next, we consider a popular neural network structure, namely, the fully connected deep neural network, as shown in Figure 8.19, as an example to demonstrate how to properly combine the previous results to derive the entire backward AD pass to compute the gradients of all network parameters.

Example 8.3.1 Fully Connected Deep Neural Networks

Considering the fully connected deep neural network shown in Figure 8.19 (copied here), assume we use the CE error as the loss function, and derive the full backward pass to compute the gradients of all network parameters for one training sample $(\mathbf{x}, \mathbf{r})$, where we use the 1-of-K encoding for $\mathbf{r}$ and use the scalar r to indicate the position of 1 in $\mathbf{r}$.

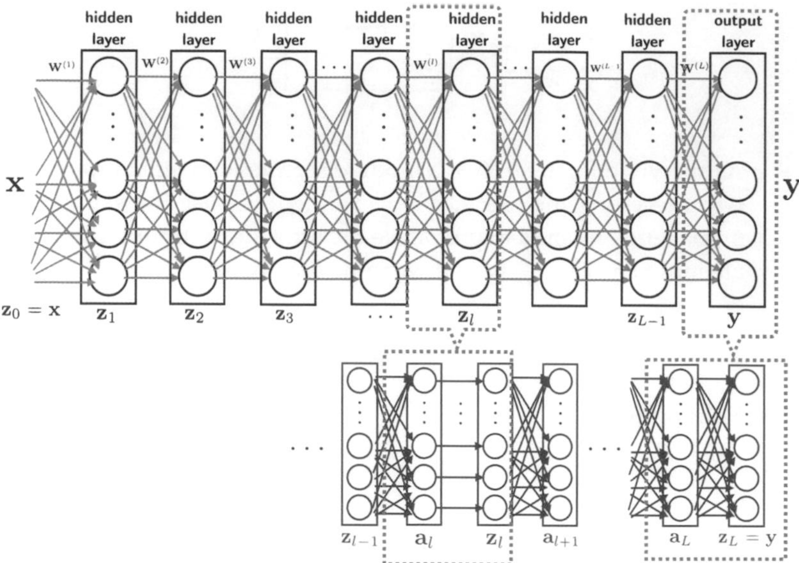

Figure 8.35: Fully connected deep neural network in Figure 8.19 is copied here.

First, we use $\mathbb{W}$ to denote all network parameters in the neural network, which include all connection-weight matrices and the biases of all layers (i.e., $\mathbb{W} = \{\mathbf{W}^{(l)}, \mathbf{b}^{(l)} \mid l = 1, 2 \cdots L\}$). Given a training sample $(\mathbf{x}, \mathbf{r})$, the objective function is derived based on the CE error as

$$Q(\mathbb{W}; \mathbf{x}) = -\ln \left[\mathbf{y}\right]_r = -\ln y_r$$

where $\mathbf{y}$ denotes the output of the neural network when $\mathbf{x}$ is fed as input. We have

$$\frac{\partial Q(\mathbb{W}; \mathbf{x})}{\partial \mathbf{y}} = \begin{bmatrix} 0 \\ \vdots \\ 0 \\ -\frac{1}{y_r} \\ 0 \\ \vdots \\ 0 \end{bmatrix}$$

where the only nonzero value $-\frac{1}{y_l}$ appears in the rth position.

In this network structure, because we only have learnable parameters in full-connection modules, we just need to maintain the error signals of all full-connection modules, denoted as

$$\mathbf{e}^{(l)} = \frac{\partial Q(\mathbb{W};\mathbf{x})}{\partial \mathbf{a}_l}$$

for all $l = L, \cdots, 2, 1$.

To derive $\mathbf{e}^{(L)}$, we just need to back-propagate $\frac{\partial Q(\mathbb{W};\mathbf{x})}{\partial \mathbf{y}}$ through the softmax module, as follows:

$$\begin{aligned}
\mathbf{e}^{(L)} &= J_{\mathrm{sm}} \frac{\partial Q(\mathbb{W};\mathbf{x})}{\partial \mathbf{y}} \\
&= \begin{bmatrix} y_1(1-y_1) & -y_1 y_2 & \cdots & -y_1 y_n \\ -y_1 y_2 & y_2(1-y_2) & \cdots & -y_2 y_n \\ \vdots & \vdots & \vdots & \vdots \\ -y_1 y_n & -y_2 y_n & \cdots & y_n(1-y_n) \end{bmatrix} \begin{bmatrix} 0 \\ \vdots \\ 0 \\ -\frac{1}{y_r} \\ 0 \\ \vdots \\ 0 \end{bmatrix} \\
&= \begin{bmatrix} y_1 \\ y_2 \\ \vdots \\ y_r - 1 \\ \vdots \\ y_n \end{bmatrix}
\end{aligned} \tag{8.21}$$

Next, to derive $\mathbf{e}^{(l)}$ from $\mathbf{e}^{(l+1)}$ for $l = L-1, \cdots, 2, 1$, we just need to back-propagate through a full-connection module of $\{\mathbf{W}^{(l+1)}, \mathbf{b}^{(l+1)}\}$ and a ReLU activation module:

$$\frac{\partial Q(\mathbb{W};\mathbf{x})}{\partial \mathbf{z}_l} = \left(\mathbf{W}^{(l+1)}\right)^{\intercal} \mathbf{e}^{(l+1)}$$

$$\mathbf{e}^{(l)} = \frac{\partial Q(\mathbb{W};\mathbf{x})}{\partial \mathbf{z}_l} \odot H(\mathbf{z}_l) = \left(\left(\mathbf{W}^{(l+1)}\right)^{\intercal} \mathbf{e}^{(l+1)}\right) \odot H(\mathbf{z}_l).$$

For the lth layer, the local gradients w.r.t. the connection-weight matrix $\mathbf{W}^{(l)}$ and the bias vector $\mathbf{b}^{(l)}$ can be derived based on $\mathbf{e}^{(l)}$ as follows:

$$\frac{\partial Q(\mathbb{W};\mathbf{x})}{\partial \mathbf{W}^{(l)}} = \mathbf{e}^{(l)} \left(\mathbf{z}_{l-1}\right)^{\intercal} \quad (l = L, \cdots, 2, 1)$$

$$\frac{\partial Q(\mathbb{W};\mathbf{x})}{\partial \mathbf{b}^{(l)}} = \mathbf{e}^{(l)} \quad (l = L, \cdots, 2, 1).$$

♦

Finally, we can summarize the entire backward pass to compute the gradients for fully connected deep neural networks as follows:

Backward Pass of Fully Connected Deep Neural Networks

Given an input–output pair $(\mathbf{x}, \mathbf{r})$, it generates the gradients of the CE error w.r.t. all network parameters.

1. For the output layer L:

$$\mathbf{e}^{(L)} = \begin{bmatrix} y_1 \; y_2 \; \cdots \; y_r - 1 \; \cdots \; y_n \end{bmatrix}^{\intercal}.$$

2. For each hidden layer $l = L-1, \cdots, 2, 1$:

$$\mathbf{e}^{(l)} = \left(\left(\mathbf{W}^{(l+1)} \right)^{\intercal} \mathbf{e}^{(l+1)} \right) \odot H(\mathbf{z}_l).$$

3. For all layers $l = L, \cdots, 2, 1$:

$$\frac{\partial Q(\mathbb{W};\mathbf{x})}{\partial \mathbf{W}^{(l)}} = \mathbf{e}^{(l)} \left(\mathbf{z}_{l-1} \right)^{\intercal}$$

$$\frac{\partial Q(\mathbb{W};\mathbf{x})}{\partial \mathbf{b}^{(l)}} = \mathbf{e}^{(l)}.$$

Here, $\mathbf{y}$ and $\mathbf{z}_l$ $(l = 0, 1, \cdots, L-1)$ are saved in the forward pass.

8.3.3 Optimization Using Stochastic Gradient Descent

Once we know how to compute the gradients of network parameters, all parameters can be iteratively learned based on any gradient descent method. The traditional method to learn neural networks is the so-called *mini-batch stochastic gradient descent (SGD) algorithm*.

As shown in Algorithm 8.8, we normally need to run the SGD algorithm through the training set many times before the learning converges. One entire pass to scan all training data is usually called an *epoch*. In each epoch, we first randomly shuffle all training data and split them into equally sized mini-batches. The size of a mini-batch must be chosen properly for the best possible result. For each mini-batch, we run both forward-pass and backward-pass algorithms as described previously to compute the gradients for every training sample in the mini-batch. These gradients from the same mini-batch are accumulated and averaged, and then the averaged gradient is used to update network parameters based on a prespecified learning rate. The updated model is used to process the next available mini-batch in the same way. After we have processed all mini-batches in the training set, we may need to adjust the learning rate at the end of every epoch. In most cases, the learning rate needs to be reduced according to a certain annealing schedule as training continues. This procedure is repeated over and over until the learning finally converges.

Algorithm 8.8 Stochastic Gradient Descent to Learn Neural Networks

randomly initialize $\mathbb{W}^{(0)}$, and set η_0
set $n = 0$ and $t = 0$
while not converged **do**
  randomly shuffle training data into mini-batches
  for each mini-batch B **do**
    for each $\mathbf{x} \in B$ **do**
      i) forward pass: $\mathbf{x} \rightarrow \mathbf{y}$
      ii) backward pass: $\{\mathbf{x}, \mathbf{y}\} \rightarrow \frac{\partial Q(\mathbb{W}^{(n)};\mathbf{x})}{\partial \mathbb{W}}$
    end for
    update model: $\mathbb{W}^{(n+1)} = \mathbb{W}^{(n)} - \frac{\eta_t}{|B|} \sum_{\mathbf{x}\in B} \frac{\partial Q(\mathbb{W}^{(n)};\mathbf{x})}{\partial \mathbb{W}}$
    $n = n + 1$
  end for
  adjust $\eta_t \rightarrow \eta_{t+1}$
  $t = t + 1$
end while

Here, η_t denotes the learning rate used in the tth epoch, and $|B|$ denotes the size of B in number of samples.

8.4 Heuristics and Tricks for Optimization

Conceptually speaking, the learning algorithm of neural networks is fairly straightforward. The key is to use a stochastic version of first-order gradient-descent-based optimization methods. The AD method systematically derives gradients for any neural network structures. However, there are two issues worth mentioning. First, the computational expenses are extremely high, especially when large-scale models are learned from an enormous amount of training data. No matter what network structures are used, both forward and backward passes usually involve a large number of matrix multiplications. Moreover, the mini-batch SGD algorithm may need to run a considerable number of epochs before it converges. These factors explain why these learning algorithms were well known several decades ago but have not shined until very recently with the advent of powerful computational resources, such as general-purpose graphics-processing units (GPUs). GPUs can significantly accelerate matrix multiplications compared with regular central processing units (CPUs). When large matrices are involved, it is normal to expect that GPUs can speed up matrix computations by orders of magnitude. This makes GPUs an ideal computational platform for neural networks. Both learning and inference algorithms can be implemented efficiently using GPUs. Second, the conceptually simple SGD learning algorithm involves many hyperparameters, which cannot be automatically learned from data and must be manually chosen based on some heuristics. Even worse, these heuristic rules are not always intuitive, and the effects of various parameters can become entangled. In many cases, the behavior of the learning algorithms becomes totally incomprehensible when these hyperparameters are changed from one combination to another. The performance of neural networks heavily relies on a good choice of these hyperparameters, but the way to find these is highly empirical, often requiring a careful trial-and-error fine-tuning process. When large-scale neural networks are learned from a large training set, this fine-tuning process may be extremely time consuming.

Here, let us first consider some important hyperparameters related to Algorithm 8.8, such as how to initialize network weights at the beginning, how many epochs we will run before termination, how large each mini-batch should be, how to initialize the learning rate, and how to adjust it during the learning process. In the discussion that follows, we will briefly explore the general principles behind selecting these hyperparameters.

- **Parameter initialization**
  In practice, it is empirically found that random initialization works well for neural networks. At the beginning of Algorithm 8.8, all network parameters are randomly set according to a uniform or Gaussian distribution centered at 0 [82].

- **Epoch number**
  In Algorithm 8.8, we need to determine how many epochs we need to run before we terminate. The termination condition usually depends on the learning curves (we will discuss this later on), and sometimes, it is also a trade-off between running time and accuracy. When the training data are limited, we may take the common approach called *early stopping* to avoid overfitting. In this case, the learning of neural networks is terminated before the performance on the training data is fully converged because further improvement in the training set may come at the expense of increased generalization errors.

- **Mini-batch size**
  When we use smaller mini-batches in Algorithm 8.8, the gradient estimates are more noisy at each model update. These noises may fluctuate in the learning process and eventually slow down the convergence of learning. On the other hand, these fluctuations may be beneficial for the learning process to escape from poor initialization or saddle points or even bad local optimums. When bigger mini-

batches are used, the learning curves are typically smoother, and the learning converges much faster. However, it does not always converge to a satisfactory local optimal point. Another advantage of using bigger mini-batches is that we can parallelize forward/backward passes of all samples within each mini-batch. If the mini-batch is big enough, we can make full use of the large number of computing cores in GPUs so that the total running time of an epoch is significantly reduced.

- **Learning rate**
A good choice of learning rate is the most crucial hyperparameter for Algorithm 8.8 to yield the best possible performance. This includes how to choose an initial learning rate at the beginning and how to adjust it at the end of every epoch. Like all first-order optimization methods, Algorithm 8.8 has no access to the curvature of the underlying loss function, and at the same time, the number of model parameters is too large to manually tune different learning rates for different model parameters. As a result, first-order optimization methods normally use the same learning rate for all model parameters at each update. This forces us to make a very conservative choice for this single learning rate at each time step because we need to ensure this learning rate is not too large for most model parameters. Otherwise, the model update will overshoot the local optimum during the learning process. On the other hand, the conservative choice of too-small learning rates at each time step will make Algorithm 8.8 converge extremely slowly because it needs to run many epochs. Moreover, as the learning proceeds and we get closer to a local optimal point, typically even smaller learning rates must be used to avoid the overshooting of the local optimum. Therefore, in Algorithm 8.8, we have to follow a prespecified annealing schedule to gradually reduce the learning rate at the end of every epoch. Normally, a multiplicative rule is used to update the learning rate; for example, the learning rate is halved or multiplied by another hyperparameter $\alpha \in (0, 1)$ at the end of each epoch when some conditions are met. Finally, another complication is that the behavior of learning algorithms under different choices of learning rates is poorly understood. When we change the learning rate from one choice to another on the same task or when we switch to work on a different task, the behavior of the learning algorithm is highly unpredictable unless we actually conduct all experiments. Therefore, it is an extremely painful and time-consuming process to look for the best learning rate for any particular task.

8.4.1 Other SGD Variant Optimization Methods: ADAM

Assuming that enough computing resources are available to fine-tune the hyperparameters, the mini-batch SGD algorithm in Algorithm 8.8 usually yields strong performance for a variety of tasks. However, many SGD variant algorithms have also been proposed to ease the potential fine-tuning efforts required in the learning of neural networks. Some typical algorithms include momentum [192], Adagrad [55], Adadelta [260], adaptive moment estimation (ADAM) [129], and AdaMax [129]. In these methods, some mechanisms are introduced to self-adjust the learning rates for SGD. By doing so, we only need to select a proper initial learning rate, and the algorithm will automatically adapt the learning rate for different model parameters according to some accumulated statistics. In the following, we introduce the popular ADAM algorithm originally proposed by Kingma and Ba [129].

Algorithm 8.9 ADAM to Learn Neural Networks

randomly initialize $\mathbb{W}^{(0)}$, and set η
set $t = 0$, $n = 0$ and $\mathbf{u}_0 = \mathbf{v}_0 = 0$
while not converged **do**
  randomly shuffle training data into mini-batches
  for each mini-batch B **do**
    for each $\mathbf{x} \in B$ **do**
      i) forward pass: $\mathbf{x} \longrightarrow \mathbf{y}$
      ii) backward pass: $\{\mathbf{x}, \mathbf{y}\} \longrightarrow \frac{\partial Q(\mathbb{W}^{(n)};\mathbf{x})}{\partial \mathbb{W}}$
    end for
    $\mathbf{g}_n = \frac{1}{|B|} \sum_{\mathbf{x} \in B} \frac{\partial Q(\mathbb{W}^{(n)};\mathbf{x})}{\partial \mathbb{W}}$
    $\mathbf{u}_{n+1} = \alpha \, \mathbf{u}_n + (1-\alpha) \, \mathbf{g}_n$
    $\mathbf{v}_{n+1} = \beta \, \mathbf{v}_n + (1-\beta) \, \mathbf{g}_n \odot \mathbf{g}_n$
    $\hat{\mathbf{u}}_{n+1} = \frac{\mathbf{u}_{n+1}}{1-\alpha^{n+1}}$ and $\hat{\mathbf{v}}_{n+1} = \frac{\mathbf{v}_{n+1}}{1-\beta^{n+1}}$
    update model: $\mathbb{W}^{(n+1)} = \mathbb{W}^{(n)} - \eta \cdot \hat{\mathbf{u}}_{n+1} \odot \left((\hat{\mathbf{v}}_{n+1} + \epsilon^2)^{-\frac{1}{2}} \right)$
    $n = n + 1$
  end for
  $t = t + 1$
end while

$\mathbf{g}_n$ denotes the averaged gradient over a mini-batch.

$\mathbf{u}_{n+1}$ and $\mathbf{v}_{n+1}$ denote the exponential moving averages of first and second moments of the gradients over time.

$\hat{\mathbf{u}}_{n+1}$ and $\hat{\mathbf{v}}_{n+1}$ denote unbiased estimates of the first and second moments.

Kingma and Ba [129] propose to use the following default values to set all hyperparameters in ADAM:

$$\eta = 0.001,$$
$$\alpha = 0.9,$$
$$\beta = 0.999,$$
$$\epsilon = 10^{-8}.$$

As shown in Algorithm 8.9, the ADAM algorithm uses exponential moving averages, $\mathbf{u}_{n+1}$ and $\mathbf{v}_{n+1}$, to estimate the first-order and second-order moments of the averaged gradients over time. And then these moving averages are normalized to derive unbiased estimates, $\hat{\mathbf{u}}_{n+1}$ and $\hat{\mathbf{v}}_{n+1}$. These unbiased estimates are used to automatically adjust the learning rate over time. As a result, we only need to set the initial learning rate η, and the ADAM algorithm will automatically anneal it as the learning proceeds. In order to see how this annealing mechanism works, let us look at the ith element of these estimates, denoted as $u_{n+1}(i)$ and $v_{n+1}(i)$. After we expand it over n, we have

$$u_{n+1}(i) = (1-\alpha)\Big(g_n(i) + \alpha \cdot g_{n-1}(i) + \alpha^2 \cdot g_{n-2}(i) + \cdots\Big)$$

$$v_{n+1}(i) = (1-\beta)\Big(g_n^2(i) + \beta \cdot g_{n-1}^2(i) + \beta^2 \cdot g_{n-2}^2(i) + \cdots\Big),$$

where $g_n(i)$ denotes the ith element of $\mathbf{g}_n$.

Furthermore, we can derive the formula to compute the ith element of the unbiased estimates as follows:

$$\hat{u}_{n+1}(i) = \frac{u_{n+1}(i)}{1-\alpha^{n+1}} = \frac{g_n(i) + \alpha \cdot g_{n-1}(i) + \alpha^2 \cdot g_{n-2}(i) + \cdots}{1 + \alpha + \alpha^2 + \cdots}$$

$$\hat{v}_{n+1}(i) = \frac{v_{n+1}(i)}{1-\beta^{n+1}} = \frac{g_n^2(i) + \beta \cdot g_{n-1}^2(i) + \beta^2 \cdot g_{n-2}^2(i) + \cdots}{1 + \beta + \beta^2 + \cdots}.$$

Moreover, we assume the averaged gradients $g_n(i)$ are slowly changing over n (i.e., $\mathbb{E}\big[g_{n-k}(i)\big] = \mathbb{E}\big[g_n(i)\big]$ for small $k = 1, 2, \cdots$). Therefore, the previous two equations clearly show that

$$\mathbb{E}\big[\hat{u}_{n+1}(i)\big] = \mathbb{E}\big[g_n(i)\big] \qquad \mathbb{E}\big[\hat{v}_{n+1}(i)\big] = \mathbb{E}\big[g_n^2(i)\big]. \tag{8.22}$$

Next, let us look at the model-update formula in Algorithm 8.9, which shows that the ith parameter in $\mathbb{W}$ is updated as follows:

$$\mathbb{W}_i^{(n+1)} = \mathbb{W}_i^{(n)} - \eta \frac{\hat{u}_{n+1}(i)}{\sqrt{\hat{v}_{n+1}(i) + \epsilon^2}},$$

where a small positive number ϵ is added to ensure numerical stability when the estimated $\hat{v}_{n+1}(i)$ becomes extremely small. We ignore ϵ and denote the update for the ith parameter as follows:

$$\Delta\mathbb{W}_i^{(n)} = \eta \frac{\hat{u}_{n+1}(i)}{\sqrt{\hat{v}_{n+1}(i)}},$$

where the numerator is an unbiased estimate of the gradient $g_n(i)$, and it is normalized by an estimate of the second-order moment. According to Eq. (8.22), its magnitude can be roughly estimated as follows:

$$\|\Delta\mathbb{W}_i^{(n)}\|^2 \simeq \eta^2 \frac{\big(\mathbb{E}\big[\hat{u}_{n+1}(i)\big]\big)^2}{\mathbb{E}\big[\hat{v}_{n+1}(i)\big]} = \frac{\eta^2\big(\mathbb{E}\big[g_n(i)\big]\big)^2}{\big(\mathbb{E}\big[g_n(i)\big]\big)^2 + \mathrm{var}\big[g_n(i)\big]}.$$

Note that

$$\mathbb{E}\big[x^2\big] = \big(\mathbb{E}[x]\big)^2 + \mathrm{var}[x]$$

As we can see in panel (a) of Figure 8.36, if the ith parameter fluctuates around an optimum, its gradients are alternatively positive and negative (i.e., $\mathbb{E}\big[g_n(i)\big] \to 0$), and $\mathrm{var}\big[g_n(i)\big]$ is large, then the ADAM algorithm will

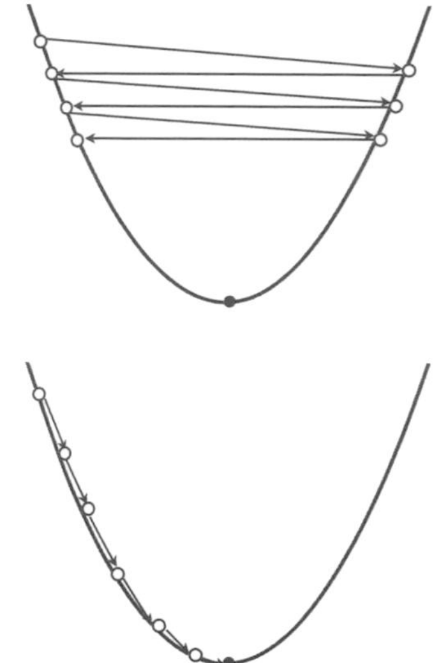

Figure 8.36: Two scenarios of parameter updates in SGD. Panel (a): Fluctuations around an optimum at top. Panel (b): Steady updates toward an optimum at bottom.

automatically reduce the update for the ith parameter as $\|\Delta \mathbb{W}_i^{(n)}\|^2 \to 0$. On the other hand, if the ith parameter is still far away from the optimum, as shown in panel (b) of Figure 8.36, all gradients are either positive or negative so that $\left(\mathbb{E}\left[g_n(i)\right]\right)^2$ tends to be large and $\mathrm{var}\left[g_n(i)\right]$ is small. As a result, the magnitude $\|\Delta \mathbb{W}_i^{(n)}\|^2$ is large in this case; namely, the update for this parameter will be relatively large as well. Hence, the ADAM algorithm will steadily update this parameter toward the optimum.

8.4.2 Regularization

Similar to other discriminative models, we can apply a variety of regularization methods in the learning of neural networks. These regularization techniques play an important role when the training set is relatively small. The following list briefly introduces several regularization methods commonly used for neural networks:

- **Weight decay**
  When we construct the objective function to learn neural networks, it is possible to add L_p norm-regularization terms. When the L_2 norm is used [133], the resultant model-update rule is colloquially called *weight decay*. In this case, the combined objective function may be represented as
  $$Q(\mathbb{W}) + \frac{\lambda}{2} \cdot \|\mathbb{W}\|^2.$$
  The model-update formula in the SGD for this objective function can be easily derived as
  $$\mathbb{W}^{(n+1)} = \mathbb{W}^{(n)} - \eta \frac{\partial Q(\mathbb{W}^{(n)})}{\partial \mathbb{W}} - \lambda \cdot \mathbb{W}^{(n)},$$
  where the extra term in the update formula (i.e., $\lambda \cdot \mathbb{W}^{(n)}$) tends to reduce the magnitude of the model parameters and push it toward the origin during the learning process. This is why this method is called *weight decay*.

- **Weight normalization**
  Zhang et al. [263] and Salimans and Kingma [209] have proposed some reparameterization methods to normalize weight vectors in neural networks. Assume $\mathbf{w}$ is a weight vector in one particular layer that generates an input to any neuron in a neural network; in Zhang et al. [263], $\mathbf{w}$ is reparameterized as
  $$\mathbf{w} = \gamma \cdot \mathbf{v} \quad \text{s.t.} \quad ||\mathbf{v}|| \leq 1,$$

where γ is a scalar parameter, and $\mathbf{v}$ is a vector constrained inside the unit sphere.
On the other hand, in Salimans and Kingma [209], the weight vector is reparameterized as

$$\mathbf{w} = \frac{\gamma}{||\mathbf{v}||}\mathbf{v},$$

where both the scalar γ and $\mathbf{v}$ are free parameters.

It is evident that these weight-normalization methods are mathematically equivalent to the original model. They are two reparameterizations that can be used to separate the norm of a weight vector from its direction without sacrificing the expressiveness of the model. They have a similar effect as batch normalization that normalizes each input by the standard deviation. Like batch normalization, these methods can facilitate the learning of neural networks by smoothing the loss function.

► **Data augmentation and dropout**
Data augmentation represents various convenient methods of generating more alternative training samples from the raw training data, for example, by injecting small noises into raw data or slightly altering raw data. It is well known that injecting small noises into training data will improve the generalization of learned models. Data augmentation is particularly convenient for images because each raw image can be slightly transformed into separate training copies by rotation, crop, translation, shear, zoom, flip, reflection, and color renormalization. When data augmentation is used, the model will see slightly different copies of the same training sample in different training epochs. This will improve the generalization ability of the model.

Srivastava et al. [230] propose a simple method called *dropout* to inject noise into the learning process of neural networks, where the activation outputs of some neurons are dropped in the forward pass, and these dropped neurons are randomly selected at each time according to a probability distribution. The dropout method is very easy to implement, and it is equally applicable to any type of training data. On the other hand, the dropout method typically slows down the convergence of the learning algorithm, so we need to run many more epochs when dropout is used.

8.4.3 Fine-Tuning Tricks

As we have discussed, it is a painful process to fine-tune all hyperparameters when learning large neural networks for the best possible performance. First of all, the high computational cost prevents us from performing a full grid search for the best combination of hyperparameters. Second, because of the high dimensionality of the learning problems, it is hard to visualize the learning process and examine what is going on. Because of the complexity of the settings, it is very challenging to pinpoint the cause of problems that arise. This section introduces some very basic rules that provide guidance during the fine-tuning process. For more fine-tuning tricks, interested readers may refer to other sources, such as Ng [174].

During the fine-tuning process, it is important to monitor the following three learning curves. By comparing these three learning curves, we can gain lots of information about the current learning process and how to further adjust the hyperparameters to improve performance.

- **The objective function**
  The first learning curve is plotted as the objective function evaluated at the end of every epoch. At each epoch, we use the latest model to compute the objective function on the training set. If the training set is too large, it is fine to use a fixed subset of the whole training data for this purpose. This learning curve gives a rough picture of how the optimization proceeds from one epoch to the next and also provides information on the suitability of many hyperparameters.

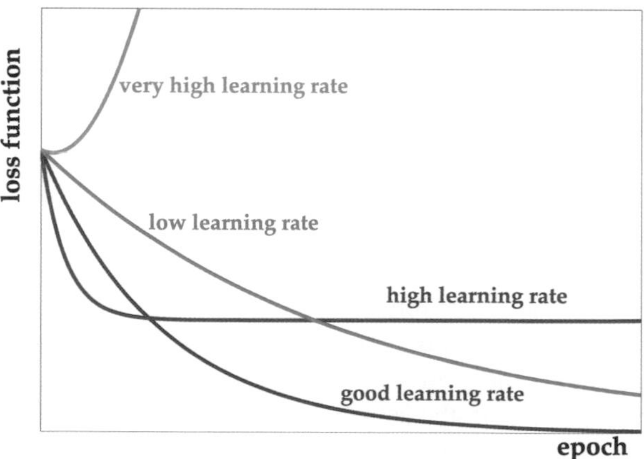

Figure 8.37: An illustration of several learning curves using different learning rates.

As shown in Figure 8.37, based on the shape of the learning curve, we may roughly know whether the used learning rate is too big or too small. We should adjust the learning rate to make it behave like the red one in Figure 8.37.

- **Performance on training data**
  The second curve is plotted by evaluating the model performance on the training set at the end of every epoch. If it is a classification task, the performance refers to the classification error rate on the training set (or a fixed subset of the training set). This learning curve should be strongly correlated with the first curve. Otherwise, it indicates that the formulation of the learning is problematic or that the implementation is buggy.

- **Performance on development data**
  The third curve is plotted by evaluating the model performance on an unseen development set at the end of every epoch. This curve is a good indicator for determining when the learning algorithm should be terminated.
  Moreover, the gap between the second and third curves provides lots of information on whether the current learned model is underfitting or overfitting. Based on how big this gap is, we may need to adjust the model size accordingly or modify the regularization method used.

8.5 End-to-End Learning

When we build a traditional machine learning system, it normally involves a pipeline of several individual steps, such as feature extraction and model construction. For a complex task, we even divide each of these steps further into some separate modules. For example, when building a conventional speech-recognition system, we usually break down the model construction into at least three modules: acoustic models, lexicon models, and language models. Acoustic models are used to represent how all phonemes in a language are distributed in the feature space and how they are affected by neighboring phonemes, a lexicon is assembled to indicate how every word is pronounced, and language models are trained to compute how likely it is that various words form a meaningful sentence. In most cases, these submodules are normally trained independently from their individually collected data by optimizing a local learning criterion only related to each module.

On the contrary, *end-to-end learning* refers to training a single model that can map directly from the raw data as input to the final targets as output for some potentially complex machine learning tasks, bypassing all the intermediate modules in the traditional pipeline design. It is understandable that end-to-end learning requires a powerful model that can handle all complex implications in a traditional pipeline. As we have learned, deep neural networks are superior in modeling capacity and very flexible in structural configuration to accommodate a variety of data types, such as static patterns and sequences. Moreover, the aforementioned standard structures in neural networks can be further customized in a special way to generate real-world data as output, for example, producing word sequences in the *encoder–decoder* structure [232], outputting dense images from the *deconvolution* layers [148], and generating audio waveforms in the *WaveNet* model [178].

Taking advantage of the highly configurable structure in neural networks, we are able to build flexible deep neural networks to conduct end-to-end learning for a variety of real-world applications, where each network layer (or a group of layers) can be learned to specialize in an intermediate task in the traditional pipeline design. End-to-end learning is appealing for many reasons. First, all components in end-to-end learning are jointly trained based on a single objective function closely related to the ultimate goal of accomplishing the underlying task. In contrast, each module in the traditional pipeline approach is normally learned separately, so it may be suboptimal in some way. Second, as long as we can collect enough end-to-end training data, we can quickly build machine learning systems for a new task without having much domain knowledge.

Here, we will use sequence-to-sequence learning [232] as an example to briefly introduce the main idea of end-to-end learning.

8.5.1 Sequence-to-Sequence Learning

Sequence-to-sequence learning refers to learning a deep neural network to map from one input sequence into an output sequence. It actually represents a very general learning framework because it covers many important applications in the real world. For example, speech-recognition systems convert speech audio streams into word sequences, and speech-synthesis systems convert word sequences back to speech audio streams. Furthermore, many natural-language-processing tasks can also be formulated as a sequence-to-sequence learning problem. Machine translation systems convert a word sequence in the source language into another word sequence in the target language. A question-answering system can be viewed as mapping a sequence of words in a question into a sequence of words in its answer.

Most sequence-to-sequence learning systems adopt the so-called *encoder–decoder* structure, as shown in Figure 8.38, where two neural networks are used: one as an encoder $\mathbb{V}$ and the other as a decoder $\mathbb{W}$. For both $\mathbb{V}$ and $\mathbb{W}$, we can choose any neural networks that are suitable to handle sequences, such as RNNs, LSTMs, or transformers. The encoder $\mathbb{V}$ aims to convert each input sequence into a compact fixed-size representation $\mathbf{z}$

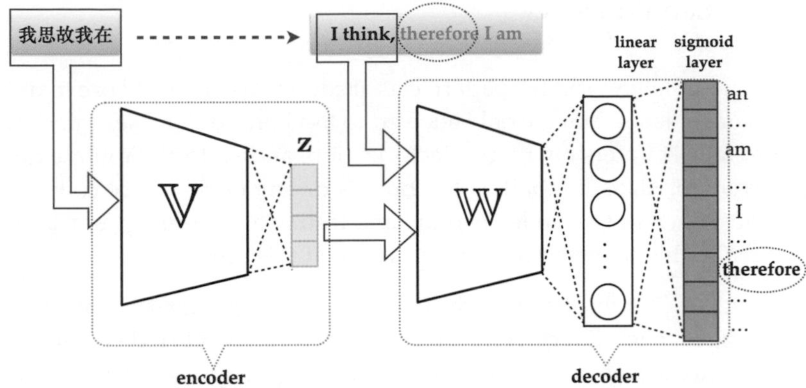

Figure 8.38: An illustration of the encoder–decoder structure for sequence-to-sequence learning in a Chinese-to-English machine translation task.

while the decoder $\mathbb{W}$ will generate an output sequence using $\mathbf{z}$ as input. As shown in Figure 8.38, the decoder is implemented in such a way that it takes $\mathbf{z}$ and a partial output sequence as input at each step and tries to predict the next word in the output sequence. The decoder normally needs to run recursively until it reaches an end-of-sequence symbol. Similar to autoencoders, both the encoder $\mathbb{V}$ and the decoder $\mathbb{W}$ are jointly learned from some pairs of input and output sequences.

Vaswani et al. [244] propose a *cross-attention* mechanism for the cases where transformers are used as the decoder $\mathbb{W}$. At each step, the partial output sequence is first processed by a regular self-attention mechanism, as shown in Figure 8.27, and then the output is forwarded to generate the query matrix $\mathbf{Q}$ in another cross-attention module that is also similar to Figure 8.27, except that the other two matrices $\mathbf{K}$ and $\mathbf{V}$ are generated from a different source (i.e., $\mathbf{z}$).

Lab Project IV

In this project, you will implement several neural networks for pattern classification. You may choose to use any programming language for your own convenience. You are only allowed to use libraries for linear algebra operations, such as matrix multiplication, matrix inversion, matrix factorization, and so forth. You are not allowed to use any existing machine learning or statistics toolkits or libraries or any open-source code for this project. You will have to implement most parts of the model learning and testing algorithms yourself for practice with the various algorithms covered in this chapter. That is the purpose of this project.

Once again, you will use the MNIST data set [142] for this project, which is a handwritten digit set containing 60,000 training images and 10,000 test images. Each image is 28 by 28 in size. The MNIST data set can be downloaded from `http://yann.lecun.com/exdb/mnist/`. In this project, for simplicity, use pixels as raw features for the following models.

a. **Fully connected deep neural network**
Implement the forward and backward passes for fully connected deep neural networks, as in Figure 8.19. Use all training data to learn a 10-class classifier with your own back-propagation implementation, investigate various network structures (e.g., different number of layers and nodes per layer), and report the best possible classification performance in the held-out test images.

b. **Convolutional neural network**
Implement the forward and backward passes for CNNs in the following figure. Use all training data to learn a 10-class classifier with your own back-propagation implementation, investigate classification accuracy by slightly varying network structures (e.g., various combinations of convolution layers of various kernel sizes, max-pooling layers, and fully connected layers), and report the best possible classification performance in the held-out test images.

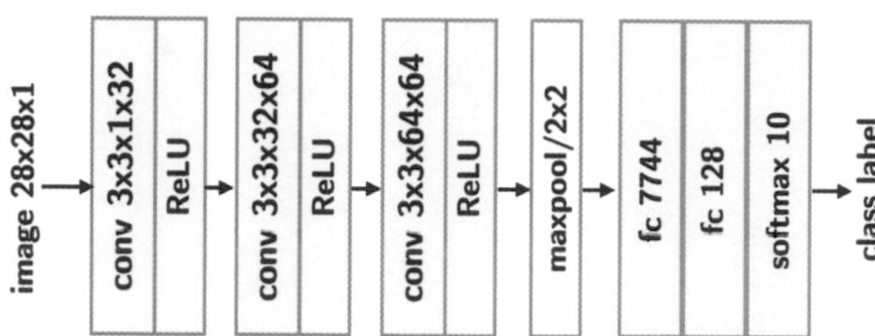

Exercises

Q8.1 Full connection and convolution are closely related:

a. Show that convolution can be viewed as a special case of full connection where **W** and **b** take a particular form. What is this particular form of **W** and **b**?
b. Show that full connection can also be viewed as a special case of convolution where the kernels are chosen in a certain way. What is this particular choice of kernels?

Q8.2 If we use the fully connected deep neural network in Figure 8.19 for a pattern-classification task that involves some nonexclusive classes, show how to configure the output layer and formulate the CE loss function to accommodate these nonexclusive classes.

Q8.3 Consider a simple CNN consisting of two hidden layers, each of which is composed of convolution and ReLU. These two hidden layers are then followed by a max-pooling layer and a softmax output layer. Assume each convolution uses K kernels of 5×5 with a stride of 1 in each direction (no zero padding). All these kernels are represented as a multidimensional array, denoted as $\mathbb{W}(f_1, f_2, p, k, l)$, where $1 \leq f_1, f_2 \leq 5$, $1 \leq k \leq K$, and l indicates the layer number $l \in \{1,2\}$, and p indicates the number of feature maps in each layer. The max-pooling layer uses 4×4 patches with a stride of 4 in each direction. Derive the back-propagation procedure to compute the gradients for all kernels $\mathbb{W}(f_1, f_2, p, k, l)$ in this network when CE loss is used.

Q8.4 In object recognition, translating an image by a few pixels in some direction should not affect the category recognized. Suppose that we consider images with an object in the foreground on top of a uniform background. Also suppose that the objects of interest are always at least 10 pixels away from the borders of the image. Is the CNN in Q8.3 invariant to the translation of at most 10 pixels in some direction? Here, the translation is applied only to the foreground object while keeping the background fixed. If your answer is yes, show that the CNN will necessarily produce the same output for two images where the foreground object is arbitrarily translated by at most 10 pixels. If your answer is no, provide a counter-example by describing a situation where the output of the CNN is different for two images where the foreground object is translated by at most 10 pixels. If your answer is no, can you find any particular translation of less than 10 pixels in which the CNN will generate an invariant output for the translation?

Q8.5 Unfold the following HORNN [228] into a feed-forward structure without using any feedback:

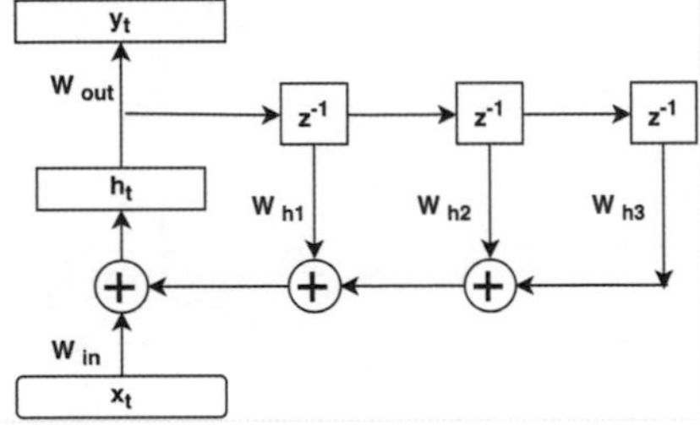

Q8.6 Use the AD rules to derive the backward-pass formulae in Eqs. (8.17) and (8.18) for multidimensional convolutions.

Q8.7 Following the derivation of batch normalization, derive the backward pass for layer normalization.

Q8.8 Using the AD rules, derive the backward pass for the following layer connections:

a. *Time-delayed feedback* in Figure 8.16
b. *Tapped delay line* in Figure 8.17
c. *Attention* in Figure 8.18

Q8.9 Suppose that we have a multihead transformer as shown in Figure 8.27, where $\mathbf{A}^{(j)}, \mathbf{B}^{(j)} \in \mathbb{R}^{l\times d}, \mathbf{C}^{(j)} \in \mathbb{R}^{o\times d}$ $(j = 1 \cdots J)$.

a. Estimate the computational complexity of the forward pass of this transformer for the input sequence $\mathbf{X} \in \mathbb{R}^{d\times T}$.
b. Derive the error back-propagation to compute the gradients for $\mathbf{A}^{(j)}, \mathbf{B}^{(j)}, \mathbf{C}^{(j)}$ when an objective function $Q(\cdot)$ is used.

Q8.10 Compared to a transformer, the *feed-forward sequential memory network* (FSMN) [262] is a more efficient model to convert a context-independent sequence into a context-dependent one. An FSMN uses the tapped delay line shown in Figure 8.17 to convert a sequence $\{\mathbf{y}_1, \mathbf{y}_2, \cdots, \mathbf{y}_T\}$ $(\mathbf{y}_i \in \mathbb{R}^n)$ into $\{\hat{\mathbf{z}}_1, \hat{\mathbf{z}}_2, \cdots, \hat{\mathbf{z}}_T\}$ $(\hat{\mathbf{z}}_i \in \mathbb{R}^o)$ through a set of bidirectional parameters $\{\mathbf{a}_i \,|\, i = -L+1, \cdots, L-1, L\}$.

a. If each $\mathbf{a}_i$ is a vector (i.e., $\mathbf{a}_i \in \mathbb{R}^n$), estimate the computational complexity of an FSMN layer. (Note that $o = n$ in this case.)
b. If each $\mathbf{a}_i$ is a matrix (i.e., $\mathbf{a}_i \in \mathbb{R}^{o\times n}$), estimate the computational complexity of an FSMN layer.
c. Assume $n = 512, o = 64, T = 128, J = 8, L = 16$; compare the total number of operations in the forward pass of one layer of such a matrix-parameterized FSMN with that of one multihead transformer in the box on page 174. How about using a vector-parameterized FSMN (assume $o = 512$ in this case)?

Ensemble Learning | 9

This chapter discusses another methodology to learn strong discriminative models in machine learning, which first builds multiple simple base models from given training data and then aims to combine them in a good way to form an ensemble for the final decision making in order to obtain better predictive performance. These methods are often called *ensemble learning* in the literature. This chapter first discusses the idea of ensemble learning in general and then introduces how to automatically learn *decision trees* for classification and regression problems because decision trees currently remain the most popular base models in ensemble learning. Next, several basic strategies to combine multiple base models are presented, such as *bagging* and *boosting*. Finally, the popular *AdaBoost* and *gradient-tree-boosting* methods and the fundamental principles behind them are introduced.

9.1 Formulation of Ensemble Learning

Even in the early days of machine learning, people had already observed the interesting phenomenon that the final predictive performance on a machine learning task could be significantly improved by combining some separately trained systems with a fairly simple method, such as averaging or majority voting, as long as there is significant diversity among these systems. These empirical observations have motivated a new machine learning paradigm, often called *ensemble learning*, where multiple base models are separately trained to solve the same problem, and then they are combined in a certain way in order to achieve more accurate or robust predictive performance on the same task [48, 90, 100, 227, 63, 179].

In ensemble learning, we normally have to address the following three fundamental issues:

- **How to choose base models for the ensemble?**
  In the early days, we often chose linear models or fully connected feed-forward neural networks as the base models in ensemble learning [48, 90]. More recently, *decision trees* have become the dominant base models in ensemble learning because of the high flexibility of using decision trees to accommodate various types of input data, as well as the great efficiency of automatically growing a decision tree

from data. Unlike the black-box neural networks, a noticeable advantage of decision trees is that the learned tree structures are highly interpretable. In the last part of this section, we will briefly explore some popular methods for learning decision trees for regression and classification tasks.

- **How to learn many base models from the same training set to maintain the diversity among them?**
  All base models in the ensemble are separately learned from the same training set, but we have to apply some tricks in the training process to ensure all base models are diverse. The final ensemble model is guaranteed to outperform these base models only when the outputs from the base models are somehow different and complementary. The common tricks include resampling the training set for each base model so that each base model uses a different subset of the training data or reweighting all training samples differently so that each base model is built to focus on a different aspect of the training data.
- **How to combine these base models to ensure the best possible performance of the ensemble model?**
  In many ensemble learning methods, the learned base models are combined in a relatively simple way, such as *bagging* [30] or *boosting* [214, 68, 215]. In these methods, we tend to use a simple additive model to combine the outputs from all base models to generate the final result for the ensemble model. For example, we can use an average (or a weighted average) of the outputs from all base models as the final result in a regression task, or we can use a majority-voting result of the decisions from all base classifiers in a classification task. In other ensemble learning methods, such as *stacking* (a.k.a. *stacked generalization*) [252, 31], we can train a high-level model, often called the *meta-model*, to make a final prediction using the predictions of all base models as its inputs. In order to alleviate overfitting, we normally use one training set to learn all base models but a separate held-out set to learn the meta-model. The common choices for the meta-model in stacking include logistic regression and neural networks.

Among these issues, the way to combine all base models is normally closely related to the way in which each base model is actually learned. In Section 9.2, we will first explore the *bagging method*, where all base models are learned independently and the resultant base models are linearly combined as the final ensemble model. In particular, we will introduce the famous *random-forest method* as a special case of bagging. In Section 9.3, we will explore the *boosting method* from the perspective of gradient boosting, where the base models are sequentially learned one by one and, at each step, a new base model is built using a gradient descent method in some model spaces. Afterward, we will focus on the popular *AdaBoost* and *gradient-tree-boosting* methods as two special cases of the gradient-boosting method.

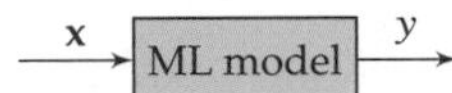

In the remainder of this section, let us briefly explore some basic concepts and learning algorithms for decision trees because they are the dominant base models in ensemble learning.

9.1.1 Decision Trees

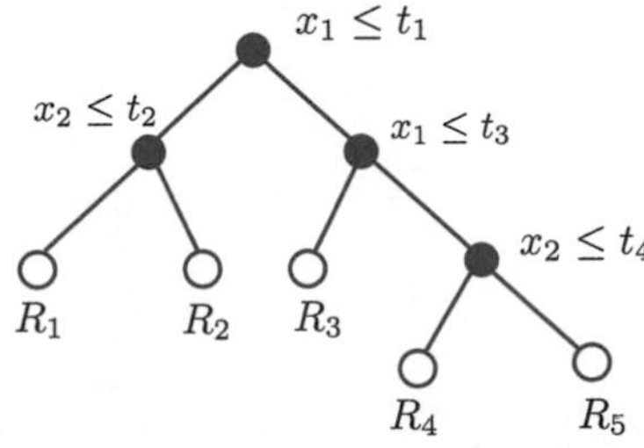

Figure 9.1: An illustration of a decision-tree model taking two features $\mathbf{x} = [x_1\ x_2]^\intercal$ as input.

Decision trees are a popular nonparametric machine learning method for regression or classification tasks, which are also called *classification and regression trees* (CARTs) [34, 193]. As shown in margin note, these tasks can normally be viewed as a system taking $\mathbf{x}$ as input and generating y as output. Assuming that the input feature vector $\mathbf{x} \in \mathbb{R}^d$ consists of a number of features as

$$\mathbf{x} = \begin{bmatrix} x_1\ x_2\ \cdots\ x_d \end{bmatrix}^\intercal,$$

a decision-tree model can be represented as a binary tree. For example, the simple example shown in Figure 9.1 uses a two-dimensional (2D) input vector $\mathbf{x} = \begin{bmatrix} x_1\ x_2 \end{bmatrix}^\intercal$. In a decision-tree model, each nonterminal node is associated with a binary question regarding a feature element x_i and a threshold t_j, taking the form $x_i \leq t_j$. Each leaf node represents a region R_l in the input space. Given any input feature vector $\mathbf{x}$, we start from the root node and ask the question associated with the node. If the answer is *TRUE*, it falls into the left child node. Otherwise, it falls into the right child node. This process continues until we reach a leaf node. As a result, each decision tree represents a particular way to partition the input space into a set of disjointed rectangle regions. For example, the decision tree in Figure 9.1 actually partitions the input space $\mathbb{R}^2$ as shown in Figure 9.2.

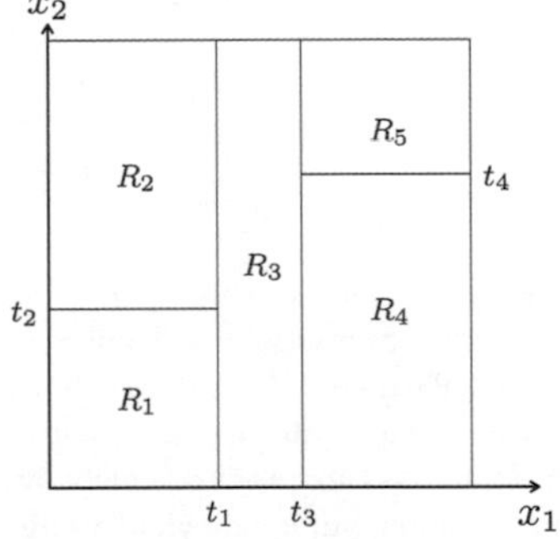

Figure 9.2: An illustration of an input space partition by the decision-tree model in Figure 9.1.

In decision-tree models, we normally fit a simple model to all y values in each region. For a regression problem, we use the constant c_l to represent all y values in each region R_l. Therefore, for regression problems, a decision-tree model essentially approximates the unknown target function between the input and output (i.e., $y = \bar{f}(\mathbf{x})$) with a piece-wise constant function, as shown in Figure 9.3. We can represent this piece-wise constant function as follows:

$$y = f(\mathbf{x}) = \sum_l c_l\, I(\mathbf{x} \in R_l), \tag{9.1}$$

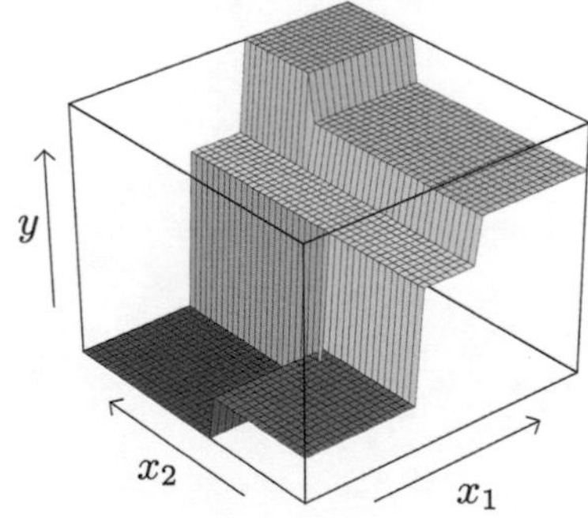

Figure 9.3: An illustration of the piece-wise constant function represented by the decision-tree model in Figure 9.1. (Image source: [92].)

where $I(\cdot)$ denotes the 0-1 indicator function as follows:

$$I(\mathbf{x} \in R_l) = \begin{cases} 1 & \text{if} \quad \mathbf{x} \in R_l \\ 0 & \text{otherwise.} \end{cases}$$

On the other hand, in a classification problem, we assign all $\mathbf{x}$ values within each region R_l into one particular class, as indicated by the different colors in Figure 9.3.

In the following, we will explore how to automatically learn a decision-tree model from a given training set of N input–output pairs:

$$\mathcal{D} = \left\{(\mathbf{x}^{(n)}, y^{(n)}) \mid n = 1, 2, \cdots, N\right\}.$$

Let's first take regression as an example; we essentially want to build a decision tree to make sure that the corresponding piece-wise constant function $y = f(\mathbf{x})$ in Eq. (9.1) minimizes the following empirical loss measured in the training set:

$$L(f;\mathcal{D}) = \frac{1}{N}\sum_{n=1}^{N} l\big(y^{(n)}, f(\mathbf{x}^{(n)})\big) = \frac{1}{N}\sum_{n=1}^{N}\big(y^{(n)} - f(\mathbf{x}^{(n)})\big)^2,$$

where $l(\cdot)$ denotes the loss function, and the square-error loss is used here for regression. From the foregoing discussion, we know that the function $y = f(\mathbf{x})$ depends on the space partition shown in Figure 9.2. Generally speaking, it is computationally infeasible to find the best partition in terms of minimizing the loss function.

In computer science, a *greedy algorithm* is any algorithm that follows some heuristics to make the locally optimal choice at each stage. Generally speaking, a greedy algorithm does not produce a globally optimal solution, but it may yield a satisfactory solution in a reasonable amount of time.

In practice, we have to rely on the greedy algorithm to construct the decision tree in a recursive manner. As we know, based on any particular binary question $x_i \le t_j$, we can always split the data set $\mathcal{D}$ into two parts as $\mathcal{D}_l = \left\{(\mathbf{x}^{(n)}, y^{(n)}) \mid x_i^{(n)} \le t_j\right\}$ and $\mathcal{D}_r = \left\{(\mathbf{x}^{(n)}, y^{(n)}) \mid x_i^{(n)} > t_j\right\}$, where $x_i^{(n)} \le t_j$ means that the ith element of the nth input sample $\mathbf{x}^{(n)}$ is not larger than a threshold t_j and similarly for $x_i^{(n)} > t_j$. As a result, $\mathcal{D}_l$ includes all training samples in $\mathcal{D}$ whose ith element is not larger than the threshold t_j, and $\mathcal{D}_r$ contains the rest.

If we only focus on one split, it is easy for us to find the best binary question (i.e., $x_i^* \le t_j^*$) by solving the following minimization problem:

$$\left\{x_i^*, t_j^*\right\} = \arg\min_{x_i, t_j}\left[\min_{c_l}\sum_{\mathbf{x}^{(n)}\in\mathcal{D}_l}\big(y^{(n)} - c_l\big)^2 + \min_{c_r}\sum_{\mathbf{x}^{(n)}\in\mathcal{D}_r}\big(y^{(n)} - c_r\big)^2\right],$$

where the inner minimization problems can be easily solved by the closed-form formulae as follows:

$$c_l^* = \arg\min_{c_l}\sum_{\mathbf{x}^{(n)}\in\mathcal{D}_l}\big(y^{(n)} - c_l\big)^2 \quad\Longrightarrow\quad c_l^* = \frac{1}{|\mathcal{D}_l|}\sum_{\mathbf{x}^{(n)}\in\mathcal{D}_l} y^{(n)}$$

$$c_r^* = \arg\min_{c_r}\sum_{\mathbf{x}^{(n)}\in\mathcal{D}_r}\big(y^{(n)} - c_r\big)^2 \quad\Longrightarrow\quad c_r^* = \frac{1}{|\mathcal{D}_r|}\sum_{\mathbf{x}^{(n)}\in\mathcal{D}_r} y^{(n)}.$$

Therefore, we can further simplify this minimization as

$$\{x_i^*, t_j^*\} = \arg\min_{x_i, t_j} \Big[\sum_{\mathbf{x}^{(n)} \in \mathcal{D}_l} \big(y^{(n)} - c_l^*\big)^2 + \sum_{\mathbf{x}^{(n)} \in \mathcal{D}_r} \big(y^{(n)} - c_r^*\big)^2 \Big].$$

We can simply go over all input elements in $\mathbf{x}$ and all possible thresholds of each element to find out the best question to locally split the data set into two subsets. The computational complexity is quadratic to the input dimension d and the total number of thresholds to be considered. If we place the two split subsets $\mathcal{D}_l$ and $\mathcal{D}_r$ as two child nodes, we can continue this process to further split these two child nodes to grow a decision tree until some termination conditions are met (e.g., some minimum node size is reached). Finally, in order to alleviate overfitting, we normally use some cost-complexity criterion (see margin note) to prune the generated tree to penalize the overly complex structures.

For example, a common cost complexity measure for regression trees is as follows:

$$Q(f;\mathcal{D}) = \sum_{n=1}^{N} \sum_{\mathbf{x}^{(n)} \in R_l} \overbrace{\big(y^{(n)} - c_l\big)^2}^{l(y^{(n)}, f(\mathbf{x}^{(n)}))} + \underbrace{\lambda \sum_l \|c_l\|^2}_{L_2 \text{ norm}} + \sum_l \alpha, \quad (9.2)$$

where $\alpha > 0$ denotes a penalty for adding a new leaf node.

We compute this complexity measure for every nonterminal node and its two child nodes. If the sum of the two child nodes is not less than that of the nonterminal node, the subtree below this nonterminal node is simply removed.

For a classification problem involving K classes (i.e., $\{\omega_1, \omega_2, \cdots, \omega_K\}$), the recursive tree-building process is also applicable, except that we need to use a different loss function for splitting the nodes and pruning the tree. For any leaf node l, representing a region R_l in the input space, we use p_{lk} (for all $k = 1, 2, \cdots, K$) to denote the portion of class k among all training samples assigned to the node l:

$$p_{lk} = \frac{1}{N_l} \sum_{\mathbf{x}^{(n)} \in R_l} I(y^{(n)} = \omega_k),$$

where N_l denotes the total number of training samples assigned to the region R_l. Once the decision tree is built, we classify all input $\mathbf{x}$ in each region R_l to the majority class as follows:

$$k_l^* = \arg\max_k \; p_{lk}.$$

When we use this recursive procedure to build decision trees for classification, the classification rule suggests that we should find the best question to split the data in such a way that two child nodes are as homogeneous as possible. In practice, we can use one of the following criteria to measure the impurity of each node l:

- Misclassification error: $\frac{1}{N_l} \sum_{\mathbf{x}^{(n)} \in R_l} I(y^{(n)} \neq \omega_{k_l^*}) = 1 - p_{lk_l^*}$.
- Gini index: $1 - \sum_{k=1}^{K} p_{lk}^2$.
- Entropy: $-\sum_{k=1}^{K} p_{lk} \log p_{lk}$.

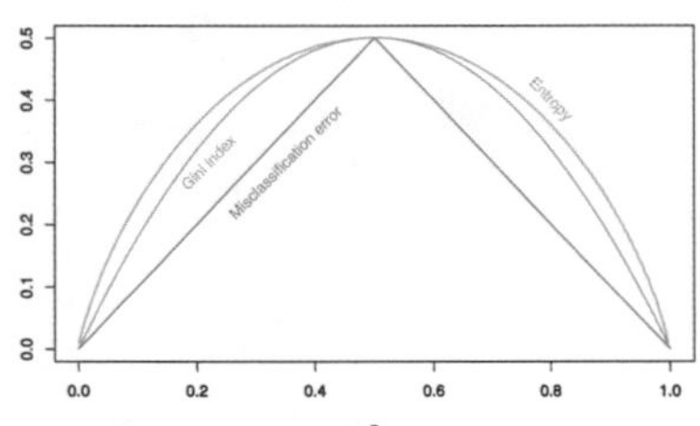

Figure 9.4: An illustration of three splitting criteria in building decision trees for binary classification problems. If p denotes the proportion of the first class, we have:

1. Misclassification error: $1 - \max(p, 1-p)$.
2. Gini index: $2p(1-p)$.
3. Entropy: $-p \log p - (1-p)\log(1-p)$.

(Image source: [92].)

These impurity measures for binary classification problems are plotted in Figure 9.4. When we build decision trees for classification, at every step, we should use one of these criteria to find the best question (i.e.,

$\{x_i^*, t_j^*\}$) that leads to the lowest impurity score summed over two split child nodes.

9.2 Bagging

Bagging (a.k.a. *bootstrap aggregating*) [30] is a simple ensemble learning method designed to improve stability and accuracy for classification and regression problems. Given a standard training set $\mathfrak{D}$, bagging generates M new subsets, each of which contains B samples, by uniformly sampling $\mathfrak{D}$ with replacement. By sampling with replacement, some training samples in $\mathfrak{D}$ may be repeated in several subsets, whereas others may never appear in any subset. Each subset is called a *bootstrap* sample in statistics. Next, we use these M bootstrap samples as separate training sets to independently learn M models. In the test stage, we just combine the results from these M models for the final decision, for example, simply averaging all M results for regression problems or conducting majority-voting among M classifiers for classification problems.

Bagging is a special case of the model-averaging method that can significantly reduce the variance in machine learning to alleviate overfitting when complex models are used, such as neural networks or decision trees. An advantage of bagging is that the training procedures of all M base models are totally independent, so bagging can be implemented in parallel across multiple processors. This allows us to efficiently build a large number of base models in the bagging method.

9.2.1 Random Forests

Random forests [99, 33] are the most popular bagging technique in machine learning, where we use decision trees as the base models. In other words, a random forest consists of a large number of decision trees, each of which is constructed using a bootstrap sample obtained from the previously described bagging procedure. The success of the bagging method largely depends on whether or not all base models are diverse enough because the combined ensemble model will surely yield a similar result if all the base models are highly correlated. In random forests, we combine the following techniques to further improve the diversity of all decision trees that are all learned from the same training set $\mathfrak{D}$:

1. *Row sampling*
   We use the bagging method to sample $\mathfrak{D}$ with replacement to generate a bootstrap sample to learn each decision-tree model.

2. *Column sampling*
   For each bootstrap sample obtained in step 1, we further sample all input elements in $\mathbf{x}$ to keep only a random subset of features used for each tree-building step.
3. *Suboptimal splitting*
   We use the random subset from step 2 to grow a decision tree. At each step, we search for the best question only from a random selection of all kept features rather than all available features.

As shown in the literature [99, 33], the feature sampling in steps 2 and 3 is crucial for random forests because it can significantly improve the diversity of all decision trees in a random forest. This is easy to understand: assuming that the input vector $\mathbf{x}$ contains some strong features and other relatively weak features, no matter how many bootstrap samples we use, they may all result in some very similar decision trees concentrating on those strong features alone. By randomly sampling features, we will be able to take advantage of those weak features in some trees so as to build a much more diverse ensemble model at the end. Generally speaking, random forests are a very powerful ensemble learning method in practice because they can significantly outperform a pure decision-tree method.

9.3 Boosting

In many ensemble learning methods, if we use a linear method to combine all base models to form the final ensemble model, it is fundamentally equivalent to learning an additive model, as follows:

$$F_m(\mathbf{x}) = w_1\, f_1(\mathbf{x}) + w_2\, f_2(\mathbf{x}) + \cdots + w_m\, f_m(\mathbf{x}),$$

where each base model $f_m(\mathbf{x}) \in \mathbb{H}$ is learned from a prespecified model space $\mathbb{H}$, and $w_m \in \mathbb{R}$ is its ensemble weight. Even when all base models are chosen from the model space $\mathbb{H}$, the ensemble model $F_m(\mathbf{x})$ does not necessarily belong to $\mathbb{H}$ but, rather, to an extended model space, denoted as $\text{lin}(\mathbb{H})$, that contains all linear combinations of any functions in $\mathbb{H}$. In general, $\text{lin}(\mathbb{H})$ does not equal to $\mathbb{H}$, but we can easily verify that $\text{lin}(\mathbb{H}) \supseteq \mathbb{H}$. Furthermore, if we treat the loss function $l\big(f(\mathbf{x}), y\big)$ as a *functional* in the function space $\text{lin}(\mathbb{H})$, the ensemble learning problem can be viewed as the following functional minimization problem:

The term *functional* is defined as a function of functions, which maps any function in a function space into a real number in $\mathbb{R}$.

$$F_m(\mathbf{x}) = \arg \min_{f \in \text{lin}(\mathbb{H})} \sum_{n=1}^{N} l\Big(f(\mathbf{x}_n), y_n\Big).$$

In this case, the functional $l(f(\mathbf{x}), y)$ is a function of all functions $f(\cdot)$ in $\text{lin}(\mathbb{H})$, and $f(\cdot)$ in turn takes $\mathbf{x} \in \mathbb{R}^d$ as input.

Boosting [214] is a special ensemble learning method that learns all base models in a sequential way. At each step, we aim to learn a new base model $f_m(\mathbf{x})$ and an ensemble weight w_m in such a way that it can further improve the ensemble model $F_{m-1}(\mathbf{x})$ after being added to the ensemble:

$$F_m(\mathbf{x}) = F_{m-1}(\mathbf{x}) + w_m\, f_m(\mathbf{x}).$$

If we can learn each new base model $f_m(\mathbf{x})$ and its weight w_m in a good way to guarantee that $F_m(\mathbf{x})$ always outperforms $F_{m-1}(\mathbf{x})$, we can repeat this sequential learning process over and over until a very strong ensemble model is finally constructed. This is the basic motivation behind all boosting techniques. As shown in the literature [214, 68], this boosting idea turns out to be an extremely powerful machine learning technique because it can eventually lead to an arbitrarily accurate ensemble model by simply combining a large number of weak base models. Each base model is said to be weak because each performs slightly better than random guessing.

In the following, we will first explore the central step in boosting, namely, how to learn a new base model at each step to ensure the ensemble model is always improved. Next, we will explore two popular boosting methods, *AdaBoost* and *gradient-tree boosting*, as case studies.

9.3.1 Gradient Boosting

As we know, boosting aims to solve the functional minimization problem sequentially. The critical issue in boosting is how to choose a new base model at each step to guarantee that the ensemble model is surely improved after the new base model is added. If we view the loss function $l\big(f(\mathbf{x}), y\big)$ as a functional on a function space, then the gradient $\frac{\partial l(f(\mathbf{x}),y)}{\partial f}$ represents a new function in the function space that points to the direction of the fastest increase of $l\big(f(\mathbf{x}), y\big)$ at f. Following the same idea of the steepest descent in regular gradient descent methods, the *gradient-boosting method* [32, 161, 72] aims to estimate the new base model along the direction of the negative gradient at the current ensemble F_{m-1}:

$$-\nabla l\big(F_{m-1}(\mathbf{x})\big) \triangleq -\frac{\partial l\big(f(\mathbf{x}), y\big)}{\partial f}\bigg|_{f=F_{m-1}}$$

However, we normally cannot directly use the negative gradient $-\nabla l\big(F_m(\mathbf{x})\big)$ as the new base model because it may not belong to the model space $\mathbb{H}$. The key idea in gradient boosting is to search for a function in $\mathbb{H}$ that resembles the specified gradient the most.

Following Mason et al. [161], we first define an inner product between any two functions $f(\cdot)$ and $g(\cdot)$ using all training samples in $\mathcal{D}$, as follows:

$$\langle f, g \rangle \triangleq \frac{1}{N} \sum_{i=1}^{N} f(\mathbf{x}_i) g(\mathbf{x}_i).$$

One way to conduct gradient boosting is to search for a base model in $\mathbb{H}$ at each step to maximize the inner product with the negative gradient:

$$f_m = \arg\max_{f \in \mathbb{H}} \left\langle f, -\nabla l\big(F_{m-1}(\mathbf{x})\big) \right\rangle. \tag{9.3}$$

The idea of gradient boosting is conceptually shown in Figure 9.5. Roughly speaking, the new base model f_m is estimated by projecting the negative gradient at F_{m-1} into the model space $\mathbb{H}$ consisting of all base models.

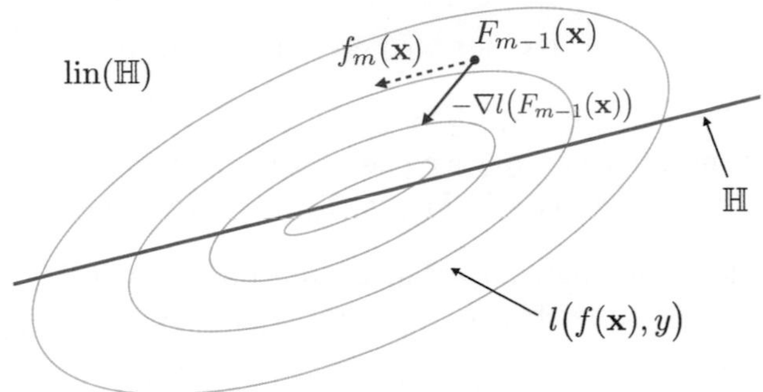

Figure 9.5: An illustration of using the gradient-boosting method to estimate a new base model f_m based on the functional gradient at the current ensemble F_{m-1}, where we use the contour plot to display the functional $l(f(\mathbf{x}), y)$ and a straight line to represent the model space $\mathbb{H}$.

Alternatively, following Friedman [72, 73], we can also define another metric between any two functions $f(\cdot)$ and $g(\cdot)$ using $\mathcal{D}$, as follows:

$$\|f - g\|^2 = \frac{1}{N} \sum_{i=1}^{N} \big(f(\mathbf{x}_i) - g(\mathbf{x}_i)\big)^2.$$

Using this distance metric, we can similarly conduct the gradient boosting at every step by searching for a base model in $\mathbb{H}$ that minimizes the distance from the negative gradient as follows:

$$\begin{aligned} f_m &= \arg\min_{f \in \mathbb{H}} \left\| f + \nabla l\big(F_{m-1}(\mathbf{x})\big) \right\|^2 \\ &= \arg\min_{f \in \mathbb{H}} \sum_{n=1}^{N} \Big(f(\mathbf{x}_n) + \nabla l\big(F_{m-1}(\mathbf{x}_n)\big)\Big)^2. \end{aligned} \tag{9.4}$$

If we can compute the second-order derivative of the functional $l(f(\mathbf{x}), y)$:

$$\nabla^2 l(f(\mathbf{x})) \triangleq \frac{\partial^2 l(f(\mathbf{x}), y)}{\partial f^2},$$

we can use the Newton method in place of gradient descent for the gradient boosting [74].
In this case, we estimate a new base model at each step, as follows:

$$f_m = \arg\min_{f \in \mathbb{H}} \left\| f + \frac{\nabla l\big(F_{m-1}(\mathbf{x})\big)}{\nabla^2 l\big(F_{m-1}(\mathbf{x})\big)} \right\|^2.$$

This method is also called *Newton boosting*.

Finally, once we have determined the new base model f_m using one of the previously described methods, we can further estimate the optimal ensemble weight by conducting the following minimization problem:

$$w_m = \arg\min_{w} \sum_{n=1}^{N} l\Big(F_{m-1}(\mathbf{x}_n) + w\, f_m(\mathbf{x}_n),\ y_n\Big). \tag{9.5}$$

Next, we'll use two examples to demonstrate how to solve the minimization problems associated with the gradient-boosting method.

9.3.2 AdaBoost

Let us apply the gradient-boosting idea to a simple binary-classification problem. Assume we are given a training set as

$$\mathcal{D} = \big\{(\mathbf{x}_1, y_1), (\mathbf{x}_2, y_2), \cdots, (\mathbf{x}_N, y_N)\big\},$$

where $\mathbf{x}_n \in \mathbb{R}^d$ and $y_n \in \{-1, +1\}$ for all $n = 1, 2, \cdots, N$. We further assume that all base models come from a model space $\mathbb{H}$ that consists of all binary functions. In other words, $\forall f \in \mathbb{H}$, $f(\mathbf{x}) \in \{-1, +1\}$ for any $\mathbf{x}$.

Moreover, let us use the exponential loss function in Table 7.1 as the loss functional for any ensemble model F [161, 74], as follows:

$$l\big(F(\mathbf{x}), y\big) = e^{-yF(\mathbf{x})}.$$

We can derive the gradient for the exponential loss functional as follows:

$$\nabla l\big(F_{m-1}(\mathbf{x})\big) \triangleq \frac{\partial l\big(f(\mathbf{x}), y\big)}{\partial f}\bigg|_{f=F_{m-1}}$$

$$= -y\, e^{-yF_{m-1}(\mathbf{x})}.$$

Following the idea in Eq. (9.3), at each step, we search for a new base model in $\mathbb{H}$ that maximizes the following inner product:

$$\begin{aligned} f_m &= \arg\max_{f\in\mathbb{H}} \big\langle f, -\nabla l\big(F_{m-1}(\mathbf{x})\big) \big\rangle \\ &= \arg\max_{f\in\mathbb{H}} \frac{1}{N} \sum_{n=1}^{N} y_n f(\mathbf{x}_n) e^{-y_n F_{m-1}(\mathbf{x}_n)}. \end{aligned}$$

If we denote $\alpha_n^{(m)} \triangleq \exp\big(-y_n F_{m-1}(\mathbf{x}_n)\big)$ for all n at step m and split the summation based on whether $y_n = f(\mathbf{x}_n)$ holds or not, we have

Due to

$$y_n \in \{-1, +1\}$$
$$f(\mathbf{x}_n) \in \{-1, +1\},$$

we have

$$y_n f(\mathbf{x}_n) = \begin{cases} 1 & \text{if } y_n = f(\mathbf{x}_n) \\ -1 & \text{if } y_n \neq f(\mathbf{x}_n). \end{cases}$$

$$\begin{aligned} f_m &= \arg\max_{f\in\mathbb{H}} \Bigg[\sum_{y_n = f(\mathbf{x}_n)} \alpha_n^{(m)} - \sum_{y_n \neq f(\mathbf{x}_n)} \alpha_n^{(m)} \Bigg] \\ &= \arg\max_{f\in\mathbb{H}} \Bigg[\sum_{n=1}^{N} \alpha_n^{(m)} - 2 \sum_{y_n \neq f(\mathbf{x}_n)} \alpha_n^{(m)} \Bigg] \\ &= \arg\min_{f\in\mathbb{H}} \sum_{y_n \neq f(\mathbf{x}_n)} \alpha_n^{(m)} \\ &= \arg\min_{f\in\mathbb{H}} \sum_{y_n \neq f(\mathbf{x}_n)} \bar{\alpha}_n^{(m)}. \end{aligned}$$

In the last step, we normalize all weights as $\bar{\alpha}_n^{(m)} = \frac{\alpha_n^{(m)}}{\sum_{n=1}^N \alpha_n^{(m)}}$ to ensure they satisfy the sum-to-1 constraint. This suggests that we should estimate the new base model f_m by learning a binary classifier from $\mathbb{H}$ that minimizes the following weighted-classification-error:

$$\epsilon_m = \sum_{y_n \neq f_m(\mathbf{x}_n)} \bar{\alpha}_n^{(m)},$$

where we have $0 \leq \epsilon_m \leq 1$ because all $\bar{\alpha}_n^{(m)}$ are normalized.

We can simply learn this binary classifier using a weighted loss function in place of the regular 0-1 loss function in constructing the learning objective function, where $\bar{\alpha}_n^{(m)}$ is treated as the incurred loss when a training sample $(\mathbf{x}_n, y_n)$ is misclassified at step m for all $n = 1, 2, \cdots, N$.

Once we have learned the new base model f_m, we can further estimate its ensemble weight by solving the minimization problem in Eq. (9.5):

$$w_m = \arg\min_w \sum_{n=1}^N e^{-y_n \left(F_{m-1}(\mathbf{x}_n) + w\, f_m(\mathbf{x}_n)\right)}.$$

By vanishing the derivative of this objective function, we can derive the closed-form solution to estimate w_m (see margin note), as follows:

$$w_m = \frac{1}{2} \ln \left(\frac{\sum_{y_n = f_m(\mathbf{x}_n)} \bar{\alpha}_n^{(m)}}{\sum_{y_n \neq f_m(\mathbf{x}_n)} \bar{\alpha}_n^{(m)}} \right) = \frac{1}{2} \ln \left(\frac{1 - \epsilon_m}{\epsilon_m} \right).$$

$$\begin{aligned} E_m &= \sum_{n=1}^N e^{-y_n \left(F_{m-1}(\mathbf{x}_n) + w\, f_m(\mathbf{x}_n)\right)} \\ &= \sum_{n=1}^N \alpha_n^{(m)} e^{-y_n w\, f_m(\mathbf{x}_n)} \\ &= \sum_{y_n = f_m(\mathbf{x}_n)} \alpha_n^{(m)} e^{-w} \\ &+ \sum_{y_n \neq f_m(\mathbf{x}_n)} \alpha_n^{(m)} e^{w}. \end{aligned}$$

$$\begin{aligned} \frac{dE_m}{dw} &= e^w \sum_{y_n \neq f_m(\mathbf{x}_n)} \alpha_n^{(m)} \\ &- e^{-w} \sum_{y_n = f_m(\mathbf{x}_n)} \alpha_n^{(m)}. \end{aligned}$$

$$\frac{dE_m}{dw} = 0 \Longrightarrow$$

$$\begin{aligned} w_m &= \frac{1}{2} \ln \left(\frac{\sum_{y_n = f_m(\mathbf{x}_n)} \alpha_n^{(m)}}{\sum_{y_n \neq f_m(\mathbf{x}_n)} \alpha_n^{(m)}} \right) \\ &= \frac{1}{2} \ln \left(\frac{\sum_{y_n = f_m(\mathbf{x}_n)} \bar{\alpha}_n^{(m)}}{\sum_{y_n \neq f_m(\mathbf{x}_n)} \bar{\alpha}_n^{(m)}} \right). \end{aligned}$$

Algorithm 9.10 AdaBoost

Input: $\{(\mathbf{x}_1, y_1), \cdots, (\mathbf{x}_N, y_N)\}$, where $\mathbf{x}_n \in \mathbb{R}^d$ and $y_n \in \{-1, +1\}$
Output: an ensemble model $F_m(\mathbf{x})$

> $m = 1$ and $F_0(\mathbf{x}) = 0$
> initialize $\bar{\alpha}_n^{(1)} = \frac{1}{N}$ for all $n = 1, 2, \cdots, N$
> **while** not converged **do**
>   learn a binary classifier $f_m(\mathbf{x})$ to minimize $\epsilon_m = \sum_{y_n \neq f_m(\mathbf{x}_n)} \bar{\alpha}_n^{(m)}$
>   estimate ensemble weight: $w_m = \frac{1}{2} \ln \left(\frac{1-\epsilon_m}{\epsilon_m} \right)$
>   add to ensemble: $F_m(\mathbf{x}) = F_{m-1}(\mathbf{x}) + w_m f_m(\mathbf{x})$
>   update $\bar{\alpha}_n^{(m+1)} = \frac{\bar{\alpha}_n^{(m)} e^{-y_n w_m f_m(\mathbf{x}_n)}}{\sum_{n=1}^N \bar{\alpha}_n^{(m)} e^{-y_n w_m f_m(\mathbf{x}_n)}}$ for all $n = 1, 2, \cdots, N$.
> $m = m + 1$
> **end while**

By definition

$$\bar{\alpha}_n^{(m+1)} = \frac{\alpha_n^{(m+1)}}{\sum_{n=1}^N \alpha_n^{(m+1)}},$$

where we have

$$\begin{aligned} \alpha_n^{(m+1)} &= \exp(-y_n F_m(\mathbf{x}_n)) \\ &= \exp\left(-y_n \left(F_{m-1}(\mathbf{x}_n) + w_m f_m(\mathbf{x}_n)\right)\right) \\ &= \alpha_n^{(m)} \exp\left(-y_n w_m f_m(\mathbf{x}_n)\right). \end{aligned}$$

If we repeat this process to sequentially estimate each base model and its ensemble weight and add them to the ensemble model one by one, it leads to the famous *AdaBoost* (a.k.a. *adaptive boosting*) algorithm [68], which is summarized in Algorithm 9.10. The AdaBoost is a general meta-learning algorithm because we can flexibly choose any binary classifiers as the base models. At each iteration, a binary classifier is learned by minimizing a weighted error on the training set, where each training sample is weighted by an adaptive coefficient $\bar{\alpha}_n^{(m)}$.

The AdaBoost algorithm has shown some nice properties in theory. For example, we have the following theorem regarding the convergence property of the AdaBoost algorithm:

Theorem 9.3.1 *Suppose the AdaBoost Algorithm 9.10 generates m base models with errors $\epsilon_1, \epsilon_2, \cdots, \epsilon_m$; the error of the ensemble model $F_m(\mathbf{x})$ is bounded as follows:*

$$\varepsilon \le 2^m \prod_{t=1}^{m} \sqrt{\epsilon_t(1-\epsilon_t)}.$$

This theorem implies another important property of the AdaBoost algorithm, which can be viewed as a general learning algorithm to combine many weak classifiers toward a strong classifier. Even though we can only estimate a weak classifier at each iteration, as long as it performs better than random guessing (i.e., $\epsilon_t \neq \frac{1}{2}$), the AdaBoost algorithm is guaranteed to yield an arbitrarily strong classifier when m is sufficiently large (i.e., $\varepsilon \to 0$ as $m \to \infty$).

In addition to this nice convergence property on the training data, many empirical results have shown that the AdaBoost algorithm generalizes very well into new, unseen data. In many cases, it has been found that AdaBoost can continue to improve the generalization error even after the training error has reached 0. A theoretical analysis [215] suggests that AdaBoost can continuously improve the margin distribution of all training samples, which may prevent AdaBoost from overfitting when more and more base models are added to the ensemble even after the training error has reached 0.

9.3.3 Gradient Tree Boosting

Here, let us look at how to apply the gradient boosting idea to regression problems, where we use decision trees as the base models in the ensemble. Assuming that we use the square error as the loss functional $l(f(\mathbf{x}), y) = \frac{1}{2}(f(\mathbf{x}) - y)^2$, we can compute the functional gradient at the ensemble model $F_{m-1}(\mathbf{x})$, as follows:

$$\nabla l\Big(F_{m-1}(\mathbf{x})\Big) = F_{m-1}(\mathbf{x}) - y.$$

Based on the idea in Eq. (9.4), we just need to build a decision tree f_m to fit to the negative gradients for all training samples. This can be easily achieved by treating each negative gradient $y_n - F_{m-1}(\mathbf{x}_n)$, also called the *residual*, as a pseudo-output for each input vector $\mathbf{x}_n$. We can run the greedy algorithm to fit to these pseudo-outputs so as to build a regression tree $f_m(\mathbf{x})$, given as

$$y = f_m(\mathbf{x}) = \sum_l c_{ml} \, I(\mathbf{x} \in R_{ml}),$$

where c_{ml} is computed as the mean of all residuals belonging to the region R_{ml}, which corresponds to the lth leaf node of the decision tree built for $f_m(\mathbf{x})$. This method is often called *gradient tree boosting*, the *gradient-boosting machine (GBM)*, or a *gradient-boosted regression tree (GBRT)* [72–74, 42].

In the gradient-tree-boosting methods, we usually do not need to conduct another optimization in Eq. (9.5) to estimate the ensemble weight for each tree. Instead, we just use a preset "shrinkage" parameter ν to control the learning rate of the boosting procedure, as follows:

In statistics, *shrinkage* refers to a method to reduce the effects of sampling variation.

$$F_m(\mathbf{x}) = F_{m-1}(\mathbf{x}) + \nu \, f_m(\mathbf{x}).$$

It has been empirically found that small values ($0 < \nu \leq 0.1$) often lead to much better generalization errors [73]. Finally, we can summarize the gradient-tree-boosting algorithm as shown in Algorithm 9.11.

Algorithm 9.11 Gradient Tree Boosting

Input: $\{(\mathbf{x}_1, y_1), \cdots, (\mathbf{x}_N, y_N)\}$
Output: an ensemble model $F_m(\mathbf{x})$

```
fit a regression tree f_0(x) to {(x_1, y_1), ··· , (x_N, y_N)}
F_0(x) = ν f_0(x)
m = 1
while not converged do
    compute the negative gradients as pseudo-outputs:
        ỹ_n = −∇l(F_{m−1}(x_n))      for all n = 1, 2, ··· , N
    fit a regression tree f_m(x) to {(x_1, ỹ_1), ··· , (x_N, ỹ_N)}
    F_m(x) = F_{m−1}(x) + ν f_m(x)
    m = m + 1
end while
```

The gradient-tree-boosting method can be easily extended to other loss functions for regression problems; see Exercise Q9.4. Moreover, we can also extend the gradient-tree-boosting procedure to classification problems, where an ensemble model is built for each class. See Exercise Q9.5 for more details on this.

Lab Project V

In this project, you will implement several tree-based ensemble learning methods for regression and classification. You may choose to use any programming language for your own convenience. You are only allowed to use libraries for linear algebra operations, such as matrix multiplication, matrix inversion, matrix factorization, and so forth. You are not allowed to use any existing machine learning or statistics toolkits or libraries or any open-source codes for this project.

In this project, you will use the Ames Housing Dataset [44] available at Kaggle (`https://www.kaggle.com/c/house-prices-advanced-regression-techniques/overview`), where each residential home is described by 79 explanatory variables on (almost) every aspect of a house. Your task is to predict the final sale price of each home as a regression problem or predict whether each home is expensive or not as a binary-classification problem (a home is said to be expensive if its sale price exceeds $150,000).

a. Use the provided training data to build a regression tree to predict the sale price. Report your best result in terms of the average square error on the test set. Use the provided training data to build a binary classification tree to predict whether each home is expensive or not. Report your best result in terms of classification accuracy on the test set.

b. Use the provided training data to build a random forest to predict the sale price. Report your best result in terms of the average square error on the test set.

c. Use the AdaBoost Algorithm 9.10 to build an ensemble model to predict whether each home is expensive or not, where you use binary classification trees as the base models. Report your best result in terms of classification accuracy on the test set.

d. Use the gradient-tree-boosting Algorithm 9.11 to learn an ensemble model to predict the sale price. Report your best result in terms of the average square error on the test set.

e. Use the gradient-tree-boosting method in Exercise Q9.5 to build an ensemble model to predict whether each home is expensive or not. Report your best result in terms of classification accuracy on the test set.

Exercises

Q9.1 In the AdaBoost Algorithm 9.10, assume we have learned a base model $f_m(\mathbf{x})$ at step m that performs worse than random guessing (i.e., its error $\epsilon_m > \frac{1}{2}$). If we simply flip it to $\bar{f}_m(\mathbf{x}) = -f_m(\mathbf{x})$, compute the error for $\bar{f}_m(\mathbf{x})$ and its optimal ensemble weight. Show that it is equivalent to use either $f_m(\mathbf{x})$ or $\bar{f}_m(\mathbf{x})$ in AdaBoost.

Q9.2 In AdaBoost, we define the error for a base model $f_m(\mathbf{x})$ as $\epsilon_m = \sum_{y_n \neq f_m(\mathbf{x}_n)} \bar{\alpha}_n^{(m)}$. We normally have $\epsilon_m < \frac{1}{2}$. We then reweight the training samples for the next round as

$$\bar{\alpha}_n^{(m+1)} = \frac{\bar{\alpha}_n^{(m)} e^{-y_n w_m f_m(\mathbf{x}_n)}}{\sum_{n=1}^{N} \bar{\alpha}_n^{(m)} e^{-y_n w_m f_m(\mathbf{x}_n)}} \qquad \forall n = 1, 2, \cdots, N.$$

Compute the error of the same base model $f_m(\mathbf{x})$ on the reweighted data, that is,

$$\tilde{\epsilon}_m = \sum_{y_n \neq f_m(\mathbf{x}_n)} \bar{\alpha}_n^{(m+1)},$$

and explain how $\tilde{\epsilon}_m$ differs from the ϵ_{m+1} that will be computed in the next round.

Q9.3 Derive the logitBoost algorithm by replacing the exponential loss in AdaBoost with the logistic loss: $l\big(F(\mathbf{x}), y\big) = \ln\big(1 + e^{-y\,F(\mathbf{x})}\big)$.

Q9.4 Derive the gradient-tree-boosting procedure for regression problems when the following loss functionals are used:

a. The least absolute deviation:

$$l\big(F(\mathbf{x}), y\big) = \big|y - F(\mathbf{x})\big|.$$

b. The Huber loss:

$$l(F(\mathbf{x}), y) = \begin{cases} \frac{1}{2}\big(y - F(\mathbf{x})\big)^2 & \text{if } |y - F(\mathbf{x})| \le \delta \\ \delta|y - F(\mathbf{x})| - \frac{\delta^2}{2} & \text{otherwise.} \end{cases}$$

Q9.5 In a classification problem of K classes (i.e., $\{\omega_1, \omega_2, \cdots, \omega_K\}$), assume that we use an ensemble model for each class ω_k (for all $k = 1, 2, \cdots, K$) as follows:

$$F_m(\mathbf{x};\, \omega_k) = f_1(\mathbf{x};\, \omega_k) + f_2(\mathbf{x};\, \omega_k) + \cdots + f_m(\mathbf{x};\, \omega_k),$$

where each base model $f_m(\mathbf{x}; \omega_k)$ is a regression tree. Derive the gradient-tree-boosting procedure to estimate the ensemble models for all K classes by minimizing the following cross-entropy loss functional:

$$l\big(F(\mathbf{x}), y\big) = -\ln\left[\frac{e^{F(\mathbf{x};y)}}{\sum_{k=1}^{K} e^{F(\mathbf{x};\omega_k)}}\right] \qquad \big(y \in \{\omega_1, \omega_2, \cdots, \omega_K\}\big).$$

Q9.6 Derive the gradient-tree-boosting procedure using Newton boosting for a twice-differentiable loss functional $l\big(F(\mathbf{x}), y\big)$. Assume that we use the L_2 norm term and the penalty α per node in Eq. (9.2) as two extra regularization terms together with the loss functional.

Generative Models

10 Overview of Generative Models

In the preceding chapters, we thoroughly discussed *discriminative models* in machine learning. In this chapter and onward, we will switch gears and explore another important school of machine learning models, namely, *generative models*. This chapter first introduces how *generative models* fundamentally differ from *discriminative models* in machine learning and then gives readers a roadmap for various generative modeling topics to be discussed in the upcoming chapters.

10.1 Formulation of Generative Models

Section 5.1 introduced the formal definition of discriminative models and also discussed a general formulation for learning discriminative models in pattern-classification problems. As we have seen, discriminative models can be viewed as a system that takes feature vectors $\mathbf{x}$ as input and generates target labels y as output (see margin note), where the input $\mathbf{x}$ is a random vector following an unknown distribution $p(\mathbf{x})$, and the relation between the input $\mathbf{x}$ and the output y is *deterministic*, specified by an unknown target function $y = \bar{f}(\mathbf{x})$. The goal in learning a discriminative model is to estimate the unknown target function within a prespecified model space based on some training samples of input–output pairs that are generated by this system.

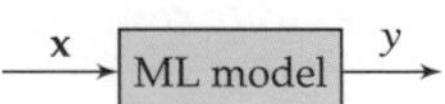

Similar to discriminative models, a generative model can also be viewed as a system that takes feature vectors $\mathbf{x}$ as input and generates target labels y as output. However, the noticeable differences in generative models include the following:

1. Both $\mathbf{x}$ and y are random variables.
2. The relation between $\mathbf{x}$ and y is not *deterministic* but *stochastic*.

In other words, the output y cannot be completely determined by the corresponding input $\mathbf{x}$. The underlying system involves some randomness that may generate different outputs even for the same input. In this case, the relation between $\mathbf{x}$ and y must be specified by a joint probability distribution between them (i.e., $p(\mathbf{x}, y)$).

Here, let us first use a simple example to elucidate the key difference between deterministic and stochastic relations.

Example 10.1.1 *Deterministic* versus *Stochastic*

1. Assume the system is linear (i.e., $y = \mathbf{w}^\intercal \mathbf{x}$), where the parameter $\mathbf{w}$ is unknown but fixed. In this case, the relation between $\mathbf{x}$ and y is *deterministic*. If we feed the same input, we always receive the same output even if we do not know it is a linear system.
2. Assume the output is corrupted by an independent Gaussian noise: $y = \mathbf{w}^\intercal \mathbf{x} + \epsilon$, where $\epsilon \sim \mathcal{N}(0, 1)$. In this case, the relation between $\mathbf{x}$ and y is *stochastic*. Even when we feed the same input to the system, the output may differ due to the additive noise.
3. Assume the parameter of this linear system (i.e., $\mathbf{w}$) is not a fixed value but a random vector following a probability distribution (i.e., $\mathbf{w} \sim p(\mathbf{w})$). In this case, the relation between $\mathbf{x}$ and y is also *stochastic* because $\mathbf{w}$ takes a different value at a different time. ♦

The discriminative models that we have discussed in the preceding chapters make sense only when the relation between $\mathbf{x}$ and y is deterministic. This is because only under this condition are those loss functions used to formulate the learning objectives, such as squared error, 0-1 loss, and margin, actually meaningful. When both $\mathbf{x}$ and y are random variables and their relation is stochastic, the mathematical tool we have to use to model them is their joint probability distribution: $p(\mathbf{x}, y)$. All generative models essentially aim to model this joint distribution.

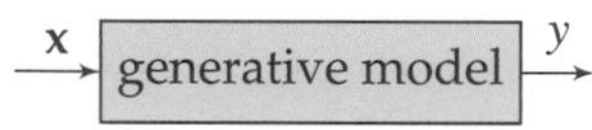

Figure 10.1: An illustration of a generative model in machine learning that is used to model the joint distribution of input and output (i.e., $p(\mathbf{x}, y)$).

When generative models are used for a machine learning problem, as in Figure 10.1, both $\mathbf{x}$ and y are random variables specified by a joint distribution $p(\mathbf{x}, y)$. The machine learning problem is normally formulated as follows: when we observe a realization of the input variable as $\mathbf{x}_0$, we want to make the best guess or estimate of the random output y conditioning on the input $\mathbf{x}_0$. Depending on whether the output y is discrete or continuous, the underlying problem is a classification or regression problem.

Of course, the joint distribution $p(\mathbf{x}, y)$ is always unknown in practice. In the next section, let us first consider some ideal cases for generative models where the joint distribution $p(\mathbf{x}, y)$ is given. As suggested by the well-known *Bayesian decision theory*, once the joint distribution $p(\mathbf{x}, y)$ is known, the *optimal* solution to estimate the output y based on any particular input $\mathbf{x}_0$ can be derived in a fairly simple way. As we will see, this theoretical result also turns the central issue in generative models into how to estimate this joint distribution if it is unknown.

10.2 Bayesian Decision Theory

Bayesian decision theory is concerned with some ideal scenarios for generative models where the joint distribution between the input and output

$p(\mathbf{x}, y)$ is given. It indicates how to make the optimal estimate for the corresponding output for any particular input in Figure 10.1 based on the given joint distribution. Bayesian decision theory forms an important theoretical foundation for generative models. In the following, we will explore the Bayesian decision theory for two important machine learning problems, that is, classification and regression, separately.

10.2.1 Generative Models for Classification

When a generative model is used for a pattern-classification problem, as in Figure 10.2, the input feature vector $\mathbf{x}$ may be continuous or discrete or even a combination of the two, but the output y must be a discrete random variable. In a K-class classification, we assume y is a discrete random variable, taking a value out of K finite values, $\{\omega_1, \omega_2, \cdots, \omega_K\}$, each of which corresponds to a class label.

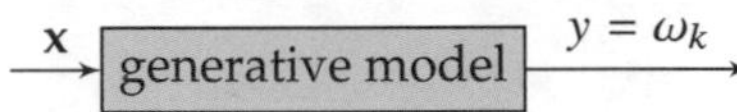

Figure 10.2: An illustration of a generative model for classification.

According to probability theory, the joint distribution $p(\mathbf{x}, y)$ can be broken down into two terms:

$$p(\mathbf{x}, y) = p(y)p(\mathbf{x}|y). \tag{10.1}$$

Because y is discrete, these two terms can be further simplified as follows:

- $p(y)$ as the *prior probabilities* of all K classes:

$$p(y = \omega_k) \stackrel{\Delta}{=} \Pr(\omega_k) \quad (\forall k = 1, 2, \cdots, K),$$

  where $\Pr(\omega_k)$ indicates the probability for class ω_k to occur prior to observing any data, so it is normally called the *prior* probability of class ω_k.
- $p(\mathbf{x}|y)$ as the *class-conditional distributions* of all K classes:

$$p(\mathbf{x} \mid y = \omega_k) \stackrel{\Delta}{=} p(\mathbf{x} \mid \omega_k) \quad (\forall k = 1, 2, \cdots, K),$$

  where the class-conditional distribution $p(\mathbf{x} \mid \omega_k)$ indicates how all data from class ω_k are distributed in the feature space, as shown in Figure 10.3.

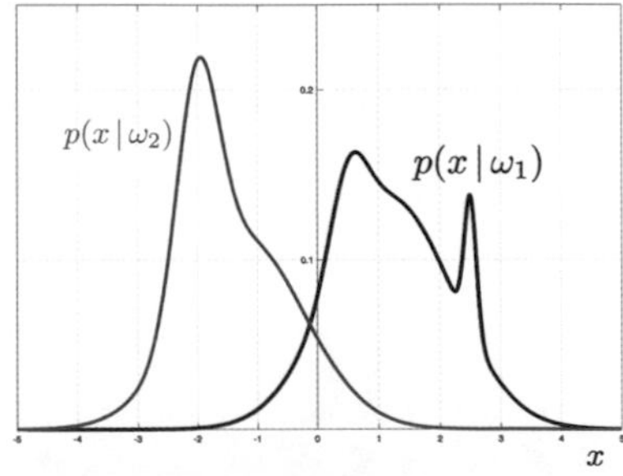

Figure 10.3: An illustration of two class-conditional distributions for classes ω_1 and ω_2 when the input feature $\mathbf{x}$ is a real value.

Because both priors $\Pr(\omega_k)$ and class-conditional distributions $p(\mathbf{x} \mid \omega_k)$ are valid probability distributions, they satisfy the sum-to-1 constraints. For all prior probabilities, we have

$$\sum_{k=1}^{K} \Pr(\omega_k) = 1.$$

For the class-conditional distributions, if the input feature vector $\mathbf{x}$ is continuous, we have

$$\int_{\mathbf{x}} p(\mathbf{x} \mid \omega_k) d\mathbf{x} = 1 \quad (\forall k = 1, 2, \cdots, K).$$

Otherwise, if $\mathbf{x}$ is discrete, we have

$$\sum_{\mathbf{x}} p(\mathbf{x} \mid \omega_k) = 1 \quad (\forall k = 1, 2, \cdots, K).$$

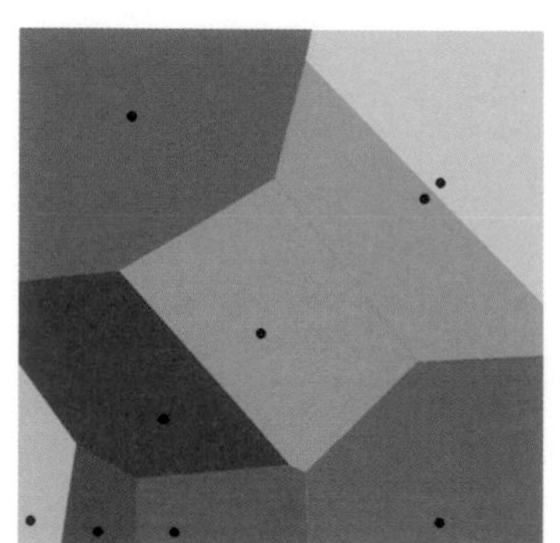

Figure 10.4: Each decision rule corresponds to a partition of the input feature space, where a color indicates a distinct O_k. Note that each O_k may consist of many disconnected pieces in the space.

In a pattern-classification problem, such as that shown in Figure 10.2, for any input feature $\mathbf{x}$, we try to use a generative model to estimate the corresponding class label ω_k. This procedure can be viewed as a decision rule $g(\mathbf{x})$ that maps any feature vector $\mathbf{x}$ into a class in $\{\omega_1, \omega_2, \cdots, \omega_K\}$:

$$g(\mathbf{x}) : \mathbf{x} \mapsto \omega_k \quad (\forall k = 1, 2, \cdots, K).$$

Also, it is easy to see that a decision rule $g(\mathbf{x})$ partitions the feature space into K disjoint regions, denoted as $O_1, O_2, \cdots, O_K$, as shown in Figure 10.4. For all $\mathbf{x} \in O_k$ $(k = 1, 2, \cdots, K)$, it implies $g(\mathbf{x}) = \omega_k$. Different decision rules partition the same input feature space in different ways.

For any classification problem, the key question is how to construct the optimal decision rule that leads to the lowest classification error. According to Bayesian decision theory, the optimal decision rule can be constructed based on a conditional probability, as follows:

$$\begin{aligned} g^*(\mathbf{x}) &= \arg\max_k \; p(\omega_k | \mathbf{x}) \\ &= \arg\max_k \; \Pr(\omega_k) \cdot p(\mathbf{x} | \omega_k), \end{aligned} \tag{10.2}$$

Based on Bayes's theorem:

$$\begin{aligned} p(\omega_k | \mathbf{x}) &= \frac{p(y = \omega_k, \mathbf{x})}{p(\mathbf{x})} \\ &= \frac{\Pr(\omega_k) \cdot p(\mathbf{x} | \omega_k)}{p(\mathbf{x})}, \end{aligned}$$

where the denominator $p(\mathbf{x})$ can be dropped because it is independent of k.

where $p(\omega_k | \mathbf{x})$ indicates the probability of class ω_k after $\mathbf{x}$ is observed and is thus called the *posterior* probability of class ω_k. As a result, this optimal decision rule $g^*(\mathbf{x})$ is often called the *maximum a posteriori (MAP)* decision rule or the *Bayes decision rule*.

The MAP decision rule is fairly simple to understand. Given any input feature $\mathbf{x}_0$, we use the prior probabilities $\Pr(\omega_k)$ and class-conditional distributions $p(\mathbf{x} \mid \omega_k)$ to compute the posterior probabilities for all K classes:

$$p(\omega_1 | \mathbf{x}_0), \; p(\omega_2 | \mathbf{x}_0), \; \ldots, \; p(\omega_K | \mathbf{x}_0),$$

and then the input $\mathbf{x}_0$ is assigned to the class that achieves the maximum posterior probability.

Regarding the optimality of the MAP decision rule, we have the following theorem:

Theorem 10.2.1 (Classification) *Assuming $p(\mathbf{x}, \omega)$ is known and ω is discrete, if $\mathbf{x}$ is used to predict ω as in pattern classification, the MAP rule in Eq. (10.2) leads to the lowest expected risk (using 0-1 loss).*

Note that the MAP rule is optimal in terms of the *expected risk*, not the *empirical loss* as in discriminative models.

Proof:

Because ω is discrete, this corresponds to a pattern-classification problem. In this case, we measure the expected risk using the 0-1 loss function:

$$l(\omega, \omega') = \begin{cases} 0 & \text{when } \omega = \omega' \\ 1 & \text{otherwise.} \end{cases}$$

We know $p(\mathbf{x}, \omega)$ is the joint distribution of any $\mathbf{x}$ and its corresponding correct class label ω. For any decision rule $g(\mathbf{x})$: $\mathbf{x} \to g(\mathbf{x}) \in \{\omega_1, \cdots, \omega_K\}$, we compute its expected risk as follows:

$$\begin{aligned} R(g) &= \mathbb{E}_{p(\mathbf{x},\omega)}\Big[l\big(\omega, g(\mathbf{x})\big)\Big] = \int_{\mathbf{x}} \sum_{\omega} l\big(\omega, g(\mathbf{x})\big) p(\mathbf{x}, \omega) d\mathbf{x} \\ &= \int_{\mathbf{x}} \sum_{k=1}^{K} l\big(\omega_k, g(\mathbf{x})\big) p(\mathbf{x}, \omega_k) d\mathbf{x} \\ &= \int_{\mathbf{x}} \underbrace{\left[\sum_{k=1}^{K} l\big(\omega_k, g(\mathbf{x})\big) p(\omega_k|\mathbf{x})\right]}_{\sum_{\omega_k \neq g(\mathbf{x})} p(\omega_k|\mathbf{x})} p(\mathbf{x}) d\mathbf{x}. \end{aligned}$$

Note that

$$p(\mathbf{x}, \omega_k) = p(\mathbf{x}) p(\omega_k|\mathbf{x})$$

$$l\big(\omega_k, g(\mathbf{x})\big) = \begin{cases} 0 & \omega_k = g(\mathbf{x}) \\ 1 & \omega_k \neq g(\mathbf{x}). \end{cases}$$

Because all posterior probabilities satisfy $\sum_{k=1}^{K} p(\omega_k|\mathbf{x}) = 1$, we have

$$\sum_{\omega_k \neq g(\mathbf{x})} p(\omega_k|\mathbf{x}) = 1 - p\big(g(\mathbf{x})|\mathbf{x}\big).$$

After substituting into the previous equation, we derive

$$R(g) = \int_{\mathbf{x}} \Big[1 - p\big(g(\mathbf{x})|\mathbf{x}\big)\Big] p(\mathbf{x}) d\mathbf{x}.$$

It is easy to see from this integral that if we can minimize $1 - p\big(g(\mathbf{x})|\mathbf{x}\big)$ for each $\mathbf{x}$ separately, we will minimize the expected risk $R(g)$ as a whole. Thus, we need to choose $g(\mathbf{x})$ in such a way to maximize $p\big(g(\mathbf{x})|\mathbf{x}\big)$ for each $\mathbf{x}$. Because $g(\mathbf{x}) \in \{\omega_1, \cdots, \omega_K\}$, $p\big(g(\mathbf{x})|\mathbf{x}\big)$ is maximized by choosing

$$g^*(\mathbf{x}) = \arg\max_k \; p(\omega_k|\mathbf{x}). \qquad \blacksquare$$

In this proof, we have managed to prove Theorem 10.2.1 without explicitly computing the expected risk $R(g)$. In a pattern-classification problem, this

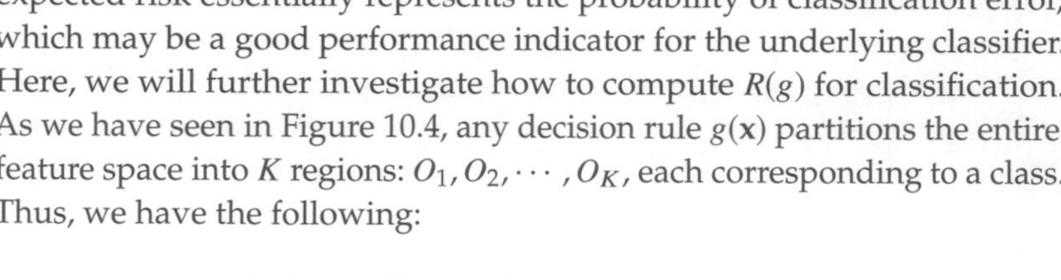

expected risk essentially represents the probability of classification error, which may be a good performance indicator for the underlying classifier. Here, we will further investigate how to compute $R(g)$ for classification. As we have seen in Figure 10.4, any decision rule $g(\mathbf{x})$ partitions the entire feature space into K regions: $O_1, O_2, \cdots, O_K$, each corresponding to a class. Thus, we have the following:

$\Pr(\mathbf{x} \in O_k, \omega_k)$ represents the probability of a pattern $\mathbf{x}$ falling inside the region O_k and, at the same time, its correct label happening to be ω_k. By definition, we classify all $\mathbf{x} \in O_k$ into ω_k. Thus, $\Pr(\mathbf{x} \in O_k, \omega_k)$ stands for the correct classification probability for class ω_k.

$$
\begin{aligned}
R(g) &= \Pr(\text{error}) = 1 - \Pr(\text{correct}) \\
&= 1 - \sum_{k=1}^{K} \Pr(\mathbf{x} \in O_k, \omega_k) \\
&= 1 - \sum_{k=1}^{K} \Pr(\omega_k) \int_{\mathbf{x} \in O_k} p(\mathbf{x}|\omega_k) d\mathbf{x}. \qquad (10.3)
\end{aligned}
$$

Among all possible decision rules, the MAP decision rule $g^*(\mathbf{x})$ yields the lowest classification-error probability $R(g^*)$, which is also called the *Bayes error*. As shown in Figure 10.5, an arbitrary decision rule always contains some reducible error, which can be eliminated by adjusting the decision boundary. The Bayes error corresponds to the minimum nonreducible error inherent in the underlying problem specification.

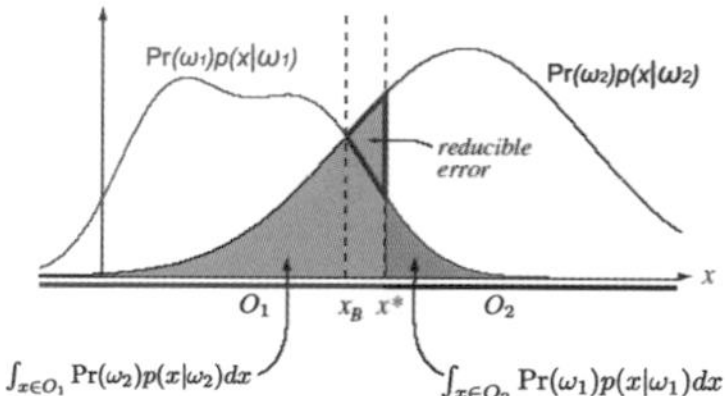

Figure 10.5: The error probability is shown for a simple two-class case. The reducible error can be eliminated by adjusting the decision boundary from x^* to x_B, which represents the MAP decision rule yielding the lowest error probability, that is, the *Bayes error*. (Source: [57].)

Of course, the integrals in Eq. (10.3) cannot be easily calculated even for many simple cases because of the discontinuous nature of the decision regions in the integral. We normally have to rely on some upper or lower bounds to analyze the Bayes error [93]. Another common approach used in practice is to empirically evaluate $R(g)$ using an independent test set.

Here, let us first use a simple example to further explore how to derive the MAP decision rule for some cases where the joint distribution can be fully specified. In the following example, we consider a two-class classification problem that only involves independent binary features:

Example 10.2.1 Classification with Independent Binary Features

Assume the prior probabilities for two classes (ω_1 and ω_2) are denoted as $\Pr(\omega_1)$ and $\Pr(\omega_2)$. We assume every sample can be evaluated by d binary questions. Based on the answers to these questions (yes/no), each sample can be represented by d independent binary (0 or 1) features, denoted as $\mathbf{x} = \left[x_1, x_2, \cdots, x_d\right]^\intercal$, where $x_i \in \{0, 1\}, \forall i = 1, 2, \cdots, d$. Derive the MAP decision rule for these two classes.

First of all, $\Pr(x_i = 1|\omega_1)$ means the probability of answering *yes* to the ith question for any sample in class ω_1, which is denoted as $\alpha_i \stackrel{\Delta}{=} \Pr(x_i = 1|\omega_1)$. The probability of answering *no* to the ith question for any sample in class ω_1 must be $1 - \alpha_i$ because all questions are binary (yes/no). Similarly, for any sample in ω_2, we denote the probability of answering *yes* to the ith question as $\beta_i \triangleq \Pr(x_i = 1|\omega_2)$. In the same way, for any sample in ω_2, the probability of answering *no* equals to $1 - \beta_i$. Given any $\mathbf{x}$, because all these features are independent, we have the following Bernoulli distribution for each class:

$$p(\mathbf{x}|\omega_1) = \prod_{i=1}^{d} \alpha_i^{x_i}(1-\alpha_i)^{1-x_i}$$

$$p(\mathbf{x}|\omega_2) = \prod_{i=1}^{d} \beta_i^{x_i}(1-\beta_i)^{1-x_i}.$$

As we know $x_i \in \{0,1\}$, we can verify:

$$\alpha_i^{x_i}(1-\alpha_i)^{1-x_i} = \begin{cases} \alpha_i & \text{if } x_i = 1 \\ 1-\alpha_i & \text{if } x_i = 0. \end{cases}$$

The MAP rule can be constructed as follows: $\mathbf{x}$ is classified as ω_1 if

$$\Pr(\omega_1) \cdot p(\mathbf{x}|\omega_1) \geq \Pr(\omega_2) \cdot p(\mathbf{x}|\omega_2),$$

and otherwise as ω_2. If we take the logarithm of both sides, we can derive the MAP rule as a **linear** decision boundary as follows:

$$g(\mathbf{x}) = \sum_{i=1}^{d} \lambda_i x_i + \lambda_0 = \begin{cases} \geq 0 & \Longrightarrow \omega_1 \\ < 0 & \Longrightarrow \omega_2, \end{cases}$$

where we have $\lambda_i = \ln \frac{\alpha_i(1-\beta_i)}{\beta_i(1-\alpha_i)}$, and $\lambda_0 = \sum_{i=1}^{d} \ln \frac{1-\alpha_i}{1-\beta_i} + \ln \frac{\Pr(\omega_1)}{\Pr(\omega_2)}$. ◆

Note that this linear classification boundary naturally arises from Bayesian decision theory because of the property of the underlying features. This is quite different from those cases in Chapter 6, where we have assumed the linearity of models in the first place.

10.2.2 Generative Models for Regression

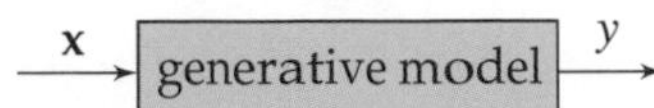

Figure 10.6: Use of generative models for regression.

If generative models are used for a regression problem, as in Figure 10.6, the output y is continuous (assuming $\mathbf{x} \in \mathbb{R}^d$ and $y \in \mathbb{R}$). Similar to previously, both $\mathbf{x}$ and y are random variables, and we assume their joint distribution is given as $p(\mathbf{x}, y)$. As in a standard regression problem, if we have observed an input sample as $\mathbf{x}_0$, we try to make the best estimate for the corresponding output y.

As we recall, this conditional distribution can be easily derived from the given joint distribution $p(\mathbf{x}, y)$:

$$p(y|\mathbf{x}_0) = \frac{p(\mathbf{x}_0, y)}{p(\mathbf{x}_0)} = \frac{p(\mathbf{x}_0, y)}{\int_y p(\mathbf{x}_0, y)\, dy}.$$

Again, Bayesian decision theory suggests that the best decision rule for this regression problem is to use the following conditional mean:

$$g^*(\mathbf{x}_0) = \mathbb{E}(y|\mathbf{x}_0) = \int_y y \cdot p(y|\mathbf{x}_0)\, dy.$$

Also, we have the following theorem to justify the optimality of using this conditional mean for regression:

Theorem 10.2.2 (Regression) *Assuming $p(\mathbf{x}, y)$ is known and y is continuous, when $\mathbf{x}$ is used to predict y, the conditional mean $\mathbb{E}(y|\mathbf{x})$ leads to the lowest expected risk (using mean-square loss).*

Proof:

Because we use the square loss function (i.e., $l(y, y') = (y - y')^2$) for any regression problem, the expected risk of any rule $\mathbf{x} \to g(\mathbf{x}) \in \mathbb{R}$:

$$
\begin{aligned}
R(g) &= \mathbb{E}_{p(\mathbf{x},y)}\Big[l\big(y, g(\mathbf{x})\big)\Big] \\
&= \int_{\mathbf{x}}\int_y \big(y - g(\mathbf{x})\big)^2 p(\mathbf{x}, y)\ d\mathbf{x}dy \\
&= \int_{\mathbf{x}} \underbrace{\left[\int_y \big(y - g(\mathbf{x})\big)^2 p(y|\mathbf{x})dy\right]}_{Q(g|\mathbf{x})} p(\mathbf{x})d\mathbf{x}.
\end{aligned}
$$

Because $p(\mathbf{x}) > 0$, if we can minimize $Q(g|\mathbf{x})$ for each $\mathbf{x}$, we will minimize $R(g)$ as a whole. Here, we compute the partial derivative of $Q(g|\mathbf{x})$ with respect to (w.r.t.) g and vanish it as follows:

$$
\frac{\partial Q(g|\mathbf{x})}{\partial g(\cdot)} = 0 \implies \int_y \big(g(\mathbf{x}) - y\big) p(y|\mathbf{x})dy = 0
$$

$$
\implies g^*(\mathbf{x}) = \int_y y \cdot p(y|\mathbf{x})dy = \mathbb{E}(y|\mathbf{x}). \qquad \blacksquare
$$

10.3 Statistical Data Modeling

As we have learned from Bayesian decision theory, as long as the true joint distribution $p(\mathbf{x}, y)$ is given, the optimal decision rule only depends on the conditional distribution, which can be easily derived from the given joint distribution. However, in any practical situation, the true joint distribution $p(\mathbf{x}, y)$ is never known to us. Normally, we do not even know the functional form of the true distribution, not to mention the true distribution itself. Therefore, the optimal Bayes decision rule is not feasible in practice. In this section, we will explore how to make the best possible decision under realistic scenarios where we do not have access to the true joint distribution of the input and output random variables. Afterward, we will consider pattern classification as an example to explain the approach, but the idea can be easily extended to other machine learning problems.

10.3.1 Plug-In MAP Decision Rule

In practice, we usually have no idea of the true joint distribution $p(\mathbf{x}, y)$, but it is possible for us to collect some training samples out of this unknown distribution. Let us denote all training samples as

$$\mathcal{D}_N = \{(\mathbf{x}_1, y_1), (\mathbf{x}_2, y_2), \cdots, (\mathbf{x}_N, y_N)\},$$

each of which is a random sample drawn from this unknown distribution, that is, $(\mathbf{x}_i, y_i) \sim p(\mathbf{x}, y)$ $(\forall i = 1, 2, \cdots, N)$. In practice, the key question we are facing is not how to construct the optimal decision based on the unknown joint distribution but how to make the best decision based on the finite set of training samples that are assumed to be randomly drawn from this distribution. The common approach is called *statistical data modeling*. In other words, we first choose some parametric probabilistic models to approximate the unknown true distribution, and then we estimate all associated parameters using the collected training samples. Once this is done, we substitute the estimated statistical models into the optimal MAP decision rule as if it were the true data distribution, which results in the so-called *plug-in MAP* decision rule [80, 81, 104]. As illustrated in Figure 10.7, the unknown data distributions are first approximated by some simpler probabilistic models (shown in red), and then the plug-in MAP decision rule is derived by substituting these estimated probabilistic models into the optimal Bayes decision rule. These *probabilistic models* are also called *generative models* or *statistical models* under this context. Hereafter, this book will use these three terms interchangeably, and all of them represent the parametric probabilistic models chosen to approximate the unknown true data distributions.

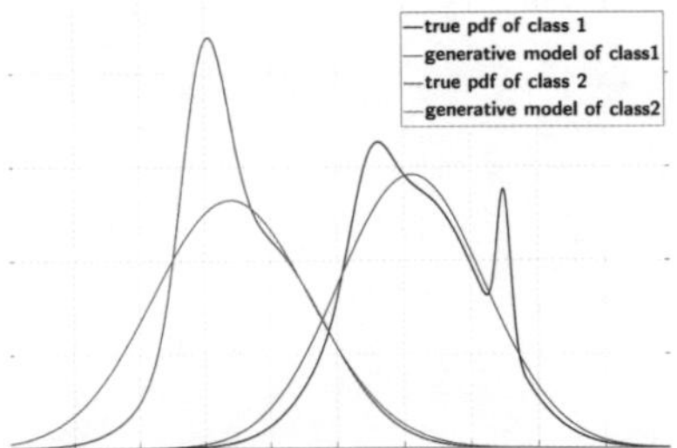

Figure 10.7: An illustration of the plug-in MAP decision rule that relies on two probabilistic models (shown in red) used to approximate the unknown true data distributions, which may be complicated.

Here, we will use pattern classification as an example to elucidate how the plug-in MAP decision rule differs from the optimal MAP rule derived from the Bayesian decision theory. As shown in Eq. (10.2), the optimal MAP decision rule for a K-class classification problem relies on the posterior probabilities, $p(\omega_k|\mathbf{x})$ $(\forall k = 1, 2 \cdots K)$, which can be computed from the prior probabilities $\Pr(\omega_k)$ and the class-conditional distributions $p(\mathbf{x}|\omega_k)$ $(\forall k = 1, 2 \cdots K)$. In practice, because we have no access to the true probability distributions $\Pr(\omega_k)$ and $p(\mathbf{x}|\omega_k)$, we use some parametric probabilistic models to approximate them as follows:

$$\Pr(\omega_k) \approx \hat{p}_{\lambda}(\omega_k)$$
$$p(\mathbf{x}|\omega_k) \approx \hat{p}_{\boldsymbol{\theta}_k}(\mathbf{x}) \quad (\forall k = 1, 2 \cdots K),$$

where $\Lambda = \{\lambda, \boldsymbol{\theta}_1, \cdots, \boldsymbol{\theta}_K\}$ denotes the model parameters of the chosen probabilistic models. The chosen models specify the functional form for the distributions. Furthermore, if we can estimate all model parameters Λ based on the collected training samples $\mathcal{D}_N$, these estimated probabilistic models can serve as an approximation to the unknown true distributions. The plug-in MAP decision rule is derived by substituting these estimated models in place of the true data distribution in the optimal Bayes decision rule as follows:

$$\hat{g}(\mathbf{x}) = \arg\max_k \ \hat{p}_{\boldsymbol{\lambda}}(\omega_k)\hat{p}_{\boldsymbol{\theta}_k}(\mathbf{x}). \tag{10.4}$$

The plug-in MAP rule $\hat{g}(\mathbf{x})$ is fundamentally different from the optimal MAP rule $g^*(\mathbf{x})$ because $\hat{g}(\mathbf{x})$ is not guaranteed to be optimal. However, as shown by Glick [80], if the chosen probabilistic models are a consistent and unbiased estimator of the true distribution, the plug-in MAP rule $\hat{g}(\mathbf{x})$ will converge to the optimal MAP decision rule $g^*(\mathbf{x})$ *almost surely* as the training sample size N increases ($N \longrightarrow \infty$).

An estimator is said to be *consistent* if it converges in probability to the true value as the number of data points used increases indefinitely.

The key steps in the statistical data-modeling procedure for pattern classification discussed thus far can be summarized as follows:

Statistical Data Modeling

Assume we have collected some training samples:

$$\mathfrak{D}_N = \{(\mathbf{x}_1, y_1), \cdots, (\mathbf{x}_N, y_N)\},$$

where each $(\mathbf{x}_i, y_i) \sim p(\mathbf{x}, y) \quad (\forall i = 1, 2, \cdots, N)$.

1. Choose some probabilistic models:

$$\Pr(\omega_k) \approx \hat{p}_{\boldsymbol{\lambda}}(\omega_k)$$

$$p(\mathbf{x}|\omega_k) \approx \hat{p}_{\boldsymbol{\theta}_k}(\mathbf{x}) \ \ (\forall k = 1, 2, \cdots, K).$$

2. Estimate the model parameters:

$$\mathfrak{D}_N \longrightarrow \{\boldsymbol{\lambda}, \boldsymbol{\theta}_1, \cdots, \boldsymbol{\theta}_K\}.$$

3. Apply the plug-in MAP rule:

$$\hat{g}(\mathbf{x}) = \arg\max_k \ \hat{p}_{\boldsymbol{\lambda}}(\omega_k) \cdot \hat{p}_{\boldsymbol{\theta}_k}(\mathbf{x}).$$

Among these three steps, the plug-in MAP rule is fairly straightforward to formulate once the chosen probabilistic models are estimated. The central issues here are how to choose the appropriate generative models for the underlying task and how to estimate the unknown model parameters in an effective way. Section 10.4 introduces how to estimate parameters for the chosen generative models, and Section 10.5 explains the basic principle behind choosing proper models for the underlying problems and provides an overview of some important model classes for generative modeling. These models will be further investigated in the following chapters as several major categories: *unimodal models* in Chapter 11, *mixture models* in Chapter 12, *entangled models* in Chapter 13, and more general *graphical models* in Chapter 15.

10.4 Density Estimation

As we have seen in the discussion of the statistical data-modeling procedure, before we can apply the plug-in MAP decision rule, the fundamental problem is how to estimate the unknown data distribution based on a finite set of training samples that are presumably drawn from this distribution. This corresponds to a standard problem in statistics, namely, *density estimation*. As we have seen, we normally take the so-called *parametric* approach to this problem. In other words, we first choose some parametric probabilistic models, and then the associated parameters are estimated from the finite set of training samples. The advantage of this approach is that we can convert an extremely challenging problem of density estimation into a relatively simple parameter-estimation problem. By estimating the parameters, we find the best fit to the unknown data distribution in the family of some prespecified generative models. Similar to discriminative models, parameter estimation for generative models can also be formulated as a standard optimization problem. The major difference here is that we need to rely on different criteria to construct the objective function for generative models. In the following, we will explore the most popular method for parametric density estimation, namely, *maximum-likelihood estimation* (MLE).

10.4.1 Maximum-Likelihood Estimation

Assume that we are interested in estimating an unknown data distribution $p(\mathbf{x})$ based on some samples randomly drawn out of this distribution; that is, $\mathcal{D}_N = \{\mathbf{x}_1, \mathbf{x}_2 \cdots, \mathbf{x}_N\}$, where each sample $\mathbf{x}_i \sim p(\mathbf{x})$ $(\forall i = 1, 2 \cdots, N)$. An important assumption in density estimation is that we assume these samples are independent and identically distributed (i.i.d.), which means that all these samples are drawn from the same probability distribution, and all of them are mutually independent. As we will see later, the i.i.d. assumption will significantly simplify the parameter-estimation problem in density estimation. In a parametric density-estimation method, we first choose a probabilistic model, $\hat{p}_{\boldsymbol{\theta}}(\mathbf{x})$, to approximate this unknown distribution $p(\mathbf{x})$, where $\boldsymbol{\theta}$ denotes the parameters of the chosen model. The unknown model parameters $\boldsymbol{\theta}$ are then estimated from the collected training samples $\mathcal{D}_N$. The most popular method for this parameter estimation problem is the so-called MLE. The basic idea of MLE is to estimate the unknown parameters $\boldsymbol{\theta}$ by maximizing the joint probability of observing all training samples in $\mathcal{D}_N$ based on the presumed probabilistic model. That is,

The last step is based on the i.i.d. assumption, which indicates that all training samples are mutually independent.

$$\begin{aligned}\boldsymbol{\theta}_{\text{MLE}} &= \arg\max_{\boldsymbol{\theta}} \hat{p}_{\boldsymbol{\theta}}(\mathcal{D}_N) \\ &= \arg\max_{\boldsymbol{\theta}} \hat{p}_{\boldsymbol{\theta}}(\mathbf{x}_1, \mathbf{x}_2, \cdots, \mathbf{x}_N) \\ &= \arg\max_{\boldsymbol{\theta}} \prod_{i=1}^{N} \hat{p}_{\boldsymbol{\theta}}(\mathbf{x}_i). \end{aligned} \tag{10.5}$$

For any probabilistic model $\hat{p}_{\boldsymbol{\theta}}(\mathbf{x})$:

a. If the model parameters $\boldsymbol{\theta}$ are given and fixed, $\hat{p}_{\boldsymbol{\theta}}(\mathbf{x})$ is viewed as a function of $\mathbf{x}$. In this case, it is a probability function over the entire feature space, where $\hat{p}_{\boldsymbol{\theta}}(\mathbf{x})$ roughly indicates the probability of observing each $\mathbf{x}$. It satisfies the sum-to-1 constraint for all $\mathbf{x}$:

$$\int_{\mathbf{x}} \hat{p}_{\boldsymbol{\theta}}(\mathbf{x})\, d\mathbf{x} = 1.$$

b. If $\mathbf{x}$ is fixed, $\hat{p}_{\boldsymbol{\theta}}(\mathbf{x})$ is viewed as a function of model parameters $\boldsymbol{\theta}$, conventionally called the *likelihood function*. Note that the likelihood function does not satisfy the sum-to-1 constraint for all $\boldsymbol{\theta}$ values in the model space, that is,

$$\int_{\boldsymbol{\theta}} \hat{p}_{\boldsymbol{\theta}}(\mathbf{x})\, d\boldsymbol{\theta} \neq 1.$$

The objective function $\hat{p}_{\boldsymbol{\theta}}(\mathbf{x}_1, \mathbf{x}_2, \cdots, \mathbf{x}_N)$ is conventionally called the *likelihood function* (see margin note for why). Intuitively speaking, MLE searches for the best model in the prespecified model family to fit the given training samples, and it provides the most likely interpretation of the observed samples. Among all density-estimation methods, MLE is the most popular approach because it always leads to the simplest solution. Furthermore, MLE also has some nice theoretical properties. For example, MLE is theoretically shown to be consistent, which means that if the model $\hat{p}_{\boldsymbol{\theta}}(\mathbf{x})$ is correct (i.e., the samples are truly generated by the underlying model), then the MLE solution converges to its true value as we have more and more samples.

In many cases, it is more convenient to work with the logarithm of the likelihood function rather than the likelihood function itself. If we denote the log-likelihood function as

$$l(\boldsymbol{\theta}) = \ln p_{\boldsymbol{\theta}}(\mathcal{D}_N) = \sum_{i=1}^{N} \ln p_{\boldsymbol{\theta}}(\mathbf{x}_i),$$

we can equivalently write the MLE as follows:

$$\begin{aligned}\boldsymbol{\theta}_{\text{MLE}} &= \arg\max_{\boldsymbol{\theta}}\ l(\boldsymbol{\theta}) \\ &= \arg\max_{\boldsymbol{\theta}}\ \sum_{i=1}^{N} \ln p_{\boldsymbol{\theta}}(\mathbf{x}_i). \end{aligned} \tag{10.6}$$

Note that the maximum-likelihood formulations in Eqs. (10.5) and (10.6) are equivalent because the logarithm function is a monotonically increasing function that does not change where the optimal points of the objective function occur. For some simple probabilistic models, the optimization problem in Eq. (10.6) can be easily solved with the differential calculus or the method of Lagrange multipliers. For other popular generative models, such as mixture models and graphical models, we can use some special optimization methods (e.g., the *expectation-maximization (EM)* method; see Section 12.2), which are much more efficient than generic gradient-descent methods for these models. We will come back to these methods in the later chapters.

Here, let us use a simple example to show how to derive a closed-form solution for the MLE of a simple Gaussian model using differential calculus.

Example 10.4.1 Assume we are given a training set of i.i.d. real scalars drawn from an unknown distribution:

$$\mathfrak{D} = \{x_1, x_2, \cdots, x_N\} \quad (x_i \in \mathbb{R}, \forall i = 1, 2, \cdots N).$$

We choose to use a univariate Gaussian to approximate the unknown distribution, as follows:

$$p_\theta(x) = \mathcal{N}(x|\mu, \sigma^2) = \frac{1}{\sqrt{2\pi\sigma^2}} e^{-\frac{(x-\mu)^2}{2\sigma^2}}.$$

Derive the MLE of the unknown parameters (i.e., μ and σ^2) based on $\mathfrak{D}$.

First of all, given $\mathfrak{D}$, the log-likelihood function can be written as

$$\begin{aligned} l(\mu, \sigma^2) &= \sum_{i=1}^{N} \ln p_\theta(x_i) \\ &= \sum_{i=1}^{N} \Big[-\frac{\ln(2\pi\sigma^2)}{2} - \frac{(x_i - \mu)^2}{2\sigma^2} \Big]. \end{aligned}$$

We solve the optimization problem in Eq. (10.6) by a simple differential calculus method:

$$\frac{\partial l(\mu, \sigma^2)}{\partial \mu} = -\frac{1}{\sigma^2} \sum_{i=1}^{N} (x_i - \mu).$$

$$\frac{\partial l(\mu, \sigma^2)}{\partial \mu} = 0 \implies \mu_{\text{MLE}} = \frac{1}{N} \sum_{i=1}^{N} x_i$$

$$\frac{\partial l(\mu, \sigma^2)}{\partial \sigma^2} = -\frac{N}{2\sigma^2} + \frac{1}{2(\sigma^2)^2} \sum_{i=1}^{N} (x_i - \mu)^2.$$

$$\frac{\partial l(\mu, \sigma^2)}{\partial \sigma^2} = 0 \implies \sigma^2_{\text{MLE}} = \frac{1}{N} \sum_{i=1}^{N} (x_i - \mu_{\text{MLE}})^2.$$

For this simple case, the MLE of the Gaussian mean and Gaussian variance equals to the sample mean and sample variance of the given training samples. ♦

10.4.2 Maximum-Likelihood Classifier

When we use the maximum-likelihood method to estimate model parameters in the statistical data-modeling procedure for a K-class pattern-classification problem, we first choose K probabilistic models $\hat{p}_{\boldsymbol{\theta}_k}(\mathbf{x})$ to approximate the class-dependent distributions $p(\mathbf{x}|\omega_k)$ for all classes $k = 1, \cdots, K$.

Second, we collect a training set for each class:

$$\mathcal{D}_k \sim p(\mathbf{x}|\omega_k) \quad (k = 1, \cdots, K).$$

Next, we apply the maximum-likelihood method to estimate the model parameters for each class:

$$\boldsymbol{\theta}_k^* = \arg\max_{\boldsymbol{\theta}_k} \hat{p}_{\boldsymbol{\theta}_k}(\mathcal{D}_k) \quad (k = 1, \cdots, K).$$

Finally, the estimated models $\hat{p}_{\boldsymbol{\theta}_k^*}(\mathbf{x})$ $(k = 1, \cdots, K)$ are used in the plug-in MAP rule in place of the unknown class-conditional distributions to classify any new pattern.

10.5 Generative Models (in a Nutshell)

As we have discussed, theoretically speaking, the plug-in MAP decision rule is not optimal because it relies on density estimators that approximate the unknown true data distribution. In practice, the performance of the plug-in MAP rule largely depends on whether we choose good probabilistic models for the underlying data distributions. Generally speaking, a good model reflects the nature of the underlying data and needs to be sophisticated enough to capture the critical dependencies in the data. On the other hand, the model structure should be simple enough to be computationally tractable. Figure 10.8 lists many popular generative models that may be used for a variety of data types. The model complexity generally increases from left to right, and each arrow indicates an extension of a simpler generative model into a more sophisticated one. In the following chapters, we will explore in detail what these models are and how to learn these models from training samples. Here, let us first have a quick overview of these generative models.

As shown in Figure 10.8, we distinguish our model choices between continuous and discrete data. *Gaussian* distributions play an essential role when we have continuous data. We can use multivariate Gaussian models for high-dimensional continuous data if they follow a unimodal distribution. For more complex distributions, we can use the idea of finite mixtures to

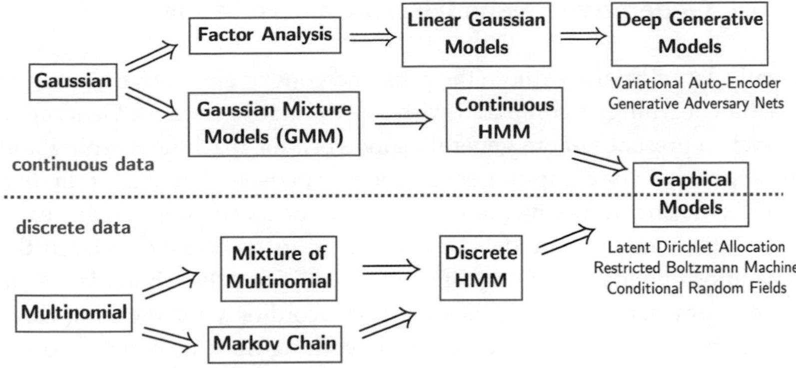

Figure 10.8: A roadmap of some important generative models for statistical data modeling. The model complexity increases from left to right, and each arrow indicates an extension of a simpler generative model into a more sophisticated model.

construct Gaussian mixture models (GMMs). Furthermore, GMMs can be extended to continuous-density hidden Markov models (HMMs) for continuous sequential data. Chapter 12 discusses these models in detail as *mixture models*. Another idea is to use some transformations of random variables to convert simple Gaussians into more sophisticated ones, such as factor analysis, linear Gaussian models, and deep generative models. Chapter 13 discusses these models as *entangled models*. Generative models can be made very general by introducing arbitrary dependency in model structure, which leads to the general Gaussian graphical models for arbitrary continuous data. Chapter 15 discusses the graphical models. On the other hand, *multinomial* distributions serve as the basic building blocks in all generative models for discrete data. A set of multinomial distributions is introduced for discrete sequential data based on the Markov assumption, leading to the Markov chains (to be discussed in Chapter 11). The complexity of these models can be enhanced with the same idea of finite mixtures, which leads to mixtures of multinomials (MMMs) and discrete-density HMMs (see Chapter 12). Furthermore, we may derive any arbitrarily dependent multinomial graphical models for discrete data (see Chapter 15).

When we go from left to right in the spectrum of models in Figure 10.8, the model power increases, so the models can be used to approximate more and more complicated distributions. However, the computational complexity of these models also generally increases from left to right. Among them, the HMM is a notable landmark in the spectrum: all models to the left of HMM (including HMMs) are normally considered to be computationally efficient, so these models can be applied to large-scale tasks without any major computational difficulties. On the other hand, all models to the right of HMM (including all general graphical models) cannot be computed in an efficient way, so they are only suitable for small-scale problems, or we have to rely on approximation schemes to derive rough solutions for larger problems.

10.5.1 Generative versus Discriminative Models

Finally, let us briefly explore the pros and cons of generative models in machine learning as compared with discriminative models. Generative models represent a more general framework for machine learning and are expected to be computationally more expensive than discriminative models in general. Taking pattern classification as an example, the learning of discriminative models only needs to focus on how to learn the separation boundaries among different classes. Once these boundaries are learned, any new pattern can be classified accordingly. On the other hand, generative models are concerned with learning the data distribution in the entire feature space. Once the data distribution is known, the decision boundaries are simply derived by the MAP rule (or the plug-in MAP rule). Conceptually speaking, density estimation is a much more difficult task than the learning of separation boundaries. At last, the advantage of generative models lies in the fact that we can explicitly model key dependencies for the underlying data based on certain fully or partially known data-generation mechanisms. By explicitly exploring these prior-knowledge sources, we are able to derive more parsimonious generative models for the data arising from certain application scenarios than with a black-box approach using discriminative models. These issues will be further discussed in Chapter 15.

Exercises

Q10.1 In the generative model $p(\mathbf{x}, \omega)$ in Figure 10.2, assume the feature vector $\mathbf{x}$ consists of two parts, $\mathbf{x} = [\mathbf{x}_g;\ \mathbf{x}_b]$, where $\mathbf{x}_b$ denotes some missing components that cannot be observed for some reason. Derive the optimal decision rule to use $p(\mathbf{x}_g, \mathbf{x}_b, \omega)$ to classify any input $\mathbf{x}$ based on its observed part $\mathbf{x}_g$ only.

Q10.2 Suppose we have three classes in two dimensions with the following underlying distributions:

- Class ω_1: $p(\mathbf{x}|\omega_1) = \mathcal{N}(\mathbf{0}, \mathbf{I})$.
- Class ω_2: $p(\mathbf{x}|\omega_2) = \mathcal{N}\left(\begin{bmatrix} 1 \\ 1 \end{bmatrix}, \mathbf{I}\right)$.
- Class ω_3: $p(\mathbf{x}|\omega_3) = \frac{1}{2}\mathcal{N}\left(\begin{bmatrix} 0.5 \\ 0.5 \end{bmatrix}, \mathbf{I}\right) + \frac{1}{2}\mathcal{N}\left(\begin{bmatrix} -0.5 \\ 0.5 \end{bmatrix}, \mathbf{I}\right)$.

Here, $\mathcal{N}(\boldsymbol{\mu}, \boldsymbol{\Sigma})$ denotes a two-dimensional Gaussian distribution with mean vector $\boldsymbol{\mu}$ and covariance matrix $\boldsymbol{\Sigma}$, and $\mathbf{I}$ is the identity matrix. Assume class prior probabilities $\Pr(\omega_i) = 1/3, i = 1, 2, 3$.

a. Classify the feature $\mathbf{x} = \begin{bmatrix} 0.25 \\ 0.25 \end{bmatrix}$ based on the MAP decision rule.
b. Suppose the first feature is missing. Classify $\mathbf{x} = \begin{bmatrix} * \\ 0.25 \end{bmatrix}$ using the optimal rule derived in Q10.1.
c. Suppose the second feature is missing. Classify $\mathbf{x} = \begin{bmatrix} 0.25 \\ * \end{bmatrix}$ using the optimal rule from Q10.1.

Q10.3 Assume that we are allowed to reject an input as unrecognizable in a pattern-classification task. For an input $\mathbf{x}$ belonging to class ω, we can define a new loss function for any decision rule $g(\mathbf{x})$ as follows:

$$l(\omega, g(\mathbf{x})) = \begin{cases} 0 & : \ g(\mathbf{x}) = \omega \\ 1 & : \ g(\mathbf{x}) \neq \omega \\ \lambda_r & : \ \text{rejection,} \end{cases}$$

where $\lambda_r \in (0, 1)$ is the loss incurred for choosing a rejection action. Derive the optimal decision rule for this three-way loss function.

Q10.4 Given a set of data samples $\{x_1, x_2, \cdots, x_n\}$, we assume the data follow an exponential distribution as follows:

$$p(x|\theta) = \begin{cases} \theta e^{-\theta x} & : \ x \geq 0 \\ 0 & : \ \text{otherwise.} \end{cases}$$

Derive the MLE for the parameter θ.

Q10.5 Given a set of training samples $\mathcal{D}_N = \{\mathbf{x}_1, \mathbf{x}_2, \cdots, \mathbf{x}_N\}$, the so-called *empirical distribution* corresponding to $\mathcal{D}_N$ is defined as follows:

$$S(\mathbf{x} \mid \mathcal{D}_N) = \frac{1}{N} \sum_{i=1}^{N} \delta(\mathbf{x} - \mathbf{x}_i),$$

where $\delta(\cdot)$ denotes Dirac's delta function. Show that the MLE is equivalent to minimizing the Kullback–Leibler (KL) divergence between the empirical distribution and the data distribution described by a generative model $\hat{p}_{\boldsymbol{\theta}}(\mathbf{x})$:

$$\boldsymbol{\theta}_{\text{MLE}} = \arg\min_{\boldsymbol{\theta}} \ \text{KL}\Big(S(\mathbf{x} \mid \mathcal{D}_N) \,\big\|\, \hat{p}_{\boldsymbol{\theta}}(\mathcal{D}_N)\Big).$$

Unimodal Models | 11

In this chapter, we first consider how to learn generative models to approximate some simple data distributions where the probability mass is concentrated only in a single region of the feature space.

For this type of data distribution, we can normally approximate it well using *unimodal* generative models. Generally speaking, a unimodal generative model represents a probability distribution that has a single peak. The unimodality is well defined for univariate functions. A univariate function is considered unimodal if it possesses a unique mode, namely, a single local maximum value (as in Figure 11.1). We can further extend this definition to include all bounded monotonic functions (as in Figure 11.2). Under this extended definition, most of the common univariate probabilistic models are unimodal, including normal distributions, binomial distributions, Poisson distributions, uniform distributions, Student's t-distributions, gamma distributions, and exponential distributions.

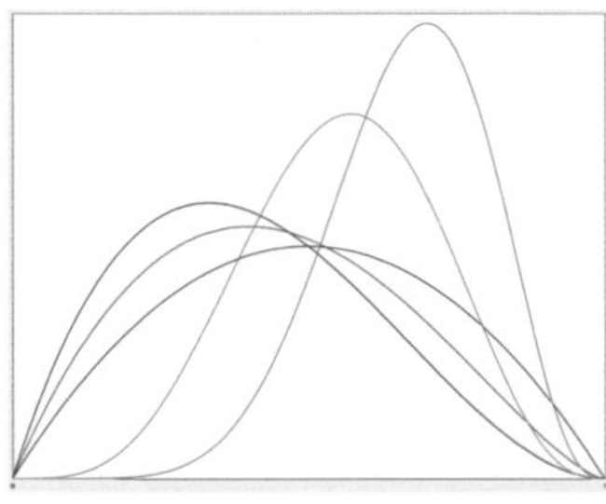

Figure 11.1: An illustration of some typical bell-shaped unimodal distributions.

On the other hand, it is not trivial to define unimodality for multivariate functions [53]. This chapter adopts a straightforward and intuitive definition: a joint probability distribution of multiple random variables is said to be unimodal if all of its univariate marginal distributions are unimodal. For example, a multinomial distribution involves a random vector, and we know the marginal distribution of each element is a binomial distribution, which is known to be unimodal. Based on this definition, we say all multinomial distributions are unimodal. Similarly, we can verify that multivariate Gaussian distributions and the so-called generalized linear models [171] are also unimodal in this sense.

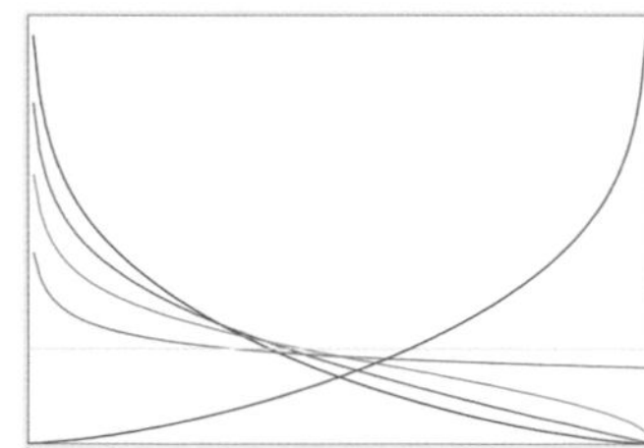

Figure 11.2: Bounded monotonic distributions are also unimodal.

The following sections introduce several unimodal generative models that have played an important role in machine learning, such as multivariate *Gaussian models* for high-dimensional continuous data in Section 11.1 and *multinomial models* for discrete data in Section 11.2. Furthermore, *Markov chain models* are introduced in Section 11.3, which adopts the Markov assumption to model discrete sequences with many multinomial distributions. Finally, we will consider a group of unimodal generative models called *generalized linear models* [171], including logistic regression, probit regression, Poisson regression, and log-linear models, as special cases.

11.1 Gaussian Models

In Example 10.4.1, we have shown how to estimate a univariate Gaussian model from a set of training samples based on maximum-likelihood estimation (MLE). Here, let us extend the MLE method to multivariate Gaussian models that can be used to approximate unimodal distributions in high-dimensional spaces.

Assume that we are given a set of independent and identically distributed (i.i.d.) samples randomly drawn from an unknown unimodal distribution in a d-dimensional space:

$$\mathcal{D} = \{\mathbf{x}_1, \mathbf{x}_2, \cdots, \mathbf{x}_N\},$$

where each $\mathbf{x}_i \in \mathbb{R}^d$ for all $i = 1, 2, \cdots, N$.

The exponent in a multivariate Gaussian:

$$\left[(\mathbf{x}-\boldsymbol{\mu})^\intercal\right]_{1\times d}\left[\ \boldsymbol{\Sigma}^{-1}\ \right]_{d\times d}\left[\mathbf{x}-\boldsymbol{\mu}\right]_{d\times 1} = [\ \cdot\ ]_{1\times 1}.$$

Here, we choose to use a multivariate Gaussian model to approximate the unknown unimodal distribution:

$$p_{\boldsymbol{\mu},\boldsymbol{\Sigma}}(\mathbf{x}) = \mathcal{N}(\mathbf{x}\,|\,\boldsymbol{\mu},\boldsymbol{\Sigma}) = \frac{1}{(2\pi)^{d/2}|\boldsymbol{\Sigma}|^{1/2}} e^{-\frac{(\mathbf{x}-\boldsymbol{\mu})^\intercal\boldsymbol{\Sigma}^{-1}(\mathbf{x}-\boldsymbol{\mu})}{2}}, \tag{11.1}$$

where $\boldsymbol{\mu} \in \mathbb{R}^d$ denotes the mean vector, and $\boldsymbol{\Sigma} \in \mathbb{R}^{d\times d}$ denotes the covariance matrix. Both of them are unknown model parameters to be estimated from the given training samples in $\mathcal{D}$. In the following, we will see how to use the MLE method to learn $\boldsymbol{\mu}$ and $\boldsymbol{\Sigma}$ from $\mathcal{D}$.

First, the log-likelihood function given $\mathcal{D}$ can be expressed as follows:

$$\begin{aligned} l(\boldsymbol{\mu},\boldsymbol{\Sigma}) &= \sum_{i=1}^{N} \ln p_{\boldsymbol{\mu},\boldsymbol{\Sigma}}(\mathbf{x}_i) \\ &= C - \frac{N}{2}\ln|\boldsymbol{\Sigma}| - \frac{1}{2}\sum_{i=1}^{N}(\mathbf{x}_i-\boldsymbol{\mu})^\intercal\boldsymbol{\Sigma}^{-1}(\mathbf{x}_i-\boldsymbol{\mu}), \end{aligned} \tag{11.2}$$

where C is a constant irrelevant to the model parameters $\boldsymbol{\mu}$ and $\boldsymbol{\Sigma}$.

Referring to the box on page 26, we have

$$\frac{\partial}{\partial\boldsymbol{\mu}}(\mathbf{x}_i-\boldsymbol{\mu})^\intercal\boldsymbol{\Sigma}^{-1}(\mathbf{x}_i-\boldsymbol{\mu}) = \boldsymbol{\Sigma}^{-1}(\boldsymbol{\mu}-\mathbf{x}_i).$$

In order to maximize the log-likelihood function $l(\boldsymbol{\mu},\boldsymbol{\Sigma})$, we compute its partial derivatives with respect to $\boldsymbol{\mu}$ and $\boldsymbol{\Sigma}$ and then derive the maximum point by vanishing the partial derivatives. We have

$$\begin{aligned} &\frac{\partial l(\boldsymbol{\mu},\boldsymbol{\Sigma})}{\partial\boldsymbol{\mu}} = 0 \\ \Longrightarrow\ &\sum_{i=1}^{N}\boldsymbol{\Sigma}^{-1}(\boldsymbol{\mu}-\mathbf{x}_i) = 0 \\ \Longrightarrow\ &\boldsymbol{\mu}_{\text{MLE}} = \frac{1}{N}\sum_{i=1}^{N}\mathbf{x}_i, \end{aligned} \tag{11.3}$$

and referring to the two formulae in the right margin, we further derive

For any square matrix $\mathbf{A}$, referring to the box on page 26, we have

$$\frac{\partial}{\partial \mathbf{A}}\left(\mathbf{x}^\intercal \mathbf{A}^{-1}\mathbf{y}\right) = -(\mathbf{A}^\intercal)^{-1}\mathbf{x}\mathbf{y}^\intercal(\mathbf{A}^\intercal)^{-1}$$

$$\frac{\partial}{\partial \mathbf{A}}\left(\ln|\mathbf{A}|\right) = (\mathbf{A}^{-1})^\intercal = (\mathbf{A}^\intercal)^{-1}.$$

$$\frac{\partial l(\boldsymbol{\mu}, \boldsymbol{\Sigma})}{\partial \boldsymbol{\Sigma}} = 0$$

$$\Longrightarrow \quad -\frac{N}{2}(\boldsymbol{\Sigma}^\intercal)^{-1} + \frac{1}{2}(\boldsymbol{\Sigma}^\intercal)^{-1}\Big[\sum_{i=1}^{N}(\mathbf{x}_i - \boldsymbol{\mu})(\mathbf{x}_i - \boldsymbol{\mu})^\intercal\Big](\boldsymbol{\Sigma}^\intercal)^{-1} = 0.$$

If we multiply $\boldsymbol{\Sigma}^\intercal$ to both the left and right sides of this equation and substitute with $\boldsymbol{\mu}_{\text{MLE}}$ in Eq. (11.3), we derive

$$\Longrightarrow \boldsymbol{\Sigma}_{\text{MLE}} = \frac{1}{N}\sum_{i=1}^{N}(\mathbf{x}_i - \boldsymbol{\mu}_{\text{MLE}})(\mathbf{x}_i - \boldsymbol{\mu}_{\text{MLE}})^\intercal. \qquad (11.4)$$

One issue with this MLE formula for the covariance matrix in Eq. (11.4) is that it estimates d^2 free parameters of $\boldsymbol{\Sigma}$, so it may end up with an ill-conditioned matrix $\boldsymbol{\Sigma}_{\text{MLE}}$ when d is large. An ill-conditioned matrix $\boldsymbol{\Sigma}_{\text{MLE}}$ may lead to unstable results when we invert $\boldsymbol{\Sigma}_{\text{MLE}}$ for the Gaussian model in Eq. (11.1). The common approach to address this issue is to impose some structural constraints on the unknown covariance matrix $\boldsymbol{\Sigma}$ rather than estimating it as a free $d \times d$ matrix. For example, we force the unknown covariance matrix $\boldsymbol{\Sigma}$ to be a diagonal matrix. In this case, we can similarly derive the MLE of this diagonal covariance matrix, whose diagonal elements happen to equal the diagonal ones in the previous $\boldsymbol{\Sigma}_{\text{MLE}}$. See Exercise Q11.2 for more details on this. For other types of structural constraints, interested readers may refer to Section 13.2 for *factor analysis* and *linear Gaussian models*.

Now, let us use an example to see how we can use Gaussian models for some pattern-classification problems involving high-dimensional feature vectors.

Example 11.1.1 Gaussian Models for Classification

In a pattern-classification problem, assume each pattern is represented by a d-dimensional continuous feature vector, and all patterns from each class follow a unimodal distribution that can be approximated by a multivariate Gaussian model. Derive the plug-in maximum a posteriori (MAP) decision rule for the classifier using Gaussian models.

Assume a classification problem involves K classes: $\{\omega_1, \cdots, \omega_K\}$. First of all, we collect a training set $\mathcal{D}_k$ for each class ω_k ($k = 1, \cdots, K$). Furthermore, we choose a multivariate Gaussian model for each class ω_k (i.e., $\mathcal{N}(\mathbf{x} \,|\, \boldsymbol{\mu}^{(k)}, \boldsymbol{\Sigma}^{(k)})$ ($k = 1, 2, \cdots, K$)).

Next, we use Eqs. (11.3) and (11.4) to estimate the unknown parameters of all Gaussian models based on the collected samples:

$$\mathcal{D}_k \longrightarrow \left\{\boldsymbol{\mu}_{\text{MLE}}^{(k)}, \boldsymbol{\Sigma}_{\text{MLE}}^{(k)}\right\} \qquad (k = 1, \cdots, K).$$

The estimated Gaussian models (i.e., $\mathcal{N}(\mathbf{x}|\boldsymbol{\mu}_{\text{MLE}}^{(k)}, \boldsymbol{\Sigma}_{\text{MLE}}^{(k)})$) can be used to approximate unknown class-conditional distributions $p(\mathbf{x}|\omega_k)$ for all classes $k = 1, \cdots, K$. As a result, for any unknown pattern $\mathbf{x}$, it is classified based on the following plug-in MAP decision rule:

$$g(\mathbf{x}) = \arg\max_k \ \Pr(\omega_k)p(\mathbf{x}|\omega_k) = \arg\max_k \ \mathcal{N}(\mathbf{x}|\boldsymbol{\mu}_{\text{MLE}}^{(k)}, \boldsymbol{\Sigma}_{\text{MLE}}^{(k)}),$$

where, for simplicity, all classes are assumed to be equiprobable; that is, $\Pr(\omega_k) = \frac{1}{K}$ for all k.

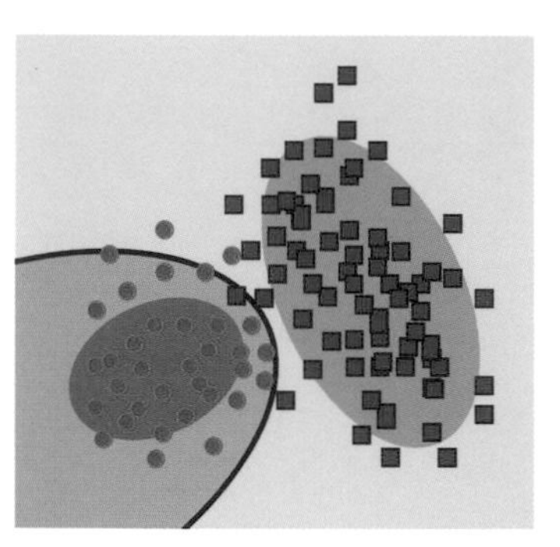

Figure 11.3: An illustration of quadratic discriminant analysis, where each class is modeled by a multivariate Gaussian model, and the decision boundary between any two classes is a parabola-like quadratic surface.

Furthermore, we investigate the properties of this classifier by examining the decision boundary between different classes. For example, let us take any two classes ω_i and ω_j; we can easily show that the decision boundary between them can be expressed as

$$\mathcal{N}(\mathbf{x}|\boldsymbol{\mu}_{\text{MLE}}^{(i)}, \boldsymbol{\Sigma}_{\text{MLE}}^{(i)}) = \mathcal{N}(\mathbf{x}|\boldsymbol{\mu}_{\text{MLE}}^{(j)}, \boldsymbol{\Sigma}_{\text{MLE}}^{(j)}).$$

After taking the logarithm of both sides, we can determine that this boundary is actually a parabola-like quadratic surface in d-dimensional space, as shown in Figure 11.3. The plug-in MAP rule corresponds to some pairwise quadratic classifiers between each pair of classes. This method is sometimes called *quadratic discriminant analysis (QDA)* in the literature. See Exercise Q11.4 for more details on QDA.

In the QDA method, we need to learn several large $d \times d$ covariance matrices for all K classes. This may lead to poor or unstable estimators when training sets are relatively small or the dimension d is high. An alternative approach is to make all K classes share a common covariance matrix, say, $\boldsymbol{\Sigma}$. Under this setting, each class is still represented by a multivariate Gaussian model that has its own mean vector $\boldsymbol{\mu}^{(k)}$ $(k = 1, \cdots, K)$, but all K Gaussian models share the same covariance matrix $\boldsymbol{\Sigma}$. In this case, we still use each training set to learn each Gaussian mean as in Eq. (11.3):

$$\mathcal{D}_k \longrightarrow \boldsymbol{\mu}_{\text{MLE}}^{(k)} \qquad (k = 1, \cdots, K).$$

Meanwhile, we pool all training sets together to estimate the common covariance matrix $\boldsymbol{\Sigma}$ as in Eq. (11.4):

$$\left\{\mathcal{D}_1, \mathcal{D}_2, \cdots, \mathcal{D}_K\right\} \longrightarrow \boldsymbol{\Sigma}_{\text{MLE}}.$$

The plug-in MAP decision rule for these models can be similarly written as follows:

$$g(\mathbf{x}) = \arg\max_k \ \mathcal{N}(\mathbf{x}|\boldsymbol{\mu}_{\text{MLE}}^{(k)}, \boldsymbol{\Sigma}_{\text{MLE}}).$$

As previously, we can examine the decision boundary of this classifier in the same way (also refer to Exercise Q11.4). We can easily show that the decision boundary between any two classes degenerates into a linear hyperplane because the common covariance matrix cancels out the quadratic terms, as shown in Figure 11.4. The previous plug-in MAP rule corresponds to some pair-wise linear classifiers. This method is also called *linear discriminant analysis*. For pattern classification, this method shares many common aspects with the linear discriminative models we have discussed in Chapter 6. The most noticeable difference in linear discriminant analysis lies in that the parameters of these linear classifiers are learned by the MLE method, whereas the linear methods in Chapter 6 are mostly learned by minimizing some error counts. ♦

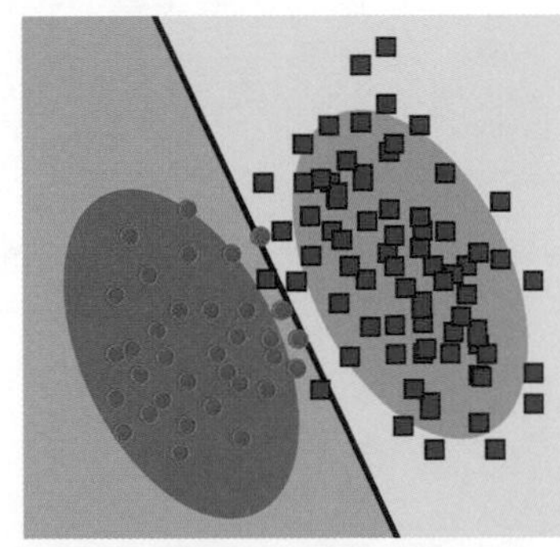

Figure 11.4: An illustration of linear discriminant analysis, where classes are modeled by some multivariate Gaussian models sharing a common covariance matrix, and the decision boundary between any two classes degenerates into a linear hyperplane.

11.2 Multinomial Models

Gaussian models are good for some problems involving continuous data, where each observation may be represented as a continuous feature vector in a normed vector space. However, they are not suitable for other data types, such as discrete or categorical data. In these problems, each sample usually consists of some distinct symbols, each of which comes from a finite set. For example, a DNA sequence consists of a sequence of only four different types of nucleotides, G, A, T, and C. No matter how long a DNA sequence is, it contains only these four nucleotides. Another example is text documents. We know that each text document may be short or long, but it can be viewed as a sequence of some distinct words. All possible words in a language come from a dictionary, which can be fairly large but definitely finite for any natural language. Among many choices, multinomial models are probably the simplest generative model for discrete or categorical data.

Discrete data normally consist of separate observations, each of which is a distinct symbol coming from a finite set. Assume there are M distinct symbols in the set, and the probability of observing each symbol is assumed to be p_i ($0 \leq p_i \leq 1$) for all $i = 1, 2, \cdots, M$. These probabilities must satisfy the sum-to-1 constraint:

$$\sum_{i=1}^{M} p_i = 1. \tag{11.5}$$

If we further assume that all observations in any sample are independent from each other, then the probability of observing a sample, denoted as $\mathbf{X}$, can be computed with the following multinomial distribution:

$$\Pr(\mathbf{X} \mid p_1, p_2, \cdots p_M) = \frac{(r_1 + r_2 + \cdots + r_M)!}{r_1! \, r_2! \, \cdots \, r_M!} \, p_1^{r_1} \, p_2^{r_2} \, \cdots \, p_M^{r_M},$$

where r_i ($i = 1, 2, \cdots, M$) denotes the frequency of the ith symbol appearing among all observations in $\mathbf{X}$. The probabilities $\{p_1, \cdots, p_M\}$ are the parameters of a multinomial model. Once we know these probabilities, we can compute the probability of observing any sample consisting of these symbols.

Example 11.2.1 Multinomial Models for DNA Sequences

If we ignore the order information, we can use a multinomial model to compute the probability of observing the following DNA sequence, which is denoted as $\mathbf{X}$:

```
GAATTCTTCAAAGAGTTCCAGATATCCACAGGCAGATTCTACAAAAGAAG
TGTTTCAATACTGCTCTATCAAAAGATGTATTCCACTCAGTTACTTTCAT
GCACACATCTCAATGAAGTTCCTGAGAAAGCTTCTGTCTAGTTTTTATGT
GAAAATATTTCCTTTTCCATCATGGGCCTCAAAGCGCTCAAAATGAACCC
TTGCAGATACTAGAGAAAGACTGTTTCAAAACTGCTCTATCCA
```

In this case, every observation in this sequence is a nucleotide. There are four types of nucleotides in DNA in total. Assume we use p_1 to denote the probability of observing G in any location, p_2 for A, p_3 for T, and p_4 for C. Obviously, we have $\sum_{i=1}^{4} p_i = 1$ in this case. If we further assume all nucleotides in the sequence are independent from each other, we can compute the probability of observing this sequence as

$$\Pr(\mathbf{X} \mid p_1, p_2, p_3, p_4) = \frac{(r_1 + r_2 + r_3 + r_4)!}{r_1! \, r_2! \, r_3! \, r_4!} \prod_{i=1}^{4} p_i^{r_i}, \tag{11.6}$$

where r_1 denotes the frequency of G appearing in this sequence, r_2 for A, r_3 for T, and r_4 for C. ♦

If we know all parameters, that is, the four probabilities $\{p_1, p_2, p_3, p_4\}$, we can use the multinomial model in Eq. (11.6) to compute the probability of observing any other DNA sequence as well. For each given DNA sequence, we just need to count how many times each nucleotide appears in the sequence. Of course, we need to estimate these probabilities from a training sequence beforehand. Next, let us consider how to estimate these probabilities from a training sequence $\mathbf{X}$ based on MLE.

Given any training sequence $\mathbf{X}$, according to Eq. (11.6), we can represent the log-likelihood function as follows:

$$l(p_1, p_2, p_3, p_4) = \ln \Pr(\mathbf{X} \mid p_1, p_2, p_3, p_4) = C + \sum_{i=1}^{4} r_i \cdot \ln p_i, \tag{11.7}$$

where C is a constant irrelevant of all parameters. The MLE method aims to estimate all four parameters by maximizing this log-likelihood function. An important point in this optimization problem is that these parameters must satisfy the sum-to-1 constraint in Eq. (11.5) to form a valid probability distribution. This constrained optimization (see margin note) can be solved by the method of Lagrange multipliers. We first introduce a Lagrange multiplier λ for this constraint and then construct the Lagrangian function:

The MLE is formulated as follows:

$$\arg \max_{p_1, p_2, p_3, p_4} l(p_1, p_2, p_3, p_4),$$

subject to

$$\sum_{i=1}^{4} p_i - 1 = 0.$$

$$\mathcal{L}(p_1, p_2, p_3, p_4, \lambda) = C + \sum_{i=1}^{4} r_i \cdot \ln p_i - \lambda \cdot \Big(\sum_{i=1}^{4} p_i - 1 \Big).$$

For all $i = 1, 2, 3, 4$, we have

$$\begin{aligned} & \frac{\partial}{\partial p_i} \mathcal{L}(p_1, p_2, p_3, p_4, \lambda) = 0 \\ \Longrightarrow \quad & \frac{r_i}{p_i} - \lambda = 0 \\ \Longrightarrow \quad & p_i = \frac{r_i}{\lambda}. \end{aligned}$$

After we substitute $p_i = \frac{r_i}{\lambda}$ $(i = 1, \cdots, 4)$ into the sum-to-1 constraint $\sum_{i=1}^{4} p_i = 1$, we can derive $\lambda = \sum_{i=1}^{4} r_i$. Substituting this back into the previous equation, we finally derive the MLE formula for this multinomial model as follows:

$$p_i^{(\text{MLE})} = \frac{r_i}{\sum_{i=1}^{4} r_i} \quad (i = 1, 2, 3, 4). \tag{11.8}$$

The MLE formula for multinomial models is fairly simple. We only need to count the frequencies of all distinct symbols in the training set, and the MLE estimates for all probabilities are computed as the ratios of these counts. Finally, these estimated probabilities can be used in Eq. (11.6) to compute the probability of observing any new sequence.

11.3 Markov Chain Models

As we have seen, when we use a multinomial model for discrete sequences, we have to assume that all observations in each sequence are independent from each other, which means that we completely ignore the order information of the sequence and simply treat it as a bag of symbols. Thus, a multinomial model is a very weak model for discrete sequences because it fails to capture any sequential information. This section introduces a sequence model based on the Markov assumption, called the *Markov chain model*, which is essentially composed of many different multinomial models.

First of all, let us consider how to model sequences in general. Given a sequence of T random variables:

$$\mathbf{X} = \left\{x_1\ x_2\ x_3 \cdots x_{t-1}\ x_t\ x_{t+1} \cdots x_T\right\},$$

we can always compute the probability of observing this sequence according to the product rule in probability theory as

$$\Pr(\mathbf{X}) = p(x_1)p(x_2|x_1)p(x_3|x_1x_2)\cdots p(x_t|x_1\cdots x_{t-1})\cdots p(x_T|x_1\cdots x_{T-1}).$$

The problem here is that this computation relies on conditional probabilities that involve more and more conditions as a sequence gets longer and longer. For example, the last term $p(x_T \mid x_1 \cdots x_{T-1})$ is essentially a probability function of T variables because it involves $T-1$ conditional variables. The complexity of such a model will explode exponentially as a sequence becomes longer and longer.

The well-known *Markov assumption* has been proposed to address this issue. Under this assumption, every random variable in a sequence only depends on its most recent history and, in turn, becomes independent from the others given the most recent history. If the recent history is defined as only the preceding variable in the sequence, it is called a *first-order Markov assumption*. If it is defined as the two immediately preceding variables, it is called a *second-order Markov assumption*. In the same way, we can extend this idea to higher-order Markov assumptions.

Under the first-order *Markov assumption*, we have

$$p(x_t \mid x_1 \cdots x_{t-1}) = p(x_t \mid x_{t-1}) \qquad \forall t = 2, 3, \cdots, T.$$

Similarly, under the second-order Markov assumption, we can derive the second-order Markov chain models as follows:

$$\Pr(\mathbf{X}) = p(x_1)p(x_2 \mid x_1)$$
$$\prod_{t=3}^{T} p(x_t \mid x_{t-2}\, x_{t-1}),$$

where none of these conditional probability distributions takes more than three variables.

Therefore, we can compute the probability of observing sequence $\mathbf{X}$ as follows:

$$\Pr(\mathbf{X}) = p(x_1) \prod_{t=2}^{T} p(x_t \mid x_{t-1}). \tag{11.9}$$

This formula represents the so-called first-order *Markov chain models*, which include a set of conditional distributions as parameters. We can see that none of these probability functions has more than two free variables.

Next, the Markov chain models can be further simplified if we adopt two more assumptions as follows:

- ► *Stationary assumption*: All conditional probabilities in Eq. (11.9) do not change for different t values. That is,

$$p(x_t \mid x_{t-1}) = p(x_{t'} \mid x_{t'-1})$$

for any two t and t' in $1, 2, \cdots T$. The stationary assumption allows us to use only a single probability function to compute all conditional probabilities in a sequence because the same function is applicable to any location t in a sequence.

- ► *Discrete observation assumption*: All observations in a sequence are discrete random variables. Furthermore, all of these discrete random variables take their values from the *same* finite set of M distinct symbols (i.e., $\{\omega_1, \omega_2, \cdots, \omega_M\}$). Hence, we can represent the previous conditional distribution $p(x_t \mid x_{t-1})$ as a matrix $\mathbf{A}$:

$$\mathbf{A} = \left[\quad a_{ij} \quad \right]_{M \times M}$$

where each element a_{ij} denotes one conditional probability: $a_{ij} = \Pr(x_t = \omega_j \mid x_{t-1} = \omega_i)$ for all $1 \leq i, j \leq M$. Each distinct symbol is also called a *Markov state* in a first-order Markov chain model. The matrix $\mathbf{A}$ is usually called a *transition matrix*. Each a_{ij} can be viewed as a transition probability from state ω_i to state ω_j.

Under these assumptions, as long as we know the transition matrix $\mathbf{A}$, we will be able to compute the probability for any discrete sequence as in Eq. (11.9). In other words, a Markov chain model is fully represented by the Markov states and the transition matrix. Furthermore, a Markov chain model can also be represented as a directed graph, where each node represents a Markov state and each arc represents a state transition, associated with a transition probability. Any sequence can be viewed as a path traversing such a graph, with the probability of observing the sequence computed based on the transition probabilities along the path.

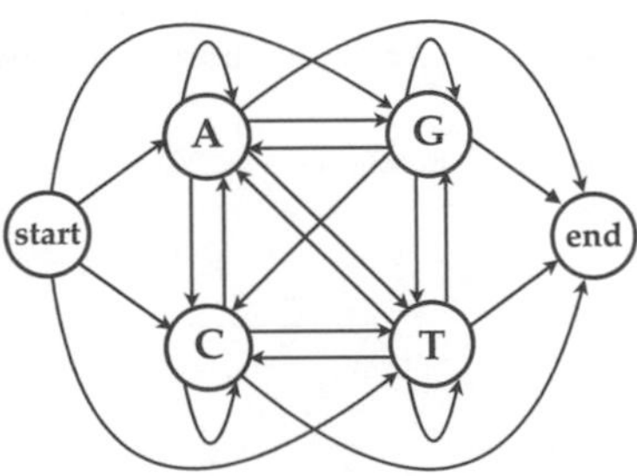

Figure 11.5: An illustration of a first-order Markov chain model for DNA sequences.

Here, let us use Example 11.2.1 again to explain how to use the first-order Markov chain model for DNA sequences. Any DNA sequence contains only four different nucleotides, G, A, T, and C. We can further add two dummy symbols, *begin* and *end*, to indicate the beginning and ending of a sequence. In this case, we end up with six Markov states in total. This Markov chain model can be represented by the directed graph in Figure 11.5. Each arc is associated with a transition probability a_{ij}, summarized in Figure 11.6.

	begin	A	C	G	T	*end*
begin	0	0.28	0.24	0.25	0.23	0
A	0	0.18	0.27	0.42	0.12	0.01
C	0	0.17	0.36	0.27	0.19	0.01
G	0	0.16	0.34	0.37	0.12	0.01
T	0	0.08	0.35	0.38	0.18	0.01
end	0	0	0	0	0	1

Figure 11.6: An illustration of the transition matrix of a first-order Markov chain model for DNA sequences.

Based on these, we will be able to compute the probability of observing any DNA sequence with this Markov chain model. For example:

$$\Pr(\text{GAATC}) = p(\text{G}|begin)p(\text{A}|\text{G})p(\text{A}|\text{A})p(\text{T}|\text{A})p(\text{C}|\text{T})p(end|\text{C})$$

$$= 0.25 \times 0.16 \times 0.18 \times 0.12 \times 0.35 \times 0.01.$$

Next, let us look at how to estimate Markov chain models, particularly the transition matrix **A**, from training samples. We can recognize that each row of the transition matrix **A** is actually a multinomial model. As a result, the transition matrix of a Markov chain model can be broken down into a number of different multinomial models, where the ith row is a multinomial model for how likely it is that each symbol appears right after the ith symbol ω_i in a sequence. After applying the same method of Lagrange multipliers, we derive the MLE formula for the Markov chain model as follows:

$$a_{ij}^{(\text{MLE})} = \frac{r(\omega_i \omega_j)}{r(\omega_i)} \quad (1 \le i, j \le M), \tag{11.10}$$

where $r(\omega_i)$ denotes the frequency of symbol ω_i appearing in training samples, and $r(\omega_i \omega_j)$ denotes the frequency of an ordered pair $\omega_i \omega_j$ appearing in the training set. This idea can be extended to higher-order Markov chain models. Refer to Exercise Q11.7 for more details.

In biology, the CpG sites are regions of DNA occurring more often in CG islands, which have a certain significance in gene expression.

Once we know how to learn Markov chain models from training data, we can use the Markov chain models to classify sequences. For example, the first-order Markov chain models can be used to determine whether an unknown DNA segment belongs to CpG or GpC sites. We just collect some DNA sequences from each category and estimate two Markov chain models for them. Any new unknown DNA segment can be classified using these estimated models.

In the following, let us introduce another example that uses Markov chain models for natural language processing. As we know, texts in any language can be viewed as discrete sequences of different words chosen from a finite set, which is usually called the *vocabulary*. The vocabulary includes all distinct words that can be used in a language. In most natural languages, the vocabulary is usually very large, and it may include tens of thousands or even up to tens of millions of distinct words. Under this setting, any text document can be viewed as a sequence of discrete symbols, each of which is a word from the predetermined vocabulary. An important topic in natural language processing, called *language modeling*, represents a group of methods that distinguish natural or meaningful sentences in a language from random word sequences that do not make any senses. To do this, a language model should be able to score any word sequence and give higher scores to meaningful sentences and lower scores to random word sequences. As a result, language models can also be used to predict the next word or any missing words in partial sentences. A good language model plays a critical role in many successful real-world applications, such as speech recognition and machine translation.

Example 11.3.1 N-Gram Language Models

Use Markov chain models to build a language model for English sentences.

When we use Markov chain models for language modeling, we adopt the Markov assumption for languages, and the resultant models are usually called *n-gram* language models. Assume we have M distinct words in the vocabulary. Each English sentence is a sequence of words from the vocabulary. For example, given the following English sentence $\mathbf{S}$:

```
I would like to fly from Toronto to San Francisco this Friday,
```

a language model should be able to calculate the probability of observing such a sequence (i.e., $\Pr(\mathbf{S})$). First, assume we adopt the first-order Markov assumption, leading to the first-order Markov chain model, normally called a *bigram* language model. In a bigram model, the probability in the previous example is computed by the following conditional probabilities:

$$\Pr(\mathbf{S}) = p(\text{I}|begin)\, p(\text{would}|\text{I})\, p(\text{like}|\text{would}) \cdots p(end|\text{Friday}).$$

Because we have M distinct words in our vocabulary, our bigram language model has $M \times M$ conditional probabilities like these. As long as we have all $M \times M$ conditional probabilities, we are able to compute the probability of observing any word sequence. A bigram language model can be similarly represented as a directed graph, as in Figure 11.5, where each vertex represents a distinct word, and each arc is associated with a conditional probability. These $M \times M$ conditional probabilities can also be organized as an $M \times M$ transition matrix, as in Figure 11.6. Meanwhile, a bigram language model can also be viewed as a set of M different multinomial models, each of which corresponds to one row of this matrix.

A bigram model can only model the dependencies between two consecutive words in a sequence. If we want to model long-span dependencies in language, a straightforward extension is to use higher-order Markov chain models. For example, in a second-order Markov chain model, usually called a *trigram* language model, the probability $\Pr(\mathbf{S})$ is computed as follows:

$$p(\text{I}|begin)\, p(\text{would}|begin, \text{I})\, p(\text{like}|\text{I}, \text{would}) \cdots p(end|\text{this}, \text{Friday}).$$

A trigram model needs to maintain $M \times M \times M$ conditional probabilities like these in order to compute the probability for any word sequence.

These naive n-gram models are bulky. Each conditional probability is usually represented by a model parameter. Assuming $M = 10^4$ (a relatively small vocabulary only suitable for some specific domains), a bigram model ends up with about 100 million (10^8) parameters, whereas a trigram model has about a trillion (10^{12}) parameters.

In language modeling, we usually collect a large number of English sentences, called a *training corpus*, to learn all of the conditional probabilities in an n-gram language model. The MLE for n-gram language models can be similarly derived using the method of Lagrange multipliers. For bigram models, we have

$$p_{\text{MLE}}(w_j|w_i) = \frac{r(w_i w_j)}{r(w_i)} \quad (1 \le i, j \le M),$$

and similarly, for trigram models, we have

$$p_{\text{MLE}}(w_k|w_i, w_j) = \frac{r(w_i w_j w_k)}{r(w_i w_j)} \quad (1 \le i, j, k \le M),$$

where $r(w_i)$ denotes the frequency of a word w_i appearing in the training corpus, $r(w_i w_j)$ denotes the frequency of a word bigram $w_i w_j$, and $r(w_i w_j w_k)$ denotes the frequency of a word trigram $w_i w_j w_k$. From these MLE formulae, it is clear that if a bigram $w_i w_j$ or a trigram $w_i w_j w_k$ never appears in the training corpus, it yields a 0 probability (i.e., $p_{\text{MLE}}(w_j|w_i) = 0$ or $p_{\text{MLE}}(w_k|w_i, w_j) = 0$). In any natural language like English, we usually have a large number of such bigrams/trigrams. If a term does not appear in the training corpus, it usually means that we have not obtained enough samples to see this infrequent term, rather than it being impossible to appear. Any such unseen term in a sequence will make the probability of observing the whole sequence be 0, which can significantly skew the prediction of it.

To fix these 0 probabilities due to data sparsity, the MLE formulae for n-gram models must be combined with some smoothing techniques. Interested readers may refer to Good–Turing discounting [83] or back-off models [125] for how to smooth the MLE estimates for n-grams. ♦

11.4 Generalized Linear Models

This section introduces another class of unimodal generative models, called *generalized linear models (GLMs)* [171], which were initially extended from ordinary linear regression in order to deal with non-Gaussian distributions. At present, GLMs are a popular method in statistics to handle binary, categorical, and count data. Here, we will first consider the basic idea behind GLMs, and then briefly explore several GLMs that are particularly important in machine learning: *probit regression*, *Poisson regression*, and *log-linear models*.

In statistics, the inputs $\mathbf{x}$ are usually called *explanatory variables*, and the output y is usually called a *response* variable.

The key idea behind GLMs is to construct a simple generative model to approximate the conditional distribution of the output y given the input random variables $\mathbf{x}$ (i.e., $p(y|\mathbf{x})$) in a general machine learning setting, as depicted in the margin note. The key components of a generalized linear model include the following:

- An underlying *unimodal probability distribution*
  We first assume that the output y follows a simple unimodal probability distribution. The choice of a probability function for this distribution mainly depends on the nature of the output y. For example, if y is binary, we may choose a binomial distribution. If y is a K-way categorical variable, we may select a multinomial distribution. Moreover, if y is count data (i.e., $y \in \{0, 1, 2, \cdots\}$), we may use a Poisson distribution.
- A *link function*
  We further assume that the mean of the chosen probability distribution is linked to a linear predictor of the input variables $\mathbf{x}$ through a link function $g(\cdot)$ as follows:

  $$\mathbb{E}\big[y\big] = g(\mathbf{w}^\intercal \mathbf{x}),$$

  where the linear coefficients (i.e., $\mathbf{w}$) are unknown parameters of the GLM, which must be estimated from some training samples. The link function must be properly chosen so that the range of the link function matches the domain of the distribution's mean. For example, if y is assumed to follow a Poisson distribution, we may choose an exponential function as the link function, namely, $\mathbb{E}\big[y\big] = \exp(\mathbf{w}^\intercal \mathbf{x})$, because the mean of a Poisson distribution is always positive.

Once we have made a choice for these two components, we are able to derive a parametric probability function for the conditional distribution of y given the input $\mathbf{x}$, denoted as $\hat{p}_{\mathbf{w}}(y|\mathbf{x})$, which is the GLM. Here $\mathbf{w}$ stands for the unknown parameters of the GLM, which need to be estimated from some training samples of input–output pairs based on MLE. For most GLMs, no closed-form solution exists to derive the MLE of the model parameters, and instead, we have to rely on iterative optimization methods, such as gradient-descent or Newton methods.

GLM	y	Distribution	$g(\cdot)$
Linear regression	$\mathbb{R}$	Gaussian	Identity
Logistic regression	Binary	Binomial	Sigmoid
Probit regression	Binary	Binomial	Probit
Poisson regression	Count	Poisson	$\exp(\cdot)$
Log-linear model	Categorical	Multinomial	Softmax

Table 11.1: Some popular GLMs and the corresponding choices for their underlying probability distributions and their link functions $g(\cdot)$.

Table 11.1 lists some popular choices for these two components that lead to several well-known GLMs in statistics. In the following, we will briefly explore some of these GLMs and their applications in the context of machine learning. As we will see, GLMs are good candidates for generative models when the output y is a discrete random variable.

11.4.1 Probit Regression

In the case where the output y is binary ($y \in \{0,1\}$), we assume that y follows a binomial distribution with one trial ($N = 1$), as follows:

As we know, the binomial distribution with one trial ($N = 1$),

$$\mathrm{B}(y \mid N = 1, p),$$

is also called the *Bernoulli distribution*.

$$y \sim \mathrm{B}(y \mid N = 1, p) = p^y (1-p)^{1-y},$$

where $0 \le p \le 1$ stands for the parameter of the binomial distribution. We know the mean of this random variable y can be computed as $\mathbb{E}[y] = p$ for this binomial distribution. For each pair of $(\mathbf{x}, y)$, we need to choose a link function to map a linear predictor $\mathbf{w}^\intercal\mathbf{x}$ to the range of $0 \le p \le 1$. One choice is to use the sigmoid function $l(\cdot)$ in Eq. (6.12), that is, $p = l(\mathbf{w}^\intercal\mathbf{x})$, which leads to logistic regression from Section 6.4. Another popular choice is to use the so-called *probit* function $\Phi(x)$, which is defined based on the error function of a Gaussian distribution (see margin note). As shown in Figure 11.7, similar to the sigmoid function, the probit function $\Phi(x)$ is also a monotonically increasing function from 0 to +1 when x goes from $-\infty$ to ∞. The range of the probit function matches with the domain of p, so we can choose

The probit function is defined as follows:

$$\Phi(x) = \frac{1}{2}\Big(1 + \mathrm{erf}(x)\Big),$$

with

$$\mathrm{erf}(x) = \frac{2}{\sqrt{\pi}} \int_0^x \exp\Big(-\frac{t^2}{2}\Big)dt.$$

$$p = \Phi(\mathbf{w}^\intercal\mathbf{x}). \tag{11.11}$$

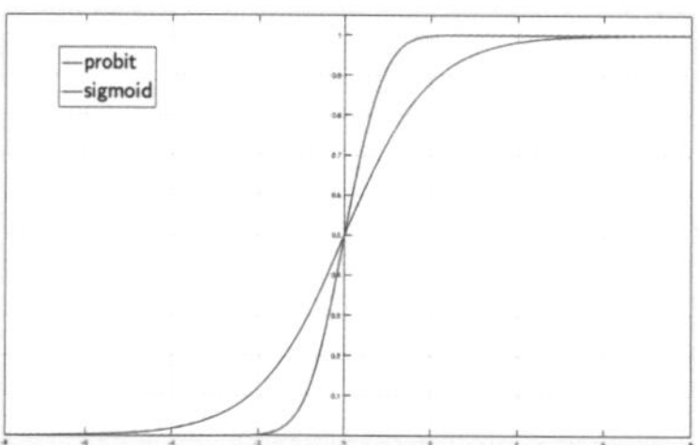

Figure 11.7: Comparison between the *probit* function $\Phi(x)$ and the *sigmoid* function $l(x)$.

Substituting Eq. (11.11) into the previous binomial distribution, we can derive the probit regression model for any input–output pair $(\mathbf{x}, y)$ as

$$\hat{p}_{\mathbf{w}}(y|\mathbf{x}) = \Big(\Phi(\mathbf{w}^\intercal\mathbf{x})\Big)^y \Big(1 - \Phi(\mathbf{w}^\intercal\mathbf{x})\Big)^{1-y} \quad y \in \{0,1\}, \tag{11.12}$$

where the model parameter $\mathbf{w}$ can be estimated from the training samples based on MLE. See Exercise Q11.8 for how to derive an MLE learning algorithm for the probit regression model.

11.4.2 Poisson Regression

In many real-world scenarios, the output y can represent some count data, such as the number of some event occurring per time unit. Some typical examples include the number of customers calling a help center per hour, visitors to a website per month, and failures in a data center per day. In these cases, we can use the input $\mathbf{x}$ to represent some measurements or observations made on the process.

Poisson regression is a very useful model for us to predict y based on some observation $\mathbf{x}$. If we assume all events happen randomly and independently and the average interval between any two consecutive events is constant, then we know y follows the Poisson distribution:

$$y \sim p(y \mid \lambda) = \frac{e^{-\lambda} \cdot \lambda^y}{y!} \quad \forall y = 0, 1, 2, \cdots,$$

Refer to the Poisson distribution in Appendix A.

where $\lambda > 0$ denotes the parameter of the Poisson distribution. We also know that $\mathbb{E}\big[y\big] = \lambda$ holds for any Poisson distribution. In this case, we use an exponential function $\exp(\cdot)$ to match the range of λ:

$$\lambda = \exp(\mathbf{w}^\intercal \mathbf{x}).$$

Substituting this into the previous Poisson distribution, we derive the Poisson regression model as follows:

$$\hat{p}_{\mathbf{w}}(y|\mathbf{x}) = \frac{1}{y!} \exp\big(-\exp(\mathbf{w}^\intercal\mathbf{x})\big) \cdot \exp\big(y\mathbf{w}^\intercal\mathbf{x}\big) \quad y = 0, 1, 2, \cdots, \tag{11.13}$$

where $\mathbf{w}$ denotes the unknown parameters of the Poisson regression model. See Exercise Q11.9 for how to derive the MLE for this model.

11.4.3 Log-Linear Models

In a K-class pattern-classification problem, the output y is a K-way category (i.e., $y \in \{\omega_1, \omega_2, \cdots \omega_K\}$). We can use the 1-of-$K$ representation to encode y as a K-dimension one-hot vector:

$$\mathbf{y} \triangleq \big[y_1 \; y_2 \; \cdots \; y_K\big]^\intercal,$$

where $y_k = \delta(y - \omega_k)$ for all $k = 1, 2, \cdots, K$ with the delta function

$$\delta(y - \omega_k) = \begin{cases} 1 & \text{when } \; y = \omega_k \\ 0 & \text{when } \; y \neq \omega_k. \end{cases}$$

We further assume each output $\mathbf{y}$ follows a multinomial distribution with one trial $N = 1$, as follows:

As we know, the multinomial distribution with one trial ($N = 1$),

$$\text{Mult}(\mathbf{y} \mid N = 1, p_1, \cdots, p_K),$$

is also called the *categorical distribution*.

$$\mathbf{y} \sim \text{Mult}(\mathbf{y} \mid N = 1, p_1, \cdots, p_K) \sim \prod_{k=1}^{K} p_k^{y_k}$$

From the property of this multinomial distribution, we have

$$\mathbb{E}\big[\mathbf{y}\big] = \big[p_1 \; p_2 \; \cdots \; p_K\big]^\intercal,$$

where $0 \le p_k \le 1$ for all k, and $\sum_{k=1}^{K} p_k = 1$.

Given any sample $(\mathbf{x}, \mathbf{y})$, we may choose the *softmax* function in Eq. (6.18) to map K different linear predictors of $\mathbf{x}$ (i.e., $\mathbf{w}_k^\intercal \mathbf{x}$ for all $k = 1, 2, \cdots, K$) to the range of the previous $\mathbb{E}[\mathbf{y}]$. In other words, we have

$$\mathbb{E}\big[\mathbf{y}\big] = \text{softmax}(\mathbf{x}) = \left[\frac{e^{\mathbf{w}_1^\intercal \mathbf{x}}}{\sum_{k=1}^{K} e^{\mathbf{w}_k^\intercal \mathbf{x}}} \;\; \frac{e^{\mathbf{w}_2^\intercal \mathbf{x}}}{\sum_{k=1}^{K} e^{\mathbf{w}_k^\intercal \mathbf{x}}} \;\; \cdots \;\; \frac{e^{\mathbf{w}_K^\intercal \mathbf{x}}}{\sum_{k=1}^{K} e^{\mathbf{w}_k^\intercal \mathbf{x}}}\right]^\intercal,$$

where we use the softmax function, along with K different linear weights (i.e., $\{\mathbf{w}_1, \cdots, \mathbf{w}_K\}$), to construct the link functions for all p_k as follows:

$$p_k = \frac{e^{\mathbf{w}_k^\intercal \mathbf{x}}}{\sum_{k=1}^{K} e^{\mathbf{w}_k^\intercal \mathbf{x}}} \qquad (k = 1, 2, \cdots, K).$$

After substituting this into the multinomial distribution, we derive the underlying GLM in this setting as follows:

$$\hat{p}_{\mathbf{w}_1,\cdots,\mathbf{w}_K}(\mathbf{y} \mid \mathbf{x}) = \prod_{k=1}^{K} \left(\frac{e^{\mathbf{w}_k^\intercal \mathbf{x}}}{\sum_{k=1}^{K} e^{\mathbf{w}_k^\intercal \mathbf{x}}}\right)^{y_k} \tag{11.14}$$

This GLM is sometimes called the *log-linear model* in machine learning, which can be viewed as a multiclass version of the logistic regression in Section 6.4. The unknown parameters $\{\mathbf{w}_1, \cdots, \mathbf{w}_K\}$ can be estimated from a set of training samples based on MLE.

Log-linear models are widely used to solve various problems in natural language processing. Here, we will consider an important topic, called *text categorization*, which represents a class of techniques that automatically classify text documents into different categories. Text categorization includes many common tasks, such as spam filtering, language identification, sentimental analysis, and news-document classification.

In the field of natural language processing, log-linear models are often called *maximum entropy models* [20].

Example 11.4.1 Log-Linear Models for Text Categorization

If we can use some predefined rules (based on keywords, syntactic patterns, etc.) to extract a fixed-size feature vector $\mathbf{x}$ to represent each text document, show that the log-linear model can be applied to text categorization.

See Berger et al. [20] for more details on how to extract fixed-size features for text documents.

Assume we have K classes in total, denoted as $\{\omega_1, \omega_2, \cdots, \omega_K\}$. As previously, if we use the one-hot vector $\mathbf{y}$ to represent the class label for each document $\mathbf{x}$, we may use the log-linear model in Eq. (11.14) to approximate the conditional probability distribution $p(\mathbf{y}|\mathbf{x})$.

Given a training set consisting of N i.i.d. samples, as follows:

$$\mathcal{D} = \left\{(\mathbf{x}^{(i)}, \mathbf{y}^{(i)}) \mid i = 1, 2, \cdots N\right\},$$

we can learn all parameters $\{\mathbf{w}_1, \mathbf{w}_2, \cdots, \mathbf{w}_K\}$ based on the MLE method.

Given $\mathcal{D}$, the log-likelihood function of the log-linear model can be expressed as

$$l(\mathbf{w}_1, \cdots \mathbf{w}_K) = \sum_{i=1}^{N} \sum_{k=1}^{K} y_k^{(i)} \ln \left(\frac{e^{\mathbf{w}_k^\intercal \mathbf{x}^{(i)}}}{\sum_{k=1}^{K} e^{\mathbf{w}_k^\intercal \mathbf{x}^{(i)}}} \right), \tag{11.15}$$

where $y_k^{(i)} \in \{0, 1\}$ denotes the kth element of the one-hot vector $\mathbf{y}^{(i)}$.

We can show that this log-likelihood function is concave with a single global maximum, which can be found by an iterative gradient-descent method.

Because we can apply the chain rule to compute the gradients (i.e., $\frac{\partial l(\cdot)}{\partial \mathbf{w}_k}$ for all $k = 1, \cdots, K$), the MLE of all parameters, denoted as $\{\mathbf{w}_1^{(\text{MLE})}, \cdots, \mathbf{w}_K^{(\text{MLE})}\}$, can be derived based on a gradient-descent algorithm. See Exercise Q11.11 for how to derive the MLE learning algorithm for this log-likelihood function.

Once we have estimated all model parameters, for any new text document $\mathbf{x}$, we classify it to class $\omega_{\hat{k}}$ based on the following plug-in MAP rule:

$$\hat{k} = \arg \max_{k=1\cdots K} \ \mathbf{x}^\intercal \mathbf{w}_k^{(\text{MLE})},$$

which is essentially a pair-wise linear classifier (see margin note). ♦

$$\begin{aligned} \hat{k} &= \arg\max_k \ \Pr(\omega_k | \mathbf{x}) \\ &= \arg\max_k \ \frac{e^{(\mathbf{w}_k^{(\text{MLE})})^\intercal \mathbf{x}}}{\sum_{k=1}^{K} e^{(\mathbf{w}_k^{(\text{MLE})})^\intercal \mathbf{x}}} \\ &= \arg\max_k \ e^{(\mathbf{w}_k^{(\text{MLE})})^\intercal \mathbf{x}} \\ &= \arg\max_k \ (\mathbf{w}_k^{(\text{MLE})})^\intercal \mathbf{x} \\ &= \arg\max_k \ \mathbf{x}^\intercal \mathbf{w}_k^{(\text{MLE})}. \end{aligned}$$

Exercises

Q11.1 Determine the condition(s) under which a beta distribution is unimodal.

Q11.2 Derive the MLE for multivariate Gaussian models with a diagonal covariance matrix, i.e. $\mathcal{N}(\mathbf{x}|\boldsymbol{\mu}, \boldsymbol{\Sigma})$ with $\mathbf{x}, \boldsymbol{\mu} \in \mathbb{R}^d$ and $\boldsymbol{\Sigma} = \begin{bmatrix} \sigma_1 & & \\ & \ddots & \\ & & \sigma_d \end{bmatrix}$. Show the MLE of $\boldsymbol{\mu}$ is the same as Eq.(11.3) and that of $\{\sigma_1, \cdots, \sigma_d\}$ equals to the diagonal elements in Eq.(11.4).

Q11.3 Given K different classes (i.e., $\{\omega_1, \omega_2, \cdots, \omega_K\}$), we assume each class ω_k $(k = 1, 2, \cdots, K)$ is modeled by a multivariate Gaussian distribution with the mean vector $\boldsymbol{\mu}_k$ and the covariance matrix $\boldsymbol{\Sigma}$; that is, $p(\mathbf{x} \,|\, \omega_k) = \mathcal{N}(\mathbf{x} \,|\, \boldsymbol{\mu}_k, \boldsymbol{\Sigma})$, where $\boldsymbol{\Sigma}$ is the common covariance matrix for all K classes. Suppose we have collected N data samples from these K classes (i.e., $\{\mathbf{x}_1, \mathbf{x}_2, \cdots, \mathbf{x}_N\}$), and let $\{l_1, l_2, \cdots, l_N\}$ be their labels so that $l_n = k$ means that the data sample $\mathbf{x}_n$ comes from the kth class ω_k. Based on the given data set, derive the MLE for all model parameters (i.e., all mean vectors $\boldsymbol{\mu}_k$ $(k = 1, 2, \cdots, K)$) and the common covariance matrix $\boldsymbol{\Sigma}$.

Q11.4 Given $\mathbf{x} \in \mathbb{R}^n$ and $y \in \{0, 1\}$, assume $\Pr(y = k) = \pi_k > 0$ for $k = 0, 1$ with $(\pi_0 + \pi_1 = 1)$, and the conditional distribution of $\mathbf{x}$ given y is $p(\mathbf{x} \,|\, y) = \mathcal{N}(\mathbf{x} \,|\, \boldsymbol{\mu}_y, \boldsymbol{\Sigma}_y)$, where $\boldsymbol{\mu}_0, \boldsymbol{\mu}_1 \in \mathbb{R}^n$ are two mean vectors (with $\boldsymbol{\mu}_0 \neq \boldsymbol{\mu}_1$), and $\boldsymbol{\Sigma}_0, \boldsymbol{\Sigma}_1 \in \mathbb{R}^{d \times d}$ are two covariance matrices.

a. What is the unconditional density of $\mathbf{x}$ (i.e., $p(\mathbf{x})$)?
b. Assume that $\boldsymbol{\Sigma}_0 = \boldsymbol{\Sigma}_1 = \boldsymbol{\Sigma}$ is a positive definite matrix. Derive the MAP decision rule. What is the nature of the separation boundary between two classes? Show the procedure.
c. Assume that $\boldsymbol{\Sigma}_0 \neq \boldsymbol{\Sigma}_1$ are two positive-definite matrices. Derive the MAP decision rule. What is the nature of the separation boundary between two classes? Show the procedure.

Q11.5 Extend the MLE in Eq. (11.8) to a generic multinomial model involving M symbols.

Q11.6 Draw a graph representation similar to Figure 11.5 for a second-order Markov chain model of the DNA sequences.

Q11.7 Derive the MLE for first-order Markov chain models in Eq. (11.10).

Q11.8 Derive the gradient for the log-likelihood function of the probit regression model in Eq. (11.12). Based on this, derive a learning algorithm for probit regression using the gradient-descent method.

Q11.9 Derive the gradient and Hessian matrix for the log-likelihood function of the Poisson regression in Eq. (11.13) and a learning algorithm for the MLE of its parameter $\mathbf{w}$ using (i) the gradient-descent method and (ii) Newton's method.

Q11.10 Prove that the log-likelihood function of log-linear models in Eq. (11.15) is concave with a single global maximum.

Q11.11 Derive the gradient-descent method for the MLE of all parameters of the log-linear models in Example 11.4.1.

Mixture Models | 12

The unimodal models discussed in the last chapter are relatively easy to learn but have strong limitations in approximating the complex data distributions abundant in real-world applications. Data generated from many physical processes tend to reveal the property of multimodality in their distributions over the feature space. For example, if we extract a major acoustic feature from speech signals collected over a large population of male and female speakers, we may observe a multimodal distribution, as shown in Figure 12.1. Obviously, we cannot use any unimodal model to approximate this type of multimodal distribution accurately.

In machine learning, we normally use unimodal models as building blocks to construct more complex generative models. Generally speaking, we have at least two different means to expand simple unimodal models. This chapter introduces the first method, which is based on the idea of finite mixture distributions [59, 239, 162], where a number of different unimodal models are combined as a mixture model to capture multiple peaks in a complex multimodal distribution. The next chapter discusses the second method, which relies on transformations of random variables to convert simpler generative models into more sophisticated ones.

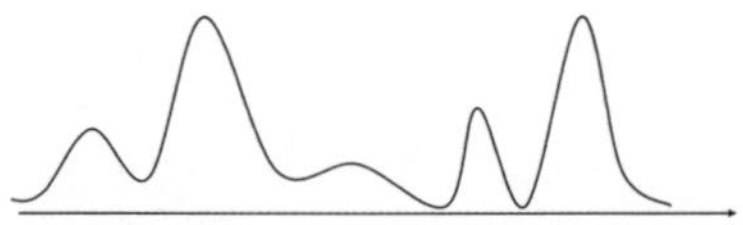

Figure 12.1: An illustration of a multimodal distribution of one major speech feature measured over a large population of speakers.

12.1 Formulation of Mixture Models

The idea of mixture models is to linearly combine a group of simpler distributions (presumably unimodal) to derive a more complex mixture distribution. The resultant model is called a *mixture model*, and each of the simpler distributions is normally called a *component model*. When we only use a finite number of component models, this leads to the so-called *finite mixture models*. Generally speaking, a finite mixture model of M ($\in \mathbb{N}$) components can be represented as follows:

$$p_{\boldsymbol{\theta}}(\mathbf{x}) = \sum_{m=1}^{M} w_m \cdot f_{\boldsymbol{\theta}_m}(\mathbf{x}), \tag{12.1}$$

where $\boldsymbol{\theta} = \{w_m, \boldsymbol{\theta}_m \mid m = 1, 2, \cdots, M\}$ denotes all model parameters of the mixture model, and $f_{\boldsymbol{\theta}_m}(\mathbf{x})$ indicates a component model with its model parameters $\boldsymbol{\theta}_m$ and w_m for its mixture weight. All mixture weights satisfy the sum-to-1 constraint: $\sum_{m=1}^{M} w_m = 1$. The mixture weights $\{w_m \mid i =$

$1, \cdots, M\}$ can be viewed as an M-value multinomial model. If every component model represents a valid distribution (self-normalized to 1), the sum-to-1 constraint for mixture weights ensures that the resultant mixture model $p_{\boldsymbol{\theta}}(\mathbf{x})$ is also a valid probability distribution over the space that also satisfies the sum-to-1 constraint (see margin note).

Given the sum-to-1 constraint

$$\sum_{m=1}^{M} w_m = 1,$$

it is trivial to prove

$$\int_{\mathbf{x}} p_{\boldsymbol{\theta}}(\mathbf{x}) d\mathbf{x} = 1.$$

In a finite mixture model, we usually choose the component models as some unimodal models according to the nature of feature vectors. For example, if we want to approximate a multimodal distribution of continuous data, we can select Gaussian models as the component models. In this case, the mixture model consists of a number of Gaussian models with different mean vectors and covariance matrices, which is usually called a *Gaussian mixture model (GMM)*. We will further discuss GMMs in detail in Section 12.3. Similarly, for discrete data, we may choose multinomial models as the component models, leading to the so-called multinomial mixture model.

See Exercise Q12.6 for more details on multinomial mixture models.

If we want to understand how a mixture model is formed, it is important to know the difference between averaging random variables and averaging probability functions.

Example 12.1.1 Averaging *Random Variables* versus *Probability Functions*

Assume two independent random variables follow two univariate Gaussian distributions: $x_1 \sim \mathcal{N}(\mu_1, \sigma_1^2)$ and $x_2 \sim \mathcal{N}(\mu_2, \sigma_2^2)$. If we generate a new random variable x by averaging x_1 and x_2 as $x = \epsilon\, x_1 + (1-\epsilon)\, x_2$ with a constant $0 < \epsilon < 1$, determine whether x follows a bimodal mixture distribution.

Because x_1 and x_2 both follow a Gaussian distribution, any linear transformation of them will result in a new random variable that follows another Gaussian distribution rather than a mixture distribution. Based on the properties of Gaussian distributions (see Exercise Q2.9), we can derive that x follows a Gaussian distribution as

$$x \sim \mathcal{N}\Big(\epsilon\mu_1 + (1-\epsilon)\mu_1,\ \epsilon^2\sigma_1^2 + (1-\epsilon)^2\sigma_2^2\Big).$$

Here, x still follows a unimodal distribution rather than a mixture distribution of two Gaussians. If we want to form a bimodal mixture model, we have to directly average the density functions as follows:

$$x' \sim \epsilon\mathcal{N}(\mu_1, \sigma_1^2) + (1-\epsilon)\mathcal{N}(x \mid \mu_2, \sigma_2^2).$$

If we properly choose ϵ and the parameters of these two Gaussians, we can approximate many bimodal distributions, such as in Figure 12.2. ♦

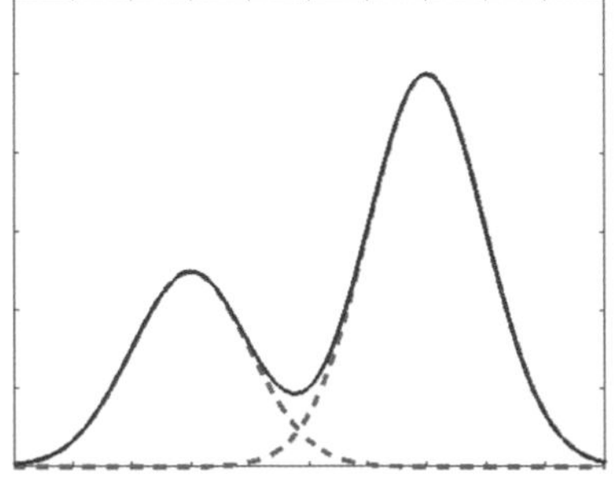

Figure 12.2: A bimodal distribution formed by averaging two different Gaussian distributions.

In fact, in addition to Gaussians and multinomials, we can choose the component models of a finite mixture model from a much broader class of probability distributions, normally called the *exponential family*. In the following, we will first consider the property of exponential family distributions before we discuss how to estimate finite mixture models from training data.

12.1.1 Exponential Family (e-Family)

As before, we use $f_{\boldsymbol{\theta}}(\mathbf{x})$ to represent a parametric probability distribution of random variable $\mathbf{x}$, where $\boldsymbol{\theta}$ denotes the regular model parameters. Generally speaking, if we can reparameterize it into the following exponential form:

$$f_{\boldsymbol{\theta}}(\mathbf{x}) = \exp\left(A(\bar{\mathbf{x}}) + \bar{\mathbf{x}}^{\intercal}\boldsymbol{\lambda} - K(\boldsymbol{\lambda})\right),$$

we say that the distribution $f_{\boldsymbol{\theta}}(\mathbf{x})$ belongs to the *exponential family* (*e-family* for short). In this canonical form, $\boldsymbol{\lambda} = g(\boldsymbol{\theta})$ is usually called the *natural parameter* of the model, and it only depends on the regular model parameters $\boldsymbol{\theta}$ (not $\mathbf{x}$) through a function $g(\cdot)$. Meanwhile, $\bar{\mathbf{x}} = h(\mathbf{x})$ is called *sufficient statistic* of the model because it only depends on $\mathbf{x}$ (not $\boldsymbol{\theta}$) through another function $h(\cdot)$. Here, $K(\boldsymbol{\lambda})$ is a normalization term to ensure that $f_{\boldsymbol{\theta}}(\mathbf{x})$ satisfies the sum-to-1 constraint.

We can derive $K(\boldsymbol{\lambda})$ as follows:

$$\int_{\mathbf{x}} f_{\boldsymbol{\theta}}(\mathbf{x}) d\mathbf{x} = 1 \implies$$

$$K(\boldsymbol{\lambda}) = \ln\left[\int_{\mathbf{x}} \exp\left(A(h(\mathbf{x})) + (h(\mathbf{x}))^{\intercal}\boldsymbol{\lambda}\right) d\mathbf{x}\right].$$

One important property of all e-family distributions is that their log-likelihood functions can be represented in a fairly simple form as the exponential cancels out the logarithm. If we take the logarithm on $f_{\boldsymbol{\theta}}(\mathbf{x})$, we have

$$\ln f_{\boldsymbol{\theta}}(\mathbf{x}) = A(\bar{\mathbf{x}}) + \bar{\mathbf{x}}^{\intercal}\boldsymbol{\lambda} - K(\boldsymbol{\lambda}),$$

which includes three separate terms: one term $A(\bar{\mathbf{x}})$ only depending on sufficient statistics $\bar{\mathbf{x}}$, one term $K(\boldsymbol{\lambda})$ only relying on natural parameters $\boldsymbol{\lambda}$, and a linear cross term $\bar{\mathbf{x}}^{\intercal}\boldsymbol{\lambda}$. This also suggests that when we estimate any e-family model with maximum likelihood estimation (MLE), it is always more convenient to work with the log-likelihood function rather than the likelihood function itself.

In spite of its fairly restricted form, the e-family represents a very broad class of parametric probability functions, which includes almost all common probability distributions we are familiar with. For example, let us explain why the multivariate Gaussian distributions belong to the e-family by reparameterizing them to derive the natural parameters $\boldsymbol{\lambda}$ and sufficient statistics $\bar{\mathbf{x}}$. Based on the original form of the multivariate Gaussian model in Eq. (11.1), we have

$$\ln \mathcal{N}(\mathbf{x}|\boldsymbol{\mu}, \boldsymbol{\Sigma}) = -\frac{d}{2}\ln(2\pi) - \frac{1}{2}\ln|\boldsymbol{\Sigma}| - \frac{1}{2}(\mathbf{x}-\boldsymbol{\mu})^{\intercal}\boldsymbol{\Sigma}^{-1}(\mathbf{x}-\boldsymbol{\mu})$$

$$= -\frac{d}{2}\ln(2\pi) + \frac{1}{2}\ln|\boldsymbol{\Sigma}^{-1}| - \frac{1}{2}\mathbf{x}^{\intercal}\boldsymbol{\Sigma}^{-1}\mathbf{x} + \mathbf{x}^{\intercal}\boldsymbol{\Sigma}^{-1}\boldsymbol{\mu} - \frac{1}{2}\boldsymbol{\mu}^{\intercal}\boldsymbol{\Sigma}^{-1}\boldsymbol{\mu}$$

$$= \underbrace{-\frac{d}{2}\ln(2\pi)}_{A(\bar{\mathbf{x}})} + \underbrace{\mathbf{x}\cdot\Big(\overbrace{\Sigma^{-1}\boldsymbol{\mu}}^{\lambda_1}\Big) + \Big(-\frac{1}{2}\mathbf{x}^\intercal\mathbf{x}\Big)\cdot\overbrace{\Sigma^{-1}}^{\lambda_2}}_{\bar{\mathbf{x}}^\intercal\boldsymbol{\lambda}} + \underbrace{\frac{1}{2}\ln|\Sigma^{-1}| - \frac{1}{2}\boldsymbol{\mu}^\intercal\Sigma^{-1}\boldsymbol{\mu}}_{K(\boldsymbol{\lambda})=\frac{1}{2}\ln|\boldsymbol{\lambda}_2|-\frac{1}{2}\boldsymbol{\lambda}_1^\intercal\boldsymbol{\lambda}_2^{-1}\boldsymbol{\lambda}_1}$$

It is easy to verify that

$$-\frac{1}{2}\mathbf{x}^\intercal\Sigma^{-1}\mathbf{x} = \Big(-\frac{1}{2}\mathbf{x}^\intercal\mathbf{x}\Big)\cdot\Sigma^{-1}$$

$$\mathbf{x}^\intercal\Sigma^{-1}\boldsymbol{\mu} = \mathbf{x}\cdot\big(\Sigma^{-1}\boldsymbol{\mu}\big),$$

where $\cdot$ denotes element-wise multiplication and summation, that is, the inner product of two vectors or matrices.

From this, we can see that the natural parameters for the multivariate Gaussian are $\boldsymbol{\lambda} = [\boldsymbol{\lambda}_1\ \ \boldsymbol{\lambda}_2] = g(\boldsymbol{\mu}, \Sigma) = \big[\Sigma^{-1}\boldsymbol{\mu}\ \ \Sigma^{-1}\big]$ and the corresponding sufficient statistics $\bar{\mathbf{x}} = h(\mathbf{x}) = \big[\mathbf{x}\ \ -\frac{1}{2}\mathbf{x}^\intercal\mathbf{x}\big]$. And the normalization term $K(\boldsymbol{\lambda})$ can also be represented as a function of $\boldsymbol{\lambda}_1$ and $\boldsymbol{\lambda}_2$ as previously. Therefore, multivariate Gaussian distributions belong to the e-family. In the same way, we can verify that binomial, multinomial, Bernoulli, Dirichlet, beta, gamma, von Mises–Fisher, and inverse-Wishart distributions can all be reparameterized into the exponential form of natural parameters and sufficient statistics. Therefore, all of these probability distributions belong to the e-family.

Table 12.1: Some distributions reparameterized as the canonical e-family form with their natural parameters and sufficient statistics.

$f_{\boldsymbol{\theta}}(\mathbf{x})$	$\boldsymbol{\lambda} = g(\boldsymbol{\theta})$	$\bar{\mathbf{x}} = h(\mathbf{x})$	$K(\boldsymbol{\lambda})$	$A(\bar{\mathbf{x}})$
Univariate Gaussian $\mathcal{N}(x \mid \mu, \sigma^2)$	$[\overbrace{\mu/\sigma^2}^{\lambda_1}, \overbrace{1/\sigma^2}^{\lambda_2}]$	$[x, -x^2/2]$	$-\frac{1}{2}\lambda_1^2/\lambda_2$ $+\frac{1}{2}\ln(\lambda_2)$	$-\frac{1}{2}\ln(2\pi)$
Multivariate Gaussian $\mathcal{N}(\mathbf{x} \mid \boldsymbol{\mu}, \Sigma)$	$[\overbrace{\Sigma^{-1}\boldsymbol{\mu}}^{\boldsymbol{\lambda}_1}, \overbrace{\Sigma^{-1}}^{\boldsymbol{\lambda}_2}]$	$[\mathbf{x}, -\frac{1}{2}\mathbf{x}\mathbf{x}^\intercal]$	$-\frac{1}{2}\boldsymbol{\lambda}_1^\intercal\boldsymbol{\lambda}_2^{-1}\boldsymbol{\lambda}_1$ $+\frac{1}{2}\ln|\boldsymbol{\lambda}_2|$	$-\frac{d}{2}\ln(2\pi)$
Gaussian (mean only) $\mathcal{N}(\mathbf{x} \mid \boldsymbol{\mu}, \Sigma_0)$	$\boldsymbol{\mu}$	$\Sigma_0^{-1}\mathbf{x}$	$-\frac{1}{2}\boldsymbol{\lambda}^\intercal\Sigma_0^{-1}\boldsymbol{\lambda}$	$-\frac{d}{2}\ln(2\pi)$ $-\frac{1}{2}\ln|\Sigma_0|$ $-\frac{1}{2}\mathbf{x}^\intercal\Sigma_0^{-1}\mathbf{x}$
Multinomial $C\cdot\prod_{d=1}^{D} p_d^{x_d}$	$\big[\ln p_1, \cdots, \ln p_D\big]$	$\mathbf{x}$	0	$\ln(C)$

Table 12.1 lists the reparameterization results for some useful distributions in machine learning. For instance, the third row considers a special multivariate Gaussian model with a known covariance matrix, where only the Gaussian mean vector is treated as the model parameter. The fourth row gives a reparameterization result for the multinomial distribution, where the natural parameters are denoted as $\boldsymbol{\lambda} = \big[\lambda_1\ \lambda_2\ \cdots\ \lambda_D\big] = g(p_1, \cdots, p_D) = \big[\ln p_1\ \ln p_2\ \cdots \ln p_D\big]$. For this reparameterization, we note that these natural parameters must satisfy the constraint $\sum_{d=1}^{D} e^{\lambda_d} = 1$, which arises from the sum-to-1 constraint of the original parameters p_i.

An important property of the e-family is that almost all e-family distributions are unimodal, with only a small number of exceptions. Therefore, all e-family distributions are considered to be mathematically tractable. Moreover, we also note that the e-family is closed under multiplication. In other words, the product of any two e-family distributions is still an e-family distribution. This property is straightforward to prove from the exponential form of the e-family distributions. On the other hand, we note that the e-family is not closed under addition. This immediately suggests that a finite mixture of e-family distributions does not belong to the e-family anymore.

12.1.2 Formal Definition of Mixture Models

We can now summarize this section with a formal definition of finite mixture models. Throughout this book, a finite mixture model is defined as a mixture model composed of M ($\in \mathbb{N}$) e-family distributions: $p_{\boldsymbol{\theta}}(\mathbf{x}) = \sum_{m=1}^{M} w_m \cdot f_{\boldsymbol{\theta}_m}(\mathbf{x})$, where $\boldsymbol{\theta} = \{w_m, \boldsymbol{\theta}_m \mid m = 1, 2, \cdots, M\}$ denotes all parameters associated with the mixture model.

Under this definition, the model $p_{\boldsymbol{\theta}}(\mathbf{x})$ is formally called a finite mixture model if the following two conditions hold:

1. All mixture weights are positive ($0 < w_m < 1,\ \forall m$) and satisfy the sum-to-1 constraint (i.e., $\sum_{m=1}^{M} w_m = 1$).
2. All component models $f_{\boldsymbol{\theta}_m}(\mathbf{x})$ ($\forall m$) belong to the e-family.

It is fine for different components to take different functional forms in the e-family. However, for simplicity, we normally assume that all component models in a mixture model have the same functional form, only with different parameters $\boldsymbol{\theta}_m$ in each component. As we have discussed, generally speaking, $p_{\boldsymbol{\theta}}(\mathbf{x})$ is not an e-family distribution when $M > 1$.

The next section discusses how to learn all parameters $\boldsymbol{\theta}$ in a mixture model based on MLE.

12.2 Expectation-Maximization Method

Assume we have a training set of N samples $\mathfrak{D} = \{\mathbf{x}_1, \mathbf{x}_2, \cdots, \mathbf{x}_N\}$, randomly drawn from a complex multimodal distribution. If we want to use a finite mixture model $p_{\boldsymbol{\theta}}(\mathbf{x})$ to approximate this unknown distribution, we need to estimate all model parameters $\boldsymbol{\theta}$ from the given training samples in $\mathfrak{D}$.

$$p_{\boldsymbol{\theta}}(\mathbf{x}) = \sum_{m=1}^{M} w_m \cdot f_{\boldsymbol{\theta}_m}(\mathbf{x}).$$

First of all, we have to determine the value for M, namely, how many components are in the mixture model. Unfortunately, there does not exist any automatic method to effectively identify the correct number of components from data. We will have to treat M as a hyperparameter and determine a good value for M based on some trial-and-error experiments.

12.2.1 Auxiliary Function: Eliminating Log-Sum

Once M is selected, we use MLE to learn all parameters in $\boldsymbol{\theta}$. As usual, we write down the log-likelihood function for the mixture model as follows:

$$l(\boldsymbol{\theta}) = \sum_{i=1}^{N} \ln p_{\boldsymbol{\theta}}(\mathbf{x}_i) = \sum_{i=1}^{N} \ln\left(\sum_{m=1}^{M} w_m \cdot f_{\boldsymbol{\theta}_m}(\mathbf{x}_i)\right). \tag{12.2}$$

Unlike what we obtained for unimodal models, we are facing a huge computational challenge here because the log-likelihood function of a mixture model consists of some *log-sum* terms (highlighted in red in the previous equation), which are mathematically awkward to handle. Given that each component model is an e-family distribution, if we could manage to switch the order of the logarithm and the summation in the previous equation, then the logarithm will directly apply to each component model so that it cancels out the exponential in each component model. The key idea in the following derivation is to use some mathematical tricks to switch the order of the logarithm and the summation to derive more mathematically tractable results.

Hereafter, we use $\boldsymbol{\theta}$ to denote model parameters as free variables of a function and $\boldsymbol{\theta}^{(n)}$ to represent one particular set of given parameters.

To do so, let us first treat index m of the mixture model in Eq. (12.1) as a *latent variable*, which is essentially an unobserved random variable that takes its value from a finite set of $\{1, 2, \cdots, M\}$. Assuming we are given a set of model parameters, denoted as

$$\boldsymbol{\theta}^{(n)} = \left\{w_m^{(n)}, \boldsymbol{\theta}_m^{(n)} \,|\, m = 1, 2, \cdots, M\right\},$$

we can compute a conditional probability distribution of the latent variable m based on each training sample $\mathbf{x}_i$ in $\mathfrak{D}$ as follows:

$$\Pr(m \,|\, \mathbf{x}_i, \boldsymbol{\theta}^{(n)}) = \frac{w_m^{(n)} \cdot f_{\boldsymbol{\theta}_m^{(n)}}(\mathbf{x}_i)}{\sum_{m=1}^{M} w_m^{(n)} \cdot f_{\boldsymbol{\theta}_m^{(n)}}(\mathbf{x}_i)} \qquad (\forall m = 1, 2, \cdots, M). \tag{12.3}$$

We have $\sum_{m=1}^{M} \Pr(m \,|\, \mathbf{x}_i, \boldsymbol{\theta}^{(n)}) = 1$ for any $\mathbf{x}_i$.

Next, let us define an auxiliary function for $\boldsymbol{\theta}$ as the following conditional expectation over the latent variable m:

Refer to the definition of *conditional expectation* in Section 2.2.

$$\begin{aligned} Q(\boldsymbol{\theta}|\boldsymbol{\theta}^{(n)}) &= \sum_{i=1}^{N} \mathbb{E}_m\Big[\overbrace{\ln\left(w_m \cdot f_{\boldsymbol{\theta}_m}(\mathbf{x}_i)\right)}^{\text{use } \boldsymbol{\theta} \text{ here}} \,\Big|\, \mathbf{x}_i, \boldsymbol{\theta}^{(n)}\Big] + C \\ &= \sum_{i=1}^{N}\sum_{m=1}^{M} \ln\left[w_m \cdot f_{\boldsymbol{\theta}_m}(\mathbf{x}_i)\right] \cdot \Pr(m \mid \mathbf{x}_i, \boldsymbol{\theta}^{(n)}) + C, \end{aligned} \tag{12.4}$$

where C is a constant defined as the sum of the entropy of the conditional probability distributions:

$$C \triangleq H(\boldsymbol{\theta}^{(n)}|\boldsymbol{\theta}^{(n)}) = -\sum_{i=1}^{N}\sum_{m=1}^{M} \ln \Pr(m \,|\, \mathbf{x}_i, \boldsymbol{\theta}^{(n)}) \Pr(m \,|\, \mathbf{x}_i, \boldsymbol{\theta}^{(n)}).$$

We can see that C is independent of the model variables $\boldsymbol{\theta}$. If we compare the highlighted parts (in red) in Eq. (12.2) and Eq. (12.4), we can see that the auxiliary function $Q(\boldsymbol{\theta}|\boldsymbol{\theta}^{(n)})$ is constructed in such a way that we have managed to switch the order of logarithm and summation to eliminate the log-sum terms. As a result, the auxiliary function $Q(\boldsymbol{\theta}|\boldsymbol{\theta}^{(n)})$ has a much simpler form than the original log-likelihood function $l(\boldsymbol{\theta})$. More importantly, we can show that $Q(\boldsymbol{\theta}|\boldsymbol{\theta}^{(n)})$ is also closely related to $l(\boldsymbol{\theta})$. The following theorem formally summarizes three important properties of the auxiliary function $Q(\boldsymbol{\theta}|\boldsymbol{\theta}^{(n)})$, clearly elucidating how it is related to the original log-likelihood function $l(\boldsymbol{\theta})$.

Theorem 12.2.1 *The auxiliary function $Q(\boldsymbol{\theta}|\boldsymbol{\theta}^{(n)})$ in Eq. (12.4) satisfies the following three properties:*

1. *$Q(\boldsymbol{\theta}|\boldsymbol{\theta}^{(n)})$ and $l(\boldsymbol{\theta})$ achieve the same value at $\boldsymbol{\theta}^{(n)}$:*

$$Q(\boldsymbol{\theta}|\boldsymbol{\theta}^{(n)})\Big|_{\boldsymbol{\theta}=\boldsymbol{\theta}^{(n)}} = l(\boldsymbol{\theta})\Big|_{\boldsymbol{\theta}=\boldsymbol{\theta}^{(n)}}.$$

2. *$Q(\boldsymbol{\theta}|\boldsymbol{\theta}^{(n)})$ is tangent to $l(\boldsymbol{\theta})$ at $\boldsymbol{\theta}^{(n)}$:*

$$\frac{\partial Q(\boldsymbol{\theta}|\boldsymbol{\theta}^{(n)})}{\partial \boldsymbol{\theta}}\Big|_{\boldsymbol{\theta}=\boldsymbol{\theta}^{(n)}} = \frac{\partial l(\boldsymbol{\theta})}{\partial \boldsymbol{\theta}}\Big|_{\boldsymbol{\theta}=\boldsymbol{\theta}^{(n)}}.$$

3. *For all $\boldsymbol{\theta} \neq \boldsymbol{\theta}^{(n)}$, $Q(\boldsymbol{\theta}|\boldsymbol{\theta}^{(n)})$ is located strictly below $l(\boldsymbol{\theta})$:*

$$Q(\boldsymbol{\theta}|\boldsymbol{\theta}^{(n)}) < l(\boldsymbol{\theta}) \quad (\forall \boldsymbol{\theta} \neq \boldsymbol{\theta}^{(n)}).$$

Proof:

Step 1: For any two random variables x and y, we can rearrange the Bayes theorem into

$$p(y|x) = \frac{p(x,y)}{p(x)} \implies p(x) = \frac{p(x,y)}{p(y|x)}.$$

Step 2: We apply this to a joint distribution of m and $\mathbf{x}$, represented by a generative model $p_{\boldsymbol{\theta}}(m, \mathbf{x})$ with model parameters $\boldsymbol{\theta}$, so we have

$$p_{\boldsymbol{\theta}}(\mathbf{x}) = \frac{p_{\boldsymbol{\theta}}(m, \mathbf{x})}{\Pr(m|\mathbf{x}, \boldsymbol{\theta})} \implies \ln p_{\boldsymbol{\theta}}(\mathbf{x}) = \ln p_{\boldsymbol{\theta}}(m, \mathbf{x}) - \ln \Pr(m|\mathbf{x}, \boldsymbol{\theta}).$$

Step 3: We multiply the conditional probability $\Pr(m|\mathbf{x}, \boldsymbol{\theta}^{(n)})$ to both sides of the previous equation and sum over all $m \in \{1, 2, \cdots, M\}$, so we have

$$\begin{aligned}\sum_{m=1}^{M} \ln p_{\theta}(\mathbf{x}) \cdot \Pr(m|\mathbf{x}, \theta^{(n)}) &= \sum_{m=1}^{M} \ln p_{\theta}(m, \mathbf{x}) \cdot \Pr(m|\mathbf{x}, \theta^{(n)}) \\ &- \sum_{m=1}^{M} \ln \Pr(m|\mathbf{x}, \theta) \cdot \Pr(m|\mathbf{x}, \theta^{(n)}).\end{aligned}$$

The left-hand side (LHS) of the equation simplifies to

$$\sum_{m=1}^{M} \ln p_{\theta}(\mathbf{x}) \cdot \Pr(m|\mathbf{x}, \theta^{(n)}) = \ln p_{\theta}(\mathbf{x})$$

because $\ln p_{\theta}(\mathbf{x})$ is independent of m, and $\sum_{m=1}^{M} \Pr(m|\mathbf{x}, \theta^{(n)}) = 1$.

Step 4: We substitute $\mathbf{x}$ with every training sample $\mathbf{x}_i$ in $\mathfrak{D}$ and sum over all N samples, so we have

$$\begin{aligned}\sum_{i=1}^{N} \ln p_{\theta}(\mathbf{x}_i) &= \sum_{i=1}^{N}\sum_{m=1}^{M} \ln p_{\theta}(m, \mathbf{x}_i) \cdot \Pr(m|\mathbf{x}_i, \theta^{(n)}) \\ &- \sum_{i=1}^{N}\sum_{m=1}^{M} \ln \Pr(m|\mathbf{x}_i, \theta) \cdot \Pr(m|\mathbf{x}_i, \theta^{(n)}).\end{aligned}$$

Step 5: Note that the LHS equals to $l(\theta)$, and we have

By definition, in Eq. (12.4), we have

$Q(\theta|\theta^{(n)}) =$

$\sum_{i=1}^{N}\sum_{m=1}^{M} \ln\left[w_m \cdot f_{\theta_m}(\mathbf{x}_i)\right] \cdot \Pr(m \mid \mathbf{x}_i, \theta^{(n)})$

$- \sum_{i=1}^{N}\sum_{m=1}^{M} \ln \Pr(m \mid \mathbf{x}_i, \theta^{(n)}) \Pr(m \mid \mathbf{x}_i, \theta^{(n)}).$

$$p_{\theta}(m, \mathbf{x}_i) = \Pr(m|\theta) p_{\theta}(\mathbf{x}_i|m) = w_m \cdot f_{\theta_m}(\mathbf{x}_i).$$

Substituting $Q(\theta|\theta^{(n)})$ in Eq. (12.4) into the previous equation, we have

$$\begin{aligned}l(\theta) &= Q(\theta|\theta^{(n)}) + \left[\sum_{i=1}^{N}\sum_{m=1}^{M} \ln \Pr(m|\mathbf{x}_i, \theta^{(n)}) \Pr(m|\mathbf{x}_i, \theta^{(n)}) \right. \\ &\left. - \sum_{i=1}^{N}\sum_{m=1}^{M} \ln \Pr(m|\mathbf{x}_i, \theta) \Pr(m|\mathbf{x}_i, \theta^{(n)})\right] \\ &= Q(\theta|\theta^{(n)}) + \sum_{i=1}^{N} \underbrace{\left[\sum_{m=1}^{M} \ln\left(\frac{\Pr(m|\mathbf{x}_i, \theta^{(n)})}{\Pr(m|\mathbf{x}_i, \theta)}\right) \Pr(m|\mathbf{x}_i, \theta^{(n)})\right]}_{\mathrm{KL}\left(\Pr(m|\mathbf{x}_i, \theta^{(n)}) \,||\, \Pr(m|\mathbf{x}_i, \theta)\right) \geq 0} \\ &\geq Q(\theta|\theta^{(n)}).\end{aligned} \tag{12.5}$$

According to Theorem 2.3.1, the Kullback–Leibler (KL) divergence is always nonnegative, and it equals to 0 only when two distributions are identical.

Based on the property of the KL-divergence, we know that equality holds only when $\theta = \theta^{(n)}$. Therefore, Properties 1 and 3 are proved.

Step 6: From Eq. (12.5), we have

$$\frac{\partial l(\boldsymbol{\theta})}{\partial \boldsymbol{\theta}} = \frac{\partial Q(\boldsymbol{\theta}|\boldsymbol{\theta}^{(n)})}{\partial \boldsymbol{\theta}} - \frac{\partial H(\boldsymbol{\theta}|\boldsymbol{\theta}^{(n)})}{\partial \boldsymbol{\theta}},$$

with

$$\begin{aligned}
\frac{\partial H(\boldsymbol{\theta}|\boldsymbol{\theta}^{(n)})}{\partial \boldsymbol{\theta}}\bigg|_{\boldsymbol{\theta}=\boldsymbol{\theta}^{(n)}} &= \sum_{i=1}^{N}\left[\sum_{m=1}^{M} \frac{\Pr(m|\mathbf{x}_i, \boldsymbol{\theta}^{(n)})}{\Pr(m|\mathbf{x}_i, \boldsymbol{\theta})} \frac{\partial \Pr(m|\mathbf{x}_i, \boldsymbol{\theta})}{\partial \boldsymbol{\theta}}\right]\bigg|_{\boldsymbol{\theta}=\boldsymbol{\theta}^{(n)}} \\
&= \sum_{i=1}^{N}\left[\sum_{m=1}^{M} \frac{\partial \Pr(m|\mathbf{x}, \boldsymbol{\theta})}{\partial \boldsymbol{\theta}}\right]\bigg|_{\boldsymbol{\theta}=\boldsymbol{\theta}^{(n)}} \\
&= \sum_{i=1}^{N} \frac{\partial}{\partial \boldsymbol{\theta}}\left[\sum_{m=1}^{M} \Pr(m|\mathbf{x}, \boldsymbol{\theta})\right]\bigg|_{\boldsymbol{\theta}=\boldsymbol{\theta}^{(n)}} \\
&= \sum_{i=1}^{N} \frac{\partial}{\partial \boldsymbol{\theta}}\left[\ 1\ \right]\bigg|_{\boldsymbol{\theta}=\boldsymbol{\theta}^{(n)}} = 0.
\end{aligned}$$

Here, we denote

$H(\boldsymbol{\theta}|\boldsymbol{\theta}^{(n)}) =$

$$\sum_{i=1}^{N}\sum_{m=1}^{M} \ln \Pr(m|\mathbf{x}_i, \boldsymbol{\theta}) \Pr(m|\mathbf{x}_i, \boldsymbol{\theta}^{(n)}).$$

This proves Property 2. ■

As we know, the log-likelihood function $l(\boldsymbol{\theta})$ is a function of model parameters $\boldsymbol{\theta}$, spanning the whole model space. At the same time, the auxiliary function $Q(\boldsymbol{\theta}|\boldsymbol{\theta}^{(n)})$ is also a function of $\boldsymbol{\theta}$, but it must be constructed based on a given model $\boldsymbol{\theta}^{(n)}$. Their relation can be intuitively illustrated in Figure 12.3, where $l(\boldsymbol{\theta})$ is presumably a complex function because of the log-sum terms, but $Q(\boldsymbol{\theta}|\boldsymbol{\theta}^{(n)})$ is a relatively simple function that eliminates those log-sum terms. We may construct an auxiliary function for any given model $\boldsymbol{\theta}^{(n)}$. As shown in Figure 12.3, the auxiliary function is tangent to $l(\boldsymbol{\theta})$ at the construction point $\boldsymbol{\theta}^{(n)}$, staying below $l(\boldsymbol{\theta})$ everywhere else.

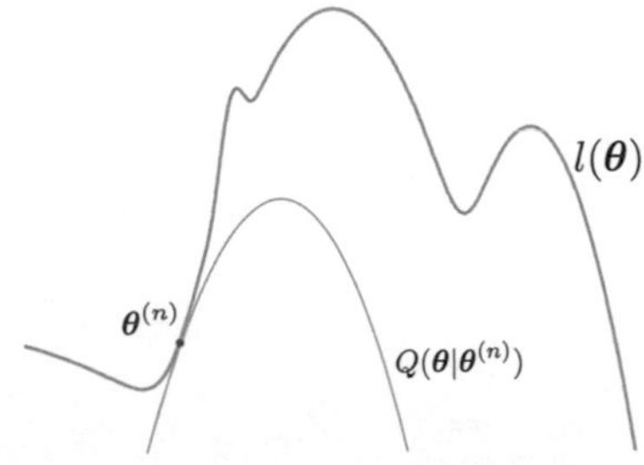

Figure 12.3: An illustration of how the auxiliary function $Q(\boldsymbol{\theta}|\boldsymbol{\theta}^{(n)})$ is related to the original log-likelihood function $l(\boldsymbol{\theta})$.

12.2.2 Expectation-Maximization Algorithm

The auxiliary function $Q(\boldsymbol{\theta}|\boldsymbol{\theta}^{(n)})$ is significantly simpler than the original log-likelihood function $l(\boldsymbol{\theta})$ because it has successfully eliminated all log-sum terms. As a result, it should be easier to maximize $Q(\boldsymbol{\theta}|\boldsymbol{\theta}^{(n)})$ than $l(\boldsymbol{\theta})$ itself. In fact, we can show that $Q(\boldsymbol{\theta}|\boldsymbol{\theta}^{(n)})$ is a concave function because all component models belong to the e-family (see Exercise Q12.4). In many cases, we can even derive a closed-form solution to explicitly solve this optimization problem:

$$\boldsymbol{\theta}^{(n+1)} = \arg\max_{\boldsymbol{\theta}} \ Q(\boldsymbol{\theta}|\boldsymbol{\theta}^{(n)}).$$

Because of the nice properties of the auxiliary function in Theorem 12.2.1, we can prove that the solution $\boldsymbol{\theta}^{(n+1)}$ is guaranteed to improve the original log-likelihood function as well. Based on this, a famous optimization method, called the *expectation-maximization (EM)* algorithm [52], has been proposed to solve MLE for mixture models. As shown in Algorithm 12.12,

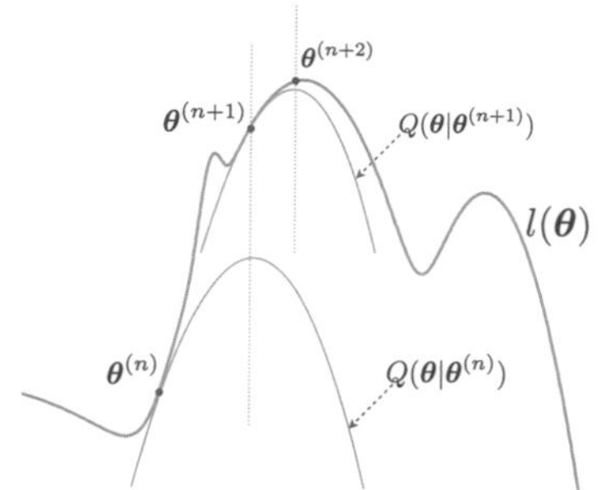

Figure 12.4: An illustration of how the EM algorithm works.

the EM algorithm is an iterative optimization method, with each iteration being composed of two steps. In the first step, we construct auxiliary function $Q(\boldsymbol{\theta}|\boldsymbol{\theta}^{(n)})$ based on the current model $\boldsymbol{\theta}^{(n)}$, as in Eq. (12.4). This step is usually called the *expectation step (E-step)* because the auxiliary function is defined based on a conditional expectation over the latent variable. In the second step, we maximize the auxiliary function to derive a new model $\boldsymbol{\theta}^{(n+1)}$. This step is usually called the *maximization step (M-step)*. Furthermore, we can construct another auxiliary function based on $\boldsymbol{\theta}^{(n+1)}$ to continue another E-step and M-step iteration, as depicted in Figure 12.4. If we continue this process over and over, the EM algorithm will eventually converge to a local maximum of the log-likelihood function.

Algorithm 12.12 EM algorithm

initialize $\boldsymbol{\theta}^{(0)}$, set $n = 0$
while not converged **do**
E-step:

$$Q(\boldsymbol{\theta}|\boldsymbol{\theta}^{(n)}) = \sum_{i=1}^{N} \mathbb{E}_m\Big[\ln\big(w_m \cdot f_{\boldsymbol{\theta}_m}(\mathbf{x}_i)\big)\,\Big|\,\mathbf{x}_i, \boldsymbol{\theta}^{(n)}\Big]$$

M-step:

$$\boldsymbol{\theta}^{(n+1)} = \arg\max_{\boldsymbol{\theta}}\; Q(\boldsymbol{\theta}|\boldsymbol{\theta}^{(n)})$$

$n = n + 1$
end while

Here, let us present some key theoretical results regarding the convergence of the EM algorithm. The important thing is to show why the new model parameters $\boldsymbol{\theta}^{(n+1)}$, derived by maximizing the auxiliary function, are guaranteed to improve the log-likelihood function.

Theorem 12.2.2 *Each EM iteration guarantees to improve* $l(\boldsymbol{\theta})$:

$$l(\boldsymbol{\theta}^{(n+1)}) \geq l(\boldsymbol{\theta}^{(n)}).$$

Furthermore, the improvement of the log-likelihood function is not less than the improvement of the auxiliary function:

$$l(\boldsymbol{\theta}^{(n+1)}) - l(\boldsymbol{\theta}^{(n)}) \geq Q(\boldsymbol{\theta}|\boldsymbol{\theta}^{(n)})\Big|_{\boldsymbol{\theta}=\boldsymbol{\theta}^{(n+1)}} - Q(\boldsymbol{\theta}|\boldsymbol{\theta}^{(n)})\Big|_{\boldsymbol{\theta}=\boldsymbol{\theta}^{(n)}}.$$

Proof:

Step 1: According to Property 1 in Theorem 12.2.1, we have

$$l(\boldsymbol{\theta}^{(n)}) = Q(\boldsymbol{\theta}|\boldsymbol{\theta}^{(n)})\Big|_{\boldsymbol{\theta}=\boldsymbol{\theta}^{(n)}}.$$

Step 2: Because we have maximized the auxiliary function in the M-step, we have

$$Q(\boldsymbol{\theta}|\boldsymbol{\theta}^{(n)})\Big|_{\boldsymbol{\theta}=\boldsymbol{\theta}^{(n+1)}} \geq Q(\boldsymbol{\theta}|\boldsymbol{\theta}^{(n)})\Big|_{\boldsymbol{\theta}=\boldsymbol{\theta}^{(n)}}.$$

Step 3: Based on Property 3 in Theorem 12.2.1, we have

$$l(\boldsymbol{\theta}^{(n+1)}) \geq Q(\boldsymbol{\theta}|\boldsymbol{\theta}^{(n)})\Big|_{\boldsymbol{\theta}=\boldsymbol{\theta}^{(n+1)}}.$$

Step 4: If we put the previous three statements together, we have

$$l(\boldsymbol{\theta}^{(n+1)}) \geq Q(\boldsymbol{\theta}|\boldsymbol{\theta}^{(n)})\Big|_{\boldsymbol{\theta}=\boldsymbol{\theta}^{(n+1)}} \geq Q(\boldsymbol{\theta}|\boldsymbol{\theta}^{(n)})\Big|_{\boldsymbol{\theta}=\boldsymbol{\theta}^{(n)}} = l(\boldsymbol{\theta}^{(n)}).$$

Therefore, we have proved $l(\boldsymbol{\theta}^{(n+1)}) \geq l(\boldsymbol{\theta}^{(n)})$.

Step 5: Based on the previous inequality, it is also easy to show that

$$l(\boldsymbol{\theta}^{(n+1)}) - l(\boldsymbol{\theta}^{(n)}) \geq Q(\boldsymbol{\theta}|\boldsymbol{\theta}^{(n)})\Big|_{\boldsymbol{\theta}=\boldsymbol{\theta}^{(n+1)}} - Q(\boldsymbol{\theta}|\boldsymbol{\theta}^{(n)})\Big|_{\boldsymbol{\theta}=\boldsymbol{\theta}^{(n)}}.$$

■

Theorem 12.2.2 ensures the correctness of the EM algorithm. In other words, it guarantees that the EM algorithm will converge to a local optimum point of the likelihood function. Furthermore, because the improvement of the log-likelihood function is guaranteed to be more than the improvement of the auxiliary function, it suggests that the convergence rate of the EM algorithm is fairly fast.

If we compare the EM algorithm with other iterative optimization methods such as gradient descent, the EM algorithm has two major advantages. First, unlike the sensitive learning rates that must be manually set in gradient-descent methods, the EM algorithm does not rely on any hyperparameters. As a result, it is much easier to implement the EM algorithm, and it normally delivers much stabler results. Second, because of Theorem 12.2.2, the convergence rate of the EM algorithm is much faster than that of gradient descent. On the other hand, gradient-descent methods are generic for any differentiable objective functions, whereas the EM algorithm is restricted to some special forms of objective functions involving log-sum terms, such as the log-likelihood functions of mixture models. Generally speaking, for all cases where the EM algorithm is applicable, the EM algorithm is strongly preferred to any other iterative optimization methods.

Note that the EM algorithm does not specify how to choose the initial model $\boldsymbol{\theta}^{(0)}$ at the beginning and how to solve the maximization problem in the M-step. In the following sections, we will use two popular mixture models, namely, *Gaussian mixture models* (GMMs) and *hidden Markov models (HMMs)*, to explain how to address these issues.

12.3 Gaussian Mixture Models

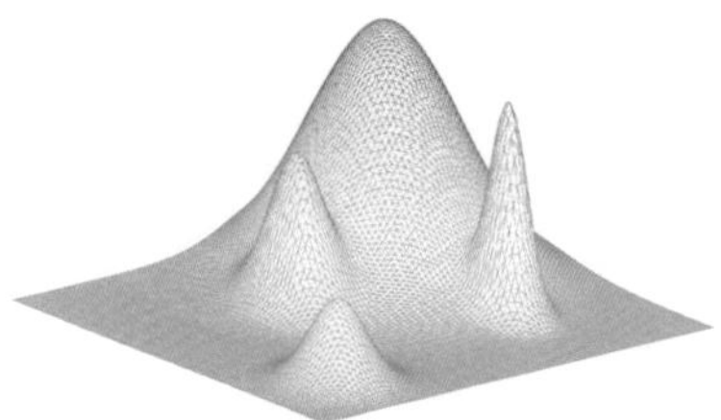

Figure 12.5: An illustration of the use of a GMM to approximate a multimodal distribution with four peaks in two-dimensional (2D) space.

GMMs are probably the most popular mixture models in machine learning, in which we choose multivariate Gaussian models as the component models. Unlike the unimodal models in Chapter 11, GMMs are very powerful generative models that are often used to approximate complex multimodal distributions in high-dimensional spaces. In a GMM, a number of different multivariate Gaussians can collectively capture multiple peaks in a complex probability distribution, as illustrated in Figure 12.5.

Generally speaking, a GMM for $\mathbf{x} \in \mathbb{R}^d$ can be represented as follows:

$$\mathcal{N}(\mathbf{x} \mid \boldsymbol{\mu}_m, \boldsymbol{\Sigma}_m) = \frac{1}{(2\pi)^{d/2}|\boldsymbol{\Sigma}_m|^{1/2}} e^{-\frac{(\mathbf{x}-\boldsymbol{\mu}_m)^\intercal \boldsymbol{\Sigma}_m{}^{-1}(\mathbf{x}-\boldsymbol{\mu}_m)}{2}}.$$

$$p_{\boldsymbol{\theta}}(\mathbf{x}) = \sum_{m=1}^{M} w_m \cdot \mathcal{N}(\mathbf{x} \mid \boldsymbol{\mu}_m, \boldsymbol{\Sigma}_m), \tag{12.6}$$

where $\boldsymbol{\theta} = \{w_m, \boldsymbol{\mu}_m, \boldsymbol{\Sigma}_m \mid m = 1, 2, \cdots, M\}$ denotes all parameters in the GMM; all mixture weights w_m satisfy $\sum_{m=1}^{M} w_m = 1$; and $\boldsymbol{\mu}_m$ and $\boldsymbol{\Sigma}_m$ denote the mean vector and the covariance matrix of the mth Gaussian component, respectively. The computational complexity of calculating $p_{\boldsymbol{\theta}}(\mathbf{x})$ for each $\mathbf{x} \in \mathbb{R}^d$ is roughly estimated as $O(M \cdot d^2)$.

This estimation assumes all determinants $|\boldsymbol{\Sigma}_m|$ and the inverse matrices $\boldsymbol{\Sigma}_m^{-1}$ are precomputed and stored.

If M is large enough, GMMs represent a rather broad class of probability distributions. According to the theoretical results of Sorenson and Alspach [229] and Plataniotis and Hatzinakos [187], for any smooth probability density function, there exists a GMM (with possibly many components) that approximates the given distribution up to any arbitrary precision. Therefore, GMMs are sometimes called a *universal approximator* of probability densities.

Given a set of training data $\mathcal{D} = \{\mathbf{x}_1, \mathbf{x}_2, \cdots, \mathbf{x}_N\}$, let us consider how to learn a GMM from these samples. Similar to any other mixture model, the number of components, M, must be manually prespecified as a hyperparameter. Once M is fixed, we will be able to use the EM algorithm to learn all model parameters $\boldsymbol{\theta}$ associated with the GMM. In the following, we will investigate how to apply the two EM steps to the MLE of GMMs.

In the E-step, we need to construct the auxiliary function as in Eq. (12.4) based on a given set of model parameters: $\boldsymbol{\theta}^{(n)} = \{w_m^{(n)}, \boldsymbol{\mu}_m^{(n)}, \boldsymbol{\Sigma}_m^{(n)} \mid m = 1, 2, \cdots, M\}$. To do this, we just need to compute the conditional probabilities of the latent variable m based on the model parameters $\boldsymbol{\theta}^{(n)}$ and each training sample (i.e., $\Pr(m \mid \mathbf{x}_i, \boldsymbol{\theta}^{(n)})$ for all $m = 1, \cdots, M$ and $i = 1, \cdots, N$). For notation convenience, we use $\xi_m^{(n)}(\mathbf{x}_i)$ to denote these conditional probabilities. Furthermore, given the GMM defined in Eq. (12.6), we compute the conditional probabilities in Eq. (12.3) as follows:

$$\xi_m^{(n)}(\mathbf{x}_i) \triangleq \Pr(m|\mathbf{x}_i, \boldsymbol{\theta}^{(n)}) = \frac{w_m^{(n)} \mathcal{N}(\mathbf{x}_i \mid \boldsymbol{\mu}_m^{(n)}, \boldsymbol{\Sigma}_m^{(n)})}{\sum_{m=1}^{M} w_m^{(n)} \mathcal{N}(\mathbf{x}_i \mid \boldsymbol{\mu}_m^{(n)}, \boldsymbol{\Sigma}_m^{(n)})} \quad (12.7)$$
$$(\forall m = 1, \cdots, M; \ \forall i = 1, \cdots, N).$$

Substituting these probabilities into Eq. (12.4), we then construct the auxiliary function for GMMs as follows:

$$Q(\boldsymbol{\theta}|\boldsymbol{\theta}^{(n)}) =$$
$$\sum_{i=1}^{N}\sum_{m=1}^{M}\left[\ln w_m - \frac{\ln|\boldsymbol{\Sigma}_m|}{2} - \frac{(\mathbf{x}_i - \boldsymbol{\mu}_m)^\intercal \boldsymbol{\Sigma}_m^{-1}(\mathbf{x}_i - \boldsymbol{\mu}_m)}{2}\right]\xi_m^{(n)}(\mathbf{x}_i) + C'. \quad (12.8)$$

Next, in the M-step, we need to maximize the auxiliary function $Q(\boldsymbol{\theta}|\boldsymbol{\theta}^{(n)})$ with respect to all model parameters $\boldsymbol{\theta} = \{w_m, \boldsymbol{\mu}_m, \boldsymbol{\Sigma}_m \mid m = 1, 2, \cdots, M\}$. As all log-sum terms have been eliminated, the auxiliary function actually has a functional form similar to the multivariate Gaussians in Eq. (11.2) with respect to all $\boldsymbol{\mu}_m$ and $\boldsymbol{\Sigma}_m$ and the multinomials in Eq. (11.7) with respect to all w_m.

For all $\boldsymbol{\mu}_m$ and $\boldsymbol{\Sigma}_m$ $(m = 1, 2, \cdots, M)$, we vanish their partial derivatives to derive their updating formulae as follows:

$$\frac{\partial Q(\boldsymbol{\theta}|\boldsymbol{\theta}^{(n)})}{\partial \boldsymbol{\mu}_m} = \sum_{i=1}^{N} \boldsymbol{\Sigma}_m^{-1}\left(\boldsymbol{\mu}_m - \mathbf{x}_i\right)\xi_m^{(n)}(\mathbf{x}_i).$$

$$\frac{\partial Q(\boldsymbol{\theta}|\boldsymbol{\theta}^{(n)})}{\partial \boldsymbol{\mu}_m} = 0 \quad (m = 1, 2, \cdots, M)$$
$$\Longrightarrow \quad \boldsymbol{\mu}_m^{(n+1)} = \frac{\sum_{i=1}^{N} \xi_m^{(n)}(\mathbf{x}_i)\,\mathbf{x}_i}{\sum_{i=1}^{N} \xi_m^{(n)}(\mathbf{x}_i)} \quad (12.9)$$
$$\frac{\partial Q(\boldsymbol{\theta}|\boldsymbol{\theta}^{(n)})}{\partial \boldsymbol{\Sigma}_m} = 0 \quad (m = 1, 2, \cdots, M)$$
$$\Longrightarrow \quad \boldsymbol{\Sigma}_m^{(n+1)} = \frac{\sum_{i=1}^{N} \xi_m^{(n)}(\mathbf{x}_i)(\mathbf{x}_i - \boldsymbol{\mu}_m^{(n+1)})(\mathbf{x}_i - \boldsymbol{\mu}_m^{(n+1)})^\intercal}{\sum_{i=1}^{N} \xi_m^{(n)}(\mathbf{x}_i)}. \quad (12.10)$$

$$\frac{\partial Q(\boldsymbol{\theta}|\boldsymbol{\theta}^{(n)})}{\partial \boldsymbol{\Sigma}_m} = -\frac{1}{2}(\boldsymbol{\Sigma}_m^\intercal)^{-1}\sum_{i=1}^{N}\xi_m^{(n)}(\mathbf{x}_i) + \frac{1}{2}(\boldsymbol{\Sigma}_m^\intercal)^{-1}\left[\sum_{i=1}^{N}\xi_m^{(n)}(\mathbf{x}_i)(\mathbf{x}_i - \boldsymbol{\mu}_m)(\mathbf{x}_i - \boldsymbol{\mu}_m)^\intercal\right](\boldsymbol{\Sigma}_m^\intercal)^{-1}.$$

As for mixture weights w_m $(m = 1, 2, \cdots, M)$, we introduce a Lagrange multiplier λ for the constraint $\sum_{m=1}^{M} w_m = 1$ and derive the updating formula for each w_m as follows:

$$\frac{\partial}{w_m}\left[Q(\boldsymbol{\theta}|\boldsymbol{\theta}^{(n)}) - \lambda\Big(\sum_{m=1}^{M} w_m - 1\Big)\right] = 0$$
$$\Longrightarrow \quad w_m^{(n+1)} = \frac{\sum_{i=1}^{N} \xi_m^{(n)}(\mathbf{x}_i)}{N}. \quad (12.11)$$

Note that $\forall i, n$

$$\sum_{m=1}^{M} \xi_m^{(n)}(\mathbf{x}_i) = 1.$$

Finally, Algorithm 12.13 summarizes the EM algorithm for GMMs. In the E-step, we use Eq. (12.7) to update all conditional probabilities based on the current model parameters $\boldsymbol{\theta}^{(n)}$. Next, in the M-step, the conditional probabilities are used to update all model parameters, as in Eqs. (12.9), (12.10), and (12.11), to derive a new set of model parameters $\boldsymbol{\theta}^{(n+1)}$. This training procedure is repeated until it converges.

Algorithm 12.13 EM Algorithm for GMMs

---

initialize $\{w_m^{(0)}, \boldsymbol{\mu}_m^{(0)}, \boldsymbol{\Sigma}_m^{(0)}\}$, set $n = 0$
while not converged **do**
  E-step: use Eq. (12.7) for all $m = 1, \cdots, M$ and $i = 1, \cdots, N$:

$$\{w_m^{(n)}, \boldsymbol{\mu}_m^{(n)}, \boldsymbol{\Sigma}_m^{(n)}\} \cup \{\mathbf{x}_i\} \longrightarrow \{\xi_m^{(n)}(\mathbf{x}_i)\}$$

  M-step: use Eqs. (12.9), (12.10), and (12.11) for all $m = 1, \cdots, M$:

$$\{\xi_m^{(n)}(\mathbf{x}_i)\} \cup \{\mathbf{x}_i\} \longrightarrow \{w_m^{(n+1)}, \boldsymbol{\mu}_m^{(n+1)}, \boldsymbol{\Sigma}_m^{(n+1)}\}$$

  $n = n + 1$
end while

12.3.1 K-Means Clustering for Initialization

As we have seen, the EM algorithm in Algorithm 12.13 does not specify how to choose the initial model parameters $\{w_m^{(0)}, \boldsymbol{\mu}_m^{(0)}, \boldsymbol{\Sigma}_m^{(0)}\}$. In practice, it is usually better to use some simple bootstrapping methods to initialize them rather than random initialization. For GMMs, we usually use the *k-means clustering* method to partition all N training samples into M homogeneous clusters. Then, each cluster is used to train a multivariate Gaussian separately, as in Section 11.1. These Gaussian models are used as the initial GMM parameters $\boldsymbol{\theta}^{(0)}$ in the EM algorithm. This section briefly introduces the k-means clustering method because it is a popular unsupervised learning algorithm in machine learning [147, 66].

Algorithm 12.14 shows a top-down version of the k-means clustering algorithm, which takes a training set $\mathfrak{D}$ of N samples as input and eventually partitions $\mathfrak{D}$ into M ($M \ll N$) disjoint clusters as output. In k-means clustering, each cluster is represented by its centroid, that is, the mean of all data samples assigned to this cluster. At the beginning, we start with one cluster by randomly initiating the centroid of the first cluster C_1. At each iteration, we first reassign all training samples to the nearest cluster based on which centroid each training sample is closest to. Then, we recompute the centroids for all clusters in the update step. These two steps are repeated until the assignments do not change anymore. After

Algorithm 12.14 Top-Down K-Means Clustering

Input: $\mathcal{D} = \{\mathbf{x}_1, \mathbf{x}_2, \cdots, \mathbf{x}_N\}$
Output: M disjoint clusters: $C_1 \cup C_2 \cdots \cup C_M = \mathcal{D}$

$k = 1$
initialize the centroid of C_1
while $k \leq M$ **do**
  repeat
    assign each $\mathbf{x}_i \in \mathcal{D}$ to the nearest cluster among $C_1, \cdots, C_k$
    update the centroids for the first k clusters: $C_1, \cdots, C_k$
  until assignments no longer change
  split: split any cluster into two clusters
  $k = k + 1$
end while

that, if the total number of current clusters is still less than M, we choose a cluster, such as the one with the largest number of samples or the largest variance, and randomly split its centroid into two. We then go back to repeat the assignment and update steps until the assignments stabilize again. The procedure is repeated until we have M stable clusters.

After this k-means bootstrapping, the training samples in each cluster are used to learn a multivariate Gaussian model separately, as in Section 11.1 (see margin note). Meanwhile, the mixture weights for all Gaussian components can be estimated from the number of samples in each cluster. These parameters are used as the initial model parameters $\{w_m^{(0)}, \boldsymbol{\mu}_m^{(0)}, \boldsymbol{\Sigma}_m^{(0)}\}$ in Algorithm 12.13, and then the EM algorithm is used to further refine all GMM parameters.

For all $m = 1, 2, \cdots, M$, we have the following:

$$\begin{aligned} w_m^{(0)} &= \frac{|C_m|}{N} \\ \boldsymbol{\mu}_m^{(0)} &= \frac{1}{|C_m|} \sum_{\mathbf{x}_i \in C_m} \mathbf{x}_i \\ \boldsymbol{\Sigma}_m^{(0)} &= \frac{1}{|C_m|} \sum_{\mathbf{x}_i \in C_m} (\mathbf{x}_i - \boldsymbol{\mu}_m^{(0)})(\mathbf{x}_i - \boldsymbol{\mu}_m^{(0)})^\intercal. \end{aligned}$$

12.4 Hidden Markov Models

As we extend Gaussian models to GMMs, the modeling capacity of generative models can be significantly enhanced. However, GMMs are only suitable for static patterns that can be represented with fixed-size feature vectors. Here, we will investigate how to use the same idea of mixture models to improve the modeling capacity for variable-length sequences. Section 11.3 introduced Markov chain models as a generative model for sequences. As we will show later, the Markov chain model is a fairly weak unimodal model for sequences because it belongs to the e-family. This section presents a more powerful generative model for sequences, called a *hidden Markov model (HMM)*. We will first consider some basic concepts related to HMMs from the perspective of finite mixture models, and then we will explore several important algorithms that efficiently solve key computation problems in HMMs.

12.4.1 HMMs: Mixture Models for Sequences

HMMs extend Markov chain models in a similar fashion as GMMs extend single Gaussian models. Let us revisit Markov chain models with a simple example of three states $\{\omega_1, \omega_2, \omega_3\}$, as shown in Figure 12.6. If we assume states are directly observed, then this Markov chain model will generate some state sequences, such as $\mathbf{s} = \{\omega_2\omega_1\omega_1\omega_3\}$. As explained in Section 11.3, we can use transition probabilities $\{a_{ij}\}$ to compute the probability of observing any sequence of this kind as

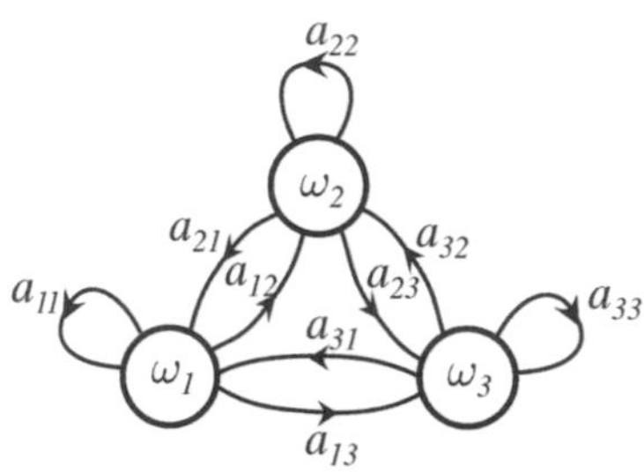

Figure 12.6: An illustration of Markov chain model of three Markov states $\{\omega_1, \omega_2, \omega_3\}$, where states can be directly observed.

$$\Pr(\mathbf{s}) = \Pr(\omega_2\omega_1\omega_1\omega_3) = \pi_2 \times a_{21} \times a_{11} \times a_{13},$$

where $\pi_2 = p(\omega_2)$ denotes the initial probability that a sequence starts from state ω_2.

Another equivalent setting for Markov chain models is that we assume states are not directly observed, but each state *deterministically* generates a unique observation symbol, such as $s_1 \to v_1, s_2 \to v_2, s_3 \to v_3$ in Figure 12.7. In this case, this Markov chain model will generate some observation sequences, such as $\mathbf{o} = \{v_2v_1v_1v_3\}$. Although we do not directly observe the underlying state sequence, we can always deduce the corresponding state sequence from each observation sequence because each state always generates a unique observation symbol. Therefore, we can similarly compute the probability of observing such an observation sequence as follows:

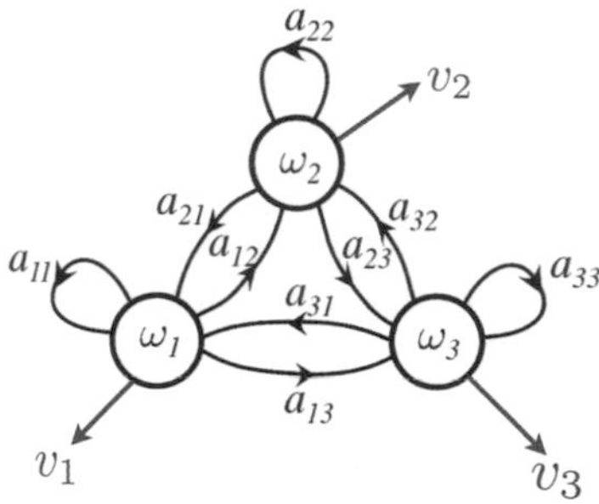

Figure 12.7: An illustration of Markov chain model of three Markov states $\{\omega_1, \omega_2, \omega_3\}$, where states are not directly observed, but each state deterministically generates a unique observation symbol $(\omega_1 \to v_1, \omega_2 \to v_2, \omega_3 \to v_3)$.

$$\Pr(\mathbf{o}) = \Pr(v_2v_1v_1v_3) = \Pr(\omega_2\omega_1\omega_1\omega_3) = \pi_2 \times a_{21} \times a_{11} \times a_{13}.$$

These examples, along with Eq. (11.9), show that the probability of observing a sequence in Markov chain models is a product of many conditional probabilities. If we choose e-family distributions for these conditional probabilities (e.g., multinomial), the overall Markov chain model is also an e-family distribution. Hence, Markov chain models are suitable for modeling sequences following some simple unimodal distributions.

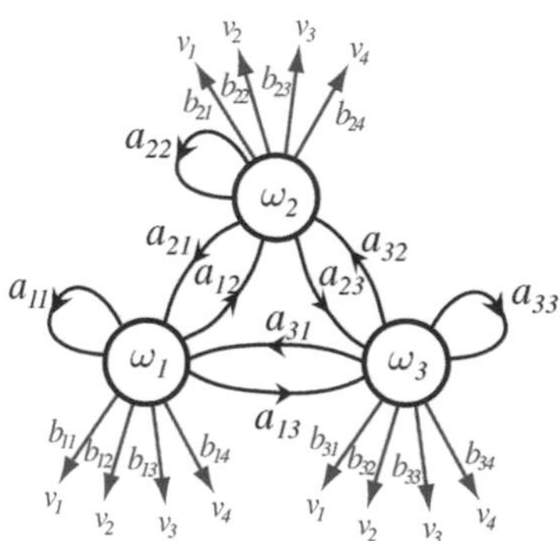

Figure 12.8: An illustration of a discrete HMM of three states and four distinct observation symbols.

Next, we will consider expanding this simple sequence model based on the idea of finite mixture models. The most important extension is to assume that each state can generate all possible symbols based on a unique probability distribution rather than always producing the same unique symbol as in Figure 12.7. This leads to a new setting, as shown in Figure 12.8. In this case, we have three states $\{\omega_1, \omega_2, \omega_3\}$ but four distinct observation symbols $\{v_1, v_2, v_3, v_4\}$. Note that the number of distinct observations is not necessarily equal to the number of unique states here. Each state may generate any symbol based on a different probability. For example, state ω_2 may generate symbol v_1 with probability b_{21}, symbol v_2 with b_{22}, and so on. Similarly, state ω_1 may also generate symbol v_1 with probability b_{11}, symbol v_2 with b_{12}, and so on. In this model, the mechanism to generate an observation sequence is a doubly embedded stochastic process, in which it first randomly traverses different states according to transition probabilities (i.e., $\{a_{ij}\}$) and then randomly generates a symbol at each state based on a probability distribution associated with the state (i.e., $\{b_{ik}\}$).

Furthermore, we adopt the following two assumptions for the stochastic process:

1. *Markov assumption*: The state transition follows a first-order Markov chain. In other words, the probability of being a state only depends on the previous state, which can be fully specified by the transition probability between them (i.e., $a_{ij} = p(\omega_j|\omega_i)$).
2. *Output independence assumption*: The probability of generating an observation only depends on the current state (i.e., $b_{ik} = p(v_k|s_i)$). Given the current state, the observation generated from this state is independent of other states as well as all other observations in the sequence.

Under these assumptions, if we observe an observation sequence $\mathbf{o} = \{v_2 v_1 v_1 v_3\}$, and meanwhile we happen to know its underlying state sequence $\mathbf{s} = \{\omega_2 \omega_1 \omega_1 \omega_3\}$, we can easily compute the probability of generating $\mathbf{o}$ along this state sequence $\mathbf{s}$ as follows:

$$\Pr(\mathbf{o}, \mathbf{s}) = \pi_2 \times b_{22} \times a_{21} \times b_{11} \times a_{11} \times b_{11} \times a_{13} \times b_{33}. \tag{12.12}$$

It is straightforward to verify that this model also belongs to the e-family, and it has no fundamental difference from the Markov chain model in Figure 12.7.

However, if we further assume that we can only observe the observation sequence $\mathbf{o} = \{v_2 v_1 v_1 v_3\}$ while its underlying state sequence is hidden from us, unlike the model in Figure 12.7, we cannot uniquely determine the underlying state sequence from an observation sequence alone. In this setting, the same observation sequence can actually be generated from many different state sequences. Each of these different state sequences may generate the same observation sequence with a different probability, similar to what is computed in Eq. (12.12) (see margin note). If the underlying state sequence is hidden, we will have to treat it as a latent variable; the probability of observing an observation sequence $\mathbf{o}$ without knowing its underlying state sequence must sum over all possible state sequences. In other words, the probability of observing any observation sequence is computed as follows:

$$\Pr(\mathbf{o}) = \sum_{\mathbf{s} \in \mathcal{S}} \Pr(\mathbf{o}, \mathbf{s}), \tag{12.13}$$

where $\mathcal{S}$ is a set of all possible state sequences that may generate $\mathbf{o}$, and each $\Pr(\mathbf{o}, \mathbf{s})$ is computed in the same way as in Eq. (12.12). The models in this equation are HMMs. In the foregoing discussion, we have assumed

Given the model in Figure 12.8, the observation sequence $\mathbf{o} = \{v_2 v_1 v_1 v_3\}$ may be generated from in total $3^4 = 81$ different state sequences, each of which has a different probability. In addition to $\mathbf{s} = \{\omega_2 \omega_1 \omega_1 \omega_3\}$, we can give two more examples here:

$$\mathbf{s}' = \{\omega_1 \omega_2 \omega_2 \omega_3\},$$

with

$$\Pr(\mathbf{o}, \mathbf{s}') = \pi_1 b_{12} a_{12} b_{21} a_{22} b_{21} a_{23} b_{33},$$

and

$$\mathbf{s}'' = \{\omega_3 \omega_1 \omega_2 \omega_1\},$$

with

$$\Pr(\mathbf{o}, \mathbf{s}'') = \pi_3 b_{32} a_{31} b_{11} a_{12} b_{21} a_{21} b_{13}.$$

each observation sequence $\mathbf{o}$ consists of discrete symbols. Thus, they are often called *discrete HMMs*. The methodology of HMMs can be extended to deal with sequences of continuous observations. As shown in Figure 12.9, each state is associated with a separate continuous density function. For example, when being in state ω_2, a continuous vector $\mathbf{x} \in \mathbb{R}^d$ is generated as an observation based on the probability density function $p_2(\mathbf{x})$. Assuming that we have observed a sequence of continuous observations $\mathbf{o} = \{\mathbf{x}_1\mathbf{x}_2\mathbf{x}_3\mathbf{x}_4\}$, along with its underlying state sequence $\mathbf{s} = \{\omega_2\omega_1\omega_1\omega_3\}$, the probability of generating $\mathbf{o}$ along $\mathbf{s}$ is similarly computed as

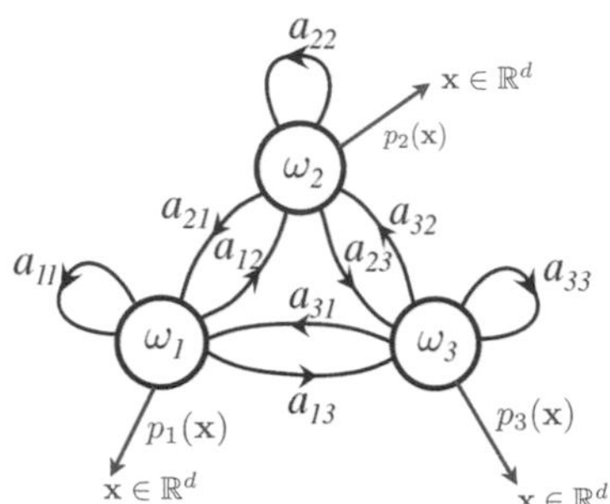

Figure 12.9: An illustration of a continuous density HMM of three states, where each state is associated with a continuous density function.

$$\Pr(\mathbf{o}, \mathbf{s}) = \pi_2 \times p_2(\mathbf{x}_1) \times a_{21} \times p_1(\mathbf{x}_2) \times a_{11} \times p_1(\mathbf{x}_3) \times a_{13} \times p_3(\mathbf{x}_4).$$

When the underlying state sequence is hidden from us, we will have to sum this probability over all possible state sequences in the same way as Eq. (12.13), which is usually called a *continuous density HMM*. In practice, we may choose any probability density function $p_i(\mathbf{x})$ for each state, such as Gaussian models or even GMMs.

In either discrete or continuous density HMMs, we can decompose the joint probability as follows:

$$\Pr(\mathbf{o}, \mathbf{s}) = \Pr(\mathbf{s}) \cdot p(\mathbf{o}|\mathbf{s}),$$

In discrete HMMs, we have

$$\Pr(\mathbf{o}, \mathbf{s}) = \underbrace{\pi_2 a_{21} a_{11} a_{13}}_{\Pr(\mathbf{s})} \times \underbrace{b_{22} b_{11} b_{11} b_{33}}_{p(\mathbf{o}|\mathbf{s})}.$$

In continuous density HMMs, we have

$$\Pr(\mathbf{o}, \mathbf{s}) = \underbrace{\pi_2 a_{21} a_{11} a_{13}}_{\Pr(\mathbf{s})} \times \underbrace{p_2(\mathbf{x}_1) p_1(\mathbf{x}_2) p_1(\mathbf{x}_3) p_3(\mathbf{x}_4)}_{p(\mathbf{o}|\mathbf{s})}.$$

where $\Pr(\mathbf{s})$ denotes the probability of traversing one particular state sequence $\mathbf{s}$, which can be computed based on the initial probabilities and transition probabilities, and $p(\mathbf{o} \mid \mathbf{s})$ indicates the probability of generating an observation sequence $\mathbf{o}$ along this state sequence $\mathbf{s}$ when $\mathbf{s}$ is already given, which is computed based on all state-dependent density functions, that is, $\{b_{ik}\}$ in discrete HMMs and $p_i(\mathbf{x})$ in continuous density HMMs. Furthermore, we can easily verify the following:

$$\sum_{\mathbf{s} \in \mathcal{S}} \Pr(\mathbf{s}) = 1.$$

Therefore, both discrete HMMs and continuous density HMMs (assume that each density function $p_i(\mathbf{x})$ is chosen from the e-family) can be viewed as finite mixture models, as defined in Section 12.1.2, because an HMM can be represented as follows:

$$\Pr(\mathbf{o}) = \sum_{\mathbf{s} \in \mathcal{S}} \Pr(\mathbf{s}) \cdot p(\mathbf{o}|\mathbf{s}), \tag{12.14}$$

where the hidden state sequence $\mathbf{s}$ is treated as the mixture index, and $\Pr(\mathbf{s})$ is treated as the mixture weights. Given any state sequence $\mathbf{s}$, the conditional distribution $p(\mathbf{o}|\mathbf{s})$ can be viewed as a component model, which belongs to the e-family because it can be expressed as a product of many simple e-family distributions.

Finally, let us summarize our discussions with a more generic definition for HMMs. As we have described, HMMs can be viewed as finite mixture models for sequences. Each observation sequence is generated from a doubly embedded stochastic process involving some hidden state sequences, and the Markov and output independence assumptions are adopted in the model. Generally speaking, an HMM, denoted as $\mathbf{\Lambda}$, consists of the following basic elements:

1. $\Omega = \{\omega_1, \omega_2, \cdots \omega_N\}$: a set of N Markov states.
2. $\boldsymbol{\pi} = \{\pi_i \,|\, i = 1, 2, \cdots, N\}$: a set of initial probabilities of all states as $\{\pi(\omega_1), \pi(\omega_2), \cdots \pi(\omega_N)\}$, each of which indicates the probability that any state sequence will start from each state. We denote $\pi(\omega_i)$ as π_i for short.
3. $\mathbf{A} = \{a_{ij} \,|\, 1 \leq i, j \leq N\}$: a set of state transition probabilities $a(\omega_i, \omega_j)$ going from state ω_i to state ω_j for any pair of states in Ω. For simplicity, we denote $a(\omega_i, \omega_j)$ as a_{ij}.
4. $\mathbb{B} = \{b_i(\mathbf{x}) \,|\, i = 1, 2, \cdots, N\}$: a set of state-dependent probability distributions $b(\mathbf{x}|\omega_i)$ for all $\omega_i \in \Omega$. We also denote $b(\mathbf{x}|\omega_i)$ as $b_i(\mathbf{x})$ for short. Each $b_i(\mathbf{x})$ specifies how likely it is for an observation to be generated from state ω_i. We will have to choose different probability functions for $b_i(\mathbf{x})$ depending on whether $\mathbf{x}$ is discrete or continuous.

Note that we have $\sum_{i=1}^{N} \pi_i = 1$.

We have

$$\sum_{j=1}^{N} a_{ij} = 1$$

for any $i = 1, 2, \cdots, N$.

The first three parameters $\{\Omega, \boldsymbol{\pi}, \mathbf{A}\}$ define a Markov chain model, and they also jointly specify the topology of an HMM. In some large HMMs involving many states, all allowed state transitions may be sparse. In other words, a valid state sequence is only allowed to start from a small subset of Ω, and meanwhile, each state can only transit to a very small subset in Ω. In these cases, it may be more convenient to represent $\{\Omega, \boldsymbol{\pi}, \mathbf{A}\}$ using a directed graph, where each node represents a state and each arc represents an allowed state transition, along with the corresponding transition probability.

The HMM $\mathbf{\Lambda} = \{\Omega, \boldsymbol{\pi}, \mathbf{A}, \mathbb{B}\}$ specified previously can be used to compute the probability of observing any sequence of T observations:

$$\mathbf{o} = \{\mathbf{x}_1, \mathbf{x}_2, \cdots, \mathbf{x}_T\}.$$

Because the underlying state sequence is hidden, we will have to sum over all possible state sequences of length T that may produce $\mathbf{o}$, denoted as $\mathbf{s} = \{s_1, s_2, \cdots, s_T\}$, with each $s_t \in \Omega$. Therefore, we have the probability distribution of $\mathbf{o}$ given by the HMM as follows:

$$\begin{aligned} p_{\mathbf{\Lambda}}(\mathbf{o}) &= \sum_{\mathbf{s}} p_{\mathbf{\Lambda}}(\mathbf{o}, \mathbf{s}) = \sum_{s_1 \cdots s_T} \pi(s_1) b(\mathbf{x}_1|s_1) \prod_{t=2}^{T} a(s_{t-1}, s_t) b(\mathbf{x}_t|s_t) \\ &= \sum_{s_1 \cdots s_T} \pi(s_1) b(\mathbf{x}_1|s_1) a(s_1, s_2) b(\mathbf{x}_2|s_2) \cdots a(s_{T-1}, s_T) b(\mathbf{x}_T|s_T). \end{aligned} \tag{12.15}$$

HMMs were originally studied in the field of statistics under the name *probabilistic functions of Markov chains* [16, 17, 15], and the terminology *hidden Markov models* was later adopted widely in engineering [194] for many real-world applications, such as speech, handwriting, gesture recognition, natural language processing, and bioinformatics. The scale of an HMM may vary from a toy example of several states to a tremendous number of states. As we will see later, because efficient algorithms for solving all computation problems in HMMs exist, the HMM is one of a few machine learning methods that can actually be applied to large-scale real-world tasks. For example, some huge HMMs consisting of over millions of states are usually used to solve large-vocabulary speech-recognition problems [256, 173, 218].

In the following, let us investigate how to solve three major computation problems for HMMs, namely, *evaluation*, *decoding*, and *training* problems. Because of the structural constraints specified by the two HMM assumptions, fortunately, we are able to derive very efficient algorithms for solving all of these problems.

12.4.2 Evaluation Problem: Forward–Backward Algorithm

The evaluation problem for HMMs is related to how to compute $p_{\mathbf{\Lambda}}(\mathbf{o})$ in Eq. (12.15) for any observation sequence $\mathbf{o}$ when all HMM parameters $\mathbf{\Lambda}$ are given. As opposed to GMMs, it is prohibitive for us to compute the summation in Eq. (12.15) by any brute-force method. The reason is that the number of different state sequences is exponential to the length of a sequence. In an ergodic HMM structure, as in Figure 12.9, we can estimate that the number of different state sequences that could generate a sequence of T observations is roughly $O(N^T)$. This number is extremely large in any meaningful case. For example, even for a small HMM of $N = 5$ states to generate a sequence of $T = 100$ observations, we will have to sum over approximately 10^{70} different state sequences in Eq. (12.15).

Note that $5^{100} \approx 10^{70}$.

However, the good news is that HMMs adopt the Markov and output independence assumptions, allowing us to factor the joint probability $p_{\mathbf{\Lambda}}(\mathbf{o}, \mathbf{s})$ into a product of many locally dependent conditional probabilities, as in Eq. (12.15). This further enables us to use an efficient dynamic programming method to compute this summation recursively from left to right, as follows:

$$\sum_{s_1 \cdots s_T} \underbrace{\pi(s_1) b(\mathbf{x}_1|s_1)}_{\alpha_1(s_1)} a(s_1, s_2) b(\mathbf{x}_2|s_2) \cdots a(s_{T-1}, s_T) b(\mathbf{x}_T|s_T)$$

$$= \sum_{s_2 \cdots s_T} \underbrace{\left(\sum_{s_1=1}^{N} \alpha_1(s_1) a(s_1, s_2) b(\mathbf{x}_2 | s_2) \right)}_{\alpha_2(s_2)} a(s_2, s_3) \cdots a(s_{T-1}, s_T) b(\mathbf{x}_T | s_T)$$

$$= \sum_{s_3 \cdots s_T} \underbrace{\left(\sum_{s_2=1}^{N} \alpha_2(s_2) a(s_2, s_3) b(\mathbf{x}_3 | s_3) \right)}_{\alpha_3(s_3)} a(s_3, s_4) \cdots a(s_{T-1}, s_T) b(\mathbf{x}_T | s_T)$$

$$\vdots$$

$$= \sum_{s_T} \underbrace{\left(\sum_{s_{T-1}=1}^{N} \alpha_{T-1}(s_{T-1}) a(s_{T-1}, s_T) b(\mathbf{x}_T | s_T) \right)}_{\alpha_T(s_T)} = \sum_{s_T=1}^{N} \alpha_T(s_T).$$

This procedure computes $p_{\mathbf{\Lambda}}(\mathbf{o})$ by repeatedly performing T rounds of summations. As a result, the computational complexity is dramatically reduced to $O(T \times N^2)$. The dynamic programming algorithm to perform this recursive computation is often called the *forward* algorithm because it proceeds from the beginning of a sequence until the end. All partial sums $\alpha_t(s_t)$ in this procedure are called *forward probabilities*. We may represent these forward probabilities for all $t = 1, \cdots, T$ and $i = 1, \cdots, N$ as

$$\alpha_t(i) \triangleq \alpha_t(s_t) \Big|_{s_t = \omega_i}$$

The physical meaning of $\alpha_t(i)$ is the probability of observing the partial observation sequence up to time t (i.e., $\mathbf{x}_1 \cdots \mathbf{x}_t$) when traversing all possible partial state sequences up to $t-1$ but stopping at state ω_i at t, namely, $\alpha_t(i) = \Pr(\mathbf{x}_1 \cdots \mathbf{x}_t, s_t = \omega_i \mid \mathbf{\Lambda})$.

This forward procedure can be represented by an $N \times T$ lattice, as shown in Figure 12.10, where each row corresponds to a state, each column corresponds to a time instance, and each node represents a forward probability $\alpha_t(i)$. We first initialize all nodes in the first column as $\alpha_1(s_1)$, and then all nodes in the next column can be computed by summing all nodes in the previous column, as follows:

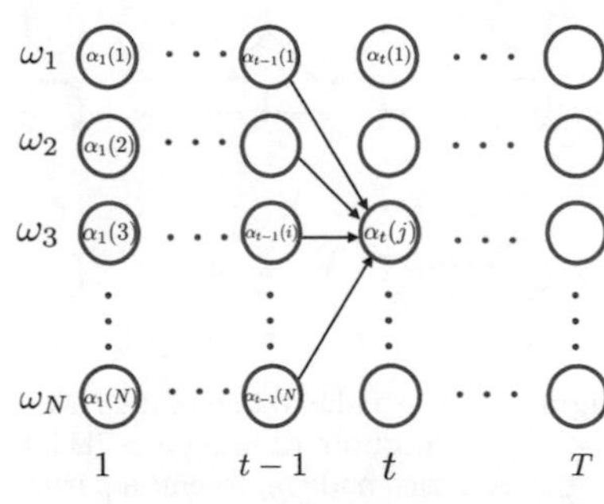

Figure 12.10: An illustration of the HMM forward algorithm running in a 2D lattice, where each node represents a partial probability $\alpha_t(j)$.

$$\alpha_t(j) = \sum_{i=1}^{N} \alpha_{t-1}(i) a_{ij} b_j(\mathbf{x}_t).$$

It proceeds recursively from left to right for all columns. At last, the evaluation probability $p_{\mathbf{\Lambda}}(\mathbf{o})$ is computed by summing all nodes in the last column:

$$p_{\mathbf{\Lambda}}(\mathbf{o}) = \sum_{i=1}^{N} \alpha_T(i). \tag{12.16}$$

Moreover, we can also conduct the recursive summation from the end of

Backward recursion is conducted as follows:

$$\sum_{s_1 \cdots s_T} \pi(s_1) b(\mathbf{x}_1 | s_1) \cdots a(s_{T-1}, s_T) \, b(\mathbf{x}_T | s_T)$$

$$= \textstyle\sum_{s_1 \cdots s_{T-1}} \pi(s_1) \cdots \underbrace{\left(\sum_{s_T} a(s_{T-1}, s_T) b(\mathbf{x}_T | s_T) \right)}_{\beta_{T-1}(s_{T-1})}$$

$$\vdots$$

$$= \textstyle\sum_{s_1} \pi(s_1) b(\mathbf{x}_1 | s_1) \underbrace{\left(\sum_{s_2} a(s_1, s_2) b(\mathbf{x}_2 | s_2) \beta_2(s_2) \right)}_{\beta_1(s_1)}$$

$$= \textstyle\sum_{s_1} \pi(s_1) b(\mathbf{x}_1 | s_1) \beta_1(s_1).$$

a sequence and move backward to the beginning (see margin note). This procedure is called the *backward* algorithm. The computational complexity of the backward algorithm is the same as that of the forward algorithm. All partial sums $\beta_t(s_t)$ in this procedure are called *backward probabilities*. We similarly denote

$$\beta_t(i) \triangleq \beta_t(s_t)\Big|_{s_t = \omega_i} \qquad \text{for all } \; t = 1, \cdots T; \; i = 1, \cdots, N.$$

The physical meaning of $\beta_t(i)$ is the probability of observing the partial sequence $\mathbf{x}_{t+1} \cdots \mathbf{x}_T$ by starting from state ω_i at t and then traversing all partial state sequences until the end of this sequence, which is usually denoted as $\beta_t(i) = \Pr(\mathbf{x}_{t+1} \cdots \mathbf{x}_T \mid s_t = \omega_i, \mathbf{\Lambda})$. Similarly, the backward algorithm can be represented by the lattice shown in Figure 12.11. In this case, we first initialize all nodes in the last column and then recursively compute all columns by working backward until the first one. After that, the evaluation probability $p_{\mathbf{\Lambda}}(\mathbf{o})$ is computed by summing all nodes in the first column as follows:

$$p_{\mathbf{\Lambda}}(\mathbf{o}) = \sum_{i=1}^{N} \pi_i b_i(\mathbf{x}_1) \beta_1(i). \tag{12.17}$$

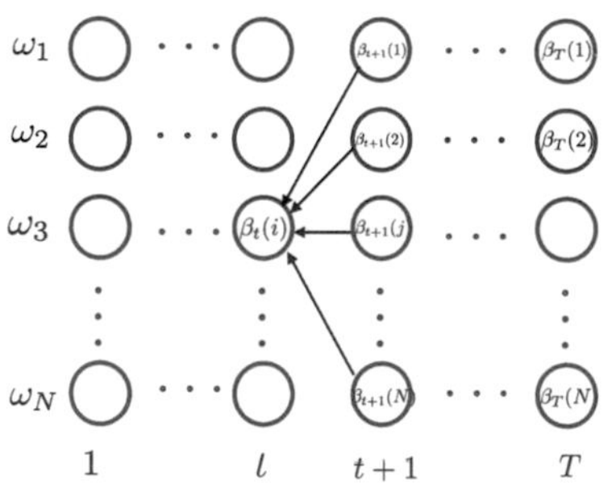

Figure 12.11: An illustration of the HMM backward algorithm running in a 2D lattice, where each node represents a partial probability $\beta_t(j)$.

Finally, we can summarize both forward and backward algorithms as shown in Algorithm 12.15. Given any HMM $\mathbf{\Lambda}$, for any observation sequence $\mathbf{o} = \{\mathbf{x}_1, \mathbf{x}_2, \cdots \mathbf{x}_T\}$, the forward–backward Algorithm 12.15 will yield all forward and backward probabilities as output:

$$\{\alpha_t(i), \beta_t(i) \mid t = 1, 2, \cdots, T, \; i = 1, 2, \cdots, N\}.$$

Once we have these partial probabilities, we can derive $p_{\mathbf{\Lambda}}(\mathbf{o})$ using either the forward probabilities, as in Eq. (12.16), or the backward probabilities, as in Eq. (12.17).

Moreover, we can also compute $p_{\mathbf{\Lambda}}(\mathbf{o})$ by combining the forward and backward probabilities at any time t as follows:

$$p_{\mathbf{\Lambda}}(\mathbf{o}) = \sum_{i=1}^{N} \alpha_t(i) \beta_t(i) \qquad (\forall t = 1, 2, \cdots, T). \tag{12.18}$$

This corresponds to the cases where we use the forward procedure to compute the initial partial sequence up to time t and then use the backward procedure to compute the remaining part of the sequence. Refer to Exercise Q12.8 for more details on this.

Algorithm 12.15 HMM Forward–Backward Algorithm

Input: an HMM $\mathbf{\Lambda} = \{\Omega, \pi, \mathbf{A}, \mathbb{B}\}$ and a sequence $\mathbf{o} = \{\mathbf{x}_1, \mathbf{x}_2, \cdots \mathbf{x}_T\}$
Output: $\{\alpha_t(i), \beta_t(i) \mid t = 1, \cdots, T, \ i = 1, \cdots, N\}$

```
initiate α_1(j) = π_j b_j(x_1) for all j = 1,2···,N
for t = 2,3,···,T do
  for j = 1,2,···,N do
    α_t(j) = Σ_{i=1}^N α_{t-1}(i) a_ij b_j(x_t)
  end for
end for
initiate β_T(j) = 1 for all j = 1,2···,N
for t = T−1,···,1 do
  for i = 1,2,···,N do
    β_t(i) = Σ_{j=1}^N a_ij b_j(x_{t+1}) β_{t+1}(j)
  end for
end for
```

12.4.3 Decoding Problem: Viterbi Algorithm

Given an HMM $\mathbf{\Lambda}$, for any observation sequence $\mathbf{o}$, there exist many different state sequences $\mathbf{s}$, which may generate $\mathbf{o}$ with a probability $p_{\mathbf{\Lambda}}(\mathbf{o}, \mathbf{s})$. Sometimes, we are interested in the most probable state sequence $\mathbf{s}^*$, which yields the largest probability of generating $\mathbf{o}$ along a single state sequence among all in $\mathcal{S}$. That is,

$$\mathbf{s}^* = \arg\max_{\mathbf{s} \in \mathcal{S}} \ p_{\mathbf{\Lambda}}(\mathbf{o}, \mathbf{s}).$$

The decoding problem in HMMs is related to how to efficiently uncover this most probable state sequence $\mathbf{s}^*$. Similarly, we cannot use any brute-force method to search for it. The most efficient way is a similar dynamic programming method that replaces sum with max in the previous forward algorithm. As shown in Figure 12.12, when we proceed from $t-1$ to t, we keep track of the maximum incoming value as $\gamma_t(j)$ for each node, rather than summing over all incoming paths in the forward algorithm. Furthermore, the maximum incoming node from the previous column is indicated by a back-tracking pointer $\delta_t(j)$. This results in the so-called *Viterbi* decoding Algorithm 12.16 [245]. The most probable state sequence $\mathbf{s}^*$ is sometimes called the *Viterbi path*. For example, if we use the three-state HMM in Figure 12.9 to run the Viterbi algorithm against an observation sequence $\mathbf{o} = \{\mathbf{x}_1\mathbf{x}_2\mathbf{x}_3\mathbf{x}_4\mathbf{x}_5\}$, as shown in Figure 12.13, we assume all back-tracking pointers $\delta_t(i)$ are kept. We also assume that $\gamma_5(2)$ is the largest outcome in the termination step. Following the back-tracking pointer at $\gamma_5(2)$ all the way back, we may recover the Viterbi path (indicated by the solid arrows) as $\mathbf{s}^* = \{\omega_1\, \omega_2\, \omega_3\, \omega_3\, \omega_2\}$.

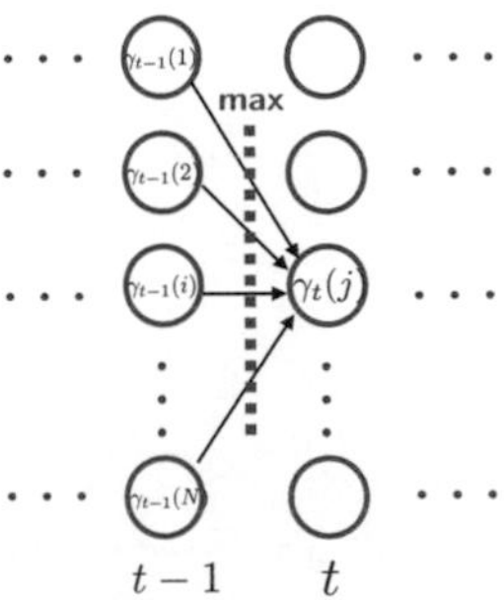

Figure 12.12: An illustration of the HMM Viterbi algorithm running from $t-1$ to t in a 2D lattice, where each node represents a partial probability $\gamma_t(j)$.

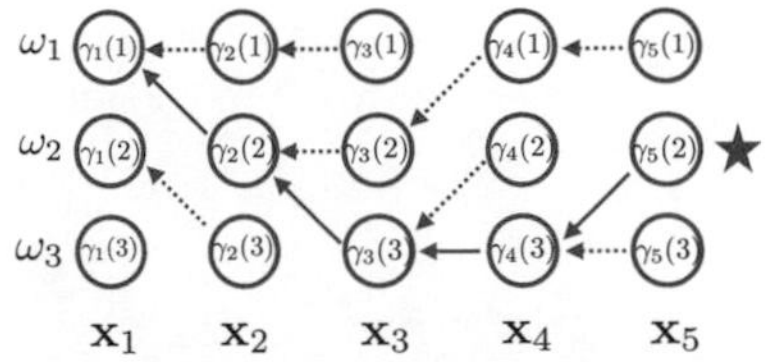

Figure 12.13: An illustration of back-tracing the Viterbi path from the back-tracking pointers. The Viterbi path $\mathbf{s}^* = \{\omega_1\, \omega_2\, \omega_3\, \omega_3\, \omega_2\}$ is uncovered by the solid arrows, whereas the dashed arrows are not used. Along the most probable path, $\mathbf{x}_1$ is generated at state ω_1 in Figure 12.9, $\mathbf{x}_2$ at ω_2, $\mathbf{x}_3$ at ω_3, $\mathbf{x}_4$ at ω_3, and $\mathbf{x}_5$ at ω_2.

Algorithm 12.16 Viterbi Algorithm for HMMs

Input: an HMM $\mathbf{\Lambda} = \{\Omega, \boldsymbol{\pi}, \mathbf{A}, \mathbb{B}\}$ and a sequence $\mathbf{o} = \{\mathbf{x}_1, \mathbf{x}_2, \cdots \mathbf{x}_T\}$
Output: Viterbi path $\mathbf{s}^*$ and $p_{\mathbf{\Lambda}}(\mathbf{o}, \mathbf{s}^*)$

initiate $\gamma_1(j) = \pi_j b_j(\mathbf{x}_1)$ for all $j = 1, 2 \cdots, N$
for $t = 2, 3, \cdots, T$ **do**
  for $j = 1, 2, \cdots, N$ **do**
    $\gamma_t(j) = \left(\max_{i=1}^N \ \gamma_{t-1}(i) a_{ij}\right) b_j(\mathbf{x}_t)$
    $\delta_t(j) = \arg\max_{i=1}^N \ \gamma_{t-1}(i) a_{ij}$
  end for
end for
termination: $p_{\mathbf{\Lambda}}(\mathbf{o}, \mathbf{s}^*) = \max_{i=1}^N \gamma_T(i)$
path backtracking: $\mathbf{s}^* = \{s_1^* s_2^* \cdots s_T^*\}$ with $s_T^* = \arg\max_{i=1}^N \gamma_T(i)$ and $s_{t-1}^* = \delta_t(s_t^*)$ for $t = T, \cdots, 2$

In speech recognition, the Viterbi algorithm is often used to uncover the most probable Viterbi path, which in turn is used to generate the final recognition result [173]. However, the 2D-lattice-based implementation in Figure 12.13 is not possible for large HMMs, which require a huge space to store this lattice. Therefore, a memory-efficient in-place implementation, called the *token-passing algorithm* [257], is often used in speech recognition.

Moreover, if the observation sequence $\mathbf{o}$ is long, the probabilities $p_{\mathbf{\Lambda}}(\mathbf{o}, \mathbf{s})$ along different state paths usually vary dramatically, often differing in the order of magnitude. As a result, the probability summation over all possible state sequences is always dominated by the maximum along the Viterbi path. This suggests that we can also use $p_{\mathbf{\Lambda}}(\mathbf{o}, \mathbf{s}^*)$ from the Viterbi algorithm as a good approximation to the previous evaluation probability instead of running the forward–backward algorithm:

$$p_{\mathbf{\Lambda}}(\mathbf{o}) \approx p_{\mathbf{\Lambda}}(\mathbf{o}, \mathbf{s}^*).$$

12.4.4 Training Problem: Baum–Welch Algorithm

The last computation problem in HMMs is how to learn an HMM for any particular task. As usual, we will have to first specify the structure of an HMM, such as the number of states in Ω and the topology of the HMM. Then we will be able to estimate all model parameters, including $\mathbf{\Lambda} = \{\boldsymbol{\pi}, \mathbf{A}, \mathbb{B}\}$, using some training samples. Because HMMs are used to model sequences, a training set for learning an HMM normally consists of many variable-length sequences:

$$\mathcal{D} = \left\{\mathbf{o}^{(1)}, \mathbf{o}^{(2)}, \cdots, \mathbf{o}^{(R)}\right\},$$

where each $\mathbf{o}^{(r)} = \{\mathbf{x}_1^{(r)}, \mathbf{x}_2^{(r)}, \cdots \mathbf{x}_{T_r}^{(r)}\}$ $(r = 1, 2 \cdots R)$ denotes an observation sequence of length T_r. Again, we will use the MLE method to learn all model parameters $\mathbf{\Lambda}$ from $\mathfrak{D}$, as follows:

$$\mathbf{\Lambda}^*_{\text{MLE}} = \arg\max_{\mathbf{\Lambda}} \sum_{r=1}^{R} \ln p_{\mathbf{\Lambda}}(\mathbf{o}^{(r)}) = \arg\max_{\mathbf{\Lambda}} \sum_{r=1}^{R} \ln \sum_{\mathbf{s}^{(r)}} p_{\mathbf{\Lambda}}(\mathbf{o}^{(r)}, \mathbf{s}^{(r)}),$$

where $\mathbf{s}^{(r)}$ represents a hidden state sequence corresponding to $\mathbf{o}^{(r)}$, denoted as $\mathbf{s}^{(r)} = \{s_1^{(r)} s_2^{(r)} \cdots s_{T_r}^{(r)}\}$, which is a sequence of states occupied at each time. Because HMMs are essentially finite mixture models, we will explain how to use the EM algorithm to solve the training problem for HMMs. This leads to the famous Baum–Welch algorithm [17, 15].

In the E-step, assume we are given a set of HMM parameters $\mathbf{\Lambda}^{(n)}$; let us look at how to construct the auxiliary function $Q(\mathbf{\Lambda}|\mathbf{\Lambda}^{(n)})$ for HMMs. Because the hidden state sequences are latent variables in HMMs, we can derive the conditional probabilities in Eq. (12.3) for HMMs as follows:

$$\begin{aligned} \Pr\left(\mathbf{s}^{(r)} \,\middle|\, \mathbf{o}^{(r)}, \mathbf{\Lambda}^{(n)}\right) &= \frac{p_{\mathbf{\Lambda}^{(n)}}\left(\mathbf{o}^{(r)}, \mathbf{s}^{(r)}\right)}{p_{\mathbf{\Lambda}^{(n)}}\left(\mathbf{o}^{(r)}\right)} \\ &= \frac{p_{\mathbf{\Lambda}^{(n)}}\left(\mathbf{o}^{(r)}, \mathbf{s}^{(r)}\right)}{\sum_{\mathbf{s}^{(r)}} p_{\mathbf{\Lambda}^{(n)}}\left(\mathbf{o}^{(r)}, \mathbf{s}^{(r)}\right)}. \end{aligned} \tag{12.19}$$

As in Eq. (12.4), we construct the auxiliary function for HMMs as follows:

$$\begin{aligned} Q(\mathbf{\Lambda}|\mathbf{\Lambda}^{(n)}) &= \sum_{r=1}^{R} \mathbb{E}_{\mathbf{s}^{(r)}}\left[\ln p_{\mathbf{\Lambda}}(\mathbf{o}^{(r)}, \mathbf{s}^{(r)}) \,\middle|\, \mathbf{o}^{(r)}, \mathbf{\Lambda}^{(n)}\right] \\ &= \sum_{r=1}^{R} \sum_{\mathbf{s}^{(r)}} \ln p_{\mathbf{\Lambda}}(\mathbf{o}^{(r)}, \mathbf{s}^{(r)}) \Pr\left(\mathbf{s}^{(r)} \,\middle|\, \mathbf{o}^{(r)}, \mathbf{\Lambda}^{(n)}\right). \end{aligned}$$

Considering the hidden state sequence $\mathbf{s}^{(r)} = \{s_1^{(r)} s_2^{(r)} \cdots s_{T_r}^{(r)}\}$, if we substitute

$$p_{\mathbf{\Lambda}}(\mathbf{o}^{(r)}, \mathbf{s}^{(r)}) = \pi(s_1^{(r)}) b(\mathbf{x}_1^{(r)} | s_1^{(r)}) \prod_{t=1}^{T_r - 1} a(s_t^{(r)}, s_{t+1}^{(r)}) b(\mathbf{x}_{t+1}^{(r)} | s_{t+1}^{(r)})$$

into the previous auxiliary function, we have

$$\begin{aligned} Q(\mathbf{\Lambda}|\mathbf{\Lambda}^{(n)}) = \sum_{r=1}^{R} \sum_{s_1^{(r)} \cdots s_{T_r}^{(r)}} & \left[\ln \pi(s_1^{(r)}) + \sum_{t=1}^{T_r-1} \ln a(s_t^{(r)}, s_{t+1}^{(r)}) + \sum_{t=1}^{T_r} \ln b(\mathbf{x}_t^{(r)} | s_t^{(r)}) \right] \\ & \Pr\left(s_1^{(r)} s_2^{(r)} \cdots s_{T_r}^{(r)} \,\middle|\, \mathbf{o}^{(r)}, \mathbf{\Lambda}^{(n)}\right). \end{aligned}$$

Because each state $s_t^{(r)} \in \Omega = \{\omega_1, \omega_2, \cdots, \omega_N\}$, we rearrange the previous summation according to different states ω_i in Ω, and we derive the

Taking $Q(\mathbf{A}|\mathbf{A}^{(n)})$ as example, considering different combinations of $s_{t-1}^{(r)}$ and $s_t^{(r)}$, we can rearrange

$$\begin{aligned}&\sum_{r=1}^{R}\sum_{s_1^{(r)}\cdots s_{T_r}^{(r)}}\sum_{t=1}^{T_r-1}\ln a(s_t^{(r)},s_{t+1}^{(r)})\\&\Pr\left(s_1^{(r)}s_2^{(r)}\cdots s_{T_r}^{(r)}|\mathbf{o}^{(r)},\mathbf{\Lambda}^{(n)}\right)\\=&\sum_{r=1}^{R}\sum_{t=1}^{T_r-1}\sum_{i=1}^{N}\sum_{j=1}^{N}\ln a_{ij}\\&\Pr\left(s_t^{(r)}=\omega_i,s_{t+1}^{(r)}=\omega_j\,\middle|\,\mathbf{o}^{(r)},\mathbf{\Lambda}^{(n)}\right)\\=&\;Q(\mathbf{A}|\mathbf{A}^{(n)}).\end{aligned}$$

We can similarly derive $Q(\boldsymbol{\pi}|\boldsymbol{\pi}^{(n)})$ and $Q(\mathbb{B}|\mathbb{B}^{(n)})$.

auxiliary function as follows (see margin note):

$$\begin{aligned}Q(\mathbf{\Lambda}|\mathbf{\Lambda}^{(n)})=&\underbrace{\sum_{r=1}^{R}\sum_{i=1}^{N}\ln\pi_i\Pr(s_1^{(r)}=\omega_i\,|\,\mathbf{o}^{(r)},\mathbf{\Lambda}^{(n)})}_{Q(\boldsymbol{\pi}|\boldsymbol{\pi}^{(n)})}\\&+\underbrace{\sum_{r=1}^{R}\sum_{t=1}^{T_r-1}\sum_{i=1}^{N}\sum_{j=1}^{N}\ln a_{ij}\Pr(s_t^{(r)}=\omega_i,s_{t+1}^{(r)}=\omega_j\,|\,\mathbf{o}^{(r)},\mathbf{\Lambda}^{(n)})}_{Q(\mathbf{A}|\mathbf{A}^{(n)})}\\&+\underbrace{\sum_{r=1}^{R}\sum_{t=1}^{T_r}\sum_{i=1}^{N}\ln b_i(\mathbf{x}_t^{(r)})\Pr(s_t^{(r)}=\omega_i\,|\,\mathbf{o}^{(r)},\mathbf{\Lambda}^{(n)})}_{Q(\mathbb{B}|\mathbb{B}^{(n)})}.\end{aligned}$$

From this, we can see that the overall auxiliary function is broken down into three independent parts, each of which is only related to one group of HMM parameters. This allows us to derive the estimation formula for each group separately. Before we look at how to maximize each of them in the M-step, let us first investigate how to compute the conditional probabilities in the previous equation.

Index notations:
n: HMM parameters at nth iteration
r: rth training sequence
t: tth observation in a sequence
i: an HMM state ω_i
j: an HMM state ω_j

First of all, we use a compact notation $\eta_t^{(r)}(i,j)$ to represent $\Pr\left(s_t^{(r)}=\omega_i,s_{t+1}^{(r)}=\omega_j\,|\,\mathbf{o}^{(r)},\mathbf{\Lambda}^{(n)}\right)$, which indicates the conditional probability of passing state ω_i at time t and state ω_j at time $t+1$ when conditioning on $\mathbf{o}^{(r)}$ and $\mathbf{\Lambda}^{(n)}$. Based on Eq. (12.19), we can express it as

$$\begin{aligned}&\eta_t^{(r)}(i,j)\triangleq\Pr\left(s_t^{(r)}=\omega_i,s_{t+1}^{(r)}=\omega_j\,|\,\mathbf{o}^{(r)},\mathbf{\Lambda}^{(n)}\right)\\=&\frac{\sum_{s_1^{(r)}\cdots s_{t-1}^{(r)}s_{t+2}^{(r)}\cdots s_{T_r}^{(r)}}p_{\mathbf{\Lambda}^{(n)}}\left(\mathbf{o}^{(r)},s_1^{(r)},\cdots s_{t-1}^{(r)},\omega_i,\omega_j,s_{t+2}^{(r)}\cdots s_{T_r}^{(r)}\right)}{\sum_{s_1^{(r)}\cdots s_{T_r}^{(r)}}p_{\mathbf{\Lambda}^{(n)}}\left(\mathbf{o}^{(r)},s_1^{(r)},s_2^{(r)}\cdots s_{T_r}^{(r)}\right)}.\end{aligned}$$

Both the numerator and the denominator can be efficiently computed with the forward–backward algorithm. We first run the forward–backward algorithm on the training sequence $\mathbf{o}^{(r)}$ using the current HMM $\mathbf{\Lambda}^{(n)}$ to derive the set of all forward and backward probabilities for $\mathbf{o}^{(r)}$, denoted as $\{\alpha_t^{(r)}(i),\beta_t^{(r)}(i)\}$. The denominator is the evaluation probability we have studied in the evaluation problem, which can be computed by Eq. (12.16) or Eq. (12.17). As shown in Figure 12.14, the numerator can be computed as three parts:

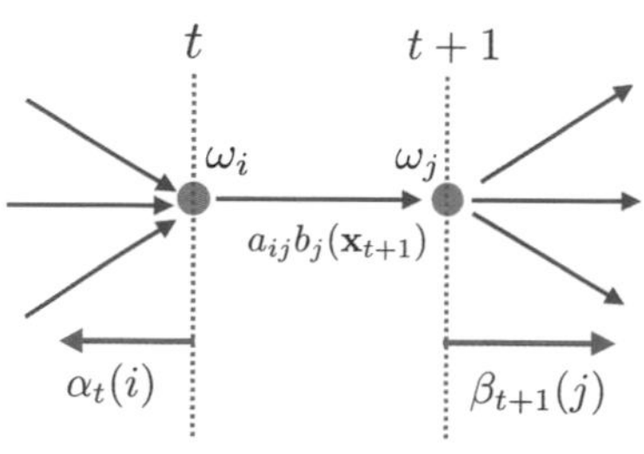

Figure 12.14: An illustration of summation of a subset of state sequences that all pass ω_i at t and ω_j at $t+1$.

1. $\alpha_t^{(r)}(i)$: a sum of all partial state sequences until t;
2. $a_{ij}b_j(\mathbf{x}_{t+1})$: a transition from ω_i to ω_j at time t; and
3. $\beta_{t+1}^{(r)}(j)$: a sum of all partial state sequences after $t+1$.

Putting them together, for each $\mathbf{o}^{(r)}$, we can compute

$$\eta_t^{(r)}(i,j) = \frac{\alpha_t^{(r)}(i) a_{ij} b_j(\mathbf{x}_{t+1}) \beta_{t+1}^{(r)}(j)}{\sum_{i=1}^N \alpha_{T_r}^{(r)}(i)} \tag{12.20}$$

for all $1 \leq t \leq T_r$ and $1 \leq i, j \leq N$.

Second, we can use $\eta_t^{(r)}(i,j)$ to compute another conditional probability, as follows:

$$\Pr(s_t^{(r)} = \omega_i \,\big|\, \mathbf{o}^{(r)}, \mathbf{\Lambda}^{(n)}) = \sum_{j=1}^N \eta_t^{(r)}(i,j)$$

Using the compact notations for all conditional probabilities, we rewrite the auxiliary functions for three groups of HMM parameters as follows:

$$Q(\boldsymbol{\pi}|\boldsymbol{\pi}^{(n)}) = \sum_{r=1}^R \sum_{i=1}^N \sum_{j=1}^N \ln \pi_i \cdot \eta_1^{(r)}(i,j)$$

$$Q(\mathbf{A}|\mathbf{A}^{(n)}) = \sum_{r=1}^R \sum_{t=1}^{T_r-1} \sum_{i=1}^N \sum_{j=1}^N \ln a_{ij} \cdot \eta_t^{(r)}(i,j)$$

$$Q(\mathbb{B}|\mathbb{B}^{(n)}) = \sum_{r=1}^R \sum_{t=1}^{T_r} \sum_{i=1}^N \sum_{j=1}^N \ln b_i(\mathbf{x}_t^{(r)}) \cdot \eta_t^{(r)}(i,j).$$

Index notations:
n: HMM parameters at nth iteration
r: rth training sequence
t: tth observation in a sequence
i: an HMM state ω_i
j: an HMM state ω_j

In the M-step, we maximize these auxiliary functions to derive the estimation formulae for all three groups of HMM parameters.

For $\boldsymbol{\pi}$, taking the constraint $\sum_{i=1}^N \pi_i = 1$ into account, we have

$$\frac{\partial}{\partial \boldsymbol{\pi}}\Big(Q(\boldsymbol{\pi}|\boldsymbol{\pi}^{(n)}) + \lambda\big(\sum_{i=1}^N \pi_i - 1\big)\Big) = 0 \implies$$

$$\pi_i^{(n+1)} = \frac{\sum_{r=1}^R \sum_{j=1}^N \eta_1^{(r)}(i,j)}{\sum_{r=1}^R \sum_{i=1}^N \sum_{j=1}^N \eta_1^{(r)}(i,j)}. \tag{12.21}$$

For $\mathbf{A}$, taking into account the constraints $\sum_j a_{ij} = 1$ for all i, we similarly derive the formula for all $i, j = 1, 2, \cdots, N$ as

$$a_{ij}^{(n+1)} = \frac{\sum_{r=1}^R \sum_{t=1}^{T_r-1} \eta_t^{(r)}(i,j)}{\sum_{r=1}^R \sum_{t=1}^{T_r-1} \sum_{j=1}^N \eta_t^{(r)}(i,j)}. \tag{12.22}$$

For $\mathbb{B}$, we will have to consider different HMM types.

1. Estimating $\mathbb{B}$ for Discrete HMMs

In discrete HMMs, all observations are discrete symbols. We assume that all discrete observation symbols come from a finite set, denoted as $\{v_1, v_2, \cdots, v_K\}$. In this case, we may choose a multinomial distribution for each state-dependent distribution $b_i(\mathbf{x})$ in an HMM state. As a result, $\mathbb{B}$ consists of all multinomial models in all HMM states $i = 1, 2, \cdots, N$:

$$\mathbb{B} = \{b_{ik} \,|\, 1 \le i \le N, 1 \le k \le K\},$$

where b_{ik} indicates the probability of generating the kth symbol v_k from state ω_i.

Substituting all probabilities $\{b_{ik}\}$ into the previous $Q(\mathbb{B}|\mathbb{B}^{(n)})$, we can derive the auxiliary function for discrete HMMs as follows:

$$\delta(\mathbf{x}_t^{(r)} - v_k) = \begin{cases} 1 & \text{if } \mathbf{x}_t^{(r)} = v_k \\ 0 & \text{otherwise.} \end{cases}$$

$$Q(\mathbb{B}|\mathbb{B}^{(n)}) = \sum_{r=1}^{R} \sum_{t=1}^{T_r} \sum_{i=1}^{N} \sum_{j=1}^{N} \sum_{k=1}^{K} \ln b_{ik} \cdot \delta(\mathbf{x}_t^{(r)} - v_k) \cdot \eta_t^{(r)}(i,j).$$

After taking into account the constraints $\sum_{k=1}^{K} b_{ik} = 1$ for all i, we derive the estimation formula for all i and k as

Index notations:
n: HMM parameters at nth iteration
r: rth training sequence
t: tth observation in a sequence
i: an HMM state ω_i
j: an HMM state ω_j
k: kth observation symbol v_k

$$b_{ik}^{(n+1)} = \frac{\sum_{r=1}^{R} \sum_{t=1}^{T_r} \sum_{j=1}^{N} \eta_t^{(r)}(i,j) \cdot \delta(\mathbf{x}_t^{(r)} - v_k)}{\sum_{r=1}^{R} \sum_{t=1}^{T_r} \sum_{j=1}^{N} \eta_t^{(r)}(i,j)}. \tag{12.23}$$

2. Estimating $\mathbb{B}$ for Continuous Density HMMs

In continuous density HMMs, all observations $\mathbf{x}_t^{(r)}$ are continuous feature vectors. In this case, we have to choose a probability density function $b_i(\mathbf{x})$ for each HMM state ω_i. Because of the universal density approximation capability of GMMs, we normally use a GMM to represent the probability density function in each state [120]. That is,

$$b_i(\mathbf{x}) = \sum_{m=1}^{M} w_{im} \cdot \mathcal{N}(\mathbf{x} \mid \boldsymbol{\mu}_{im}, \boldsymbol{\Sigma}_{im}),$$

where $\boldsymbol{\mu}_{im}$ and $\boldsymbol{\Sigma}_{im}$ denote the mean vector and covariance matrix of the mth Gaussian component in state ω_i, and w_{im} is its mixture weight. We have $\sum_{m=1}^{M} w_{im} = 1$ for all i.

In this case, $\mathbb{B}$ is composed of all of these GMM parameters:

$$\mathbb{B} = \{\boldsymbol{\mu}_{im}, \boldsymbol{\Sigma}_{im}, w_{im} \,|\, 1 \le i \le N, 1 \le m \le M\}.$$

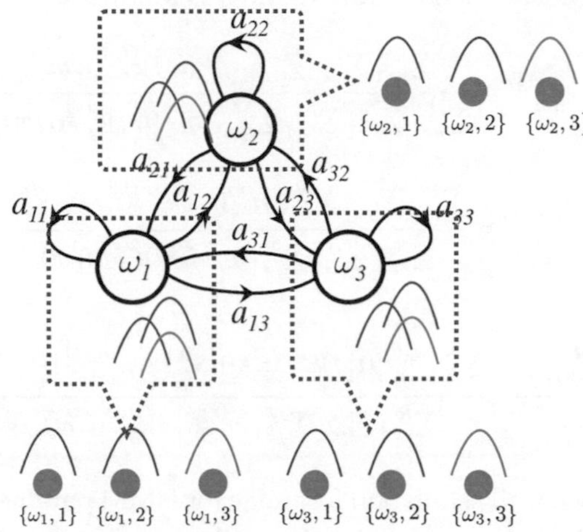

Figure 12.15: An illustration of expanding each state in a Gaussian mixture HMM into several compound states of $\{\omega_i, m\}$.

For Gaussian mixture HMMs, we can expand each HMM state into the product space of Ω and $\{1, \cdots, M\}$, as in Figure 12.15. Each compound state $\{\omega_i, m\}$ contains only one Gaussian $\mathcal{N}(\mathbf{x} \mid \boldsymbol{\mu}_{im}, \boldsymbol{\Sigma}_{im})$. If we treat the compound state sequences $\{s_t^{(r)}, l_t^{(r)}\}$, where $s_t^{(r)} \in \Omega$ and $l_t^{(r)} \in \{1, \cdots, M\}$, as latent variables, we can construct the auxiliary function for $\mathbb{B}$ in Gaussian mixture HMMs as follows:

Here we use $s_t^{(r)}$ and $l_t^{(r)}$ to indicate the state and Gaussian component, from which $\mathbf{x}_t^{(r)}$ may be generated.

$$\begin{aligned} Q(\mathbb{B}|\mathbb{B}^{(n)}) \;\; = \;\; & \sum_{r=1}^{R} \sum_{t=1}^{T_r} \sum_{i=1}^{N} \sum_{m=1}^{M} \Big[\ln w_{im} + \ln \mathcal{N}(\mathbf{x} \mid \boldsymbol{\mu}_{im}, \boldsymbol{\Sigma}_{im}) \Big] \\ & \Pr\big(s_t^{(r)} = \omega_i, l_t^{(r)} = m \,\big|\, \mathbf{o}^{(r)}, \boldsymbol{\Lambda}^{(n)}\big). \end{aligned}$$

The conditional probability may be computed as

$$\begin{aligned} & \Pr\big(s_t^{(r)} = \omega_i, l_t^{(r)} = m \,\big|\, \mathbf{o}^{(r)}, \boldsymbol{\Lambda}^{(n)}\big) \\ = \;\; & \underbrace{\Pr\big(s_t^{(r)} = \omega_i \,\big|\, \mathbf{o}^{(r)}, \boldsymbol{\Lambda}^{(n)}\big)}_{= \sum_{j=1}^{N} \eta_t^{(r)}(i,j)} \; \underbrace{\Pr\big(l_t^{(r)} = m \,\big|\, s_t^{(r)} = \omega_i, \mathbf{o}^{(r)}, \boldsymbol{\Lambda}^{(n)}\big)}_{\triangleq \; \xi_t^{(r)}(i,m)}, \end{aligned}$$

where $\xi_t^{(r)}(i, m)$ is called the *occupancy probability* of each Gaussian component, which is computed similar to Eq. (12.7), as follows:

$$\begin{aligned} \xi_t^{(r)}(i, m) \;\; &= \;\; \Pr(l_t^{(r)} = m \mid s_t^{(r)} = \omega_i, \mathbf{x}_t^{(r)}, \boldsymbol{\Lambda}^{(n)}) \\ &= \;\; \frac{w_{im}^{(n)} \mathcal{N}(\mathbf{x}_t^{(r)} \mid \boldsymbol{\mu}_{im}^{(n)}, \boldsymbol{\Sigma}_{im}^{(n)})}{\sum_{m=1}^{M} w_m^{(n)} \mathcal{N}(\mathbf{x}_t^{(r)} \mid \boldsymbol{\mu}_{im}^{(n)}, \boldsymbol{\Sigma}_{im}^{(n)})}. \end{aligned} \tag{12.24}$$

After we substitute these occupancy probabilities into the previous auxiliary function and maximize it with respect to mixture weights, Gaussian mean vectors, and covariance matrices, we finally derive the estimation formula for the Gaussian mixture HMMs, as follows:

$$w_{im}^{(n+1)} = \frac{\sum_{r=1}^{R} \sum_{t=1}^{T_r} \sum_{j=1}^{N} \eta_t^{(r)}(i,j)\xi_t^{(r)}(i,m)}{\sum_{r=1}^{R} \sum_{t=1}^{T_r} \sum_{j=1}^{N} \sum_{m=1}^{M} \eta_t^{(r)}(i,j)\xi_t^{(r)}(i,m)} \tag{12.25}$$

Index notations:
n: HMM parameters at nth iteration
r: rth training sequence
t: tth observation in a sequence
i: an HMM state ω_i
j: an HMM state ω_j
m: mth Gaussian component

$$\boldsymbol{\mu}_{im}^{(n+1)} = \frac{\sum_{r=1}^{R} \sum_{t=1}^{T_r} \sum_{j=1}^{N} \eta_t^{(r)}(i,j)\xi_t^{(r)}(i,m) \cdot \mathbf{x}_t^{(r)}}{\sum_{r=1}^{R} \sum_{t=1}^{T_r} \sum_{j=1}^{N} \eta_t^{(r)}(i,j)\xi_t^{(r)}(i,m)} \tag{12.26}$$

$$\boldsymbol{\Sigma}_{im}^{(n+1)} = \frac{\sum_{r=1}^{R} \sum_{t=1}^{T_r} \sum_{j=1}^{N} \eta_t^{(r)}(i,j)\xi_t^{(r)}(i,m)\left(\mathbf{x}_t^{(r)} - \boldsymbol{\mu}_{im}^{(n+1)}\right)\left(\mathbf{x}_t^{(r)} - \boldsymbol{\mu}_{im}^{(n+1)}\right)^\intercal}{\sum_{r=1}^{R} \sum_{t=1}^{T_r} \sum_{j=1}^{N} \eta_t^{(r)}(i,j)\xi_t^{(r)}(i,m)}. \tag{12.27}$$

Taking Eq. (12.26) as an example:

$$\boldsymbol{\mu}_{im}^{(n+1)} = \frac{\overbrace{\sum_{r=1}^{R} \sum_{t=1}^{T_r} \sum_{j=1}^{N} \eta_t^{(r)}(i,j)\xi_t^{(r)}(i,m) \cdot \mathbf{x}_t^{(r)}}^{\text{numerator statistics}}}{\underbrace{\sum_{r=1}^{R} \sum_{t=1}^{T_r} \sum_{j=1}^{N} \eta_t^{(r)}(i,j)\xi_t^{(r)}(i,m)}_{\text{denominator statistics}}}.$$

As we have seen, all estimation formulae for HMM parameters are represented as a ratio between two statistics in the numerator and denominator (see margin note). In each iteration, we just need to use the current HMM parameter $\boldsymbol{\Lambda}^{(n)}$ to accumulate these statistics over the entire training set. At the end of each iteration, a new set of HMM parameters $\boldsymbol{\Lambda}^{(n+1)}$ is derived as the ratios between these statistics. The EM algorithm guarantees that the new parameters will improve the likelihood function over the old ones. This training process is repeated over and over until it converges. Finally, we summarize the Baum–Welch algorithm in Algorithm 12.17.

As for how to initialize $\boldsymbol{\Lambda}^{(0)}$ for HMMs, interested readers may refer to the uniform segmentation in Young et al. [258] and the segmental k-means method in Juang and Rabiner [121].

Algorithm 12.17 Baum–Welch Algorithm for HMMs

Input: a training set of observation sequences $\{\mathbf{o}^{(r)} \mid r = 1, 2, \cdots, R\}$
Output: HMM parameters $\boldsymbol{\Lambda} = \{\boldsymbol{\pi}, \mathbf{A}, \mathbb{B}\}$

set $n = 0$
initialize $\boldsymbol{\Lambda}^{(0)} = \{\boldsymbol{\pi}^{(0)}, \mathbf{A}^{(0)}, \mathbb{B}^{(0)}\}$
while not converged **do**
  zero numerator/denominator accumulators for all parameters
  for $r = 1, 2, \cdots, R$ **do**
    1. run forward–backward algorithm on $\mathbf{o}^{(r)}$ using $\boldsymbol{\Lambda}^{(n)}$:
    $\{\mathbf{o}^{(r)}, \boldsymbol{\Lambda}^{(n)}\} \longrightarrow \{\alpha_t^{(r)}(i), \beta_t^{(r)}(i)\}$
    2. use Eqs. (12.20) and (12.24):
    $\{\alpha_t^{(r)}(i), \beta_t^{(r)}(i)\} \longrightarrow \{\eta_t^{(r)}(i,j), \xi_t^{(r)}(i,m)\}$
    3. accumulate all numerator/denominator statistics
  end for
  update all parameters as the ratios of statistics $\longrightarrow \boldsymbol{\Lambda}^{(n+1)}$
  $n = n + 1$
end while

Lab Project VI

In this project, you will solve a simple binary classification problem (class A vs. class B) using multivariate Gaussian models. Assume two classes have equal prior probabilities. Each observation feature is a three-dimensional (3D) vector. You can download the data set from

`http://www.eecs.yorku.ca/~hj/MLF-gaussian-dataset.zip.`

You will use several different methods to build such a classifier based on the provided training set, and then the estimated models will be evaluated on the provided test set. You can use any programming language of your preference, but you will have to implement all training and test methods from scratch.

a. First of all, build a simple classifier using multivariate Gaussian models. Each class is modeled by a single 3D Gaussian distribution. You should consider the following structures for the covariance matrices:
   - Each Gaussian uses a separate diagonal covariance matrix.
   - Each Gaussian uses a separate full covariance matrix.
   - Two Gaussians share a common diagonal covariance matrix.
   - Two Gaussians share a common full covariance matrix.

   Use the provided training data to estimate the Gaussian mean vector and covariance matrix for each class based on MLE. Report the classification accuracy of the MLE-trained models as measured by the test set for each choice of the covariance matrix.

b. Improve the Gaussian classifier from the previous step by using a GMM to model each class. You need to use the k-means clustering method to initialize all parameters in the GMMs, and then improve the GMMs based on the EM algorithm. Investigate GMMs that have 2, 4, 8, or 16 Gaussian components, respectively.

c. Assume each class is modeled by a *factorial GMM*, where all feature dimensions are assumed to be independent, and each dimension is separately modeled by a 1-dimensional Gaussian mixture. Use the k-means clustering method and the EM algorithm to estimate these two factorial GMMs. Investigate the performance of two factorial GMMs on the test data for the cases where each dimension has 2, 4, or 8 Gaussian components, respectively.

d. Determine the best model configuration in terms of the number of Gaussian components and the covariance matrix structure for this data set.

The csv data format: All training samples are given in the file *train-gaussian.csv*, and all test samples are given in the file *test-gaussian.csv*. Each line represents a feature vector in the format as follows:

$$y, \; x1, \; x2, \; x3,$$

where $y \in \{A, B\}$ is class label, and $[x1 \;\; x2 \;\; x3]$ is a 3D feature vector.

Exercises

Q12.1 Determine whether the following distributions belong to the exponential family:

a. Dirichlet distribution
b. Poisson distribution
c. Inverse-Wishart distribution
d. von Mises–Fisher distribution

Derive the natural parameters, sufficient statistics, and normalization term for those distributions that belong to the exponential family.

Q12.2 Determine whether the following generalized linear models belong to the exponential family:

a. Logistic regression
b. Probit regression
c. Poisson regression
d. Log-linear models

Q12.3 Prove that the exponential family is close under multiplication.

Q12.4 Prove that the auxiliary function $Q(\boldsymbol{\theta}|\boldsymbol{\theta}^{(n)})$ is concave—namely, $-Q(\boldsymbol{\theta}|\boldsymbol{\theta}^{(n)})$ is convex—if we choose all component models in a finite mixture model as one of the following e-family distributions:

a. Multivariate Gaussian distribution
b. Multinomial distribution
c. Dirichlet distribution
d. von Mises–Fisher distribution

Q12.5 The index m in finite mixture models, as in Eq. (12.1), can be extended to be a continuous variable $y \in \mathbb{R}$:

$$p(\mathbf{x}) = \int w(y)\, p(\mathbf{x} \,|\, \boldsymbol{\theta}, y)\, dy.$$

This is called an *infinite mixture model* if $\int w(y)\, dy = 1$ and $\int p(\mathbf{x} \,|\, \boldsymbol{\theta}, y)\, d\mathbf{x} = 1$ $(\forall \boldsymbol{\theta}, y)$ hold. Extend the EM algorithm to the infinite mixture models:

a. Define the auxiliary function for an infinite mixture model.
b. Design the E-step and M-step for an infinite mixture model.

Q12.6 Consider an m-dimensional variable $\mathbf{r}$, whose elements are nonnegative integers. Suppose its distribution is described by a mixture of multinomial distributions:

$$p(\mathbf{r}) = \sum_{k=1}^{K} \pi_k \text{ Mult}(\mathbf{r} \,|\, \boldsymbol{p}_k) \propto \sum_{k=1}^{K} \pi_k \prod_{i=1}^{m} p_{ki}^{r_i}$$

where the parameter p_{ki} denotes the probability of ith dimension in the kth component, subject to $0 \le p_{ki} \le 1$ $(\forall k, i)$ and $\sum_i p_{ki} = 1$ $(\forall k)$. Assume a set of training samples is given as $\{\mathbf{r}^{(n)} \,|\, n = 1, \cdots, N\}$. Derive the E-step and M-step of the EM algorithm to optimize the mixing weights $\{\pi_k\}$ $(\sum_k \pi_k = 1)$ and all component parameters $\{p_{ki}\}$ based on the MLE.

Q12.7 Assume a GMM is given as follows:

$$p(\mathbf{x}) = \sum_{m=1}^{M} w_m \, \mathcal{N}\big(\mathbf{x} \,|\, \boldsymbol{\mu}_m, \boldsymbol{\Sigma}_m\big).$$

If we partition the vector $\mathbf{x}$ into two parts as $\mathbf{x} = \big[\mathbf{x}_a \,;\, \mathbf{x}_b\big]$, then do the following:

a. Show that the marginal distribution $p(\mathbf{x}_a)$ is also a GMM, and find expressions for the mixture weights and all Gaussian means and covariance matrices.
b. Show that the conditional distribution $p(\mathbf{x}_a \,|\, \mathbf{x}_b)$ is also a GMM, and find expressions for the mixture weights and all Gaussian means and covariance matrices.
c. Find the expression for the conditional mean $\mathbb{E}\big[\mathbf{x}_a \,|\, \mathbf{x}_b\big]$.

Q12.8 Prove that $\alpha_t(i)$ and $\beta_t(i)$ in an HMM satisfy Eq. (12.18) for any t.

Q12.9 Run the Viterbi algorithm on a left-to-right HMM, where the transitions only go from one state to itself or to a higher-indexed state. Use a diagram as in Figure 12.13 to show how the HMM topology affects the Viterbi algorithm.

Q12.10 Derive the update formula in Eq. (12.23) for $\mathbb{B}$ in discrete HMMs.

Q12.11 Derive the update formulae in Eqs. (12.25), (12.26), and (12.27) for $\mathbb{B}$ in Gaussian mixture HMMs.

Q12.12 Derive an efficient method to compute the gradient of the log-likelihood function for the following mixture models:

a. Gaussian mixture models: $\frac{\partial}{\partial \boldsymbol{\theta}} \ln p_{\boldsymbol{\theta}}(\mathbf{x})$, where $p_{\boldsymbol{\theta}}(\mathbf{x})$ is given in Eq.(12.6).
b. Hidden Markov models: $\frac{\partial}{\partial \boldsymbol{\Lambda}} \ln p_{\boldsymbol{\Lambda}}(\mathbf{o})$, where $p_{\boldsymbol{\Lambda}}(\mathbf{o})$ is given in Eq.(12.15).

Q12.13 When the HMM algorithms are run on long sequences, *underflow* errors often occur because we need to multiply many small positive numbers. To address this issue, we often represent all forward and backward probabilities in the logarithm domain. In this case, we can do arithmetic operations as follows:

$$\log(ab) = \log(a) + \log(b) \qquad \log(a/b) = \log(a) - \log(b)$$

$$\log(a \pm b) = \log(a) + \log\Big[1 \pm \exp\big(\log(b) - \log(a)\big)\Big].$$

Use these routines to rewrite the forward–backward Algorithm 12.15 in the logarithm domain. In other words, use $\tilde{\alpha}_t(i) = \log\big(\alpha_t(i)\big)$ and $\tilde{\beta}_t(i) = \log\big(\beta_t(i)\big)$ in place of $\alpha_t(i)$ and $\beta_t(i)$.

Entangled Models | 13

In addition to finite mixture models, there exists another methodology in machine learning that can expand simple generative models into more sophisticated ones. This method results in a large chunk of popular machine learning methods, which are all referred to as *entangled models* throughout this book. As we will see, this category includes the traditional *factor analysis, probabilistic PCA*, and *independent component analysis* (ICA), as well as the more recent deep generative models, such as *variational autoencoders* (VAEs) and *generative adversarial nets* (GANs). This chapter first introduces the key idea behind all entangled models and then briefly discusses some representative models in this category.

13.1 Formulation of Entangled Models

In finite mixture models, we superpose many different simple generative models to form a mixture distribution to approach any arbitrarily complex distribution. In contrast, entangled models take a rather different approach to construct more advanced generative models. The key idea behind all entangled models is that we can rely on a transformation of random variables to convert a simple probability distribution into any arbitrary distribution. The theoretical justification is formally stated in the following theorem:

Theorem 13.1.1 *Given a normally distributed random variable $z \sim \mathcal{N}(0,1)$, for any smooth probability distribution $p(\mathbf{x})$ ($\mathbf{x} \in \mathbb{R}^d$), there exist some L^p functions: $f_1(z), f_2(z), \cdots, f_d(z)$ to convert z into a vector $f(z) = \begin{bmatrix} f_1(z) & \cdots & f_d(z) \end{bmatrix}^\intercal$ so that $f(z)$ follows this distribution (i.e., $f(z) \sim p(\mathbf{x})$).*

A general form of this theorem is called the *Borel isomorphism* theorem in measure theory [126].

Moreover, this theorem can be easily extended to any other continuous distributions rather than a univariate normal distribution. This theorem suggests that we can apply some transformations to a simple generative model to construct complicated generative models for any arbitrary data distributions. As shown in Figure 13.1, we can always start with a fairly simple generative model $p(\mathbf{z})$ in a low-dimensional space $\mathbb{R}^n$ and meanwhile find a *deterministic* vector-valued function from $\mathbb{R}^n$ to a higher-dimensional space $\mathbb{R}^d$ $(d > n)$ (i.e., $\mathbf{x} = f(\mathbf{z})$) to derive an arbitrarily complex generative model $p(\mathbf{x})$ in $\mathbb{R}^d$. The resultant models $p(\mathbf{x})$ are all called *entangled models*.

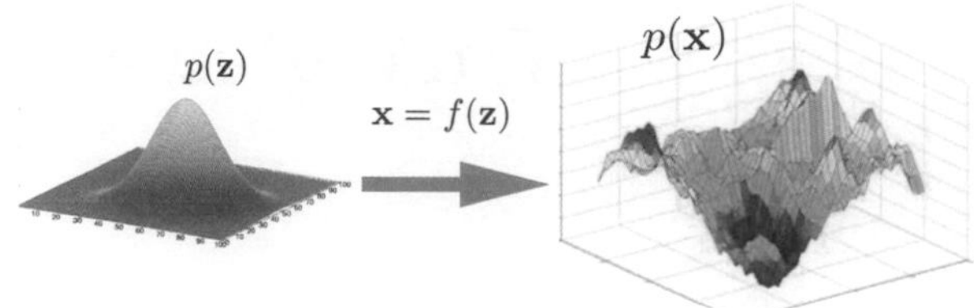

Figure 13.1: Entangled models are constructed by applying a transformation to a simple generative model to convert it into a more sophisticated one.

This idea of *entangled models* is well aligned with a popular viewpoint regarding the data-generation process in the physical world. As we know, most real-world data we observe in practice are often complicated in nature, and they often follow a very complex distribution in a high-dimensional space. However, in most cases, what we are really concerned with in these high-dimensional data can usually be abstracted into some high-level key messages, whereas most fine details in the raw data are irrelevant. These key messages in fact can be determined by a small number of independent factors. For instance, if we take a photo of someone's face as an example, the raw data compose a fairly complex high-dimensional image. However, the key information we perceive from this image can actually be specified by only a small number of main factors, such as the person's identity, face orientation, illumination, wearing glasses or not, and so on. Accordingly, we may assume that this image is generated from a simple two-stage stochastic process:

1. All of these key factors, denoted as $\mathbf{z}$, are randomly sampled from a simple distribution. It makes sense to assume this distribution to be simple because all of these key factors are statistically independent.
2. These sampled factors are entangled by a fixed mixing function $\mathbf{x} = f(\mathbf{z})$ to generate the final observed image, whereas the underlying sampled factors $\mathbf{z}$ are unknown to us.

As suggested by Theorem 13.1.1, we can assume this mixing function is deterministic because a deterministic function is already sufficient to derive any complex distribution to model any data. Because all independent factors are entangled by a presumably complicated mixing function, the underlying key factors $\mathbf{z}$ usually become imperceptible from the observed data $\mathbf{x}$.

13.1.1 Framework of Entangled Models

In machine learning, we usually adopt a general framework for entangled models, as shown in Figure 13.2. Within this framework, $\mathbf{z}$ is often called *factors* (a.k.a. *continuous latent variables* in the literature), which follows a simple distribution $p_\lambda(\mathbf{z})$ with parameters λ. And the deterministic mapping $\mathbf{x} = f(\mathbf{z}; \mathbf{W})$ is called the *mixing function* with some parameters

W. Furthermore, we assume that the output of the mixing function is corrupted by an independent additive noise $\boldsymbol{\varepsilon}$, called the *residual*. The residual is introduced here to accommodate some observation or measurement errors in the process, and we assume the residual $\boldsymbol{\varepsilon}$ follows another simple distribution (usually a Gaussian distribution), that is, $p_{\boldsymbol{\nu}}(\boldsymbol{\varepsilon})$ with parameters $\boldsymbol{\nu}$.

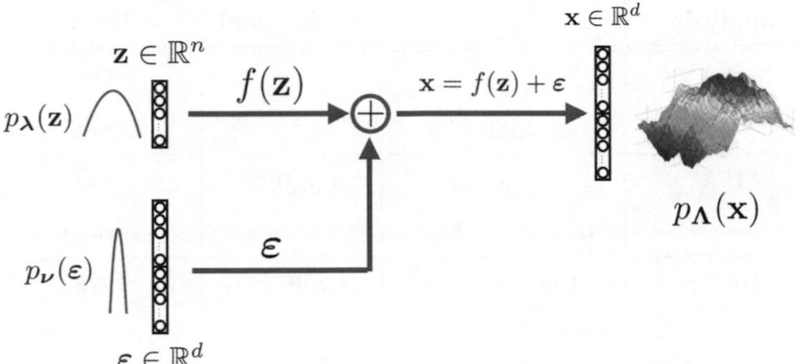

Figure 13.2: An illustration of a generally accepted framework for entangled models in machine learning, involving three components:
1. The factor distribution $p_{\lambda}(\mathbf{z})$
2. The residual distribution $p_{\boldsymbol{\nu}}(\boldsymbol{\varepsilon})$
3. The mixing function $f(\mathbf{z})$

After the deterministic mapping $\mathbf{x} = f(\mathbf{z}) + \boldsymbol{\varepsilon}$, we can derive an entangled model as $p_{\boldsymbol{\Lambda}}(\mathbf{x})$, where $\boldsymbol{\Lambda} = \{\mathbf{W}, \lambda, \boldsymbol{\nu}\}$ denote all model parameters of the underlying entangled model. The entangled models actually depend on the choices of the factor distribution $p_{\lambda}(\mathbf{z})$, the residual distribution $p_{\boldsymbol{\nu}}(\boldsymbol{\varepsilon})$, and the mixing function $f(\mathbf{z}; \mathbf{W})$. When we choose these components in a different way, we end up with different entangled models. Table 13.1 lists some representative entangled models well known in the literature, along with their corresponding choices of these three components. Generally speaking, we can organize all entangled models into three main categories. In the first category, we choose Gaussian models for both $p_{\lambda}(\mathbf{z})$ and $p_{\boldsymbol{\nu}}(\boldsymbol{\varepsilon})$ and a linear function for $f(\mathbf{z})$. This leads to the so-called *linear Gaussian models*, including factor analysis [231] and probabilistic principal component analysis (PCA) [238] as two special cases. In the second category, we still use a linear function for $f(\mathbf{z})$ but choose some non-Gaussian models for $p_{\lambda}(\mathbf{z})$, such as some heavy-tail distributions or mixture models. This leads to some important machine learning methods, such as ICA [18, 107], *independent factor analysis* (IFA) [4], and *hybrid orthogonal projection and estimation* (HOPE) [261]. In the third category, we choose the mixing function $f(\mathbf{z})$ as an L^p function as specified in Theorem 13.1.1. Due to the well-known universal approximator theorem, neural networks can serve as a good candidate for more general nonlinear mixing functions in this category. Hence, the entangled models in this category are often called *deep generative models*; these models includes two recently popular methods: VAEs [130] and GANs [84]. The following sections introduce some representative entangled models from these three categories. The rest of this section first briefly discusses some general issues related to

Table 13.1: A summary of some representative entangled models, along with their corresponding choices for the three components, including *probabilistic PCA* [238], *factor analysis* [231], ICA [18, 107], IFA [4], HOPE [261], VAEs [130], and GANs [84]. GMM = Gaussian mixture model. movMF = mixtures of *von Mises–Fisher* (vMF) distributions.

Entangled models	**Factor** $\mathbf{z} \sim p(\mathbf{z})$	**Residual** $\boldsymbol{\varepsilon} \sim p(\boldsymbol{\varepsilon})$	**Mixing** $f(\mathbf{z})$
Probabilistic PCA	$\mathcal{N}(\mathbf{z}\|\mathbf{0},\mathbf{I})$	$\mathcal{N}(\boldsymbol{\varepsilon}\|\mathbf{0},\sigma^2\mathbf{I})$	$\mathbf{Wz}$ linear
Factor analysis	$\mathcal{N}(\mathbf{z}\|\mathbf{0},\mathbf{I})$	$\mathcal{N}(\boldsymbol{\varepsilon}\|\mathbf{0},\mathbf{D})$ D: diagonal	$\mathbf{Wz}$ linear
ICA	$\prod_i p_i(z_i)$ non-Gaussian	—	$\mathbf{Wz}$ linear
IFA	$\prod_i p_i(z_i)$ factorial GMM	$\mathcal{N}(\boldsymbol{\varepsilon}\|\mathbf{0},\boldsymbol{\Lambda})$	$\mathbf{Wz}$ linear
HOPE	Mixture model (movMF/GMM)	$\mathcal{N}(\boldsymbol{\varepsilon}\|\mathbf{0},\sigma^2\mathbf{I})$	$\mathbf{Wz}$ **W**: orthogonal
VAE	$\mathcal{N}(\mathbf{z}\|\mathbf{0},\mathbf{I})$	$\mathcal{N}(\boldsymbol{\varepsilon}\|\mathbf{0},\sigma^2\mathbf{I})$	$f(\cdot) \in L^p$ neural nets
GAN	$\mathcal{N}(\mathbf{z}\|\mathbf{0},\mathbf{I})$	—	$f(\cdot) \in L^p$ neural nets

all entangled models to give a high-level overview about all topics to be discussed in the remainder of this chapter.

13.1.2 Learning of Entangled Models in General

Generally speaking, we have two different methods to explicitly derive the underlying entangled model in Figure 13.2 from the three components: $p_\lambda(\mathbf{z})$, $p_\nu(\boldsymbol{\varepsilon})$, and $f(\mathbf{z};\mathbf{W})$. First of all, if the mixing function $f(\mathbf{z};\mathbf{W})$ is invertible and differentiable, we can derive the entangled model using the Jacobian matrix of the mixing function as follows:

$$p_\Lambda(\mathbf{x}) = \big|\,\mathbf{J}\,\big|\, p_\lambda\big(f_1^{-1}(\mathbf{x})\big)\, p_\nu\big(f_2^{-1}(\mathbf{x})\big), \tag{13.1}$$

where $f_1^{-1}(\mathbf{x})$ denotes the inverse of the mixing function transforming from $\mathbf{x}$ back to $\mathbf{z}$, $f_2^{-1}(\mathbf{x})$ denotes the inverse function from $\mathbf{x}$ to $\boldsymbol{\varepsilon}$, and $\mathbf{J}$ denotes the Jacobian matrix of these inverse transformations. This Jacobian-based method is particularly useful when the mixing function is linear.

The joint distribution of $\mathbf{z}$ and $\boldsymbol{\varepsilon}$ is

$$p(\mathbf{z},\boldsymbol{\varepsilon}) = p(\mathbf{z})p(\boldsymbol{\varepsilon}),$$

where $p(\mathbf{x})$ is derived by treating $\mathbf{x}$ as a transformation of $\mathbf{z}$ and $\boldsymbol{\varepsilon}$:

$$\mathbf{x} = f(\mathbf{z}) + \boldsymbol{\varepsilon}.$$

Refer to Eq. (2.3) for how to derive $p(\mathbf{x})$ from $p(\mathbf{z},\boldsymbol{\varepsilon})$.

Second, if the mixing function is not invertible or the Jacobian matrix is not computable, we can use a marginalization method to derive the entangled model as follows:

$$p_{\Lambda}(\mathbf{x}) = \int_{\mathbf{z}} p_{\lambda}(\mathbf{z}) p_{\nu}\big(\mathbf{x} - f(\mathbf{z};\mathbf{W})\big)\, d\mathbf{z} \tag{13.2}$$

Unfortunately, this formulation requires us to integrate over the factor $\mathbf{z}$, which may be computationally difficult in many cases.

Following the marginalization over a joint distribution of $\mathbf{x}$ and $\mathbf{z}$:

$$\begin{aligned} p(\mathbf{x}) &= \int_{\mathbf{z}} p(\mathbf{x}, \mathbf{z})\, d\mathbf{z} \\ &= \int_{\mathbf{z}} p(\mathbf{z}) p(\mathbf{x} \mid \mathbf{z})\, d\mathbf{z}. \end{aligned}$$

Because we have $\boldsymbol{\varepsilon} = \mathbf{x} - f(\mathbf{z};\mathbf{W})$, then

$$p(\mathbf{x} \mid \mathbf{z}) = p_{\nu}\big(\mathbf{x} - f(\mathbf{z};\mathbf{W})\big).$$

Once we know all the three components in Figure 13.2, we can determine the underlying entangled models using one of the two previously described methods. Like any other generative model, entangled models can also be used to model complex data distributions for the purposes of classification or regression. Moreover, in some circumstances, we may be interested in inferring the unobserved factor $\mathbf{z}$ based on an observation $\mathbf{x}$. This procedure is often called *disentangling* because it aims to uncover the unknown independent key factor $\mathbf{z}$, which may be used as an intuitive representation to interpret the raw data $\mathbf{x}$. This is usually called *disentangled representation learning* in machine learning. Assuming we have known all parameters of an entangled model, this disentangling process can be done through either the inverse function $\mathbf{z} = f_1^{-1}(\mathbf{x})$ when the mixing function is invertible or through the conditional distribution derived from the entangled model as follows:

$$p(\mathbf{z}|\mathbf{x}) = \frac{p(\mathbf{z}, \mathbf{x})}{p(\mathbf{x})} = \frac{p_{\lambda}(\mathbf{z}) p_{\nu}\big(\mathbf{x} - f(\mathbf{z};\mathbf{W})\big)}{\int_{\mathbf{z}} p_{\lambda}(\mathbf{z}) p_{\nu}\big(\mathbf{x} - f(\mathbf{z};\mathbf{W})\big)\, d\mathbf{z}}. \tag{13.3}$$

Another interesting application of entangled models is to generate new data samples, such as image generation in Goodfellow et al. [84] and Gregor et al. [85]. In this case, we first randomly sample the distributions of the factor and the residual, and then we apply the mixing function to map these samples to generate a new observation $\mathbf{x}$. This data-generation strategy has recently drawn a great deal of attention in many computer vision applications [123, 2].

The final issue in entangled models is how to estimate all model parameters $\boldsymbol{\Lambda} = \{\mathbf{W}, \lambda, \nu\}$ from a training set of observed samples (i.e., $\mathcal{D}_N = \{\mathbf{x}_1, \mathbf{x}_2, \cdots, \mathbf{x}_n\}$). As with other generative models, we can use the maximum-likelihood estimation (MLE) method, as follows:

$$\boldsymbol{\Lambda}_{\text{MLE}} = \arg\max_{\boldsymbol{\Lambda}} \sum_{i=1}^{N} \ln p_{\boldsymbol{\Lambda}}(\mathbf{x}_i).$$

We can substitute either Eq. (13.1) or Eq. (13.2) into the entangled model $p_{\boldsymbol{\Lambda}}(\mathbf{x})$ and apply some suitable optimization methods to solve this maximization problem. However, for deep generative models, it is unfortunate that we cannot explicitly express $p_{\boldsymbol{\Lambda}}(\mathbf{x})$ because neither the Jacobian matrix in Eq. (13.1) nor the integral in Eq. (13.2) is computable for neural networks. Some alternative approaches must be used to learn deep generative models. We will briefly consider them in Section 13.4.

13.2 Linear Gaussian Models

As mentioned, *linear Gaussian models* represent a subset of the entangled models in Figure 13.2 when we choose Gaussian models for the factor and residual distributions and use a linear mapping for the mixing function. Without losing generality, let us assume that the factor $\mathbf{z}$ follows a zero-mean multivariate Gaussian distribution as

$$p(\mathbf{z}) = \mathcal{N}(\mathbf{z} \,|\, \mathbf{0}, \mathbf{\Sigma}_1),$$

where $\mathbf{\Sigma}_1 \in \mathbb{R}^{n\times n}$ denotes its covariance matrix, and the residual $\boldsymbol{\varepsilon}$ follows another multivariate Gaussian distribution as

$$p(\boldsymbol{\varepsilon}) = \mathcal{N}(\boldsymbol{\varepsilon} \,|\, \boldsymbol{\mu}, \mathbf{\Sigma}_2),$$

where $\boldsymbol{\mu} \in \mathbb{R}^d$ and $\mathbf{\Sigma}_2 \in \mathbb{R}^{d\times d}$ stand for the mean vector and the covariance matrix, respectively. The mixing function is assumed to be linear, taking the following form:

$$f(\mathbf{z}; \mathbf{W}) = \mathbf{W}\mathbf{z},$$

where $\mathbf{W} \in \mathbb{R}^{d\times n}$ denotes the parameters of the linear mixing function. Based on the property of Gaussian random variables, we can explicitly derive the linear Gaussian models as another Gaussian model:

Refer to Exercise Q13.2 for how to derive Eq.(13.4) for linear Gaussian models.

$$p_{\mathbf{\Lambda}}(\mathbf{x}) = \mathcal{N}(\mathbf{x} \,|\, \boldsymbol{\mu}, \mathbf{W}\mathbf{\Sigma}_1\mathbf{W}^\intercal + \mathbf{\Sigma}_2), \tag{13.4}$$

where $\mathbf{\Lambda} = \{\mathbf{W}, \mathbf{\Sigma}_1, \boldsymbol{\mu}, \mathbf{\Sigma}_2\}$ denotes all parameters of the linear Gaussian models. Furthermore, we can also derive that the conditional distribution in Eq. (13.3) is also another multivariate Gaussian for all linear Gaussian models. As a result, linear Gaussian models represent a group of entangled models that are highly tractable. In the following, we will use *probabilistic PCA* [238] and *factor analysis* [231] as two examples to explain how to handle linear Gaussian models.

13.2.1 Probabilistic PCA

In probabilistic PCA methods, we assume the factor distribution is a zero-mean unit-covariance Gaussian as

$$p(\mathbf{z}) = \mathcal{N}(\mathbf{z} \,|\, \mathbf{0}, \mathbf{I}),$$

where we have no parameters in the factor distribution. Meanwhile, we assume that the residual distribution is an isotropic covariance Gaussian as

$$p_\sigma(\boldsymbol{\varepsilon}) = \mathcal{N}(\boldsymbol{\varepsilon} \,|\, \boldsymbol{\mu}, \sigma^2\mathbf{I}),$$

where σ^2 is the only parameter representing the variance in each dimension. According to Eq. (13.4), we can derive the following formula for a probabilistic PCA model:

$$p_{\mathbf{\Lambda}}(\mathbf{x}) = \mathcal{N}\big(\mathbf{x} \,|\, \boldsymbol{\mu}, \mathbf{W}\mathbf{W}^\intercal + \sigma^2\mathbf{I}\big),$$

where $\mathbf{\Lambda} = \{\mathbf{W}, \boldsymbol{\mu}, \sigma^2\}$ denotes all parameters of a probabilistic PCA model.

Next, we will consider how to estimate the model parameters $\mathbf{\Lambda}$ based on the MLE method. Given a set of training data, denoted as $\mathfrak{D}_N = \{\mathbf{x}_i \,|\, i = 1, 2, \cdots, N\}$, we can express the log-likelihood function as follows:

$$l(\mathbf{W}, \boldsymbol{\mu}, \sigma^2) =$$
$$C - \frac{N}{2}\ln\big|\mathbf{W}\mathbf{W}^\intercal + \sigma^2\mathbf{I}\big| - \frac{1}{2}\sum_{i=1}^{N}(\mathbf{x}_i - \boldsymbol{\mu})^\intercal\big(\mathbf{W}\mathbf{W}^\intercal + \sigma^2\mathbf{I}\big)^{-1}(\mathbf{x}_i - \boldsymbol{\mu}).$$

Here, $C = -\frac{dN}{2}\ln(2\pi)$ is a constant.

If we compute the partial derivative of this log-likelihood function with respect to (w.r.t.) $\boldsymbol{\mu}$ and vanish it to 0, we can derive the formula to estimate $\boldsymbol{\mu}$ as

$$\boldsymbol{\mu}_{\text{MLE}} = \bar{\mathbf{x}} = \frac{1}{N}\sum_{i=1}^{N}\mathbf{x}_i. \tag{13.5}$$

Substituting $\boldsymbol{\mu}_{\text{MLE}}$ into the previous equation, we may derive the log-likelihood function for the remaining parameters as follows:

$$l(\mathbf{W}, \sigma^2) = C - \frac{N}{2}\Big[\ln\Big|\mathbf{W}\mathbf{W}^\intercal + \sigma^2\mathbf{I}\Big| + \text{tr}\Big(\big(\mathbf{W}\mathbf{W}^\intercal + \sigma^2\mathbf{I}\big)^{-1}\mathbf{S}\Big)\Big], \tag{13.6}$$

$$\mathbf{S} = \frac{1}{N}\sum_{i=1}^{N}(\mathbf{x}_i - \bar{\mathbf{x}})(\mathbf{x}_i - \bar{\mathbf{x}})^\intercal.$$

where $\mathbf{S}$ is the $d \times d$ sample covariance matrix computed in the same way as in the PCA in Section 4.2.1, and tr denotes the trace of a matrix.

As shown in Tipping and Bishop [237], there exists a closed-form solution to derive the global maximum of the log-likelihood function, as follows:

$$\mathbf{W}_{\text{MLE}} = \mathbf{U}_n(\mathbf{\Lambda}_n - \sigma^2_{\text{MLE}})^{1/2}\mathbf{R},$$

where $\mathbf{\Lambda}_n$ is an $n \times n$ diagonal matrix consisting of the top n largest eigenvalues of $\mathbf{S}$, each column of the $d \times n$ matrix $\mathbf{U}_n$ is the corresponding eigenvector of $\mathbf{S}$, and $\mathbf{R}$ is an arbitrary $n \times n$ orthogonal rotation matrix. Furthermore, σ^2_{MLE} can also be computed by averaging the remaining $d - n$

smallest eigenvalues, as follows:

$$\sigma^2_{\text{MLE}} = \frac{1}{d-n} \sum_{j=n+1}^{d} \lambda_j$$

For any $n \times n$ rotation matrix $\mathbf{R}$, we have

$$\mathbf{R}\mathbf{R}^\intercal = \mathbf{I}.$$

Therefore, any $\mathbf{R}$ will lead to the same likelihood value in Eq. (13.6) because $\mathbf{R}$ is canceled out in $\mathbf{W}\mathbf{W}^\intercal$.

These formulae show that the estimation for $\mathbf{W}_{\text{MLE}}$ is not unique under this setting because we can choose any rotation matrix $\mathbf{R}$. When we choose $\mathbf{R} = \mathbf{I}$, the column vectors $\mathbf{W}_{\text{MLE}}$ correspond to the top n principal components in the standard PCA procedure as described in Section 4.2.1, scaled by the variance parameter $\lambda_j - \sigma^2_{\text{MLE}}$. Therefore, the resultant models are often called *probabilistic PCA*. The probabilistic PCA can be viewed as a generative model that stochastically extends the traditional PCA method. The introduction of the likelihood function allows a formal treatment of PCA, as with other generative models. For example, more advanced models, such as the mixtures of probabilistic PCA in Tipping and Bishop [237], can be formulated in a principled way like the regular mixture models in Chapter 12.

Finally, in probabilistic PCA models, we can explicitly express the conditional distribution in Eq. (13.3) for the purpose of disentangling as the following Gaussian distribution:

$$p(\mathbf{z} \,|\, \mathbf{x}) = \mathcal{N}\Big(\mathbf{z} \,\Big|\, \mathbf{M}^{-1}\mathbf{W}^\intercal(\mathbf{x} - \boldsymbol{\mu}), \sigma^{-2}\mathbf{M}\Big), \tag{13.7}$$

where $\mathbf{M}$ is an $n \times n$ matrix computed as $\mathbf{M} = \mathbf{W}^\intercal\mathbf{W} + \sigma^2\mathbf{I}$. Note that the mean vector of this conditional distribution depends on $\mathbf{x}$, but the covariance matrix is totally independent of $\mathbf{x}$. How to derive this conditional distribution is left as Exercise Q13.3.

13.2.2 Factor Analysis

Factor analysis [231] is a traditional data-analysis method in statistics and is normally used to describe variability among observed variables in terms of a lower number of unobserved latent variables called *factors*. Factor analysis can also be formulated as a linear Gaussian model, which is closely related to the aforementioned probabilistic PCA method. The only difference between factor analysis and probabilistic PCA is that we replace the isotropic covariance Gaussian in the residual distribution with a *diagonal* covariance Gaussian distribution, as follows:

$$p(\boldsymbol{\varepsilon}) = \mathcal{N}(\boldsymbol{\varepsilon} \,|\, \boldsymbol{\mu}, \mathbf{D}),$$

where $\mathbf{D} \in \mathbb{R}^{d \times d}$ denotes an unknown diagonal covariance matrix. Similarly, we can derive the data distribution in factor analysis models as

$$p_{\Lambda}(\mathbf{x}) = \mathcal{N}\big(\mathbf{x} \,\big|\, \boldsymbol{\mu}, \mathbf{W}\mathbf{W}^{\intercal} + \mathbf{D}\big),$$

where $\Lambda = \{\mathbf{W}, \boldsymbol{\mu}, \mathbf{D}\}$ denotes all parameters in factor analysis.

We can also use the MLE method to learn all unknown parameters from some training samples. Given the training set $\mathcal{D}_N = \{\mathbf{x}_i \,|\, i = 1, 2, \cdots, N\}$, we express the log-likelihood function in factor analysis as follows:

$$l(\mathbf{W}, \boldsymbol{\mu}, \mathbf{D}) =$$
$$C - \frac{N}{2} \ln \left| \mathbf{W}\mathbf{W}^{\intercal} + \mathbf{D} \right| - \frac{1}{2} \sum_{i=1}^{N} (\mathbf{x}_i - \boldsymbol{\mu})^{\intercal} \left(\mathbf{W}\mathbf{W}^{\intercal} + \mathbf{D}\right)^{-1} (\mathbf{x}_i - \boldsymbol{\mu}).$$

First of all, we can similarly derive the maximum-likelihood estimate for $\boldsymbol{\mu}$ that is the same as Eq. (13.5). After substituting $\boldsymbol{\mu}_{\text{MLE}}$ in Eq. (13.5), we represent the log-likelihood function of $\mathbf{W}$ and $\mathbf{D}$ as follows:

$$\boldsymbol{\mu}_{\text{MLE}} = \bar{\mathbf{x}} = \frac{1}{N} \sum_{i=1}^{N} \mathbf{x}_i.$$

$$l(\mathbf{W}, \mathbf{D}) = C - \frac{N}{2} \left[\ln \left| \mathbf{W}\mathbf{W}^{\intercal} + \mathbf{D} \right| + \operatorname{tr}\left(\left(\mathbf{W}\mathbf{W}^{\intercal} + \mathbf{D}\right)^{-1} \mathbf{S} \right) \right].$$

Algorithm 13.18 Alternating MLE for Factor Analysis

Input: the sample covariance matrix $\mathbf{S}$
Output: $\mathbf{W}$ and $\mathbf{D}$

randomly initialize $\mathbf{D}_0$; set $t = 1$
while not converged **do**
1. construct $\mathbf{P}_t$ using the n leading eigenvectors of $\mathbf{D}_{t-1}^{-\frac{1}{2}} \mathbf{S} \mathbf{D}_{t-1}^{-\frac{1}{2}}$
2. $\mathbf{W}_t = \mathbf{D}_{t-1}^{\frac{1}{2}} \mathbf{P}_t$
3. $\mathbf{D}_t = \operatorname{diag}\left(\mathbf{S} - \mathbf{W}_t \mathbf{W}_t^{\intercal}\right)$
4. $t = t + 1$

end while

However, because of the change made to the covariance matrix of the residual distribution, there is no closed-form solution to maximize the log-likelihood function. We have to rely on some iterative optimization methods to estimate $\mathbf{W}$ and $\mathbf{D}$ for factor analysis. Here, we consider an alternating method, as shown in Algorithm 13.18, to estimate $\mathbf{W}$ and $\mathbf{D}$ one by one in an alternative fashion. We first randomly initialize the diagonal covariance matrix $\mathbf{D}$. Then, we maximize $l(\mathbf{W}, \mathbf{D})$ with respect to $\mathbf{W}$ only. According to Bartholomew [14], when $\mathbf{D}$ is fixed, the optimal $\mathbf{D}^{-\frac{1}{2}}\mathbf{W}$ is given by the $d \times n$ matrix whose columns are the n leading eigenvectors of the matrix $\mathbf{D}^{-\frac{1}{2}} \mathbf{S} \mathbf{D}^{-\frac{1}{2}}$. After we derive a new $\mathbf{W}$ from the optimal $\mathbf{D}^{-\frac{1}{2}}\mathbf{W}$, we maximize $l(\mathbf{W}, \mathbf{D})$ with respect to $\mathbf{D}$ alone. It can be shown that the optimal choice of $\mathbf{D}$ is given by the diagonal elements of $\mathbf{S} - \mathbf{W}\mathbf{W}^\intercal$ when $\mathbf{W}$ is fixed. As shown in Algorithm 13.18, we can alternatively optimize over $\mathbf{W}$ and $\mathbf{D}$ until it converges.

Similar to probabilistic PCA, the MLE found by this numerical method is not unique because the likelihood function of factor analysis is also invariant to any rotation in the space of $\mathbf{z}$. Finally, we can also use an extended expectation-maximization (EM) algorithm to solve the MLE estimation for $\mathbf{W}$ and $\mathbf{D}$ in factor analysis. See Exercise Q13.5 for more details on this approach.

13.3 Non-Gaussian Models

In the second category of entangled models, we still use a linear mixing function and a Gaussian model for the residual distribution, but we consider some non-Gaussian models for the factor distribution. This leads to many interesting machine learning methods, and some of them have been successfully applied to several important real-world tasks. In this section, we will briefly consider some representative methods in this category.

13.3.1 Independent Component Analysis (ICA)

Many real-world applications require the solution of a blind source-separation problem. For example, assume that several people are simultaneously speaking aloud in a room. If we place several microphones in the same room and each microphone can only capture a mixed signal from all speakers, the blind source-separation problem aims to recover the voices of all speakers based on the recordings of all microphones, as shown in Figure 13.3. This problem can be formulated as an entangled model like that shown in Figure 13.2. In this case, we use each element in the factor $\mathbf{z}$ to represent the original voice from one speaker. And it is reasonable to assume that all factor elements are statistically independent, and these independent elements are mixed through a linear function to generate all mixed signals, which are captured by the microphones as the observation $\mathbf{x}$. The key problem in ICA is to learn an entangled model to disentangle any observation $\mathbf{x}$ to derive all independent components in $\mathbf{z}$. For simplicity, we usually assume that the dimension of the observations is equal to that of the hidden factor elements in ICA (i.e., $n = d$). Furthermore, we also ignore the residual in the following ICA discussion.

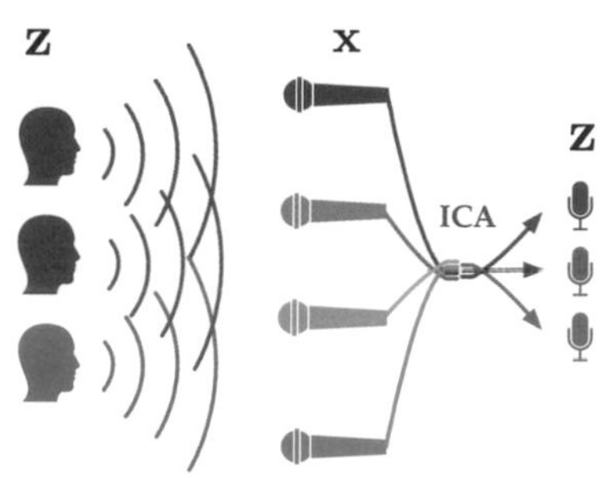

Figure 13.3: An illustration of a blind source-separation task, where four microphones are used to capture mixed signals from three independent speakers.

For the factor distribution $p(\mathbf{z})$, we can assume that it is factorized into each component because all factor components are assumed to be independent in the first place. Therefore, we have

$$p(\mathbf{z}) = \prod_{j=1}^{n} p(z_j), \tag{13.8}$$

where $p(z_j)$ indicates the probability distribution of one element in $\mathbf{z}$. According to Hyvärinen and Oja [107], it is crucial to use some non-Gaussian models for $p(z_j)$. As we know from the previous section, the likelihood function of a linear Gaussian model is invariant to any arbitrary rotation of $\mathbf{z}$. In other words, if these independent components follow any Gaussian distribution, we cannot disentangle them using any linear transformation. In practice, a common choice for each $p(z_j)$ is a heavy-tail distribution, as follows:

$$p(z_j) = \frac{2}{\pi \cosh(z_j)} = \frac{4}{\pi(e^{z_j} + e^{-z_j})}.$$

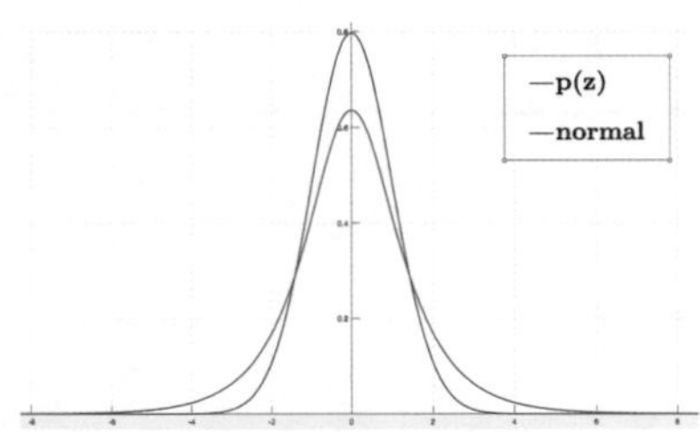

Figure 13.4: Comparison between the normal distribution with the heavy-tail distribution commonly used for ICA.

For comparison, Figure 13.4 plots this heavy-tail distribution along with a standard normal distribution. Note that there is no unknown parameter for this distribution.

Given a training set of some observation samples (i.e., $\mathcal{D}_N = \{\mathbf{x}_i \mid i = 1, 2, \cdots, N\}$), we can use MLE to learn the linear mixing function $\mathbf{x} = \mathbf{W}\mathbf{z}$. When $n = d$ and $\mathbf{W}$ is invertible, we have $\mathbf{z} = \mathbf{W}^{-1}\mathbf{x}$. According to Eq. (13.1), the log-likelihood function of the inverse matrix $\mathbf{W}^{-1}$ can be expressed as follows:

$$l(\mathbf{W}^{-1}) = \sum_{i=1}^{N} \sum_{j=1}^{n} \ln p(\mathbf{w}_j^\intercal \mathbf{x}_i) + N \ln \left|\mathbf{W}^{-1}\right|, \tag{13.9}$$

where the Jacobian matrix for the inverse mapping from $\mathbf{x}$ to $\mathbf{z}$ is equal to $\mathbf{W}^{-1} \in \mathbb{R}^{n \times n}$, and $\mathbf{w}_j$ denotes the jth row vector of $\mathbf{W}^{-1}$. We can easily compute the gradient of this objective function and use any gradient-descent method to maximize $l(\mathbf{W}^{-1})$ with respect to $\mathbf{W}^{-1}$. Once the matrix $\mathbf{W}^{-1}$ is estimated, we can disentangle any observation $\mathbf{x}$ to uncover all independent components in $\mathbf{z}$ as $\mathbf{z} = \mathbf{W}^{-1}\,\mathbf{x}$.

In addition to the MLE method, there are many different methods for estimating the mixing function for ICA available in the literature. Interested readers may refer to Hyvärinen and Oja [107] for other ICA methods.

13.3.2 Independent Factor Analysis (IFA)

Attias [4] proposes a new entangled model, called IFA, to extend the traditional ICA methods. In IFA, each component of $\mathbf{z}$ is assumed to follow a Gaussian mixture model (GMM) as

$$p(z_j) = \sum_{m=1}^{M} w_{jm} \mathcal{N}(z_j \,|\, \mu_{jm}, \sigma_{jm}^2)$$

for all $j = 1, 2, \cdots n$. If we substitute these GMMs into Eq. (13.8), we can show that $p(\mathbf{z})$ is also a larger GMM, where each component corresponds to a combination of Gaussians from all dimensions in $\mathbf{z}$. This large GMM is called a *factorial* GMM. In IFA, all unknown parameters can also be learned based on MLE. If we substitute the factorial GMM and the linear mixing function into Eq. (13.2), the log-likelihood function in IFA is very similar to those in the regular mixture models. Therefore, we can use the EM algorithm to iteratively learn all unknown parameters of the factorial GMM and the mixing function from any given training set. Interested readers can refer to Attias [4] for more details on IFA. Compared with the ordinary ICA methods, the IFA model can deal with more general scenarios in blind source separation (e.g., when the dimensions of $\mathbf{x}$ and $\mathbf{z}$ are different or when a residual distribution must be used for noisy observations).

13.3.3 Hybrid Orthogonal Projection and Estimation (HOPE)

Zhang et al. [261], propose another entangled model, called HOPE, to model the data distributions in a high-dimensional space. In HOPE, we assume the factor distribution $p(\mathbf{z})$ is a mixture model in $\mathbb{R}^n$, and the residual $\boldsymbol{\varepsilon}$ follows a simple zero-mean isotropic covariance Gaussian (i.e., $p(\boldsymbol{\varepsilon}) = \mathcal{N}(\boldsymbol{\varepsilon} \,|\, \mathbf{0}, \sigma^2\mathbf{I})$) in a separate space $\mathbb{R}^{d-n}$. The factor $\mathbf{z}$ and the residual $\boldsymbol{\varepsilon}$ are statistically independent, and they are mixed by an *orthogonal* linear function to generate the final observation $\mathbf{x}$ in a higher-dimensional space $\mathbb{R}^d$:

$$\mathbf{x} = \mathbf{W} \begin{bmatrix} \mathbf{z} \\ \boldsymbol{\varepsilon} \end{bmatrix},$$

where $\mathbf{W} \in \mathbb{R}^{d \times d}$ is a full-rank orthogonal matrix (i.e., $\mathbf{W}\mathbf{W}^\intercal = \mathbf{I}$).

Substituting all of these into Eq. (13.1), we can derive the HOPE model as follows:

$$p(\mathbf{x}) = p(\mathbf{z})\, p(\boldsymbol{\varepsilon}).$$

Note that the Jacobian matrix is equal to $\mathbf{W}^\intercal$ in this case and $|\mathbf{W}^\intercal| = 1$ for all orthogonal matrices (see Example 2.2.4).

Under this setting, we can easily formulate the likelihood function for any observed data $\mathbf{x}$. As a result, all HOPE model parameters can be efficiently learned using a simple gradient-descent algorithm to explicitly maximize the log-likelihood. Zhang et al. [261] have shown that this entangled model is equivalent in model structure to a hidden layer in regular neural networks when we choose mixtures of the *von Mises–Fisher* (vMF) distribution for the factor distribution $p(\mathbf{z})$. As a result, the MLE of the HOPE models can be applied to unsupervised learning of neural networks in a layer-wise fashion.

13.4 Deep Generative Models

In all the aforementioned entangled models, we have stuck to a linear mixing function for computational convenience. However, linear mixing functions strongly limit the power of the resultant entangled models. In this section, we will consider more general nonlinear mixing functions for entangled models.

Similar to discriminative models, we can use deep neural networks to model the underlying nonlinear mixing functions in entangled models. Theoretically speaking, we can use neural networks to approximate any L^p function. This configuration of the mixing functions leads to a category of powerful entangled models, which are often called *deep generative models* in the literature. As suggested by Theorem 13.1.1, as long as the underlying neural network is large enough, the deep generative models are very powerful generative models, and in principle, they can be used to model any data distribution, even when the factor and residual distributions are very simple. As a result, for deep generative models, we usually choose a zero-mean and unit-covariance Gaussian for the factor distribution (i.e., $p(\mathbf{z}) = \mathcal{N}(\mathbf{z} \,|\, \mathbf{0}, \mathbf{I})$) and a zero-mean and isotropic covariance Gaussian for the residual distribution (i.e., $p(\boldsymbol{\varepsilon}) = \mathcal{N}(\boldsymbol{\varepsilon} \,|\, \mathbf{0}, \sigma^2\mathbf{I})$), where σ^2 denotes the unknown variance parameter. Meanwhile, we assume the mixing function is modeled by a deep neural network as $f(\mathbf{z}; \mathbb{W})$, where $\mathbb{W}$ stands for all parameters associated with the underlying neural network.

Despite the superior model capacity in theory, deep neural networks are faced with huge computational challenges in practice. The major difficulty is that the likelihood function of deep generative models cannot be explicitly evaluated. This is clear because neither the Jacobian matrix in Eq. (13.1) nor the integral in Eq. (13.2) is computable when a neural network is used for the mixing function. Therefore, it is basically intractable to use MLE for deep generative models. In the following, we will consider two interesting methods that have managed to bypass this difficulty so that deep generative models can be learned in some alternative ways.

13.4.1 Variational Autoencoders (VAE)

Because the likelihood function $p_{\Lambda}(\mathbf{x})$ of deep generative models cannot be explicitly evaluated, the basic idea behind the VAE method is to construct a proxy objective function to replace the intractable likelihood function for parameter estimation. The proxy function is constructed based on the idea of approximating the true conditional distribution $p(\mathbf{z}|\mathbf{x})$ with a Gaussian distribution. In deep generative models, the true conditional distribution $p(\mathbf{z}|\mathbf{x})$ in Eq. (13.3) cannot be explicitly evaluated either because it also involves the integral over the factor $\mathbf{z}$, just like the likelihood function itself. As motivated by the conditional distribution of linear Gaussian models, such as Eq. (13.7), we may use a similar $\mathbf{x}$-dependent multivariate Gaussian distribution to approximate the true conditional distribution $p(\mathbf{z}|\mathbf{x})$ in a deep generative model:

$$p(\mathbf{z}|\mathbf{x}) \approx q(\mathbf{z}|\mathbf{x}),$$

with

$$q(\mathbf{z}|\mathbf{x}) = \mathcal{N}(\mathbf{z} \,|\, \boldsymbol{\mu}_{\mathbf{x}}, \boldsymbol{\Sigma}_{\mathbf{x}}), \tag{13.10}$$

where the Gaussian mean vector $\boldsymbol{\mu}_{\mathbf{x}}$ and covariance matrix $\boldsymbol{\Sigma}_{\mathbf{x}}$ both depend on the given $\mathbf{x}$. To make it more flexible, we assume both $\boldsymbol{\mu}_{\mathbf{x}}$ and $\boldsymbol{\Sigma}_{\mathbf{x}}$ can be computed from $\mathbf{x}$ by another deterministic L^p function $h(\cdot)$, which is modeled by another deep neural network as follows:

$$\left[\boldsymbol{\mu}_{\mathbf{x}} \; \boldsymbol{\Sigma}_{\mathbf{x}}\right] = h(\mathbf{x}; \mathbb{V}),$$

where $\mathbb{V}$ denotes all model parameters of this neural network. This neural network maps any observation $\mathbf{x}$ into the mean vector and covariance matrix of the approximate conditional distribution. Hence, this neural network $\mathbb{V}$ is called a *probabilistic encoder*.

Using this Gaussian distribution $q(\mathbf{z}|\mathbf{x})$, after some simple arrangements, we can represent the intractable log-likelihood as follows:

$$\overbrace{\ln p(\mathbf{x})}^{l(\mathbb{W},\sigma|\mathbf{x})} = \overbrace{\mathrm{KL}\Big(q(\mathbf{z}|\mathbf{x}) \| p(\mathbf{z}|\mathbf{x})\Big)}^{\geq 0} + \overbrace{\Big\{\mathbb{E}_{q(\mathbf{z}|\mathbf{x})}\big[\ln p(\mathbf{x}|\mathbf{z})\big] - \mathrm{KL}\Big(q(\mathbf{z}|\mathbf{x}) \| p(\mathbf{z})\Big)\Big\}}^{L(\mathbb{W},\mathbb{V},\sigma|\mathbf{x})}.$$

Expand all three terms in the right-hand side as follows:

1. $\mathrm{KL}\Big(q(\mathbf{z}|\mathbf{x}) \| p(\mathbf{z}|\mathbf{x})\Big) = \int_{\mathbf{z}} \ln q(\mathbf{z}|\mathbf{x}) q(\mathbf{z}|\mathbf{x}) d\mathbf{z} - \int_{\mathbf{z}} \ln p(\mathbf{z}|\mathbf{x}) q(\mathbf{z}|\mathbf{x}) d\mathbf{z}.$
2. $\mathbb{E}_{q(\mathbf{z}|\mathbf{x})}\big[\ln p(\mathbf{x}|\mathbf{z})\big] = \int_{\mathbf{z}} \ln p(\mathbf{x}|\mathbf{z}) q(\mathbf{z}|\mathbf{x}) d\mathbf{z}.$
3. $-\mathrm{KL}\Big(q(\mathbf{z}|\mathbf{x}) \| p(\mathbf{z})\Big) = \int_{\mathbf{z}} \ln p(\mathbf{z}) q(\mathbf{z}|\mathbf{x}) d\mathbf{z} - \int_{\mathbf{z}} \ln q(\mathbf{z}|\mathbf{x}) q(\mathbf{z}|\mathbf{x}) d\mathbf{z}.$

(The $\int_{\mathbf{z}} \ln q(\mathbf{z}|\mathbf{x}) q(\mathbf{z}|\mathbf{x}) d\mathbf{z}$ terms in 1 and 3 are struck through.)

Adding these three equations together, we have

$$\Longrightarrow \int_{\mathbf{z}} \ln \frac{p(\mathbf{z})p(\mathbf{x}|\mathbf{z})}{p(\mathbf{z}|\mathbf{x})} q(\mathbf{z}|\mathbf{x}) d\mathbf{z} = \int_{\mathbf{z}} \ln \frac{p(\mathbf{x},\mathbf{z})}{p(\mathbf{z}|\mathbf{x})} q(\mathbf{z}|\mathbf{x}) d\mathbf{z} = \int_{\mathbf{z}} \ln p(\mathbf{x}) \, q(\mathbf{z}|\mathbf{x}) d\mathbf{z} = \ln p(\mathbf{x}).$$

First of all, we can easily verify this equation by expanding all three terms on the right-hand side and adding them together to arrive at the log-likelihood function on the left-hand side (see margin note).

Second, we can sort out several key messages from this equation:

1. The first two terms, namely, $\ln p(\mathbf{x})$ and $\mathrm{KL}(q(\mathbf{z}|\mathbf{x}) \,\|\, p(\mathbf{z}|\mathbf{x}))$, are not actually computable because they both involve some intractable

integrals with respect to some unknown distributions depending on the neural network in the entangled model.
2. The third term, $L(\mathbb{W}, \mathbb{V}, \sigma|\mathbf{x})$, is totally computable because all integrals are only based on the earlier approximate Gaussian distribution $q(\mathbf{z}|\mathbf{x})$, and this term is a function of all model parameters.
3. Moreover, $L(\mathbb{W}, \mathbb{V}, \sigma|\mathbf{x})$ is actually a lower bound of the true log-likelihood function, so it can be used as a proxy function for model learning.

We have

$$L(\mathbb{W}, \mathbb{V}, \sigma\,|\mathbf{x}) \leq \ln p(\mathbf{x})$$

because

$$\mathrm{KL}\Big(q(\mathbf{z}|\mathbf{x}) \| p(\mathbf{z}|\mathbf{x})\Big) \geq 0.$$

Kingma and Welling [130] propose an empirical learning procedure to learn deep generative models by maximizing this proxy function instead of the intractable likelihood function. Because the proxy function is often called the *variational bound* of the log-likelihood function, the corresponding learning method is usually called a *variational autoencoder* (VAE).

Given a training set (i.e., $\mathcal{D}_N = \{\mathbf{x}_i \,|\, i = 1, 2, \cdots, N\}$), the VAE aims to learn all model parameters, including the original entangled model as well as the newly introduced encoder, by maximizing the proxy function $L(\mathbb{W}, \mathbb{V}, \sigma|\mathbf{x})$, as follows:

$$\arg\max_{\mathbb{W},\mathbb{V},\sigma} \sum_{i=1}^{N} L(\mathbb{W}, \mathbb{V}, \sigma|\mathbf{x}_i)$$

$$\Longrightarrow \arg\max_{\mathbb{W},\mathbb{V},\sigma} \sum_{i=1}^{N} \Big\{ \mathbb{E}_{q(\mathbf{z}|\mathbf{x}_i)}\big[\ln p(\mathbf{x}_i|\mathbf{z})\big] - \mathrm{KL}\Big(q(\mathbf{z}|\mathbf{x}_i) \| p(\mathbf{z})\Big) \Big\}.$$

As with other neural networks, we will have to rely on the stochastic gradient-descent method to solve this optimization. The key is how to compute the gradient of this proxy function with respect to all model parameters. Because both $q(\mathbf{z}|\mathbf{x}_i)$ and $p(\mathbf{z})$ are Gaussian models, we can express the Kullback–Leibler (KL) divergence between them in a closed form so that the gradient of this term can be easily computed (see margin note).

Given the factor distribution

$$p(\mathbf{z}) = \mathcal{N}(\mathbf{0}, \mathbf{I})$$

and the approximate Gaussian distribution

$$q(\mathbf{z}|\mathbf{x}) = \mathcal{N}(\mathbf{z} \,|\, \boldsymbol{\mu}_\mathbf{x}, \boldsymbol{\Sigma}_\mathbf{x}),$$

we can compute the KL divergence between them as

$$\mathrm{KL}\Big(q(\mathbf{z}|\mathbf{x}) \,\|\, p(\mathbf{z})\Big) =$$

$$C + \frac{1}{2}\Big(\mathrm{tr}(\boldsymbol{\Sigma}_\mathbf{x}) + \boldsymbol{\mu}_\mathbf{x}^\intercal \boldsymbol{\Sigma}_\mathbf{x}^{-1} \boldsymbol{\mu}_\mathbf{x} - \ln|\boldsymbol{\Sigma}_\mathbf{x}|\Big),$$

where C is a constant.

However, the other term is an expectation of $\ln p(\mathbf{x}_i|\mathbf{z})$ over the approximate Gaussian distribution. We have no closed-form solution for it, and instead we will have to rely on a sampling-based method.

We first randomly sample from this Gaussian distribution, and the expectation is approximately computed as an average of these samples. For $j = 1, 2, \cdots G$, we sample $\mathbf{z}_j$ as follows:

$$\mathbf{z}_j \sim q(\mathbf{z}|\mathbf{x}_i) = \mathcal{N}(\mathbf{z} \,|\, \boldsymbol{\mu}_{\mathbf{x}_i}, \boldsymbol{\Sigma}_{\mathbf{x}_i}),$$

and we have

$$\mathbb{E}_{q(\mathbf{z}|\mathbf{x}_i)}\big[\ln p(\mathbf{x}_i|\mathbf{z})\big] \approx \frac{1}{G} \sum_{j=1}^{G} \ln p(\mathbf{x}_i|\mathbf{z}_j).$$

However, one difficulty in this procedure is that the samples are drawn from a distribution that depends on the neural network $\mathbb{V}$. This makes it hard to explicitly compute the gradient for error back-propagation.

Kingma and Welling [130] use a reparameterization trick to reformulate the procedure into an equivalent sampling process that does not depend on any model parameters. As we know, for any sample $\boldsymbol{\epsilon}$ from a zero-mean unit-covariance Gaussian (i.e., $\boldsymbol{\epsilon} \sim \mathcal{N}(\boldsymbol{\epsilon} \,|\, \mathbf{0}, \mathbf{I})$), the linear transformation $\boldsymbol{\Sigma}^{\frac{1}{2}}\boldsymbol{\epsilon} + \boldsymbol{\mu}$ will make it follow the Gaussian distribution $\mathcal{N}(\mathbf{z} \,|\, \boldsymbol{\mu}, \boldsymbol{\Sigma})$.

For $j = 1, 2, \cdots, G$, we sample as $\boldsymbol{\epsilon}_j \sim \mathcal{N}(\boldsymbol{\epsilon} \,|\, \mathbf{0}, \mathbf{I})$, and then we have

Based on the residual distribution

$$\mathcal{N}(\boldsymbol{\varepsilon} \,|\, \mathbf{0}, \sigma^2\mathbf{I})$$

and the mixing function

$$\mathbf{x} = f(\mathbf{z}; \mathbb{W}) + \boldsymbol{\varepsilon},$$

we have

$$p(\mathbf{x}|\mathbf{z}) = \mathcal{N}(\mathbf{x} - f(\mathbf{z}; \mathbb{W}) \,|\, \mathbf{0}, \sigma^2\mathbf{I}).$$

Therefore, we have

$$\ln p(\mathbf{x}|\mathbf{z}) = -\ln\sigma - \frac{(\mathbf{x} - f(\mathbf{z}; \mathbb{W}))^2}{2\sigma^2}.$$

$$\begin{aligned}
\mathbb{E}_{q(\mathbf{z}|\mathbf{x}_i)}\big[\ln p(\mathbf{x}_i \,|\, \mathbf{z})\big] &\approx \frac{1}{G}\sum_{j=1}^{G} \ln p(\mathbf{x}_i \,|\, \boldsymbol{\Sigma}_{\mathbf{x}_i}^{\frac{1}{2}}\boldsymbol{\epsilon}_j + \boldsymbol{\mu}_{\mathbf{x}_i}) \\
&= -\ln\sigma - \frac{1}{G}\sum_{j=1}^{G} \frac{\left(\mathbf{x}_i - f(\boldsymbol{\Sigma}_{\mathbf{x}_i}^{\frac{1}{2}}\boldsymbol{\epsilon}_j + \boldsymbol{\mu}_{\mathbf{x}_i}; \mathbb{W})\right)^2}{2\sigma^2},
\end{aligned}$$

where $\boldsymbol{\mu}_{\mathbf{x}_i}$ and $\boldsymbol{\Sigma}_{\mathbf{x}_i}^{\frac{1}{2}}$ are computed from the encoder based on $\mathbf{x}_i$ as $h(\mathbf{x}_i; \mathbb{V})$. Therefore, we can easily compute the gradient of the sum with respect to all model parameters (i.e., $\{\mathbb{W}, \mathbb{V}, \sigma\}$) using the automatic differentiation method discussed in Chapter 8.

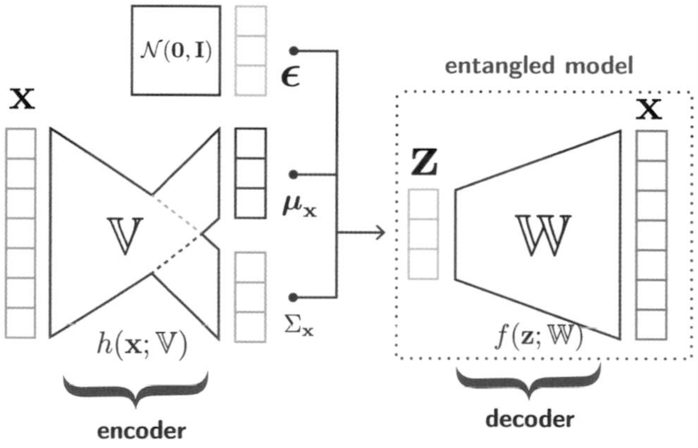

Figure 13.5: An illustration of the VAE training procedure to learn deep generative models [199].

Figure 13.5 summarizes the whole VAE-based training procedure to learn entangled models by maximizing the previous proxy function $L(\mathbb{W}, \mathbb{V}, \sigma|\mathbf{x})$. As noted earlier, we have introduced another neural network $\mathbb{V}$ as a supplementary module to compute the proxy function. At each iteration, we take any training sample $\mathbf{x}$ to feed into $\mathbb{V}$ to compute the mean and covariance of the approximate Gaussian distribution. Along with some random samples from a normal distribution, they are in turn fed to the entangle model to generate the output. After this, the gradient of the proxy function with respect to all model parameters (i.e., $\{\mathbb{W}, \mathbb{V}, \sigma\}$) can be computed from the output all the way back to the input using the standard error back-propagation method. The gradients are then used to update the model parameters. This procedure is repeated over and over until it converges. Compared with the autoencoder method in Figure 4.15, we can see that the first neural network $\mathbb{V}$ serves as an encoder to generate some codes for each sample $\mathbf{x}$, and the second neural network works like a decoder to convert the codes back to an estimate of the sample. The expectation term in the proxy function may be viewed as a distortion measure between the initial input $\mathbf{x}$ and the recovered output from the decoder.

Finally, it is important to note some fundamental differences between the proxy function in the VAE training method and the auxiliary function in the EM algorithm discussed in the last chapter. Unlike the auxiliary function in the EM method, increasing the proxy function $L(\mathbb{W}, \mathbb{V}, \sigma|\mathbf{x})$ does not necessarily lead to the growth of the likelihood function, not to mention maximizing the likelihood function. The proxy function and the log-likelihood function are closely related only when this lower bound is sufficiently tight. As we can see, the gap between them depends on the KL divergence between the approximate Gaussian and the true conditional distribution. Therefore, the VAE training method is highly heuristic, and the final performance largely depends on how much we can effectively close this gap in the VAE training, which implicitly relies on whether the configuration of two neural networks fits well with the given data.

13.4.2 Generative Adversarial Nets (GAN)

As we have seen, the learning of deep generative models is fundamentally difficult because the likelihood function cannot be explicitly evaluated. In the VAE training procedure, we attempt to learn all model parameters by maximizing a tractable proxy function that is a variational lower bound of the log-likelihood function.

Goodfellow et al. [84] propose a pure sampling-based training procedure to learn deep generative models, which completely abandons the intractable likelihood function. This training procedure is often called *generative adversarial nets* (GANs) because it relies on the competition between two adversarial neural networks. As shown in Figure 13.6, in order to learn the deep generative model $\mathbb{W}$, another neural network $\mathbb{V}$ has been introduced for the GAN as a supplementary module. On the one hand, we can sample the factor distribution $p(\mathbf{z})$ to get many samples of the factor $\mathbf{z}$, which are sent to the mixing function $\mathbf{x} = f(\mathbf{z}; \mathbb{W})$ to generate some so-called "fake" data samples. On the other hand, we can directly sample the training set to get the so-called "true" samples. Both the true and fake samples, along with their corresponding true/fake binary labels, are used to train the neural network $\mathbb{V}$ in order to discriminate between true and

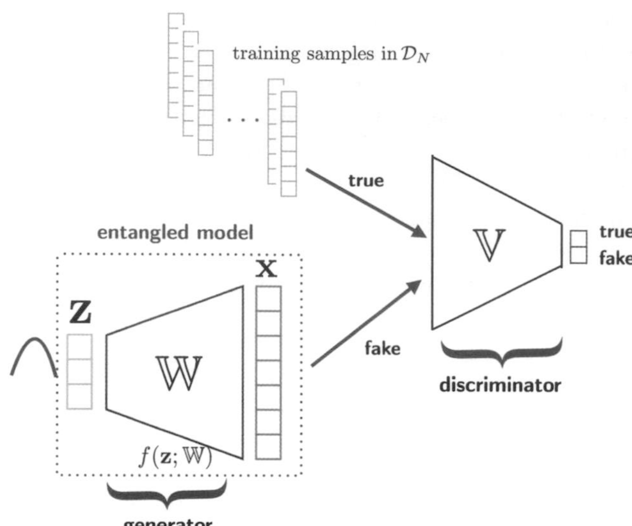

Figure 13.6: An illustration of a training procedure for entangled models based on GANs.

fake samples. As a result, the neural network $\mathbb{V}$ is also called *discriminator*; meanwhile, $\mathbb{W}$ is called *generator* because it aims to generate fake samples to fool the discriminator. In the training process, both the generator $\mathbb{W}$ and the discriminator $\mathbb{V}$ are learned jointly. As stated in Goodfellow et al. [84], if the training reaches an equilibrium—namely, the discriminator cannot distinguish fake samples from the true ones in the training set—it means that we have learned a successful entangled model, working as the generator $\mathbb{W}$, to generate good samples following the same distribution as the training data. The learned entangled model can be used to generate more data samples $\mathbf{x}$ from the learned distribution. The fine part of GANs is that a discriminator is introduced so that the entangled models can be learned in a way that has nothing to do with the likelihood function.

As a final remark, the GAN training procedure has drawn lots of attention in many image-generation applications. As we know, the GAN training is irrelevant to the likelihood function. However, it still lacks a fundamental understanding of what information is actually learned by the entangled models in the adversarial competition process. More theoretical works are needed to answer this fundamental question for all GAN-based methods.

Exercises

Q13.1 Assume a joint distribution $p(\mathbf{x}, \mathbf{y})$ of two random vectors $\mathbf{x} \in \mathbb{R}^n$ and $\mathbf{y} \in \mathbb{R}^n$ is a linear Gaussian model defined as follows:

$$p(\mathbf{x}) = \mathcal{N}\left(\mathbf{x} \mid \boldsymbol{\mu}, \boldsymbol{\Delta}^{-1}\right),$$

where $\boldsymbol{\mu} \in \mathbb{R}^n$ is the mean vector; $\boldsymbol{\Delta} \in \mathbb{R}^{n \times n}$ is the precision matrix; and

$$p(\mathbf{y} \mid \mathbf{x}) = \mathcal{N}\left(\mathbf{y} \mid \mathbf{A}\mathbf{x} + \mathbf{b}, \mathbf{L}^{-1}\right),$$

where $\mathbf{A} \in \mathbb{R}^{n \times n}$, $\mathbf{b} \in \mathbb{R}^n$, and $\mathbf{L} \in \mathbb{R}^{n \times n}$ is the precision matrix. Derive the mean vector and covariance matrix of the marginal distribution $p(\mathbf{y})$ in which the variable $\mathbf{x}$ has been integrated out.

Hints:

$$\begin{bmatrix} \mathbf{A} & \mathbf{B} \\ \mathbf{C} & \mathbf{D} \end{bmatrix}^{-1} = \begin{bmatrix} \mathbf{M} & -\mathbf{M}\mathbf{B}\mathbf{D}^{-1} \\ -\mathbf{D}^{-1}\mathbf{C}\mathbf{M} & \mathbf{D}^{-1} + \mathbf{D}^{-1}\mathbf{C}\mathbf{M}\mathbf{B}\mathbf{D}^{-1} \end{bmatrix}$$

with $\mathbf{M} = \left(\mathbf{A} - \mathbf{B}\mathbf{D}^{-1}\mathbf{C}\right)^{-1}$.

Q13.2 Show the procedure to derive Eq.(13.4) for liner Gaussian models.

Q13.3 Derive the conditional distribution in Eq. (13.7) for probabilistic PCA models.

Q13.4 Derive the conditional distribution $p(\mathbf{z}|\mathbf{x})$ for factor analysis.

Q13.5 Factor analysis can be viewed as an infinite mixture model in Q12.5, where the factor $\mathbf{z}$ is considered to be the continuous mixture index, and $p(\mathbf{z})$ and $p(\mathbf{x}|\mathbf{z})$ are viewed as mixture weights and component models, respectively. Extend the EM algorithm for infinite mixture models in Q12.5 to derive another MLE method for factor analysis.

Q13.6 Compute the gradient for the ICA log-likelihood function in Eq. (13.9), and derive a gradient-descent method for the MLE of ICA.

Q13.7 Derive a stochastic gradient-descent (SGD) algorithm for VAE to train a convolutional neural network (CNN)–based deep generative model for image generation, using a convolution-layer-based encoder and a deconvolution-layer-based decoder [148].

Q13.8 Derive an SGD algorithm for a GAN to train a CNN-based deep generative model for image generation, using a convolution-layer-based encoder and a deconvolution-layer-based decoder [148].

14 Bayesian Learning

In the previous chapters, we have thoroughly discussed various types of generative models in machine learning. As we have seen, generative models are essentially parametric probability functions that are used to model data distributions, denoted as $p_{\boldsymbol{\theta}}(\mathbf{x})$. In the previous setting, we first choose a functional form for $p_{\boldsymbol{\theta}}(\mathbf{x})$ according to the nature of the data and then estimate the unknown parameters $\boldsymbol{\theta}$ based on some training samples. A common approach for parameter estimation is maximum likelihood estimation (MLE). An important implication in this setting is that we only treat data $\mathbf{x}$ as random variables, whereas model parameters $\boldsymbol{\theta}$ are viewed as some unknown but fixed quantities. The MLE method provides some particular statistical estimates for these unknown quantities by maximizing the likelihood function. In this chapter, we will consider a totally different treatment for generative models, which leads to another school of machine learning approaches parallel to what we have learned in the previous chapters. These methods are normally referred to as *Bayesian learning* because they are all founded on the well-known Bayes's theorem in statistics. This chapter introduces Bayesian learning as an alternative strategy to learn generative models and discusses how to make inferences under the Bayesian setting.

14.1 Formulation of Bayesian Learning

In the Bayesian learning framework, the most important premise is that the model parameters $\boldsymbol{\theta}$ of generative models are also treated as random variables. Similar to data $\mathbf{x}$, the model parameters $\boldsymbol{\theta}$ of a generative model may randomly take different values according to a particular probability distribution, denoted as $p(\boldsymbol{\theta})$. In this case, there is no fundamental distinction between the data $\mathbf{x}$ and the model parameters $\boldsymbol{\theta}$. Therefore, in the Bayesian setting, we prefer to rewrite a generative model $p_{\boldsymbol{\theta}}(\mathbf{x})$ as a conditional distribution $p(\mathbf{x} \mid \boldsymbol{\theta})$, which describes how the data $\mathbf{x}$ are distributed when the model parameters $\boldsymbol{\theta}$ are given. Putting these together, we can represent the joint distribution of the data $\mathbf{x}$ and the model parameters $\boldsymbol{\theta}$ as follows:

$$p(\mathbf{x}, \boldsymbol{\theta}) = p(\boldsymbol{\theta})\, p(\mathbf{x} \mid \boldsymbol{\theta}).$$

Because $p(\boldsymbol{\theta})$ is a valid probability density function (p.d.f.), it satisfies the sum-to-1 constraint:

$$\int_{\boldsymbol{\theta}} p(\boldsymbol{\theta})\, d\boldsymbol{\theta} = 1.$$

Substituting this into the well-known Bayes's theorem, we have

$$p(\boldsymbol{\theta} \mid \mathbf{x}) = \frac{p(\mathbf{x}, \boldsymbol{\theta})}{p(\mathbf{x})} = \frac{p(\boldsymbol{\theta})\, p(\mathbf{x}|\boldsymbol{\theta})}{p(\mathbf{x})}.$$

If we focus on the model parameters $\boldsymbol{\theta}$, we can see that the denominator $p(\mathbf{x})$, often called *evidence*, has nothing to do with $\boldsymbol{\theta}$, and it is just a normalization factor to ensure that $p(\boldsymbol{\theta} \mid \mathbf{x})$ satisfies the sum-to-1 constraint (see margin note). Therefore, we may simplify the previous formula as

The denominator $p(\mathbf{x})$ is computed as

$$p(\mathbf{x}) = \int_{\boldsymbol{\theta}} p(\boldsymbol{\theta})\, p(\mathbf{x} \mid \boldsymbol{\theta})\, d\boldsymbol{\theta}.$$

This ensures the sum-to-1 constraint:

$$\int_{\boldsymbol{\theta}} p(\boldsymbol{\theta}|\mathbf{x}) d\boldsymbol{\theta} = 1.$$

$$p(\boldsymbol{\theta}|\mathbf{x}) \propto p(\boldsymbol{\theta})\, p(\mathbf{x}|\boldsymbol{\theta}).$$

This formula highlights the fundamental principle of Bayesian learning. In the Bayesian setting, model parameters are treated as random variables. As we have seen, the best way to describe random variables is to specify their probability distribution. Here, $p(\boldsymbol{\theta})$ is the probability distribution of the model parameters at an initial stage before any data are observed. As a result, $p(\boldsymbol{\theta})$ is normally called the *prior distribution* of the model parameters, which represents our initial belief and background knowledge about the model parameters. On the other hand, once some data $\mathbf{x}$ are observed, this new information will convert the prior distribution into another distribution (i.e., $p(\boldsymbol{\theta}|\mathbf{x})$), based on the previously described learning rule. The new distribution of model parameters is normally called the *posterior distribution*, which fully specifies our knowledge about the model parameters after some new information is added in. As we have learned previously, the term $p(\mathbf{x} \mid \boldsymbol{\theta})$ is the likelihood function. The Bayesian learning rule indicates that the optimal way to combine our prior knowledge and the new information is to follow a multiplication rule, conceptually represented as follows:

$$\text{posterior} \propto \text{prior} \times \text{likelihood}.$$

Moreover, the Bayesian learning rule can also be similarly applied to a set of data samples instead of one. For example, if we are given a set of independent and identically distributed (i.i.d.) training samples as $\mathcal{D} = \{\mathbf{x}_1, \mathbf{x}_2, \cdots, \mathbf{x}_N\}$, we may apply Bayesian learning as follows:

$$p(\boldsymbol{\theta}|\mathcal{D}) \propto p(\boldsymbol{\theta})\, p(\mathcal{D}|\boldsymbol{\theta}) = p(\boldsymbol{\theta}) \prod_{i=1}^{N} p(\mathbf{x}_i|\boldsymbol{\theta}), \tag{14.1}$$

where $p(\boldsymbol{\theta}|\mathcal{D})$ denotes the posterior distribution of the model parameters after we have observed the entire training set $\mathcal{D}$. Bayesian theory states that $p(\boldsymbol{\theta}|\mathcal{D})$ optimally combines the initial knowledge in the prior distribution with the new information provided by the training set. In the Bayesian setting, the optimal inference for any new data must solely rely on this posterior distribution.

Here, let us summarize three key steps in any Bayesian approach for machine learning:

1. **Prior specification**
   In any Bayesian approach, we always need to first specify a prior distribution (i.e., $p(\boldsymbol{\theta})$) for any generative models that we are interested in. The prior distribution is used to describe our prior knowledge of the model used for a machine learning task. Theoretically speaking, the prior distributions should be flexible and powerful enough to reflect our prior knowledge of or initial beliefs about the underlying models. However, in practice, the priors are often chosen in such a way to ensure computational convenience. We will discuss this issue in detail in Section 14.2.

2. **Bayesian learning**
   Once any new data $\mathfrak{D}$ are observed, we follow the multiplication rule of Bayesian learning to update our belief on the underlying model, converting the prior distribution $p(\boldsymbol{\theta})$ into a new posterior distribution $p(\boldsymbol{\theta}|\mathfrak{D})$. As shown previously, Bayesian learning itself is conceptually simple because it only involves a multiplication between the prior distribution and the likelihood function, then a renormalization operation to ensure the sum-to-1 constraint, as shown in Figure 14.1. However, the posterior distribution derived from the Bayesian learning may get very complicated in nature, except in some simple scenarios. The central issue in practice is how to approximate the true posterior distribution in such a way that the following inference step is mathematically tractable. We will come back to discuss these approximation methods in Section 14.3.

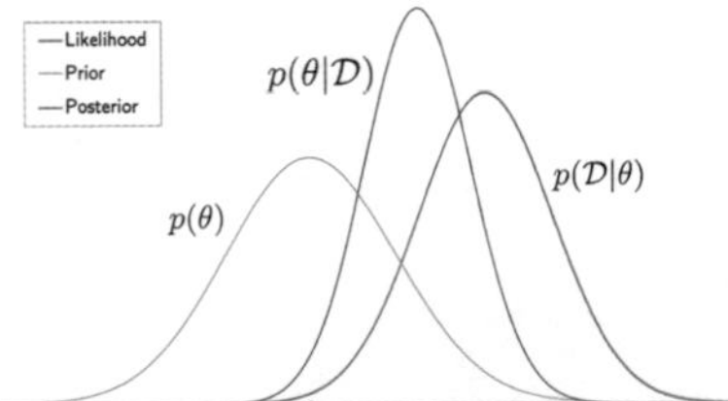

Figure 14.1: An illustration of the Bayesian learning rule as multiplying prior with likelihood, followed by renormalization.

3. **Bayesian inference**
   After the Bayesian learning step, it is believed that all available information on the underlying model has been contained in the posterior distribution $p(\boldsymbol{\theta}|\mathfrak{D})$. Bayesian theory suggests that any inference or decision making must solely rely on $p(\boldsymbol{\theta}|\mathfrak{D})$, including classification, regression, prediction, and so on. In the remainder of this section, we will continue to discuss the general principles on how to use this posterior distribution for Bayesian inference.

14.1.1 Bayesian Inference

In the Bayesian setting, we start with a prior distribution of the model parameters $p(\boldsymbol{\theta})$. Once some training samples $\mathfrak{D}$ are observed, we can update the prior distribution into a posterior distribution using the Bayesian learning rule in Eq. (14.1). Bayesian inference is concerned with how to make a decision for any new data $\mathbf{x}$ based on the updated posterior distribution

$p(\boldsymbol{\theta} \,|\, \mathfrak{D})$. Bayesian theory suggests that the optimal decision must be made based on the so-called *predictive distribution* [78] , which is computed as follows:

$$p(\mathbf{x} \,|\, \mathfrak{D}) = \int_{\boldsymbol{\theta}} p(\mathbf{x} \,|\, \boldsymbol{\theta})\, p(\boldsymbol{\theta} \,|\, \mathfrak{D})\, d\boldsymbol{\theta}, \tag{14.2}$$

where $p(\mathbf{x} \,|\, \boldsymbol{\theta})$ denotes the likelihood of the underlying model. Because the model parameters $\boldsymbol{\theta}$ are random variables rather than some fixed quantities, we will have to average over all possible values based on the posterior distribution derived from the Bayesian learning stage.

As an example, let us consider how to apply this Bayesian reference to a pattern-classification task. Assume we have K classes, denoted as $\{\omega_1, \omega_2, \cdots, \omega_K\}$. The prior probabilities for all classes are denoted as $\Pr(\omega_k)$ $(k = 1, 2, \cdots, K)$. Each class-conditional distribution is modeled by a generative model θ_k as $p(\mathbf{x} \,|\, \omega_k, \theta_k)$. For each class ω_k $(k = 1, 2, \cdots, K)$, the model parameters θ_k are assumed to be random variables, and we specify a prior distribution $p(\theta_k)$ to encode our prior knowledge of each model. Assume we collect a training set for each class, denoted as $\mathfrak{D}_k$, for all $k = 1, 2, \cdots, K$. We first conduct Bayesian learning for each model θ_k to convert the prior $p(\theta_k)$ into the posterior $p(\theta_k \,|\, \mathfrak{D}_k)$, as follows:

$$p(\theta_k \,|\, \mathfrak{D}_k) = \frac{p(\theta_k)\, p(\mathfrak{D}_k \,|\, \omega_k, \theta_k)}{p(\mathfrak{D}_k)} \propto p(\theta_k)\, p(\mathfrak{D}_k \,|\, \omega_k, \theta_k).$$

Given any new data $\mathbf{x}$, we classify the data to a class according to the predictive distributions of all classes, as follows:

$$\begin{aligned} g(\mathbf{x}) &= \arg\max_{k=1}^{K}\; p(\mathbf{x} \,|\, \mathfrak{D}_k) \\ &= \arg\max_{k=1}^{K}\; \Pr(\omega_k) \int_{\theta_k} p(\mathbf{x}|\omega_k, \theta_k)\, p(\theta_k \,|\, \mathfrak{D}_k)\, d\theta_k. \end{aligned}$$

This approach is normally called *Bayesian classification*.

14.1.2 Maximum a Posterior Estimation

As we know, the central cornerstone in Bayesian learning is the posterior distribution of model parameters because it represents the full knowledge about the underlying model by optimally combining our prior knowledge with the new information from the observed data. However, in practice, it is computationally challenging to make use of the posterior distribution because it involves some intractable integrals in several stages of the pipeline. First, we need to solve an integral to compute $p(\mathbf{x})$ for the renormalization in Bayesian learning. Second, we also have to solve an integral in Eq. (14.2) to compute the predictive density for Bayesian inference. Unfortunately, these integrals are intractable in most cases.

$$p(\mathbf{x}) = \int_{\boldsymbol{\theta}} p(\boldsymbol{\theta}) p(\mathbf{x}|\boldsymbol{\theta})\, d\boldsymbol{\theta}.$$

Given the fact that the posterior distribution is the only means to fully specify our beliefs about the underlying models in any Bayesian setting, sometimes it may be convenient to use point estimation to represent the model parameters even though they are random variables. In other words, we want to use the posterior distribution to calculate a single value to represent each model parameter, which is normally called a *point estimate* because it identifies a point in the whole space of model parameters. Analogous to the maximum-likelihood estimate, a common approach is to find the maximum value of the posterior distribution as a point estimate for model parameters, as follows:

$$\boldsymbol{\theta}_{\text{MAP}} = \arg\max_{\boldsymbol{\theta}} \; p(\boldsymbol{\theta} \mid \mathfrak{D}) = \arg\max_{\boldsymbol{\theta}} \; p(\boldsymbol{\theta})\, p(\mathfrak{D} \mid \boldsymbol{\theta}). \tag{14.3}$$

This approach is normally called *maximum a posteriori* (MAP) estimation. The MAP estimate of model parameters (i.e., $\boldsymbol{\theta}_{\text{MAP}}$) can be used in the same way as the maximum-likelihood estimate (i.e., $\boldsymbol{\theta}_{\text{MLE}}$), as discussed in the previous chapters. The MAP estimation can be viewed as an alternative approach to MLE. The difference between MAP and maximum-likelihood estimates is intuitively shown in Figure 14.2. As opposed to the maximum-likelihood estimate that solely depends on the likelihood function, the MAP estimate is derived from a mode of the posterior distribution, which in turn depends on both the prior distribution and the likelihood function.

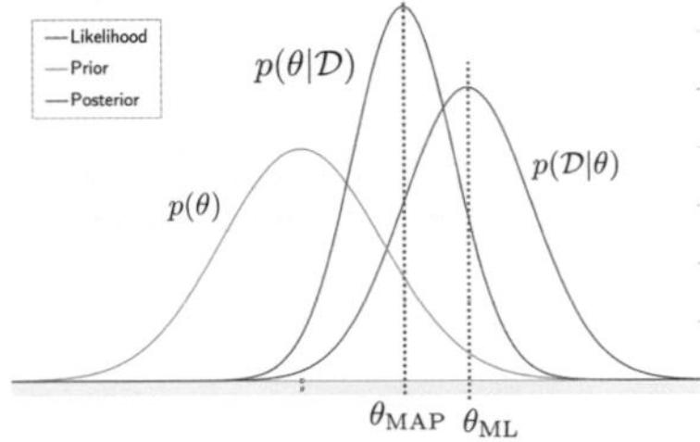

Figure 14.2: Comparison between MAP and maximum-likelihood estimates is illustrated in a simple case involving a single model parameter.

Once a prior distribution is properly chosen, we can choose some standard optimization methods to derive the MAP estimation in Eq. (14.3). For example, we can obtain closed-form solutions for many simple models, and we can also use the expectation-maximization (EM) algorithm in Section 12.2 to derive the MAP estimation for mixture models [52]. Refer to Exercise Q14.7 for the MAP estimation of Gaussian mixture models (GMMs).

14.1.3 Sequential Bayesian Learning

Bayesian learning is also an excellent tool for online learning, where the data are coming one by one rather than all training data being obtained as a chunk. As shown in Figure 14.3, we still start from a prior distribution $p(\boldsymbol{\theta})$ before any data are observed. After the first sample $\mathbf{x}_1$ is observed, we can apply the Bayesian learning rule to update it into the posterior distribution $p(\boldsymbol{\theta} \mid \mathbf{x}_1)$, as follows:

$$p(\boldsymbol{\theta} \mid \mathbf{x}_1) \propto p(\boldsymbol{\theta}) p(\mathbf{x}_1 \mid \boldsymbol{\theta}),$$

which can be used to make any decision at this point. When another sample $\mathbf{x}_2$ comes in, we treat $p(\boldsymbol{\theta} \mid \mathbf{x}_1)$ as a new prior, and we repeatedly apply the same Bayesian learning rule to derive a new posterior distribution $p(\boldsymbol{\theta}|\mathbf{x}_1, \mathbf{x}_2)$, as follows:

$$p(\boldsymbol{\theta} \mid \mathbf{x}_1, \mathbf{x}_2) \propto p(\boldsymbol{\theta} \mid \mathbf{x}_1)\, p(\mathbf{x}_2 \mid \boldsymbol{\theta}),$$

which is accordingly used to make any decision at this time. This process may continue whenever any new data arrive. At any time, the updated posterior distribution serves as the foundation for us to make any decision because it essentially combines all knowledge and information available at each time instance. Under some minor conditions, this sequential Bayesian learning converges to the same posterior distribution in Eq. (14.1) that uses all data only once.

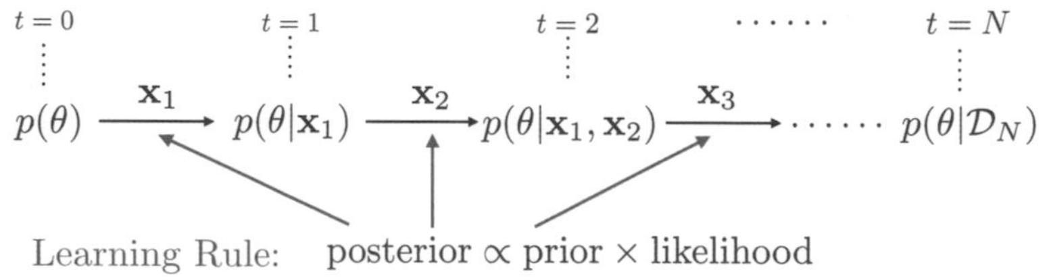

$t=0$ $t=1$ $t=2$ ...... $t=N$

$p(\theta) \xrightarrow{\mathbf{x}_1} p(\theta|\mathbf{x}_1) \xrightarrow{\mathbf{x}_2} p(\theta|\mathbf{x}_1, \mathbf{x}_2) \xrightarrow{\mathbf{x}_3} \cdots\cdots\ p(\theta|\mathcal{D}_N)$

Learning Rule: posterior $\propto$ prior $\times$ likelihood

Figure 14.3: An illustration of sequential Bayesian learning in an online learning setting, where the Bayesian learning rule is repeatedly applied to update the posterior distribution of the model parameters.

In many practical scenarios, sequential Bayesian learning is a good strategy to dynamically adapt the underlying models to cope with a slowly changing environment, such as in robot navigation.

Example 14.1.1 Sequential Bayesian Learning

Assume we use a univariate Gaussian model with a known variance to represent a data distribution as $p(x \mid \mu) = \mathcal{N}(x \mid \mu, \sigma_0^2)$, where the mean μ is the only model parameter, and σ_0^2 is a given constant. If some training samples arrive one by one at each time instance as $x_1, x_2, x_3, \cdots$, use the sequential Bayesian learning method to update the model at each time when each new sample arrives.

First of all, we represent the underlying model as

$$p(x \mid \mu) = \mathcal{N}(x \mid \mu, \sigma_0^2) = \frac{1}{\sqrt{2\pi\sigma_0^2}} e^{-\frac{(x-\mu)^2}{2\sigma_0^2}},$$

where μ is the only parameter in the model, which is assumed to be a random variable. We assume the prior distribution $p(\mu)$ is another univariate Gaussian distribution, as follows:

We have a good reason to choose a Gaussian distribution for the prior in this case, which will be explained later.

$$p(\mu) = \mathcal{N}(\mu \mid \nu_0, \tau_0^2) = \frac{1}{\sqrt{2\pi\tau_0^2}} e^{-\frac{(\mu-\nu_0)^2}{2\tau_0^2}},$$

where the mean ν_0 and variance τ_0^2 are the parameters of the prior distribution, which are often called the *hyperparameters*. They are normally set according to our initial beliefs about the model parameter μ. For example, if we are quite uncertain about μ, the variance τ_0^2 should be large, and the prior tends to be a relatively flat distribution to reflect the uncertainty.

Once we observe the first sample x_1, we apply the Bayesian learning as follows:

$$p(\mu|x_1) \propto p(\mu)p(x_1|\mu) = \frac{1}{\sqrt{2\pi\tau_0^2}} e^{-\frac{(\mu-\nu_0)^2}{2\tau_0^2}} \times \frac{1}{\sqrt{2\pi\sigma_0^2}} e^{-\frac{(x_1-\mu)^2}{2\sigma_0^2}}.$$

After we renormalize it (see margin note), we can represent the posterior distribution as another Gaussian distribution, which has the same functional form as the prior but takes a different mean and variance, as follows:

$$p(\mu \mid x_1) = \mathcal{N}(\mu \mid \nu_1, \tau_1^2) = \frac{1}{\sqrt{2\pi\tau_1^2}} e^{-\frac{(\mu-\nu_1)^2}{2\tau_1^2}}, \tag{14.4}$$

with

$$\nu_1 = \frac{\sigma_0^2}{\tau_0^2 + \sigma_0^2}\nu_0 + \frac{\tau_0^2}{\tau_0^2 + \sigma_0^2}x_1 \tag{14.5}$$

$$\tau_1^2 = \frac{\tau_0^2\sigma_0^2}{\tau_0^2 + \sigma_0^2}. \tag{14.6}$$

Similarly, after observing another sample x_2, the posterior is again another univariate Gaussian taking a different mean and variance, as follows:

$$\nu_2 = \frac{\sigma_0^2}{\tau_1^2 + \sigma_0^2}\nu_1 + \frac{\tau_1^2}{\tau_1^2 + \sigma_0^2}x_2$$

$$\tau_2^2 = \frac{\tau_1^2\sigma_0^2}{\tau_1^2 + \sigma_0^2}.$$

After observing n samples $\{x_1, x_2, \cdots x_n\}$, we can realize that the posterior distribution $p(\mu|x_1, \cdots x_n)$ is still a Gaussian distribution, denoted as $\mathcal{N}(\mu|\nu_n, \tau_n^2)$, with the updated mean and variance as follows:

$$\nu_n = \frac{n\tau_0^2}{n\tau_0^2 + \sigma_0^2}\bar{x}_n + \frac{\sigma_0^2}{n\tau_0^2 + \sigma_0^2}\nu_0 \tag{14.7}$$

$$\tau_n^2 = \frac{\tau_0^2\sigma_0^2}{n\tau_0^2 + \sigma_0^2}, \tag{14.8}$$

As for

$$p(\mu|x_1) \propto e^{-\frac{(\mu-\nu_0)^2}{2\tau_0^2} - \frac{(x_1-\mu)^2}{2\sigma_0^2}},$$

we complete the square with respect to (w.r.t.) μ for the exponent as follows:

$$-\frac{1}{2}\left[\frac{(\mu-\nu_0)^2}{\tau_0^2} + \frac{(x_1-\mu)^2}{\sigma_0^2}\right]$$

$$= -\frac{(\tau_0^2+\sigma_0^2)\mu^2 - 2\mu(\nu_0\sigma_0^2 + x_1\tau_0^2)}{2\tau_0^2\sigma_0^2} + C$$

$$= -\frac{\tau_0^2+\sigma_0^2}{2\tau_0^2\sigma_0^2}\left(\mu^2 - 2\mu\frac{\nu_0\sigma_0^2 + x_1\tau_0^2}{\tau_0^2+\sigma_0^2}\right) + C'$$

$$= -\frac{\tau_0^2+\sigma_0^2}{2\tau_0^2\sigma_0^2}\left(\mu - \frac{\nu_0\sigma_0^2 + x_1\tau_0^2}{\tau_0^2+\sigma_0^2}\right)^2 + C''.$$

After renormalizing, we have

$$p(\mu|x_1) = \mathcal{N}(\mu|\nu_1, \tau_1^2),$$

as specified in Eq. (14.4), where the mean ν_1 and the variance τ_1^2 are given in Eqs.(14.5) and (14.6).

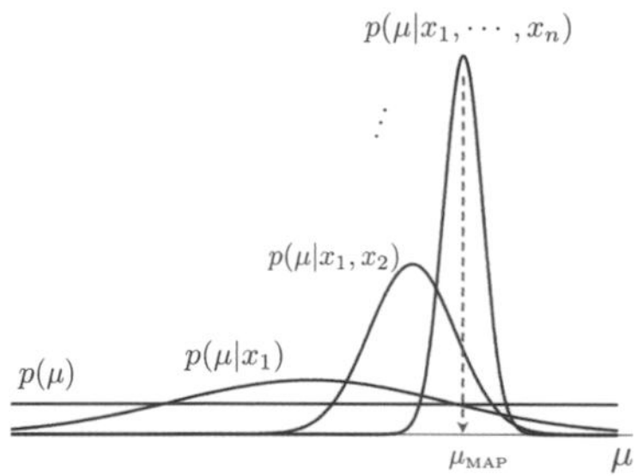

Figure 14.4: An illustration of how the posterior distributions evolve in the sequential Bayesian learning of a univariate Gaussian model.

where $\bar{x}_n = \frac{1}{n}\sum_{i=1}^{n} x_i$ denotes the sample mean of all observed data.

As shown in Figure 14.4, we can see that the posterior distribution is gradually updated whenever a new data sample is available. The posterior distribution gets sharper and sharper as we observe more and more data because we can see the variance $\tau_n^2 \to 0$ as $n \to \infty$ from the previous formula. This indicates that we are becoming more certain of the model parameter after observing more data samples. Moreover, we can also verify that the MAP estimate $\mu_{\text{MAP}} = \nu_n$ will converge to the maximum-likelihood estimation $\mu_{\text{MLE}} = \bar{x}_n$ as $n \to \infty$. ♦

14.2 Conjugate Priors

As we have discussed, even though Bayesian learning follows a simple multiplication rule, it still can make the resulting posterior distribution significantly more complicated than the prior distribution because of the complexity of the underlying likelihood function as well as the intractability of the integral in renormalization. On the other hand, Example 14.1.1 shows a good scenario of Bayesian learning from the perspective of computation. In that case, if we choose the prior distribution as a univariate Gaussian, we have seen that the posterior distribution derived from the Bayesian learning rule happens to take the same functional form as the prior (i.e., another univariate Gaussian), only taking updated parameters. This choice for a prior distribution allows us to enjoy great computational convenience in Bayesian learning because the multiplication of the prior and likelihood function ends up with the same functional form as the prior. Furthermore, we can even repeatedly apply the Bayesian learning rule as in the previous sequential learning case without complicating the functional form of any posterior at all.

Generally speaking, given a generative model, if we can find a particular functional form for the prior distribution so that the resultant posterior distribution from the Bayesian learning in Eq. (14.1) also takes the same functional form as the prior, we call this prior distribution a *conjugate prior* of the underlying generative model. In Example 14.1.1, the univariate Gaussian is the conjugate prior of the underlying model in that example, namely, a Gaussian model with known variance. However, the conjugate prior does not exist for all generative models, and in fact, only a small fraction of generative models have a conjugate prior. Once conjugate priors exist for the underlying models, we almost always choose the conjugate priors in Bayesian learning because of the huge computational advantage it offers. The well-established results in statistics [51, 26] have shown that a conjugate prior exists for all generative models in the e-family, and the exact form of the conjugate priors varies with the corresponding models.

Model $p(\mathbf{x}\|\boldsymbol{\theta})$	Conjugate prior $p(\boldsymbol{\theta})$
1D Gaussian (known variance) $\mathcal{N}(x \mid \mu, \sigma_0^2)$	1D Gaussian $\mathcal{N}(\mu \mid \nu, \tau^2)$
1D Gaussian (known mean) $\mathcal{N}(x \mid \mu_0, \sigma^2)$	Inverse-gamma $\text{gamma}^{-1}(\sigma^2 \mid \alpha, \beta)$
Gaussian (known covariance) $\mathcal{N}(\mathbf{x} \mid \boldsymbol{\mu}, \boldsymbol{\Sigma}_0)$	Gaussian $\mathcal{N}(\boldsymbol{\mu} \mid \boldsymbol{\nu}, \Phi)$
Gaussian (known mean) $\mathcal{N}(\mathbf{x} \mid \boldsymbol{\mu}_0, \boldsymbol{\Sigma})$	Inverse-Wishart $\mathcal{W}^{-1}(\boldsymbol{\Sigma} \mid \Phi, \nu)$
Multivariate Gaussian $\mathcal{N}(\mathbf{x} \mid \boldsymbol{\mu}, \boldsymbol{\Sigma})$	Gaussian-inverse-Wishart $\text{GIW}(\boldsymbol{\mu}, \boldsymbol{\Sigma} \mid \boldsymbol{\nu}, \Phi, \lambda, \nu) = \mathcal{N}(\boldsymbol{\mu} \mid \boldsymbol{\nu}, \frac{1}{\lambda}\boldsymbol{\Sigma})\, \mathcal{W}^{-1}(\boldsymbol{\Sigma} \mid \Phi, \nu)$
Multinomial $\text{Mult}(\mathbf{r} \mid \mathbf{w}) = C(\mathbf{r}) \cdot \prod_{i=1}^{M} w_i^{r_i}$ with $C(\mathbf{r}) = \frac{(r_1+\cdots+r_M)!}{r_1!\cdots r_M!}$	Dirichlet $\text{Dir}(\mathbf{w} \mid \boldsymbol{\alpha}) = B(\boldsymbol{\alpha}) \cdot \prod_{i=1}^{M} w_i^{\alpha_i - 1}$ with $B(\boldsymbol{\alpha}) = \frac{\Gamma(\alpha_1+\cdots+\alpha_M)}{\Gamma(\alpha_1)\cdots\Gamma(\alpha_M)}$

Table 14.1: A list of conjugate priors for some common e-family models used in machine learning. 1D = one-dimensional.

Note that the inverse-gamma distribution takes the following form:

$$\text{gamma}^{-1}(x \mid \alpha, \beta) = \frac{\beta^\alpha}{\Gamma(\alpha)} x^{-\alpha-1} e^{-\frac{\beta}{x}}$$

for all $x > 0$.

Table 14.1 lists the corresponding conjugate priors for several e-family distributions that play an important role in machine learning. For example, the conjugate prior of a multinomial model is a Dirichlet distribution. For a Gaussian model, if we know its covariance matrix, the conjugate priors are also Gaussian. If we know its mean vector, the conjugate priors are the so-called inverse-Wishart distributions (see margin note). If both the mean and covariance are unknown parameters, the conjugate priors are a product of Gaussian and inverse-Wishart distributions, which is normally called a *Gaussian-inverse-Wishart (GIW) distribution*.

Note that the inverse-Wishart distribution takes the following form:

$$\mathcal{W}^{-1}(\boldsymbol{\Sigma} \mid \Phi, \nu) =$$

$$\frac{|\Phi|^{\nu/2}}{2^{\nu d/2}\Gamma(\frac{\nu}{2})} |\boldsymbol{\Sigma}|^{-\frac{\nu+d+1}{2}} e^{-\frac{1}{2}\text{tr}(\Phi\boldsymbol{\Sigma}^{-1})},$$

where $\boldsymbol{\Sigma} \in \mathbb{R}^{d\times d}$, $\Phi \in \mathbb{R}^{d\times d}$, $\nu \in \mathbb{R}^+$, and $\Gamma(\cdot)$ represent the multivariate *gamma* function, and tr denotes the matrix trace.

The following two examples explain how to use conjugate priors for Bayesian learning of simple generative models in the e-family. In particular, they will show how the choice of conjugate priors can lead to some closed-form solutions to the MAP estimation of these models.

Example 14.2.1 Multinomial Models

If we use a multinomial model (i.e., $\text{Mult}(\mathbf{r} \mid \mathbf{w})$) to represent a distribution of some counts of M distinct symbols (i.e., $\mathbf{r} = [r_1\, r_2 \cdots r_M]$, where $r_i \in \mathbb{N} \cup \{0\}$ for all $i = 1, 2, \cdots M$), we can use the conjugate prior to derive the MAP estimation of the model parameters $\mathbf{w} = [w_1 \cdots w_M]$.

For example, the *bag-of-words* feature in Figure 4.1 is a set of counts of distinct words in a text document.

From Table 14.1, we choose the conjugate prior for the multinomial model, which is a Dirichlet distribution, given as follows:

$$p(\mathbf{w}) = \text{Dir}(\mathbf{w} \mid \boldsymbol{\alpha}^{(0)}) = B(\boldsymbol{\alpha}^{(0)}) \cdot \prod_{i=1}^{M} w_i^{\alpha_i^{(0)}-1},$$

where the hyperparameters $\boldsymbol{\alpha}^{(0)} = \left[\alpha_1^{(0)}\, \alpha_2^{(0)}\, \cdots \alpha_M^{(0)}\right]$ are manually set based on our prior knowledge of the model parameter $\mathbf{w}$.

Given a sample of some counts (i.e., $\mathbf{r} = \left[r_1\, r_2\, \cdots r_M\right]$), we compute the likelihood function of $\mathbf{w}$ as

$$p(\mathbf{r} \mid \mathbf{w}) = \text{Mult}(\mathbf{r} \mid \mathbf{w}) = C(\mathbf{r}) \cdot \prod_{i=1}^{M} w_i^{r_i}.$$

We apply the Bayesian learning rule in Eq. (14.1) as follows:

$$p(\mathbf{w} \mid \mathbf{r}) \propto p(\mathbf{w})\, p(\mathbf{r} \mid \mathbf{w}) \propto \prod_{i=1}^{M} w_i^{\alpha_i^{(0)}+r_i-1}.$$

If we denote $\boldsymbol{\alpha}^{(1)} = \left[\alpha_1^{(1)}\, \cdots\, \alpha_M^{(1)}\right]$ with each element as

$$\alpha_i^{(1)} = \alpha_i^{(0)} + r_i \quad \text{for all } i = 1, 2, \cdots, M$$

and renormalize the equation, we derive the posterior distribution as follows:

$$p(\mathbf{w} \mid \mathbf{r}) = \text{Dir}(\mathbf{w} \mid \boldsymbol{\alpha}^{(1)}) = B(\boldsymbol{\alpha}^{(1)}) \cdot \prod_{i=1}^{M} w_i^{\alpha_i^{(1)}-1}.$$

The MAP estimation of model parameter $\mathbf{w}$ is computed by solving the following constrained optimization problem:

$$\mathbf{w}^{(\text{MAP})} = \arg\max_{\mathbf{w}}\; p(\mathbf{w} \mid \mathbf{r}) \qquad \text{subject to} \;\; \sum_{i=1}^{M} w_i = 1.$$

It is clear that the MAP estimate depends on both the prior $\boldsymbol{\alpha}^{(0)}$ and the training data $\mathbf{r}$.

Using the method of Lagrange multipliers, we can solve $\mathbf{w}^{(\text{MAP})}$ in a closed-form solution. Each element in $\mathbf{w}^{(\text{MAP})}$ is computed as

$$w_i^{(\text{MAP})} = \frac{\alpha_i^{(1)} - 1}{\sum_{i=1}^{M} \alpha_i^{(1)} - M} = \frac{r_i + \alpha_i^{(0)} - 1}{\sum_{i=1}^{M} \left(r_i + \alpha_i^{(0)}\right) - M} \quad \text{for all } i = 1, 2, \cdots, M.$$

♦

Next, let us investigate how to use the conjugate prior for Bayesian learning of multivariate Gaussian models.

Example 14.2.2 Multivariate Gaussian Models

We use a multivariate Gaussian to represent a data distribution in $\mathbb{R}^d$ as $p(\mathbf{x}\,|\,\boldsymbol{\mu},\boldsymbol{\Sigma}) = \mathcal{N}(\mathbf{x}\,|\,\boldsymbol{\mu},\boldsymbol{\Sigma})$, where both the mean vector $\boldsymbol{\mu} \in \mathbb{R}^d$ and the covariance matrix $\boldsymbol{\Sigma} \in \mathbb{R}^{d\times d}$ are unknown model parameters. Given a training set of N samples as $\mathcal{D}_N = \{\mathbf{x}_1, \mathbf{x}_2, \cdots \mathbf{x}_N\}$, use the conjugate prior to derive the MAP estimation of all model parameters ($\boldsymbol{\mu}$ and $\boldsymbol{\Sigma}$).

First of all, from Table 14.1, we choose the conjugate prior for this multivariate Gaussian model, which is a GIW distribution, shown as follows:

$$
\begin{aligned}
p(\boldsymbol{\mu},\boldsymbol{\Sigma}) &= \mathrm{GIW}\big(\boldsymbol{\mu},\boldsymbol{\Sigma}\,\big|\,\boldsymbol{\nu}_0,\boldsymbol{\Phi}_0,\lambda_0,\nu_0\big) \\
&= \mathcal{N}\Big(\boldsymbol{\mu}\,\Big|\,\boldsymbol{\nu}_0,\frac{1}{\lambda_0}\boldsymbol{\Sigma}\Big)\,\mathcal{W}^{-1}\Big(\boldsymbol{\Sigma}\,\Big|\,\boldsymbol{\Phi}_0,\nu_0\Big) \\
&= \frac{\lambda_0^{1/2}}{(2\pi)^{d/2}|\boldsymbol{\Sigma}|^{1/2}}\, e^{-\frac{\lambda_0(\boldsymbol{\mu}-\boldsymbol{\nu}_0)^\intercal\boldsymbol{\Sigma}^{-1}(\boldsymbol{\mu}-\boldsymbol{\nu}_0)}{2}}\;\frac{\big|\boldsymbol{\Phi}_0\big|^{\nu_0/2}}{2^{\nu_0 d/2}\,\Gamma(\frac{\nu_0}{2})}\big|\boldsymbol{\Sigma}\big|^{-\frac{\nu_0+d+1}{2}}\;e^{-\frac{1}{2}\mathrm{tr}(\boldsymbol{\Phi}_0\boldsymbol{\Sigma}^{-1})} \\
&= c_0\,\big|\boldsymbol{\Sigma}^{-1}\big|^{\frac{\nu_0+d+2}{2}}\exp\Big[-\frac{1}{2}\lambda_0(\boldsymbol{\mu}-\boldsymbol{\nu}_0)^\intercal\boldsymbol{\Sigma}^{-1}(\boldsymbol{\mu}-\boldsymbol{\nu}_0)-\frac{1}{2}\mathrm{tr}(\boldsymbol{\Phi}_0\boldsymbol{\Sigma}^{-1})\Big],
\end{aligned}
$$

Note that the normalization factor

$$c_0 = \frac{\lambda_0^{1/2}\cdot\big|\boldsymbol{\Phi}_0\big|^{\nu_0/2}}{(2\pi)^{d/2}\cdot 2^{\nu_0 d/2}\cdot\Gamma(\frac{\nu_0}{2})}$$

is a constant independent of $\boldsymbol{\mu}$ and $\boldsymbol{\Sigma}$.

where the hyperparameters $\{\boldsymbol{\nu}_0,\boldsymbol{\Phi}_0,\lambda_0,\nu_0\}$ will have to be manually set based on our prior knowledge of the Gaussian model parameters.

Second, if we denote the sample mean, $\bar{\mathbf{x}}$, and the sample covariance matrix, $\mathbf{S}$, of all training samples in $\mathcal{D}_N$ as

$$\bar{\mathbf{x}} = \frac{1}{N}\sum_{i=1}^N \mathbf{x}_i \quad\text{and}\quad \mathbf{S} = \frac{1}{N}\sum_{i=1}^N(\mathbf{x}_i-\bar{\mathbf{x}})(\mathbf{x}_i-\bar{\mathbf{x}})^\intercal,$$

we can compute the likelihood function as follows:

See Exercise Q14.2 for

$$
\begin{aligned}
&\sum_{i=1}^N(\mathbf{x}_i-\boldsymbol{\mu})^\intercal\boldsymbol{\Sigma}^{-1}(\mathbf{x}_i-\boldsymbol{\mu}) \\
&= \sum_{i=1}^N(\mathbf{x}_i-\bar{\mathbf{x}})^\intercal\boldsymbol{\Sigma}^{-1}(\mathbf{x}_i-\bar{\mathbf{x}}) \\
&\quad + N(\boldsymbol{\mu}-\bar{\mathbf{x}})^\intercal\boldsymbol{\Sigma}^{-1}(\boldsymbol{\mu}-\bar{\mathbf{x}}).
\end{aligned}
$$

$$
\begin{aligned}
p(\mathcal{D}_N\,|\,\boldsymbol{\mu},\boldsymbol{\Sigma}) &= \prod_{i=1}^N p(\mathbf{x}_i\,|\,\boldsymbol{\mu},\boldsymbol{\Sigma}) \\
&= \frac{\big|\boldsymbol{\Sigma}^{-1}\big|^{\frac{N}{2}}}{(2\pi)^{Nd/2}}\exp\Big[-\frac{1}{2}\underbrace{\sum_{i=1}^N(\mathbf{x}_i-\boldsymbol{\mu})^\intercal\boldsymbol{\Sigma}^{-1}(\mathbf{x}_i-\boldsymbol{\mu})}_{\text{see margin note}}\Big] \\
&= \frac{\big|\boldsymbol{\Sigma}^{-1}\big|^{\frac{N}{2}}}{(2\pi)^{Nd/2}}\exp\Big[-\frac{1}{2}\underbrace{\sum_{i=1}^N(\mathbf{x}_i-\bar{\mathbf{x}})^\intercal\boldsymbol{\Sigma}^{-1}(\mathbf{x}_i-\bar{\mathbf{x}})}_{\mathrm{tr}\left(\left(\sum_{i=1}^N(\mathbf{x}_i-\bar{\mathbf{x}})(\mathbf{x}_i-\bar{\mathbf{x}})^\intercal\right)\boldsymbol{\Sigma}^{-1}\right)}-\frac{N}{2}(\boldsymbol{\mu}-\bar{\mathbf{x}})^\intercal\boldsymbol{\Sigma}^{-1}(\boldsymbol{\mu}-\bar{\mathbf{x}})\Big].
\end{aligned}
$$

See Exercise Q14.2 for

$$
\begin{aligned}
&\sum_{i=1}^N(\mathbf{x}_i-\bar{\mathbf{x}})^\intercal\boldsymbol{\Sigma}^{-1}(\mathbf{x}_i-\bar{\mathbf{x}}) \\
&= \mathrm{tr}\Big(\Big(\sum_{i=1}^N(\mathbf{x}_i-\bar{\mathbf{x}})(\mathbf{x}_i-\bar{\mathbf{x}})^\intercal\Big)\boldsymbol{\Sigma}^{-1}\Big) \\
&= \mathrm{tr}\Big(N\mathbf{S}\,\boldsymbol{\Sigma}^{-1}\Big).
\end{aligned}
$$

Furthermore, we can represent the previous likelihood function of the multivariate Gaussian model with the sample mean vector, $\bar{\mathbf{x}}$, and the sample covariance matrix, $\mathbf{S}$, as follows:

$$p(\mathfrak{D}_N \mid \boldsymbol{\mu}, \boldsymbol{\Sigma}) = \frac{\left|\boldsymbol{\Sigma}^{-1}\right|^{\frac{N}{2}}}{(2\pi)^{Nd/2}} \exp\Big[-\frac{1}{2}\mathrm{tr}\big(N\mathbf{S}\,\boldsymbol{\Sigma}^{-1}\big) - \frac{N}{2}(\boldsymbol{\mu}-\bar{\mathbf{x}})^\intercal\boldsymbol{\Sigma}^{-1}(\boldsymbol{\mu}-\bar{\mathbf{x}})\Big].$$

Next, when we apply the Bayesian learning rule, we can derive the posterior distribution as follows:

$$p(\boldsymbol{\mu}, \boldsymbol{\Sigma} \mid \mathfrak{D}_N) \propto \mathrm{GIW}(\boldsymbol{\mu}, \boldsymbol{\Sigma} \mid \boldsymbol{\nu}_0, \Phi_0, \lambda_0, \nu_0) \cdot p(\mathfrak{D}_N \mid \boldsymbol{\mu}, \boldsymbol{\Sigma}).$$

For how to merge the two terms with respect to $\boldsymbol{\mu}$:

$$\lambda_0(\boldsymbol{\mu}-\boldsymbol{\nu}_0)^\intercal\boldsymbol{\Sigma}^{-1}(\boldsymbol{\mu}-\boldsymbol{\nu}_0) + N(\boldsymbol{\mu}-\bar{\mathbf{x}})^\intercal\boldsymbol{\Sigma}^{-1}(\boldsymbol{\mu}-\bar{\mathbf{x}})$$

$$\begin{aligned}
&= (\lambda_0+N)\boldsymbol{\mu}^\intercal\boldsymbol{\Sigma}^{-1}\boldsymbol{\mu} - 2\boldsymbol{\mu}^\intercal\boldsymbol{\Sigma}^{-1}(\lambda_0\boldsymbol{\nu}_0 + N\bar{\mathbf{x}}) \\
&\quad + \lambda_0\boldsymbol{\nu}_0^\intercal\boldsymbol{\Sigma}^{-1}\boldsymbol{\nu}_0 + N\bar{\mathbf{x}}^\intercal\boldsymbol{\Sigma}^{-1}\bar{\mathbf{x}} \\
&= (\lambda_0+N)\Big[\boldsymbol{\mu}^\intercal\boldsymbol{\Sigma}^{-1}\boldsymbol{\mu} - 2\boldsymbol{\mu}^\intercal\boldsymbol{\Sigma}^{-1}\frac{\lambda_0\boldsymbol{\nu}_0 + N\bar{\mathbf{x}}}{\lambda_0+N}\Big] \\
&\quad + \lambda_0\boldsymbol{\nu}_0^\intercal\boldsymbol{\Sigma}^{-1}\boldsymbol{\nu}_0 + N\bar{\mathbf{x}}^\intercal\boldsymbol{\Sigma}^{-1}\bar{\mathbf{x}} \\
&= \lambda_1(\boldsymbol{\mu}-\boldsymbol{\nu}_1)^\intercal\boldsymbol{\Sigma}^{-1}(\boldsymbol{\mu}-\boldsymbol{\nu}_1) \\
&\quad - \frac{(\lambda_0\boldsymbol{\nu}_0 + N\bar{\mathbf{x}})^\intercal\boldsymbol{\Sigma}^{-1}(\lambda_0\boldsymbol{\nu}_0 + N\bar{\mathbf{x}})}{\lambda_0+N} \\
&\quad + \lambda_0\boldsymbol{\nu}_0^\intercal\boldsymbol{\Sigma}^{-1}\boldsymbol{\nu}_0 + N\bar{\mathbf{x}}^\intercal\boldsymbol{\Sigma}^{-1}\bar{\mathbf{x}} \\
&= \lambda_1(\boldsymbol{\mu}-\boldsymbol{\nu}_1)^\intercal\boldsymbol{\Sigma}^{-1}(\boldsymbol{\mu}-\boldsymbol{\nu}_1) \\
&\quad + \frac{\lambda_0 N}{\lambda_0+N}\underbrace{(\bar{\mathbf{x}}-\boldsymbol{\nu}_0)^\intercal\boldsymbol{\Sigma}^{-1}(\bar{\mathbf{x}}-\boldsymbol{\nu}_0)}_{\mathrm{tr}\left((\bar{\mathbf{x}}-\boldsymbol{\nu}_0)(\bar{\mathbf{x}}-\boldsymbol{\nu}_0)^\intercal\boldsymbol{\Sigma}^{-1}\right)}.
\end{aligned}$$

We can further denote the following:

$$\lambda_1 = \lambda_0 + N \tag{14.9}$$

$$\nu_1 = \nu_0 + N \tag{14.10}$$

$$\boldsymbol{\nu}_1 = \frac{\lambda_0\boldsymbol{\nu}_0 + N\bar{\mathbf{x}}}{\lambda_0 + N} \tag{14.11}$$

$$\Phi_1 = \Phi_0 + N\mathbf{S} + \frac{\lambda_0 N}{\lambda_0 + N}(\bar{\mathbf{x}}-\boldsymbol{\nu}_0)(\bar{\mathbf{x}}-\boldsymbol{\nu}_0)^\intercal. \tag{14.12}$$

After substituting the prior and likelihood function into the previous equation and merging the terms (see margin note), we finally derive

$$p(\boldsymbol{\mu}, \boldsymbol{\Sigma} \mid \mathfrak{D}_N) \propto \left|\boldsymbol{\Sigma}\right|^{-\frac{\nu_1+d+2}{2}} \exp\Big[-\frac{1}{2}\lambda_1(\boldsymbol{\mu}-\boldsymbol{\nu}_1)^\intercal\boldsymbol{\Sigma}^{-1}(\boldsymbol{\mu}-\boldsymbol{\nu}_1) - \frac{1}{2}\mathrm{tr}\big(\Phi_1\boldsymbol{\Sigma}^{-1}\big)\Big].$$

According to Haff [89], we can explicitly solve the integral of the previous equation w.r.t. $\boldsymbol{\mu}$ and $\boldsymbol{\Sigma}$ and properly normalize it as a valid probability distribution:

$$p(\boldsymbol{\mu}, \boldsymbol{\Sigma} \mid \mathfrak{D}_N) = c_1\left|\boldsymbol{\Sigma}^{-1}\right|^{\frac{\nu_1+d+2}{2}} \exp\Big[-\frac{1}{2}\lambda_1(\boldsymbol{\mu}-\boldsymbol{\nu}_1)^\intercal\boldsymbol{\Sigma}^{-1}(\boldsymbol{\mu}-\boldsymbol{\nu}_1) - \frac{1}{2}\mathrm{tr}\big(\Phi_1\boldsymbol{\Sigma}^{-1}\big)\Big]$$

with a new normalization factor

$$c_1 = \frac{\lambda_1^{1/2}\cdot\left|\Phi_1\right|^{\nu_1/2}}{(2\pi)^{d/2}\cdot 2^{\nu_1 d/2}\cdot\Gamma(\frac{\nu_1}{2})}.$$

We can see that the posterior distribution is still a GIW distribution with all hyperparameters updated in Eqs. (14.9)–(14.12):

$$p(\boldsymbol{\mu}, \boldsymbol{\Sigma} \mid \mathfrak{D}_N) = \mathrm{GIW}(\boldsymbol{\mu}, \boldsymbol{\Sigma} \mid \boldsymbol{\nu}_1, \Phi_1, \lambda_1, \nu_1). \tag{14.13}$$

The MAP estimation of Gaussian model parameters is computed as

$$\{\boldsymbol{\mu}_{\text{MAP}}, \boldsymbol{\Sigma}_{\text{MAP}}\} = \arg\max_{\boldsymbol{\mu},\boldsymbol{\Sigma}} \; p(\boldsymbol{\mu}, \boldsymbol{\Sigma} \,|\, \mathfrak{D}_N).$$

According to Kendall et al. [127], the mode of the Gaussian-inverse-distribution can be derived in the following closed-form solution:

We can see that the MAP estimation depends on both the prior and the training data. As $N \to \infty$, the MAP estimate approaches the MLE.

$$\boldsymbol{\mu}_{\text{MAP}} = \boldsymbol{\nu}_1 = \frac{\lambda_0 \boldsymbol{\nu}_0 + N\bar{\mathbf{x}}}{\lambda_0 + N}$$

$$\begin{aligned} \boldsymbol{\Sigma}_{\text{MAP}} &= \frac{\boldsymbol{\Phi}_1}{\nu_1 + d + 1} \\ &= \frac{\boldsymbol{\Phi}_0 + N\mathbf{S} + \frac{\lambda_0 N}{\lambda_0 + N}\left(\bar{\mathbf{x}} - \boldsymbol{\nu}_0\right)\left(\bar{\mathbf{x}} - \boldsymbol{\nu}_0\right)^{\mathsf{T}}}{\nu_0 + N + d + 1}. \end{aligned}$$

♦

14.2.1 Maximum-Marginal-Likelihood Estimation

Another issue related to the prior specification is how to set the hyperparameters in the chosen prior distribution. The strict Bayesian theory argues that the prior specification is a subject matter and that all hyperparameters should be set based on our prior knowledge of and initial beliefs about the model parameters. In these cases, setting the hyperparameters is more an art than a science.

On the other hand, in the so-called *empirical Bayes methods* [158], we aim to estimate the prior distribution from the data. Assume we have chosen the prior distribution as $p(\boldsymbol{\theta} \,|\, \boldsymbol{\alpha})$, where $\boldsymbol{\theta}$ denotes the model parameters, and $\boldsymbol{\alpha}$ denotes the unknown hyperparameters. Given a training set $\mathfrak{D}$ of some data samples, we may compute the so-called *marginal likelihood* by marginalizing out the model parameters in the standard likelihood function as follows:

$$p(\mathfrak{D} \,|\, \boldsymbol{\alpha}) = \int_{\boldsymbol{\theta}} p(\mathfrak{D} \,|\, \boldsymbol{\theta})\, p(\boldsymbol{\theta} \,|\, \boldsymbol{\alpha})\; d\boldsymbol{\theta}.$$

In this case, we may choose the hyperparameters that maximize the marginal likelihood $p(\mathfrak{D} \,|\, \boldsymbol{\alpha})$ as

$$\boldsymbol{\alpha}^* = \arg\max_{\boldsymbol{\alpha}} \; p(\mathfrak{D} \,|\, \boldsymbol{\alpha}).$$

This method of setting the hyperparameters for a prior distribution is usually called *maximum-marginal-likelihood estimation*.

14.3 Approximate Inference

As we have seen from the previous sections, conjugate priors are a very convenient tool to facilitate computation in Bayesian learning. However, the conjugate priors exist only for a small number of relatively simple generative models. For most generative models popular in machine learning, we cannot rely on the concept of conjugate priors to simplify Bayesian learning. For these generative models, the Bayesian learning rule will inevitably yield very complicated and even intractable posterior distributions. In practice, a well-adopted strategy is to use some manageable probability functions to approximate the true but intractable posterior distributions in Bayesian learning. In the following, we will consider two widely used approximate inference methods in Bayesian learning. The first method aims to approximate the true posterior distributions using tractable Gaussian distributions, which leads to the traditional *Laplace's method* [139]. Second, a convenient computational framework called the *variational Bayesian (VB)* method [5] has been recently proposed to approximate the true posterior distributions using a family of more manageable probability functions that can be factorized among various model parameters.

14.3.1 Laplace's Method

The key idea behind Laplace's method is to approximate the true posterior distribution using a multivariate Gaussian distribution. Let's discuss how to construct such a Gaussian distribution to approximate an arbitrary posterior distribution. We first find a MAP estimate $\boldsymbol{\theta}_{\text{MAP}}$ at a mode of the true posterior distribution $p(\boldsymbol{\theta} \mid \mathcal{D})$. Second, we expand the logarithm of the true distribution, denoted as $f(\boldsymbol{\theta}) = \ln p(\boldsymbol{\theta} \mid \mathcal{D})$, around $\boldsymbol{\theta}_{\text{MAP}}$ according to Taylor's theorem:

$$f(\boldsymbol{\theta}) = f(\boldsymbol{\theta}_{\text{MAP}}) + \nabla(\boldsymbol{\theta}_{\text{MAP}})(\boldsymbol{\theta} - \boldsymbol{\theta}_{\text{MAP}}) + \frac{1}{2!}(\boldsymbol{\theta} - \boldsymbol{\theta}_{\text{MAP}})^{\intercal}\mathbf{H}(\boldsymbol{\theta}_{\text{MAP}})(\boldsymbol{\theta} - \boldsymbol{\theta}_{\text{MAP}}) + \cdots,$$

where $\nabla(\boldsymbol{\theta}_{\text{MAP}})$ and $\mathbf{H}(\boldsymbol{\theta}_{\text{MAP}})$ denote the gradient and Hessian matrix, respectively, of the function $f(\boldsymbol{\theta})$ evaluated at $\boldsymbol{\theta}_{\text{MAP}}$.

Because the MAP estimate $\boldsymbol{\theta}_{\text{MAP}}$ is a maximum point of the true posterior distribution, we have $\nabla(\boldsymbol{\theta}_{\text{MAP}}) = 0$, and $\mathbf{H}(\boldsymbol{\theta}_{\text{MAP}})$ is a negative definite matrix. *Laplace's method* [153, 6] aims to approximate $f(\boldsymbol{\theta})$ using the second-order Taylor series around a stationary point $\boldsymbol{\theta}_{\text{MAP}}$:

$$f(\boldsymbol{\theta}) \approx f(\boldsymbol{\theta}_{\text{MAP}}) + \frac{(\boldsymbol{\theta} - \boldsymbol{\theta}_{\text{MAP}})^{\intercal}\mathbf{H}(\boldsymbol{\theta}_{\text{MAP}})(\boldsymbol{\theta} - \boldsymbol{\theta}_{\text{MAP}})}{2}.$$

After we take the exponent of both sides and properly normalize the right-hand side, it yields a multivariate Gaussian distribution well approximating the true posterior distribution around $\boldsymbol{\theta}_{\text{MAP}}$, as shown in Figure 14.5:

$$p(\boldsymbol{\theta} \mid \mathcal{D}) \approx \underbrace{C \cdot \exp\left(\frac{1}{2}(\boldsymbol{\theta} - \boldsymbol{\theta}_{\text{MAP}})^\intercal \mathbf{H}(\boldsymbol{\theta}_{\text{MAP}})(\boldsymbol{\theta} - \boldsymbol{\theta}_{\text{MAP}})\right)}_{\mathcal{N}\left(\boldsymbol{\theta}_{\text{MAP}}, -\mathbf{H}^{-1}(\boldsymbol{\theta}_{\text{MAP}})\right)}.$$

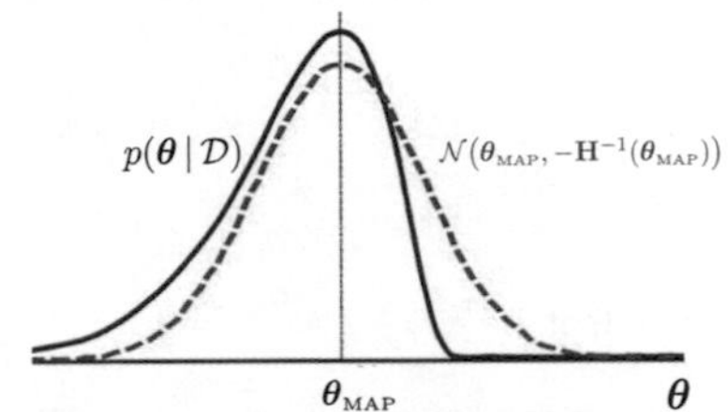

Figure 14.5: An illustration of how to construct a multivariate Gaussian distribution to approximate the true posterior distributions in Laplace's method.

In summary, Laplace's method requires us to find a MAP estimation and then evaluate the Hessian matrix at this point to construct the approximating Gaussian distribution. In the following, we will use Bayesian learning of logistic regression as an example to show how to construct the approximating Gaussian with Laplace's method.

As shown in Section 11.4, logistic regression is a generative model for binary-classification problems. Given a training set of input–output pairs, $\mathcal{D} = \{(\mathbf{x}_1, y_1), (\mathbf{x}_2, y_2), \cdots, (\mathbf{x}_N, y_N)\}$, where each $\mathbf{x}_i \in \mathbb{R}^d$ and $y_i \in \{0, 1\}$, the likelihood function of logistic regression is expressed as

$$p(\mathcal{D} \mid \mathbf{w}) = \prod_{i=1}^{N} \left(l(\mathbf{w}^\intercal \mathbf{x}_i)\right)^{y_i} \left(1 - l(\mathbf{w}^\intercal \mathbf{x}_i)\right)^{1-y_i},$$

where $\mathbf{w} \in \mathbb{R}^d$ denotes the parameters of the logistic regression model, and $l(\cdot)$ is the sigmoid function in Eq. (6.12).

There exist no conjugate priors for any generalized linear models in Section 11.4, including logistic regression. For computational convenience, we choose a Gaussian distribution as the prior distribution of model parameters $\mathbf{w}$:

$$p(\mathbf{w}) = \mathcal{N}\left(\mathbf{w} \mid \mathbf{w}_0, \boldsymbol{\Sigma}_0\right),$$

where the hyperparameters $\mathbf{w}_0$ and $\boldsymbol{\Sigma}_0$ denote the mean vector and covariance matrix of the prior distribution, respectively.

After we apply the Bayesian learning rule, the posterior distribution of $\mathbf{w}$ is derived as follows:

$$p(\mathbf{w} \mid \mathcal{D}) \propto p(\mathbf{w})\, p(\mathcal{D} \mid \mathbf{w}).$$

In this case, the posterior distribution takes a fairly complex form. Here, let us explore how to use Laplace's method to obtain a Gaussian approximation to this posterior distribution.

If we take the logarithm of both sides, we obtain

$$\begin{aligned}\ln p(\mathbf{w}\,|\,\mathcal{D}) &= C - \frac{1}{2}(\mathbf{w}-\mathbf{w}_0)^\mathsf{T}\boldsymbol{\Sigma}_0^{-1}(\mathbf{w}-\mathbf{w}_0) \\ &+ \sum_{i=1}^{N}\Big(y_i \ln l(\mathbf{w}^\mathsf{T}\mathbf{x}_i) + (1-y_i)\ln\big(1-l(\mathbf{w}^\mathsf{T}\mathbf{x}_i)\big)\Big).\end{aligned}$$

Here, C is a constant, independent of $\mathbf{w}$.

First of all, we need to maximize the posterior distribution to derive the MAP estimation $\mathbf{w}_{\text{MAP}}$, which will define the mean of the Gaussian approximation. There is no closed-form solution to derive the MAP estimation from the posterior distribution. We need to compute the gradient as

Recall that

$$1 - l(x) = l(-x)$$

$$\frac{d}{dx} l(x) = l(x)(1 - l(x)).$$

$$\nabla(\mathbf{w}) = \nabla \ln p(\mathbf{w}\,|\,\mathcal{D}) = -\boldsymbol{\Sigma}_0^{-1}(\mathbf{w}-\mathbf{w}_0) + \sum_{i=1}^{N}\big(y_i - l(\mathbf{w}^\mathsf{T}\mathbf{x}_i)\big)\mathbf{x}_i$$

and use a gradient-descent method to iteratively derive the MAP estimation $\mathbf{w}_{\text{MAP}}$.

Furthermore, we may compute the Hessian matrix for the previous function as follows:

$$\mathbf{H}(\mathbf{w}) = \nabla\nabla \ln p(\mathbf{w}\,|\,\mathcal{D}) = -\boldsymbol{\Sigma}_0^{-1} - \sum_{i=1}^{N} l(\mathbf{w}^\mathsf{T}\mathbf{x}_i)\big(1-l(\mathbf{w}^\mathsf{T}\mathbf{x}_i)\big)\,\mathbf{x}_i\mathbf{x}_i^\mathsf{T}.$$

Finally, the Gaussian approximation to the posterior distribution of the logistic regression takes the following form:

$$p(\mathbf{w}\,|\,\mathcal{D}) \approx \mathcal{N}\Big(\mathbf{w}\,\Big|\,\mathbf{w}_{\text{MAP}}, -\mathbf{H}^{-1}(\mathbf{w}_{\text{MAP}})\Big).$$

This approximate Gaussian can be further used in Eq. (14.2) to derive an approximate predictive distribution for Bayesian inference [151].

Laplace's method is a convenient way to approximate the true posterior distributions in Bayesian learning. However, it is only applicable to unconstrained real-valued model parameters because the functional form is restricted to be Gaussian. The next section introduces a more general approximation strategy, which is based on the variational bound used in the variational autoencoders (VAEs) described in Section 13.4.

14.3.2 Variational Bayesian (VB) Methods

In the VB method [247, 213, 109, 5], we aim to approximate the true posterior distribution $p(\boldsymbol{\theta}\,|\,\mathcal{D})$ with a so-called *variational distribution* $q(\boldsymbol{\theta})$ from a family of tractable probability functions. The key idea is to search for the best fit within the tractable family by minimizing the Kullback–Leibler (KL) divergence between these two distributions:

$$q^*(\boldsymbol{\theta}) = \arg\min_q \ \mathrm{KL}\Big(q(\boldsymbol{\theta}) \,\|\, p(\boldsymbol{\theta} \,|\, \mathfrak{D})\Big).$$

Similar to the variational bound of the VAE , we rearrange the KL divergence and represent it as follows [170]:

$$\mathrm{KL}\Big(q(\boldsymbol{\theta}) \,\|\, p(\boldsymbol{\theta} \,|\, \mathfrak{D})\Big) = \ln p(\mathfrak{D}) - \underbrace{\int_{\boldsymbol{\theta}} q(\boldsymbol{\theta}) \ln \frac{p(\mathfrak{D}, \boldsymbol{\theta})}{q(\boldsymbol{\theta})} \, d\boldsymbol{\theta},}_{L(q)}$$

Substituting $p(\boldsymbol{\theta}|\mathfrak{D}) = \frac{p(\mathfrak{D},\boldsymbol{\theta})}{p(\mathfrak{D})}$ into

$$\mathrm{KL}\Big(q(\boldsymbol{\theta}) \,\|\, p(\boldsymbol{\theta}|\mathfrak{D})\Big)$$

$$= \int_{\boldsymbol{\theta}} q(\boldsymbol{\theta}) \ln \frac{q(\boldsymbol{\theta})}{p(\boldsymbol{\theta}|\mathfrak{D})} d\boldsymbol{\theta}$$

$$= \underbrace{\int_{\boldsymbol{\theta}} q(\boldsymbol{\theta}) \ln p(\mathfrak{D}) d\boldsymbol{\theta}}_{= \ln p(\mathfrak{D})} - \int_{\boldsymbol{\theta}} q(\boldsymbol{\theta}) \ln \frac{p(\mathfrak{D},\boldsymbol{\theta})}{q(\boldsymbol{\theta})} \, d\boldsymbol{\theta}.$$

where $p(\mathfrak{D})$ is the evidence of the data, and $L(q)$ is also called the *evidence lower bound* because it is a lower bound on the evidence. We can easily verify this equation by expanding all these terms (see margin note). Because the evidence $p(\mathfrak{D})$ is independent of $q(\boldsymbol{\theta})$, we have the following:

$$\min_q \ \mathrm{KL}\Big(q(\boldsymbol{\theta}) \,\|\, p(\boldsymbol{\theta} \,|\, \mathfrak{D})\Big) \iff \max_q \ L(q).$$

In other words, we may instead look for the best-fit variational distribution $q^*(\boldsymbol{\theta})$ by maximizing the evidence lower bound. As we will see, under some conditions, we can even solve this maximization problem analytically so as to derive the best-fit $q^*(\boldsymbol{\theta})$ explicitly.

An important condition under which this maximization problem can be analytically solved is that the variational distribution $q(\boldsymbol{\theta})$ can be factorized among various model parameters in $\boldsymbol{\theta}$. Assume we can partition all model parameters in $\boldsymbol{\theta}$ into some disjoint subsets $\boldsymbol{\theta} = \boldsymbol{\theta}_1 \cup \boldsymbol{\theta}_2 \cup \cdots \cup \boldsymbol{\theta}_I$, and $q(\boldsymbol{\theta})$ can be factorized accordingly as follows:

$$q(\boldsymbol{\theta}) = q_1(\boldsymbol{\theta}_1)\, q_2(\boldsymbol{\theta}_2) \,\cdots\, q_I(\boldsymbol{\theta}_I). \tag{14.14}$$

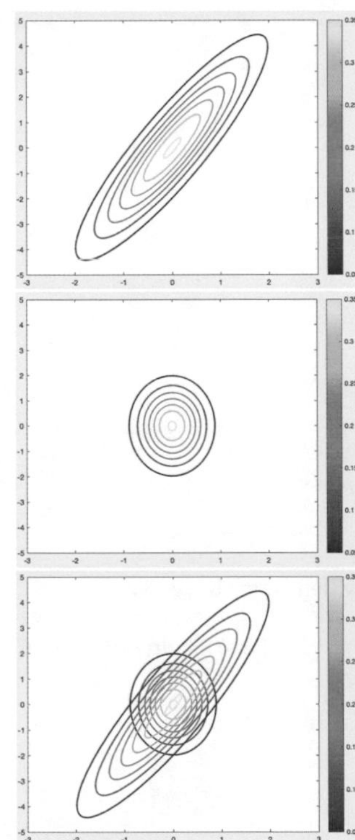

Figure 14.6: An illustration of the approximation scheme in the mean field theory. Top image: A two-dimensional (2D) Gaussian with the covariance matrix $\boldsymbol{\Sigma} = \begin{bmatrix} 1 & 2 \\ 2 & 5 \end{bmatrix}$. Middle image: The best-fit factorized 2D Gaussian $\begin{bmatrix} \sigma_1^2 & 0 \\ 0 & \sigma_2^2 \end{bmatrix}$ is found by minimizing the KL divergence. Bottom image: Both distributions are plotted together to show that the mean field theory may give a rough approximation when two components are strongly correlated.

Note that the true posterior distribution $p(\boldsymbol{\theta} \,|\, \mathfrak{D})$ usually cannot be factorized in any way. However, we may choose to use any parameter partition to factorize the variational distribution $q(\boldsymbol{\theta})$ in many different ways. Each partition usually results in one particular approximation scheme. The more we partition $\boldsymbol{\theta}$ in Eq. (14.14), the easier it usually is to solve the maximization problem. Meanwhile, this means we try to approximate $p(\boldsymbol{\theta} \,|\, \mathfrak{D})$ from a more restricted family of probability functions. In practice, we should partition $\boldsymbol{\theta}$ in a proper way to ensure a good trade-off between approximation accuracy and the ease of solving the maximization problem.

This factorization corresponds to the concept of *mean field theory* in physics [40], where the effect of all other components on any given component is approximated by a single averaged effect. In doing so, the correlation among these components is essentially ignored. As shown in Figure 14.6, a joint distribution of two correlated Gaussian random variables is approximated by a factorized model of two independent Gaussian variables. As we can see, the mean field theory is not always a good approximation method, and it may provide a rough approximation if the correlation between variables is strong.

If we substitute the previously factorized $q(\boldsymbol{\theta})$ in Eq. (14.14) into the evidence lower bound $L(q)$, we have

$$\begin{aligned} L(q) &= \int_{\boldsymbol{\theta}} \prod_{i=1}^{I} q_i(\boldsymbol{\theta}_i) \Big[\ln p(\mathfrak{D}, \boldsymbol{\theta}) - \sum_{i=1}^{I} \ln q_i(\boldsymbol{\theta}_i) \Big] \, d\boldsymbol{\theta} \\ &= \int_{\boldsymbol{\theta}} \prod_{i=1}^{I} q_i(\boldsymbol{\theta}_i) \ln p(\mathfrak{D}, \boldsymbol{\theta}) d\boldsymbol{\theta} - \sum_{i=1}^{I} \int_{\boldsymbol{\theta}_i} q_i(\boldsymbol{\theta}_i) \ln q_i(\boldsymbol{\theta}_i) d\boldsymbol{\theta}_i. \end{aligned}$$

Let us consider maximizing $L(q)$ w.r.t. each factor $q_i(\boldsymbol{\theta}_i)$ separately. For any $i = 1, 2, \cdots, I$, we have

$$\max_{q_i} \int_{\boldsymbol{\theta}_i} q_i(\boldsymbol{\theta}_i) \underbrace{\Big[\int_{\boldsymbol{\theta}_{j \neq i}} \prod_{j \neq i} q_j(\boldsymbol{\theta}_j) \ln p(\mathfrak{D}, \boldsymbol{\theta}) d\boldsymbol{\theta}_{j \neq i} \Big]}_{\mathbb{E}_{j \neq i} \left[\ln p(\mathfrak{D}, \boldsymbol{\theta}) \right]} d\boldsymbol{\theta}_i - \int_{\boldsymbol{\theta}_i} q_i(\boldsymbol{\theta}_i) \ln q_i(\boldsymbol{\theta}_i) d\boldsymbol{\theta}_i.$$

Using the expectation term $\mathbb{E}_{j \neq i} \big[\ln p(\mathfrak{D}, \boldsymbol{\theta}) \big]$, we can define a new distribution for $\boldsymbol{\theta}_i$ as follows:

$$\widetilde{p}(\boldsymbol{\theta}_i; \mathfrak{D}) \propto \exp\Big(\mathbb{E}_{j \neq i} \big[\ln p(\mathfrak{D}, \boldsymbol{\theta}) \big] \Big).$$

Equivalently, we have

$$\mathbb{E}_{j \neq i} \big[\ln p(\mathfrak{D}, \boldsymbol{\theta}) \big] = \ln \widetilde{p}(\boldsymbol{\theta}_i; \mathfrak{D}) + C.$$

Based on this new distribution, we can equivalently represent the maximization problem as follows:

$$\begin{aligned} & q_i^*(\boldsymbol{\theta}_i) = \arg\max_{q_i} \int_{\boldsymbol{\theta}_i} q_i(\boldsymbol{\theta}_i) \ln \frac{\widetilde{p}(\boldsymbol{\theta}_i; \mathfrak{D})}{q_i(\boldsymbol{\theta}_i)} d\boldsymbol{\theta}_i \\ \Longrightarrow \quad & q_i^*(\boldsymbol{\theta}_i) = \arg\min_{q_i} \ \mathrm{KL}\Big(q_i(\boldsymbol{\theta}_i) \, \| \, \widetilde{p}(\boldsymbol{\theta}_i; \mathfrak{D}) \Big). \end{aligned}$$

Because the KL divergence is nonnegative and it achieves the minimum only when two distributions are identical, we can derive that

$$q_i^*(\boldsymbol{\theta}_i) = \widetilde{p}(\boldsymbol{\theta}_i; \mathfrak{D}) \propto \exp\Big(\mathbb{E}_{j \neq i} \big[\ln p(\mathfrak{D}, \boldsymbol{\theta}) \big] \Big). \tag{14.15}$$

Or equivalently,

$$\ln q_i^*(\boldsymbol{\theta}_i) = \mathbb{E}_{j \neq i} \big[\ln p(\mathfrak{D}, \boldsymbol{\theta}) \big] + C, \tag{14.16}$$

where C is a constant, independent of model parameters $\boldsymbol{\theta}_i$.

We can repeat this process for all factors q_i so as to derive the equations for the optimal $q_i^*(\boldsymbol{\theta}_i)$ for all $i = 1, 2, \cdots, I$. Unfortunately, these equations will usually create circular dependencies among various partitions of parameters so that no closed-form solution can be derived for the optimal $q^*(\boldsymbol{\theta})$. In practice, we have to rely on some iterative methods for this. We first randomly guess all q_i and then compute $\mathbb{E}_{j \neq i}\big[\ln p(\mathfrak{D}, \boldsymbol{\theta})\big]$ based on the initial q_i. Next, all q_i are updated using all computed $\mathbb{E}_{j \neq i}\big[\ln p(\mathfrak{D}, \boldsymbol{\theta})\big]$, as in Eq. (14.15). This process is repeated over and over. Like the normal EM algorithm, it is guaranteed to converge to at least a local optimal point.

Interestingly enough, the variational Bayesian method does not assume the functional form for a variational distribution $q(\boldsymbol{\theta})$, but any presumed factorization form in Eq. (14.14) will automatically lead to some proper functional forms for $q(\boldsymbol{\theta})$. This significantly differs from Laplace's method, which assumes Gaussians for the approximate distribution in the first place.

Next, let us consider how to obtain the best-fit variational distribution using an intriguing example, namely, Bayesian learning of GMMs.

Example 14.3.1 Variational Bayesian GMM

Assume a GMM is given as follows:

$$p(\mathbf{x} \,|\, \boldsymbol{\theta}) = \sum_{m=1}^{M} w_m \cdot \mathcal{N}\big(\mathbf{x} \,|\, \boldsymbol{\mu}_m, \boldsymbol{\Sigma}_m\big),$$

where $\boldsymbol{\theta} = \big\{w_m, \boldsymbol{\mu}_m, \boldsymbol{\Sigma}_m \,|\, m = 1, 2, \cdots, M\big\}$ denotes all parameters. After observing a data sample $\mathbf{x} \in \mathbb{R}^d$, use the variational Bayesian method to approximate the posterior distribution $p(\boldsymbol{\theta}|\mathbf{x})$.

First of all, let's follow the ideas in Examples 14.2.1 and 14.2.2 to specify the prior distribution for all GMM parameters as

$$p(\boldsymbol{\theta}) = p(w_1, \cdots, w_M) \prod_{m=1}^{M} p(\boldsymbol{\mu}_m, \boldsymbol{\Sigma}_m), \tag{14.17}$$

with

$$p(w_1, \cdots, w_M) = \text{Dir}(w_1, \cdots, w_M \,|\, \alpha_1^{(0)}, \cdots, \alpha_M^{(0)})$$

$$p(\boldsymbol{\mu}_m, \boldsymbol{\Sigma}_m) = \text{GIW}\big(\boldsymbol{\mu}_m, \boldsymbol{\Sigma}_m \,|\, \boldsymbol{\nu}_m^{(0)}, \boldsymbol{\Phi}_m^{(0)}, \lambda_m^{(0)}, \nu_m^{(0)}\big),$$

where $\big\{\alpha_m^{(0)}, \boldsymbol{\nu}_m^{(0)}, \boldsymbol{\Phi}_m^{(0)}, \lambda_m^{(0)}, \nu_m^{(0)} \,|\, m = 1, \cdots, M\big\}$ are the hyperparameters that are preset based on our prior knowledge of the parameters $\boldsymbol{\theta}$.

Second, let us introduce a 1-of-M vector for $\mathbf{x}$, denoted as $\mathbf{z}$, to indicate which mixture component $\mathbf{x}$ belongs to. Treating $\mathbf{z}$ as a latent variable, we can represent the joint distribution of the GMM as

The latent variable

$$\mathbf{z} = \begin{bmatrix} z_1 \, z_2 \, \cdots z_M \end{bmatrix}$$

may take one of the following values:

$$[1\,0 \cdots 0]$$
$$[0\,1 \cdots 0]$$
$$\vdots$$
$$[0\,0 \cdots 1]$$

$$p(\mathbf{x}, \mathbf{z} \,|\, \boldsymbol{\theta}) = \prod_{m=1}^{M} (w_m)^{z_m} \Big(\mathcal{N}(\mathbf{x} \mid \boldsymbol{\mu}_m, \boldsymbol{\Sigma}_m)\Big)^{z_m}. \tag{14.18}$$

Because the latent variable $\mathbf{z}$ and the model parameter $\boldsymbol{\theta}$ are both unobserved random variables, we treat them in the same way in the following variational Bayesian method. We propose to use a variational distribution $q(\mathbf{z}, \boldsymbol{\theta})$ to approximate the posterior distribution $p(\mathbf{z}, \boldsymbol{\theta}|\mathbf{x})$. And we further assume $q(\mathbf{z}, \boldsymbol{\theta})$ is factorized as follows:

$$q(\mathbf{z}, \boldsymbol{\theta}) = q(\mathbf{z})q(\boldsymbol{\theta}) = q(\mathbf{z})\, q(w_1, \cdots, w_M) \prod_{m=1}^{M} q(\boldsymbol{\mu}_m, \boldsymbol{\Sigma}_m).$$

Here, we assume $q(\boldsymbol{\theta})$ is factorized in the same way as the prior $p(\boldsymbol{\theta})$ in Eq. (14.17).

In the following, we will use Eq. (14.16) to derive the best-fit variational distribution $q^*(\mathbf{z}, \boldsymbol{\theta})$. Let us consider the first factor $q^*(\mathbf{z})$:

$$\ln q^*(\mathbf{z}) = \mathbb{E}_{\boldsymbol{\theta}}\big[\ln p(\mathbf{x}, \mathbf{z}, \boldsymbol{\theta})\big] + C = \mathbb{E}_{\boldsymbol{\theta}}\big[\ln p(\boldsymbol{\theta}) + \ln p(\mathbf{x}, \mathbf{z}|\boldsymbol{\theta})\big] + C.$$

Substituting Eq. (14.17) and Eq. (14.18) into the previous equation, we have

$$\ln q^*(\mathbf{z}) = \sum_{m=1}^{M} z_m \underbrace{\left(\mathbb{E}\big[\ln w_m\big] - \mathbb{E}\Big[\frac{\ln|\boldsymbol{\Sigma}_m|}{2}\Big] - \mathbb{E}\Big[\frac{(\mathbf{x}-\boldsymbol{\mu}_m)^\intercal \boldsymbol{\Sigma}_m^{-1}(\mathbf{x}-\boldsymbol{\mu}_m)}{2}\Big]\right)}_{\ln \rho_m} + C'.$$

For all $m = 1, 2, \cdots, M$:

$$\rho_m = \exp\Big(\mathbb{E}\big[\ln w_m\big] - \mathbb{E}\Big[\frac{\ln|\boldsymbol{\Sigma}_m|}{2}\Big] - \mathbb{E}\Big[\frac{(\mathbf{x}-\boldsymbol{\mu}_m)^\intercal \boldsymbol{\Sigma}_m^{-1}(\mathbf{x}-\boldsymbol{\mu}_m)}{2}\Big]\Big) \tag{14.19}$$

$$\Longrightarrow\ r_m = \frac{\rho_m}{\sum_{m=1}^{M} \rho_m}.$$

If we take the exponential of both sides, it yields

$$q^*(\mathbf{z}) \propto \prod_{m=1}^{M} (\rho_m)^{z_m} \propto \prod_{m=1}^{M} (r_m)^{z_m},$$

where $r_m = \frac{\rho_m}{\sum_{m=1}^{M}\rho_m}$ for all m. From this, we can recognize that $q^*(\mathbf{z})$ is a multinomial distribution, and the expectation for z_m can be computed as follows:

$$\mathbb{E}\big[z_m\big] = r_m = \frac{\rho_m}{\sum_{m=1}^{M} \rho_m} \tag{14.20}$$

Next, we consider the factor $q^*(w_1, \cdots, w_M)$ as

$$\begin{aligned} \ln q^*(w_1, \cdots, w_M) &= \mathbb{E}_{\mathbf{z}, \boldsymbol{\mu}_m, \boldsymbol{\Sigma}_m}\Big[\ln p(\boldsymbol{\theta}) + \ln p(\mathbf{x}, \mathbf{z}|\boldsymbol{\theta})\Big] \\ &= \sum_{m=1}^{M} (\alpha_m^{(0)} - 1) \ln w_m + \sum_{m=1}^{M} r_m \ln w_m + C. \end{aligned}$$

After taking the exponential of both sides and normalizing it properly, we recognize that it is a Dirichlet distribution, as follows:

$$q^*(w_1, \cdots, w_M) = \text{Dir}\big(w_1, \cdots, w_M \mid \alpha_1^{(1)}, \cdots, \alpha_M^{(1)}\big), \tag{14.21}$$

where $\alpha_m^{(1)} = \alpha_m^{(0)} + r_m$ for all $m = 1, 2, \cdots, M$.

Furthermore, we consider the factor $q^*(\boldsymbol{\mu}_m, \boldsymbol{\Sigma}_m)$ for each m as

$$\begin{aligned} \ln q^*(\boldsymbol{\mu}_m, \boldsymbol{\Sigma}_m) &= \mathbb{E}_{\mathbf{z},w_m}\Big[\ln p(\boldsymbol{\theta}) + \ln p(\mathbf{x}, \mathbf{z}|\boldsymbol{\theta})\Big] + C \\ &= \ln p(\boldsymbol{\mu}_m, \boldsymbol{\Sigma}_m) + \mathbb{E}\big[z_m\big] \ln \mathcal{N}(\mathbf{x}|\boldsymbol{\mu}_m, \boldsymbol{\Sigma}_m) + C'. \end{aligned}$$

After substituting Eq. (14.20) and rearranging for $\boldsymbol{\mu}_m$ and $\boldsymbol{\Sigma}_m$, we can show that $q^*(\boldsymbol{\mu}_m, \boldsymbol{\Sigma}_m)$ is also a GIW distribution:

$$q^*(\boldsymbol{\mu}_m, \boldsymbol{\Sigma}_m) = \text{GIW}\big(\boldsymbol{\mu}_m, \boldsymbol{\Sigma}_m \mid \boldsymbol{\nu}_m^{(1)}, \boldsymbol{\Phi}_m^{(1)}, \lambda_m^{(1)}, \nu_m^{(1)}\big), \tag{14.22}$$

with the updated hyperparameters given as follows:

$$\begin{aligned} \lambda_m^{(1)} &= \lambda_m^{(0)} + r_m \\ \nu_m^{(1)} &= \nu_m^{(0)} + r_m \\ \boldsymbol{\nu}_m^{(1)} &= \frac{\lambda_m^{(0)} \boldsymbol{\nu}_m^{(0)} + r_m \mathbf{x}}{\lambda_m^{(0)} + r_m} \\ \boldsymbol{\Phi}_m^{(1)} &= \boldsymbol{\Phi}_m^{(0)} + \frac{\lambda^{(0)} r_m}{\lambda_m^{(0)} + r_m} \big(\mathbf{x} - \boldsymbol{\nu}_m^{(0)}\big)\big(\mathbf{x} - \boldsymbol{\nu}_m^{(0)}\big)^\intercal. \end{aligned}$$

Finally, we will have to solve the circular dependencies because all of the updating formulae make use of r_m, which is in turn defined through ρ_m in Eq. (14.19). Using the derived variational distributions in Eqs. (14.21) and (14.22), we may compute these required expectations in Eq. (14.19) as follows:

$$\begin{aligned} \ln \pi_m &\stackrel{\Delta}{=} \mathbb{E}\big[\ln w_k\big] = \psi\big(\alpha_m^{(1)}\big) - \psi\Big(\sum_{m=1}^{M} \alpha_m^{(1)}\Big) \\ \ln B_m &\stackrel{\Delta}{=} \mathbb{E}\big[\ln|\boldsymbol{\Sigma}_m|\big] = \sum_{i=1}^{d} \psi\Big(\frac{\lambda_m + 1 - i}{2}\Big) - \ln\big|\boldsymbol{\Phi}_m^{(1)}\big| \\ \mathbb{E}\Big[(\mathbf{x} - \boldsymbol{\mu}_m)^\intercal \boldsymbol{\Sigma}_m^{-1}(\mathbf{x} - \boldsymbol{\mu}_m)\Big] &= \frac{d}{\nu_m^{(1)}} + \lambda_m^{(1)}\big(\mathbf{x} - \boldsymbol{\nu}_m^{(1)}\big)^\intercal \big(\boldsymbol{\Phi}_m^{(1)}\big)^{-1}\big(\mathbf{x} - \boldsymbol{\nu}_m^{(1)}\big). \end{aligned}$$

Refer to the property of Dirichlet distributions in Abramowitz and Stegun [1]. Here, $\psi(\cdot)$ denotes the digamma function.

Refer to the property of the inverse-Wishart distributions in Appendix A and that of the GIW distributions in Abramowitz and Stegun [1].

Putting these back into Eq. (14.19) and normalizing to 1, we may derive

Algorithm 14.19 Variational Bayesian GMMs

Input: $\{\alpha_m^{(0)}, \boldsymbol{\nu}_m^{(0)}, \boldsymbol{\Phi}_m^{(0)}, \lambda_m^{(0)}, \nu_m^{(0)} \mid m = 1, \cdots, M\}$

set $n = 0$
while not converge **do**
E-step: use Eq. (14.23) to collect statistics:

$$\{\alpha_m^{(n)}, \boldsymbol{\nu}_m^{(n)}, \boldsymbol{\Phi}_m^{(n)}, \lambda_m^{(n)}, \nu_m^{(n)}\} + \mathbf{x} \longrightarrow \{r_m\}$$

M-step: use Eqs. (14.21) and (14.22) to update all hyperparameters:

$$\{\alpha_m^{(n)}, \boldsymbol{\nu}_m^{(n)}, \boldsymbol{\Phi}_m^{(n)}, \lambda_m^{(n)}, \nu_m^{(n)}\} + \{r_m\} + \mathbf{x}$$

$$\longrightarrow \{\alpha_m^{(n+1)}, \boldsymbol{\nu}_m^{(n+1)}, \boldsymbol{\Phi}_m^{(n+1)}, \lambda_m^{(n+1)}, \nu_m^{(n+1)}\}$$

$n = n + 1$
end while

the updating formula for r_m as follows:

$$r_m \propto \pi_m B_m^{1/2} \exp\left(-\frac{d}{2\nu_m^{(1)}} - \frac{\lambda_m^{(1)}}{2} (\mathbf{x} - \boldsymbol{\nu}_m^{(1)})^\intercal (\boldsymbol{\Phi}_m^{(1)})^{-1} (\mathbf{x} - \boldsymbol{\nu}_m^{(1)}) \right). \tag{14.23}$$

In summary, we can use the EM-like algorithm shown in Algorithm 14.19 to iteratively update all hyperparameters to derive the best-fit variational distribution for a GMM. In this algorithm, we first use the current hyperparameters to compute the statistics $\{r_m\}$ in the so-called E-step. Next, the statistics $\{r_m\}$ are used to derive a new set of hyperparameters in the M-step. This process repeats until it converges. ♦

14.4 Gaussian Processes

In the previous sections, we have discussed how to conduct Bayesian learning for parametric models, which belong to a family of presumed-form probability functions with a fixed number of parameters. For parametric models, as we have seen, Bayesian learning focuses on parameter estimation, where our initial belief is encoded in a prior distribution of the underlying model parameters, and the outcome of Bayesian learning is a posterior distribution of the same model parameters.

In this section, we will discuss Bayesian learning for the so-called nonparametric models, whose modeling capacity is not constrained by any fixed number of parameters but can be dynamically adjusted along with the amount of given data. These methods are normally called *nonparametric*

Bayesian methods in the literature. The key idea behind all nonparametric Bayesian methods is to use some stochastic processes as conjugate prior distributions for the underlying nonparametric models. For example, *Gaussian processes* are used as prior distributions over all possible nonlinear functions that can be used to fit the training data in a machine learning problem, including both regression and classification [152, 196]. In addition, *Dirichlet processes* are used as prior distributions of all possible discrete probability distributions for up to a countable infinite number of categories, which can be used for clustering or density estimation [61, 169].

In the following, we will use Gaussian processes as an example to explore the basic idea of nonparametric priors as well as the key steps in conducting nonparametric Bayesian learning for regression and classification problems.

14.4.1 Gaussian Processes as Nonparametric Priors

For all parametric models, we have to first choose a particular functional form for the underlying distribution $p(\mathbf{x}|\boldsymbol{\theta})$, such as Gaussian, logistic regression, or mixture models. Each of these probability functions usually involves a fixed number of parameters $\boldsymbol{\theta}$. Accordingly, in the Bayesian setting, we just need to specify a prior distribution for these parameters (i.e., $p(\boldsymbol{\theta})$).

For nonparametric models, we do not specify any functional form for the underlying model or its involved parameters. The first crucial question in nonparametric Bayesian methods is how to specify a prior distribution for some functions or models when we do not know their exact forms. The answer here is to use some stochastic processes as nonparametric priors. Among others, Gaussian processes are the most popular tool to specify nonparametric prior distributions for a class of fairly powerful nonlinear functions.

Assume we have an arbitrary function $f(\mathbf{x})$ mapping an input feature in $\mathbb{R}^d$ to a real value in $\mathbb{R}$. If we use $f(\mathbf{x})$ to evaluate any N points in $\mathbb{R}^d$ (i.e., $\mathfrak{D} = \{\mathbf{x}_1, \mathbf{x}_2, \cdots, \mathbf{x}_N\}$), their corresponding function values form an N-dimensional real-valued vector, denoted as $\mathbf{f} = \left[f(\mathbf{x}_1)\, f(\mathbf{x}_2) \cdots f(\mathbf{x}_N)\right]^\intercal$. Despite that we do not know the exact form of the underlying function $f(\mathbf{x})$, if we know the vector $\mathbf{f}$ always follows a multivariate Gaussian distribution as

$$\mathbf{f} = \left[f(\mathbf{x}_1)\, f(\mathbf{x}_2) \cdots f(\mathbf{x}_N)\right]^\intercal \sim \mathcal{N}\left(\boldsymbol{\mu}_{\mathfrak{D}}, \boldsymbol{\Sigma}_{\mathfrak{D}}\right),$$

this may play a similar role as the prior distribution for $f(\mathbf{x})$ because it has implicitly imposed some constraints on the underlying function $f(\mathbf{x})$.

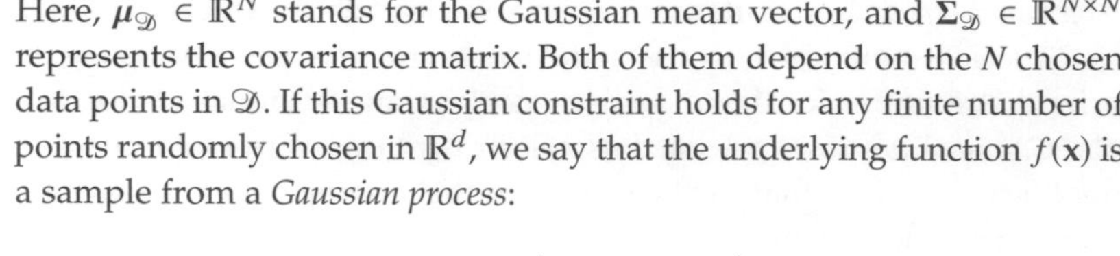

Here, $\boldsymbol{\mu}_{\mathcal{D}} \in \mathbb{R}^N$ stands for the Gaussian mean vector, and $\boldsymbol{\Sigma}_{\mathcal{D}} \in \mathbb{R}^{N \times N}$ represents the covariance matrix. Both of them depend on the N chosen data points in $\mathcal{D}$. If this Gaussian constraint holds for any finite number of points randomly chosen in $\mathbb{R}^d$, we say that the underlying function $f(\mathbf{x})$ is a sample from a *Gaussian process*:

$$f(\mathbf{x}) \sim \text{GP}\Big(\mathbf{m}(\mathbf{x}), \Phi(\mathbf{x}, \mathbf{x}')\Big),$$

where $\mathbf{m}(\mathbf{x})$ is called the *mean function* of the Gaussian process, which specifies the way to compute the Gaussian mean $\boldsymbol{\mu}_{\mathcal{D}}$ from any finite number of data points in $\mathcal{D}$. Similarly, $\Phi(\mathbf{x}, \mathbf{x}')$ is called the *covariance function*, which specifies the way to compute all elements in the covariance matrix $\boldsymbol{\Sigma}_{\mathcal{D}}$ for any given $\mathcal{D}$. If we randomly draw many samples from a Gaussian process, we end up with many different functions, as shown in Figure 14.7. We do not even know the exact functional form for each of these samples, but we do know that all of these functions follow a probability distribution specified by the given Gaussian process.

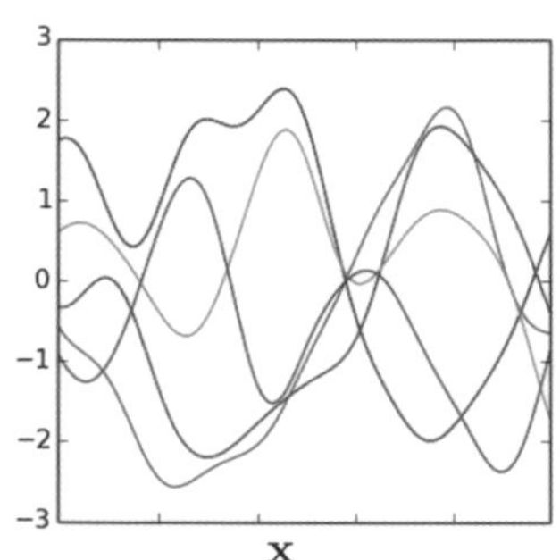

Figure 14.7: An illustration of many different nonparametric functions randomly sampled from a given Gaussian process. (Image credit: Cdipaolo96/CC-BY-SA-4.0.)

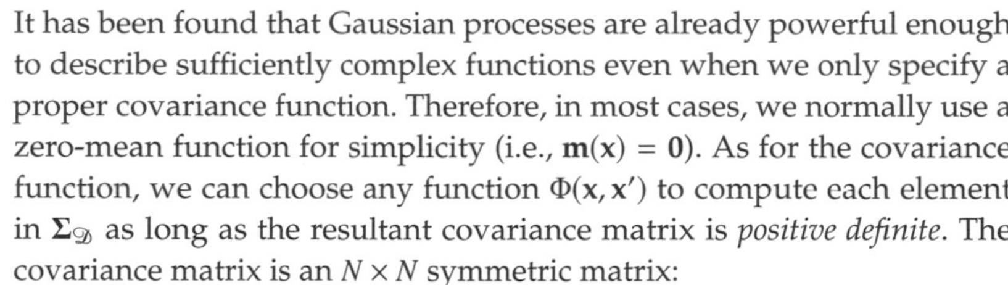

It has been found that Gaussian processes are already powerful enough to describe sufficiently complex functions even when we only specify a proper covariance function. Therefore, in most cases, we normally use a zero-mean function for simplicity (i.e., $\mathbf{m}(\mathbf{x}) = \mathbf{0}$). As for the covariance function, we can choose any function $\Phi(\mathbf{x}, \mathbf{x}')$ to compute each element in $\boldsymbol{\Sigma}_{\mathcal{D}}$ as long as the resultant covariance matrix is *positive definite*. The covariance matrix is an $N \times N$ symmetric matrix:

$$\boldsymbol{\Sigma}_{\mathcal{D}} = \Big[\; \boldsymbol{\Sigma}_{ij} \; \Big]_{N \times N},$$

where $\boldsymbol{\Sigma}_{ij}$ is used to denote the element located at the ith row and jth column. As we know, it represents the covariance between $f(\mathbf{x}_i)$ and $f(\mathbf{x}_j)$, and we can assume that it is specified by the chosen covariance function as follows:

$$\boldsymbol{\Sigma}_{ij} = \text{cov}\Big(f(\mathbf{x}_i), f(\mathbf{x}_j)\Big) = \Phi(\mathbf{x}_i, \mathbf{x}_j).$$

As we may recall from the *kernel functions* in nonlinear support vector machines (SVMs) in Section 6.5, $\Phi(\mathbf{x}_i, \mathbf{x}_j)$ must satisfy the *Mercer* condition on page 124 to ensure the positive definiteness of $\boldsymbol{\Sigma}_{\mathcal{D}}$. If a covariance function is translation invariant, it is said to be *stationary*. A stationary covariance function only depends on the difference between two points (i.e., $\Phi(\mathbf{x}_i - \mathbf{x}_j)$). In principle, any kernel function in Section 6.5 can be used as the covariance function for Gaussian processes. In machine learning, we often use the following radial basis function (RBF) kernel for the covariance function:

$$\Phi(\mathbf{x}_i, \mathbf{x}_j) = \sigma^2 \, e^{-\frac{\|\mathbf{x}_i - \mathbf{x}_j\|^2}{2l^2}}, \tag{14.24}$$

where $\{\sigma^2, l^2\}$ denote two hyperparameters: σ is called the *vertical scale*, and l is called the *horizontal scale*. The vertical scale σ roughly describes the dynamic range of the underlying functions, and the horizontal scale l roughly describes the smoothness of the underlying functions. A high l gives some relatively smooth functions, whereas a lower l results in some wiggly functions. Figure 14.8 gives some examples of Gaussian processes with different choices of these hyperparameters.

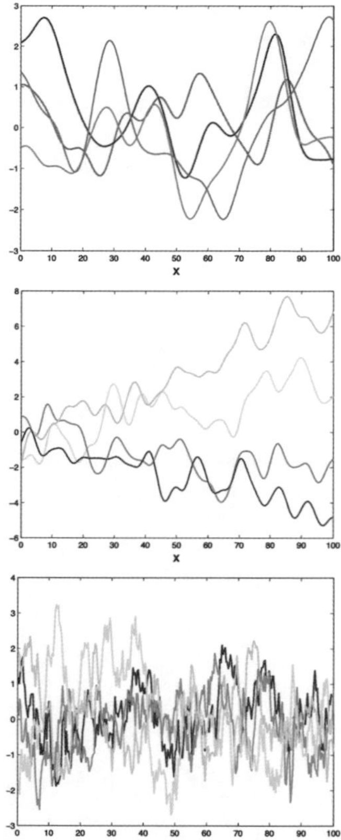

Figure 14.8: An illustration of some functions randomly drawn from three Gaussian processes with various hyperparameters: (top) lower σ and high l; (middle) high σ and high l; (bottom) lower σ and lower l. (Courtesy of Zoubin Ghahramani [79].)

At last, let us consider why a Gaussian process can be used as a prior distribution for those random functions whose exact forms and parameters are unknown. The key here is that the prior distribution can be implicitly computed based on any set $\mathcal{D}$ of N data points. When we apply any randomly sampled function $f(\cdot)$ to all data points in $\mathcal{D}$, we know that their function values $\mathbf{f}$ follow a multivariate Gaussian distribution, as specified in the definition of Gaussian processes. As a result, we can use this Gaussian distribution to indirectly compute the prior distribution for each underlying function as

$$p(f \mid \mathcal{D}) = \mathcal{N}(\mathbf{f} \mid \mathbf{0}, \boldsymbol{\Sigma}_{\mathcal{D}}), \tag{14.25}$$

where we use the zero-mean function and the covariance function in Eq. (14.24) for the Gaussian process. As long as we know the two hyperparameters, we can explicitly compute the Gaussian distribution, which can serve as a prior distribution for all nonparametric functions following this distribution.

Next, we will continue to explore how to conduct Bayesian learning based on this prior for two typical machine learning problems.

14.4.2 Gaussian Processes for Regression

In a regression problem, we aim to learn a model to map a feature vector $\mathbf{x} \in \mathbb{R}^d$ to an output $y \in \mathbb{R}$. Here, we will use Gaussian processes to learn a nonparametric function $f(\cdot)$ for this regression problem. We assume the underlying function $f(\cdot)$ is a random sample from a Gaussian process and that the function value is corrupted by an independent Gaussian noise to yield the final output y:

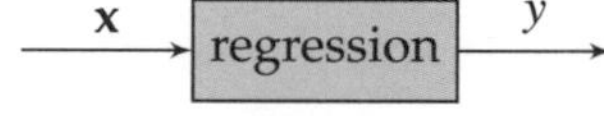

$$f(\mathbf{x}) \sim \mathrm{GP}\Big(\mathbf{0}, \Phi(\mathbf{x}, \mathbf{x}')\Big)$$

$$y = f(\mathbf{x}) + \epsilon, \qquad \text{where} \quad \epsilon \sim \mathcal{N}(0, \sigma_0^2).$$

Suppose that we are given some training samples of input–output pairs: all input vectors are denoted as $\mathcal{D} = \{\mathbf{x}_1, \mathbf{x}_2, \cdots, \mathbf{x}_N\}$, and their corresponding outputs are represented as a vector $\mathbf{y} = \big[y_1\, y_2\, \cdots\, y_N\big]^\intercal$. We first consider how to learn the parameters of this model, including the hyperparameters of the covariance function $\Phi(\mathbf{x}, \mathbf{x}')$ in Eq. (14.24) and the variance of the residual noise ϵ.

Let us denote the function values of all input vectors in $\mathfrak{D}$ as

$$\mathbf{f} = \left[f(\mathbf{x}_1) \cdots f(\mathbf{x}_N)\right]^\intercal.$$

According to the nonparametric prior specified by the Gaussian process in Eq. (14.25), we have

$$p(f \mid \mathfrak{D}) = \mathcal{N}(\mathbf{f} \mid \mathbf{0}, \mathbf{\Sigma}_{\mathfrak{D}}).$$

Furthermore, because the residual noise ϵ follows a Gaussian distribution, we have

$$p(\mathbf{y} \mid f, \mathfrak{D}) = \mathcal{N}(\mathbf{y} \mid \mathbf{f}, \sigma_0^2 \mathbf{I}).$$

Putting them together, we can derive the marginal-likelihood function as follows:

$$\begin{aligned} p(\mathbf{y} \mid \mathfrak{D}) &= \int_f p(\mathbf{y}, f \mid \mathfrak{D})\, df = \int_f p(\mathbf{y} \mid f, \mathfrak{D}) p(f \mid \mathfrak{D})\, df \\ &= \int_{\mathbf{f}} \mathcal{N}(\mathbf{y} \mid \mathbf{f}, \sigma_0^2 \mathbf{I}) \mathcal{N}(\mathbf{f} \mid \mathbf{0}, \mathbf{\Sigma}_{\mathfrak{D}})\, d\mathbf{f} \\ &= \mathcal{N}(\mathbf{y} \mid \mathbf{0}, \mathbf{\Sigma}_{\mathfrak{D}} + \sigma_0^2 \mathbf{I}) = \mathcal{N}(\mathbf{y} \mid \mathbf{0}, \mathbf{C}_N). \end{aligned} \tag{14.26}$$

We can see that this marginal-likelihood function is Gaussian, with a zero-mean vector and an $N \times N$ covariance matrix, denoted as

$$\mathbf{C}_N = \mathbf{\Sigma}_{\mathfrak{D}} + \sigma_0^2 \mathbf{I}.$$

Furthermore, we can see that this marginal likelihood is a function of all model parameters, including σ, l and σ_0. Thus, we explicitly express it as $p(\mathbf{y} \mid \mathfrak{D}, \sigma, l, \sigma_0)$. Based on the idea of maximum-marginal-likelihood estimation, we can estimate all model parameters by maximizing the marginal-likelihood function as follows:

$$\{\sigma^*, l^*, \sigma_0^*\} = \arg\max_{\sigma, l, \sigma_0} \; p(\mathbf{y} \mid \mathfrak{D}, \sigma, l, \sigma_0) = \arg\max_{\sigma, l, \sigma_0} \; \ln \mathcal{N}(\mathbf{y} \mid \mathbf{0}, \mathbf{C}_N).$$

For most choices of the covariance function, there is no closed-form solution to solve the maximization problem. We normally have to rely on some iterative gradient-descent methods to solve it because the gradients w.r.t. all parameters can be easily derived (see margin note).

If we denote

$$\begin{aligned} l &= \ln \mathcal{N}(\mathbf{y} \mid \mathbf{0}, \mathbf{C}_N) \\ &= -\frac{1}{2} \ln |\mathbf{C}_N| - \frac{1}{2} \mathbf{y}^\intercal \mathbf{C}_N^{-1} \mathbf{y} - \frac{N}{2} \ln 2\pi \end{aligned}$$

for any parameter θ, we can compute its gradient as follows:

$$\begin{aligned} \frac{\partial l}{\partial \theta} &= -\frac{1}{2} \mathrm{tr}\left(\mathbf{C}^{-1} \frac{\partial \mathbf{C}_N}{\partial \theta}\right) \\ &+ \frac{1}{2} \mathbf{y}^\intercal \mathbf{C}_N^{-1} \frac{\partial \mathbf{C}_N}{\partial \theta} \mathbf{C}_N^{-1} \mathbf{y}. \end{aligned}$$

Once we have learned all model parameters as previously described, we can use the Gaussian process model to predict the corresponding output $\tilde{y}$ for any new input vector $\tilde{\mathbf{x}}$. Following the same idea as in Eq. (14.26), we can derive the marginal-likelihood function for all available data as

$$p(\mathbf{y}, \tilde{y} \mid \mathcal{D}, \mathbf{x}) = \mathcal{N}(\mathbf{y}, \tilde{y} \mid \mathbf{0}, \mathbf{C}_{N+1}),$$

where the covariance matrix $\mathbf{C}_{N+1}$ is an $(N+1) \times (N+1)$ matrix taking the following format:

$$\mathbf{C}_{N+1} = \begin{bmatrix} \mathbf{C}_N & \mathbf{k} \\ \mathbf{k}^\intercal & \kappa^2 \end{bmatrix}$$

where $\kappa^2 = \Phi(\tilde{\mathbf{x}}, \tilde{\mathbf{x}}) + \sigma_0^2$, and each element in $\mathbf{k}$ is computed as $\mathbf{k}_i = \Phi(\mathbf{x}_i, \tilde{\mathbf{x}})$.

Moreover, we can derive the following conditional distribution, which is also Gaussian, for the final inference in regression:

$$p(\tilde{y} \mid \mathcal{D}, \mathbf{y}, \tilde{\mathbf{x}}) = \frac{p(\mathbf{y}, \tilde{y} \mid \mathcal{D}, \tilde{\mathbf{x}})}{p(\mathbf{y} \mid \mathcal{D})} = \mathcal{N}\left(\tilde{y} \mid \mathbf{k}^\intercal \mathbf{C}_N^{-1} \mathbf{y}, \kappa^2 - \mathbf{k}^\intercal \mathbf{C}_N^{-1} \mathbf{k}\right). \quad (14.27)$$

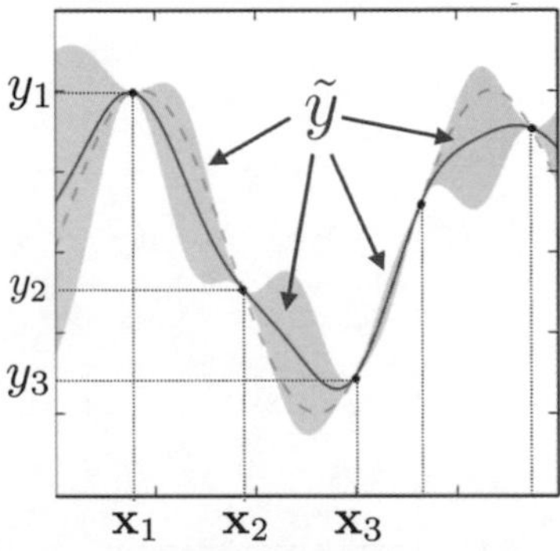

Figure 14.9: An illustration of the conditional distribution of a Gaussian process model. The shaded area shows the range of all highly probable outputs for each input, and the blue curve indicates a point estimation. (Image credit: Cdipaolo96/CC-BY-SA-4.0.)

See Exercise Q14.9 for how to derive the conditional distribution in Eq. (14.27). This conditional distribution specifies a probability distribution of the output $\tilde{y}$ for each given input $\tilde{\mathbf{x}}$. On some occasions, we prefer to use a point estimation of $\tilde{y}$ for each input $\tilde{\mathbf{x}}$, such as the conditional mean or the MAP estimation. Because the conditional distribution is Gaussian, both point estimates are the same, and they are given as follows:

$$\mathbb{E}\left[\tilde{y} \mid \mathcal{D}, \mathbf{y}, \tilde{\mathbf{x}}\right] = \tilde{y}_{\text{MAP}} = \mathbf{k}^\intercal \mathbf{C}_N^{-1} \mathbf{y}.$$

As shown in Figure 14.9, the shaded area highlights the range of all highly probable outputs for each input $\tilde{\mathbf{x}}$, and the blue curve indicates the point estimation for each $\tilde{\mathbf{x}}$.

Let us summarize the basic idea of nonparametric Bayesian learning. Based on a set of input samples in $\mathcal{D}$, we may represent the nonparametric prior $p(f|\mathcal{D})$ as in Eq. (14.25), which can be viewed as the Gaussian process shown in the left part of Figure 14.10. After we observe all corresponding function values in $\mathbf{y}$, we may derive the conditional distribution in Eq. (14.27), which can be viewed as a nonparametric posterior distribution $p(f|\mathcal{D}, \mathbf{y})$ represented by another Gaussian process, as shown in the right part of Figure 14.10. We can see that all nonparametric functions from this Gaussian process are clamped on the observed samples because the probability distribution in Eq. (14.27) is conditioned on all these input–output pairs.

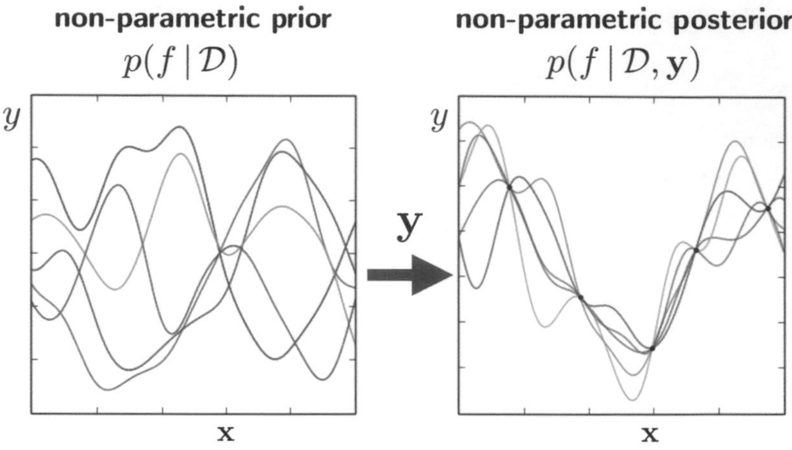

Figure 14.10: An illustration of how the nonparametric Bayesian learning updates a nonparametric prior into a nonparametric posterior, which are both represented by Gaussian processes. (Image credit: Cdipaolo96/CC-BY-SA-4.0.)

As we have seen, all Gaussian process methods require us to invert an $N \times N$ covariance matrix in either the training or the inference stage. This operation is extremely expensive in computation because the complexity of any exact algorithm is $O(N^3)$. This major drawback makes it impractical to apply Gaussian processes to any large-scale tasks where N exceeds a few hundreds of thousands.

14.4.3 Gaussian Processes for Classification

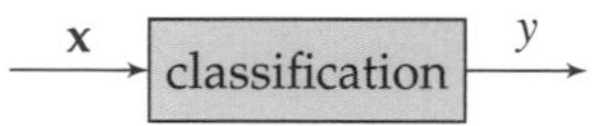

Gaussian processes can also be used for classification problems, where output y is discrete. Because any nonparametric function drawn from a Gaussian process yields an unconstrained real-valued output, we have to introduce another function to map the real values into some probability-like outputs for each class. Taking a binary-classification problem as an example, where the output is binary as $y \in \{0, 1\}$, we may use the sigmoid function $l(\cdot)$ in Eq. (6.12) for this purpose:

$$\Pr\left(y = 1 \mid \mathbf{x}\right) = l\big(f(\mathbf{x})\big) = \frac{1}{1 + e^{-f(\mathbf{x})}}. \tag{14.28}$$

This method is very similar to logistic regression, where $f(\mathbf{x})$ is chosen as a linear function $\mathbf{w}^\intercal \mathbf{x}$. However, in this case, we assume $f(\mathbf{x})$ is a nonparametric function randomly drawn from a Gaussian process as

$$f(\mathbf{x}) \sim \text{GP}\Big(\mathbf{0}, \Phi(\mathbf{x}, \mathbf{x}')\Big).$$

Suppose we have some training samples of input–output pairs: all input vectors are denoted as $\mathfrak{D} = \big\{\mathbf{x}_1, \mathbf{x}_2, \cdots, \mathbf{x}_N\big\}$, and their corresponding binary outputs are represented as a vector $\mathbf{y} = \big[y_1 \; y_2 \; \cdots \; y_N\big]^\intercal$, where $y_i \in$

$\{0, 1\}$ for all $i = 1, 2, \cdots N$. Assume we still use $\mathbf{f}$ to represent the function values of all input vectors in $\mathfrak{D}$. We can still obtain the nonparametric prior in Eq. (14.25), which is Gaussian.

In this case, we can represent the likelihood function as follows:

$$p(\mathbf{y} \,|\, f, \mathfrak{D}) = \prod_{i=1}^{N} \Big(l\big(f(\mathbf{x}_i)\big)\Big)^{y_i} \Big(1 - l\big(f(\mathbf{x}_i)\big)\Big)^{1-y_i}. \tag{14.29}$$

After this, we can follow the same ideas in Eqs. (14.26) and (14.27) to derive the marginal-likelihood function $p(\mathbf{y} \,|\, \mathfrak{D})$ for model learning and the conditional distribution $p(\tilde{y} \,|\, \mathfrak{D}, \mathbf{y}, \tilde{\mathbf{x}})$ for inference. However, the major difficulty here is that we cannot derive them analytically because the likelihood function in Eq. (14.29) is non-Gaussian. In practice, we will have to rely on some approximation methods. A common solution is to use Laplace's method, as described in Section 14.3, to approximate these intractable distributions by some Gaussians. Interested readers may refer to Williams and Barber [251] and Rasmussen and Williams [196] for more details on Gaussian process classification.

Exercises

Q14.1 Show the procedure to derive the updating formulae in Eqs. (14.7) and (14.8) for the mean ν_n and variance τ_n^2 of Example 14.1.1.

Q14.2 Show the procedure to derive the following two steps in Bayesian learning of a multivariate Gaussian model:

a. Completing the square:

$$\sum_{i=1}^{N}(\mathbf{x}_i-\boldsymbol{\mu})^\intercal\boldsymbol{\Sigma}^{-1}(\mathbf{x}_i-\boldsymbol{\mu})=\sum_{i=1}^{N}(\mathbf{x}_i-\bar{\mathbf{x}})^\intercal\boldsymbol{\Sigma}^{-1}(\mathbf{x}_i-\bar{\mathbf{x}})+N(\boldsymbol{\mu}-\bar{\mathbf{x}})^\intercal\boldsymbol{\Sigma}^{-1}(\boldsymbol{\mu}-\bar{\mathbf{x}}),$$

with $\bar{\mathbf{x}}=\frac{1}{N}\sum_{i=1}^{N}\mathbf{x}_i$.

b. $\sum_{i=1}^{N}(\mathbf{x}_i-\bar{\mathbf{x}})^\intercal\boldsymbol{\Sigma}^{-1}(\mathbf{x}_i-\bar{\mathbf{x}})=\mathrm{tr}\Big(\big(\sum_{i=1}^{N}(\mathbf{x}_i-\bar{\mathbf{x}})(\mathbf{x}_i-\bar{\mathbf{x}})^\intercal\big)\boldsymbol{\Sigma}^{-1}\Big)=\mathrm{tr}\Big(N\mathbf{S}\,\boldsymbol{\Sigma}^{-1}\Big),$
with $\mathbf{S}=\frac{1}{N}\sum_{i=1}^{N}(\mathbf{x}_i-\bar{\mathbf{x}})(\mathbf{x}_i-\bar{\mathbf{x}})^\intercal$.

Q14.3 Consider a linear regression model from $\mathbf{x}\in\mathbb{R}^n$ to $y\in\mathbb{R}$: $y=\mathbf{w}^\intercal\mathbf{x}+\varepsilon$, where $\mathbf{w}\in\mathbb{R}^n$ is the model parameter, and ε is an independent zero-mean Gaussian noise $\varepsilon\sim\mathcal{N}(0,\sigma^2)$. Assume we choose a Gaussian distribution as the prior of the model parameter $\mathbf{w}$: $p(\mathbf{w})=\mathcal{N}(\mathbf{w}_0,\boldsymbol{\Sigma}_0)$. Assuming we have obtained the training set $\mathcal{D}=\big\{(\mathbf{x}_1,y_1),(\mathbf{x}_2,y_2),\cdots,(\mathbf{x}_N,y_N)\big\}$, derive the posterior distribution $p(\mathbf{w}|\mathcal{D})$, and give the MAP estimation of the model parameter $\mathbf{w}_{\mathrm{MAP}}$.

Q14.4 Use Laplace's method to conduct Bayesian learning for the probit regression in Section 11.4.

Q14.5 Use Laplace's method to conduct Bayesian learning for the log-linear models in Section 11.4.

Q14.6 Following the ideas in Example 14.3.1, derive a variational distribution for a multivariate Gaussian model using the variational Bayesian method. Compare the derived variational distribution with the exact posterior distribution in Example 14.2.2.

Q14.7 Assume we choose the same prior distribution for a GMM as in Example 14.3.1. Use the EM algorithm to derive the MAP estimation for GMMs:

a. Give the formulae to update all GMM parameters $\boldsymbol{\theta}_{\mathrm{MAP}}$ iteratively.
b. If we approximate the true posterior distribution of a GMM $p(\boldsymbol{\theta}|\mathbf{x})$ by another approximate distribution $\tilde{q}(\boldsymbol{\theta})$ as

$$\tilde{q}(\boldsymbol{\theta})\propto p(\boldsymbol{\theta})\,Q(\boldsymbol{\theta}|\boldsymbol{\theta}_{\mathrm{MAP}}),$$

where $Q(\cdot)$ is the auxiliary function in the EM algorithm, derive this approximate posterior distribution $\tilde{q}(\boldsymbol{\theta})$, and compare it with the variational distribution $q(\boldsymbol{\theta})$ in Example 14.3.1.

Q14.8 Following the ideas in Example 14.3.1, derive the variational Bayesian learning procedure for the Gaussian mixture hidden Markov models (HMMs) in Section 12.4, as shown in Figure 12.15.

Q14.9 Show the procedure to derive the conditional distribution in Eq. (14.27).

Q14.10 Derive Laplace's method for a Gaussian process in binary classification.

Q14.11 Replace the sigmoid function in Eq. (14.28) with a softmax function, and formulate a Gaussian process for a multiclass pattern-classification problem.

Graphical Models 15

This chapter introduces a pictorial representation for generative models, normally called *graphical models* [118, 22, 13] in the literature. Graphical models aim to represent generative models with some graphs consisting of nodes and arcs. As we will see, graphical models are a very flexible way to visually represent generative models. The graphical representation can intuitively display inherent dependencies among all underlying variables in a generative model and also help to develop some generic graph-based inference algorithms for generative models. Moreover, a graphical representation is also very useful in analyzing different types of relationships among random variables, such as correlation, causality, and mediation. The following discussion will first introduce some basic concepts of graphical models and then present two different types of graphical models, namely, *directed graphical models* and *undirected graphical models*, along with some representative models from each category as case studies.

15.1 Concepts of Graphical Models

As we have seen, a generative model essentially represents a probabilistic distribution of some random variables. The idea behind the graphical representation for generative models is simple: we use each node to represent a random variable in generative models and each link to express a probabilistic relationship between random variables. The links between the nodes can be either directed or undirected. If we use all directed links, each generative model ends up with a directed acyclic graph, and each directed link represents a conditional distribution between the linked random variables. For example, if there exists a directed link from a random variable x to another y, it is said that x is a parent of y, and this link essentially represents a conditional distribution $p(y|x)$; see Figure 15.1. The graphical models using all directed links are called *directed graphical models*, also known as *Bayesian networks* in the literature [181, 113, 182]. In general, each directed graphical model represents one particular way to factorize the joint distribution of all underlying random variables:

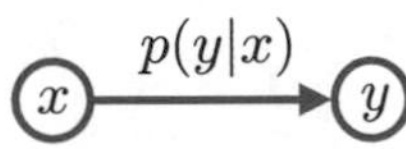

Figure 15.1: An illustration of a directed link between two random variables in a Bayesian network.

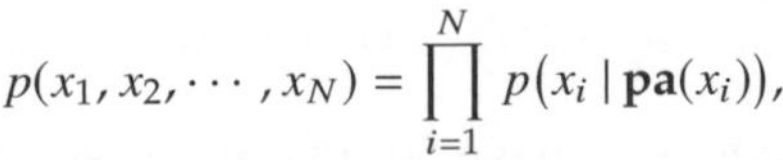

$$p(x_1, x_2, \cdots, x_N) = \prod_{i=1}^{N} p(x_i \mid \mathbf{pa}(x_i)),$$

where $\mathbf{pa}(x_i)$ denotes all parents of x_i in the graph.

On the other hand, if we use all undirected links to connect random variables, each undirected link just represents some mutual dependency between the variables because the conditioning is not explicitly shown as a result of the undirectedness of the link. The graphical models using all undirected links are called *undirected graphical models* or *Markov random fields* [128, 203]. As we will see, directed and undirected graphical models require different treatments in the formulation, but they are closely related and complementary in machine learning.

Let's first take a simple directed graphical model as an example, where we use a Bayesian network to graphically represent a generative model of five random variables (i.e., $p(x_1, x_2, x_3, x_4, x_5)$). If we do not make any assumption on this joint distribution, we can still factorize it according to the product rule in probability, as follows:

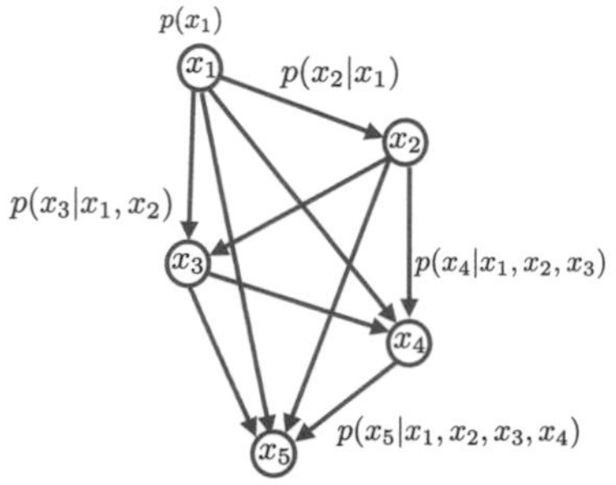

Figure 15.2: An illustration of a fully connected Bayesian network to represent a joint distribution of five random variables, $p(x_1, x_2, x_3, x_4, x_5)$.

$$\begin{aligned} & p(x_1, x_2, x_3, x_4, x_5) \\ = \; & p(x_1) \cdot p(x_2|x_1) \cdot p(x_3|x_1, x_2) \cdot p(x_4|x_1, x_2, x_3) \cdot p(x_5|x_1, x_2, x_3, x_4). \end{aligned}$$

If we use a node to represent each variable and use some directed links to properly represent all of the conditional distributions, we end up with a fully connected graph, as shown in Figure 15.2. However, a fully connected graphical model is not particularly interesting because it does not provide extra information or any convenience beyond the algebraic representation of $p(x_1, x_2, x_3, x_4, x_5)$. A fully connected graphical model simply means that all underlying variables are mutually dependent, and there are no possible independence implications among the variables that could be further explored to simplify the computation of such a model.

In fact, all sensible generative models used in practice can usually be represented by a sparsely connected graphical model, where many links are missing between some nodes in the graph. These missing links indicate certain independence implications among the variables. If we can explore them properly, it will significantly simplify the computation of the underlying generative models. For example, given the generative model of seven random variables, $p(x_1, x_2, x_3, x_4, x_5, x_6, x_7)$, that is represented by a Bayesian network in Figure 15.3, we can easily identify that this is not a fully connected graph because there are many missing links between some nodes. Based on the previous definition of a directed graphical model, we can factorize the joint distribution based on all directed links in Figure 15.3 as follows:

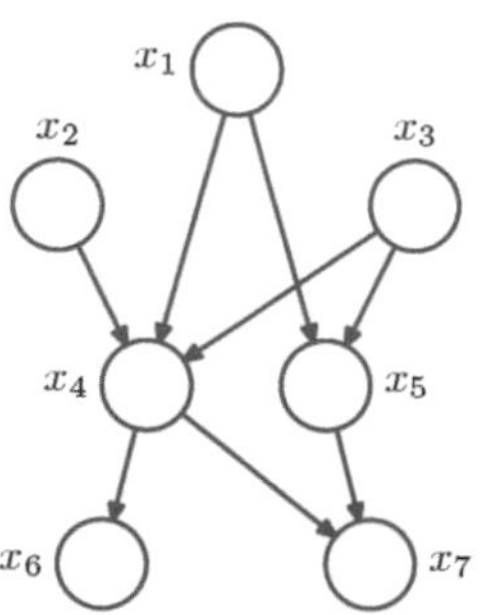

Figure 15.3: An illustration of a sparsely connected Bayesian network to represent a joint distribution of seven random variables, $p(x_1, x_2, x_3, x_4, x_5, x_6, x_7)$. (Source: Bishop [22].)

$$\begin{aligned} & p(x_1, x_2, x_3, x_4, x_5, x_6, x_7) \\ = \; & p(x_1)p(x_2)p(x_3)p(x_4|x_1, x_2, x_3)p(x_5|x_1, x_3)p(x_6|x_4)p(x_7|x_4, x_5), \end{aligned}$$

where $p(x_1)$, $p(x_2)$, and $p(x_3)$ have no conditions because these nodes do not have any parent nodes, and we write $p(x_4|x_1, x_2, x_3)$ because the node

x_4 has three parent nodes, and so on. When we compare the two Bayesian networks in Figures 15.2 and 15.3, we can see that the sparse structure in Figure 15.3 suggests one particular way to factorize the joint distribution as previously done. If we take advantage of this factorization, it will dramatically simplify the computation over the generic method using the product rule. Moreover, this sparse structure also suggests some potential independence implications among the underlying random variables. We will come back to this topic and discuss how to identify them in the next section.

Here, let us discuss how to choose all conditional distributions for a Bayesian network. Generally speaking, we normally prefer to choose a relatively simple model for each conditional distribution in Bayesian networks, for example, an e-family distribution. If we choose an e-family distribution for each conditional distribution in a Bayesian network, we can see that the joint distribution of all random variables also belongs to the e-family because it is a product of many e-family distributions. Furthermore, if the random variables in a Bayesian network are continuous, we normally assume their conditional distributions are Gaussian models with different mean and covariance parameters. This choice leads to the so-called *Gaussian Bayesian networks*, which are basically complicated versions of the *linear Gaussian models* we discussed in Section 13.2.

Refer to Section 12.1 for the definition of the *e-family distributions*.

In this chapter, we will focus more on Bayesian networks of all discrete random variables. Assume that x is a discrete random variable taking M distinct values. For notation convenience, we usually use a 1-of-M vector $\mathbf{x}$ to encode this random variable, denoted as $\mathbf{x} = \left[x_1\, x_2\, \cdots\, x_M\right]^\intercal$ (see margin note). Similarly, for another discrete random variable y taking N distinct values, we can use another 1-of-N vector $\mathbf{y} = \left[y_1\, y_2\, \cdots\, y_N\right]^\intercal$ to represent it. In this case, a conditional distribution $p(x|y)$ can be represented by the $M \times N$ table shown in Figure 15.4, where each element μ_{ij} ($1 \leq i \leq M$ and $1 \leq j \leq N$) denotes a conditional probability, as follows:

The 1-of-M vector $\mathbf{x}$ takes one of the following M different values:

$$[1\,0\,\cdots\,0]$$
$$[0\,1\,\cdots\,0]$$
$$\vdots$$
$$[0\,0\,\cdots\,1]$$

$$\mu_{ij} \triangleq \Pr(x = i \mid y = j) = \Pr(x_i = 1 \mid y_j = 1),$$

where x_i denotes the ith element of the 1-of-M vector $\mathbf{x}$ and y_j for the jth element of $\mathbf{y}$. We can quickly recognize that each column of the table forms a multinomial distribution, and it satisfies the sum-to-1 constraint: $\sum_{i=1}^{M} \mu_{ij} = 1$ for all $j = 1, 2, \cdots, N$. Using this notation, we can conveniently represent the conditional distribution as follows:

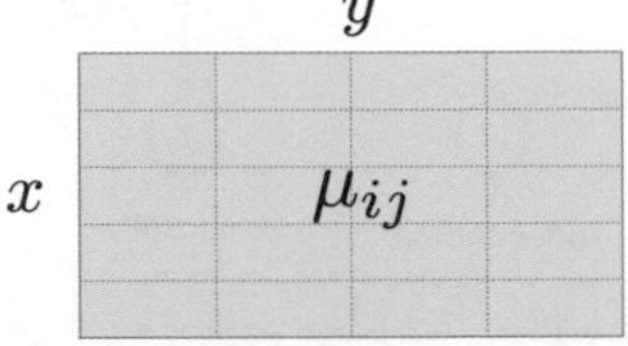

Figure 15.4: An illustration of a conditional distribution $p(x|y)$ between two discrete random variables.

$$p(x \mid y) = p(\mathbf{x} \mid \mathbf{y}) = \prod_{i=1}^{M} \prod_{j=1}^{N} \mu_{ij}^{x_i y_j}.$$

Similarly, we can extend the previous notation to conditional distributions involving more discrete random variables. For example, $p(x \mid y, z)$ can

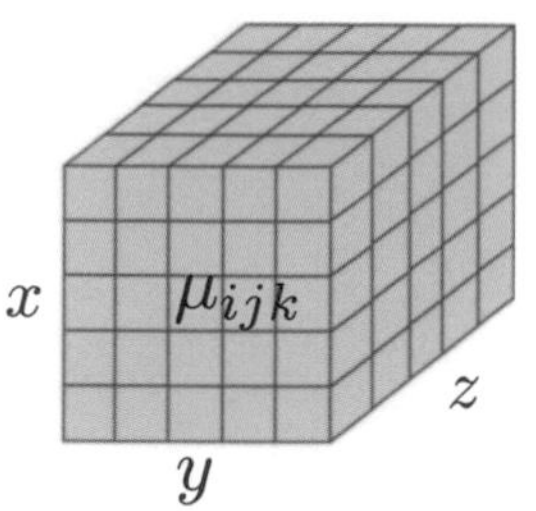

Figure 15.5: An illustration of a conditional distribution $p(x|y,z)$ involving three discrete random variables.

It is easy to verify that the conditional distribution $p(x_1 \mid x_2, x_3, x_4)$ can be represented as a four-dimensional (4D) table $\{\mu_{ijkl}\}$, and so on.

be encoded in a three-dimensional (3D) table, as shown in Figure 15.5, denoted as $\{\mu_{ijk}\}$. Therefore, we can represent this conditional distribution as

$$p(x \mid y, z) = p(\mathbf{x} \mid \mathbf{y}, \mathbf{z}) = \prod_{i=1}^{M} \prod_{j=1}^{N} \prod_{k=1}^{K} \mu_{ijk}^{x_i y_j z_k}.$$

On the other hand, an unconditional probability distribution $p(x)$ can be encoded in a one-dimensional (1D) table, denoted as $\{\mu_i\}$. Therefore, we have

$$p(x) = p(\mathbf{x}) = \prod_{i=1}^{M} \mu_i^{x_i}.$$

Finally, regarding how to formulate the joint distributions for undirected graphical models, we will consider this topic in Section 15.3.

15.2 Bayesian Networks

This section continues the discussion of several topics related to Bayesian networks, including how to interpret conditional dependencies in Bayesian networks, how to use Bayesian networks to represent generative models, and how to learn and make inferences for Bayesian networks.

15.2.1 Conditional Independence

Before we consider any general rules for identifying independence implications in Bayesian networks, let us discuss some basic junction patterns commonly used in Bayesian networks.

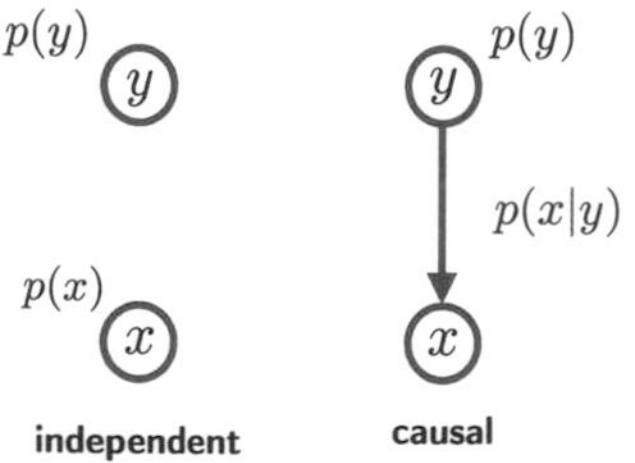

Figure 15.6: Two basic patterns involving two variables in a Bayesian network:
1. x and y are independent.
2. x and y are causal.

We first start with two simple networks of only two random variables. As shown in the left half of Figure 15.6, if two random variables x and y are not connected, they are statistically *independent* because of the implied factorization $p(x, y) = p(x)p(y)$, which is normally denoted as $x \perp y$. This can be extended to any disconnected random variables in a Bayesian network. If two random variables are not connected by any paths, we can immediately claim that they are independent. On the other hand, as shown in the right half of Figure 15.6, if two variables x and y are connected by a directed link from y to x, representing a conditional distribution $p(x|y)$, it indicates that they are mutually dependent. In a regular Bayesian network, the direction of a link is not critical because we can flip the direction of the link into "from x to y" by representing the reverse conditional distribution $p(y|x) = \frac{p(y)p(x|y)}{p(x)}$. In this case, either directed link leads to a valid Bayesian network, and they actually represent the same generative model. However, in some cases, we prefer to use the direction of the links to indicate the causal relation between two random variables; this results in a special type of Bayesian network, normally called a *causal Bayesian network* [184]. In a causal Bayesian network, a directed link from y to x indicates that the random variable x causally depends on y. In other words, it means that y is the cause and x is the effect in the physical interaction between these two variables. Note that the causation cannot be learned only from the data distribution, and it normally requires extra information on the physical process to correctly specify the direction of links in causal Bayesian networks [183, 186].

Next, we will continue to consider some basic junction patterns involving three variables in causal Bayesian networks. Assume that we focus on two variables x and y; let us investigate how a third variable z may affect their relationship in the following three different cases.

Confounding

As shown in Figure 15.7, in a so-called *fork* junction pattern, $x \leftarrow z \rightarrow y$, random variables x and y have a common cause variable z, which is commonly called a *confounder*. In this fork junction, we can factorize the joint distribution as follows:

$$p(x, y, z) = p(z) \cdot p(x|z) \cdot p(y|z). \tag{15.1}$$

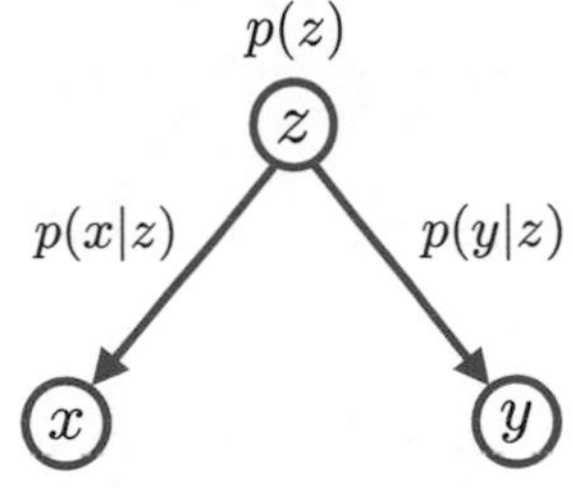

Figure 15.7: An illustration of how a confounding variable z affects the relation of its two different effects x and y in a so-called *fork* junction pattern, $x \leftarrow z \rightarrow y$.

In this case, it is easy to show that the confounder z causes a spurious association between x and y because they are not independent, as implied by $p(x, y) \neq p(x)p(y)$ (see margin note), usually denoted as $x \not\perp y$.

$$x \not\perp y \iff p(x, y) \neq p(x)\, p(y).$$

From Eq. (15.1), we can compute the marginal distributions $p(x)$, $p(y)$, and $p(x, y)$ separately. It is easy to verify:

$$\begin{aligned} p(x, y) &= \sum_z p(z)p(x|z)p(y|z) \\ &\neq p(x)p(y). \end{aligned}$$

However, once the confounder z is given, x and y become independent under this condition. This can be easily proved because we can derive $p(x, y \mid z) = p(x|z)p(y|z)$ from the confounding factorization in Eq. (15.1) (see margin note). In this case, it is said that x and y are *conditionally independent* given z, denoted as $x \perp y \mid z$:

$$x \perp y \mid z \iff p(x, y \mid z) = p(x|z)\, p(y|z).$$

For the confounding in Eq. (15.1), we have

$$\begin{aligned} p(x, y \mid z) &= \frac{p(x, y, z)}{p(z)} \\ &= \frac{\cancel{p(z)}p(x|z)p(y|z)}{\cancel{p(z)}} \\ &= p(x|z)p(y|z). \end{aligned}$$

As we know, a confounder causes some spurious association (or correlation) between two random variables, and even worse, the underlying confounders are often hidden in practice. As a result, we often misinterpret the spurious association due to some hidden confounders as the direct causation between the observed variables. This is a common mistake in data analysis. For example, it has been observed that when the number of people who drown in swimming pools in a region goes up, ice-cream sales tend to jump in the same region. Of course, we should not draw

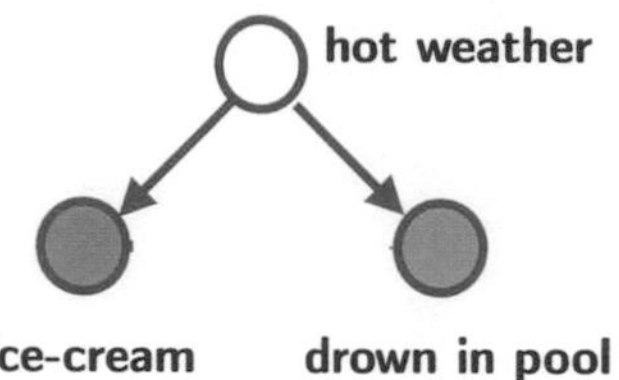

Figure 15.8: An illustration of how a hidden confounder associates two independent effect variables, where the two shaded variables are observed, but the confounder is often not observed.

the absurd conclusion that eating ice cream causes drowning in swimming pools. The correct interpretation is that these two variables are not causal but indirectly associated by some hidden confounder(s), such as hot weather, as shown in Figure 15.8. When the weather becomes hot, more people want to eat ice cream, and meanwhile, more people go swimming. More drowning accidents are caused by the hot weather rather than eating ice cream. On the other hand, if we only look at the data from some hot days (or some cool days), we can quickly realize that ice-cream sales and drowning deaths are in fact independent. This is the so-called *conditional independence* we have discussed.

Chain

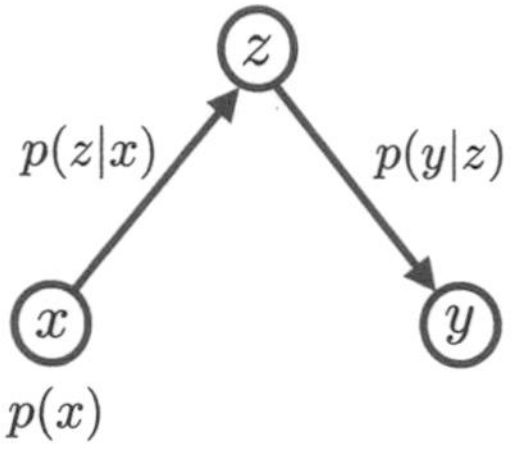

Figure 15.9: An illustration of how a mediator z affects the relation of two variables x and y in a so-called *chain* junction pattern, $x \to z \to y$.

As shown in Figure 15.9, in a *chain* junction pattern, $x \to z \to y$, the variable z is called a *mediator* that transmits the effect of x to y. In a chain junction, we can factorize the joint distribution as follows:

$$p(x, y, z) = p(x) \cdot p(z|x) \cdot p(y|z). \tag{15.2}$$

Similar to confounders, a mediator z also creates a spurious association between x and y because we can easily verify that x and y are not independent from the chain factorization in Eq. (15.2) (see margin note). In other words, we have

$$p(x,y) = \sum_z p(x)p(z|x)p(y|z)$$
$$= p(x)\sum_z p(z|x)p(y|z) \neq p(x)p(y).$$

$$x \not\perp y \iff p(x,y) \neq p(x)p(y).$$

However, if the mediator z is given (or controlled), it blocks information from x to y, and vice versa. This is true because we can derive the following conditional independence from Eq. (15.2) (see margin note) as follows:

$$\begin{aligned} p(x,y\,|\,z) &= \frac{p(x,y,z)}{p(z)} \\ &= \frac{p(x)p(z|x)p(y|z)}{p(z)} \\ &= \frac{p(x,z)p(y|z)}{p(z)} \\ &= p(x|z)p(y|z). \end{aligned}$$

$$x \perp y \,\big|\, z \iff p(x,y\,|\,z) = p(x|z)p(y|z).$$

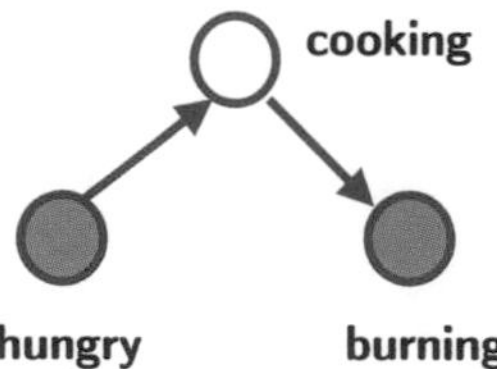

Figure 15.10: An illustration of how a mediator variable may associate two random variables. The two shaded variables are observed.

A mediator can also create a spurious association between two observed variables. In practice, relying on common sense or our intuition, it is usually much easier to identify the spurious association caused by a mediator than that caused by a confounder. For example, as shown in Figure 15.10, if someone feels hungry, he may start to cook food. When he is cooking, he may cut his fingers. From this observation, obviously, few people will draw the conclusion that hunger causes cutting of the fingers. However, if we control the mediator, the two observed variables become independent. If you do not cook, no matter how hungry you are, you will not cut your fingers. On the other hand, as long as you cook, you may cut your fingers, no matter whether you are hungry or not. This is the *conditional independence* similar to the confounding cases.

Colliding

As shown in Figure 15.11, in a so-called *colliding* junction pattern, $x \to z \leftarrow y$, two random variables x and y have a common effect z, which is usually called a *collider*. In a colliding junction, we can factorize the joint distribution as follows:

$$p(x, y, z) = p(x) \cdot p(y) \cdot p(z \mid x, y). \tag{15.3}$$

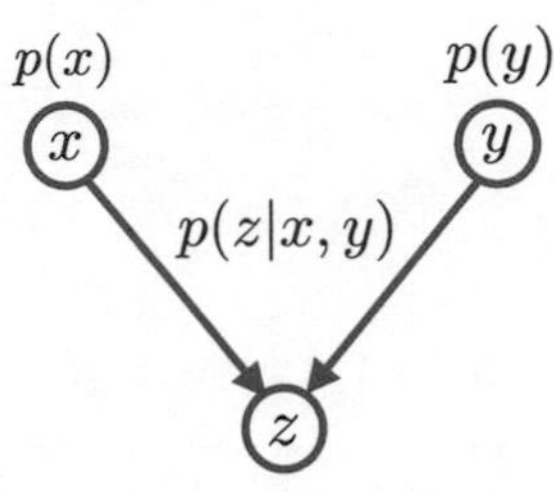

Figure 15.11: An illustration of how a collider z (common effect) affects the relation of its two independent causes x and y in a so-called *colliding* junction pattern, $x \to z \leftarrow y$.

Interestingly enough, under this colliding factorization, we can easily show that x and y are actually independent because we can prove that $p(x, y) = p(x)p(y)$ (see margin note). Therefore, we have

$$x \perp y \iff p(x, y) = p(x)p(y).$$

$$\begin{aligned} p(x,y) &= \sum_z p(x,y,z) \\ &= \sum_z p(x)p(y)p(z|x,y) \\ &= p(x)p(y) \sum_z p(z|x,y) = p(x)p(y). \end{aligned}$$

On the other hand, once the collider z is given, x and y are not independent anymore because we can show that $p(x, y \mid z) \neq p(x|z)p(y|z)$ holds for the colliding junction (see margin note), which is normally denoted as follows:

$$x \not\perp y \mid z \iff p(x, y \mid z) \neq p(x|z)p(y|z).$$

$$\begin{aligned} p(x,y|z) &= \frac{p(x,y,z)}{p(z)} \\ &= \frac{p(x)p(y)p(z|x,y)}{p(z)} \\ &\neq p(x|z)p(y|z). \end{aligned}$$

An interesting phenomenon in machine learning, called *explain away*, is attributed to the colliding junction. Assuming there exists a common effect (collider) z that may be caused by two independent causes x or y, if we only observe z, we know it may be caused by either x or y or both. However, if we observe z and also know one cause x happens, this will explain away the other cause y. In other words, the conditional probability of y given both z and x is always smaller than that of y given only z. Let us use a simple example to further explain this interesting phenomenon of *explain away*.

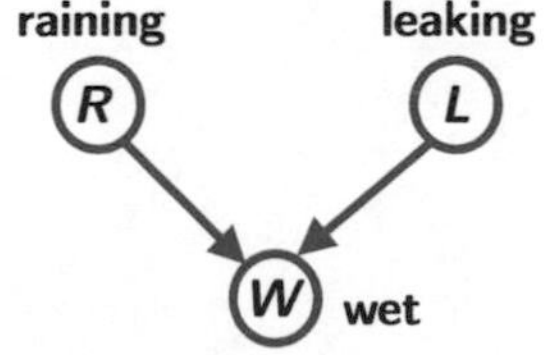

Figure 15.12: An illustration of the explain-away phenomenon, where a common effect may be caused by two independent causes.
R: It was raining.
L: The water pipe was leaking.
W: The driveway is wet.

Example 15.2.1 Explain Away

As shown in Figure 15.12, a wet driveway (W) may be caused by two independent reasons: (1) it was raining (R), or (2) the water pipe was leaking (L). Show how the observation of one cause, L, can explain away the other cause, R.

Let us assume that the three random variables in Figure 15.12 are all binary (yes/no) (i.e., $R, L, W \in \{0, 1\}$). We further assume all conditional distributions are given as follows:

$$\Pr(R = 1) = 0.1 \quad \Pr(L = 1) = 0.01$$

$$\Pr(W = 1 \mid R = 1, L = 1) = 0.90 \quad \Pr(W = 1 \mid R = 1, L = 0) = 0.80$$

$$\Pr(W = 1 \mid R = 0, L = 1) = 0.50 \quad \Pr(W = 1 \mid R = 0, L = 0) = 0.20.$$

Obviously, we have

$$\begin{aligned} &\Pr(R = 0) = 1 - \Pr(R = 1) = 0.9 \\ &\Pr(L = 0) = 1 - \Pr(L = 1) = 0.99 \\ &\Pr(W = 0 \mid R = 1, L = 1) \\ &= 1 - \Pr(W = 1 \mid R = 1, L = 1) \\ &= 0.10, \end{aligned}$$

and so on.

First of all, before we observe anything, the prior probability of raining is given as $\Pr(R = 1) = 0.1$.

Second, assume we have observed that the driveway is wet (i.e., $W = 1$). Let us compute the conditional probability of raining (see margin note):

$$\Pr(R = 1 \mid W = 1) = \frac{\Pr(W = 1, R = 1)}{\Pr(W = 1)} = \mathbf{0.3048}.$$

$\Pr(W = 1, R = 1) =$
$\Pr(W{=}1,L{=}1,R{=}1) + \Pr(W{=}1,L{=}0,R{=}1)$
$= 0.1 \times 0.01 \times 0.9 + 0.99 \times 0.1 \times 0.8$
$= 0.0801.$

$\Pr(W = 1, R = 0) =$
$\Pr(W{=}1,L{=}1,R{=}0) + \Pr(W{=}1,L{=}0,R{=}0)$
$= 0.01 \times 0.9 \times 0.5 + 0.99 \times 0.9 \times 0.2$
$= 0.1827.$

$\Pr(W = 1) =$
$\Pr(W = 1, R = 1) + \Pr(W = 1, R = 0)$
$= 0.2628.$

$\Pr(W = 1, L = 1) =$
$\Pr(W{=}1,L{=}1,R{=}1) + \Pr(W{=}1,L{=}1,R{=}0)$
$= 0.1 \times 0.01 \times 0.9 + 0.9 \times 0.01 \times 0.5$
$= 0.0054.$

As we can see, the observation of the effect ($W = 1$) significantly increases the probability of any possible cause. The probability that it was raining has gone up from 0.1 to 0.3048.

Third, assume that after we have observed that the driveway is wet, we have also found out that the water pipe was leaking ($L = 1$). Let us compute the conditional probability of raining in this case, as follows:

$$\Pr(R = 1 \mid W = 1, L = 1) = \frac{\Pr(W = 1, L = 1, R = 1)}{\Pr(W = 1, L = 1)} = \mathbf{0.1667}.$$

This shows that after we know that the water pipe was leaking (one cause), the probability of raining (another cause) is largely reduced from 0.3048 to 0.1667. In other words, the observation of one cause has significantly *explained away* the possibility of all other independent causes, whereas normally, these two factors (raining and leaking water pipe) are totally independent. ♦

Finally, we can extend the previous discussion of conditional independence from three simple cases into more general Bayesian networks so as to derive the famous *d-separation* rule [182]. Generally speaking, given any three disjoint subsets of variables A, B and C, for any path from A to B in a Bayesian network, we say that the path is blocked by C if the following two conditions hold at the same time:

1. All confounders and mediators along the path belong to C.
2. Neither any collider nor any of its descendants belongs to C.

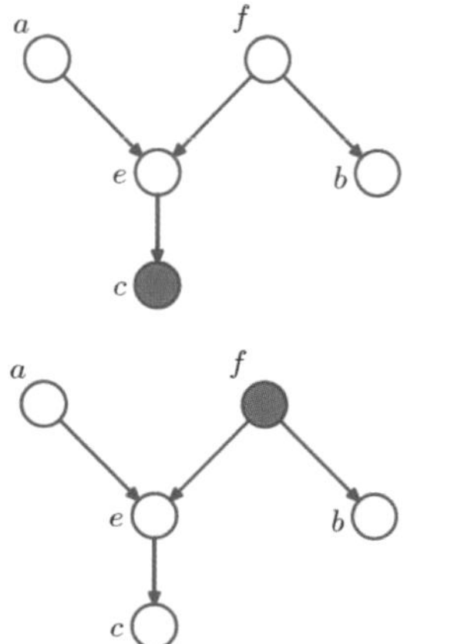

Figure 15.13: An simple example to explain the d-separation rule. (Source: Bishop [22].)

If all paths from A to B are blocked by C, it is said that A and B are d-separated by C, denoted as $A \perp B \mid C$. In other words, any random variables in A are conditionally independent from all variables in B given all variables in C. Otherwise, if any path is not blocked, A and B are not conditionally independent given C, denoted as $A \not\perp B \mid C$.

For example, given the simple causal Bayesian network in Figure 15.13, after we apply the d-separation rule to it, we can verify the following:

$$a \not\perp f \mid c \qquad a \not\perp b \mid c$$

$$a \not\perp c \mid f \qquad a \perp b \mid f \qquad e \perp b \mid f.$$

15.2.2 Representing Generative Models as Bayesian Networks

An important use of graphical models in machine learning is to intuitively represent many generative models with a graphical representation to explicitly display the underlying dependency structure of various random variables. In the following, we will discuss how to represent some popular generative models as Bayesian networks. Remember that the basic rule in a Bayesian network is that we use a node to represent a random variable and a directed link for a conditional distribution between some variables. Note that some random variables are labeled as "observed," and the others as "missing," which are treated as latent variables. We have to explicitly differentiate these two types of nodes in a Bayesian network.

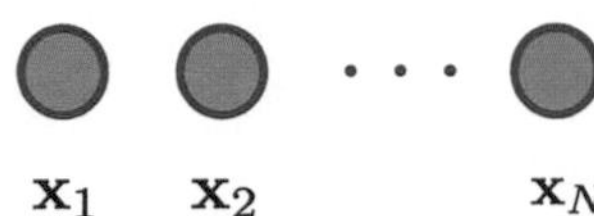

Figure 15.14: Representing Gaussian models as a Bayesian network for N i.i.d. data samples. The observed random variables are represented with shaded nodes.

Let us start with multivariate Gaussian models. As shown in Figure 15.14, a Gaussian model can be represented by a Bayesian network of some disconnected nodes, each of which stands for an independent and identically distributed (i.i.d.) data sample $\mathbf{x}_i$. All nodes are shaded in blue to indicate that they all represent some observed random variables. Each node represents a distribution specified by the Gaussian model as $p(\mathbf{x}_i) = \mathcal{N}(\mathbf{x}_i \mid \boldsymbol{\mu}, \Sigma)$ for all $i = 1, 2, \cdots, N$. In practice, we usually adopt the compact plate notation shown in Figure 15.15 to simplify the Bayesian network in Figure 15.14. In this case, the plate notation represents a repetition of N copies of the same network structure.

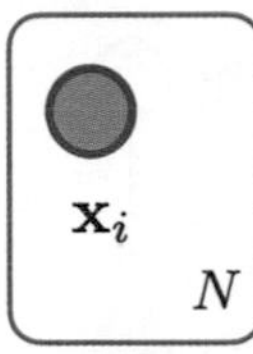

Figure 15.15: Using the plate notation to represent Gaussian models as a Bayesian network for N i.i.d. data samples.

Furthermore, we can also use the Bayesian network shown in Figure 15.16 to represent the Bayesian learning of a Gaussian model with a known covariance matrix Σ_0. As we know, all unknown model parameters are treated as random variables in Bayesian learning. Therefore, we have to add a new node to represent the unknown Gaussian mean vector $\boldsymbol{\mu}$, and this node is not shaded to indicate that it is unobserved in the Bayesian learning, so we will have to treat the Gaussian mean as a latent variable. In this Bayesian network, the prior distribution $p(\boldsymbol{\mu})$ is specified for the node of $\boldsymbol{\mu}$. The directed link represents the conditional distribution $p(\mathbf{x}_i \mid \boldsymbol{\mu}) = \mathcal{N}(\mathbf{x}_i \mid \boldsymbol{\mu}, \Sigma_0)$. Based on the rule of Bayesian networks, this structure implies the following way to factorize the joint distribution:

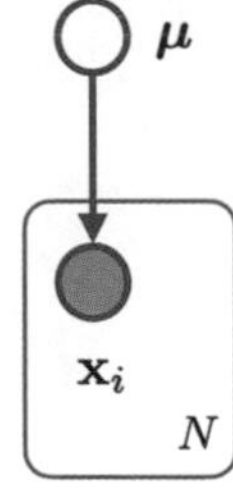

Figure 15.16: Using a Bayesian network to represent the Bayesian learning of Gaussian models (with a known covariance matrix) with N i.i.d. data samples. The observed variables are represented by shaded nodes and latent variables by unshaded nodes.

$$p(\boldsymbol{\mu}, \mathbf{x}_1, \cdots \mathbf{x}_N) = p(\boldsymbol{\mu}) \prod_{i=1}^{N} p(\mathbf{x}_i | \boldsymbol{\mu}).$$

We can verify that this factorization is identical to the Bayesian learning rule in Eq. (14.1).

Next, let us consider how to use a Bayesian network to represent a Gaussian mixture model (GMM) of M Gaussian components. For each data sample $\mathbf{x}_i$, we introduce a 1-of-M latent variable $\mathbf{z}_i$ to indicate which component $\mathbf{x}_i$ belongs to. Each $\mathbf{z}_i$ can take one of M distinct values. We can represent the GMM for N i.i.d. data samples with the Bayesian network shown in Figure 15.17. We use an unshaded node to represent each latent variable $\mathbf{z}_i$. Furthermore, we can specify a distribution for each node of $\mathbf{z}_i$ as follows:

The latent variable

$$\mathbf{z}_i = \begin{bmatrix} z_{i1} & z_{i2} & \cdots & z_{iM} \end{bmatrix}$$

may take one of the following values:

$$\begin{bmatrix} 1 & 0 & \cdots & 0 \end{bmatrix}$$
$$\begin{bmatrix} 0 & 1 & \cdots & 0 \end{bmatrix}$$
$$\vdots$$
$$\begin{bmatrix} 0 & 0 & \cdots & 1 \end{bmatrix}$$

$$p(\mathbf{z}_i) = \prod_{m=1}^{M} \left(w_m\right)^{z_{im}},$$

where w_m denotes the mixture weight of the mth Gaussian component. Moreover, the directed link represents the following conditional distribution:

$$p(\mathbf{x}_i \mid \mathbf{z}_i) = \prod_{m=1}^{M} \Big(\mathcal{N}(\mathbf{x}_i \mid \boldsymbol{\mu}_m, \Sigma_m)\Big)^{z_{im}},$$

where $\mathcal{N}(\boldsymbol{\mu}_m, \Sigma_m)$ denotes the mth Gaussian component. The model structure in Figure 15.17 indicates the following factorization for the joint distribution:

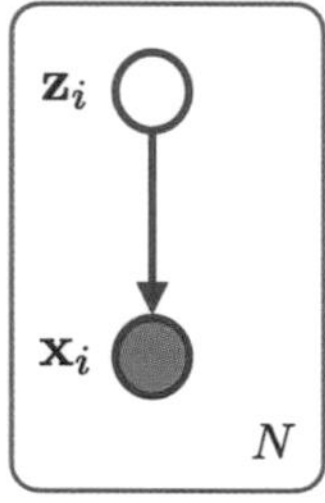

Figure 15.17: An illustration of a Bayesian network to represent a GMM of M Gaussian mixture components.

$$p(\mathbf{x}_1, \cdots, \mathbf{x}_N, \mathbf{z}_1, \cdots, \mathbf{z}_N) = \prod_{i=1}^{N} p(\mathbf{z}_i) p(\mathbf{x}_i | \mathbf{z}_i).$$

If we marginalize out all latent variables $\{\mathbf{z}_1, \cdots, \mathbf{z}_N\}$, we derive the following marginal distribution of all data samples:

$$p(\mathbf{x}_1, \cdots, \mathbf{x}_N) = \prod_{i=1}^{N} \Big(\underbrace{\sum_{\mathbf{z}_i} p(\mathbf{z}_i) p(\mathbf{x}_i | \mathbf{z}_i)}_{p(\mathbf{x}_i)} \Big).$$

Considering that each $\mathbf{z}_i$ takes only M distinct values. as described previously, we can verify that this $p(\mathbf{x}_i)$ is identical to the original definition of GMMs in Eq. (12.6).

Furthermore, we can extend the graphical representation for the Bayesian learning of GMMs discussed in Example 14.3.1. In this case, we need to add some unshaded nodes to represent all GMM parameters: a vector of all mixture weights as $\mathbf{w} = [w_1 \cdots w_M]^\intercal$ and all Gaussian mean vectors and covariance matrices $\{\boldsymbol{\mu}_m, \Sigma_m\}$. If we specify the dependency among all random variable as shown in Figure 15.18 and choose the following conditional distributions for all directed links:

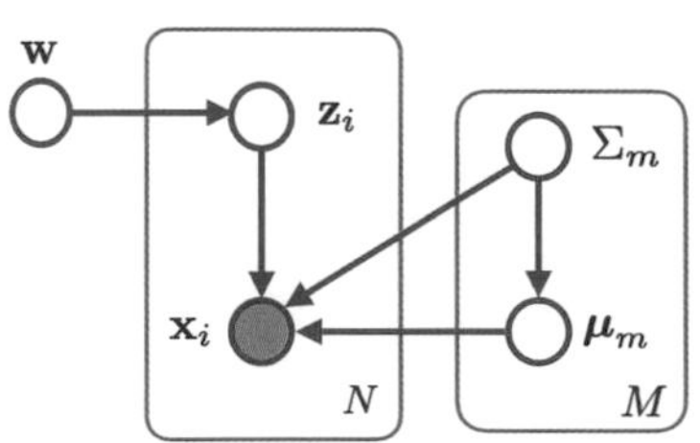

Figure 15.18: An illustration of a Bayesian network to represent the Bayesian learning of the GMM of M Gaussian mixture components in Example 14.3.1.

$$p(\mathbf{w}) = \text{Dir}(\mathbf{w} \,|\, \alpha^{(0)})$$

$$p(\mathbf{z}_i \mid \mathbf{w}) = \prod_{m=1}^{M} \left(w_m\right)^{z_{im}} \quad \forall i = 1, 2, \cdots N$$

$$p(\Sigma_m) = \mathcal{W}^{-1}\left(\Sigma_m \,\middle|\, \Phi_m^{(0)}, \nu_m^{(0)}\right) \quad \forall m = 1, 2, \cdots M$$

$$p(\boldsymbol{\mu}_m \,|\, \Sigma_m) = \mathcal{N}\left(\boldsymbol{\mu}_m \,\middle|\, \boldsymbol{\nu}_m^{(0)}, \frac{1}{\lambda_m^{(0)}}\Sigma_m\right) \quad \forall m = 1, 2, \cdots M$$

$$p(\mathbf{x}_i \,|\, \mathbf{z}_i, \{\boldsymbol{\mu}_m, \Sigma_m\}) = \prod_{m=1}^{M} \left(\mathcal{N}(\mathbf{x}_i \,|\, \boldsymbol{\mu}_m, \Sigma_m)\right)^{z_{im}} \quad \forall i = 1, 2, \cdots N,$$

then we can verify that these specifications lead to exactly the same formulation as in Example 14.3.1.

Along the same line of thought, we can represent the Markov chain models discussed in Section 11.3 for any sequence $\{x_1, x_2, x_3, x_4 \cdots\}$ with the Bayesian networks shown in Figure 15.19. In a first-order Markov chain model, each state only depends on its previous state as $p(x_i|x_{i-1})$, which is represented by a directed link from one observation to the next. In a second-order Markov chain model, each state depends on the two preceding states as $p(x_i|x_{i-1}, x_{i-2})$, which is reflected by the directed links from two parent nodes. As we can see, there are no latent variables in Markov chain models.

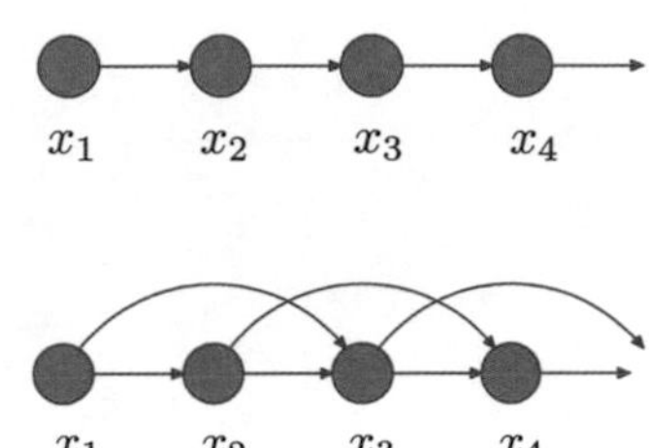

Figure 15.19: An illustration of Bayesian networks to represent Markov chain models for a sequence:
1. First-order Markov chain
2. Second-order Markov chain

On the other hand, the hidden Markov models (HMMs) discussed in Section 12.4 can be represented by the Bayesian network shown in Figure 15.20 for an observation sequence $\{\mathbf{x}_1, \mathbf{x}_2 \cdots, \mathbf{x}_T\}$. Here, we introduce all corresponding Markov states s_t as latent variables for all $t = 1, 2, \cdots, T$. As in the definition of HMMs, each observation $\mathbf{x}_t$ only depends on the current Markov state s_t, which in turn depends on the previous state s_{t-1}. The model structure in Figure 15.20 suggests the following factorization for the joint distribution:

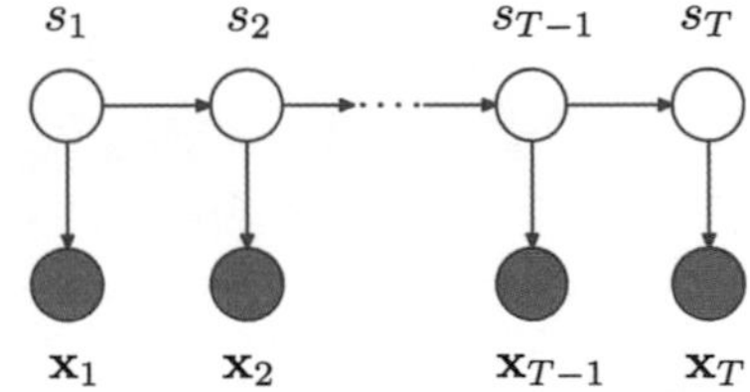

Figure 15.20: An illustration of Bayesian networks to represent HMMs for a sequence of $\{\mathbf{x}_1, \cdots, \mathbf{x}_T\}$.

$$p(s_1, \cdots, s_T, \mathbf{x}_1, \cdots, \mathbf{x}_T) = p(s_1)p(\mathbf{x}_1|s_1)\prod_{t=2}^{T} p(s_t|s_{t-1})p(\mathbf{x}_t|s_t).$$

If we marginalize out all latent variables $\{s_1, \cdots, s_T\}$, we can derive the following marginal distribution for all observations:

$$p(\mathbf{x}_1, \cdots, \mathbf{x}_T) = \sum_{s_1, \cdots, s_T} p(s_1, \cdots, s_T, \mathbf{x}_1, \cdots, \mathbf{x}_T).$$

This computation results in the same formulation in Eq. (12.15) as the original definition of HMMs in Section 12.4.

15.2.3 Learning Bayesian Networks

As we have seen, Bayesian networks are a flexible graphical representation for a variety of generative models. An interesting question is how we can automatically learn Bayesian networks from available training data. This learning problem usually includes two different parts:

1. **Structure learning**
   In structure learning, we need to answer some questions related to the graph structure. For example, how many latent variables are actually involved? Which random variables in a model are linked, and which variables are not? How do we determine the direction of the links for those connected nodes? Unfortunately, structure learning is largely an open problem in machine learning. The model structure relies much on the underlying data-generation mechanism, and it is generally believed that the data distribution alone does not provide enough information to infer the correct model structure. For a given data distribution, we often can come up with a vast number of differently structured models that yield the same data distribution (see Exercises Q15.1 and Q15.2). In practice, the model structure has to be manually specified based on the understanding of the given data, as well as some general assumptions about the physical data-generation process.

2. **Parameter estimation**
   How do we learn the conditional distributions for all directed links in a given model structure? Assuming that all random variables are discrete, these conditional distributions are essentially many different multinomial distributions. In this case, this step reduces to a parameter-estimation problem, that is, how to estimate all parameters in these multinomial distributions. In contrast, parameter estimation is a well-solved problem in machine learning. As we have seen in the previous chapters, unknown parameters can be estimated by optimizing various objective functions, such as maximum-likelihood estimation (MLE) or maximum a posteriori (MAP) estimation.

Once the structure is specified, a Bayesian network usually represents a particular way to factorize the joint distribution of many different random variables:

$$p_{\boldsymbol{\theta}}(x_1, x_2, x_3, \cdots),$$

where $\boldsymbol{\theta}$ denotes all unknown parameters.

If we can observe all random variables in the joint distribution, the parameter estimation is actually a fairly simple problem. Assume we have collected a training set of many samples of these random variables as follows:

$$\left\{ \left(x_1^{(1)}, x_2^{(1)}, x_3^{(1)}, \cdots\right), \left(x_1^{(2)}, x_2^{(2)}, x_3^{(2)}, \cdots\right), \cdots \left(x_1^{(i)}, x_2^{(i)}, x_3^{(i)}, \cdots\right), \cdots \right\}.$$

As we have seen, the unknown model parameter $\boldsymbol{\theta}$ can be estimated by maximizing the following log-likelihood function:

$$l(\boldsymbol{\theta}) = \sum_i \ln p_{\boldsymbol{\theta}}(x_1^{(i)}, x_2^{(i)}, x_3^{(i)}, \cdots).$$

After we factorize the joint distribution, it results in some simple expressions because the logarithm can be directly applied to each conditional distribution, which is usually assumed to belong to the e-family. In this case, we normally can derive a closed-form solution to the MLE for all unknown parameters $\boldsymbol{\theta}$, such as the Markov chain models in Section 11.3.

In many other cases where the underlying model contains some latent variables, we cannot fully observe all random variables in the joint distribution. For example, we can only observe a subset of random variables in the available training samples:

$$\Big\{(x_1^{(1)}, *, x_3^{(1)}, \cdots), (x_1^{(2)}, *, x_3^{(2)}, \cdots), \cdots, (x_1^{(i)}, *, x_3^{(i)}, \cdots), \cdots\Big\},$$

where we assume the latent variable x_2 is not observed in the training set. In this case, we have to marginalize out all latent variables to derive the following log-likelihood function for parameter estimation:

$$l(\boldsymbol{\theta}) = \sum_i \ln \sum_{x_2} p_{\boldsymbol{\theta}}(x_1^{(1)}, x_2, x_3^{(1)}, \cdots).$$

Similar to the mixture models described in Chapter 12, this log-likelihood function contains some log-sum terms. In this case, we can use the expectation-maximization (EM) method to estimate all model parameters $\boldsymbol{\theta}$ in an iterative fashion.

15.2.4 Inference Algorithms

Once a Bayesian network is learned, it fully specifies a joint distribution of all underlying random variables as follows:

$$p(\underbrace{x_1, x_2, x_3,}_{\text{observed } \mathbf{x}} \underbrace{x_4, x_5, x_6}_{\text{interested } \mathbf{y}}, \underbrace{x_7, x_8, \cdots}_{\text{missing } \mathbf{z}}).$$

As shown previously, we can always categorize all random variables into three different groups:

1. All observed variables, denoted as $\mathbf{x}$;
2. Some unobserved variables that we are interested in, denoted as $\mathbf{y}$;
3. The remaining unobserved variables, denoted as $\mathbf{z}$.

The central inference problem lies in that we want to use the given Bayesian network to make some decisions regarding the variables of interest $\mathbf{y}$ based on the observed variables $\mathbf{x}$. As we have seen in the discussion of Bayesian decision theory in Chapter 10, the optimal decision must be made based on the conditional distribution $p(\mathbf{y} \mid \mathbf{x})$. The Bayesian network specifies the joint distribution $p(\mathbf{x}, \mathbf{y}, \mathbf{z})$, and the required conditional distribution can be readily computed as follows:

We assume all random variables are discrete here. For continuous random variables, we just need to replace all summations with the integrals over $\mathbf{y}$ or $\mathbf{z}$.

$$p(\mathbf{y} \mid \mathbf{x}) = \frac{p(\mathbf{x}, \mathbf{y})}{p(\mathbf{x})} = \frac{\sum_{\mathbf{z}} p(\mathbf{x}, \mathbf{y}, \mathbf{z})}{\sum_{\mathbf{y},\mathbf{z}} p(\mathbf{x}, \mathbf{y}, \mathbf{z})}. \tag{15.4}$$

Once the Bayesian network is given, at least in principle, we can sum over all combinations of $\mathbf{y}$ and $\mathbf{z}$ to compute the numerator and denominator so as to derive the required conditional distribution. However, any brute-force method is extremely expensive in computation. Assume the total number of variables in $\mathbf{y}$ and $\mathbf{z}$ is T, and each discrete random variable can take up to K distinct values. The computational complexity to sum for the denominator is exponential (i.e., $O(K^T)$), which is prohibitive in practical scenarios. Therefore, when we use any Bayesian network to make inferences, the critical question is how to design more efficient algorithms to compute the summations in a smarter way.

Table 15.1 lists the popular inference algorithms proposed for graphical models in the literature. Generally speaking, these inference algorithms are broken into two major categories: exact or approximate inference.

Table 15.1: A summary of some representative inference algorithms for a variety of graphical models:

1. Brute-force method
2. Forward–backward method
3. Sum-product algorithm (a.k.a. belief propagation)
4. Max-sum algorithm
5. Junction-tree algorithm
6. Loopy belief propagation
7. Variational inference
8. Expectation propagation
9. Monte Carlo sampling

Here, T denotes the total number of random variables in a discrete graphical model, and K denotes the maximum number of distinct values each discrete variable can take, and p is the tree width of a graph.

	Inference algorithm	**Applicable graphs**	**Complexity**
Exact inference	Brute force	All	$O(K^T)$
	Forward–backward	Chain	$O(T \cdot K^2)$
	Sum-product (belief propagation)	Tree	$O(T \cdot K^2)$
	Max-sum	Tree	$O(T \cdot K^2)$
	Junction tree	All	$O(K^p)$
Approximate inference	Loopy belief propagation	All	—
	Variational inference	All	—
	Expectation propagation	All	—
	Monte Carlo sampling	All	—

All exact-inference algorithms aim to precisely compute the conditional distribution in an efficient way. The basic idea behind these exact-inference methods is to use dynamic programming to compute the summations locally and recursively by exploring the structure of a graph, such as the *forward–backward* algorithm [194] for chain-structured graphs and the *sum-product* algorithm (a.k.a. *belief propagation*) [180, 140, 134, 22] and the *max-sum* algorithm [245, 22] for tree-structured graphs. In general, these algorithms are fairly efficient because the summations can be computed by some local operations in an acyclic graph, such as message passing between two neighboring nodes. Therefore, the computational complexity of these algorithms is usually quadratic (i.e., $O(T \cdot K^2)$).

However, for more general graphs, dynamic programming leads to the famous junction-tree algorithm [140, 13]. The computational cost of the junction-tree algorithm will grow exponentially with the tree width (denoted as p) of a graph, which is defined as the largest number of mutually connected nodes in the graph. Therefore, the junction-tree algorithm normally becomes impractical for large and densely connected graphs.

On the other hand, approximate-inference methods aim to approximate the conditional distribution using different strategies. In the so-called *loopy belief propagation* method [182, 71], the computationally cheap sum-product algorithm is directly run on a general graph that may contain loops. This method will not produce the correct result for any cyclic graph, but it has been found that it may yield acceptable results in some applications [70, 154].

In the *variational inference* [119, 5] and *expectation propagation* [164, 22] methods, some variational distributions $q(\mathbf{y})$ are used to approximate the true conditional distribution $p(\mathbf{y} \,|\, \mathbf{x})$. Similar to Section 14.3.2, under some factorization assumptions, the best-fit variational distribution can be derived using some iterative methods. After that, the inference will be made based on the best-fit variational distribution instead of the true conditional distribution.

Finally, in the *Monte Carlo* method [155], we directly sample the joint distribution specified by a graphical model to generate many independent samples. The conditional distribution is then estimated from all randomly drawn samples. This method normally results in fairly accurate estimates if we have resources to generate a large number of samples.

In this chapter, we will not fully cover the inference algorithms in Table 15.1 but just want to use some simple cases to highlight the key ideas behind them. For example, we will briefly introduce the forward–backward algorithm to explain how to perform message passing on a chain-structured graph, and we will use a simple example to show how to implement Monte Carlo sampling to generate samples to estimate the required conditional distribution. Interested readers need to refer to the given references for more details on other inference algorithms.

Forward–Backward Inference: Message Passing on a Chain

Given a Bayesian network of T discrete random variables, each of which takes up to K distinct values, as shown in Figure 15.21, the chain structure suggests the following factorization for the joint distribution of these variables:

$$p(x_1, x_2, \cdots, x_T) = p(x_1)p(x_2|x_1)\cdots p(x_n|x_{n-1})\cdots p(x_T|x_{T-1}). \qquad (15.5)$$

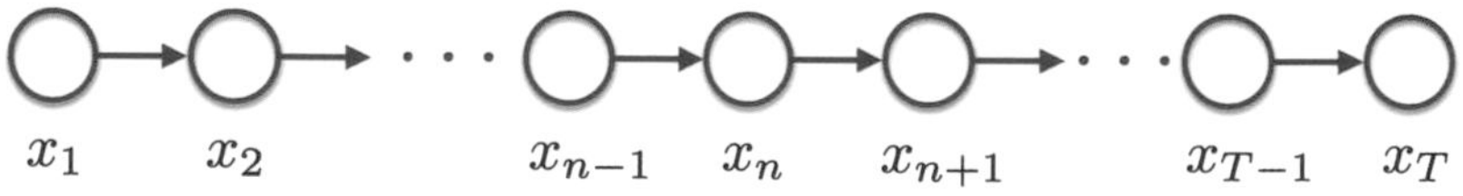

Figure 15.21: An illustration of a chain-structured Bayesian network of T random variables (i.e., $x_1, x_2, \cdots, x_T$).

Let us consider how to compute the summations in this Bayesian network as required by the conditional distribution in Eq. (15.4). As an example, we will compute the marginal distribution $p(x_n)$ of one arbitrary variable x_n. By definition, we need to marginalize out all other variables in the joint distribution as follows:

$$p(x_n) = \sum_{x_1}\cdots\sum_{x_{n-1}}\sum_{x_{n+1}}\cdots\sum_{x_T} p(x_1, x_2, \cdots, x_T).$$

This summation involves K^{T-1} different terms, and the computational complexity is generally exponential. However, if we explore the chain structure of the network, we can significantly facilitate the computation.

After we substitute the chain factorization in Eq.(15.5) into the previous summation, we can group the summation into a product of two parts; one is the summation from x_1 to x_{n-1}, and the other is from x_{n+1} to x_T, as follows:

$$\begin{aligned} p(x_n) &= \sum_{x_1}\cdots\sum_{x_{n-1}}\sum_{x_{n+1}}\cdots\sum_{x_T} p(x_1)p(x_2|x_1)p(x_3|x_2)\cdots p(x_T|x_{T-1}) \\ &= \Bigg(\sum_{x_1\cdots x_{n-1}} p(x_1)\cdots p(x_n|x_{n-1})\Bigg)\Bigg(\sum_{x_{n+1}\cdots x_T} p(x_{n+1}|x_n)\cdots p(x_T|x_{T-1})\Bigg). \end{aligned}$$

Furthermore, this chain factorization allows us to use dynamic programming to recursively sum over each individual variable one by one for both parts, as follows:

$$p(x_n) = \overbrace{\Big(\sum_{x_{n-1}} p(x_n|x_{n-1}) \cdots \overbrace{\Big(\sum_{x_2} p(x_3|x_2) \overbrace{\Big(\sum_{x_1} \overbrace{p(x_1)}^{\alpha_1(x_1)} p(x_2|x_1)\Big)}^{\alpha_2(x_2)}\Big)}^{\alpha_3(x_3)}\Big)}^{\alpha_n(x_n)}$$

$$\underbrace{\Big(\sum_{x_{n+1}} p(x_{n+1}|x_n) \cdots \underbrace{\Big(\sum_{x_{T-1}} p(x_{T-1}|x_{T-2}) \underbrace{\Big(\sum_{x_T} p(x_T|x_{T-1})\Big)}_{\beta_{T-1}(x_{T-1})}\Big)}_{\beta_{T-2}(x_{T-2})}\Big)}_{\beta_n(x_n)}$$

Note that this recursive summation technique is the same, in principle, as the forward–backward algorithm for HMMs discussed in Section 12.4.

All summations for each $\alpha_t(x_t)$ and $\beta_t(x_t)$ can be recursively computed as follows:

$$\alpha_t(x_t) = \sum_{x_{t-1}} p(x_t|x_{t-1})\,\alpha_{t-1}(x_{t-1}) \quad (\forall t = 2, \cdots, n)$$
$$\beta_t(x_t) = \sum_{x_{t+1}} p(x_{t+1}|x_t)\,\beta_{t+1}(x_{t+1}) \quad (\forall t = T-1, \cdots, n).$$

If we use the matrix form in Figure 15.4 to represent each conditional distribution $p(x_t|x_{t-1})$ as a $K \times K$ matrix $\left[\ \mu_{ij}^{(t)}\ \right]$, and we use two $K \times 1$ vectors (i.e., $\boldsymbol{\alpha}_t$ and $\boldsymbol{\beta}_t$) to represent $\alpha_t(x_t)$ and $\beta_t(x_t)$ for K different values of x_t, the previous two equations can be compactly represented with matrix multiplication as follows:

$$\boldsymbol{\alpha}_t = \left[\ \mu_{ij}^{(t)}\ \right] \boldsymbol{\alpha}_{t-1} \qquad (\forall t = 2, \cdots, n)$$

$$\boldsymbol{\beta}_t = \left[\ \mu_{ij}^{(t+1)}\ \right]^{\intercal} \boldsymbol{\beta}_{t+1} \qquad (\forall t = T-1, \cdots, n).$$

It is easy to verify that the computational complexity of each of these updates is $O(K^2)$. Each of these local updates can be represented as shown in Figure 15.22.

Interestingly enough, the previous computation can be conveniently implemented as some local operations on the graph. Assume we maintain a message, vector $\boldsymbol{\alpha}_t$, for each node x_t in the graph. After we initialize for the first node x_1 on the chain as $\boldsymbol{\alpha}_1 = \left[\ p(x_1)\ \right]$, we can use the previous formula to recursively update all messages on the chain one by one from left to right, as shown in Figure 15.23. These local graph operations are

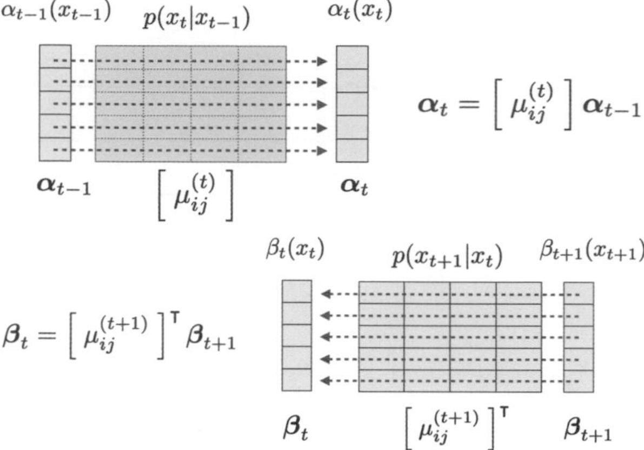

Figure 15.22: An illustration of using matrix multiplication to locally update messages for each node on a chain: (top) forward updating from left to right; (bottom) backward updating from right to left.

often called *message passing* (a.k.a. *belief propagation*). The idea of message passing can also be applied to all vectors $\boldsymbol{\beta}_t$ in the graph. We first initialize it for the last node on the chain x_T as $\boldsymbol{\beta}_T = \mathbf{1}$, and we use the previous formula to similarly pass the messages backward one by one all the way to x_1, as shown in Figure 15.23.

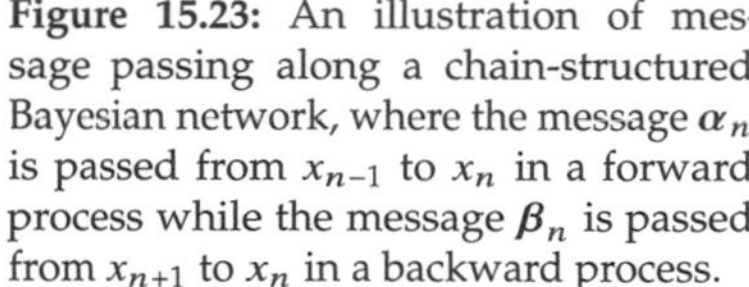

Figure 15.23: An illustration of message passing along a chain-structured Bayesian network, where the message $\boldsymbol{\alpha}_n$ is passed from x_{n-1} to x_n in a forward process while the message $\boldsymbol{\beta}_n$ is passed from x_{n+1} to x_n in a backward process.

Once we have obtained both $\boldsymbol{\alpha}_t$ and $\boldsymbol{\beta}_t$ for all nodes in the graph, we can use them to compute many marginal distributions, for example, $p(x_n) = \alpha_n(x_n)\beta_n(x_n)$ and $p(x_n, x_{n+1}) = \alpha_n(x_n)p(x_{n+1}|x_n)\beta_{n+1}(x_{n+1})$, and so on.

The message-passing mechanism can be easily modified to accommodate observed variables. For example, if we have observed a variable $x_t = \omega_k$, which belongs to the group of $\mathbf{x}$ in Eq. (15.4), when we pass messages on the graph, we do not need to sum over all different values for x_t but just replace the sum with the observed value ω_k, as follows:

$$\alpha_{t+1}(x_{t+1}) = p(x_{t+1}|x_t)\alpha_t(x_t)\Big|_{x_t=\omega_k}$$

$$\beta_{t-1}(x_{t-1}) = p(x_t|x_{t-1})\beta_t(x_t)\Big|_{x_t=\omega_k}.$$

Finally, the local operation of message passing on a graph can be extended to deal with more general graphical models. However, for non-chain structures, we usually cannot directly run the message-passing algorithm on the original graph of a given model but have to create some intermediate proxy graphs for message passing, for example, the so-called *factor graphs* built for tree-structured models [134] or the *junction trees* for cyclic graphical models [140]. After that, the same message-passing operations between neighboring nodes can be similarly implemented over a proxy graph to derive an exact-inference algorithm for these graphical models.

Monte Carlo Sampling

The Monte Carlo–based sampling method can be used to estimate any conditional distribution in Eq. (15.4) for any arbitrarily structured graph [155]. The concept of sampling methods is straightforward. Here, we consider a simple example to show how to conduct sampling to generate samples that are suitable for estimating a particular conditional distribution. Let us consider a simple Bayesian network of seven discrete random variables, as shown in Figure 15.24, where all conditional distributions are given. Assume three variables x_1, x_3, and x_5 are observed, whose values are denoted as $\hat{x}_1$, $\hat{x}_3$, and $\hat{x}_5$. We are interested in making an inference on x_6 and x_7. Let us consider how to sample this Bayesian network to estimate the conditional distribution $p(x_6, x_7 \mid \hat{x}_1, \hat{x}_3, \hat{x}_5)$.

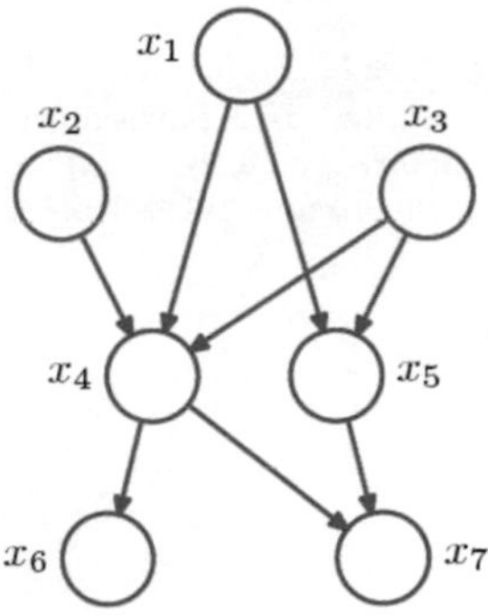

Figure 15.24: An illustration of a Bayesian network of seven discrete random variables, $p(x_1, x_2, x_3, x_4, x_5, x_6, x_7)$, which is defined by the following conditional distributions:
$p(x_1)$, $p(x_2)$, $p(x_3)$
$p(x_4|x_1, x_2, x_3)$
$p(x_5|x_1, x_3)$
$p(x_6|x_4)$
$p(x_7|x_4, x_5)$

We can design the sampling scheme in Algorithm 15.20 to generate N training samples for this conditional distribution. In each step, we just randomly generate a sample from a multinomial distribution. Based on the given conditions, each multinomial distribution basically corresponds to one column in Figure 15.4 or one slice in Figure 15.5. After all random samples are obtained in $\mathfrak{D}$, we just use $\mathfrak{D}$ to estimate a joint distribution of x_6 and x_7, which will be a good estimate of $p(x_6, x_7 \mid \hat{x}_1, \hat{x}_3, \hat{x}_5)$ as long as N is sufficiently large.

Algorithm 15.20 Monte Carlo Sampling for $p(x_6, x_7 \mid \hat{x}_1, \hat{x}_3, \hat{x}_5)$

$\mathfrak{D} = \emptyset$; $n = 0$
while $n < N$ **do**
1. sampling $\hat{x}_2^{(n)} \sim p(x_2)$
2. sampling $\hat{x}_4^{(n)} \sim p(x_4 \mid \hat{x}_1, \hat{x}_2^{(n)}, \hat{x}_3)$
3. sampling $\hat{x}_6^{(n)} \sim p(x_6 \mid \hat{x}_4^{(n)})$
4. sampling $\hat{x}_7^{(n)} \sim p(x_7 \mid \hat{x}_4^{(n)}, \hat{x}_5)$
5. $\mathfrak{D} \Leftarrow \mathfrak{D} \cup \{(\hat{x}_6^{(n)}, \hat{x}_7^{(n)})\}$
6. $n = n + 1$

end while

15.2.5 Case Study I: Naive Bayes Classifier

In a pattern-classification task, we aim to classify an unknown object into one of K predefined classes, denoted as $y \in \{\omega_1, \omega_2, \cdots, \omega_K\}$, based on a number of observed features regarding this object, denoted as $\{x_1, x_2, \cdots x_d\}$. The so-called naive Bayes assumption [159] states that all these features are conditionally independent given the class label y. This conditional independence assumption leads to the *naive Bayes classifiers* shown in Figure 15.25, which are among the simplest Bayesian networks in machine learning. The naive Bayes assumption is implied in this model structure because the class label y is a confounder of all observed features, which suggests the following factorization to the joint distribution:

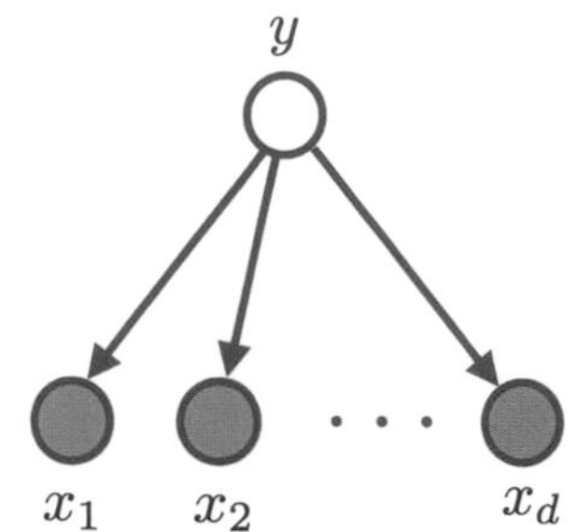

Figure 15.25: Naive Bayes classifiers can be represented as a Bayesian network, where all observed features $\{x_i\}$ are used to infer the unknown class label y.

$$\begin{aligned} p(y, x_1, x_2, \cdots, x_d) &= p(y)p(x_1|y)p(x_2|y)\cdots p(x_d|y) \\ &= p(y)\prod_{i=1}^{d} p(x_i|y). \end{aligned}$$

In a naive Bayesian classifier, all observed features are used to infer the unknown class label y as follows:

$$y^* = \arg\max_y \; p(y|x_1, x_2, \cdots, x_d) = \arg\max_y \; p(y)\prod_{i=1}^{d} p(x_i|y).$$

Naive Bayes classifiers are very flexible in dealing with a variety of feature types. For example, we can separately choose each conditional distribution $p(x_i|y)$ according to the property of a feature x_i, for example, a Bernoulli distribution for a binary feature, a multinomial distribution for a nonbinary discrete feature, and a Gaussian distribution for a continuous feature. The total number of parameters in a naive Bayes classifier is linear in the number of features. The learning and inference of naive Bayes classifiers can be done with some closed-form solutions, which are also linear in the number of different features. As a result, naive Bayes classifiers are highly scalable to large problems that involve a tremendous number of different features, such as information retrieval [159] and text-document classification.

15.2.6 Case Study II: Latent Dirichlet Allocation

How to model text documents is an important application in machine learning. The simple bag-of-words model is normally considered to be a shallow model because it treats all words in a document equally without taking into account the text structure of the document. An ideal generative model for documents should be able to explore the inherent text structure because the text structure is crucial in conveying semantic meanings in natural language. *Topic modeling* is a well-known technique along these lines for exploring some finer structures in documents. The key observation behind the topic models is that each document usually touches only a small number of coherent topics, and some words are used to describe one topic much more often than the others. In other words, a document can be described by a distribution of topics, and each topic can be described by a skewed distribution of all words. On the other hand, because we can only observe the words in a document but not the underlying topics, the topics must be treated as latent variables in a topic model.

The William Randolph Hearst Foundation will give $1.25 million to Lincoln Center, Metropolitan Opera Co., New York Philharmonic and Juilliard School. "Our board felt that we had a real opportunity to make a mark on the future of the performing arts with these grants an act every bit as important as our traditional areas of support in health, medical research, education and the social services," Hearst Foundation President Randolph A. Hearst said Monday in announcing the grants. Lincoln Center's share will be $200,000 for its new building, which will house young artists and provide new public facilities. The Metropolitan Opera Co. and New York Philharmonic will receive $400,000 each. The Juilliard School, where music and the performing arts are taught, will get $250,000. The Hearst Foundation, a leading supporter of the Lincoln Center Consolidated Corporate Fund, will make its usual annual $100,000 donation, too.

Figure 15.26: An illustration of how to model a text document using a topic model, such as LDA. All words labeled by the same color are assumed to come from the same topic. (Image source: Blei et al. [23].)

Latent Dirichlet allocation (LDA) [23] is a popular topic model that takes a hierarchical modeling approach for each word in a document. As shown in Figure 15.26, in LDA, we assume that each document has a unique distribution of all possible topics, and each word in a document comes from one particular topic (labeled by a color). In this case, all words from the same topic (with the same color) come from the same word distribution, whereas a different topic usually has a different distribution of words. In the following, we will briefly consider LDA as a case study of Bayesian networks because LDA is one of the most popular Bayesian networks widely used in practical applications.

Assume we have a corpus of M documents, and each document contains N_i $(i = 1, 2, \cdots, M)$ words. Furthermore, assume that there are K different topics in total, and all documents in the corpus contain V distinct words in total. In LDA, we assume that these text documents are generated from the following stochastic process:

1. For each document $i = 1, 2, \cdots, M$, we first sample a topic distribution $\boldsymbol{\theta}_i$ from a Dirichlet distribution:

$$\boldsymbol{\theta}_i \sim p(\boldsymbol{\theta}) = \text{Dir}(\boldsymbol{\theta} \mid \boldsymbol{\alpha}),$$

   where $\boldsymbol{\alpha} \in \mathbb{R}^K$ denotes the unknown parameters of the Dirichlet distribution. Here, $\boldsymbol{\theta}_i$ essentially denotes the model parameters of a topic distribution, which is a multinomial distribution of K categories (one category for each topic). Furthermore, if we restrict all parameters in $\boldsymbol{\alpha}$ to be less than 1, the Dirichlet distribution concentrates more at the corners of the K-simplex, as shown in Figure 2.9; namely, it favors sparse values over dense ones for $\boldsymbol{\theta}$. In LDA, a sparse Dirichlet distribution is always preferable because usually only smaller numbers of coherent topics are touched in a document.

We choose a multinomial distribution for the topic distribution or the word distributions because both topics and words are viewed as discrete random variables. A Dirichlet distribution is chosen as a distribution of various topic distributions because Dirichlet distributions are the conjugate prior of multinomial distributions.

2. For each location $j = 1, 2, \cdots, N_i$ in the ith document,
   a. We first sample a topic $\mathbf{z}_{ij}$ from the multinomial distribution with model parameters $\boldsymbol{\theta}_i$:

   $$\mathbf{z}_{ij} \sim p(\mathbf{z} \,|\, \boldsymbol{\theta}_i) = \text{Mult}(\mathbf{z} \,|\, \boldsymbol{\theta}_i),$$

   where each $\mathbf{z}_{ij} = [z_{ij1} \cdots z_{ijK}]$ is represented as a 1-of-K vector, taking one of K distinct values for each topic.

   b. In LDA, we maintain K different word distributions for all K different topics. Each word distribution is essentially a multinomial distribution of V categories (i.e., $\text{Mult}(\mathbf{w} \,|\, \boldsymbol{\beta}_k)$), where $\boldsymbol{\beta}_k$ denotes the unknown parameters for the word distribution of the kth topic ($k = 1, 2, \cdots, K$). According to $\mathbf{z}_{ij}$, we further sample the word distribution associated with this topic to generate a word $\mathbf{w}_{ij}$ for this location:

   $$\mathbf{w}_{ij} \sim \prod_{k=1}^{K} \Big(\text{Mult}(\mathbf{w}_{ij} \,|\, \boldsymbol{\beta}_k)\Big)^{z_{ijk}},$$

   where we also represent each $\mathbf{w}_{ij} = [w_{ij1} \cdots w_{ijV}]$ as a 1-of-V vector, taking one of V distinct values for each unique word.

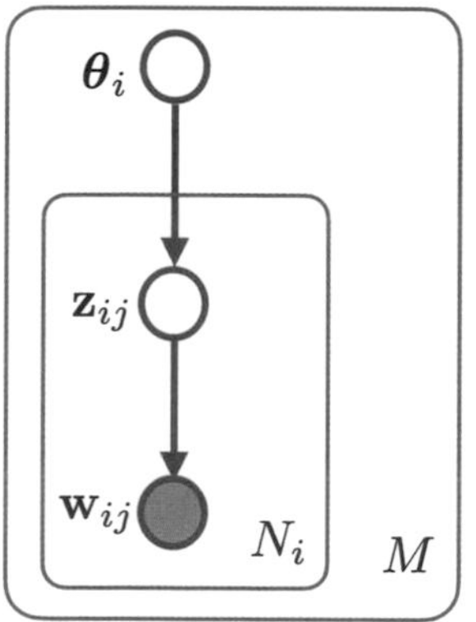

Figure 15.27: Representing an LDA as a Bayesian network, where each document samples a topic distribution $\boldsymbol{\theta}_i$ from a Dirichlet distribution and then at each location of document, a topic $\mathbf{z}_{ij}$ is first sampled from this topic, and a word $\mathbf{w}_{ij}$ is sampled from the word distribution associated with this topic.

Putting it all together, we can represent the LDA model as a Bayesian network, as shown in Figure 15.27. If we denote all topic distributions as $\boldsymbol{\Theta} = \{\boldsymbol{\theta}_i \,|\, 1 \le i \le M\}$, all words in all documents as $\mathbf{W} = \{\mathbf{w}_{ij} \,|\, 1 \le i \le M; 1 \le j \le N_i\}$, and all sampled topics as $\mathbf{Z} = \{\mathbf{z}_{ij} \,|\, 1 \le i \le M; 1 \le j \le N_i\}$, the model structure in Figure 15.27 suggests the following way to factorize the joint distribution:

$$p(\boldsymbol{\Theta}, \mathbf{Z}, \mathbf{W}) = \prod_{i=1}^{M} p(\boldsymbol{\theta}_i) \prod_{j=1}^{N_i} p(\mathbf{z}_{ij} \,|\, \boldsymbol{\theta}_i)\, p(\mathbf{w}_{ij} \,|\, \mathbf{z}_{ij}),$$

where each conditional distribution is further represented as follows:

$$p(\boldsymbol{\theta}_i) = \text{Dir}(\boldsymbol{\theta}_i \,|\, \boldsymbol{\alpha})$$

$$p(\mathbf{z}_{ij} \,|\, \boldsymbol{\theta}_i) = \text{Mult}(\mathbf{z}_{ij} \,|\, \boldsymbol{\theta}_i)$$

$$p(\mathbf{w}_{ij} \,|\, \mathbf{z}_{ij}) = \prod_{k=1}^{K} \Big(\text{Mult}(\mathbf{w}_{ij} \,|\, \boldsymbol{\beta}_k)\Big)^{z_{ijk}}.$$

In most tasks involving natural language processing, the number of distinct words (i.e., V) is usually very large. As suggested in Blei et al. [23], it is better to add a symmetric Dirichlet distribution as a universal background to smooth out 0 probabilities for unseen words in $p(\mathbf{w}_{ij} \mid \mathbf{z}_{ij})$. Therefore, we can modify the previous $p(\mathbf{w}_{ij} \mid \mathbf{z}_{ij})$ as follows:

$$p(\mathbf{w}_{ij} \mid \mathbf{z}_{ij}) = \text{Dir}(\mathbf{w}_{ij} \mid \eta \cdot \mathbf{1}) \prod_{k=1}^{K} \Big(\text{Mult}(\mathbf{w}_{ij} \mid \boldsymbol{\beta}_k)\Big)^{z_{ijk}}$$

A Dirichlet distribution is said to be symmetric if all of its parameters are equal, such as

$$\text{Dir}(\mathbf{w} \mid \eta \cdot \mathbf{1})$$

where $\mathbf{1} = [1 \cdots 1]^{\intercal}$.

If we substitute these conditional distributions into the previous factorization equation, we can represent the joint distribution as follows:

$$p(\boldsymbol{\Theta}, \mathbf{Z}, \mathbf{W} \,;\, \boldsymbol{\alpha}, \boldsymbol{\beta}, \eta),$$

where $\boldsymbol{\alpha} \in \mathbb{R}^K$, $\boldsymbol{\beta} \in \mathbb{R}^{K \times V}$, and $\eta \in \mathbb{R}$ denote all unknown parameters in an LDA model. These model parameters are estimated by maximizing the likelihood function of the observed documents, given as follows:

$$p(\mathbf{W} \,;\, \boldsymbol{\alpha}, \boldsymbol{\beta}, \eta) = \iiint_{\boldsymbol{\theta}_1 \cdots \boldsymbol{\theta}_M} \prod_{i=1}^{M} p(\boldsymbol{\theta}_i) \prod_{j=1}^{N_i} \sum_{\mathbf{z}_{ij}} p(\mathbf{z}_{ij} \mid \boldsymbol{\theta}_i)\, p(\mathbf{w}_{ij} \mid \mathbf{z}_{ij})\, d\boldsymbol{\theta}_1 \cdots d\boldsymbol{\theta}_M.$$

On the other hand, the inference problem in LDA lies in how to infer the underlying topic distribution $\boldsymbol{\theta}_i$ for each document and the most probable topic $\mathbf{z}_{ij}$ for each word in all documents. These inference decisions rely on the following conditional distribution:

$$p(\boldsymbol{\Theta}, \mathbf{Z} \,\big|\, \mathbf{W}) = \frac{p(\boldsymbol{\Theta}, \mathbf{Z}, \mathbf{W})}{p(\mathbf{W})} = \frac{p(\boldsymbol{\Theta}, \mathbf{Z}, \mathbf{W})}{\iiint_{\boldsymbol{\Theta}} \sum_{\mathbf{Z}} p(\boldsymbol{\Theta}, \mathbf{Z}, \mathbf{W}) d\boldsymbol{\Theta}}.$$

Unfortunately, both learning and inference problems in LDA are computationally intractable because both require us to compute some complicated multiple integrals. Some approximate-inference methods must be used here to alleviate the computational difficulty. Blei et al. [23] have proposed a variational inference method to use the following variational distribution:

$$q(\boldsymbol{\Theta}, \mathbf{Z}) = \prod_{i=1}^{M} q(\boldsymbol{\theta}_i \,|\, \boldsymbol{\gamma}) \prod_{j=1}^{N_i} q(\mathbf{z}_{ij} \,|\, \boldsymbol{\phi}_{ij}) \qquad (15.6)$$

to approximate the true conditional distribution $p(\boldsymbol{\Theta}, \mathbf{Z} \,|\, \mathbf{W})$. Following the same variational Bayesian procedure as in Section 14.3.2, we can show that $q(\boldsymbol{\theta}_i \,|\, \boldsymbol{\gamma})$ turns out to be a Dirichlet distribution, each $q(\mathbf{z}_{ij} \,|\, \boldsymbol{\phi}_{ij})$ is a multinomial distribution, and all variational parameters $\boldsymbol{\gamma}$ and $\boldsymbol{\phi}_{ij}$ can be iteratively estimated from the observed $\mathbf{W}$. Relying on the estimated variational distribution, we can derive an iterative algorithm to learn all of the LDA parameters $\{\boldsymbol{\alpha}, \boldsymbol{\beta}, \eta\}$ by maximizing a variational lower bound of the previous $p(\mathbf{W} \,;\, \boldsymbol{\alpha}, \boldsymbol{\beta}, \eta)$, and we can also derive a MAP estimate for

The iterative training procedure to learn $\{\boldsymbol{\alpha}, \boldsymbol{\beta}, \eta\}$ is similar to that for variational autoencoders (VAEs) in Section 13.4.

all $\boldsymbol{\theta}_i$ and $\mathbf{z}_{ij}$. Interested readers can refer to Blei et al. [23] for more details on this.

15.3 Markov Random Fields

This section introduces the second class of graphical models, namely, *undirected graphical models* (a.k.a. *Markov random fields*) [128, 203], which use undirected links between nodes in a graph to indicate the relation of various random variables. Moreover, it briefly introduces two representative models in this category, namely, *conditional random fields* [138, 233] and *restricted Boltzmann machines* [226, 97].

15.3.1 Formulation: Potential and Partition Functions

Similar to Bayesian networks, Markov random fields (MRFs) are another graphical representation that is used to describe a joint distribution of random variables. In MRFs, we still use a node to represent a random variable, but we use undirected links to represent dependency between random variables. Unlike Bayesian networks, the striking difference here is that each link does not directly represent a conditional distribution but just some mutual dependency among the linked variables. For example, Figure 15.28 shows a simple MRF that represents a joint probability distribution of seven random variables (i.e., $p(x_1, x_2, \cdots, x_7)$). From the graph, we can immediately recognize that x_3 and x_6 are statistically independent (i.e., $x_3 \perp x_6$) because they are not connected by any links. On the other hand, x_4 must be dependent on x_5 (i.e., $x_4 \not\perp x_5$) because of the undirected link between them.

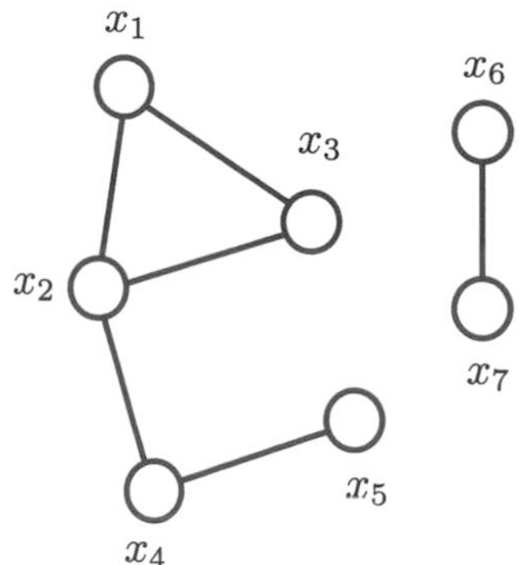

Figure 15.28: An example MRF representing a joint distribution of seven random variables, $\{x_1, x_2, \cdots, x_7\}$.

First of all, let us discuss how to formulate the joint distribution in MRFs. We first define a *clique* in an MRF as a subset of nodes that are mutually connected in the graph. In other words, there exists a link between all pairs of nodes in a clique. For example, $\{x_1, x_2\}$, $\{x_1, x_2, x_3\}$, and $\{x_2, x_4\}$ are three cliques in the MRF shown in Figure 15.28. Furthermore, a clique is said to be a *maximum clique* if it is not contained by another larger clique. In Figure 15.28, $\{x_1, x_2\}$ is not a maximum clique because it is a subset of another larger clique $\{x_1, x_2, x_3\}$. On the other hand, both $\{x_1, x_2, x_3\}$ and $\{x_2, x_4\}$ are maximum cliques because we cannot enlarge them into a larger clique. After some inspection, we can recognize that the MRF in Figure 15.28 has a total of four maximum cliques (i.e,. $c_1 = \{x_1, x_2, x_3\}$, $c_2 = \{x_2, x_4\}$, $c_3 = \{x_4, x_5\}$, and $c_4 = \{x_6, x_7\}$).

In general, each MRF contains a finite number of maximum cliques. When we formulate a joint probability distribution for an MRF, we need to define a so-called *potential function* $\psi(\cdot)$ over all random variables in each maximum clique c, denoted as $\mathbf{x}_c$. The joint distribution of an MRF is defined as a product of the potential functions of all maximum cliques in the graph, divided by a normalization term:

$$p(\mathbf{x}) = \frac{1}{Z} \prod_c \psi_c(\mathbf{x}_c), \tag{15.7}$$

where the term Z is the normalization term, often called the *partition function*, which is computed by summing the product of all potential functions over the entire space of all random variables:

The summation in Z is replaced by integrals for continuous random variables.

$$Z = \sum_{\mathbf{x}} \prod_c \psi_c(\mathbf{x}_c).$$

Moreover, we always choose nonnegative potential functions $\psi_c(\mathbf{x}_c) \geq 0$ to ensure that $p(\mathbf{x}) \geq 0$ holds for any $\mathbf{x}$. By doing so, we can see that the previous $p(\mathbf{x})$ defined in Eq. (15.7) is always a valid probability distribution of $\mathbf{x}$ because it is nonnegative for any $\mathbf{x}$, and it satisfies the sum-to-1 constraint over the entire space of $\mathbf{x}$.

As an example, we can see that the MRF in Figure 15.28 defines a joint distribution as follows:

$$p(x_1, x_2, \cdots, x_7) = \frac{\psi_1(x_1, x_2, x_3)\psi_2(x_2, x_4)\psi_3(x_4, x_5)\psi_4(x_6, x_7)}{\sum_{x_1 \cdots x_7} \psi_1(x_1, x_2, x_3)\psi_2(x_2, x_4)\psi_3(x_4, x_5)\psi_4(x_6, x_7)},$$

where $\psi_1(\cdot)$, $\psi_2(\cdot)$, $\psi_3(\cdot)$, and $\psi_4(\cdot)$ are four potential functions that we may choose arbitrarily.

Because the potential functions must be nonnegative, it is convenient to express them as exponentials:

$$\psi_c(\mathbf{x}_c) = \exp\Big(- E(\mathbf{x}_c)\Big),$$

where $E(\mathbf{x}_c)$ is called an *energy function*, which can be defined in many ways (e.g., a linear function, a quadratic function, or a higher-order polynomial function). We will further explore how to choose energy functions for an MRF in the following case studies. The joint distribution $p(\mathbf{x})$ expressed by the previous exponentially-formed potential functions is often called a *Boltzmann distribution*.

Compared with Bayesian networks, a major advantage of using MRFs is that we can simply rely on graph separation to quickly determine the conditional independence of random variables in the joint distribution defined in Eq. (15.7). Given any three disjoint subsets of nodes in an MRF (e.g., A, B and C), we can determine the following conditional independence property:

$$A \perp B \,\big|\, C$$

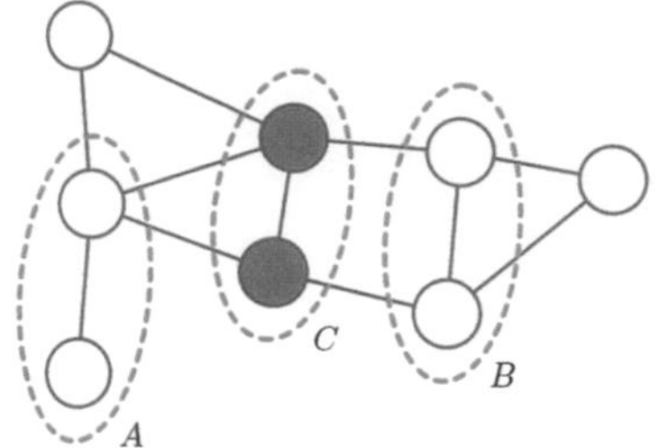

Figure 15.29: An illustration of conditional independence in an MRF:

$$A \perp B \,|\, C.$$

(Source: Bishop [22].)

by inspecting whether all paths from A to B are blocked by at least a node in C. In other words, after we remove all nodes in C, along with all links that connect to these nodes from the graph, if there still exists a path connecting any node in A to any node in B, we say A and B are not conditionally independent given C. Otherwise, if there are no such paths left, then the conditional independence property holds. For example, in the MRF shown in Figure 15.29, we can verify that A and B are conditionally independent given C.

When we learn model parameters of an MRF from some training samples, we can still use the MLE method in the same way as in Bayesian networks. However, because the log-likelihood function of any MRF needs to be constructed from the joint distribution in Eq. (15.7), it always contains the partition function Z. The partition function is awkward to handle because it requires us to sum over the entire input space. Generally speaking, the learning of MRFs is much harder than that of Bayesian networks. The partition function becomes the major limitation of using MRFs in practice. In the following case studies, we will briefly explore how to use sampling methods to deal with the intractable partition function when learning an MRF.

On the other hand, MRFs generally do not impose any difficulty in the inference stage. When we compute the conditional distribution in Eq. (15.4) for an MRF, we can see that the intractable partition function Z actually cancels out from the numerator and denominator. As a result, all inference algorithms in Table 15.1 are equally applicable to MRFs.

15.3.2 Case Study III: Conditional Random Fields

Assume that we consider two groups of random variables, namely, $\mathbf{X} = \{\mathbf{x}_1, \mathbf{x}_2, \cdots, \mathbf{x}_T\}$ and $\mathbf{Y} = \{\mathbf{y}_1, \mathbf{y}_2, \cdots, \mathbf{y}_T\}$. A regular MRF aims to establish a joint distribution $p(\mathbf{X}, \mathbf{Y})$ for these random variables. Alternatively, *conditional random fields* (CRFs) [138] are undirected graphical models that aim to specify the conditional distribution $p(\mathbf{Y} \,|\, \mathbf{X})$. In the CRF setting, one group of random variables $\mathbf{X}$ is always assumed to be given, and a CRF model aims to establish a probability distribution only for the other group of random variable $\mathbf{Y}$ based on the same idea of potential functions in a regular MRF. In a graph of any CRF, we can first imagine removing all nodes in $\mathbf{X}$, along with all links associated with any node in $\mathbf{X}$. Then we consider all maximum cliques in the leftover graph of only all $\mathbf{Y}$ nodes, where a potential function is defined for each maximum clique. Based on these potential functions, we define the conditional distribution for a CRF as follows:

$$p(\mathbf{Y} \,|\, \mathbf{X}) = \frac{\prod_c \psi_C(\mathbf{Y}_c, \mathbf{X})}{\sum_{\mathbf{Y}} \prod_c \psi_C(\mathbf{Y}_c, \mathbf{X})},$$

where the numerator is the product of the potential functions for all maximum cliques. Note that each CRF potential function is applied to all **Y** nodes in a maximum clique of the leftover graph, as well as all removed nodes in **X**. This is possible in CFRs because all randoms variables in **X** are always assumed to be given in the first place.

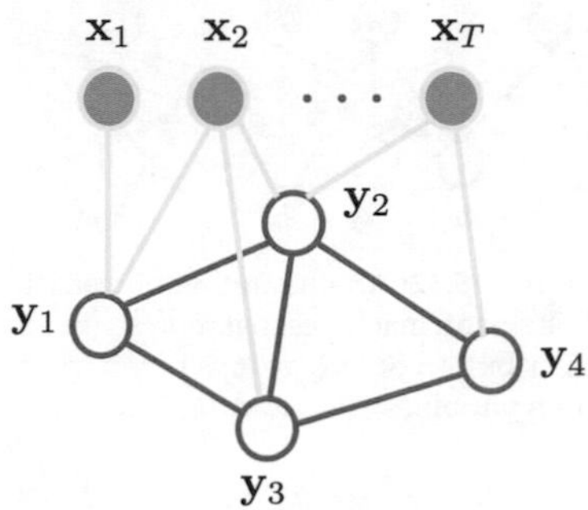

Figure 15.30: An illustration of a CRF that defines a conditional distribution $p(\mathbf{Y}\,|\,\mathbf{X})$.

For example, in the CRF in Figure 15.30, the leftover graph of **Y** (labeled in red) contains two maximum cliques, $c_1 = \{\mathbf{y}_1, \mathbf{y}_2, \mathbf{y}_3\}$ and $c_2 = \{\mathbf{y}_2, \mathbf{y}_3, \mathbf{y}_4\}$. Therefore, the conditional distribution of this CRF can be expressed as follows:

$$p(\mathbf{Y}\,|\,\mathbf{X}) = \frac{\psi_1(\mathbf{y}_1, \mathbf{y}_2, \mathbf{y}_3, \mathbf{X})\,\psi_2(\mathbf{y}_2, \mathbf{y}_3, \mathbf{y}_4, \mathbf{X})}{\sum_{\mathbf{y}_1\mathbf{y}_2\mathbf{y}_3\mathbf{y}_4} \psi_1(\mathbf{y}_1, \mathbf{y}_2, \mathbf{y}_3, \mathbf{X})\,\psi_2(\mathbf{y}_2, \mathbf{y}_3, \mathbf{y}_4, \mathbf{X})}.$$

The most popular CRF is the so-called *linear-chain conditional random field* [138, 233], where all **Y** nodes form a chain structure. As shown in Figure 15.31, the maximum cliques of the leftover graph of **Y** are the pairs of consecutive variables on the chain, that is, $\{\mathbf{y}_1, \mathbf{y}_2\}, \{\mathbf{y}_2, \mathbf{y}_3\}, \cdots, \{\mathbf{y}_{T-1}, \mathbf{y}_T\}$. Based on the previous definition, the conditional distribution of a linear-chain CRF is given as follows:

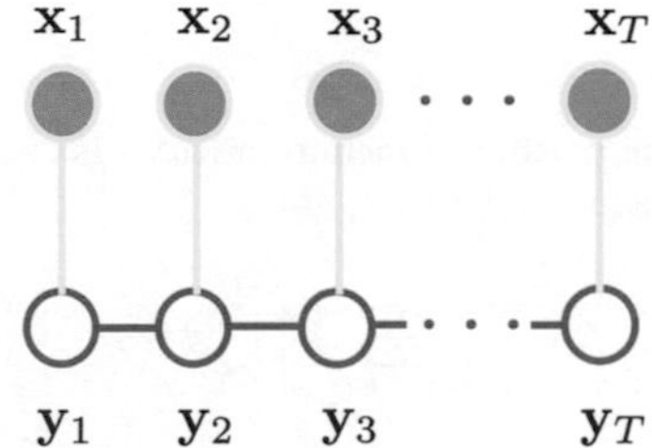

Figure 15.31: An illustration of a linear-chain CRF that defines a conditional distribution for two sequences.

$$p(\mathbf{Y}\,|\,\mathbf{X}) = \frac{\prod_{t=1}^{T-1} \psi(\mathbf{y}_t, \mathbf{y}_{t+1}, \mathbf{X})}{\sum_{\mathbf{Y}} \prod_{t=1}^{T-1} \psi(\mathbf{y}_t, \mathbf{y}_{t+1}, \mathbf{X})}.$$

Furthermore, we can use some feature functions to specify a linear energy function for the previous potential function as follows:

$$\psi(\mathbf{y}_t, \mathbf{y}_{t+1}, \mathbf{X}) = \exp\left(\sum_{k=1}^{K} w_k \cdot f_k(\mathbf{y}_t, \mathbf{y}_{t+1}, \mathbf{X})\right),$$

where $f_k(\cdot)$ denotes the kth feature function that is normally manually specified to reflect one particular aspect of the input–output pair at a location on the chain, and w_k is an unknown weight for kth feature function. Usually, all feature functions $f_k(\cdot)$ do not have any learnable parameters, and all weights $\{w_k \,|\, 1 \leq k \leq K\}$ constitute the model parameters of a linear-chain CRF model. The model parameters can be estimated based on MLE. Under this setting, the log-likelihood function of a linear-chain CRF is concave, and it can be iteratively optimized by some gradient-descent algorithms. Moreover, we can use the forward–backward inference algorithm described on page 358 to make inferences for any linear-chain CRF in a very efficient manner. As a result, the linear-chain CRFs are widely used for many large-scale sequence-labeling problems in natural language processing and bioinformatics [233].

15.3.3 Case Study IV: Restricted Boltzmann Machines

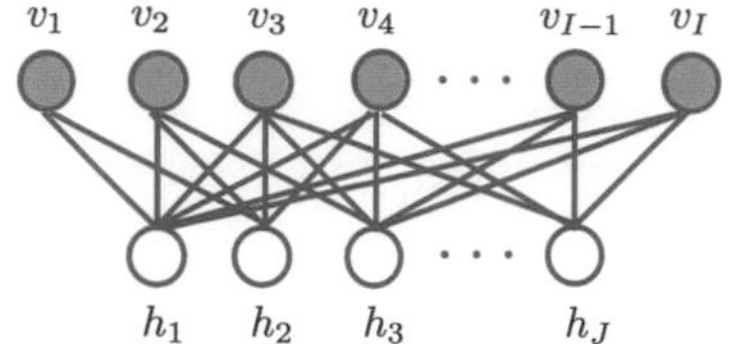

Figure 15.32: An illustration of restricted Boltzmann machines that represent a joint distribution of two groups of binary random variables, $\{v_i\}$ and $\{h_j\}$.

Restricted Boltzman machines (RBMs) [226, 97] are another class of popular MRFs in machine learning and can specify a joint distribution of two groups of binary random variables, that is, some *visible* variables v_i and some *hidden* variables h_j, where each $v_i \in \{0,1\}$ and $h_j \in \{0,1\}$ for all $1 \le i \le I$ and $1 \le j \le J$. As shown in Figure 15.32, these binary random variables form a bipartite graph, where every pair of nodes from each of these two groups is linked, and there are no connections between nodes within a group. We can see that the maximum cliques of this graph include all pairs of nodes $\{v_i, h_j\}$ for all i and j. Assume we define a potential function for each of these maximum cliques as follows:

$$\psi(v_i, h_j) = \exp\left(a_i v_i + b_j h_j + w_{ij} v_i h_j\right),$$

where a_i, b_j, and w_{ij} are some learnable parameters of an RBM model. Putting the potential functions of all maximum cliques together, the joint distribution of these random variables can be expressed as

$$p(v_1, \cdots, v_I, h_1, \cdots, h_J) = \frac{1}{Z} \prod_{i=1}^{I} \prod_{j=1}^{J} \psi(v_i, h_j),$$

The partition function in RBMs is computed as follows:

$$\begin{aligned} Z &= \sum_{v_1 \cdots v_I} \sum_{h_1 \cdots h_J} \prod_{i=1}^{I} \prod_{j=1}^{J} \psi(v_i, h_j) \\ &= \sum_{v_1 \cdots v_I} \sum_{h_1 \cdots h_J} \exp\Big(\sum_{i=1}^{I} a_i v_i + \\ &\quad \sum_{j=1}^{J} b_j h_j + \sum_{i=1}^{I} \sum_{j=1}^{J} w_{ij} v_i h_j \Big) \\ &= \sum_{\mathbf{v}} \sum_{\mathbf{h}} \exp\left(\mathbf{a}^\intercal \mathbf{v} + \mathbf{b}^\intercal \mathbf{h} + \mathbf{v}^\intercal \mathbf{W} \mathbf{h}\right). \end{aligned}$$

where Z denotes the partition function (see margin note). After substituting the previous potential functions, we can derive the joint distribution of an RBM model as follows:

$$p(v_1, \cdots, v_I, h_1, \cdots, h_J) = \frac{1}{Z} \exp\left(\sum_{i=1}^{I} a_i v_i + \sum_{j=1}^{J} b_j h_j + \sum_{i=1}^{I} \sum_{j=1}^{J} w_{ij} v_i h_j \right).$$

If we represent all variables with the following vectors and matrix:

$$\mathbf{a} = \begin{bmatrix} a_1 \\ \vdots \\ a_I \end{bmatrix} \quad \mathbf{b} = \begin{bmatrix} b_1 \\ \vdots \\ b_J \end{bmatrix} \quad \mathbf{v} = \begin{bmatrix} v_1 \\ \vdots \\ v_I \end{bmatrix} \quad \mathbf{h} = \begin{bmatrix} h_1 \\ \vdots \\ h_J \end{bmatrix} \quad \mathbf{W} = \Big[\; w_{ij} \; \Big]_{I \times J}$$

we can represent an RBM model with the following matrix form:

$$p(\mathbf{v}, \mathbf{h}) = \frac{1}{Z} \exp\left(\mathbf{a}^\intercal \mathbf{v} + \mathbf{b}^\intercal \mathbf{h} + \mathbf{v}^\intercal \mathbf{W} \mathbf{h}\right), \tag{15.8}$$

where **a**, **b** and **W** denote the model parameters of an RBM that need to be estimated from training samples.

The RBMs are often used for representation learning. For example, if we feed all binary pixels of a black-and-white image into an RBM as the visible variables, we may wish to learn the RBM in such a way that it can extract some meaningful features in its hidden variables. The RBM parameters can be learned by maximizing the log-likelihood function of all visible variables:

$$\arg\max_{\mathbf{a},\mathbf{b},\mathbf{W}} \prod_{\mathbf{v}_i \in \mathcal{D}} p(\mathbf{v}_i) = \arg\max_{\mathbf{a},\mathbf{b},\mathbf{W}} \prod_{\mathbf{v}_i \in \mathcal{D}} \frac{\sum_{\mathbf{h}} \exp\left(\mathbf{a}^\intercal \mathbf{v}_i + \mathbf{b}^\intercal \mathbf{h} + \mathbf{v}_i^\intercal \mathbf{W} \mathbf{h}\right)}{\sum_{\mathbf{h}} \sum_{\mathbf{v}} \exp\left(\mathbf{a}^\intercal \mathbf{v} + \mathbf{b}^\intercal \mathbf{h} + \mathbf{v}^\intercal \mathbf{W} \mathbf{h}\right)}$$

$$\begin{aligned} p(\mathbf{v}_i) &= \sum_{\mathbf{h}} p(\mathbf{v}_i, \mathbf{h}) \\ &= \frac{1}{Z} \sum_{\mathbf{h}} \exp\left(\mathbf{a}^\intercal \mathbf{v}_i + \mathbf{b}^\intercal \mathbf{h} + \mathbf{v}_i^\intercal \mathbf{W} \mathbf{h}\right) \\ &= \frac{\sum_{\mathbf{h}} \exp\left(\mathbf{a}^\intercal \mathbf{v}_i + \mathbf{b}^\intercal \mathbf{h} + \mathbf{v}_i^\intercal \mathbf{W} \mathbf{h}\right)}{\sum_{\mathbf{h}} \sum_{\mathbf{v}} \exp\left(\mathbf{a}^\intercal \mathbf{v} + \mathbf{b}^\intercal \mathbf{h} + \mathbf{v}^\intercal \mathbf{W} \mathbf{h}\right)} \end{aligned}$$

where $\mathbf{h}$ and $\mathbf{v}$ are summed over all possible values in their entire spaces.

where $\mathcal{D}$ denotes a training set of some samples of visible nodes $\{\mathbf{v}_i\}$. Hinton [96] proposes the so-called *contrastive divergence* algorithm to learn the RBM parameters by embedding random sampling into a gradient-descent procedure. The sampling method is used to deal with the intractable summations in the objective function.

Once the RBM is given, the inference problem in RBMs is fairly simple. Because the RBM has the shape of a bipartite graph shown in Figure 15.32, we can verify that all hidden nodes are conditionally independent given all visible nodes, and conversely, all visible nodes are conditionally independent given all hidden nodes. In other words, we have

$$p(\mathbf{h} \,|\, \mathbf{v}) = \prod_{j=1}^{J} p(h_j \,|\, \mathbf{v})$$

$$p(\mathbf{v} \,|\, \mathbf{h}) = \prod_{i=1}^{I} p(v_i \,|\, \mathbf{h}).$$

After substituting the RBM distribution in Eq. (15.8) into the previous equation, we can further derive

$$\Pr(h_j = 1 \,|\, \mathbf{v}) = l\Big(b_j + \sum_{i=1} w_{ij} v_i\Big),$$

$$\Pr(v_i = 1 \,|\, \mathbf{h}) = l\Big(a_i + \sum_{j=1} w_{ij} h_j\Big),$$

where $l(\cdot)$ stands for the sigmoid function in Eq. (6.12).

Once all RBM parameters are learned, for any new sample of visible variables $\mathbf{v}$, we can use this formula to compute the conditional probabilities for all hidden nodes (i.e., $\Pr(h_j = 1 \,|\, \mathbf{v})$ for all $j = 1, 2, \cdots, J$). These probabilities are then used to estimate all hidden variables $\mathbf{h}$, which can be used as some feature representations for $\mathbf{v}$.

Exercises

Q15.1 Assume three binary random variables $a, b, c \in \{0, 1\}$ have the following joint distribution:

a	b	c	$p(a, b, c)$
0	0	0	0.024
0	0	1	0.056
0	1	0	0.108
0	1	1	0.012
1	0	0	0.120
1	0	1	0.280
1	1	0	0.360
1	1	1	0.040

By direct evaluation, show that this distribution has the property that a and c are marginally dependent (i.e., $p(a, c) \neq p(a)p(c)$), but a and c become independent when conditioned on b (i.e., $p(a, c|b) = p(a|b)p(c|b)$). Based on this joint distribution, draw all possible directed graphs for a, b, c, and compute all conditional probabilities for each graph.

Q15.2 Assume three binary random variables $a, b, c \in \{0, 1\}$ have the following joint distribution:

a	b	c	$p(a, b, c)$
0	0	0	0.072
0	0	1	0.024
0	1	0	0.008
0	1	1	0.096
1	0	0	0.096
1	0	1	0.048
1	1	0	0.224
1	1	1	0.432

By direct evaluation, show that this distribution has the property that a and c are marginally independent (i.e., $p(a, c) = p(a)p(c)$), but a and c become dependent when conditioned on b (i.e., $p(a, c|b) \neq p(a|b)p(c|b)$). Based on this joint distribution, draw all possible directed graphs for a, b, c, and compute all conditional probabilities for each graph.

Q15.3 Given the causal Bayesian network in Figure 15.12, calculate the following probabilities:

a. $\Pr(W = 1)$
b. $\Pr(L = 1 \mid W = 1)$ and $\Pr(L = 1 \mid W = 0)$
c. $\Pr(L = 1 \mid R = 1)$ and $\Pr(R = 0 \mid L = 0)$

Q15.4 If all conditional probabilities of the causal Bayesian network in Figure 15.12 are unknown, what types of data do you need to estimate these probabilities? How will you collect them?

Q15.5 For the Bayesian network in Figure 15.24, design a sampling scheme to generate samples to estimate the following conditional distributions:

- $p(x_1, x_2 \mid \hat{x}_6, \hat{x}_7)$
- $p(x_3, x_7 \mid \hat{x}_4, \hat{x}_5)$

Q15.6 Following the idea of the VAEs in Section 13.4, use the variational distribution in Eq. (15.6) to derive a proxy function for the likelihood function of the LDA model (i.e., $p(\mathbf{W}; \boldsymbol{\alpha}, \boldsymbol{\beta}, \eta)$). By maximizing this proxy function iteratively, derive a learning algorithm for all LDA parameters.

Q15.7 Use the joint distribution of RBMs in Eq. (15.8) to prove the conditional independence of RBMs, and further derive that both $\Pr(h_j = 1 \mid \mathbf{v})$ and $\Pr(v_i = 1 \mid \mathbf{h})$ can be computed with a sigmoid function.

Appendix

Other Probability Distributions A

This appendix, in addition to what we have reviewed in Section 2.2.4, further introduces a few more probability distributions that are occasionally used in some machine learning methods.

1. Uniform Distribution

The uniform distribution is often used to describe a random variable that equiprobably takes any value inside a constrained region in the space. For example, the uniform distribution inside an n-dimensional hypercube $[a,b]^n$ takes the following form:

$$U(\mathbf{x} \mid [a,b]^n) = \begin{cases} \frac{1}{(b-a)^n} & \mathbf{x} \in [a,b]^n \\ 0 & \text{otherwise.} \end{cases}$$

2. Poisson Distribution

The Poisson distribution is often used to describe a discrete random variable X that can take any nonnegative integers, such as counting data. The Poisson distribution takes the following form:

$$\text{Poisson}(n \mid \lambda) \triangleq \Pr(X = n) = \frac{e^{-\lambda} \cdot \lambda^n}{n!} \quad \forall n = 0, 1, 2 \cdots,$$

where λ is the parameter of the distribution. We can summarize the key results for the Poisson distribution as follows:

- Parameter: $\lambda > 0$
- Support: The domain of the random variable

$$n = 0, 1, 2, \cdots$$

- Mean and variance:

$$\mathbb{E}[X] = \lambda \quad \text{and} \quad \text{var}(X) = \lambda$$

- The sum-to-1 constraint:

$$\sum_{n=0}^{\infty} \text{Poisson}(n \mid \lambda) = 1$$

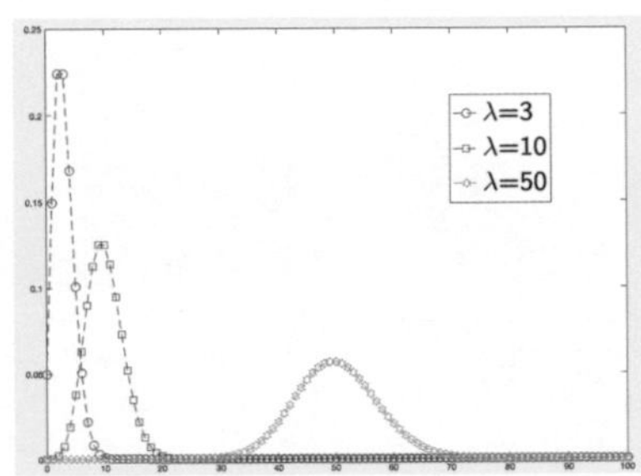

Figure A.1: An illustration of the Poisson distribution for three choices of the parameter λ.

As shown in Figure A.1, the Poisson distribution is a unimodal distribution, and the parameter λ specifies the center and concentration of the distribution.

3. Gamma Distribution

The gamma distribution is used to describe a continuous random variable X that can take any positive real value. In machine learning, the gamma distribution is mainly used as the prior distribution for the variance parameter σ^2, which must be positive, in Bayesian learning. The general form for the gamma distribution is given as follows:

$$\text{gamma}(x \,|\, \alpha, \beta) = \frac{\beta^\alpha}{\Gamma(\alpha)} x^{\alpha-1} e^{-\beta x} \qquad \forall x > 0,$$

where α and β are two parameters of the distribution. We can summarize the key results for the gamma distribution as follows:

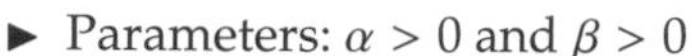

- Parameters: $\alpha > 0$ and $\beta > 0$
- Support: The domain of the random variable is $x > 0$.
- Mean, variance, and mode:

  $$\mathbb{E}[X] = \frac{\alpha}{\beta} \quad \text{and} \quad \text{var}(X) = \frac{\alpha}{\beta^2}$$

  The gamma distribution is a unimodal bell-shaped curve when $\alpha > 1$. The mode of the distribution is $\frac{\alpha-1}{\beta}$ when $\alpha \geq 1$.
- The sum-to-1 constraint:

  $$\int_0^\infty \text{gamma}(x \,|\, \alpha, \beta)\, dx = 1$$

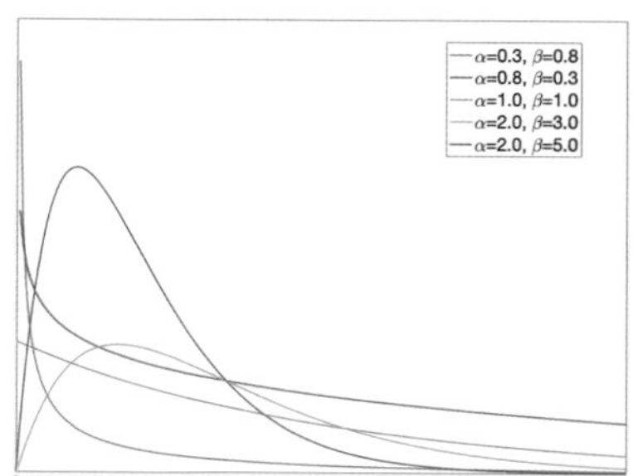

Figure A.2: An illustration of the gamma distribution for several choices of parameters α and β.

The shape of the gamma distribution depends on the choice of two parameters α and β. Figure A.2 plots the gamma distribution for several typical choices of the parameters.

4. Inverse-Wishart Distribution

The inverse-Wishart distribution is a multivariate generalization of the gamma distribution [191, 116]. It can be used to describe a multidimensional continuous random variable that takes a value on all positive definite matrices $\mathbf{X} \in \mathbb{R}^{d \times d}$. In machine learning, the inverse-Wishart distribution is mainly used as the prior distribution for the precision matrix Σ^{-1} of the multivariate Gaussian model in Bayesian learning. As we know, the precision matrix must be positive definite. The inverse-Wishart distribution takes the following form:

$$\mathcal{W}^{-1}(\mathbf{X}\,|\,\Phi,\nu) = \frac{|\Phi|^{\nu/2}}{2^{\nu d/2}\,\Gamma_d\left(\frac{\nu}{2}\right)}\,|\mathbf{X}|^{-\frac{\nu+d+1}{2}}\; e^{-\frac{1}{2}\mathrm{tr}(\Phi\mathbf{X}^{-1})},$$

where $\Phi \in \mathbb{R}^{d\times d}$ and $\nu \in \mathbb{R}^+$ are two parameters of the distribution, $\Gamma_d(\cdot)$ is the multivariate gamma function [1], and $\mathrm{tr}(\cdot)$ denotes the matrix trace. We can summarize several key results for the inverse-Wishart distribution as follows:

- Parameters: $\Phi \in \mathbb{R}^{d\times d}$ is positive definite ($\Phi \succ 0$), and $\nu \in \mathbb{R}$ is larger than $d-1$ ($\nu > d-1$).
- Support: The domain of the random variable is $\mathbf{X} \succ 0$.
- Mean and mode:

$$\mathbb{E}\big[\mathbf{X}\big] = \frac{\Phi}{\nu - d - 1}$$

  The mode of the distribution is $\frac{\Phi}{\nu+d+1}$.
- The sum-to-1 constraint:

$$\int\cdots\int_{\mathbf{X}\succ 0} \mathcal{W}^{-1}(\mathbf{X}\,|\,\Phi,\nu)\; d\mathbf{X} = 1$$

5. von Mises–Fisher Distribution

The von Mises–Fisher (vMF) distribution is an extension of the multivariate Gaussian distribution to describe a random vector $\mathbf{x} \in \mathbb{R}^d$ that only takes a value on the surface of a unit hyper-sphere. In machine learning, the vMF distribution is useful in dealing with high-dimensional feature vectors whose norms are noisy and unreliable [12, 261]. The von Mises–Fisher (vMF) distribution takes the following form:

$$\mathrm{vMF}\big(\mathbf{x}\,|\,\mathbf{u}\big) = \frac{\|\mathbf{u}\|^{d/2-1}}{(2\pi)^{d/2} I_{d/2-1}\big(\|\mathbf{u}\|\big)}\;\exp\big(\mathbf{u}^\intercal\mathbf{x}\big),$$

where $\mathbf{u} \in \mathbb{R}^d$ denotes the parameter of the distribution, and $I_\nu(\cdot)$ is the modified Bessel function of the first kind at order ν [1].
Some key results for the vMF distribution can be summarized as follows:

- Parameters: $\mathbf{u} \in \mathbb{R}^d$
- Support: The domain of the random vector is the surface of the unit hyper-sphere (i.e., $\mathbf{x} \in \mathbb{R}^d$ and $\|\mathbf{x}\| = 1$).
- Mean and mode:

$$\mathbb{E}\big[\,\mathbf{x}\,\big] = \frac{\mathbf{u}}{\|\mathbf{u}\|}$$

  The mode of the distribution is the same as the mean.

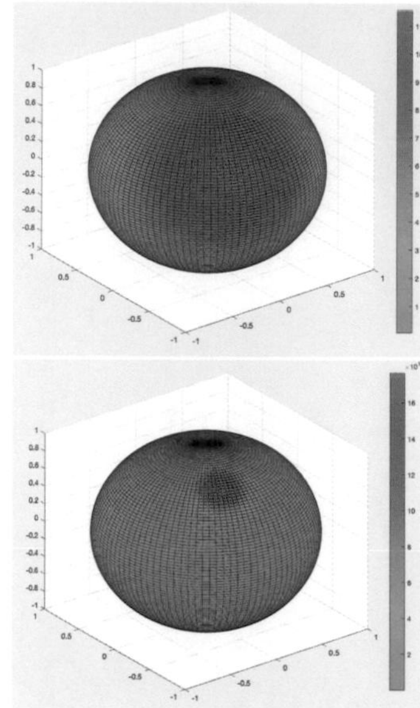

Figure A.3: An illustration of two vMF distributions in a three-dimensional (3D) space. Top panel: $\mathbf{u} = \begin{bmatrix} -1 & -2 & 1 \end{bmatrix}^\intercal$. Bottom panel: $\mathbf{u} = \begin{bmatrix} -10 & -20 & 30. \end{bmatrix}^\intercal$

- The sum-to-1 constraint:

$$\int \cdots \int_{\|\mathbf{x}\|=1} \text{vMF}\big(\mathbf{x} \,|\, \mathbf{u}\big)\, d\mathbf{x} = 1$$

As shown in Figure A.3, the vMF specifies a distribution on the surface of the unit hyper-sphere, where the mean $\frac{\mathbf{u}}{\|\mathbf{u}\|}$ indicates the center of the distribution, and the norm $\|\mathbf{u}\|$ indicates the concentration of the distribution.

Bibliography

[1] Milton Abramowitz and Irene A. Stegun. *Handbook of Mathematical Functions with Formulas, Graphs, and Mathematical Tables*. Mineola, NY: Dover, 1964 (cited on pages 331, 379).

[2] Martin Arjovsky, Soumith Chintala, and Léon Bottou. 'Wasserstein Generative Adversarial Networks'. In: *Proceedings of the 34th International Conference on Machine Learning*. Ed. by Doina Precup and Yee Whye Teh. Vol. 70. Sydney, Australia: PMLR, 2017, pp. 214–223 (cited on page 295).

[3] Behnam Asadi and Hui Jiang. 'On Approximation Capabilities of ReLU Activation and Softmax Output Layer in Neural Networks'. In: *CoRR* abs/2002.04060 (2020) (cited on page 155).

[4] Hagai Attias. 'Independent Factor Analysis'. In: *Neural Computation* 11.4 (1999), pp. 803–851. DOI: 10.1162/089976699300016458 (cited on pages 293, 294, 301, 302).

[5] Hagai Attias. 'A Variational Bayesian Framework for Graphical Models'. In: *Advances in Neural Information Processing Systems 12*. Cambridge, MA: MIT Press, 2000, pp. 209–215 (cited on pages 324, 326, 357).

[6] Adriano Azevedo-Filho. 'Laplace's Method Approximations for Probabilistic Inference in Belief Networks with Continuous Variables'. In: *Uncertainty in Artificial Intelligence*. Ed. by Ramon Lopez de Mantaras and David Poole. San Francisco, CA: Morgan Kaufmann, 1994, pp. 28–36 (cited on page 324).

[7] Lei Jimmy Ba, Jamie Ryan Kiros, and Geoffrey E. Hinton. 'Layer Normalization'. In: *CoRR* abs/1607.06450 (2016) (cited on page 160).

[8] Dzmitry Bahdanau, Kyunghyun Cho, and Yoshua Bengio. 'Neural Machine Translation by Jointly Learning to Align and Translate'. In: *3rd International Conference on Learning Representations, ICLR 2015, San Diego, CA, May 7–9, 2015, Conference Track Proceedings*. ICLR, 2015 (cited on page 163).

[9] James Baker. 'The DRAGON System—An Overview'. In: *IEEE Transactions on Acoustics, Speech, and Signal Processing* 23.1 (1975), pp. 24–29 (cited on pages 2, 3).

[10] Gükhan H. Bakir et al. *Predicting Structured Data (Neural Information Processing)*. Cambridge, MA: MIT Press, 2007 (cited on page 4).

[11] P. Baldi and K. Hornik. 'Neural Networks and Principal Component Analysis: Learning from Examples without Local Minima'. In: *Neural Networks* 2.1 (Jan. 1989), pp. 53–58. DOI: 10.1016/0893-6080(89)90014-2 (cited on page 91).

[12] Arindam Banerjee et al. 'Clustering on the Unit Hypersphere Using von Mises-Fisher Distributions'. In: *Journal of Machine Learning Research* 6 (Dec. 2005), pp. 1345–1382 (cited on page 379).

[13] David Barber. *Bayesian Reasoning and Machine Learning*. Cambridge, England: Cambridge University Press, 2012 (cited on pages 343, 357).

[14] David Bartholomew. *Latent Variable Models and Factor Analysis. A Unified Approach*. Chichester, England: Wiley, 2011 (cited on page 299).

[15] Leonard E. Baum. 'An Inequality and Associated Maximization Technique in Statistical Estimation for Probabilistic Functions of Markov Processes'. In: *Inequalities* 3 (1972), pp. 1–8 (cited on pages 276, 281).

[16] Leonard E. Baum and Ted Petrie. 'Statistical Inference for Probabilistic Functions of Finite State Markov Chains'. In: *Annals of Mathematical Statistics* 37.6 (Dec. 1966), pp. 1554–1563. DOI: 10.1214/aoms/1177699147 (cited on page 276).

[17] Leonard E. Baum et al. 'A Maximization Technique Occurring in the Statistical Analysis of Probabilistic Functions of Markov Chains'. In: *Annals of Mathematical Statistics* 41.1 (Feb. 1970), pp. 164–171. DOI: 10.1214/aoms/1177697196 (cited on pages 276, 281).

[18] A. J. Bell and T. J. Sejnowski. 'An Information Maximization Approach to Blind Separation and Blind Deconvolution.' In: *Neural Computation* 7 (1995), pp. 1129–1159 (cited on pages 293, 294).

[19] Shai Ben-David et al. 'A Theory of Learning from Different Domains'. In: *Machine Learning* 79.1–2 (May 2010), pp. 151–175. DOI: 10.1007/s10994-009-5152-4 (cited on page 16).

[20] Adam L. Berger, Stephen A. Della Pietra, and Vincent J. Della Pietra. 'A Maximum Entropy Approach to Natural Language Processing'. In: *Computational Linguistics* 22 (1996), pp. 39–71 (cited on page 254).

[21] Dimitri Bertsekas and John Tsitsiklis. *Introduction to Probability*. Nashua, NH: Athena Scientific, 2002 (cited on page 40).

[22] Christopher M. Bishop. *Pattern Recognition and Machine Learning (Information Science and Statistics)*. 1st ed. New York, NY: Springer, 2007 (cited on pages 343, 344, 350, 357, 368).

[23] David M. Blei, Andrew Y. Ng, and Michael I. Jordan. 'Latent Dirichlet Allocation'. In: *Journal of Machine Learning Research* 3 (Mar. 2003), pp. 993–1022 (cited on pages 363, 365, 366).

[24] Léon Bottou. 'On-Line Learning and Stochastic Approximations'. In: *On-Line Learning in Neural Networks*. Ed. by D. Saad. Cambridge, England: Cambridge University Press, 1998, pp. 9–42 (cited on page 61).

[25] Olivier Bousquet, Stéphane Boucheron, and Gábor Lugosi. 'Introduction to Statistical Learning Theory'. In: *Advanced Lectures on Machine Learning*. Ed. by Olivier Bousquet, Ulrike von Luxburg, and Gunnar Rätsch. Vol. 3176. Springer, 2003, pp. 169–207 (cited on pages 102, 103).

[26] G. E. P. Box and G. C. Tiao. *Bayesian Inference in Statistical Analysis*. Reading, MA: Addison-Wesley, 1973 (cited on page 318).

[27] M. J. Box, D. Davies, and W. H. Swann. *Non-Linear Optimisation Techniques*. Edinburgh, Scotland: Oliver & Boyd, 1969 (cited on page 71).

[28] Stephen Boyd and Lieven Vandenberghe. *Convex Optimization*. Cambridge, England: Cambridge University Press, 2004 (cited on page 50).

[29] Stephen Boyd et al. 'Distributed Optimization and Statistical Learning via the Alternating Direction Method of Multipliers'. In: *Foundations and Trends in Machine Learning* 3.1 (Jan. 2011), pp. 1–122. DOI: 10.1561/2200000016 (cited on page 71).

[30] Leo Breiman. 'Bagging Predictors'. In: *Machine Learning* 24.2 (1996), pp. 123–140 (cited on pages 204, 208).

[31] Leo Breiman. 'Stacked Regressions'. In: *Machine Learning* 24.1 (July 1996), pp. 49–64. DOI: 10.1023/A:1018046112532 (cited on page 204).

[32] Leo Breiman. 'Prediction Games and Arcing Algorithms'. In: *Neural Computation* 11.7 (Oct. 1999), pp. 1493–1517. DOI: 10.1162/089976699300016106 (cited on page 210).

[33] Leo Breiman. 'Random Forests'. In: *Machine Learning* 45.1 (2001), pp. 5–32. DOI: 10.1023/A:1010933404324 (cited on pages 208, 209).

[34] Leo Breiman et al. *Classification and Regression Trees*. Monterey, CA: Wadsworth and Brooks, 1984 (cited on pages 7, 205).

[35] John S. Bridle. 'Probabilistic Interpretation of Feedforward Classification Network Outputs, with Relationships to Statistical Pattern Recognition'. In: *Neurocomputing*. Ed. by Françoise Fogelman Soulié and Jeanny Hérault. Berlin, Germany: Springer, 1990, pp. 227–236 (cited on pages 115, 159).

[36] John S. Bridle. 'Training Stochastic Model Recognition Algorithms as Networks Can Lead to Maximum Mutual Information Estimation of Parameters'. In: *Advances in Neural Information Processing Systems (NIPS)*. Vol. 2. San Mateo, CA: Morgan Kaufmann, 1990, pp. 211–217 (cited on pages 115, 159).

[37] Peter Brown, Chin-Hui Lee, and J. Spohrer. 'Bayesian Adaptation in Speech Recognition'. In: *ICASSP '83. IEEE International Conference on Acoustics, Speech, and Signal Processing*. Vol. 8. Washington, D.C.: IEEE Computer Society, 1983, pp. 761–764 (cited on page 16).

[38] Peter Brown et al. 'A Statistical Approach to Language Translation'. In: *Proceedings of the 12th Conference on Computational Linguistics—Volume 1*. COLING '88. Budapest, Hungary: Association for Computational Linguistics, 1988, pp. 71–76. DOI: 10.3115/991635.991651 (cited on pages 2, 3).

[39] E. J. Candès and M. B. Wakin. 'An Introduction to Compressive Sampling'. In: *IEEE Signal Processing Magazine* 25.2 (2008), pp. 21–30 (cited on page 146).

[40] P. M. Chaikin and T. C. Lubensky. *Principles of Condensed Matter Physics*. Cambridge, England: Cambridge University Press, 1995 (cited on page 327).

[41] Chih-Chung Chang and Chih-Jen Lin. 'LIBSVM: A Library for Support Vector Machines'. In: *ACM Transactions on Intelligent Systems and Technology* 2.3 (2011). Software available at http://www.csie.ntu.edu.tw/~cjlin/libsvm, 27:1–27:27 (cited on page 125).

[42] Tianqi Chen and Carlos Guestrin. 'XGBoost: A Scalable Tree Boosting System'. In: *Proceedings of the 22nd ACM SIGKDD International Conference on Knowledge Discovery and Data Mining*. Ed. by Balaji Krishnapuram. New York, NY: Association for Computing Machinery, Aug. 2016. DOI: 10.1145/2939672.2939785 (cited on page 215).

[43] Kyunghyun Cho et al. 'Learning Phrase Representations Using RNN Encoder-Decoder for Statistical Machine Translation.' In: *EMNLP*. Ed. by Alessandro Moschitti, Bo Pang, and Walter Daelemans. Stroudsburg, PA: Association for Computational Linguistics, 2014, pp. 1724–1734 (cited on page 171).

[44] Dean Cock. 'Ames, Iowa: Alternative to the Boston Housing Data as an End of Semester Regression Project'. In: *Journal of Statistics Education* 19 (Nov. 2011). DOI: 10.1080/10691898.2011.11889627 (cited on page 216).

[45] Corinna Cortes and Vladimir Vapnik. 'Support-Vector Networks'. In: *Machine Learning* 20.3 (Sept. 1995), pp. 273–297. DOI: 10.1023/A:1022627411411 (cited on page 124).

[46] Koby Crammer and Yoram Singer. 'On the Algorithmic Implementation of Multiclass Kernel-Based Vector Machines'. In: *Journal of Machine Learning Research* 2 (Mar. 2002), pp. 265–292 (cited on page 127).

[47] G. Cybenko. 'Approximation by Superpositions of a Sigmoidal Function'. In: *Mathematics of Control, Signals, and Systems (MCSS)* 2.4 (Dec. 1989), pp. 303–314. DOI: 10.1007/BF02551274 (cited on page 154).

[48] B. V. Dasarathy and B. V. Sheela. 'A Composite Classifier System Design: Concepts and Methodology'. In: *Proceedings of the IEEE*. Vol. 67. Washington, D.C.: IEEE Computer Society, 1979, pp. 708–713 (cited on page 203).

[49] Steven B. Davis and Paul Mermelstein. 'Comparison of Parametric Representations for Monosyllabic Word Recognition in Continuously Spoken Sentences'. In: *IEEE Transactions on Acoustics, Speech and Signal Processing* 28.4 (1980), pp. 357–366 (cited on page 77).

[50] Scott Deerwester et al. 'Indexing by Latent Semantic Analysis'. In: *Journal of the American Society for Information Science* 41.6 (1990), pp. 391–407 (cited on page 142).

[51] M. H. DeGroot. *Optimal Statistical Decisions*. New York, NY: McGraw-Hill, 1970 (cited on page 318).

[52] A. P. Dempster, N. M. Laird, and D. B. Rubin. 'Maximum Likelihood from Incomplete Data via the EM Algorithm'. In: *Journal of the Royal Statistical Society, Series B* 39.1 (1977), pp. 1–38 (cited on pages 265, 315).

[53] S. W. Dharmadhikari and Kumar Jogdeo. 'Multivariate Unimodality'. In: *Annals of Statistics* 4.3 (May 1976), pp. 607–613. DOI: `10.1214/aos/1176343466` (cited on page 239).

[54] Pedro Domingos. 'A Few Useful Things to Know about Machine Learning'. In: *Communications of the ACM* 55.10 (Oct. 2012), pp. 78–87. DOI: `10.1145/2347736.2347755` (cited on pages 14, 15).

[55] John Duchi, Elad Hazan, and Yoram Singer. 'Adaptive Subgradient Methods for Online Learning and Stochastic Optimization'. In: *Journal of Machine Learning Research* 12 (July 2011), pp. 2121–2159 (cited on page 192).

[56] Richard O. Duda and Peter E. Hart. *Pattern Classification and Scene Analysis*. New York, NY: John Wiley & Sons, 1973 (cited on page 2).

[57] Richard O. Duda, Peter E. Hart, and David G. Stork. *Pattern Classification*. 2nd ed. New York, NY: Wiley, 2001 (cited on pages 7, 11, 226).

[58] Mehdi Elahi, Francesco Ricci, and Neil Rubens. 'A Survey of Active Learning in Collaborative Filtering Recommender Systems'. In: *Computer Science Review* 20.C (May 2016), pp. 29–50. DOI: `10.1016/j.cosrev.2016.05.002` (cited on page 17).

[59] B. Everitt and D. J. Hand. *Finite Mixture Distributions*. Monographs on Applied Probability and Statistics. New York, NY: Springer, 1981 (cited on page 257).

[60] Scott E. Fahlman. *An Empirical Study of Learning Speed in Back-Propagation Networks*. Tech. rep. CMU-CS-88-162. Pittsburgh, PA: Computer Science Department, Carnegie Mellon University, 1988 (cited on page 63).

[61] Thomas S. Ferguson. 'A Bayesian Analysis of Some Nonparametric Problems'. In: *The Annals of Statistics* 1 (1973), pp. 209–230 (cited on page 333).

[62] Lev Finkelstein et al. 'Placing Search in Context: The Concept Revisited'. In: *Proceedings of the 10th International Conference on World Wide Web*. New York, NY: Association for Computing Machinery, 2001, pp. 406–414. DOI: `10.1145/503104.503110` (cited on page 149).

[63] Jonathan Fiscus. 'A Post-Processing System to Yield Reduced Word Error Rates: Recognizer Output Voting Error Reduction (ROVER)'. In: *IEEE Workshop on Automatic Speech Recognition and Understanding Proceedings*. Washington, D.C.: IEEE Computer Society, Aug. 1997, pp. 347–354 (cited on page 203).

[64] R. A. Fisher. 'The Use of Multiple Measurements in Taxonomic Problems'. In: *Annals of Eugenics* 7.7 (1936), pp. 179–188 (cited on page 85).

[65] R. Fletcher. *Practical Methods of Optimization*. 2nd ed. Hoboken, NJ: Wiley-Interscience, 1987 (cited on page 63).

[66] E. Forgy. 'Cluster Analysis of Multivariate Data: Efficiency versus Interpretability of Classification'. In: *Biometrics* 21.3 (1965), pp. 768–769 (cited on pages 5, 270).

[67] Simon Foucart and Holger Rauhut. *A Mathematical Introduction to Compressive Sensing*. Basel, Switzerland: Birkhäuser, 2013 (cited on page 146).

[68] Yoav Freund and Robert E Schapire. 'A Decision-Theoretic Generalization of On-Line Learning and an Application to Boosting'. In: *Journal of Computer and System Sciences* 55.1 (Aug. 1997), pp. 119–139. DOI: 10.1006/jcss.1997.1504 (cited on pages 204, 210, 214).

[69] Yoav Freund and Robert E. Schapire. 'Large Margin Classification Using the Perceptron Algorithm'. In: *Proceedings of the Eleventh Annual Conference on Computational Learning Theory*. COLT' 98. Madison, Wisconsin: ACM, 1998, pp. 209–217. DOI: 10.1145/279943.279985 (cited on page 111).

[70] Brendan J. Frey. *Graphical Models for Machine Learning and Digital Communication*. Cambridge, MA: MIT Press, 1998 (cited on page 357).

[71] Brendan J. Frey and David J. C. MacKay. 'A Revolution: Belief Propagation in Graphs with Cycles'. In: *Advances in Neural Information Processing Systems 10*. Ed. by M. I. Jordan, M. J. Kearns, and S. A. Solla. Cambridge, MA: MIT Press, 1998, pp. 479–485 (cited on page 357).

[72] Jerome H. Friedman. 'Greedy Function Approximation: A Gradient Boosting Machine'. In: *Annals of Statistics* 29 (2000), pp. 1189–1232 (cited on pages 210, 211, 215).

[73] Jerome H. Friedman. 'Stochastic Gradient Boosting'. In: *Computational Statistics and Data Analysis* 38.4 (Feb. 2002), pp. 367–378. DOI: 10.1016/S0167-9473(01)00065-2 (cited on pages 211, 215).

[74] Jerome Friedman, Trevor Hastie, and Rob Tibshirani. 'Additive Logistic Regression: a Statistical View of Boosting'. In: *The Annals of Statistics* 38.2 (2000) (cited on pages 211, 212, 215).

[75] Jerome Friedman, Trevor Hastie, and Rob Tibshirani. 'Regularization Paths for Generalized Linear Models via Coordinate Descent'. In: *Journal of Statistical Software* 33.1 (2010), pp. 1–22. DOI: 10.18637/jss.v033.i01 (cited on page 140).

[76] Kunihiko Fukushima. 'Neocognitron: A Self-Organizing Neural Network Model for a Mechanism of Pattern Recognition Unaffected by Shift in Position'. In: *Biological Cybernetics* 36 (1980), pp. 193–202 (cited on page 157).

[77] J. Gauvain and Chin-Hui Lee. 'Maximum a Posteriori Estimation for Multivariate Gaussian Mixture Observations of Markov Chains'. In: *IEEE Transactions on Speech and Audio Processing* 2.2 (1994), pp. 291–298 (cited on page 16).

[78] S. Geisser. *Predictive Inference: An Introduction*. New York, NY: Chapman & Hall, 1993 (cited on page 314).

[79] Zoubin Ghahramani. *Non-Parametric Bayesian Methods*. 2005. URL: http://mlg.eng.cam.ac.uk/zoubin/talks/uai05tutorial-b.pdf (visited on 03/10/2020) (cited on page 335).

[80] Ned Glick. 'Sample-Based Classification Procedures Derived from Density Estimators'. In: *Journal of the American Statistical Association* 67 (1972), pp. 116–122 (cited on pages 229, 230).

[81] Ned Glick. 'Sample-Based Classification Procedures Related to Empiric Distributions'. In: *IEEE Transactions on Information Theory* 22 (1976), pp. 454–461 (cited on page 229).

[82] Xavier Glorot and Yoshua Bengio. 'Understanding the Difficulty of Training Deep Feedforward Neural Networks'. In: *Proceedings of the International Conference on Artificial Intelligence and Statistics (AISTATS'10)*. Society for Artificial Intelligence and Statistics, 2010, pp. 249–256 (cited on pages 153, 190).

[83] I. J. Good. 'The Population Frequencies of Species and the Estimation of Population Parameters'. In: *Biometrika* 40.3–4 (Dec. 1953), pp. 237–264. DOI: 10.1093/biomet/40.3-4.237 (cited on page 250).

[84] Ian Goodfellow et al. 'Generative Adversarial Nets'. In: *Advances in Neural Information Processing Systems 27*. Ed. by Z. Ghahramani et al. Red Hook, NY: Curran Associates, Inc., 2014, pp. 2672–2680 (cited on pages 293–295, 307, 308).

[85] Karol Gregor et al. 'DRAW: A Recurrent Neural Network for Image Generation'. In: *Proceedings of the 32nd International Conference on Machine Learning*. Ed. by Francis Bach and David Blei. Vol. 37. Proceedings of Machine Learning Research. Lille, France: PMLR, July 2015, pp. 1462–1471 (cited on page 295).

[86] F. Grezl et al. 'Probabilistic and Bottle-Neck Features for LVCSR of Meetings'. In: *2007 IEEE International Conference on Acoustics, Speech and Signal Processing*. Vol. 4. Washington, D.C.: IEEE Computer Society, 2007, pp. 757–760 (cited on page 91).

[87] M. H. J. Gruber. *Improving Efficiency by Shrinkage: The James–Stein and Ridge Regression Estimators*. Boca Raton, FL: CRC Press, 1998, pp. 7–15 (cited on page 139).

[88] Isabelle Guyon and André Elisseeff. 'An Introduction to Variable and Feature Selection'. In: *Journal of Machine Learning Research* 3 (Mar. 2003), pp. 1157–1182 (cited on page 78).

[89] L. R. Haff. 'An Identity for the Wishart Distribution with Applications'. In: *Journal of Multivariate Analysis* 9.4 (Dec. 1979), pp. 531–544 (cited on page 322).

[90] L. K. Hansen and P. Salamon. 'Neural Network Ensembles'. In: *IEEE Transactions on Pattern Analysis and Machine Intelligence* 12.10 (Oct. 1990), pp. 993–1001. DOI: 10.1109/34.58871 (cited on page 203).

[91] Zellig Harris. 'Distributional Structure'. In: *Word* 10.23 (1954), pp. 146–162 (cited on pages 5, 77, 142).

[92] Trevor Hastie, Robert Tibshirani, and Jerome Friedman. *The Elements of Statistical Learning*. Springer Series in Statistics. New York, NY: Springer, 2001 (cited on pages 138, 205, 207).

[93] Martin E. Hellman and Josef Raviv. 'Probability of Error, Equivocation and the Chernoff Bound'. In: *IEEE Transactions on Information Theory* 16 (1970), pp. 368–372 (cited on page 226).

[94] H. Hermansky, D. P. W. Ellis, and S. Sharma. 'Tandem Connectionist Feature Extraction for Conventional HMM Systems'. In: *2000 IEEE International Conference on Acoustics, Speech, and Signal Processing. Proceedings*. Vol. 3. Washington, D.C.: IEEE Computer Society, 2000, pp. 1635–1638 (cited on page 91).

[95] Salah El Hihi and Yoshua Bengio. 'Hierarchical Recurrent Neural Networks for Long-Term Dependencies'. In: *Advances in Neural Information Processing Systems 8*. Ed. by D. S. Touretzky, M. C. Mozer, and M. E. Hasselmo. Cambridge, MA: MIT Press, 1996, pp. 493–499 (cited on page 171).

[96] Geoffrey E. Hinton. 'Training Products of Experts by Minimizing Contrastive Divergence'. In: *Neural Computation* 14.8 (2002), pp. 1771–1800. DOI: 10.1162/089976602760128018 (cited on page 371).

[97] Geoffrey E. Hinton. 'A Practical Guide to Training Restricted Boltzmann Machines.' In: *Neural Networks: Tricks of the Trade*. Ed. by Grégoire Montavon, Genevieve B. Orr, and Klaus-Robert Müller. 2nd ed. Vol. 7700. New York, NY: Springer, 2012, pp. 599–619 (cited on pages 366, 370).

[98] Geoffrey Hinton and Sam Roweis. 'Stochastic Neighbor Embedding'. In: *Advances in Neural Information Processing Systems*. Ed. by S. Thrun S. Becker and K. Obermayer. Vol. 15. Cambridge, MA: MIT Press, 2003, pp. 833–840 (cited on page 89).

[99] Tin Kam Ho. 'Random Decision Forests'. In: *Proceedings of the Third International Conference on Document Analysis and Recognition (Volume 1)*. ICDAR '95. Washington, D.C.: IEEE Computer Society, 1995, p. 278 (cited on pages 208, 209).

[100] Tin Kam Ho, Jonathan J. Hull, and Sargur N. Srihari. 'Decision Combination in Multiple Classifier Systems'. In: *IEEE Transactions on Pattern Analysis and Machine Intelligence* 16.1 (Jan. 1994), pp. 66–75. DOI: 10.1109/34.273716 (cited on page 203).

[101] Sepp Hochreiter and Jürgen Schmidhuber. 'Long Short-Term Memory'. In: *Neural Computation* 9.8 (Nov. 1997), pp. 1735–1780. DOI: 10.1162/neco.1997.9.8.1735 (cited on page 171).

[102] Kurt Hornik. 'Approximation Capabilities of Multilayer Feedforward Networks'. In: *Neural Networks* 4.2 (Mar. 1991), pp. 251–257. DOI: 10.1016/0893-6080(91)90009-T (cited on pages 154, 155).

[103] H. Hotelling. 'Analysis of a Complex of Statistical Variables into Principal Components.' In: *Journal of Educational Psychology* 24.6 (1933), pp. 417–441. DOI: 10.1037/h0071325 (cited on page 80).

[104] Qiang Huo. 'An Introduction to Decision Rules for Automatic Speech Recognition'. In: *Technical Report TR-99-07*. Hong Kong: Department of Computer Science and Information Systems, University of Hong Kong, 1999 (cited on page 229).

[105] Qiang Huo and Chin-Hui Lee. 'On-Line Adaptive Learning of the Continuous Density Hidden Markov Model Based on Approximate Recursive Bayes Estimate'. In: *IEEE Transactions on Speech and Audio Processing* 5.2 (1997), pp. 161–172 (cited on page 17).

[106] Ahmed Hussein et al. 'Imitation Learning: A Survey of Learning Methods'. In: *ACM Computing Surveys* 50.2 (Apr. 2017). DOI: 10.1145/3054912 (cited on page 17).

[107] Aapo Hyvärinen and Erkki Oja. 'Independent Component Analysis: Algorithms and Applications'. In: *Neural Networks* 13 (2000), pp. 411–430 (cited on pages 293, 294, 301).

[108] Sergey Ioffe and Christian Szegedy. 'Batch Normalization: Accelerating Deep Network Training by Reducing Internal Covariate Shift'. In: *Proceedings of the 32nd International Conference on International Conference on Machine Learning—Volume 37*. ICML'15. Lille, France: Journal of Machine Learning Research, 2015, pp. 448–456 (cited on page 160).

[109] Tommi S. Jaakkola and Michael I. Jordan. *A Variational Approach to Bayesian Logistic Regression Models and Their Extensions*. 1996. URL: https://people.csail.mit.edu/tommi/papers/aistat96.ps (visited on 11/10/2019) (cited on page 326).

[110] Peter Jackson. *Introduction to Expert Systems*. 2nd ed. USA: Addison-Wesley Longman Publishing Co., Inc., 1990 (cited on page 2).

[111] Kevin Jarrett et al. 'What Is the Best Multi-Stage Architecture for Object Recognition?' In: *2009 IEEE 12th International Conference on Computer Vision*. Washington, D.C.: IEEE Computer Society, 2009, pp. 2146–2153 (cited on page 153).

[112] F. Jelinek, L. R. Bahl, and R. L. Mercer. 'Design of a Linguistic Statistical Decoder for the Recognition of Continuous Speech'. In: *IEEE Transactions on Information Theory* 21 (1975), pp. 250–256 (cited on pages 2, 3).

[113] Finn V. Jensen. *Introduction to Bayesian Networks*. 1st ed. Berlin, Germany: Springer-Verlag, 1996 (cited on page 343).

[114] J. L. W. V. Jensen. 'Sur les fonctions convexes et les inégalités entre les valeurs moyennes'. In: *Acta Mathematica* 30.1 (1906), pp. 175–193 (cited on page 46).

[115] Hui Jiang. 'A New Perspective on Machine Learning: How to Do Perfect Supervised Learning'. In: *CoRR* abs/1901.02046 (2019) (cited on page 13).

[116] Richard Arnold Johnson and Dean W. Wichern. *Applied Multivariate Statistical Analysis*. 5th ed. Upper Saddle River, NJ: Prentice Hall, 2002 (cited on page 378).

[117] Karen Spärck Jones. 'A Statistical Interpretation of Term Specificity and Its Application in Retrieval'. In: *Journal of Documentation* 28 (1972), pp. 11–21 (cited on page 78).

[118] Michael I. Jordan, ed. *Learning in Graphical Models*. Cambridge, MA: MIT Press, 1999 (cited on page 343).

[119] Michael I. Jordan et al. 'An Introduction to Variational Methods for Graphical Models'. In: *Learning in Graphical Models*. Ed. by Michael I. Jordan. Dordrecht, Netherlands: Springer, 1998, pp. 105–161. DOI: 10.1007/978-94-011-5014-9_5 (cited on page 357).

[120] B. H. Juang. 'Maximum-Likelihood Estimation for Mixture Multivariate Stochastic Observations of Markov Chains'. In: *AT&T Technical Journal* 64.6 (July 1985), pp. 1235–1249. DOI: 10.1002/j.1538-7305.1985.tb00273.x (cited on page 284).

[121] B. H. Juang and L. R. Rabiner. 'The Segmental K-Means Algorithm for Estimating Parameters of Hidden Markov Models'. In: *IEEE Transactions on Acoustics, Speech, and Signal Processing* 38.9 (Sept. 1990), pp. 1639–1641. DOI: 10.1109/29.60082 (cited on page 286).

[122] Rudolph Emil Kalman. 'A New Approach to Linear Filtering and Prediction Problems'. In: *Journal of Basic Engineering* 82.1 (1960), pp. 35–45 (cited on page 69).

[123] Tero Karras, Samuli Laine, and Timo Aila. 'A Style-Based Generator Architecture for Generative Adversarial Networks.' In: *CoRR* abs/1812.04948 (2018) (cited on page 295).

[124] William Karush. 'Minima of Functions of Several Variables with Inequalities as Side Conditions'. MA thesis. Chicago, IL: Department of Mathematics, University of Chicago, 1939 (cited on page 57).

[125] Slava M. Katz. 'Estimation of Probabilities from Sparse Data for the Language Model Component of a Speech Recognizer'. In: *IEEE Transactions on Acoustics, Speech and Signal Processing*. 1987, pp. 400–401 (cited on page 250).

[126] Alexander S. Kechris. *Classical Descriptive Set Theory*. Berlin, Germany: Springer-Verlag, 1995 (cited on page 291).

[127] M. G. Kendall, A. Stuart, and J. K. Ord. *Kendall's Advanced Theory of Statistics*. Oxford, England: Oxford University Press, 1987 (cited on page 323).

[128] R. Kinderman and S. L. Snell. *Markov Random Fields and Their Applications*. Ann Arbor, MI: American Mathematical Society, 1980 (cited on pages 344, 366).

[129] Diederik P. Kingma and Jimmy Ba. 'ADAM: A Method for Stochastic Optimization.' In: *CoRR* abs/1412.6980 (2014) (cited on page 192).

[130] Diederik P. Kingma and Max Welling. 'Auto-Encoding Variational Bayes'. In: *2nd International Conference on Learning Representations, ICLR 2014, Banff, AB, Canada, April 14-16, 2014, Conference Track Proceedings*. ICLR, 2014 (cited on pages 293, 294, 305, 306).

[131] Yehuda Koren, Robert Bell, and Chris Volinsky. 'Matrix Factorization Techniques for Recommender Systems'. In: *Computer* 42.8 (Aug. 2009), pp. 30–37. DOI: 10.1109/MC.2009.263 (cited on page 143).

[132] Mark A. Kramer. 'Nonlinear Principal Component Analysis Using Autoassociative Neural Networks'. In: *AIChE Journal* 37.2 (1991), pp. 233–243. DOI: 10.1002/aic.690370209 (cited on page 90).

[133] Anders Krogh and John A. Hertz. 'A Simple Weight Decay Can Improve Generalization'. In: *Advances in Neural Information Processing Systems 4*. Ed. by J. E. Moody, S. J. Hanson, and R. P. Lippmann. Burlington, MA: Morgan-Kaufmann, 1992, pp. 950–957 (cited on page 194).

[134] F. R. Kschischang, B. J. Frey, and H. A. Loeliger. 'Factor Graphs and the Sum-Product Algorithm'. In: *IEEE Transactions on Information Theory* 47.2 (Sept. 2006), pp. 498–519. DOI: 10.1109/18.910572 (cited on pages 357, 360).

[135] H. W. Kuhn and A. W. Tucker. 'Nonlinear Programming'. In: *Proceedings of the Second Berkeley Symposium on Mathematical Statistics and Probability*. Berkeley, CA: University of California Press, 1951, pp. 481–492 (cited on page 57).

[136] Brian Kulis. 'Metric Learning: A Survey'. In: *Foundations and Trends in Machine Learning* 5.4 (2013), pp. 287–364. DOI: 10.1561/2200000019 (cited on page 13).

[137] S. Kullback and R. A. Leibler. 'On Information and Sufficiency'. In: *Annals of Mathematical Statistics* 22.1 (1951), pp. 79–86 (cited on page 41).

[138] John D. Lafferty, Andrew McCallum, and Fernando C. N. Pereira. 'Conditional Random Fields: Probabilistic Models for Segmenting and Labeling Sequence Data'. In: *Proceedings of the Eighteenth International Conference on Machine Learning*. ICML '01. San Francisco, CA: Morgan Kaufmann Publishers Inc., 2001, pp. 282–289 (cited on pages 366, 368, 369).

[139] Pierre Simon Laplace. 'Memoir on the Probability of the Causes of Events'. In: *Statistical Science* 1.3 (1986), pp. 364–378 (cited on page 324).

[140] S. L. Lauritzen and D. J. Spiegelhalter. 'Local Computations with Probabilities on Graphical Structures and Their Application to Expert Systems'. In: *Journal of the Royal Statistical Society. Series B (Methodological)* 50.2 (1988), pp. 157–224 (cited on pages 357, 361).

[141] Yann LeCun and Yoshua Bengio. 'Convolutional Networks for Images, Speech, and Time Series'. In: *The Handbook of Brain Theory and Neural Networks*. Ed. by Michael A. Arbib. Cambridge, MA: MIT Press, 1998, pp. 255–258 (cited on page 157).

[142] Yann LeCun et al. 'Gradient-Based Learning Applied to Document Recognition'. In: *Proceedings of the IEEE* 86.11 (1998), pp. 2278–2324 (cited on pages 92, 129, 200).

[143] Chin-Hui Lee and Qiang Huo. 'On Adaptive Decision Rules and Decision Parameter Adaptation for Automatic Speech Recognition'. In: *Proceedings of the IEEE* 88.8 (2000), pp. 1241–1269 (cited on page 16).

[144] C. J. Leggetter and P. C. Woodland. 'Maximum Likelihood Linear Regression for Speaker Adaptation of Continuous Density Hidden Markov Models'. In: *Computer Speech & Language* 9.2 (1995), pp. 171–185. DOI: https://doi.org/10.1006/csla.1995.0010 (cited on page 16).

[145] Seppo Linnainmaa. 'Taylor Expansion of the Accumulated Rounding Error'. In: *BIT Numerical Mathematics* 16.2 (June 1976), pp. 146–160. DOI: 10.1007/BF01931367 (cited on page 176).

[146] Quan Liu et al. 'Learning Semantic Word Embeddings Based on Ordinal Knowledge Constraints'. In: *Proceedings of the 53rd Annual Meeting of the Association for Computational Linguistics and the 7th International Joint Conference on Natural Language Processing (Volume 1: Long Papers)*. Beijing, China: Association for Computational Linguistics, July 2015, pp. 1501–1511. DOI: 10.3115/v1/P15-1145 (cited on page 149).

[147] Stuart P. Lloyd. 'Least Squares Quantization in PCM'. In: *IEEE Transactions on Information Theory* 28 (1982), pp. 129–137 (cited on page 270).

[148] Jonathan Long, Evan Shelhamer, and Trevor Darrell. 'Fully Convolutional Networks for Semantic Segmentation'. In: *The IEEE Conference on Computer Vision and Pattern Recognition (CVPR)*. Washington, D.C.: IEEE Computer Society, June 2015 (cited on pages 198, 309).

[149] David G. Lowe. 'Object Recognition from Local Scale-Invariant Features'. In: *Proceedings of the International Conference on Computer Vision*. ICCV '99. Washington, D.C.: IEEE Computer Society, 1999, p. 1150 (cited on page 77).

[150] Laurens van der Maaten and Geoffrey Hinton. 'Visualizing Data Using t-SNE'. In: *Journal of Machine Learning Research* 9 (2008), pp. 2579–2605 (cited on page 89).

[151] David J. C. MacKay. 'The Evidence Framework Applied to Classification Networks'. In: *Neural Computation* 4.5 (1992), pp. 720–736. DOI: 10.1162/neco.1992.4.5.720 (cited on page 326).

[152] David J. C. MacKay. 'Introduction to Gaussian Processes'. In: *Neural Networks and Machine Learning*. Ed. by C. M. Bishop. NATO ASI Series. Amsterdam, Netherlands: Kluwer Academic Press, 1998, pp. 133–166 (cited on page 333).

[153] David J. C. MacKay. *Information Theory, Inference, and Learning Algorithms*. Cambridge, England: Cambridge University Press, 2003 (cited on page 324).

[154] David J. C. MacKay. 'Good Error-Correcting Codes Based on Very Sparse Matrices'. In: *IEEE Transactions on Information Theory* 45.2 (Sept. 2006), pp. 399–431. DOI: 10.1109/18.748992 (cited on page 357).

[155] David J. C. Mackay. 'Introduction to Monte Carlo Methods'. In: *Learning in Graphical Models*. Ed. by Michael I. Jordan. Dordrecht, Netherlands: Springer, 1998, pp. 175–204. DOI: 10.1007/978-94-011-5014-9_7 (cited on pages 357, 361).

[156] Matt Mahoney. *Large Text Compression Benchmark*. 2011. URL: http://mattmahoney.net/dc/textdata.html (visited on 11/10/2019) (cited on page 149).

[157] Julien Mairal et al. 'Online Learning for Matrix Factorization and Sparse Coding'. In: *Journal of Machine Learning Research* 11 (Mar. 2010), pp. 19–60 (cited on page 145).

[158] J. S. Maritz and T. Lwin. *Empirical Bayes Methods*. London, England: Chapman & Hall, 1989 (cited on page 323).

[159] M. E. Maron. 'Automatic Indexing: An Experimental Inquiry'. In: *Journal of the ACM* 8.3 (July 1961), pp. 404–417. DOI: 10.1145/321075.321084 (cited on page 362).

[160] James Martens. 'Deep Learning via Hessian-Free Optimization'. In: *Proceedings of the 27th International Conference on International Conference on Machine Learning*. ICML'10. Haifa, Israel: Omnipress, 2010, pp. 735–742 (cited on page 63).

[161] Llew Mason et al. 'Boosting Algorithms as Gradient Descent'. In: *Proceedings of the 12th International Conference on Neural Information Processing Systems*. NIPS'99. Denver, CO: MIT Press, 1999, pp. 512–518 (cited on pages 210, 212).

[162] G. J. McLachlan and D. Peel. *Finite Mixture Models*. New York, NY: Wiley, 2000 (cited on page 257).

[163] A. Mead. 'Review of the Development of Multidimensional Scaling Methods'. In: *Journal of the Royal Statistical Society. Series D (The Statistician)* 41.1 (1992), pp. 27–39 (cited on page 88).

[164] T. P. Minka. 'Expectation Propagation for Approximate Bayesian Inference'. In: *Uncertainty in Artificial Intelligence*. Vol. 17. Association for Uncertainty in Artificial Intelligence, 2001, pp. 362–369 (cited on page 357).

[165] Tom M. Mitchell. *Machine Learning*. New York, NY: McGraw-Hill, 1997 (cited on page 2).

[166] Volodymyr Mnih et al. 'Playing Atari with Deep Reinforcement Learning'. In: *arXiv* (2013). arXiv:1312.5602 (cited on page 15).

[167] Volodymyr Mnih et al. 'Human-Level Control through Deep Reinforcement Learning'. In: *Nature* 518.7540 (Feb. 2015), pp. 529–533 (cited on page 16).

[168] Vinod Nair and Geoffrey E. Hinton. 'Rectified Linear Units Improve Restricted Boltzmann Machines'. In: *Proceedings of the 27th International Conference on Machine Learning (ICML-10)*. ICML, 2010, pp. 807–814 (cited on page 153).

[169] Radford M. Neal. 'Bayesian Mixture Modeling'. In: *Maximum Entropy and Bayesian Methods: Seattle, 1991*. Ed. by C. Ray Smith, Gary J. Erickson, and Paul O. Neudorfer. Dordrecht, Netherlands: Springer, 1992, pp. 197–211. DOI: 10.1007/978-94-017-2219-3_14 (cited on page 333).

[170] Radford M. Neal and Geoffrey E. Hinton. 'A View of the EM Algorithm That Justifies Incremental, Sparse, and Other Variants'. In: *Learning in Graphical Models*. Ed. by Michael I. Jordan. Dordrecht, Netherlands: Springer, 1998, pp. 355–368. DOI: 10.1007/978-94-011-5014-9_12 (cited on page 327).

[171] J. A. Nelder and R. W. M. Wedderburn. 'Generalized Linear Models'. In: *Journal of the Royal Statistical Society, Series A, General* 135 (1972), pp. 370–384 (cited on pages 239, 250).

[172] Yurii Nesterov. *Introductory Lectures on Convex Optimization: A Basic Course*. 1st ed. New York, NY: Springer, 2014 (cited on pages 49, 50).

[173] H. Ney and S. Ortmanns. 'Progress in Dynamic Programming Search for LVCSR'. In: *Proceedings of the IEEE* 88.8 (Aug. 2000), pp. 1224–1240. DOI: 10.1109/5.880081 (cited on pages 276, 280).

[174] Andrew Ng. *Machine Learning Yearning*. 2018. URL: http://www.deeplearning.ai/machine-learning-yearning/ (visited on 12/10/2019) (cited on page 196).

[175] Jorge Nocedal and Stephen J. Wright. *Numerical Optimization*. 2nd ed. Springer Series in Operations Research and Financial Engineering. New York, NY: Springer, 2006, pp. XXII, 664 (cited on page 63).

[176] A. B. Novikoff. 'On Convergence Proofs on Perceptrons'. In: *Proceedings of the Symposium on the Mathematical Theory of Automata*. Vol. 12. New York, NY: Polytechnic Institute of Brooklyn, 1962, pp. 615–622 (cited on page 108).

[177] Christopher Olah. *Understanding LSTM Networks*. 2015. URL: http://colah.github.io/posts/2015-08-Understanding-LSTMs/ (visited on 11/10/2019) (cited on page 171).

[178] Aäron van den Oord et al. 'WaveNet: A Generative Model for Raw Audio'. In: *CoRR* abs/1609.03499 (2016) (cited on page 198).

[179] David Opitz and Richard Maclin. 'Popular Ensemble Methods: An Empirical Study'. In: *Journal of Artificial Intelligence Research* 11.1 (July 1999), pp. 169–198 (cited on page 203).

[180] Judea Pearl. 'Reverend Bayes on Inference Engines: A Distributed Hierarchical Approach'. In: *Proceedings of the National Conference on Artificial Intelligence*. Menlo Park, CA: Association for the Advancement of Artificial Intelligence, 1982, pp. 133–136 (cited on page 357).

[181] Judea Pearl. 'Bayesian Networks: A Model of Self-Activated Memory for Evidential Reasoning'. In: *Proceedings of the Cognitive Science Society (CSS-7)*. 1985 (cited on page 343).

[182] Judea Pearl. *Probabilistic Reasoning in Intelligent Systems: Networks of Plausible Inference*. San Francisco, CA: Morgan Kaufmann Publishers Inc., 1988 (cited on pages 343, 350, 357).

[183] Judea Pearl. 'Causal Inference in Statistics: An Overview'. In: *Statistics Surveys* 3 (Jan. 2009), pp. 96–146. DOI: 10.1214/09-SS057 (cited on pages 16, 347).

[184] Judea Pearl. *Causality: Models, Reasoning and Inference*. 2nd ed. Cambridge, MA: Cambridge University Press, 2009 (cited on pages 16, 347).

[185] Karl Pearson. 'On Lines and Planes of Closest Fit to Systems of Points in Space'. In: *Philosophical Magazine* 2 (1901), pp. 559–572 (cited on page 80).

[186] Jonas Peters, Dominik Janzing, and Bernhard Schlkopf. *Elements of Causal Inference: Foundations and Learning Algorithms*. Cambridge, MA: MIT Press, 2017 (cited on pages 16, 347).

[187] K. N. Plataniotis and D. Hatzinakos. 'Gaussian Mixtures and Their Applications to Signal Processing'. In: *Advanced Signal Processing Handbook: Theory and Implementation for Radar, Sonar, and Medical Imaging Real Time Systems*. Ed. by Stergios Stergiopoulos. Boca Raton, FL: CRC Press, 2000, Chapter 3 (cited on page 268).

[188] John C. Platt. 'Fast Training of Support Vector Machines Using Sequential Minimal Optimization'. In: *Advances in Kernel Methods*. Ed. by Bernhard Schölkopf, Christopher J. C. Burges, and Alexander J. Smola. Cambridge, MA: MIT Press, 1999, pp. 185–208 (cited on page 127).

[189] John C. Platt, Nello Cristianini, and John Shawe-Taylor. 'Large Margin DAGs for Multiclass Classification'. In: *Advances in Neural Information Processing Systems 12*. Ed. by S. A. Solla, T. K. Leen, and K. Müller. Cambridge, MA: MIT Press, 2000, pp. 547–553 (cited on page 127).

[190] L. Y. Pratt. 'Discriminability-Based Transfer between Neural Networks'. In: *Advances in Neural Information Processing Systems 5*. Ed. by S. J. Hanson, J. D. Cowan, and C. L. Giles. Burlington, MA: Morgan-Kaufmann, 1993, pp. 204–211 (cited on page 16).

[191] S. James Press. *Applied Multivariate Analysis*. 2nd ed. Malabar, FL: R. E. Krieger, 1982 (cited on page 378).

[192] Ning Qian. 'On the Momentum Term in Gradient Descent Learning Algorithms'. In: *Neural Networks* 12.1 (Jan. 1999), pp. 145–151. DOI: `10.1016/S0893-6080(98)00116-6` (cited on page 192).

[193] J. R. Quinlan. 'Induction of Decision Trees'. In: *Machine Learning* 1.1 (Mar. 1986), pp. 81–106. DOI: `10.1023/A:1022643204877` (cited on page 205).

[194] Lawrence R. Rabiner. 'A Tutorial on Hidden Markov Models and Selected Applications in Speech Recognition'. In: *Proceedings of the IEEE* 77.2 (1989), pp. 257–286 (cited on pages 276, 357).

[195] Piyush Rai. *Matrix Factorization and Matrix Completion*. 2016. URL: `https://cse.iitk.ac.in/users/piyush/courses/ml_autumn16/771A_lec14_slides.pdf` (visited on 11/10/2019) (cited on page 144).

[196] Carl Edward Rasmussen and Christopher K. I. Williams. *Gaussian Processes for Machine Learning (Adaptive Computation and Machine Learning)*. Cambridge, MA: MIT Press, 2005 (cited on pages 333, 339).

[197] Francesco Ricci, Lior Rokach, and Bracha Shapira. 'Introduction to Recommender Systems Handbook'. In: *Recommender Systems Handbook*. Ed. by Francesco Ricci et al. Boston, MA: Springer, 2011, pp. 1–35. DOI: `10.1007/978-0-387-85820-3_1` (cited on page 141).

[198] Jorma Rissanen. 'Modeling by Shortest Data Description.' In: *Automatica* 14.5 (1978), pp. 465–471 (cited on page 11).

[199] Joseph Rocca. *Understanding Variational Autoencoders (VAEs)*. 2019. URL: `https://towardsdatascience.com/understanding-variational-autoencoders-vaes-f70510919f73` (visited on 03/03/2020) (cited on page 306).

[200] F. Rosenblatt. 'The Perceptron: A Probabilistic Model for Information Storage and Organization in the Brain'. In: *Psychological Review* (1958), pp. 65–386 (cited on pages 2, 108).

[201] Sam T. Roweis and Lawrence K. Saul. 'Nonlinear Dimensionality Reduction by Locally Linear Embedding'. In: *Science* 290.5500 (2000), pp. 2323–2326. DOI: `10.1126/science.290.5500.2323` (cited on page 87).

[202] R. Rubinstein, A. M. Bruckstein, and M. Elad. 'Dictionaries for Sparse Representation Modeling'. In: *Proceedings of the IEEE* 98.6 (June 2010), pp. 1045–1057. DOI: 10.1109/JPROC.2010.2040551 (cited on page 145).

[203] Havard Rue and Leonhard Held. *Gaussian Markov Random Fields: Theory and Applications (Monographs on Statistics and Applied Probability)*. Boca Raton, FL: Chapman & Hall/CRC, 2005 (cited on pages 344, 366).

[204] David E. Rumelhart, Geoffrey E. Hinton, and Ronald J. Williams. 'Learning Representations by Back-Propagating Errors'. In: *Nature* 323.6088 (1986), pp. 533–536. DOI: 10.1038/323533a0 (cited on pages 153, 176).

[205] David E. Rumelhart, James L. McClelland, and et al., eds. *Parallel Distributed Processing: Explorations in the Microstructure of Cognition, Vol. 2: Psychological and Biological Models*. Cambridge, MA: MIT Press, 1986 (cited on page 2).

[206] David E. Rumelhart, James L. McClelland, and PDP Research Group, eds. *Parallel Distributed Processing: Explorations in the Microstructure of Cognition, Vol. 1: Foundations*. Cambridge, MA: MIT Press, 1986 (cited on page 2).

[207] Stuart Russell and Peter Norvig. *Artificial Intelligence: A Modern Approach*. 3rd ed. Upper Saddle River, NJ: Prentice Hall, 2010 (cited on pages 1, 2).

[208] Sumit Saha. *A Comprehensive Guide to Convolutional Neural Networks*. 2018. URL: http://towardsdatascience.com/a-comprehensive-guide-to-convolutional-neural-networks-the-eli5-way-3bd2b1164a53 (visited on 11/10/2019) (cited on page 169).

[209] Tim Salimans and Diederik P. Kingma. 'Weight Normalization: A Simple Reparameterization to Accelerate Training of Deep Neural Networks'. In: *Proceedings of the 30th International Conference on Neural Information Processing Systems*. NIPS'16. Barcelona, Spain: Curran Associates Inc., 2016, pp. 901–909 (cited on pages 194, 195).

[210] Mostafa Samir. *Machine Learning Theory—Part 2: Generalization Bounds*. 2016. URL: https://mostafa-samir.github.io/ml-theory-pt2/ (visited on 11/10/2019) (cited on page 103).

[211] John W. Sammon. 'A Nonlinear Mapping for Data Structure Analysis'. In: *IEEE Transactions on Computers* 18.5 (1969), pp. 401–409 (cited on page 88).

[212] A. L. Samuel. 'Some Studies in Machine Learning Using the Game of Checkers'. In: *IBM Journal of Research and Development* 3.3 (July 1959), pp. 210–229. DOI: 10.1147/rd.33.0210 (cited on page 2).

[213] Lawrence K. Saul, Tommi Jaakkola, and Michael I. Jordan. 'Mean Field Theory for Sigmoid Belief Networks'. In: *Journal of Artificial Intelligence Research* 4 (1996), pp. 61–76 (cited on page 326).

[214] Robert E. Schapire. 'The Strength of Weak Learnability'. In: *Machine Learning* 5.2 (1990), pp. 197–227. DOI: 10.1023/A:1022648800760 (cited on pages 204, 209, 210).

[215] Robert E. Schapire et al. 'Boosting the Margin: A New Explanation for the Effectiveness of Voting Methods'. In: *Proceedings of the Fourteenth International Conference on Machine Learning*. ICML '97. San Francisco, CA: Morgan Kaufmann Publishers Inc., 1997, pp. 322–330 (cited on pages 204, 214).

[216] Bernhard Schölkopf, Alexander Smola, and Klaus-Robert Müller. 'Nonlinear Component Analysis as a Kernel Eigenvalue Problem'. In: *Neural Computation* 10.5 (July 1998), pp. 1299–1319. DOI: 10.1162/089976698300017467 (cited on page 125).

[217] M. Schuster and K. K. Paliwal. 'Bidirectional Recurrent Neural Networks'. In: *IEEE Transactions on Signal Processing* 45.11 (Nov. 1997), pp. 2673–2681. DOI: 10.1109/78.650093 (cited on page 171).

[218] Frank Seide, Gang Li, and Dong Yu. 'Conversational Speech Transcription Using Context-Dependent Deep Neural Networks'. In: *Proceedings of Interspeech*. Baixas, France: International Speech Communication Association, 2011, pp. 437–440 (cited on page 276).

[219] Burr Settles. *Active Learning Literature Survey*. Computer Sciences Technical Report 1648. Madison, WI: University of Wisconsin–Madison, 2009 (cited on page 17).

[220] Shai Shalev-Shwartz and Shai Ben-David. *Understanding Machine Learning: From Theory to Algorithms*. Cambridge, England: Cambridge University Press, 2014 (cited on pages 11, 14).

[221] Shai Shalev-Shwartz and Yoram Singer. 'A New Perspective on an Old Perceptron Algorithm'. In: *International Conference on Computational Learning Theory*. New York, NY: Springer, 2005, pp. 264–278 (cited on page 111).

[222] C. E. Shannon. 'A Mathematical Theory of Communication'. In: *Bell System Technical Journal* 27.3 (1948), pp. 379–423. DOI: 10.1002/j.1538-7305.1948.tb01338.x (cited on page 41).

[223] N. Z. Shor, Krzysztof C. Kiwiel, and Andrzej Ruszcayński. *Minimization Methods for Non-Differentiable Functions*. Berlin, Germany: Springer-Verlag, 1985 (cited on page 71).

[224] David Silver et al. 'Mastering the Game of Go with Deep Neural Networks and Tree Search'. In: *Nature* 529.7587 (Jan. 2016), pp. 484–489. DOI: 10.1038/nature16961 (cited on page 16).

[225] Morton Slater. *Lagrange Multipliers Revisited*. Cowles Foundation Discussion Papers 80. New Haven, CT: Cowles Foundation for Research in Economics, Yale University, 1959 (cited on page 57).

[226] P. Smolensky. 'Information Processing in Dynamical Systems: Foundations of Harmony Theory'. In: *Parallel Distributed Processing: Explorations in the Microstructure of Cognition, Vol. 1: Foundations*. Ed. by David E. Rumelhart, James L. McClelland, and PDP Research Group. Cambridge, MA: MIT Press, 1986, pp. 194–281 (cited on pages 366, 370).

[227] Peter Sollich and Anders Krogh. 'Learning with Ensembles: How Overfitting Can Be Useful.' In: *Advances in Neural Information Processing Systems 7*. Ed. by David S. Touretzky, Michael Mozer, and Michael E. Hasselmo. Cambridge, MA: MIT Press, 1995, pp. 190–196 (cited on page 203).

[228] Rohollah Soltani and Hui Jiang. 'Higher Order Recurrent Neural Networks'. In: *CoRR* abs/1605.00064 (2016) (cited on pages 171, 201).

[229] H. W. Sorenson and D. L. Alspach. 'Recursive Bayesian Estimation Using Gaussian Sums'. In: *Automatica* 7.4 (1971), pp. 465–479. DOI: https://doi.org/10.1016/0005-1098(71)90097-5 (cited on page 268).

[230] Nitish Srivastava et al. 'Dropout: A Simple Way to Prevent Neural Networks from Overfitting'. In: *Journal of Machine Learning Research* 15.1 (Jan. 2014), pp. 1929–1958 (cited on page 195).

[231] W. Stephenson. 'Technique of Factor Analysis'. In: *Nature* 136.297 (1935). DOI: https://doi.org/10.1038/136297b0 (cited on pages 293, 294, 296, 298).

[232] Ilya Sutskever, Oriol Vinyals, and Quoc V Le. 'Sequence to Sequence Learning with Neural Networks'. In: *Advances in Neural Information Processing Systems 27*. Ed. by Z. Ghahramani et al. Red Hook, NY: Curran Associates, Inc., 2014, pp. 3104–3112 (cited on page 198).

[233] C. Sutton and A. McCallum. 'An Introduction to Conditional Random Fields for Relational Learning'. In: *Introduction to Statistical Relational Learning*. Ed. by Lise Getoor and Ben Taskar. Cambridge, MA: MIT Press, 2007 (cited on pages 366, 369).

[234] Richard S. Sutton and Andrew G. Barto. *Reinforcement Learning: An Introduction*. 2nd ed. Cambridge, MA: MIT Press, 2018 (cited on page 15).

[235] Joshua B. Tenenbaum, Vin de Silva, and John C. Langford. 'A Global Geometric Framework for Nonlinear Dimensionality Reduction'. In: *Science* 290.5500 (2000), p. 2319 (cited on page 88).

[236] Robert Tibshirani. 'Regression Shrinkage and Selection Via the LASSO'. In: *Journal of the Royal Statistical Society, Series B* 58 (1994), pp. 267–288 (cited on page 140).

[237] M. E. Tipping and Christopher Bishop. 'Mixtures of Probabilistic Principal Component Analyzers'. In: *Neural Computation* 11 (Jan. 1999), pp. 443–482 (cited on pages 297, 298).

[238] Michael E. Tipping and Chris M. Bishop. 'Probabilistic Principal Component Analysis'. In: *Journal of the Royal Statistical Society, Series B* 61.3 (1999), pp. 611–622 (cited on pages 293, 294, 296).

[239] D. M. Titterington, A. F. M. Smith, and U. E. Makov. *Statistical Analysis of Finite Mixture Distributions*. New York, NY: Wiley, 1985 (cited on page 257).

[240] Peter D. Turney and Patrick Pantel. 'From Frequency to Meaning: Vector Space Models of Semantics'. In: *Journal of Artificial Intelligence Research* 37.1 (Jan. 2010), pp. 141–188 (cited on pages 142, 149).

[241] Joaquin Vanschoren. 'Meta-Learning'. In: *Automated Machine Learning: Methods, Systems, Challenges*. Ed. by Frank Hutter, Lars Kotthoff, and Joaquin Vanschoren. Cham, Switzerland: Springer International Publishing, 2019, pp. 35–61. DOI: 10.1007/978-3-030-05318-5_2 (cited on page 16).

[242] Vladimir N. Vapnik. *The Nature of Statistical Learning Theory*. Berlin, Germany: Springer-Verlag, 1995 (cited on pages 102, 103).

[243] Vladimir N. Vapnik. *Statistical Learning Theory*. Hoboken, NJ: Wiley-Interscience, 1998 (cited on pages 102, 103).

[244] Ashish Vaswani et al. 'Attention Is All You Need'. In: *Advances in Neural Information Processing Systems 30*. Ed. by U. Von Luxburg. Red Hook, NY: Curran Associates, Inc., 2017, pp. 5998–6008 (cited on pages 164, 172, 173, 199).

[245] Andrew J. Viterbi. 'Error Bounds for Convolutional Codes and an Asymptotically Optimum Decoding Algorithm.' In: *IEEE Transactions on Information Theory* 13.2 (1967), pp. 260–269 (cited on pages 279, 357).

[246] Alexander Waibel et al. 'Phoneme Recognition Using Time-Delay Neural Networks'. In: *IEEE Transactions on Acoustics, Speech, and Signal Processing* 37.3 (1989), pp. 328–339 (cited on page 161).

[247] Steve R. Waterhouse, David MacKay, and Anthony J. Robinson. 'Bayesian Methods for Mixtures of Experts'. In: *Advances in Neural Information Processing Systems 8*. Ed. by D. S. Touretzky, M. C. Mozer, and M. E. Hasselmo. Cambridge, MA: MIT Press, 1996, pp. 351–357 (cited on page 326).

[248] C. J. C. H. Watkins. 'Learning from Delayed Rewards'. PhD thesis. Oxford, England: King's College, 1989 (cited on page 15).

[249] P. J. Werbos. 'Beyond Regression: New Tools for Prediction and Analysis in the Behavioral Sciences'. PhD thesis. Cambridge, MA: Harvard University, 1974 (cited on pages 153, 176).

[250] J. Weston and C. Watkins. 'Support Vector Machines for Multiclass Pattern Recognition'. In: *Proceedings of the Seventh European Symposium on Artificial Neural Networks*. European Symposium on Artificial Neural Networks, Apr. 1999 (cited on page 127).

[251] C. K. I. Williams and D. Barber. 'Bayesian Classification with Gaussian Processes'. In: *IEEE Transactions on Pattern Analysis and Machine Intelligence* 20.12 (1998), pp. 1342–1351 (cited on page 339).

[252] David H. Wolpert. 'Stacked Generalization'. In: *Neural Networks* 5.2 (1992), pp. 241–259. DOI: https://doi.org/10.1016/S0893-6080(05)80023-1 (cited on page 204).

[253] David H. Wolpert. 'The Lack of a Priori Distinctions between Learning Algorithms'. In: *Neural Computation* 8.7 (Oct. 1996), pp. 1341–1390. DOI: 10.1162/neco.1996.8.7.1341 (cited on page 11).

[254] Kouichi Yamaguchi et al. 'A Neural Network for Speaker-Independent Isolated Word Recognition'. In: *First International Conference on Spoken Language Processing (ICSLP 90)*. International Symposium on Computer Architecture, 1990, pp. 1077–1080 (cited on page 159).

[255] Liu Yang and Rong Jin. *Distance Metric Learning: A Comprehensive Survey*. 2006. URL: https://www.cs.cmu.edu/~liuy/frame_survey_v2.pdf (cited on page 13).

[256] Steve Young. 'A Review of Large Vocabulary Continuous Speech Recognition'. In: *IEEE Signal Processing Magazine* 13.5 (Sept. 1996), pp. 45–57. DOI: 10.1109/79.536824 (cited on page 276).

[257] Steve J. Young, N. H. Russell, and J. H. S Thornton. *Token Passing: A Simple Conceptual Model for Connected Speech Recognition Systems*. Tech. rep. Cambridge, MA: Cambridge University Engineering Department, 1989 (cited on page 280).

[258] Steve Young et al. *The HTK Book*. Tech. rep. Cambridge, MA: Cambridge University Engineering Department, 2002 (cited on page 286).

[259] Kevin Zakka. *Deriving the Gradient for the Backward Pass of Batch Normalization*. 2016. URL: http://kevinzakka.github.io/2016/09/14/batch_normalization/ (visited on 11/20/2019) (cited on page 183).

[260] Matthew D. Zeiler. 'ADADELTA: An Adaptive Learning Rate Method'. In: *CoRR* abs/1212.5701 (2012) (cited on page 192).

[261] Shiliang Zhang, Hui Jiang, and Lirong Dai. 'Hybrid Orthogonal Projection and Estimation (HOPE): A New Framework to Learn Neural Networks'. In: *Journal of Machine Learning Research* 17.37 (2016), pp. 1–33. DOI: http://jmlr.org/papers/v17/15-335.html (cited on pages 293, 294, 302, 303, 379).

[262] Shiliang Zhang et al. 'Feedforward Sequential Memory Networks: A New Structure to Learn Long-Term Dependency'. In: *CoRR* abs/1512.08301 (2015) (cited on pages 161, 202).

[263] Shiliang Zhang et al. 'Rectified Linear Neural Networks with Tied-Scalar Regularization for LVCSR'. In: *INTERSPEECH 2015, 16th Annual Conference of the International Speech Communication Association, Dresden, Germany, September 6–10, 2015*. International Speech Communication Association, 2015, pp. 2635–2639 (cited on page 194).

[264] Shiliang Zhang et al. 'The Fixed-Size Ordinally-Forgetting Encoding Method for Neural Network Language Models'. In: *Proceedings of the 53rd Annual Meeting of the Association for Computational Linguistics and the 7th International Joint Conference on Natural Language Processing*. Beijing, China: Association for Computational Linguistics, July 2015, pp. 495–500. DOI: 10.3115/v1/P15-2081 (cited on page 78).

[265] Shiliang Zhang et al. 'Nonrecurrent Neural Structure for Long-Term Dependence'. In: *IEEE/ACM Transactions on Audio, Speech, and Language Processing* 25.4 (2017), pp. 871–884 (cited on page 161).

Index